A TREASURY OF

AFRO-AMERICAN FOLKLORE

Also by Harold Courlander

Novels and Novellas
The Master of the Forge
The Bordeaux Narrative
The African
The Mesa of Flowers
The Big Old World of Richard Creeks
The Son of the Leopard
The Caballero

Nonfiction
A Treasury of African Folklore
A Treasury of Afro-American Folklore
Tales of Yoruba Gods and Heroes
The Heart of the Ngoni, Heroes of the African Kingdom of
    Segu (with Ousmana Sako)
The Drum and the Hoe, Life and Lore of the Haitian People
Negro Folk Music, U.S.A.
Haiti Singing
Big Falling Snow (with Albert Yava)
Hopi Voices: Recollections, Traditions and Narratives of the
    Hopi Indians
Negro Songs from Alabama
The Fourth World of the Hopis

Folklore and Folk Tales
The Hat-Shaking Dance and Other Ashanti Tales from Ghana
Olode the Hunter and Other Tales from Nigeria
The King's Drum and Other African Stories
The Crest and the Hide and Other African Stories of Heroes,
    Chiefs, Bards, Hunters, Sorcerers and Common People
The Cow-Tail Switch and Other West African Stories (with
    George Herzog)
The Fire on the Mountain and Other Ethiopian Stories (with
    Wolf Leslau)
People of the Short Blue Corn: Tales and Legends of the Hopi
    Indians
The Tiger's Whisker and Other Tales from Asia and the Pacific
Terrapin's Pot of Sense
The Piece of Fire and Other Haitian Tales
Kantchil's Lime Pit and Other Sources from Indonesia
Uncle Bouqui of Haiti
Ride with the Sun

A TREASURY OF

AFRO-AMERICAN FOLKLORE

*THE ORAL LITERATURE, TRADITIONS,
RECOLLECTIONS, LEGENDS, TALES,
SONGS, RELIGIOUS BELIEFS,
CUSTOMS, SAYINGS, AND HUMOR
OF PEOPLES OF AFRICAN DESCENT
IN THE AMERICAS*

by
HAROLD COURLANDER
Decorations by Enrico Arno

SMITHMARK

© 1976, 1996 by Harold Courlander

This edition published in 1996 by
SMITHMARK Publishers
a division of US Media Holdings, Inc.
16 East 32nd Street, New York, NY 10016

SMITHMARK books are available for bulk purchase for sales,
promotion, and premium use. For details, write or call the
manager of special sales, SMITHMARK Publishers
16 East 32nd Street, New York, NY 10016 (212)-532-6600.

Library of Congress data is available upon request

Printed in the United States of America

ISBN: 0-7651-9733-2

10 9 8 7 6 5 4 3 2 1

FOR FOUR FRIENDS,
BOB, DORIE, HAL, STEPHIE

CONTENTS

PHOTO ILLUSTRATIONS

(Photos follow page 298)

PHOTO CREDITS

ACKNOWLEDGMENTS
AND
APPRECIATION

I am much indebted to numerous persons and organizations for their help in assembling the contents of this book, for guidance of various kinds, and for permission to use previously published or unpublished materials. In particular, I want to express my thanks to:

Dr. George E. Simpson, of Oberlin, for his valuable guidance on cults and traditions in Jamaica, and for his kind permission to include in this book portions of some of his studies and writings.

Dr. Luis Felipe Ramon y Rivera, of Caracas, for his generous assistance in locating materials from Venezuela relating to the central theme of this anthology, including songs, stories and photographs.

Dr. Robert A. Hall, Jr., of Cornell University, for permission to use some of his Haitian Creole texts.

Dr. Douglas MacRae Taylor, of Dominica, for permission to include portions of his important studies on the Black Caribs.

Dr. Richard Dorson, Director of the Folklore Institute, Indiana University, for permission to reprint some of his previously published American Negro tales.

Mr. John Benson Brooks, of New York, for his transcriptions of numerous songs in this book.

Dr. Alan P. Merriam, of Indiana University, for both his suggestions and help in the assembling of these materials, as well as for his permission to use his transcription of a Brazilian cult song.

Mr. Carl Carmer for his kind permission to reprint the story, "The Knee-High Man," from *Stars Fell on Alabama*.

Miss Katherine Dunham for permission to use extracts from her book, *Journey to Accompong*.

Dr. Donald W. Hogg, of the University of Puerto Rico, for his help and advice on the Maroon and Kumina cults of Jamaica.

Dr. John Figueroa, of the Centro Caribeño de Estudios Postgraduados, Carolina, Puerto Rico, for his kindness in checking the accuracy of transcriptions of some Jamaican tape recordings.

Dr. Pedro Escabí, of the University of Puerto Rico, for his generosity in making available some of his personally gathered Puerto Rican materials.

Mr. Moses Asch for his kindness in making accessible the music and text resources of Folkways Records and the Ethnic Folkways Library.

Mr. Bayard Rustin, Justice Wade H. McCree, Mr. Roy Wilkins and Mrs. Mildred Bond Roxborough for advice and suggestions concerning the use of the terms "black," "Negro" and "Afro-American."

Mr. Fernando Galvan and Mr. Esteban MacCragh for their much valued help in the translation of Latin-American texts.

Dr. Angelina Pollak-Eltz, of Caracas, for her suggestions about Venezuelan and other South American folkloric materials.

Mr. Malcolm Bell, Jr., and Mrs. Muriel Bell, of Savannah, for their generous and greatly appreciated help in the procuring of photographic materials documenting traditions in Georgia, and in particular for their permission to use their photographs of scenes in the Sea Islands.

Mr. William E. Birdsong, of Atlanta, for his extraordinary kindness in photographing for me the Belali Document in the archives of the Georgia State Library.

Mr. Frank J. Gillis, of the Indiana University Archives of Traditional Music, for making available to me the Herskovits texts of Bahian secular songs.

Mr. Frederic Ramsey, Jr., for his generosity in making available some of his unique photographic materials.

Mme. Odette Mennesson Rigaud, of Port-au-Prince, for her kind permission to use two scenes from her unequalled collection of photographs of cult life in Haiti.

Miss Helanie Mandell for her generous help in the securing of out-of-print source materials.

My son, Michael Courlander, for his invaluable aid in procuring hard-to-find publications; and my daughter, Susan Courlander, for typing assistance.

Mrs. Ruth Walsh, to whom fell the difficult task of copyreading the manuscript of this book, for her dedicated effort to make things right.

Miss Mara Lurie for her many acts of help in times of need.

And Mr. David McDowell, my editor, whose interest, support and friendship greatly facilitated the making of this book.

I also wish to thank the following institutions and professional groups for their generous cooperation and assistance:

The Association for the Study of Negro Life and History
The Wenner-Gren Foundation for Anthropological Research
The American Anthropological Association
The American Folklore Society
The Institute of Social and Economic Research, University of the West Indies
The Archives of Traditional Music, Indiana University
The Venezuelan National Institute of Folklore
Georgia State Library
Creole Petroleum Corporation, Caracas
Central Photograph Unit, Columbus Memorial Library, Organization of American States

And I am of course grateful to numerous publishing houses for their permissions to use stories and descriptive excerpts from their publications. Acknowledgments for specific items are made on the pages where the excerpts appear, but I want to express my special thanks here to:

Columbia University Press
University of California Press
Harcourt Brace Jovanovich

Holt, Rinehart and Winston
University of Georgia Press
Harper & Row
Thames and Hudson
Crown Publishers
Dodd, Mead and Company
Farrar, Straus and Giroux
Creative Age Press
St. Martin's Press
Academy Editions
Every possible effort has been made to locate authors or others with rights and interests in the selections included in this book, so that the customary permissions requests could be made. In some instances, regrettably, these efforts were unsuccessful, but the sources of the materials are clearly cited in every case.

Ajo ajo,
Ajo mi re.
Kini l'awa o?
Ajo ajo.

Journey journey,
This is my journey.
What are we?
Journey journey.
                    —Shango song from Trinidad

AFRICA'S MARK IN THE WESTERN HEMISPHERE

Among the Africans transported as slaves to the New World, beginning early in the sixteenth century, were people from the Sudanic regions, the Guinea Coast, the Zaire (Congo) River watershed and even from the eastern side of the African continent. There is no complete or even adequate record of all the tribes, cultures and linguistic groups represented in the slave cargoes carried to the Americas during four hundred years of the slave trade. The preponderant part of the shipments was from the Atlantic side of Africa. European vessels roamed from port to port gathering the thousands of captives who had been marched to the sea as objects of commerce. Some of the victims of the trade came from regions readily accessible to the coast, others from villages and kingdoms in the interior of the continent. Some of the slaves were the booty of conflicts between states or political struggles within kingdoms. On the Guinea Coast, for example, Dahomean and Yoruban armies in combat took prisoners from each other and sold them to slave entrepreneurs or to European traders. In the far interior, Arab or black Islamic raiders swept through rural areas and villages gathering the human substance of the trade. Certain non-Islamic tribes such as the Ovimbundu of Angola established commercial relations with people in the interior with the primary purpose of acquiring captives to be disposed of at coastal ports. From the east coast of Africa, large numbers of slaves were sent to Arab lands and to South Asia. From the west coast ports they went largely to Spanish, Portuguese, Dutch, French and English settlements in the Western Hemisphere, including, of course, the United States after it became independent from Britain.

The slave trade did not distinguish between animist and Moslem, farmer and craftsman, prince and serf, priest and servitor. The slave merchants disposed of them—Sudanic, West Coast Guinean, Bantu and Nilotic—in whatever proportions and mixes they happened to come, usually hawking their cargoes as the best available. The ethnic mix of a slave cargo generally reflected the points along the African coast where a ship had called. Thus, British slave carriers had a high percentage of Yoruban, Ibo, Mahi and Akan slaves, while Portuguese vessels, loading at ports near the mouth of the Zaire River, had large numbers of slaves from the Zaire watershed. But because of the diverse ways in which the slaves had been procured, any single cargo could have within it Africans of varied tribal and linguistic backgrounds. In the New World, the Africans were scattered through the West Indies, the North American mainland, and those parts of Central and South America we now know as Mexico, Honduras, Panama, Surinam, Guiana, Brazil, Venezuela, Colombia and Argentina, as well as elsewhere.

In some places—as in the British and French North American colonies (and, later, in the United States)—the Africans were further mixed and distributed on the plantations, as a matter of policy, in a manner that assured a withering of tribal and cultural ties. In certain other regions, however, Africans of common or similar ethnic backgrounds

1

lived in close proximity and preserved some of the traditions, concepts and even institutions of their cultural past. Where Africans far outnumbered the Europeans, they retained more of their old traditions than where they were few in number. The pace as well as the character of cultural assimilation differed from one place to another. In a number of New World locales Africans preserved traditions whose core was explicitly Yoruban, Fon or Bantu. Elsewhere, Akan, Efik, Ekoi, Ibo or Congolese institutions survived. In still other settings the general African inheritance was muted, blurred, or disguised under a heavy overlay of dominant European customs, or almost totally obliterated.

Looking at the Western Hemisphere as a whole, it is abundantly evident that many tangible elements of African ways, customs, attitudes, values and views of life survived the Atlantic crossing. In differing degrees, according to the complex of social forces at work, numerous Negro communities in the Americas continue to draw from the African wellspring. In the upriver jungle country of Surinam, for example, descendants of African slaves live in a style reminiscent of the West African bush village. Haiti, though overlaid with a heavy veneer of French custom, manifests many characteristics of African life. Black communities in Cuba, the English-speaking West Indies, Brazil, Venezuela, Guiana, the French Caribbean and the United States—all preserve something of the African past, and sufficiently so that it is possible to perceive the shared African inheritance. The entire region is properly seen as an area of significant African cultural influence, even as an outer edge of the African culture complex.

This does not mean that Haitians, black Cubans or black North Americans are Africans, for they are products not only of their African past but of the European cultures on which they have so heavily drawn and, most important of all, of their unique collective experience in the New World. The fact that certain African traditions, viewpoints and ways of doing things, in varying degrees of visibility, live on is not a characterization of New World Negro communities, but rather a special observable phenomenon. In short, it is a body of Africanisms, not Africans, that has survived in the New World.

What, then, is the nature of the African inheritance? The anthropologist Melville J. Herskovits in his book, *The Myth of the Negro Past,* noted numerous aspects of Negro New World life that reflect African influence and survivals. In the United States, where the survivals have generally been more muted than in the Caribbean and South America, African tradition and influence are found in baptismal, burial and mourning rites, in the naming of children, attitudes toward elders and family, group work conventions, music and music making, dance (postures, movement and concept), vocabulary and grammar retentions, African motifs in religious activities, and, of course, in stories and storytelling. Elements that are blended, submerged, disguised or lost among blacks in the United States become more evident and explicit in Jamaica, Haiti, Cuba, Surinam and other Negro cultures to the south.

Material objects of African derivation are less visible, less readily encountered than nonmaterial elements. Where they do exist they are most likely to be associated with music and cult life, or with work traditions. The evidence is there, waiting to be recognized. Throughout the Caribbean, and in Negro communities on the South American mainland, one finds wooden implements and utensils of African design, musical instruments made to an African pattern, and styles of decoration reminiscent of African prototypes. In Surinam is to be found woodcarving that is stylistically related to Ashanti or other Akan tradition. Haitians make wari (munkala) gameboards, and play the game much as it is played in Africa. Haitian ironsmiths forge paraphernalia for the cult centers in a tradition that is clearly related to that of the Yoruba. Some of the old ritual objects in the collection of the Museo Nacional in Havana—once used by the Lucumi (Yoruba), Arara (Dahomey) and Mayombe cults and the Abakwa fraternal society— could well have been fabricated on the African continent. They include elaborately carved drums, Shango wands, forged iron bells and costumes representing various spirits. Mortars for pulverizing grain were used throughout Negro America, and wooden grave markers that stood not long ago in a burial ground in the southeastern United States were astonishingly similar in concept to markers seen in various regions of Africa (see Illus. 2).

One conspicuous material survival is that of musical instruments, whose wide distribution in the Americas exemplifies the geographical extent, as well as the conceptual importance, of African tradition. Here is a brief picture of how African-style instruments have persevered, usually but not exclusively in connection with religious ritual, in Afro-American communities:

Drums: African-style drums are found today throughout most of the West Indies, in various scattered regions of Brazil, in Venezuela, Surinam, Guiana and elsewhere. Haiti has a peg-style hollow log drum called Arada (named after Allada in Dahomey), used in Fon-related religious rites and dances; another peg-type drum called Nago (i.e., Yoruba); a drum with a hoop-mounted head, called Congo, of Bantu origin; a drum called Loango, after the Kingdom of Loango; various permutations of these types, all designed in the African manner; and drumsticks of African pattern, all carrying their original Fon names. Similar kinds of drums are found in Venezuela, among them the tambor Mina (taking its name from the Amine people) and others named after, and in the tradition of, the Calabar region of West Africa. In Cuba, various cults and fraternal societies have drums patterned after those of the Fon, the Yoruba, the Efik and the Yombe. In Brazil, African-type drums are employed in Yoruba, Congo and Fon-derived religious rituals. Negro communities in remote areas of Surinam have drums of Akan and Dahomean design. And until fairly recent times, hollow-log drums patterned after the African have been made and used in the southeastern United States and Louisiana.

The earth bow: Sometimes called a ground harp, the earth bow is an African device developed from an animal snare. It consists of a hole in the ground covered with a skin or leaf membrane to which one end of a cord is attached. The other end of the cord is fastened to a bent stick embedded in the ground. The taut cord is played by plucking, and different tones are achieved by slight pressure on the bent stick. This device, known as a mosquito drum in Haiti, is found in various islands of the West Indies and in Venezuela. Portable variants of the earth bow, made of a large can, have been documented in Haiti and elsewhere. In the United States, a portable version, called a washtub bass or a gutbucket, is made of an inverted washtub and a broomstick. (See pp. 505–6.)

Stamping tubes: Bamboo stamping tubes, played by striking the closed ends on the earth, have been found in diverse parts of Afro-America, including Haiti, where they are called dikambos, and Venezuela, where they are known as quitiplas.

Metal percussion: In Haiti, Cuba, other Caribbean islands, Venezuela and Brazil, as well as in other New World regions where descendants of Africans live, iron bells of African design and function are commonly used to produce percussion effects for religious and secular music. In a number of such places, the instrument retains its Yoruba name, ogan. The bell is sounded by striking it with a stick or bit of metal. It is somewhat flat and has a flare at the edge reminiscent of the African original, although numerous variant patterns are known. Where it is difficult to acquire the traditional bell, alternate objects such as plowpoints or automobile springs may be used. In the United States, bells or metal substitutes were commonly used well into the nineteenth century in Louisiana, and even today the cowbell, its internal clapper removed, is frequently seen in Negro street bands.

Scrapers: Metal scrapers, scraping sticks, and notched gourds and bones, all in the African tradition, are found throughout Afro-America. In the United States, the common kitchen grater and the washboard were, and continue to be, used as musical devices by street performers and organized jazz bands.

Rattles: Numerous types of African-style rattles are found throughout Latin America, where they are used as musical or ritual devices. The common hollow gourd with pebbles or seeds inside and a stick handle is a commonplace musical instrument found in almost any singing or orchestral setting. The calabash rattle with an external network of beads, nuts or seeds as strikers is known in Cuba, Haiti and other islands of the Caribbean as well as on the South, Central and North American mainland wherever African cults are found. Metal substitutes for one or both of these types are used in Cuba, Brazil, Haiti and Venezuela. The rattles with basket type handles, often woven of basket materials and sometimes made of wood or cloth, are known in Cuba in connection with the Abakwa society's rituals, and have been reported from mainland South America.

The marimba, or marimbula: Known most commonly in Africa in the form of a small hollow or solid board with metal or reed keys attached, and widely referred to as a sansa although its name varies from region to region, the marimba is widely dispersed throug[ ] bean area and along its mainland shores. Although small [ ] marimbas have been noted in Cuba, most of the New Wo[ ] are larger, usually about the size of a soap box. In Jamai[ ] English-speaking islands it is called a rhumba box. The instrument makes its appearance almost everywhere in the Western Hemisphere that Latin American music is heard. In its smaller, more African form, the marimba was once used for music making in Louisiana.

Other: In addition to the instruments already noted, others of African origin such as the mouth bow, wooden clappers and sounders, quills, bull roarers and friction drums have been reported from numerous New World Negro communities. The banjo, so well known to folk musicians in the southern part of the United States, is generally believed to have developed out of an earlier African instrument.

This widespread retention of African musical instruments, along with the musical concepts associated with them, is only one indicator of the strength of certain African traditions in the Americas. Another is the persevering, and in some settings the flourishing, of African religious concepts and rites, which are found today in the Caribbean region and South America. Cults and rituals of Dahomeyan, Yoruba, Akan and various Bantu peoples persist in Brazil, Haiti, Cuba, Jamaica, Martinique, Guadaloupe, Trinidad, Grenada, Surinam and other places where Negro communities exist. In some of these cults African religious ideas are veneered with Christian beliefs, and essentially African deities may have the names of Christian saints. In the United States, numerous eighteenth- and nineteenth-century chroniclers recorded the existence of African religious activities in Louisiana, though most of these writers failed to grasp the real meanings of what they had observed.

The intention here is not to detail our accumulated knowledge about African cultural survivals in the Western Hemisphere, nor to suggest a predominance of the African inheritance over the non-African, but merely to take those survivals into account. It is equally evident that Negroes in the New World are the inheritors of Spanish, Portuguese, French, Dutch, English and other traditions as well. A devotee of the Macumba cult in Brazil may be, and probably is, a Catholic; if he speaks some ritual words in Yoruba, his native language is Brazilian Portuguese; if he holds a number of superstitions, a good many of them probably came from Europe; if he responds to African-style music, he also responds to music more in the Caboclo and Iberian traditions. Although he is a devotee of Macumba, so are countless whites. And as has been pointed out by various studies of this cult, Macumba today is compounded of African, European, Catholic, Indian, spiritualist and even more diverse and exotic elements. Similarly, in Venezuela we have the example of the Maria Lionza cult, built around the myth of an ancient water deity of the original Indian inhabitants. To this Indian mythological core have been added African, Afro-American, Spanish, Catholic and other beliefs having to do with gods, demigods, spirits, curing practices, charms, rituals and magic. (See pp. 229–30.)

We need to caution ourselves now and again, at this particular time in our social development when so much stress is given to *black* literature, *black* traditions and *black* ideas, that oral literature and customs are products of environment, history and culture, and not of race. Compare, for example, the ways of the Appalachian hill people with those of the equally white Ainus of Japan. Or look at the Seminoles, the Athabascans, the Maya and the Fuegians, Indians all: their life systems vary one from the other as widely as do those of the Lapps and the southern Europeans. In speaking broadly and familiarly of Afro-America, therefore, we are not referring to a common genetic inheritance but to cultural inheritance, which is to say an inheritance of experience. For this reason it is somewhat misleading to talk of black culture (or cultures) unless it is clearly understood that this nomenclature is merely a matter of convenience, and that we are speaking of social groups that happen to be, among other things, dark-skinned. It is of course true that having a dark skin and other distinguishing racial attributes was a particular disability to slaves and their descendants in the Western Hemisphere. The fact of their being black had a direct bearing on their experience, which, in turn, left a mark on their lives and their literature. But the culture (or cultures) that was partly shaped by New World experience has no genetic base. Skin color is an absolute measure of nothing that is consequential. While it may help to distinguish one large group from another, it has little to do with the almost numberless ways in which humans have sought to adjust to their environment, create institutions, develop art and literature and live in some kind of social equilibrium. The term Afro-American is merely an offhand, ready-made way of identifying people of African descent and inheritance in the Americas.

And so we come to the question of what is meant by Afro-American (or Negro or black) folklore and oral literature. As the term is used in the pages that follow, it merely refers to myths, tales, recollections, songs and other orally transmitted lore of the various, sometimes disparate, Negro cultures in the New World. It includes narratives and traditions unique to particular communities as well as those that are shared by many or all, and themes of European as well as African origin. It is obvious that much of the Afro-American oral literature has a distinctly New World character. Some old traditional themes persist stubbornly while others fade, but the literature as a whole is renewed by the creative genius of untold numbers of narrators, by conscious or unconscious borrowing, and by innovation. In the end, the narrative, the song, the poem or the myth must stand on its own, and our knowledge about origins becomes academic and incidental.

Negro folklore in the United States is usually treated separately from that of the Caribbean and Latin America as though it were something distinct and apart. It is true that the Negro in the United States possesses an oral literature readily distinguishable from others—as, indeed, do Brazilian, Venezuelan, Cuban and Haitian blacks. Yet many

threads of the common inheritance run through the music and literature of all Negro America, and it is only in juxtaposition that the shared
inheritance can be perceived and measured. Religious belief systems
of the Cumina and other cults in Jamaica add a little light for our per-
ception and appreciation of certain traditional Negro religious attitudes and practices in the United States. An understanding of Caribbean dancing and of the relationship between sound and motion puts
traditional U.S. Negro dancing in broader perspective. Our total concept of U.S. folklore and oral tradition is larger and more profound as
we come to realize that some elements of U.S. Negro speech are found
in the idioms of black communities of the Bahamas, Jamaica, Trinidad
and Guiana; that traditional group work techniques and worksongs
have much in common; and that story themes commonplace in the repertoire of American blacks are likewise known to peoples of the Caribbean and Afro-Americans on the Central and South American mainland. And although the Negro folk music of mainland North America
developed a distinct direction of its own, while the music of the Caribbean moved in another, they continue to share elements of a common
past, as in their structure and the nature of their lyrics. In short, all of
Afro-America can be seen as the inheritor of various combinations of
the cultural legacy.

The concept of folklore, oral literature and traditions put forward in
this book is broad. It includes myths, myth-legends, human tales, animal tales, songs, near-epics and recollections of historical happenings.
There are descriptions of cult life, around which so many traditions
and beliefs flow; of music and dance, which have an integral connection with traditional singing; and of the social scene in places where
African and European, or white and black, ideas and ways were inter-
mingling and in the process of becoming Afro-American. Some regions
of Afro-America are better represented than others, and some, unfortunately, get little more than brief mention, but it would not be possible
in a work this size to do more than pause here and there to look upon
what waits to be seen. What is more important than what any particular
scene has to offer is the total view of the Afro-American culture area
with its local variations and its interconnections. Beginning sections of
the book survey the traditions of Spanish-, French- and English-speaking islands of the Caribbean, after which there are visits to some of the
Central and South American regions inhabited by people of African
descent. Oral traditions of Negroes in the United States comprise the
last portion of this anthology, an order that is arbitrary but which may
help to underline the connections between one part of Afro-America
and another. For those who care for some specifics as to African origins
of one tale or another, the Appendices include a number of African stories that we may regard as prototypes of tales told today in the New
World.

THE INHERITANCE IN CUBA

The Africans who came to Cuba as slaves during Spanish colonial times were from many different tribes along the Gulf of Guinea and in the Congo River basin. Old records enumerate dozens of different Bantu-speaking groups represented among the colony's slave population, and from West Africa came Ibo, Efik, Yoruba, Mahi, Fon (Dahomean), Bambara, Foula, Wolof and other peoples. Contraband slaves continued to flow into Cuba until relatively late in the nineteenth century, and in the first third of the twentieth century there were still some old people living in Cuba who had been born on the African continent.

While the Afro-Cuban community absorbed much of the mainstream Hispanic-American culture, it demonstrated a remarkable capacity for preserving African beliefs and customs. Social and political institutions of African derivation survived and even flourished. Various Congo peoples—Loango, Mondongo, Bafiote, Mosondi and others—grouped themselves around the Kimbisa or Mayombe cult. Yoruba religious and musical traditions, elements of the Yoruba language, and Yoruba oral literature survived in the traditions of the Lucumi (Yoruba) cult. Dahomean religious practices and beliefs were preserved in the Arara (i.e., Allada) rites, with which many Haitian immigrants identified themselves. Old Efik and Ekoi traditions persevered with astonishing fidelity in the context of the Abakwa secret fraternal society. And manifestations of other cultural traditions came to the surface during the seasonal *comparsas* that filled the streets of Havana with African-style masquerades. After the end of slavery in Cuba, blacks and whites—even those sharing the same economic level—tended to maintain separate communities, particularly so in the countryside. This separateness, to the extent that it existed, undoubtedly contributed to the survival of old traditional ideas. Just as the white *guajiros*— peasant farmers—were the preservers of Spanish folk traditions, Afro-Cubans were the preservers of African ways in their New World environment. At some points these separate traditions met and merged, producing unique phenomena such as Afro-Cuban music—rhumbas, congas and other distinctive musical forms that were compounded out of European and African musical instruments and Spanish and African melodies and rhythms.

SOME YORUBA LEGENDS IN CUBA

Numerous Yoruba tales and legends have survived in Cuba, among them stories whose protagonists are orishas, or deities. Separated by distance from the mainstream of Yoruba oral literature, the Cuban orisha stories have undergone change. They have adapted to the Cuban environment and, no doubt inadvertently, the personalities, roles and activities of some of the deities have been altered. The supreme Yoruba sky god, Olorun, is called Olofin. The important male orisha Obatala becomes a female deity who owns the thunderbolt which, in the older tradition, is properly the possession of Shango. Shango, usually characterized among the African Yoruba as a hot-tempered and stern ruler of Oyo, is often portrayed among Afro-Cubans as a growing boy or young man. But the orisha tales nevertheless remain essentially Yoruba and continue to draw primarily on the traditions brought to the New World from what is now southwestern Nigeria. Here are some of the old orisha stories as they are remembered in Cuba.

These examples of Cuban Yoruba tales are taken in free translation from "El Sistema Religioso de los Lucumis y Otras Influencias Africanas en Cuba," by Rómulo Lachatañeré, Estudios Afrocubanos, Havana, 1945–1946. In English translation they first appeared in Tales of Yoruba Gods and Heroes, *1972 by Harold Courlander, New York, © Crown Publishers. Reprinted by permission of Crown Publishers.*

The Distribution of the Orishas' Powers

In the earliest days only the orishas lived on the earth. Their paramount ruler was an old man called Olofin [Olorun], who lived on the summit of a mountain so steep that only one person had ever succeeded in reaching him. A woman by the name of Obatala knew of a twisting but safe path by which she could get to the Father of Heaven and Earth. The path was known as the way to Osanquiriyan. Whenever Obatala felt the desire to do so she went up the mountain to visit Olofin, who, although he ruled, was never seen by the other orishas.

It happened one time that things on earth began to go wrong. There was a drought, and the cattle began to die and the crops failed. Hunger came among the orishas. They assembled in a crowd at the foot of the mountain and called out to Olofin, "Father, we are dying! We have hardly the strength to meet death!" But from Olofin there was no answer. The orishas grew desperate. Finally they went to Obatala and entreated her to climb the mountain to make contact with Olofin. Obatala agreed. She climbed the trail known as the way to Osanquiriyan. She reached the place where Olofin lived, and she found him lying on the ground.

Obatala called his name several times, but Olofin did not answer. Obatala shook him, whereupon Olofin said, "I am too tired. I can't go on."

Obatala went down the mountain to the plain. She called all the orishas together and said, "The old man is too tired to go on."

On hearing this the orishas said, "If he can not go on he should turn over his powers to us. Then we will know how to deal with things."

Again Obatala went up the mountain and spoke to Olofin. She said, "The people are asking you to make a supreme effort."

Olofin answered, "I can't go on."

Obatala said, "In that case the people want you to share your powers with them."

The Father of Heaven and Earth said, "That is fair."

"Do it, then," Obatala said.

Olofin said to her, "Summon an assembly under the ceiba tree."

Obatala descended. She went to the ceiba tree. She gathered food. She cooked it with cocoa butter, which was known to soothe impatience. Then she called the assembly. The orishas came. They ate, argued and waited for Olofin. Early in the evening they saw him coming down the mountain. When he arrived he said once again, "I am tired. I can't go on."

"Father," the orishas said, "if you cannot go on give us something to help us, because we cannot go on either."

Olofin said, "I will give each person what is due to him."

"Yes," the orishas said, "but do not keep us waiting too long."

Whereupon Olofin reached for a thunderbolt and gave it to Shango. He reached for the lightning and gave it to Oya, saying, "You are the owner of the light that goes with the thunder." He picked up the river and placed it in the hands of Oshun, saying, "You are the mistress of the river." He embraced the sea and gave it to Yemaja [Yemoja], telling her, "You are the owner of the sea." In this way, one by one, Olofin gave each orisha his power. And at last he told Obatala, "You are mistress of all the heads."

Olofin remained the Supreme Orisha, but Obatala became his deputy on earth. She became the one who protects those who fall under the anger of Ogun. She also possesses great healing powers. When somebody has been sick for a long time he goes to the Lucumi priest. The priest takes a pigeon, plucks from it a few feathers, wraps them in a white cloth and rubs the sick person with them, while reciting the following prayer [to Obatala]:

> Sara yeye bakuro,
> Sara yeye bakuro. . . .

The sick person recovers.
(For an African comparison see Appendix I, pp. 566–68.)

Olofin Punishes Babaluaye

When Olofin [Olorun] gave out the powers to the various orishas he gave to Babaluaye [i.e., Obaluaye, or Sonponno] inordinate sexual strength. Babaluaye was profuse in the use of the strength given him by Olofin and was constantly lying with women.

Olofin sent his assistant, Orumbila [Orunmila], with a message for Babaluaye. Orumbila said to Babaluaye, "As tomorrow is Good Friday, Olofin wants you to keep your sexual impulses under control."

But Babaluaye answered, "Olofin gave me the power of sexual intercourse, therefore I will use it whenever I wish."

"Do what you like," Orumbila said, and he went away.

During the evening of Good Thursday, Babaluaye had intercourse with Oshun. The next day he awoke with his body full of sores, and a few days after that he died of syphilis. This was the punishment that Olofin had sent him.

Oshun felt that the punishment was severe and unjust. She prayed to Olofin, asking him to restore Babaluaye to life. But Olofin refused to undo what he had done. So Oshun went to Olofin's assistant, Orumbila, and asked him to participate in a trick on Olofin. Orumbila agreed. Oshun gave Orumbila a magic honey she possessed, and instructed him to sprinkle it all through Olofin's house. This Orumbila did. When that was done, Olofin felt himself under a very pleasant power. He called Orumbila and asked him, "Who has sprinkled my house with such a pleasant thing?"

Orumbila said, "I don't know."

Olofin said, "I want you to get some of that tasty honey for me."

Orumbila replied, "No, I cannot do it."

Olofin said, "Who then can do it?"

Orumbila answered laconically, "A woman."

Olofin asked all the women around his house, "Who has sprinkled my place with this pleasant honey?"

Each of the women answered, "I don't know."

At last Olofin, observing closely who was present, noted that Oshun was absent. He sent for her, and she was brought before him. He asked her, as he had the others, "Who has sprinkled my place with that pleasant honey?"

Oshun answered, "The thing that pleases you so much, it is mine."

Olofin said, "It is very good. I want you to provide me with more of it."

But Oshun replied, "Yes, I have the knowledge of providing this pleasant honey. You have the power to take life away from Babaluaye. If you have the power to kill, you also have the power to restore to life. Bring life back to Babaluaye and I will provide you with the honey."

Olofin agreed. He brought Babaluaye back to life. Oshun gave Olofin the honey that he wanted. And Babaluaye continued the same pursuits and enjoyments that he had had before.

(For an African comparison, see Appendix II, pp. 568–70.)

Ogun Traps Orumbila

One day Olofin [Olorun] sent his assistant, Orumbila [Orunmila], into the woods to get coconuts for him. Orumbila took a bag and went out to get the coconuts. After Orumbila had gone into the woods, Ogun learned where he was and what he was doing. He went at once to the trails leading from the woods and dug deep holes in them—that is to say, traps—which he covered over and disguised with straw.

Orumbila finished gathering coconuts and began to return to Olofin's house. Passing along one of the trails he fell into one of Ogun's traps. He tried to get out, but the hole was too deep. He was unable to escape, and it seemed that there was nothing for him to do but stay where he was. He remained in the trap for several days, and when he felt his strength leaving his body he accepted the inevitability of death, and he waited for life to leave him.

Meanwhile, three sisters—Oshun, Yemaja [Yemoja] and Obatala—went to the woods together to find medicinal herbs. They heard Orumbila making sounds in the place where he was awaiting death. They went to the trap in which he was imprisoned. They heard death sounds in Orumbila's throat—*r-r-r-r. . . . r-r-r-r. . . .*

Oshun said, "Oh, my sisters, that is Orumbila!"

Yemaja said, "Oh my sisters, Orumbila has fallen into the trap of Ogun Arere!"

Obatala said, "Let us rescue Orumbila!"

Oshun took off the five kerchiefs that she wore. She tied them together and made a strong rope. She made a loop in the rope and it it down into the hole. Orumbila put it around his body and the three sisters pulled him out. They gave him some brandy to revive him, and after that they took him home to Olofin.

Why Obatala Trembles at the River

It is said that Ogun of Arere [Onire] used the women who went into the woods, where he lived, in a violent and angry way. He took them roughly, had intercourse with them, and afterwards drove them out of his domain.

A beautiful woman by the name of Yemaya [Yemoja] Saramagua, her curiosity excited by the tales told about Ogun, once went to the woods intending for Ogun to possess her. Ogun took her and had intercourse with her, and then ordered her to depart. But Yemaya did not wish to go. She asked Ogun to give her more pleasure. Ogun ignored her wish and drove her from the woods. Full of anguish, Yemaya went to her sister Oshun and asked for her help, for she had fallen in love with the brutal Ogun.

Oshun said to her, "Wait in your house for Ogun tonight." She tied her five kerchiefs around her waist, and taking a dish of her magic honey she went to the woods. There she encountered the savage Ogun. Ogun tried to hold Oshun in his arms, but she broke away from him, her body slipping through his rough hands. She removed the five kerchiefs from around her waist and began to dance. And while dancing she poured some of the magic honey over her body. She danced close to Ogun and he tried to catch her but he was unable to do it. She poured some of the magic honey on Ogun's body. Overcome by the power of the honey and enraptured by Oshun, Ogun followed her meekly. She went to the edge of the woods. There she lay down and let Ogun have intercourse with her.

Soon Ogun said, "Woman, let us do it again."

Oshun answered, "Let us go to my house. It will be better there."

Ogun agreed. He followed her. She led him not to her own place but to the house of Yemaya. It was now very dark. Oshun put Ogun in Yemaya's bed and lay down with him. Later she slipped away and Yemaya took her place. Without suspecting anything, Ogun enjoyed himself with Yemaya, thinking she was Oshun.

But when day came he discovered the deception and he was overcome with rage. He beat Yemaya furiously and left the house. Outside he met Obatala, and in his fury he began to beat her also. Obatala ran away, with Ogun in pursuit. She came to the river. Seeing no other escape, she threw herself into the water. Shivering with cold and struggling against the current, Obatala remained in the water until Ogun went away. Then she came out, her body shaking with cold. She went looking for a blanket to put around her. In time she found one. Thus ended the episode.

This story explains why a person possessed by the orisha Obatala trembles and shakes when he approaches the river, and searches for a shawl to cover himself.

Shango Looks for His Father

The orisha Agayu was the father of Shango, and Obatala was Shango's mother. But Obatala had never told Shango who his father was. As Shango grew up he was moved by a desire to know his father. So one day he left his mother's house and went looking for the father he did not know. After a long journey he came upon Agayu in the woods.

Agayu asked him, "Child, what are you looking for?"

Shango answered, "I am looking for my father."

Agayu said, "And who are you?"

Shango replied, "I am the child of Baba," meaning, "the child of my father."

Agayu's answer was to pick up a piece of wood and hit the boy with it.

Shango did not complain. He said, "You are my father."

Agayu said, "Don't come to me with such a ridiculous story."

But Shango persisted, saying, "You are my father."

Agayu gathered some sticks and made a fire. He said, "I am going to roast you and eat you."

Shango said nothing. When the fire was going well Agayu threw the boy into it with the expectation that he would die in the flames. But the fire lapped at Shango's body without doing him any harm.

The orisha Oya happened to be passing through the woods, and she saw Shango in the flames. She ran to where Obatala lived, crying out, "Agayu is burning your child!"

Obatala took her thunderbolt and handed it to Oya. She said, "Use my thunderbolt. Set the woods afire."

Oya did as she was told. She returned to the woods and hurled the thunderbolt, setting the trees aflame. Agayu was frightened. He fled from the place, and some distance from there he took shelter under a palm tree.

Oyo took Shango from the fire where Agayu had placed him. She was surprised to find that Shango had not been harmed in any way. After that she brought Shango safely back to his mother Obatala.

Out of these events come the explanation of three facts that are known:

Whereas it was Obatala who originally owned the thunderbolt, Oya received the power to use it because Obatala gave it to her.

Because Shango was immune to the flames he became the master and owner of fire.

And because Agayu found refuge under the palm tree, palm trees ever since have been his sanctuary.

Obatala's Yams

The woman named Obatala owned an extensive plantation of yams. She had the knowledge of making these sacred yams grow and flourish, but the secret was known to no one else. Obatala wanted to employ a man to plant and cultivate her plantation, but she wanted to make sure that such a person would be discreet and not reveal her secret. Anyone to whom she divulged the knowledge had to have the capability of keeping silent about what he knew. Now, it was Obatala's opinion that when a man has women in his life he is inclined not to be reliable in such matters, and so she sought to find a man who was sexually indifferent. She heard of a person named Orisha-Oko who, it was said, had never had or desired sexual relations with a woman. She sent for him, and after lengthy questioning she appointed him chief of her plantation and instructed him in the magic of making the yams grow. He learned quickly. He planted and he cultivated, and Obatala's yams continued to grow well. Many people sought to find out the secret of Obatala's yams and what made them flourish, but they were unable to do so. If they tried to get Orisha-Oko to say something about it, he kept his silence.

The young man named Shango had on numerous occasions implored Obatala to give him possession of her ritual drums, but Obatala's answer had always been to refuse him. Shango's mother Yemaya [Yemoja] wanted very much to help her son fulfill his desire. And so she plotted as follows: "If I can get from Orisha-Oko the secret of the yams, I can give the secret to Shango. If I can ruin Obatala's plantation, she will have no more yams. Then Shango can exchange his yams for the drums he wants."

So Yemaya went to Orisha-Oko and tried to make him divulge the secret of the cultivation of the yams. But Orisha-Oko's answer was silence. Yemaya persisted. She came back day after day, but his answer was always the same, silence. Then one day she said to Orisha-Oko, "let us go and have intercourse." Orisha-Oko said nothing. She went to him again the next day and proposed that they have intercourse, but Orisha-Oko ignored her. Day after day she went to where Orisha-Oko was working and tried to arouse him. And then, at last, she succeeded in making desire flow in his body. Together they lay on the ground and had intercourse.

"Ah!" Orisha-Oko said. "This is a very pleasant thing we have done. We are going to do it every day."

But Yemaya demanded that he give her, in exchange, the secret of the yams, which he did. She gave the secret to Shango, who began to grow yams. And while he grew yams, Yemaya continued to meet with Orisha-Oko and have repeated intercourse with him. Orisha-Oko was so preoccupied with his new discovery that he neglected Obatala's plantation. He failed to do what he was supposed to do, and a time came when Obatala's yams were withered and exhausted. Her plantation was barren.

Then Shango brought a sack of his own yams to Obatala, saying, "This is a present for you."

Obatala said, "How did you acquire these yams?"

Shango said, "My mother has the secret of growing them."

When Yemaya was certain that Obatala had no more yams left she went to visit her. She began to negotiate for the ritual drums that Shango wanted. And in the end it was agreed that Obatala would get the yams grown by Shango, and that Obatala would give him the drums.

Shango acquired the drums, and he was acknowledged thereafter as their owner and master.

As for Orisha-Oko, he left Obatala's plantation and disappeared in the wilderness.

LUCUMI (YORUBA) LITURGICAL MUSIC IN CUBA

The customary orchestra for Lucumi ritual music consists of three drums, iron percussion devices and a large rattle. The drums, usually called bata, are goblet-shaped and have goatskin heads at both ends. The two heads of the bata drum are mounted on hoops, around which the skins are wrapped, and are held in place by cords or leather thongs laced from one hoop to another. At an early stage in the lacing, the cords have a multiple V appearance. They are drawn tight, and further tension on the skins, as required, is achieved by interlacing another cord around the circumference of the drum near one or both heads. Surplus cord is finally wound around the drum at the middle narrow part, giving the appearance of a belt. Inasmuch as one head is larger than the other, a considerable range of tones is possible on each instrument. Sometimes a bata contains a large nut within it, said to be an "African" palm nut. The three bata are of different sizes, varying from about eighteen to thirty inches in length. The longest is called Iya. Its larger head usually has a thick circular patch of a red resinlike substance applied to the surface near the center, the function of which is considered to be moderate damping. Around the body of the Iya near the large head is a belt of harness-type bells which is called tchaworo. The second drum, called Itotele, may or may not have a damping patch on its larger head. The smallest drum is called Okonkolo or Amele. The

The substance of this introduction to the musical examples is extracted from "Musical Instruments of Cuba," by Harold Courlander, The Musical Quarterly, July 1941. Music notations are from Los Bailes y el Teatro de los Negros en el Folklore de Cuba, *by Fernando Ortiz, Havana, 1951.*

sacred name of the Lucumi drums is Ana, and the profane name Ilu.

Each bata is firmly held in the lap of its drummer (called olori) by a cord passing around and under the knees, and the right hand usually plays the deep tones—that is, on the larger drumhead. The Iya is always in the center, flanked by the smaller instruments, and its player—designated as kpuataki—is considered to be the chief.

The traditionally made bata is carved from a length of log, but stave and barrel drums are frequently substituted. A usual part of the instrumental ensemble is a large oblong rattle made of a calabash, with an external network of bead strikers. The beads are sometimes glass, sometimes made of mani nuts. The technique of playing consists of striking the base of the rattle sharply against the free hand, producing in addition to the sound of the strikers a musical tone. The rattle sounds are not indicated in the following examples of Lucumi liturgical music.

TWO LITURGICAL SONGS OF THE LUCUMI

In the Eya Aranla cycle of liturgical pieces, the Lucumi deities, each in his turn, are praised and invoked by drumming, singing and dancing. While some cycles of Lucumi music are performed in nonpublic settings, the Eya Aranla performance is public and has a festive atmosphere. Normally, more than one honoring song can be sung to an orisha, or deity. The following notations are for songs to the deities Legba and Ogun.

Lucumi Dance-Song for Eleggua (Legba)

FIRST PIECE OF THE EYA ARANLA CYCLE

Andante – Tempo: 6 X 8

Y ba ra go o mo yu ba

Okonkolo

Itotele

Iya

Lucumi Dance-Song for Ogun

FOURTH PIECE OF THE EYA ARANLA CYCLE

y__ le gbon gbon lo ku a___ o gun

gua ni__ le___ o gun gua lo na___

__ y__ le gbon gbon lo ku__ a é.

RITES OF THE ABAKWA SECRET SOCIETY

The Abakwa cabildo, or lodge, in Cuba is a direct and explicit inheritance from the Efik and Ekoi peoples of West Africa's Calabar Coast. The term Abakwa refers to the region and people of Akwa, where this secret society flourished in West Africa. Because of the Calabar origin of the society it is also called (with an inversion of the l and the r) Carabali. The Ekoi-Efik antecedent of the Cuban Abakwa lodge was called Egbo. It wielded considerable influence and power in Calabar even as late as the beginning of the twentieth century. What is most remarkable is that its offspring in Cuba preserved so much of the Calabar tradition and so much vitality. The Abakwa society has an impressive Ekoi-Efik vocabulary, in which some of the most learned members are able to carry on conversations. A good many words in Carabali correspond exactly with terms used by the Egbo group. For example, the chief functionary is called, in both Calabar and Cuba, iyámba; the carrier of the ritual rattle is called morwá; and other officials, isué. Many of the rites are virtually identical. And the costumes of the participants in the Cuban ceremonies and rites remain remarkably similar to those of the West African Egbo. Cuban Abakwa music—singing and drumming—is distinctive and readily recognized; there is hardly any doubt that members of the Egbo society in West Africa would recognize it as their own.

The Cuban Abakwa society is a fraternal order whose membership may cut through the various religious cults. A devotee of the Lucumí cult, for example, may also be an Abakwa ocobío, or brother. Membership confers prestige, and it offers various kinds of mutual aid. An ocobío's funeral arrangements and all the associated rites and ceremonies are taken care of by the society. If an ocobío finds himself in personal difficulty, he may appeal to the society for help. Membership requires a period of "testing" and instruction, initiation, and a complex of responsibilities and obligations.

The Abakwa structure is rigid and formal, and the functions of its officialdom are clearly delineated. The topmost authority is the iyámba, the "king" or chief, under whom serve numerous officers with specific duties. There are the isué eribó, or deputy chief; avasóngu, or subchiefs; the macongo, or war chief; the anasaco, doctor and diviner; the empeco, scribe and secretary; the mosongo, who assists the war chief; the embacara, or judge; and a variety of others. Followers of the supreme chief are called abanekwe.

Abakwa ceremonies are constructed out of esoteric symbolism understood only by members of the brotherhood, dancing (only for principal performers), mimicry and pantomime, drumming and singing, ritualistic drama, sacrifices on special occasions, the theatrical appearance of representatives of the world of the dead, and, above all, mystery. The cast includes a priestly authority called morwa and a variety of costumed figures representing visitors from the dead, called ireme (or, in Spanish, diablitos), each with a particular character and function. One is an ireme of discipline and order, another an ireme of peacekeeping. Still others have such roles as instructing initiates or enforcing Abakwa law. There is a warrior ireme, an executioner ireme, and an ireme who rules in the woods and mountains.

One of the important functions of the priestly authority known as the morwa is to guide and control the visiting demonlike figures who come from "the invisible side of the world." The morwa leads the iremes out of the lodge or "temple," controlling them by ritual words, by songs, by use of the sacred quadruple gourd rattle called erikunde, and above all by the magical powers he has within him. The morwa makes the dead spirit perform all of the actions required of him. Compelled by the powers of the priest, the ireme moves and acts in dancelike postures and motions to the accompaniment of music made by four drums, an iron or brass bell, and a set of basket rattles. When a particular ireme's part in a ceremony is ended, the priest compels him to return to the lodge. There the ireme vanishes and returns once more to the invisible side of the world.

In Africa this belief in visitors from the land of the dead was once widespread, and it is still prevalent in some tribal traditions. The Yoruba, for example, traditionally regarded their Egunguns as visitors or messengers from the dead. Like the Egungun of the Yoruba, the Cuban ireme is feared by spectators, even by the fraternal brothers who are privy to the Abakwa ritual.

At least as early as the mid-nineteenth century the Abakwa diablitos made public appearances in the streets of Havana and other cities at certain festival times. As representatives of dead African ancestors they were subjects of awe and terror. In 1880 the Abakwa society and others as well were banned from making public appearances, and their secret activities were proscribed. But the Abakwas continued their rites underground until early in the present century when the ban was rescinded, and once again, from time to time, the visitors from the land of the dead were seen in public places.

An Abakwa Initiation

The initiation ceremony took place in a rectangular court about a hundred feet long and lined on two sides by unpainted weather-beaten houses. At one end of the court was the lodge, a large wooden building with a white six-pointed star just below the ridge and doors painted in checkered patterns. About two hundred persons were present in the court, some of them spectators, others ocobios (brothers), members of the Abakwa society. The only light came from oil lamps hung at various places and from wooden torches carried back and forth, from one

Based on "Abakwa Meeting in Guanabacoa," by Harold Courlander, Journal of Negro History, Vol. XXIX, 1944. The ceremony described took place in 1941 in Guanabacoa, a suburb of Havana.

strategic place to another, by several designated participants. While the most secret portions of the ritual were conducted within the lodge itself, the court was filled with movement and the din of drums.

Four drummers and an ekon (bell) player stood under a palm to one side of the court. Ocobios encircled them tightly and sang Abakwa songs. Behind the ocobios male spectators pressed close to get a view of the scene in the dim light. Women spectators stood at one side of the court. The singers dramatized the words of their songs by gesticulating, posturing, and sometimes pointing fingers at one another. From time to time a new singing leader took over. One of the singers close to the drums broke into a dance. His movements suggested mimicry, though the meaning was apparent only to the other ocobios, who encouraged him with rhythmic hand clapping. While most of the participants were black, there were a number of whites among them.

Suddenly the lodge doors swung wide open and a solemn-faced personage in a turban, walking backwards, descended the stairs to the court. In front of him he held the erikunde, the cruciform gourd rattle used for controlling the "demons" or spirits from the dead. As he reached the ground level the rattle carrier, called morwa, watched the doorway intently. For a moment the doorway was empty, then it was filled by the masked and costumed figure of the ireme. This "diablito," as the ireme is sometimes called, had a cone-shaped head surmounted by a small tassel. Affixed tightly to the back of the conical head was a small disk-shaped hat. A single green eye glared from the forehead. He wore a full raffia skirt and had raffia cuffs around his wrists and ankles. Around his waist was a heavy leather belt strung with numerous small bells that sounded as he moved. Only his feet and hands were uncovered. In one hand he clenched a cylindrical bundle of straws.

The ireme crouched, postured and hesitated, then he sprang forward, following the morwa who controlled him with the erikunde. He bounded down the stairs three or four at a time, conveying the sense of a wild force. He advanced and retreated, his green eye fixed on the morwa who drew him along yet kept him at a distance. The ireme followed the morwa to the drums. There he performed a wild and unrestrained dance for a few moments, after which, knees far apart and toes pointed outward, he fled back into the lodge.

The drummers and other musicians now moved across the court to a small rectangle at the side of the lodge. With them was a player of the Abakwa basket rattles, who had joined the group unnoticed. Occasionally, when the drumming stopped for brief periods, the weird and unearthly sound of the uyo, a friction drum, could be heard coming from somewhere within the lodge.

Again the doors of the lodge opened. Six blindfolded men were brought out, their legs and chests bared. An Abakwa official, title unknown, marked their bodies in yellow chalk with a pattern of x's, after which he sprayed rum on them from his mouth. Someone came with a tile tray of burning incense which he held in turn before each of them.

The six initiates kneeled in a row and put their heads to the ground.

The ireme appeared from the lodge again, a baton in one hand and, in the other, a large live rooster held by the legs. He danced around the first prostrated man, rubbed the rooster lightly across his back, encircled him again, and finally stood astride him, going through highly stylized but immediately recognizable motions of a copulating rooster. He ended by swishing his raffia tail. He danced away through the crowd, but reappeared almost instantly, going through the same movements with the second man. Again he danced away through the crowd, returning soon to the third man, then the fourth, fifth and sixth. Afterwards they all retired inside the lodge. The friction drum kept roaring and wailing throughout the night. The drummers and singers moved back again to their original place under the palm tree.

Very late in the night a second ireme danced out of the building and across the court to the palm tree. He sat at the base and rubbed his back against it, trembled, seemed to doze, then he arose and followed the morwa back through the doors.

The first ireme, with the green eye, appeared again in the center of a procession which came from the lodge. In the group were the initiates, their backs and chests marked with blood. Their heads were now covered with yellow symbols in chalk. Some of the ocobios carried candles and torches. One of them carried a ceremonial drum dressed with the tail feathers of a rooster. Another carried a tile of burning incense. Still another held between his teeth the head of the sacrificed cock. The morwa carried a plush upholstered tray, at each corner of which was an upright quiver of feathers. He walked backward, leading the ireme. He seemed to be protecting the initiates from the ireme. This ireme went to a second tree in the court, where he sat for a moment. Then he arose and the procession retired to the lodge. It was then four o'clock in the morning.

(For an African comparison see Appendix III, p. 570 ff.)

Abakwa Drumming

From La Africanía de la Música Folklorica de Cuba, by Femando Ortiz, Havana, 1950

Some Passages from Abakwa Songs

SACRIFICE SONG

From Los Bailes y el Teatro de los Negros en el Folklore de Cuba, *by Fernando Ortiz, Havana, 1950.*

FUNERAL SONG

E kue kue cha bia__ ka mo kon go ma che be re____ e
kue kue o mo kon go ma che be re____ e
kue kue cha bia ka mo kon go ma che be re.

PROCESSIONAL, REENTERING THE LODGE

O yao se se ri bo ya o__ o yao
Ba ro ko nan sa o o yao se se ri bo ya o.

PROCESSIONAL, COMING OUT OF THE LODGE

San ga ka ñon bo ne kuen tu ma san ga ma
ñon e ku i ton go.

HAITIAN RELIGIOUS TRADITIONS: VODOUN

When the African slaves stepped ashore in the New World they brought with them highly developed religious beliefs and attitudes toward life. But Africa was a continent of many cultures and nations, and its belief systems varied. The Congo African did not have the same view of the natural and supernatural as the Senegalese, for example; and even neighboring peoples such as the Ibos, the Yorubas, and the Mahis did not have common religious traditions. Yet in the strange new land that was Haiti, the common elements in their religious beliefs were accented. In time a new composite religious system emerged. It was called Vodoun.

The preponderance of Africans in Haiti came from the region of Dahomey, Togo, Nigeria, and the Congo River basin. Among them the

Extracted, with minor changes, from The Drum and the Hoe, Life and Lore of the Haitian People, © *1960 by Harold Courlander. Reprinted by permission of the Regents of the University of California.*

Dahomeans seem to have been the most influential, and it was they who provided the framework for the Afro-Haitian religious system.

The word Vodoun itself is Dahomean in origin. Among the Fon-speaking people of West Africa it signified "spirit," or "deity." In Haiti the word came to be applied in a general sense to all the activities of cult life, from the ritual of the "temple" to the songs and dances, though in some old songs it still applies specifically to the idea of a supernatural spirit. However, the Congo word *loa* came to be used to designate the deities.

In a literal sense, Vodoun in Haiti consists of the rites, beliefs, and practices of the Vodoun cult, built around the similar religious systems of the Dahomeans and the Nagos. In a wider sense it applies to similar but distinct ritual activities of other cults. The Ibo-Kanga rites and dances are in a specific sense "not quite" Vodoun. The rites in the Congo-Guinée cult group—made up of Congo, Bambarra, "Guinée," and miscellaneous elements—have separate practices and deities of their own, and are often regarded as not Vodoun at all. Yet the term Vodoun is used in a generic sense to include all these rites, and examination of the beliefs and activities of these cult groups shows that they have drawn in considerable measure upon a common inheritance.

Vodoun is clearly more than ritual of the cult temple. It is an integrated system of concepts concerning human behavior, the relation of mankind to those who have lived before, and to the natural and supernatural forces of the universe. It relates the living to the dead and to those not yet born. It "explains" unpredictable events by showing them to be consistent with established principles. In short, it is a true religion which attempts to tie the unknown to the known and thus create order where chaos existed before.

As in Dahomey, it is not a system imposed from above but one which pushes out from below. It is bred and nurtured in the family, in the towns and in the fields. It is common law, with deep roots in an unbroken and continuous past. The priests of Vodoun do not control it and direct its course. They, like the least fortunate peasant, simply move about within it and make use of its resources. They are its servants and its interpreters. In their cult centers, the principles of Vodoun are brought into sharp focus and dramatized. Vodoun is democratic in concept. Any man or woman may have direct contact with the deities or dead ancestors without the intervention of the cult priest. There is no place or situation beyond the influence of the loa or beyond the limits of Vodoun. At every crossroads is the spirit of the crossroads guardian, Legba, and on every long trail is the spirit of the Master of the Highway.

The cult priest nevertheless plays a significant and essential role. He translates beliefs that otherwise might tend to become amorphous into formalized action. He is a teacher, a repository of cult learning, and a vital catalyst. He gives form to abstraction, and practical meaning to symbols. He is the intellectualizing agency of a tremendous emotional force. Through his knowledge of the substance and forms of Vodoun, his experience in dealing with the loa, and in some instances his capacity to set magical forces into action, the cult priest is a dynamic power within his community.

Though the making of ritual magic and ouangas (aggressive magic directed against individuals) is within the realm of the cult priest's activities, these things are part of Vodoun only in a subsidiary sense. Magic lurks on the periphery of Vodoun. It has little or no place in the placating of the deities or the dead. It concerns the relationship of the living with one another and with loups-garous and baka (demons). Although cult rituals include various pouin (magic) ceremonies, the cult priest draws upon magic as he draws upon other mystic arts and fields of learning—leaf doctoring, divination, Catholic ritual, and Masonic symbolism. He attempts to bring together all thinking that widens the scope of Vodoun, in order to strengthen his hand to deal with all aspects of the natural and supernatural. But the reputable cult priest does not dabble in "black" magic—the kind that maims or destroys human beings. One who does so is said to "work with two hands": one for the loa and one for evil. (The expression "serving with two hands" is also applied to a cult chief who deals with deities of more than one "nation.") Many a cult priest in making his ritual flour drawings on the earth holds his left hand behind his back and draws with his right, giving testimony that he "works with one hand" only.

Each cult priest maintains his own cult temple, or hounfor. There are no cult officials above him, as there is no formal religious organization beyond the hounfor itself. Within his own special community he is therefore the chief religious functionary, the apex of an intratemple social organization. Under the cult priest, ordinarily, there are two grades of assistants, and below them two classes of servitors.

The cult priest is usually referred to as a houngan, a Fon (Dahomean) title signifying "spirit chief." Sometimes he is called gangan (a Bantu word meaning "conjuror" or "doctor") or capla. He also is known by the title boco or bocor, which seems to be derived from bocono, the diviner or priest of the Dahomean Fa cult. The bocor is, in fact, sometimes referred to as a divineur, and he is regarded by some Haitians as a clairvoyant and a practitioner of magic. As in Dahomey, the bocor in Haiti fortells fate through the throwing of shells or chips, much in the manner of the secular game mayamba. He also reads destiny with small sticks or ashes. In earlier days the cult priest was sometimes known by the Yoruba name babalao, a title which has been corrupted to papaloi. A female cult leader is known as a mambo. She is presumed to have, in a general way, the same powers as the houngan, though in some quarters her connaissance, or "understanding," is not regarded so highly, and her status is believed to be somewhat lower.

Directly under the houngan is his chief assistant, the laplace, and perhaps a little below him on the ladder, the mambo caille. The laplace is regarded as the vice-houngan, and he assumes responsibility for running the hounfor in the absence of his chief. The mambo caille, a woman, runs the cult center in the absence of both the houngan and the laplace. One step farther down the ladder is the houngénicon, who acts as a sort of chief of the main body of devotees. These high-ranking assistants to the houngan are sometimes called badjicans, or keepers of the altar.

The servitors of the cult are known as hounsi, or "spirit wives," a name that was given to certain categories of cult servants in Dahomey. There are two main groups of hounsi: kanzo (those who have passed through a ritual fire test) and bossale (those whose loa are wild or untamed). The loa makes his appearance in Vodoun ritual by possessing ("mounting") one or more of the participants. When these possessions first occur, the possessed persons lapse into a kind of frenzy without controls or direction. They may stagger, fall, and go into convulsions. The deity must be controlled so that he will not harm the person whose body he takes over. The houngan eventually establishes a conditioned, formalized response to possession; and once this is achieved, the loa is regarded as having been tamed. The hounsi bossale then becomes eligible for elevation to the status of kanzo. The term kanzo means "to tie fire," that is, to conquer or show mastery over fire. Demonstrations of supremacy of possessed persons over flames, hot coals, and red-hot metal characterize many Vodoun rituals. In the kanzo ritual the initiate must undergo the test of boiling oil.

Among the hounsi there are some who have special duties or functions. There is the reine silence, for example, whose job is to maintain order. The one assigned to cook the various sacrifices is called the hounsi cuisinière, and so on.

There is no single, clear-cut process for becoming a Vodoun priest. A man with special talents may rise from the rank of hounsi and eventually become a houngan by succession. Or a person with a strong connaissance may simply feel the call—sometimes in a dream—and establish himself as a houngan or bocor. If such a man demonstrates that he is "strong," a following will gather around him to constitute his société.

When a houngan dies, his cult center may be abandoned, or it may be taken over by another established houngan or by the deceased man's protege. Frequently the laplace will inherit the cult temple and all that goes with it. Acquisition of a cult center by inheritance is looked upon as a means of keeping an established hounfor intact. The man who wishes to achieve the rank of houngan applies to the oldest and most venerable cult priest in the district and announces that he wishes to receive the asson (the ritual rattle) that is, to become a houngan. If the elder priest approves and wishes to sponsor the younger man's elevation, he consults other reputable houngans and arranges for a special service for purification and investiture. The elder cult priest conducts the ceremonies. He is regarded as especially wise because of his age and long experience in dealing with the loa, whose approval of the candidate's elevation is needed. He is also regarded as being on more intimate terms with the family ancestors who, likewise, must be in accord with the proceedings. The candidate for the asson is confined within the hounfor for a number of days, during which he takes purification baths and participates in other rituals. The rites that take place during this period are prescribed by the elder priest who has assumed responsibility. When the purification is ended, the candidate emerges into the peristyle (roofed court) to participate in the general service, and to undergo further tests.

Present during the ceremonies are all the principal houngans of the region—men who will be friendly associates of the new priest or, possibly, unfriendly competitors. The candidate is tested on his knowledge of how to use the asson and the tiny hand bell, and in the course of the service he is mounted by the loa who is the chief protector of the cult temple. Animals are sacrificed, and all the loa sacred to the hounfor are invoked and asked for their approval and support. But it is not only the loa and the dead who must indicate their approval. The elder houngan polls the hounsi kanzo on whether they will accept their new cult chief and follow him. He also asks the chief drummer, who polls his assistant drummers. It is taken for granted that the decision is in the hands of the hounsi. The consensus is known before the actual service, but the formality of asking the question is observed. Should the hounsi refuse to accept the candidate for the asson, the elevation cannot take place.

It is easily observed that no two hounfors are exactly alike. They differ in many details. But, in general, the cult establishment consists of a central building of one or more rooms with an adjoining court, or peristyle, over which there is a covering—usually a straw roof. The covering, called the tonnelle, is supported by a number of poles, one of which is placed squarely in the center of the court. This center pole is the focus of most of the ritual activities. The loa who descend upon the service enter by way of this pole. The ritual vèvès, or flour paintings are made at its foot. Around it all the dancing takes place. On certain rare occasions when rituals are held in the open, a carefully selected tree becomes the center post—though it is by no means certain that the po'teau mitan is not, in fact, a symbolic tree.

The building adjoining the peristyle contains the inner sanctum. Here are deposited the paraphernalia of the cult, such as ritual bottles and jars, flags of the société, and the iron kettles used in various ceremonies. On the walls there may be primitive paintings of the special loa of the hounfor, or perhaps of his symbol. The loa of the sea, Agwé, may be represented by a ship. Damballa, the serpent-rainbow loa, may be represented by a snake or a rainbow. Usually there are colored lithographs of Catholic saints, who have both Catholic and African names. And there are hand-beaten iron crosses, dishes containing Indian celts in which loa are believed to reside, gourd bowls, and carved wooden double and triple bowls used for services to dead twins and triplets. Upon the altar place, called badji, there are the criches or govis, earthen jars or bottles in which rest the loa removed from the heads of people who have died. Sometimes special niches are built on the hounfor grounds for the deities. Each cult priest designs his hounfor in his own way.

Many services are held outside the hounfor and the peristyle. Some rituals, such as animal sacrifices and "talking to the loa below the water," may take place some distance from the cult buildings. Indeed, various Vodoun ceremonies may be held at waterfalls, at the seashore, in sacred groves, in ordinary homes, in a boat at sea, or under a sacred tree.

The rites of the hounfor are almost without number. They are associated with the supplication or conciliation of virtually countless deities, each of which has his own special service. There are services in multitudinous combinations and permutations for the dead, for twins, for albinos, and for unborn children. There are ceremonies for the elevation of hounsi and for initiation, smoke and fire ordeals, and tests of other kinds. There are mangé loa (feasts for the deities) and mangé morts (feasts for the dead). There are services for the sick, for the crops, and for the harvest. In one context or another, Vodoun relates to nearly every aspect and phase of life—and its counterpart, death. Since every region, every locality, and, in fact, almost every hounfor has developed its own ritual out of the common materials, it is possible to see hundreds of ceremonies without ever seeing precisely the same one twice. Yet the common elements bind them all together.

A Hounfor Seen at the Turn of the Century

In 1906 the French writer Eugène Aubin saw and described a hounfor in the Cul-de-Sac Plain, a few miles from Port-au-Prince. His description suggests that the physical characteristics and concept of the hounfor have changed little in the intervening years.

[The] hounfor is fronted by a peristyle, which is used for the Vodoun dances and services; it is a large area, with a floor of beaten earth, covered with a straw roof. On three sides the walls rise to support the roof; on the fourth there is the inscription:

Société la Fleur de Guinée

Roi d'Engole

[Flower of Africa Society

King of Angola]

indicating the name of the patron of the society [the loa Roi Angole, or Wangol], over which the houngan presides. The hounfor is an ordinary

From En Haiti, *by Eugène Aubin, Paris, 1910.*

house, a little larger than average. The sanctuary contains a principal pé [altar], running the whole length of the room on one side, and another altar, a little smaller, in one of the corners. These pés are altars largely made of brick, in which the underpart is decorated with hearts and stars in relief; above, draperies hang from the ceiling. The lateral pé is divided into three compartments. There are, therefore, four sections in all, consecrated to each of the loa served in the hounfor: Aguay Aoyo [Agwé Woyo], Damballa, Ogoun Badagry, and Loco [Loko], Nago King, Maître Aguay is represented by the customary little boat; a medallion is consecrated to Monsieur Damballa, shown holding two snakes in his hand; a figure on horseback represents Ogoun Badagry, with a woman at one side holding a flag; Papa Loco is pictured in full uniform, smoking a pipe and fanning himself. The walls are covered with religious paintings [Catholic lithographs]. The back of the altar is occupied by numerous carafes in baked clay, called canaris, which contain the . . . mystères [spirits taken from the heads of the dead] gathered in the hounfor; in front are bottles of wine, liqueurs and vermouth presented to them in homage; then the plates, the cups for the mangers-marassas [feasts for the twin spirit], crucifixes, hand bells, assons for directing the dance or calling the loa; plates filled with polished stones [celts] inherited from the Indians—"thunder stones," symbols of Damballa, which Saugo [Sobo] the god of lightning hurls from the sky into the enclosure of his favorite papaloi [houngan]. Beside these miraculous stones are many coins of copper or silver [property of the loa]. The loa . . . possess coins of Joseph Bonaparte, King of Spain, minted in 1811; of Frederick VII of Denmark, 1859; of Charles IV of Spain, 1783, and of President Boyer, dated year 27 and year 30 of Haitian Independence. On the ground there is placed a coconut-oil lamp; in the corner, the flags of the hounfor and the saber of [the] laplace, the man who acts as master of ceremonies in the services. In the court, the bases of four sacred trees . . . are surrounded by circles of masonry [low brick walls]. These reposoirs are inhabited by the loa Legba, Ogoun, Loco and Saugo [Sobo or Sogbo].

TWO VODOUN RITUALS

Service for Agwé, God of the Sea

This is a description by Maya Deren of the
final stage of a long service honoring the god
of the sea, Agwé Woyo—the launching of a

Extracted from Divine Horsemen, the Living Gods of Haiti, by Maya Deren.
London, Thames and Hudson, 1953. By permission of the publishers.

**miniature sailing vessel heavily loaded with
sacrificial offerings, and the sacrifice of a ram.**

The first sounds of preparation began at three in the morning. The offerings and all the enormous quantity of paraphernalia were packed in baskets of every shape and size. At four the two large open trucks, of the kind used for carting gravel, arrived, and benches were lined up in them. Then the loading began: the drums and the ram and the barque d'Agwé and a huge seven-tiered white wedding cake, and the chickens and the pigeons and the baskets of food and the ceremonial flags and much more; and finally, after that, the people, who seemed, by then, to number several hundred, but probably added up to about fifty. Then, with the more agile hanging on to the framework, the trucks lumbered off down the road.

The drums set up the initial beats, and the blowers of the trumpet and the conch shell, who were perched on the roof of the cab, picked it up, and the voices lifted into the cold dawn. In every small community clustered along the road, the people ran out and cheered us on. Eventually the trucks left the highway and turned down a tiny, rutted, mud road which cut directly toward the sea. It was obvious, soon, that the mud would make it impossible to reach the shore by truck. We pulled to a stop and unloaded at a point which turned out to be a good two miles from our destination. The barque, the baskets of food, everything was hoisted up on the heads, and, in single file, safari fashion, we started out for the sea on foot. The sun was rapidly growing hotter, while the mud gave way to a gray, oozing clay in which one sank deeper and deeper with each step. When it no longer seemed humanly possible to go any farther, the screen of trees which we had been approaching thinned out, and there, anchored a good distance from shore (for the ocean floor sloped gradually here), was the sailboat which awaited us, its bright trimmings dancing in the wind. On the shore we gathered once more for ritual, vevers [vèvès], salutations, songs. And again everything was hoisted to the heads of the people, even the ram had to be carried this time, and the safari waded into the water.

It was over five feet deep at the boat, but, as they said, the gods were with us, for nothing was lost and everyone managed to clamber in and set about arranging things in·the impossibly small space. It was already ten o'clock, and, there being no shade from the sun, the heat was soon unendurable. Those who had no hats wrapped handkerchiefs around their heads, moistening them from time to time. The clothes, initially wet from the wading, were kept wet now by the perspiration which poured from everyone. Those who were responsible for arranging the barque were particularly unfortunate, since they worked in the deep open hold of the ship, into which no breeze penetrated.

In the flurry of ritual preparation no one had thought to bring fresh drinking water, and within a short time every face seemed rigid with the effort of endurance. Lips were painfully parched. There was practically no conversation. Those who were concerned with the final arrangement of the barque communicated by gestures. Grouped together, silently passing the things from hand to hand, or indicating placement to one another, they seemed to be dancing a strange, cryptic ballet in slow motion, seen through the shimmering veil of rising heat.

But they sang, and the drums beat and the trumpet and conch shell called, over and over. In the intervals between songs, the grating and ringing of the mambo's rattle and bell was the only sound. She stood near the mast, apparently oblivious of everything, sounding her rattle, and from time to time she lifted the two white chickens which she held in one hand, toward the cardinal points, signaling Agwé. They made no protest, and the ram, too, had been stunned into silence by the heat.

Again they chanted—songs on behalf of sailors, and in praise of La Sirène, and, for Agassou, and, above all, in praise of Agwé and the mighty thunder of his cannon, the flash of his lightning strokes. . . .

Apparently we were nearing, now, the island beneath the water, although I was never to discover exactly how this was determined. Suddenly a certain haste was made to complete the preparations. The barque was now piled high with every conceivable food and delicacy, arranged to make the finest possible display, and topped with the huge white wedding cake. The houngan who was assisting her took the chickens from the mambo, killed them with a deft movement, and laid them also on the barque.

At this first offering, two women were almost simultaneously possessed by Agwé. The initial convulsive movement occurred so suddenly that almost no one had remarked it, and now their faces, which had been normally feminine, planed off, imperceptibly, into a masculine nobility. Water was drawn up from the sea in a pail and poured over them, since normally Agwé, being a water divinity, would have immediately immersed himself in the basin. Those who were near saluted the arrival of the divinity, and, through each of the women, Agwé spoke a few words of greeting in a voice which gurgled as if with rising air bubbles, and seemed truly to come from the waters. His mood was not displeased, but it was sober. The houngan, conscience-stricken, began to explain that he, too, would soon make a ceremony. The two Agwés listened to him, their eyes at once forgiving and somehow detached. One thought: perhaps they forgive because they are detached. And, with the same air of noble, gentle sadness, they looked slowly from person to person, from the barque of food, to the mambo. There was something in their regard which stilled everyone. One had seen it in the faces of those who prepare to leave and wish to remember that to which they will no longer return. They met each other's eyes, and as a way was cleared for them, approached each other, and crouched down in an embrace of mutual consolation, their arms about each other's shoulders, their foreheads lowered, each on the other's shoulder. So mirrored, they wept.

The people in the boat were accustomed, now, to the fact that their great gods wept, and they accepted it, sometimes saying to them, as one would to a child, that they mustn't weep. Yet, after all, one could not hope to understand all the moods of the gods, and there was work to be done, and the ceremony to be continued. The houngenikon began a song, the drums, trumpet and shell joined in, and the chorus. The preparations gathered speed, and, with everyone moving deftly so as not to disturb or intrude upon the Agwés, the ram was passed forward. One hardly had time to observe it before the animal was lifted to the rail, where it balanced for a moment, and then plunged into the water.

Apparently we were now directly over the sacred "zilet" for the last ritual consecration of the barque was accomplished with almost frantic speed. It was so heavily laden that six men were required to lift it to the rail. A cry of "Attention!" went up, the boom swung widely in the opposite direction, the boat swerved and tilted sharply on its side. In that split second, when the water lay almost level with the rail, the men slid the barque on to the surface of the sea. Our boat lurched and righted itself and there, below us, and already behind, the barque was drifting swiftly away in our backwash. It looked incredibly lovely, the high-piled offerings, crowned with the sparkling white cake, drifting in the deep blue of the sea. As we all watched it silently, it seemed to hesitate to a stop, and then, as if a great hand had reached up from below and grasped it, it disappeared abruptly into the quiet water.

The houngenikon, the drums, the chorus burst forth all at once, into a vivid song of "réjouissance." It was the first song of joyous nature since the beginning of the trip. Beside me stood the painter, his eyes fixed on the spot where his barque had disappeared. He was singing joyously. Everyone had worked hard, and had given, each in his own fashion; but for the painter there must have existed an image of special pride in his mind's eye, as he saw the fabulous submarine palace where the great Papa Agwé, pleased with his servant's labor, was already motioning his illustrious guests toward his banquet table.

The Degradation Ceremony

> The anthropologist George Eaton Simpson here describes the ritual of removing a "spirit" from the head of a dead person, in this instance a dead houngan or cult priest. If not removed, the "spirit" can cause trouble and difficulties for the living.

The Haitian peasant believes that those who have some unusual ability or some special skill in dealing with the supernatural world are inspired and assisted by a "spirit." In northern Haiti the term "l'esprit" may be used to indicate a loa, but it may also mean a special talent of any kind. It is the latter concept to which we refer here. At death the "spirit" must be removed and transferred to another person. In this way the deceased is reduced to the common level. The ordinary grand-don (prosperous peasant) is not degraded; but a good singer, a père-savanne (a peasant who has memorized parts of Catholic rituals), a

Extracted from "Four Vodun Ceremonies," by George Eaton Simpson, Journal of American Folklore, *April–June, 1946. By permission of Dr. Simpson and the American Folklore Society.*

houngan or any one who possesses some special ability must be given a degradation ceremony. The more important the dead man the more elaborate the rites. There is no notion at all of disgrace in this ceremony as there is in the military procedure of demoting or degrading an officer. . . .

While the news of a houngan's death is spreading through the countryside, the members of his family occupy themselves with arrangements for the wake. Finally the crowd assembles in the tonnelle (a shelter erected near the house for this occasion) and the yard. The women weep and cry out praises for the dead man, and both men and women partake freely of the cassava cakes, meat, coffee, and tafia (cheap rum) distributed by the servingwomen. In a large room of the house the regular religious ceremony is taking place: prayers for the dead, morning prayers, evening prayers, litanies for the saints, prayers with beads. The père-savanne sees to it that nothing he knows about is omitted. Catholic chants of all sorts, interspersed with prayers, are included by the singers. In an adjoining room the principal ceremony is being performed by the family, the relatives, close friends, flag-bearers, children carrying rattles and a handbell, and the houngan's entourage of petites feuilles (children cured by the dead man), badjicans (assistants), and pupils. There may be two or three houngans present to share the obligation and the pleasure of conducting this service for their colleague, their former rival, and perhaps their former enemy.

There are so many people in the small room that it is almost impossible for anyone to move at all. Near the body, which is covered with a sheet, are placed a jug and a new canari (a large earthen jar). The officiating houngan makes the sign of the cross, mumbles a few ritual formulas, and taking a spoon puts some "manger les morts" (special food for the dead) in the canari: plantains, yams, bananas, tairauts, sweet potatoes, corn meal, roasted corn, bread, cakes, rice, millet, meat, chicken, pistachio, chopped coconut, and other kinds of food. He then adds some water and stirs this mixture. A few drops of water are put in the jug. The other houngans perform the same rite. The family, friends, and others in the room imitate the acts of the houngans with the green branches which they hold in their hands. In a grave voice and with solemn gestures the officiant then appeals to the loas with songs and prayers. He invites them to come to the aid of their faithful servant, to protect him in the other world as they have protected him in this world. Following the songs and prayers the leader pronounces these words:

> Innocent! A good man has left us!
> Mother of children weep!
> Weep, console yourselves.
> Accelon lived among us.
> He is dead!
> Master Pierre Jean-Baptiste lived
> among us.
> He is dead!

General Baptiste lived among us.
He is dead!
Marius who survived them
Has just died!
But Brother Joseph is still with us.
We weep but we console ourselves
    because of him!

The weeping and the cries redouble, but the père-savanne and the houngan carry on. In the other room the père-savanne solemnly intones:

I have only one soul
That it is necessary to save.
By the eternal flame,
I must preserve it.

The officiating houngan speaks directly to the dead man:

Boss Marius, here is a canari that your heirs have especially prepared for you so that in the future you will not have any trouble and demand other sacrifices of them. You others, the dead, you are always unreasonable. Because you have peace you forget that the times are hard and that on this earth we unfortunate men are crushed by suffering. Leave your family in peace after this service, Boss Marius. Do not torment them, and do not send illnesses to their children or misery to their older people. You were always a good father when you were living. Continue to protect your family after death. If you need other services give abundantly to your heirs in order to obtain satisfaction. Oh, good father, good servant, good parent, good friend! Good-bye! Do not forget us as we shall not forget you.

Then he goes to the canari, strikes it three times with a piece of palm bark and chants:

I advise all the loas.
Legba-qui-Sous-Miroi,
La oué! La oué!
In the "capitol of the loas"
A great event has occurred!
Let us pray to God who is in Heaven,
Let us pray to "the loas below."
There is God, our Good Father
Who protects us!

The members of the family respond by dancing in their places and by shaking green branches. The others present dance as well as they can in the crowded room. Another houngan begins a chant:

> Mother in Heaven and Mother below,
> Hé lou-hé! Hé lou-hé!
> None no matter how great he may be is superior to God!

After all sorts of variations the couplet is discontinued and the ceremony for the twins [a special category of the dead] is begun:

> Twins, here is the food
> That we give you.
> Twins, you are accustomed,
> After you have received food from us,
> To say you have not eaten!

This song inspires another houngan:

> Twins-Marassa, the devil cries.
> Dossi! Dossi-dossa! the devil cries!
> Credo, Mother of Twins.
> The devil cries!

This chant is repeated many times and the dance becomes more animated. A badjican takes his turn:

> I say, Mother of Twins,
> Please leave us this room!
> Marassa Twins,
> Please leave us this room!

This is followed by the chant of another houngan:

> Twins, I bring you food and drink,
> Twins, I bring you food and drink,
> Dossi-dossa, Marassa Twins,
> My life is in the hands of God!

The ceremony continues with the officiating houngan chanting and calling the loas. Songs and prayers are interwoven as he again supplicates the saints and the loas, asking them to assist the deceased and the members of his family:

Oh, Mary, Mother of God, Mother of Mercy, Mary Apolita, Mother of Mothers, Mother of Grace! All the Saints, all the Angels, Angels of Heaven, Zanges (loas) of the water, Zanges of the woods, Zanges known and unknown, all the Saints, open the door for this poor man.

Saint Mary, Mother of God,
Pray for all the children.
Aradas, our friend has departed!
Pardon for all of the children!
Say good evening to me, Haitians!
Say good evening to me, Haitians!
It is a mistake to have too much confidence.
Say good evening to me, Haitians!
It is a mistake to have too much confidence.
Laoka, prepare the charms.
Laoka, good dancer,
Prepare the charms, Laoka!

The loas do not fail to respond to these appeals. All of the loas whom Boss Marius served during his life invade the room as person after person becomes possessed by loas Arada, loas Congo, loas known and unknown. All come weeping to pay their tribute to the dead man. It is necessary now to find out how the houngan died, what his last wishes were and what his loas demand. An assistant brings the sacred shells of the dead houngan. The officiant murmurs ritualistic words, throws the shells on the floor, pours tafia three times and lights a candle. The shells are now eagerly consulted.

[There are two more throwings and readings of the shells. In the third reading, the houngan identifies three indifferent men, four loas to whom offerings must be given, two enemies who are plotting against the family, three children of the dead houngan, two curious men, a thunder stone, and a relative seeking protection because he is in danger. The houngan now draws a chart containing symbols for the crossroads and the four cardinal points, for four family loa-protectors, and for liberty and peace.]

The family is praying and declares itself ready to make any sacrifice as the members cry "Pardon! Grace! Save us, Zanges (loas) of our father." This brings the response from the ceremonial leader that the death of Boss Marius is not the death of an ordinary man, that he is now resting in La Ville-au-Camp (capital of the loas which is located "under the water"), and that the loas will continue to protect his descendants provided that they show themselves worthy of protection.

The houngan now goes to the middle of the room and improvises a chant with dolorous rhythm.

Bassin-canari, I am going
To seek a new charm.

The participants repeat the couplet, shaking green branches to the cadence of the song. The officiant continues:

Canari of the houmfort! Canari of the houmfort!
I am going to take a wife
In a balance, canari of the houmfort!

After a few moments he sings:

> Loas-Bolodjoré, seek some leaves
> To cover the canari!

With appropriate gestures the houngan chants:

> Ah! Legba San-Yan, San-Yan!
> We shall break the canari
> To serve all the living!

Houngans, badjicans, petites-feuilles and other participants now pretend to cover the canari while the relatives and friends put pieces of money on top of it. It is time for the officiant to give the signal of adoration:

> Adore, adore, adore!
> All children come and adore!

He makes a cross on the canari and hands his pencil to each member of the family, to the badjicans, and to the others who are in the room, and each one traces the sign of a cross on the canari. It is this act which will constitute proof against the dead in the future in case a new demand is made. Then all kneel. The houngan strikes the front of the canari three times and his act is imitated by everyone. Finally the group marches around the canari with springing steps, and then the direction of the march is reversed.

The rites require several hours and at this point in the ceremony it is about four o'clock in the morning. The serving of food and drink enables the participants to continue although some are now noticeably hoarse. Food for the loas is placed under the trees which are sacred for them, and food for the dead is chosen with care. The time for sending the loas away has arrived. The assistants sing:

> Everything is vanity,
> Lies, fragility.

This couplet is followed by another:

> Come back, sinner.
> It is God who calls you.

Still other songs announce the departure of the loas. Those in the degradation room also give the signal for the sending away of the loas. The leader intones:

> Spirits of Guinea,
> Today we renounce you.

> Seek again a rock
> Which is suitable for you,
> Where you may put your garde (charm).

The procession begins to move with the officiating houngan at the head of it, followed by two badjicans carrying the canari, by a member of the family bearing the jug of water and a little cornmeal, and then by the rest of the assistants and participants. The group in the other room joins them and they all sing:

> Let us send away papa-loi
> To seek the place he must find.

This chant is continued until the procession reaches the crossroads. After an impressive silence, all sorts of gestures to the four cardinal points, invocations, and genuflexions, the houngan chants:

> Congo, open paradise,
> That paradise,
> For us to enter!
> We send away all loas.
> If you continue to disturb,
> You must tell us what you desire.
> We have no further relations with you,
> On earth
> Until we come before God,
> Good courage, friends!
> Peace for the living and the dead!

This chant stimulates new cries and lamentations. Then the houngan asks for and obtains silence. He continues:

> Now we shall dance!
> We shall dance around the broken canari.

Clasping hands they dance around the canari, and the voice of the houngan becomes graver as the solemn moment draws near. He lifts the canari, balances it to the right, balances it to the left, shows it to the stars, incorruptible witnesses of the sacrifice. He starts the final song in a loud voice:

> Simbi! All of you Simbi-loas!
> What must I do?
> I send away the loas!
> Caya! Caya!
> Where may I find refuge?

The participants do an about-face while the houngan raises the canari as high as possible, almost as high as his face, as he repeats the last line:

Where may I find refuge?

With a quick movement the canari is shattered. The food is scattered, the loas are satisfied, and the crowd breaks into a disorderly flight. Great misfortune would befall anyone who was foolish enough to look behind, for the loa-protecteur of the dead houngan would certainly plague the offender until he went to the expense of sending him away again. Misfortune would also come to anyone who was imprudent enough to gather up the few pieces of money left by the houngans for the loas. Surely such a person would not live until the end of the year.

Several hours later the body is placed in its coffin, and the scene which is enacted in the house almost defies description. All the loas (i.e., persons possessed by their loas) responding to the appeals of the houngan jump and whirl, for the loas are not sad in their mourning. Roasted corn, chopped coconut, bread, and cake cut into small pieces are thrown like confetti. The flags salute the body, the coffin is covered again, and the crying is intensified. Four badjicans hoist the coffin to their shoulders. Then the procession forms itself again and starts towards the mysterious spring whose waters have cured many sicknesses which physicians had pronounced incurable.

Oh, Congo! Congo loas!
Oh, loas Arada! All you loas,
Open the door, open the road,
Open the road for us to pass.

But first the coffin is taken to the trees of the loas, and to all of the sacred places. Finally they arrive at the last station. The bearers of the coffin circle the spring several times. The coffin is swung for each of the four cardinal points. The rain of roasted corn is repeated. The houngan has performed the complicated rite and the cortege returns to the house. The père-savanne now takes charge of the participants, and in the midst of piercing cries leads the funeral procession to the village. Those who remain in the house throw water to the left, to the front, and to the right at all the entrances.

Everything has been done properly and the houngan may be proud of his last ceremonies. Nothing can prevent him from enjoying happiness in Ville-au-Camp, the residence of the loas.

TWO HAITIAN DRUM RHYTHMS

Kitta Mouillé, or "Wet" Kitta

This dance associated with the rites of the Congo cult, and takes its name from the loa, or deity, for whom it is performed.

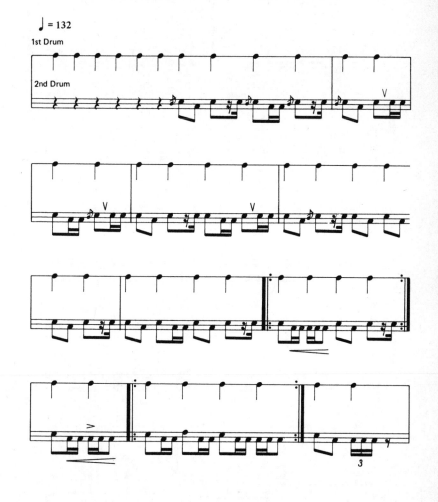

Notated by George Herzog. From Haiti Singing, ©1939, 1967 by Harold Courlander.

Ibo Dance

This Ibo dance takes place in connection with cult rituals held for deities of the Ibo pantheon. The cult centers on religious traditions inherited from the Ibo people of West Africa.

Notated by Mieczslaw Kolinski. From The Drum and the Hoe, Life and Lore of the Haitian People, by Harold Courlander. Berkeley, University of California Press, 1960.

HAITI'S POLITICAL SONGS:
COMMENTS ON THE MIGHTY

The African-style song of social criticism has found no worthier subjects than the historic political figures of Haiti. There is no doubt that the African slaves used this art form to express their feelings toward the white masters as they had used it to comment upon the behavior of their own chiefs and fellow tribesmen. The worthy leaders were praised in song; the unworthy were castigated and their sins, failures, and social misdemeanors publicized in folk songs. By the beginning of the nineteenth century, slavery had come to an end in Haiti. The deep democratic sense of human dignity had outlasted the colonial masters and emerged tempered and sharp. The songs of criticism became not only comments upon political figures but campaign propaganda as well. They dwelt upon the accomplishments or faults of the candidates for political office. Friendly songs sought out every virtue, and invented others, in the man or woman being praised. Unfriendly songs lashed out and lacerated or poked biting fun at the subject, not even sparing his physical deformities.

Yet the political songs are more than statements of merit or fault. Cumulatively they are a kind of folk history of Haiti. No political aspirant ever went unsung by his peasant army, or unridiculed by his opponent's followers. The songs the people sang about their heroes and their enemies recall events and details that formal history has forgotten or ignored. The memory of the folk song is powerful and long. Some of the recollections go back more than a century.

History books tell us that in December, 1843, Major Charles Hérard âiné Rivière was elected to the office of the presidency, and that a new constitution was drawn up by the Constituent Assembly. The new constitution was an accomplishment of the liberal and democratic forces of the nation. It guaranteed certain civil rights to the people. It provided that judges be elected instead of appointed, abolished life terms for presidents, and emphatically declared the army to be within and under the law.

The new President, finding his office without the prerogatives he had expected it to have, openly complained of the restraints imposed on him by the new constitution. He broke campaign promises he had made to the peasants in the south and stirred up antagonisms on every side. Finally, while he was on a military expedition in the Spanish part of the island, revolution broke out at home. His army was beaten by the Dominicans, too, which completely shattered his morale. He fled by ship to Jamaica, the traditional refuge of outgoing Haitian presidents. In memory of his administration the peasants sang:

President Rivière was cross-eyed!
He said that he was going to pillage Belanton's army!
Loot for treasure!
Loot for treasure!
Loot for treasure!
They sent everyone from Lowinsor to Lambam!

The Constitution was founded by Columbus
When the country suffered too much misery!
He said he would do like Henry [Christophe]!
He said he would do like Henry!
He said he would do like Henry!
Make blood run to poison the countryside!

From Colonel Déro to Private Diplaro,
They marched with fanfare, a great army of foot soldiers!
He thought that he was king!
He thought that he was king!
He thought that he was king!
The Spaniards chased him, he ran like a dog after fresh carrion!

Forty-five years later, in 1888, there was a big political rally in Port-au-Prince. The two presidential candidates were General Séide Télémaque and Déus Légitime. Their supporters clashed near the palace, and Télémaque was killed in an exchange of gunfire. Légitime naturally was accused of having murdered his rival, though his supporters would not believe that he had committed such a crime. Evidence for a trial was entirely lacking, and Déus Légitime became president. But feeling ran high, and the followers of Télémaque began to sing:

Listen my friends to the story of Légitime!
Assassin of Séide, and he is President!
Listen well to the story, the people of the north will march
On Port-au-Prince one day to avenge the death of Séide!
Go to the devil, bandit Déus!
Escape, ingrate Déus!
If you lose time, Déus,
Florvil will have you shot!

Légitime had this possibility clearly in his mind. And the next year, when Florvil Gélin Hippolyte marched from the north with an army of *cacos* (peasant troops who hired out to political aspirants), Légitime hurriedly boarded a steamer in the harbor and sailed for Jamaica. Séide Télémaque was considered avenged, as the army bugles still bear wit-

Extracted from The Drum and the Hoe, Life and Lore of the Haitian People,© *1960 by Harold Courlander. Reprinted by permission of the University of California Press and the Regents of the University of California.*

ness. For now when the bugle plays reveille it is supposed to be saying:

> Séide Télémaque, Légitime has fled!
> Séide Télémaque, Légitime has fled!

The new President, Florvil Hippolyte, died in office in 1896. J. N.
Leger, a Haitian historian, tells soberly of Hippolyte's end in the following words.

> For some time the President, who was sixty-nine years old, had
> not been in good health, and disregarding the friendly warning of
> those who were interested in his welfare he refused to give up his
> hard work and to take the rest of which he was in sore need.
> Against the advice of his doctor he decided to undertake a long
> journey to Jacmel. He started on the 24th of March, 1896, at three
> o'clock in the morning, but before he even had time to leave Port-
> au-Prince, he fell from his horse dead in a fit of apoplexy, at a short
> distance from the executive mansion.

The legend of Hippolyte's death passed on in song is not nearly so
dispassionate. It is told that Hippolyte was going out on a drastic puni-
tive trip to Jacmel, where there were rumblings of political opposition
and revolution. Among other things, the President was going to seize
the powerful Vodoun priest Mérisier, regarded as a powerful force in
the opposition. Hippolyte also had sworn to reduce Jacmel to ashes
and wipe out the entire population except one male and one female to
repopulate the land. As he prepared to leave on his mission, his wife
and his son stood by the door to see him off.

> He arose early on Tuesday morning,
> He saddled his horse.
> As he climbed on his horse,
> His hat came off and fell.
>
> L'Hérison [Hippolyte's son] called out, "Papa!"
> He said to him, "Father,
> Your hat has come off and fallen.
> That is already a bad omen."
>
> He replied to him, "My child,
> I have already sent the army ahead,
> My army is already at the city gate,
> I have to go."
>
> Arrived at Pont Gentil,
> He fell unconscious.
> They sent for Dr. Jules,
> "Come to save Florvil Gélin."

Dr. Jules fell on his knees.
He called Mother St. Anne,
He called St. Augustin,
"Come to save Florvil Gélin!"

St. Anne said, "He has to die."
St. Augustin said, "He has to die."
He called St. Jacques Majeur,
"Come to save Florvil Gélin."

Mérisier waited at Jacmel.
He shook his sacred rattle.
He knew what was going on.
All the small holes were filled.[1]

Victoire said
When Florvil dies
She will hold a beautiful party
With all the young people.

CHORUS

We are going to dance
We are going to dance!
We are going this evening
To the house of beautiful Victoire [Hippolyte's young wife]!

The legend of Hippolyte's falling hat is preserved in another folk song called "Panama'm Tombé":

My hat fell down,
My hat fell down,
My hat fell down; whoever is behind,
Pick it up for me!

Mérisier, the Vodoun priest whom Hippolyte regarded as an enemy, was not pleased with the rumors and talk about him that was going the rounds in the capital. His displeasure is recorded in a protest song with a familiar theme:

Mérisier [says] they come to see me to go away and talk, *wo wa é!*
Mérisier [says] they come to see it and go away to talk about it!
What is mine you see!
What is yours you evilly hide!
Mérisier isn't there, sound the salute, wa wa é!

Seven days after Hippolyte's death, General Simon Sam was elected to the presidency. His friends and his enemies had different things to

---

1. *That is, the affair was finished.*

say about him. One song makes a tart comment on Sam's administration.

There was a president,
He was Tirésius Augustin Simon Sam.
If they were all like him,
Haiti would be finished!

In 1902 General Nord Alexis became the chief executive of Haiti. His abilities and accomplishments are still being debated, but he appears to have been a rather lovable old man whom everyone called by the affectionate term Uncle. His administration was fairly stable and prosperous—as prosperity is known in Haiti—and in large measure peaceful. When his election was confirmed, the people were convinced that the nation was in for a period of law and order, and that the constant threat of cacos and brigandage would come to an end. One of the election-year songs goes:

Tin-tin ci-la, tin-tin ci-la, tin-tin ci-la va fi-ni!
Bas-sin Vo-doun, Bas-sin Vo-doun, Bas-sin Vo-doun c'est pou' nous!

We cry long live Nord's army!
The chaos will be ended!
We cry long live Nord's soldiers!
The chaos will be ended!
The chaos, the chaos, the chaos will be ended!
Bassin Vodoun,[2] Bassin Vodoun, Bassin Vodoun is for us!

One of the serious problems confronting Nord Alexis after his election was that of a disappearing national currency. Haitian paper money
was circulating elsewhere in the West Indies and in South America and
was becoming increasingly scarce in Haiti itself. Nord Alexis called in
all the old currency and issued new, with the happy result that large
quantities of money were again seen in the Republic. The common
people who made the songs seem to have been very grateful:

Original pitch — 2 st. ♩ = ±144

A-le-xis Nord Pa-pa ou bon chef— oh! Ou bas nous mo-né,
ou bas nous pa-pier! A-le-xis Nord Pa-pa ou bon chef— oh!
Ou bas nous mo-né, Ou bas nous pa-pier! Nous
pas man-dé ou a-nyien! Nous pas man-dé l'a-gent en-co'! Papa Nord ça nous té man-dé oh chef, C'est bam-boche nous man-dé ou!

2. *Probably a place-name.*

Alexis Nord, Papa, you are a good chief, oh!
You gave us money, you gave us paper!
Alexis Nord, Papa, you are a good chief, oh!
You gave us money, you gave us paper!
We don't ask you for anything more!
We don't ask you again for money!
Papa Nord, only one thing we are going to ask you, chief,
It is a big celebration we ask for!

The president's wife, Çéçé, seems to have been very proud of him and very sure of his talents. When the army bugles blow a general assembly call, they are supposed to be saying:

Çéçé said Alexis Nord is a thoroughly fine man!
Çéçé said Alexis Nord is a thoroughly fine man!
Çéçé said he will quit his office whenever he sees fit!
Çéçé said Uncle Nord is a thoroughly fine man!

Another bugle call, with words attributed to Nord's wife, contains a note of complaint:

Çéçé said waille!
Çéçé said that, said that!
Çéçé said if you don't have any money you can't have a woman!
Çéçé said waille!
Çéçé said that, said that!
Çéçé said we are working our guts out!
Çéçé said waille!

Çéçé said that, said that!
Çéçé said Alexis Nord is president!

Çéçé was not the only one in Haiti who had confidence in Nord's staying power. One popular song of the period goes:

> Alexis Nord, Papa,
> It is God who put you there!
> Take care of those
> Who wish to make trouble for you!
>
> Alexis Nord is a good papa!
> You didn't put him there, you can't take him away!
> Don't try to remove him, don't try to remove him!
> Don't try to remove Alexis Nord!

Nord Alexis remained as president until 1909. He was then more than eighty years old, and he planned to turn the government over to General Jean-Gilles, who would carry on the policies of the administration. But Antoine Simon, an assembly delegate from the south, had other plans. He marched on Port-au-Prince with an army of three hundred cacos, who sang:

> Dear Uncle, Antoine is not joking!
> He brings the army of the south, my friend,
> He will make you go zigzag.
> *Débor débor débor!*
> *Nord's men are asking for gunfire!*
> *Débor débor débor!*
> Nord's men are asking for a lesson!

After Nord Alexis had vacated the palace and embarked for Jamaica, Antoine Simon became president. Historians often refer to the period that followed as the "Epoch of Ephemeral Presidents." Simon was not in the palace long before a man named Cincinnatus Leconte was successfully stirring up a new caco movement in the north, and people were singing:

Original pitch — 12 st. ♩ = 132

1. An - toine Si - mon pres - sé   oh   pou al - lé!   Ou

pas ten - dé   l'ar - mée Le - conte Go - na - ïves?   2. An -

conte Go - na - ïves?   3. An - toine Si - mon pres - sé   oh

pou' al - lé!   Ou pas ten-dé   l'ar-mée Le - conte Go-na-ïves?   4. An -

Antoine Simon, you'd better leave!
Haven't you heard Leconte's army is at Gonaïves?

In August, 1912, Leconte marched on the capital, and Antoine Simon sailed for Jamaica. General Leconte was duly elected to the presidency; but less than a year after he took office a terrific explosion wrecked the palace, killing Leconte, his son, and a number of militia. It was believed by many that this disaster was an act of vengeance by Antoine Simon:

The bells ring, I ask what is going in?
It is Chapuzette now who has revolted.
But Maribaroux he comes again,
What he is looking for is revenge.

In Ouanaminthe the guns are quiet,
What was the reason for this pillage?
They have carried off the donkeys, mules,
    and even the iron roofing,
Everything that was worth more than three centimes.

Leconte's soldiers are stronger than a jalap [a purgative],
It is with them that Chapuzette gives medicine.
If you want to know how to give the "stomach-hand-nose"
Ask Oreste and Antoine Simon.

Antoine Simon said before he left
That he would leave a bomb in the middle of the palace.
When it went off he was already in Kingston.
He will pay for laughing at a sovereign people.

In Aux Cayes du Fond, I heard of the Mapou Simon,
In Léogane I heard of the Mapou Danpisse
When we arrive there we'll see what will happen.
Bowl covers bowl, Antoine will turn over on his back.

REFRAIN
Honor to Chapuzette, St. Juste and Delphin,
Ducasse and Corvoisier, long live Cincinnatus.

Two more presidents—Tancrede Auguste and Michele Oreste—divided the next eighteen months between them. Two caco movements to remove Oreste started simultaneously, one under the leadership of Davilmar Théodore, the other under the Zamor brothers, Charles and Oreste. The Zamor cacos first chased Théodore's army into the mountains and then marched on the capital. Oreste Zamor was elected to the presidency on a reform program, which quickly evaporated into thin air. One song describes the arrival of the President's brother Charles and his "Réform" at the gates of Port-au-Prince, where a crowd of enthusiasts had gathered:

Hail the Reform! It is the young men of Port-au-Prince,
The young men of Port-au-Prince, and the Reform turns its back on them.
They arose early Tuesday morning, dressed all in white,
They dressed all in white to meet Charles Zamor.
At the gates of Port-au-Prince the Reform reversed itself,
The Reform reversed itself and turned its back on them.

The Zamors and the reform administration held the palace less than nine months before Davilmar Théodore's cacos were marching on the capital singing the song that other presidents had heard.

Oreste Zamor, you'd better embark!
Oreste Zamor, you'd better embark!
Haven't you heard Davilmar's army has entered Gonaïves?

Gonaïves seems to have been the crucial point for invading armies from the north. Whenever revolutionary troops entered this town, the president holding office prepared to leave. True to the tradition, the Zamors sailed for a foreign shore, and Davilmar Théodore became the new executive. Although his tenure was to last only three months, there was much excitement when he entered the capital:

Celebrations and dancing!
Tooting horns to right and left!
The city is in an uproar,
It is Davilmar who is coming in!
Davilmar, hard, hard!
The cacos were nothing to laugh at!
Papa Da is hard, hard!
Leconte's army was nothing to laugh at!
Davilmar is hard, hard!

In 1915 came the United States intervention in Haiti, with the prime objective of freezing out German commercial and political interests. A president named Guillaume Sam had assassinated his political enemies in the prison at Port-au-Prince and had, in turn, been dragged out of the French consulate and killed. The benefits of the American occupation of Haiti are hotly debated to this day, though it is more than forty years since the United States military forces were withdrawn. Some Haitians think the occupation was a good lesson in politics, and that Haiti benefited in many ways. Others continue to look upon it as an overt expression of American diplomacy by force. One of the early assignments of the U.S. Marines in Haiti was the destruction of the roaming bands of cacos, generally regarded as bandit elements. Caco chiefs were imprisoned or killed as outlaws, though much of their activity was directed against the American occupation rather than the civil government. Many of the injustices of the occupation were the result of inadequate understanding of the Haitian people and their way of life. There was much unspoken bitterness against the occupation forces, and in some popular songs the Marines were referred to by the peaceful peasantry as "cacos in khaki." During President Borno's administration the people in the north were singing:

> Grand Prevost, didn't you hear the cacos are at the Bottle Gate?
> Grand Prevost, we are going to see the cacos at the Bottle Gate!
> Now we have two species:
> The Americans are the worst, the cacos come second!

When President Borno's tenure of office came to an end, it was felt in some quarters that Madame Borno was taking the prospective change of residence very hard:

> Madame Borno, what is the matter, why are you crying?
> You always knew one day you would have to leave the palace!
> Madame Borno, what is the matter, why are you crying?
> You always knew one day you'd have to give it up!

In 1930 Sténio Vincent came into office. He was a generally unpopular executive who managed to hold on to the presidency by suppressing the political opposition. When he was elected, the progressives were hopeful, and his supporters were singing: "Sténio Vincent bon garçon." But public sentiment shifted. Times were hard for the Haitian people during the Vincent administration. The darker citizens felt Vincent was "too light" to have their interests at heart. They were violently aroused, too, by his gingerly handling of the massacre of Haitians in the Dominican Republic in 1937. During his administration there were a number of abortive caco demonstrations and an unsuccessful revolt of high-ranking army officers. But in the early days a Meringue piece called "Merci Papa Vincent" was very popular. According to the song, the noteworthy achievement of the president was the law he sponsored to drive the "Syrians" out of the retail trades:

> We know the man who loves the people,
> He is President Vincent!
> We know the man who loves the people,
> He is President Vincent!

> We know the man who loves the people,
> He is President Vincent!
> We know the man who loves the people,
> He is President Vincent!
> We call out, thank you, Papa Vincent!
> We call out, thank you, Papa Vincent!
> We call out, thank you, Papa Vincent!
>
> Who is the man who gave us the retail business?
> It is President Vincent!
> Who is the man who gave us the retail business?
> It is President Vincent!
> Who is the man who gave us the retail business?
> It is President Vincent!
> We call out, thank you, Papa Vincent!
> We call out, thank you, Papa Vincent!

This song soon became the "official" musical theme of the president and was heard in the carnival festivities, at salon dances, and at military functions. But as discontent with Vincent grew, less adulatory versions of "Merci Papa Vincent" sprang up in the side streets of Port-au-Prince. One rendition (as translated) went:

> We know the man who loves the people,
> He is Sténio Vincent!
> Who made my wife leave me to go to her family?
> He is President Vincent!
> Who made my skin show through my worn out pants?
> He is President Vincent!
> Who is the man who made my house fall down?
> He is President Vincent!
> Oh, we call out, thank you, Papa Vincent!

So widespread did the burlesques on the original become that the tune itself became suspect. One never knew which versions were running through the minds of the listeners.

In 1950, during the administration of President Estimé, there was a new public works program which provided employment for a good many needy people in the Port-au-Prince area, and a coumbite song of the period went:

> President Estimé waille, oh!
> Hold on to the country, don't let go, oh!
> It is God in heaven who gave me this president!
> It is God in heaven who gave me this president!
> Hold on to the country, don't let go, oh!
> Port-au-Prince, oh, is turning into a Havana, oh!

When Estimé was overthrown by a military coup, the melody lingered on, but the name of the protagonist was changed.

No president of Haiti has served his term of office, either for good or bad, without providing the raw materials for a folk song. His heroic deeds, his failures, and his foibles are as likely as not to be perpetuated in the music of the people.

As for the presidency itself, it is held in the highest esteem. A rousing salute song, reminiscent of the Marseillaise, sends every new president-elect on the way to the palace:

> The President passes by,
> He is taking over the government!
> The President passes by,
> He is taking over the government!

It is not only great political events that are perpetuated in songs like these; many are the comments on little people in the government, such as a legislator named Daniel Fignolé. One of Fignolé's deeds, probably apocryphal, which is recorded in folk song has to do with an act of justice in a hospital in Port-au-Prince. According to the song, Fignolé entered the hospital and found the rich patients on beds and the poor patients on mats on the floor. He promptly ordered the rich patients placed on the floor and the poor patients placed on the beds. (A few years later, after serving as president for less than three weeks, Fignolé became a political exile in the United States.)

There is also an old song about a government engineer named Louis Gentil Tippenhauer—or Ti 'Benhauer (Little 'Benhauer), as he was commonly known. When he was young he was in charge of the construction of a section of the Haitian narrow-gauge railway. There was an accident in which a smoking locomotive jumped the tracks. Though small in stature, Tippenhauer had a forceful personality. He quickly assembled his workmen, and with chains, ropes, and crowbars they wrestled the locomotive back on the rails. The song commemorating the dramatic event was born at the height of the rescue operation. It is marked with concern for the feelings of Engineer Tippenhauer:

> Ti 'Benhauer shouts "Bring a rope to tie it!"
> Ti 'Benhauer shouts, "Bring a chain to chain it!"
> If you tie it, it unties itself, before God!
> Poor devil, poor 'Benhauer, the machine is derailed!
> Poor devil, poor 'Benhauer, the machine is derailed!

It is seventy or more years since the affair of the derailed locomotive, and the railroad itself is not much longer for this world. But the song is still sung, and mostly by people who have no personal knowledge of the man named Tippenhauer.

HAITIAN TALES: GODS,
TRICKSTERS AND OTHERS

The folklore of the Haitian people—their tales, legends, contes (a narrative form in which the story is told with the aid of interspersed songs), proverbs, sayings, and songs—is partly of Old World (Europe and Africa) origin and partly of Haitian creation. For four and a half centuries Haitians have been drawing on their own life experience to build around the lore brought to the island by Africans, Spaniards, Frenchmen, and others. The precise origins of some stories are difficult to establish, but others can be readily traced to tales told in Eastern Europe, the British Isles, Nigeria, Ghana, Dahomey, and other regions of Africa. Many of the older stories have undergone considerable change in the New World, while some retain a remarkable likeness to European and African versions.

There is an almost endless repertoire of animal tales, trickster tales, stories that account for the beginning of things or the characteristics of certain animals or natural phenomena, tall tales, tales of contests between the strong and the weak, and stories in which participative singing is the most important feature.

Among many characters who appear again and again in Haitian stories are Jean Sot and Jean l'Esprit (Foolish John and Smart John, of European beginnings) and Brise Montaigne, or Break Mountain, Haiti's enfant terrible. Probably the most popular of the characters are Uncle Bouki and his perpetual antagonist, Ti Malice. Bouki is ineffective, boastful, sometimes greedy, continually hungry, foolish, and often gently touching. Ti Malice is quick, conniving, and ready to deceive either for an advantage or a joke. Together, Uncle Bouki and Ti Malice form a combination for plot and counterplot, usually funny, sometimes with amoral humor. Existing evidence suggests that Bouki evolved out of an original animal character. In some old tales, for example, he is a member of an all-animal cast. In some of the Creole-speaking islands of the Caribbean and in Louisiana, he has been described as having feathers. As for Ti Malice, Haitians would roughly translate the name as meaning "Mischief." But the Ti in the name could well have come from *tio*, meaning "Uncle" in Spanish. Like Uncle Bouki, Ti Malice may also have developed from an animal character. According to the Haitian scholar Jean Price-Mars, some country people refer occasionally to Ti Malice as lapin, the rabbit. Both Bouki and Ti Malice play roles in tales that in West Africa had only animal participants. Central to the West African stories were animal tricksters such as the hare, the spider, and the tortoise.

The Ashanti spider trickster, Anansi, and the Yoruba tortoise trickster, Ijapa, are very similar in character. Each of them is a curious combination of the clever and the stupid, the predator and the victim. Ti Malice seems to have inherited their sharp and relentless traits and their desire to outwit and take advantage of others, while Bouki appears to be heir to their silliness and greed.

When God appears as a character in Haitian tales, he is represented as an ultimate, benign authority, but one who has moods and impulses, who can be argued with and persuaded, and who reacts in situations very much as humans do. This easy familiarity with God in tales is a characteristic of West African storytelling. Among the Ashanti, for example, Nyame, the Sky God, appears as a character in numerous tales featuring animals and humans, and in some instances he is outwitted by the spider trickster.

Much Haitian lore has to do with supernatural beings and demons. Such stories are usually interesting to Haitians more for the emotional experience involved than for humor or story line.

Like true folk tales anywhere, Haitian tales are meant to be told and dramatized rather than read. The narrator impersonates his characters, mimicks their actions, moves around, gestures, dwells on and expands elements that seem to intrigue his audience, and generally treats his performance as a production. In some regions the accomplished storyteller is called a maît' conte—a "story chief" or master of ceremonies—

and elsewhere he is called a samba. While his audience is theoretically one of children, in fact it frequently includes adults. There are any number of formalized endings and beginnings for a narration. The storyteller may begin with something like: "Ladies and gentlemen, good evening. Tonight we shall have a story. It will be a story that is not too long. It will be a story that is not too short." In another convention, the storyteller begins by saying, "Crick!" to which the audience replies, "Crack!" A formula ending to a story may be some variant of: "I was there and I saw it, and Bouki gave me a kick and sent me from there to here to tell you about it." Or again: "He gave me a blow, and I have just come to my senses."

Nananbouclou and the Piece of Fire

In ancient times only the deities lived in the world. There were Shango, the god of lightning; Ogoun, the god of ironsmiths; Agwé, the god of the sea; Legba, the messenger god; and others. Their mother was Nananbouclou; she was the first of all the gods.

One day Legba came to the city and said: "A strange thing has happened. A great piece of fire has fallen from the sky." The gods went out with Legba, and he showed them where the piece of fire lay, scorching the land on all sides. Because Agwé was god of the sea, he brought the ocean in to surround the piece of fire and prevent it from burning up the world. Then they approached the fire and began to discuss how they could take it back to the city. Because Ogoun was the god of ironsmiths, he forged a chain around the great piece of fire and captured it. But there remained the problem of how to transport it. So Shango, the god of lightning, fastened it to a thunderbolt and hurled it to the city. Then they returned.

Nananbouclou, the mother of the gods, admired what they had found. And she said, "This is indeed a great thing." But the gods began to quarrel over who should have it.

Legba, the messenger god, said: "It was I who discovered it. Therefore, it belongs to me."

Agwé, the god of the sea, said: "I brought the ocean to surround it and keep it from eating up the earth. Therefore, it should be mine."

Ogoun, the ironworker, said: "Did I not forge a chain to wrap around the fire and capture it? Therefore, I am the proper owner."

And Shango, the god of lightning, said: "Who brought the piece of fire home? It was I who transported it on a thunderbolt. Therefore, there is no doubt whatsoever, it is mine."

This story and the four that follow—"*The Voyage Below the Water,*" "*Mérisier, Stronger Than the Elephants,*" "*Jean Britisse, the Champion,*" *and* "*Charles Legoun and His Friend*"—*are from* The Piece of Fire and Other Haitian Tales, © 1942, 1964 by Harold Courlander. *Reprinted by permission of Harcourt Brace Jovanovich.*

They argued this way back and forth. They became angry with one another.

At last Nananbouclou halted the argument. She said: "This thing that has been brought back is beautiful. But before it came, there was harmony, and now there are bad words. This person claims it, that person claims it. Therefore, shall we continue to live with it in our midst?"

Nananbouclou took hold of the piece of fire and hurled it high into the sky.

There it has remained ever since. It is known by the name of Baiacou. It is the evening star.

(For an African comparison see Appendix IV, pp. 576–77.)

The Voyage Below the Water

There was a country man named Bordeau. He had worked hard all his life, and he became wealthy. He had many children. He was happy. Then, one day, his wife died.

There were the ceremonies. He had a mahogany coffin made. She was buried.

Bordeau hardly said a word. He sat in his house silently. If the children spoke, he did not seem to hear. The sons went out to take care of the fields, but Bordeau did not go with them. His old friends came to pass an hour or two with him in the evening, but he said nothing. When food was brought to him, he refused to eat. He didn't seem to know whether it was day or night.

The time went by. The evening arrived for the saying of last prayers for the dead woman. Relatives and friends came from the villages, the houngan, or Vodoun priest, came and the drummers came. And as they were preparing for the customary praying, dancing, and singing in the courtyard, Bordeau came out of the house and asked them all to go home.

"Bordeau," one of his old friends said, "this is the night for last prayers. Do not send the people home. Let us hold the service."

Bordeau answered: "For the praying, the singing, the dancing, and the feast, I care nothing. What does all this mean to me now that my wife is gone? Go away. I cannot bear the sound of music. I will not dance, I will not eat. My grief is too great."

"Bordeau," one of his friends said, "death comes to every family. It spares no one. Today it is there. Tomorrow it is here."

Another one said, "Bordeau, the dead cannot return. Do not treat yourself this way. Let the last prayers be said. Let the people dance. And let the feast be held."

"No," Bordeau said. "My house shall remain silent."

"Bordeau," the Vodoun priest said, "your wife now lives beneath the water with the ancestors. We do not give ourselves to silence and grief forever because one we love has gone there."

But Bordeau would not be persuaded.

So the Vodoun priest said "Bordeau, I will go beneath the water to find your wife. I will try to speak with her."

"Very well," Bordeau said. "But if you do not bring her back, then I will not speak again, I will not eat, my land can grow back to wild grass, and my house can rot and fall where it stands."

The Vodoun priest made preparations. He took his sacred beaded rattle in his hand and went down to the edge of the river. The people brought animals to sacrifice. There was a ceremony. They sang. And at midnight the Vodoun priest walked slowly into the river, deeper and deeper, until he disappeared.

The people waited on the bank of the river for three days, and at midnight of the third day, the Vodoun priest came out of the river, shaking his sacred rattle. There was great excitement. The people took him to Bordeau's house. They entered. Bordeau was sitting there.

"He has returned!" the people shouted to Bordeau. "Our Vodoun priest has gone below the water and come back!"

"Where is my wife?" Bordeau said.

"Listen, Bordeau," the Vodoun priest said. "I went below the water. I went far. There was a long road. I followed it. There were hills, and I crossed them. There was a forest, and I passed through it. I came to the City of the Ancestors. There were many, many people there. My father was among them. My mother was among them. Your father and mother were there. Your grandfathers were there. Everyone who was ever here before us was there. I searched for your wife. I went everywhere. I came to the marketplace, and there I found her selling beans. I said, 'Your husband Bordeau is grieving. He does not eat, he does not sleep, he does not speak. He says, "If my wife does not return from the dead, may my house fall in upon me." I have come to bring you back.' Your wife said this, Bordeau. She said, 'It is pleasant to have someone grieve for you. But I live here now, below the water. When one dies, he does not return. Tell Bordeau to bring the grief to an end. Tell him to eat. For when one is dead, he is dead, but when one is alive, he must live.' Bordeau, your wife gave me one of the gold earrings she wore. She said it was for you."

The Vodoun priest took his kerchief from his pocket, and from the kerchief he took an earring, which he gave to Bordeau.

Bordeau looked at the earring, saying, "Yes, this is my wife's earring."

He sat silently then for a long while, looking at the earring. At last he said:

"My wife has sent me a message from below the water. She said, 'When one is alive, he must live.' So it shall be. Let us hold the service of the last prayers. Let the food be prepared. Let the drummers drum. I will eat. I will dance."

(For an African comparison see Appendix V, pp. 577–79.)

Mérisier, Stronger Than the Elephants

There was an old man with three sons. One day he fell ill, and he sent a message to his sons, asking them to come to his house. When they arrived, he said to them, "I am an old man, I am sick. If I should die, how will you bury me?"

One son answered, "Father, may you grow strong again. But if you should die, I would have you buried in a mahogany coffin."

Another son answered, "Father, may you live long. But if you should die, I would make you a coffin of brass."

And the third son, named Brisé, replied, "Father, I would bury you in the great drum of the king of the elephants."

"The great drum of the king of the elephants! Who before now has ever been buried so magnificently!" the old man said. "Yes, that is the way it should be." And he asked the son who had suggested it to bring him the drum of the king of the elephants.

Brisé went home. He told his wife: "I said I would do this thing for my father, but it is impossible. Why didn't I say I would make him a coffin of silver? Even that would have been more possible. How shall I ever be able to do what I have promised?"

His wife prepared food for him and gave him his knapsack. Brisé began his journey. But he didn't know where to find the elephants. He asked here, he asked there, but no one knew where the elephants were to be found. As evening came on, he met a blind beggar who was being led by a small boy. The beggar said, "Man, give me a little of whatever you have, a piece of bread or a taste of rice."

Brisé took a piece of cornbread from his pocket and gave it to the beggar. "If you were not blind," he said, "I would ask you if you had ever seen the elephants."

"Even men with eyes have not seen the elephants," the beggar answered.

Brisé went on. When it was dark, he slept in the grass by the edge of the road. When day came, he walked again, asking everywhere for information about the elephants.

When the sun became hot, Brisé went to sit in the shade of a large tree. There, sitting on a stone, he saw a crippled man with only one foot and a crutch. "Give me a little of what you have in your knapsack," the man said. "I have a great hunger in my stomach."

Brisé gave him a piece of cornbread. They talked. Brisé said, "I have two feet, while you have only one. You go slowly, and I travel far. But what good is that when I don't know where to find the great drum of the king of the elephants?"

He continued on his way. And as night came on, he saw an old man sitting before a little fire at the edge of the road. The old man said, "Come and rest here."

Brisé sat down and opened his knapsack. There were only two pieces of cornbread left. He gave one to the old man and ate the other one himself. After a while the old man said: "I thank you for the third piece of cornbread, which I have just finished. I thank you for the second piece. I thank you for the first piece."

Brise said, "Papa, you are mistaken. I gave you only one."

The old man said, "No, it is you who are mistaken. At noon I was a man with one foot and a crutch, and yesterday I was a blind beggar. My name is Mérisier."

Then Brisé understood that the old man was a houngan, a Vodoun priest with magical powers. The old man took out his bead-covered rattle. He shook it and went into a trance and talked with the gods. At last he put the rattle away and said: "Go that way, to the north, across the grassland. There is a great mapou tree, called Mapou Plus Grand Passe Tout. Wait there. The elephants come there with the drum. They dance until they are tired, then they fall asleep. When they sleep, take the drum. Travel fast. Here are four wari nuts for protection. If you are pursued, throw a wari nut behind you and say, 'Mérisier is stronger than the elephants.' "

When day came, Brisé went north across the grasslands. He came to the tree called Mapou Plus Grand Passe Tout. He climbed into the tree and waited. As the sun was going down, he saw a herd of elephants coming, led by their king. They gathered around the mapou tree. The king's drummer began to play on the great drum. The elephants began to dance. The ground shook with their stamping. The dancing went on and on, all night. They danced until the first cocks began to crow. Then they stopped, lay down on the ground, and slept.

Brisé came down from the tree. He was in the middle of a large circle of elephants. He took the great drum and placed it on his head. He climbed first over one sleeping elephant, then another, until he was outside the circle. He traveled as fast as he could with his heavy load.

When he was halfway across the grassland, he heard the enraged elephant herd coming after him. When they were very close, he took one of the wari nuts the old man had given him and threw it behind him, saying, "Mérisier is stronger than the elephants!" And where the nut fell, a tremendous pine forest grew up instantly. The elephants stopped running and began to work their way slowly through the trees. Brisé went on.

He walked a great distance. Again he heard the sound of the elephants coming. He took another wari nut and threw it behind him, saying, "Mérisier is stronger than the elephants!" And where the nut fell, there was suddenly a large fresh-water lake. The elephants stopped at its shore.

The king of the elephants commanded, "Drink up the water, so that we can pass!" The elephants began drinking, and slowly, very slowly, the level of the lake went down.

Brisé traveled far. He was almost across the grassland. He heard the elephants coming again. He threw a third wari nut on the ground behind him, saying, "Mérisier is stronger than the elephants!" This time there appeared a large salt-water lake.

The king of the elephants commanded, "Drink it up so that we can pass!" The elephants began drinking. The salt water made them sick. But their king commanded, "Drink, drink!" So they continued to drink, and one by one they fell dying. Only the king of the elephants did not drink, and at last he alone of the herd was alive.

Brisé came out of the grassland. He followed the trails. He went to his father's house with the drum. When he arrived, his father was not dead; he was not sick; he was working with his hoe in the fields.

"Put the drum away," the father said. "I don't need it yet. I am feeling fine."

Brisé took the drum to his own house. He ate and slept. When he awoke, he heard a loud noise in the courtyard. He saw the king of elephants coming. The elephant ran straight toward the great drum and seized hold of it.

Brisé took the last wari nut that the Vodoun priest had given him and threw it on the ground, saying, "Mérisier is stronger than the elephants!"

Instantly the great drum broke into small pieces, and each piece became a small drum. The king of elephants broke into many pieces, and each piece became a drummer. The drummers went everywhere, each one taking a drum with him.

Thus it is that there are drums everywhere in the country. Thus it is that people have a proverb which says: "Every drum has a drummer."

And thus it is, also, that no one has ever been buried in a drum.

(For a U.S. comparison see "The Mojo," pp. 432–33. For an African prototype, see Appendix VI, pp. 579–82.)

Jean Britisse, the Champion

Jean Britisse said to his mother, "Mamma, I am going to Martinique to make my fortune."

His mother said to him, "Jean, that is fine. But without money how are you going to get there? You'll have to swim."

Jean Britisse went down to the wharf. He asked people where this ship was going and that ship was going. When he found one that was going to Martinique, he went aboard and hid himself under a pile of crates. The ship went out to sea. After two days, just before dawn, Jean Britisse heard the Captain say, "Men, as soon as we reach port, unload all these crates." Jean Britisse worried that he would be found. So he made his way to the back of the ship in the dark. Then, just as the sun was rising and the ship was sailing into port, he jumped into the water and began to swim.

"Captain, Captain!" he called out.

"Did I hear someone calling me?" the Captain said.

"Captain, Captain, slow the ship down and take me aboard!" Jean Britisse shouted.

The Captain looked over the stern.

"Who's that down there?" he said.

"Captain, take me aboard!" Jean Britisse called. "I'm getting a little tired!"

"Stop the ship!" the Captain shouted. "Take this man aboard!"

They stopped the ship. They hauled Jean Britisse out of the water.

"Wherever did you come from?" the Captain asked.

"Captain," Jean Britisse said, "I was going to Martinique, but I missed the boat. I jumped in the water, but I couldn't quite catch you. I've been swimming for two days and two nights, and at last I've made it."

"Do you mean to say you swam all the way from Haiti?" the Captain said.

"Yes," Jean Britisse said, "and now I can buy a ticket and ride to Martinique with you."

"Man," the Captain said, "you don't need a ticket because you are already in Martinique."

Jean Britisse went ashore with the other passengers. Everywhere he went people said. "That's Jean Britisse, the world's champion swimmer! He swam from Haiti to Martinique, and he arrived at the same time as the ship!"

Now there were some good swimmers in Martinique, but the best of them was a man named Coqui. The people went to Coqui and asked him to race against Jean Britisse. Coqui said he would race him for five hundred gourdes. The people went back to Jean Britisse and said that Coqui challenged him. Jean Britisse said he would accept the challenge but not for such a little bit of money. So the people went back again, and Coqui said he would bet one thousand gourdes. And they agreed to meet on the seashore at dawn.

When daylight came, there was a crowd at the beach. Coqui arrived in his swimming suit. When Jean Britisse arrived, he was wearing a white suit, a new Panama hat and new shoes, and he was carrying a heavy bundle. The crowd laughed.

"Is that the way you expect to swim?" people asked him.

"Just a minute," Jean Britisse said. "I am the man who was challenged, so I can set the conditions for the race, isn't that right?"

The crowd agreed.

"Very well," Jean Britisse said. "The race is to be from here to Cuba. Coqui can swim a straight line if he wishes, but I have a few things here in this bundle that I bought for my mother, so I'd like to drop them off in Haiti. Since I wouldn't want to meet my old friends there in my swimming suit, I'll just go the way I am. I hope Coqui will bring enough food along to last for five or six days."

Coqui listened. He took off his swimming suit and put on his street clothes.

"Here's the thousand gourdes," he said. "I'm not going to race a man who wants to swim to Cuba."

When the carnival season arrived, there were wrestling matches in the town. The French wrestler Dumee La Farge was there. He won all the matches. They were going to give him the grand prize when someone said, "Wait, he's not the champion yet. He hasn't beaten Jean Britisse."

So Dumée LaFarge challenged him.

"Very well," Jean Britisse said. "Tomorrow morning at the wrestling court." It was arranged.

Jean Britisse didn't know how to wrestle. He sat and thought for a long time. At last he figured it out. First he went to a carpenter and ordered a coffin to be made. Then he went to a brickmason and ordered a tomb to be constructed. Then he went to the parish priest. He gave him fifty gourdes and made arrangements for him to give the last sacrament.

After that, when it was dark, Jean Britisse went to the wrestling court. There were two trees standing there, side by side. Jean Britisse dug down around the trees and chopped off all the roots. Then he put back the dirt and stamped it flat and made it look natural.

When morning came, Jean Britisse went again to the wrestling court. There was a crowd. Dumée LaFarge was waiting. Dumée LaFarge took off his shirt. He took off his shoes. Jean Britisse took off his shirt. He took off his shoes.

Just then the carpenter arrived. He was carrying a new coffin on his head. On the side of the coffin was painted the name "Dumée LaFarge."

"What kind of joke is this?" Dumée LaFarge shouted.

The carpenter put the coffin down. And he said, as he had been instructed: "What must be must be."

At that moment the brickmason came along. He went up to Dumée LaFarge and said, "Where shall I build the tomb?"

"What is going on here?" Dumée LaFarge shouted. He began to sweat.

The mason shook his head and said, "What must be must be."

And then the parish priest came walking along, reading from the Scripture in Latin. He sprinkled holy water on Dumée LaFarge.

"Stop it! I am not dead!" Dumée LaFarge said. But his legs were getting weak.

"Let the wrestling begin," the people called out.

"One moment, I must warm up a little," Jean Britisse said.

First he crouched and jumped and raced around the wrestling court. He did exercises. Then he went between the two trees he had fixed. He began to push them, one in one direction, one in the other. They leaned, and the crowd watched in astonishment. Jean Britisse pushed harder. The trees started to fall. Dumée LaFarge put on his shirt and shoes. The trees crashed to the ground. Dumée LaFarge put on his hat.

"Give him the prize money," Dumée LaFarge said. "I'm not going to wrestle a man who knocks down trees just for exercise."

"Wait," Jean Britisse said. "I'm not warmed up yet."

Dumée walked away. The parish priest followed him, sprinkling him with holy water. The carpenter followed, carrying the coffin. Behind him was the brickmason. Dumée LaFarge began to run. He went over the hill. It was the last time he was ever seen in Martinique.

Charles Legoun and His Friend

There was a farmer named Charles Legoun. Wherever he was, he referred to his friend God. Out in the garden he said things like, "Oh, God, this is your friend Charles Legoun talking. I'm planting yams and peas here. I hope you'll see to it that they grow properly." When he went to the market, he would talk right up, saying, "Papa God, your old friend Charles Legoun is here selling cotton. I guess you're going to get me a good price for all this cotton." If he was hungry, Charles Legoun said, "Well, you know me, friend God. I hope you fix things so I get a big dinner tonight." If he went fishing, he'd sit in his boat and say, "Here I am, Papa God—Charles Legoun, just in case you missed me. You can fill my net right up with fish." If he was in a shop in town, he might say, "Well, this is Charles Legoun speaking, God. Don't let this man charge me too much."

People got pretty tired of hearing Charles Legoun talk about his friend God.

One night after dark a man went to Charles Legoun's house and knocked on the door. Charles Legoun was sitting inside with his lamp on. He called out, "Who's that?"

The man said, "I'm looking for my friend Charles Legoun."

"Who is it, who is looking for Charles Legoun?" Charles Legoun answered.

"Charles Legoun knows who I am," the man said. "We have a big conversation every day."

"What's your name?" Charles Legoun demanded.

"This is Charles Legoun's friend, Papa God," the man said. Charles Legoun sat straight up.

"Papa God? What are you doing here?"

"Well, Charles Legoun has been talking to me a long time," the man answered. "He's been asking me to do this and do that. I haven't always been able to oblige him. But there's one last thing I can do for him."

"What's that?" Charles Legoun said.

"Well, Charles Legoun is getting to be a pretty old man now, and his time is about up. So I've come to take him."

Charles Legoun jumped. He pinched out the lamp flame with his fingers.

"It's a shame," he said. "You've come all this way, but Charles Legoun isn't here. Nobody's here. I'll tell him if I ever see him, but for all I know, old Charles Legoun isn't coming back at all."

The man went away.

When Charles Legoun came out of the house in the morning, he looked carefully in all directions. He told his neighbors: "In case you hear anyone asking for me and saying he's my friend, you just tell him there's been a mistake, and I'm just somebody else by the same name."

The Singing Tortoise

A tortoise was crawling along slowly one day when he came to a fine garden where many birds were eating. They were eating the peas and millet of a farmer named Pierre Jean. The turkey, the chicken, the pigeon, the duck, and even the nightingale were there. They invited the tortoise to eat with them. But he replied: "Oh, no. If the farmer who owns the garden surprises us, you can fly away. But where would I be? He would catch me and beat me."

The birds said, "We will give you wings." And each of the birds took some of its feathers and attached them to the tortoise. So he came and ate with them. But while they were eating, the nightingale called out, "Habitant 'rivé! Habitant 'rivé!" (The farmer is coming! The farmer is coming!). And in a panic they all grabbed the feathers they had given the tortoise and flew away. Tortoise crawled, crawled, crawled; but he was too slow. Uncle Pierre Jean caught him. He was going to beat him. But the tortoise began to sing:

> Colico Pierre Jean oh!
> Colico Pierre Jean oh!
> Si'm capab' m'pito volé, enhé!
> C'est regrettant ça, m'pas gainyain zel!
>
> Colico Pierre Jean, oh!
> Colico Pierre Jean, oh!
> If I could I would fly, enhé!
> What a tragedy, I have no wings!

The farmer was amazed to hear a tortoise sing. He liked the tortoise's song, and he asked him to sing again. Tortoise sang his song again. Pierre Jean took the tortoise home and put him in a box. Then he went to Port-au-Prince and asked the people to make bets with him. He said he would bet them any amount of money he had a tortoise that could sing. Some people bet one gourde, some people bet five gourdes. And then the President came along in his carriage. When he saw the crowd he stopped and said, "Ça nous gainyain icite?" ("What is going on here?")

When he heard about Pierre Jean's singing tortoise, the President said, "This man is a Ti Malice; there aren't any tortoises that sing. I will bet you one hundred thousand gourdes." But Pierre Jean said, "I can't bet that much. I am a poor man." The President said. "Nevertheless, you are a vagabond trying to cheat the people. I will bet you one

---

This story and the four that follow—"Bouki and Ti Malice Go Fishing," "Baptizing the Babies," "Bouki and Ti Bef," and "Uncle Bouki Gets Whee-ai"—are from The Drum and the Hoe, Life and Lore of the Haitian People, © *1960 by Harold Courlander. Reprinted by permission of the University of California Press and the Regents of the University of California.*

hundred thousand gourdes. If you lose the bet I will have you shot."

Meanwhile Madame Pierre Jean heard rumors that her husband had a talking tortoise in the house. She searched until she found the tortoise, and she asked him to sing. "I can only sing by the edge of the river," the tortoise said. So she took him to the edge of the river. "My feet must be wet," the tortoise said. So she put him in the water by the bank of the river. And then he crawled into the water quickly and swam away. Madame Pierre Jean heard the crowd coming up to the house from the city. She was frightened. She ran home, and on the way she caught a small lizard. She put the lizard in the box and closed the lid. When the men from the city arrived, Pierre Jean took them to the box. The President said, "Let the singing begin."

Pierre Jean said then, "Sing, tortoise, sing." The lizard replied from inside the box, "Cric!" Pierre Jean said again, "Sing, tortoise sing!" And the lizard replied, "Crac!" The President was angry and said, "You call that singing? Open the box!" They opened the box and found only the small zandolite. The President said, "You are a cheat. Take this man down to the river to have him shot." So they took Pierre Jean down to the river and stood him by a tree to shoot him. And just at that moment the tortoise stuck his head out of the water and sang:

> Colico Pierre Jean oh!
> Colico Pierre Jean oh!
> Si ou capab' ou pito volé enhé!
> C'est regrettant ça, ou pas gainyain zel!
>
> Colico Pierre Jean, oh!
> Colico Pierre Jean, oh!
> If you could you would fly, enhé!
> What a tragedy you have no wings!

"Ah, that is my tortoise!" Pierre Jean said. "Listen to him sing!" And the tortoise continued to sing.

> Colico Président, oh!
> Colico Président, oh!
> Nonc' Pierre Jean pa'lé trop enhé!
> Sotte pas tuyé Haitien, fai li siè!
>
> Colico Président, oh!
> Colico Président, oh!
> Uncle Pierre Jean talks too much, enhé!
> Stupidity doesn't kill a Haitian, it makes him sweat!

When the President heard that, he turned Pierre Jean loose and paid him the hundred thousand gourdes. But it was the last they saw of the singing tortoise.

(For an African comparison see Appendix VII, pp. 582–83.)

Bouki and Ti Malice Go Fishing

Bouki and Ti Malice went into the fishing business together. Ti Malice painted the name St. Jacques on the front of the boat, poured some rum over it and christened it. Bouki took some rum and poured it over the back end of the boat and christened it Papa Pierre. They went out to sea and caught fish. When they came home, Ti Malice counted the fish. "There are eighteen fish," he said. "How shall we divide?"

"I'll take one and you take one until they're gone," Bouki said.

Malice said: "There are so few fish it isn't worth while. You take all the fish today and I'll take all the fish tomorrow."

"Oh, no," Bouki said, "I'm not totally stupid. You take all today and I'll take all tomorrow." Sc Malice took all the fish.

They went out again the next day, and when they came home Malice counted again and said, "There are so few, you take all today and I'll take all tomorrow."

"Oh, no," Bouki said, "you're trying to cheat me. You take all today and I'll take all tomorrow." So Malice took all.

The next day they went out again. And when they were returning Ti Malice said, "Waille, such a small catch! I'm glad it's your turn to take all today."

Bouki became angry and said, "Are you trying to break my head? I'm no fool. You take the catch today and I'll take it tomorrow."

Every day Ti Malice took the whole catch. Every day Bouki got nothing. Malice got fatter and Bouki got thinner. Every day it was this way, until one day Bouki looked at Malice and saw how fat he was getting. It came to him suddenly that he had been cheated. He shouted at Ti Malice and began to chase him. They ran through the peristyle of the town hounfor [cult house] and Ti Malice said "cata-cata," imitating the sound of a drum, and called on Ogoun and Damballa to save him.

They ran through the church, where the priest was holding a service. Malice crossed himself and said a quick prayer, without stopping for a second, and ran out again. They ran, ran, ran, and Bouki was getting closer. Ti Malice came to a limekiln with a hole in it. He tried to crawl through, but he stuck at the hips. No matter how hard he tried, he couldn't get through. Finally Bouki came along. He stopped and looked in all directions. There was no Ti Malice, only the behind facing him from the limekiln.

Bouki put on his best manners, and said, "Behind, have you seen Ti Malice?"

The behind replied, "Take off your hat when you address me."

Bouki took off his hat to Ti Malice's behind. He said politely, "Why are you smiling at me? I only asked if you saw Ti Malice?"

"I smile when I please," the behind said.

"Have you seen Ti Malice?" Bouki said.

"Push me and I'll tell you," the behind said.

Bouki pushed.

"Harder," the behind said.

Bouki pushed harder.

"Harder yet," the behind said.

Bouki gave a big push, and Ti Malice went through the hole into the limekiln. And that was the way he made his escape.

(For an African comparison see Appendix VIII, pp. 584–85.)

Baptizing the Babies

One day Ti Malice and Bouki decided to make a coumbite [work their fields] together. First they were going to cultivate Ti Malice's garden; afterward Bouki's garden. So they took their machetes and started to work cultivating Ti Malice's peas and yams.

Ti Malice said, "Did you hear someone calling me?" Bouki replied, "I didn't hear anything."

They chopped weeds some more, and Ti Malice said, "Someone is definitely calling me." He put down his machete and went over the hill. He went to Bouki's house and took down Bouki's honey gourd. He sat in the shade of Bouki's house and drank as much honey as he could. Then he hung the gourd up and went back to his field, where Bouki was working, working, working.

"Who was it?" Bouki asked. "Oh, those people wanted me to be godfather to their baby." Bouki asked, "What did you name the baby?" Ti Malice said, "I named him Coummencé (Beginning)."

They chopped more weeds, and Ti Malice said, "Excuse me, someone is calling me again." He put down his machete and went over the hill back to Bouki's house. He took down the honey gourd and sat in the shade and drank as much as he could. Bouki was still in Ti Malice's garden, working, working, working. Ti Malice put the honey gourd back and returned to his garden.

"Some important people wanted me for godfather," Ti Malice said. Bouki asked, "What did you name the baby?" Ti Malice answered, "I called this one Dé Fois (Two Times)."

They worked some more, and Ti Malice said, "Waille, they are calling me again!" He put his machete down and went over the hill to Bouki's house and got the honey gourd down again. He drank, drank, drank until it was all gone. Then he came back.

Bouki had finished weeding Ti Malice's garden. "What did you call this baby?" Bouki asked. "Oh, this one was the last, so I called him Ai Bobo (Finish)," Ti Malice said.

Ti Malice's garden was all cultivated. He said to Bouki, "Now we will cultivate your garden." But Bouki was exhausted from doing Ti Malice's work as well as his own. He said, "I'll have to let my own weeds grow. I'm done in."

He went home and took his honey gourd down for a drink, but it was empty. He was so angry he kicked me all the way here to tell you about it.

Bouki and Ti Bef

Bouki and Ti Bef (Calf). The calf's mother had died. He was an orphan. Bouki was crossing the fields one day and he saw Ti Bef grazing all by himself. Bouki's mouth watered. He wanted to eat Ti Bef. So he said, "Ti Bef, I haven't seen you for a long time. Where do you live these days?" But the calf knew Bouki. So he said, "I sleep over there on top of the hill."

That night Bouki took a sack and crept to the top of the hill; but he couldn't find Ti Bef. Ti Bef was sleeping in the woods. Bouki looked all night without finding him, and when he went home his children said, "Where is Ti Bef?" Bouki just slapped them and told them to keep quiet. The next day Bouki saw Ti Bef grazing, and he asked, "Ti Bef, where were you last night? I dropped by and I didn't find you home."

Ti Bef said: "Oh, last night I found a place in the woods. That is where I sleep now."

The next night Bouki searched in the woods, but he didn't find the calf. The next day, he said to Ti Bef, "Oh Ti Bef, I just happened to drop by the woods last night, but I didn't find you home. Where were you?" And the calf replied, "Last night I found a nice place by the spring. That's where I sleep now."

So the next night Bouki took his sack and searched by the spring, but he didn't find Ti Bef. He began to get very angry.

When he saw Ti Bef the next day he said, "Ti Bef, you have been telling me lies. Where do you really live?" Ti Bef said to him, "Nonc' Bouki, I really live in that cave there in the mountain."

The cave belonged to a tiger. That night Bouki took his sack and went up to the cave. He said, "Are you there?" And the tiger replied, "Of course I'm here." So Bouki went into the dark cave, took hold of the tiger, and tried to put him in the sack. But the tiger knocked Bouki down. He tore his clothes off, he bit him, and he mauled him. Bouki ran home. His children wanted to know where Ti Bef was. Bouki said, "Woy, that Ti Bef is a devil! He is so small and weak in the daytime, but at night he's as ferocious as a tiger! So if you happen to meet him anywhere, show him the greatest respect."

Uncle Bouki Gets Whee-ai

Uncle Bouki went down to the city to market, to sell some yams, and while he was there he got hungry. He saw an old man squatting by the side of the road, eating something. The old man was enjoying his food tremendously, and Bouki's mouth watered. Bouki tipped his hat and said to the old man, "Where can I get some of whatever you are eating?" But the old man was deaf. He didn't hear a word Bouki said. Bouki asked him then, "What do you call that food?" Just then the old man bit into a hot pepper, and he said loudly, "Whee-ai!" Bouki thanked him and went into the market. He went everywhere asking for five centimes worth of whee-ai. The people only laughed. Nobody had any whee-ai.

He went home thinking about whee-ai. He met Ti Malice on the way. Ti Malice listened to him and said, "I will get you some whee-ai." Malice went down and got some cactus leaves. He put them in a sack. He put some oranges on top of the cactus leaves. He put a pineapple on top. Then a potato. Then he brought the sack to Bouki. Bouki reached in and took out a potato. "That's no whee-ai," he said. He reached in and took out a pineapple. "That's no whee-ai," Bouki said. He reached in and took out oranges. "That's no whee-ai," he said. Then he reached way to the bottom and grabbed the cactus leaves. The needles stuck into his hand. He jumped into the air. He shouted, *"Whee-ai!"*

"That's your whee-ai," Malice said.

HAITIAN ANIMAL TALES

Who Is the Older?

This tale recalls the Sudanese proverb: "A beard would befit the bull, but God gave it to the goat."

A goat and a bull met one time in the field. The bull ignored the goat. But the goat stood before him and said, "I'm an older man than you."

The bull looked at the goat with amazement. He said, "No, I am older than you."

The goat said, "Son, run home to your father."

The bull said, "Does your mother know you are out here alone?"

The goat said, "Your big sister ought to be taking care of you."

The bull said, "Why are you always saying baa, baa? Are you calling for your grandmother?"

The goat said, "Don't talk to your elders that way. Don't you see I have a beard?"

The bull replied, "Good Lord! What is the country coming to? The

From The Piece of Fire and Other Haitian Tales, ©*1942, 1964 by Harold Courlander. Reprinted by permission of Harcourt Brace Jovanovich.*

little ones have beards, but I, who am big, big, big, have no beard!"
Tears came to his eyes.

"One side," the goat said, "and let an elderly gentleman pass."

The Dogs Pay a Visit to God

One day all the dogs in the world gathered and decided to pay a visit
to God. They started off through the woods together, but one of their
number was distracted by the smell of carrion. He left his friends for a
brief time, found the carrion and ate some of it. Then he hurriedly
joined his companions again. Together they arrived at God's house and
were admitted to the parlor, where they sat around making polite conversation with God and one another. But after a while God caught the
scent of the carrion which was still smeared on the nose of the dog that
had eaten it. God sniffed the air several times to test the unpleasant
odor. Misjudging it, he decided that one of the dogs had defecated in
his parlor, and he demanded to know who had done this impolite
thing. The dogs were deeply concerned that one of their party had
desecrated God's house. They immediately began to run around smelling each other to determine the culprit. But they never found the evidence, because it was on a dog's nose. The dogs are still, to this day, attempting to discover who committed a deed that never actually happened.

Frog, Chief of the Well

One time there was a drought, and there was no place for the animals
to get water. So God provided a well where all the animals could come
to drink, and he put Frog in charge. Frog was to receive the animals
who came to quench their thirst. But when the animals came, the frog
refused to provide them with water. When the cow came to drink, the
frog sang from inside the well:

> M'apé mandé ça qui là donc, enhé, ça qui là?
> M'apé mandé ça qui là donc, enhé, ça qui là?
>
> I am asking who is there, enhé, who is there?
> I am asking who is there, enhé, who is there?

From "The Loa of Haiti: New World African Deities," by Harold Courlander,
in Miscelánia de Estudios Dedicados a Fernando Ortiz por sus Discipulos,
Colegas y Amigos, Vol. I, Havana, 1955.

From The Drum and the Hoe, Life and Lore of the Haitian People, © 1960 by
Harold Courlander. Used by permission of the Regents of the University of
California.

And the cow sang back:

> C'est moin bèf qui nan pi à!
>
> It is I, the cow, at the well!

And the frog replied:

> Moin dit bèf allez donc,   I say, cow, go away,
> Pi à chêche!   The well is dry!

The cow went away and died from thirst. Then the horse came and asked for water, and the frog conversed in the same way with him as he had with the cow:

> M'apé mandé ça qui là donc, enhé, ça qui là?
> M'apé mandé ça qui là donc, enhé, ça qui là?
>
> C'est moin ch'wal qui nan pi à!
>
> Moin dit ch'wal nen point dleau,
> Pi à chêche!

> I am asking who is there, enhé, who is there?
> I am asking who is there, enhé, who is there?
> It is I, the horse, at the well!
> I say, horse, there is no water,
> The well is dry!

The horse went away suffering, and he died of thirst. The other animals came in turn: the donkey, the goat, the dog, the cat, and the birds. The frog turned them all away in the same manner, and they suffered and died of thirst.

So, one day, God said: "What is this? I put Frog in charge of the water. I will have to go and see what is the matter." So he went to the well, and when he got there the frog called out:

> M'apé mandé ça qui là, enhé, ça qui là?
> M'apé mandé ça qui là, enhé, ça qui là?

And God replied:

> C'est moin Papa Bondieu qui nan pi à!
>
> It is I, Father God, who is at the well!

And Frog answered:

> Papa Bondieu nen point dleau,
> Pi à chêche!

> Father God, there is no water,
> The well is dry!

So God cut off the frog's tail. From that time on, the frog has had no tail; but you still find him in the well.

The Lizard Bocor

> In this tale the zandolite—a small climbing lizard—is portrayed as a bocor (another designation for a houngan, or cult priest). The thrust of the tale is that Bocor Zandolite is so powerful that whoever attends his services is overcome by a possession. That is to say, one of the deities of the Afro-Haitian pantheon "mounts" him. The climax comes when God goes down to put an end to the disruptive service.

Bocor Zandolite once held a great ritual service. People came from the whole countryside. It was a long service, scheduled to last for seven weeks. Chickens, goats and bulls were sacrificed. The finest drummers in the country were drumming. Everyone danced, and the celebration went on day after day, night after night without stopping. The noise was deafening. God heard it. It kept him from sleeping at night, and in the daytime he could not concentrate on his work. Finally God decided he would have to put a stop to it. So he called St. John and instructed him to go down and order Bocor Zandolite to bring the service to an end. St. John went down and approached the gate of Bocor Zandolite's hounfor [cult house]. Bocor Zandolite met him at the gate. He took St. John by the hand. St. John sang:

Factionnaire ouv'é bayè pou' moin passé! [Guard, open the gate
   for me to enter.]

And Bocor Zandolite replied by singing:

Wa wa ilé londja londja!
Bocor Zandolite wa wa ilé londja londja! [Ritual language.]

From "The Loa of Haiti: New World African Deities," by Harold Courlander, in Miscelânia de Estudios Dedicados a Fernando Ortiz por sus Discipulos, Colegas y Amigos, *Vol. I, Havana, 1955.*

Then he shook St. John's hands three times and pirouetted him around, first to the left and then to the right. Suddenly St. John staggered and began to talk language. He grasped the center pole of the dance court and twirled around and around it. Then Bocor Zandolite gave him a lighted candle and a glass of water, and St. John spilled a bit of the water on the ground in honor of the loa who had entered his head.

When a week went by and St. John didn't come back, God became angry. The noise of the drumming and singing was getting worse. So he called St. Patrick and sent him down to stop the ceremony. St. Patrick approached the hounfor and sang:

Factionnaire ouv'é bayè pou' moin passé!

And again Bocor Zandolite came to the gate and sang:

Wa wa ilé londja londja!
Bocor Zandolite wa wa ilé londja londja!

He took St. Patrick by the hands, pirouetted him around, and a loa came into St. Patrick's head too.

Another week went by, and when St. Patrick didn't return God sent St. Michael. The same thing happened to St. Michael. God then sent St. Anthony, and later he sent St. Peter. But when St. Peter didn't return, God became very angry indeed. He hadn't slept for weeks. So he decided to go down himself and put an end to the affair. He approached the hounfor singing:

Factionnaire ouv'é bayè pou' moin passé!

And Bocor Zandolite replied as he had before. He took God by the hands to greet him. He shook his hands downward three times, then he pirouetted God to the right and the left. God suddenly staggered and reeled from one end of the habitation to the other. The drummers beat a special salute and the singers sang loudly and clapped their hands, for God had a loa in his head.

THE CREOLE LANGUAGE

The language spoken throughout Haiti is called Creole. It is not a patois of French, though a preponderant part of its vocabulary consists of

Examples are from the previously cited study by Robert A. Hall, Jr. Reproduced by permission of The Society for Applied Anthropology and Dr. Hall from Monographs of the Society for Applied Anthropology, Vol. 55, No. 74, 1953.

modified, truncated or elided French words. Language specialists tend
to agree that Creole relates to French much as, for example, modern
Italian does to Latin. A study made by Robert A. Hall, Jr.,[1] concludes
that in its morphology Creole must be classed with the Romance Languages. While it is the language spoken by most Haitians, it exists in
various dialects in other West Indian islands such as Martinique,
Guadeloupe, Trinidad, Marie Galante and St. Lucia, among others. It
was once commonplace in Louisiana, and may still be heard there. Its
distribution, therefore, relates mainly, though not exclusively, to the
patterns of French colonial settlement in the Caribbean and the southern reaches of the Mississippi. It is also heard in some of the islands
that were never under French rule—Cuba, for example, where numerous Haitians settled early in the twentieth century. Creole vocabulary
includes numerous words borrowed from English and Spanish, and a
good many African words as well. A person speaking good continental
French is usually surprised that his speech is not always readily understood in the Haitian countryside, and because Creole *sounds* so French
he is also surprised that he does not readily grasp it. Elisions, trunca-
tions, the manner of conjugating verbs, verb-plus-verb phrases, some
words from archaic French, and constructions of African rather than
European character give Creole a nature all its own.

The following examples of Creole speech, given in the McConnell-
Laubach orthography, are in the dialect heard in the region of Port-au-
Prince. Apart from offering a taste of Creole, they are documents of tra-
ditional beliefs and customs concerning death.

Removing a Loa from the Head of a Person Who Has Died

Moun-nâ mouri. Apré ké yo fini
êstalé li sou-bèl kabân li, ké souvâ
yo rélé: "badlékê-tèt-brodé"
paské sé you grâ é-gro kabân ak-
kònichô, kabân arâjé ak-dé-bèl
rido dâtèl tout o-li. Oûsi-a fè tout
moun lâ-kay-la sòti. Sèl li-mêm
ak-kèk piti fèy li é-pitit mò si-l-
gâgnê. Alò pitit yo vlé lwa-a râtré
lâ-tèt li-a, kêbé lâ-mê li you gro
kòk zêga ou blâch a tè dévâ kabân-la yo râjé you bèl sèvièt
blâch, â-ro li gê dlo siro, bouji
limê sou-tèt boutèy, tafia é-òt

The person has died. After they
have finished installing him on a
fine bed, which they often call
"baldequin with embroidered
head," because it's a great big bed
with a canopy; the bed is arranged with two fine lace curtains
all around. The hounsi [servitor
of the Vodoun cult] makes everybody in the house go out. Only he
and some little acolytes of his,
and the dead man's child, if there
is one. Then the child they want
to have the loa [deity] enter the

---

1. Haitian Creole, *by Robert A. Hall, Jr., The American Anthropological Association,
Vol. 55, No. 2, Part 2, Memoir No. 74, April–June 1953.*

choz. Apré ké yo fin jété dlo, bat mê, châté lwa, yo fè tout tou ka-bân mò-a, pitit-la, kòk a-lamê, fè tou-a ak oûsi-a. Yo pasé kòk-la yo répasé li, dé, twa, kat, sêk, sis fwa sou tèt mò-a. Pâdâ tâ sa-a, tout asistâs-lâ ap-môté lwa, châté, bat mê, kâbân mò-a prâ kraké. Voup, oûsi-a môté sou kabân-la, kêbé dé bra mò-a, lâ-pla mê li. Li mété li chita, pitit ké-yo vlé lwâ râtré là-tèt li-a frapé poul-la twa fwa lâ-tèt mò-a, li fè li kâpé sou-tèt mò-a, li lagé poul-la, poul-la volé, li mété kouri lâ-tout châm-la, krazé, brizé pòt, vésèl, you kèbé poul-la, yo voyé li â-lè twa fwa â-kriâ: "Ai bobo lwa-a." O-sito lwa-a râtré lâ-tèt pitit mò-a. Yo tòdié kou poul, yo dékapé li, sâ-plîmê, yo mété li lâ-you kwi ki gâgnê tout kalité viv raché, you ti-pôgnê pwa dé-chak kalité, grên mai, gren roroli, grên pistach, grên kafé, pimâ pwav avèk dlo plat marasa kay-la. Yo fè you mâjé yo rélé diak ké-tout pitit yo mâjé âvâ âtèmâ-â.

head of, grasps in his hand a black-and-white or white cock; on the ground in front of the bed they arrange a fine white napkin, on top of it there is syrup, candles lit on the head of bottles, taffia, and other things. After they have finished sprinkling water, clapping their hands, singing to the loa, they go all around the bed of the dead person; the child, cock in hand, makes the rounds with the hounsi. They wave the rooster, they wave it back and forth two, three, four, five, six times over the dead person's head. During this time, all those present get possessed by loas, sing, clap their hands; the dead person's bed begins to creak. The hounsi climbs on the bed, [and] grabs the dead person's two arms in the palms of his hands. He pulls him to a sitting position; the child whom they want the loa to go into the head of, strikes the chicken three times on the head of the dead person; he lets go the chicken, the chicken flies up, he starts to run all around the room, smashing, breaking pots [and] vessels; they grab the chicken [and] they let it go into the air three times, yelling "Ai bobo loa a." ["End it, loa"]. Immediately the loa goes into the head of the dead person's child. They wring the chicken's neck, they cut off its head; without plucking [it], they put it into a stew which has all kinds of foods chopped up: a little handful of beans of each kind, a bit of corn, a bit of roroli, a bit of peanut, a bit of coffee, pimiento pepper, with water from the twins' plate of the house. They make a food they call diak, which all the children eat before the burial.

Brother Lédan's Return

Mò kôn bay jou pou-yo fè dènié priè li, li kônê lésé bèt pouyo touyé pou-li. Lè kô-sa, si-yo pa-fè sa li vlé malè ap-rivé moun-nâ ki gê chajé laprič-a.

Yô jou, frè Lédâ trouvé mouri, li toujou di madâm li, li mèt mouri yô dimâch, sé-madi pou-li fè dènié priè li.

Sé-trouvé yô madi frè Lédâ mouri. Yo fè lâtèmâ-â nâ-aprémidi. Kòm yo kômâsé priè-a mèkrédi, dènié, prié-a ap-fini mèkrédi â-wit. Mê kòm frè Lédâ toujou di sé-pou yo fè dènié prié li yô madi, madâm ni biê kôsâti fè li madi. You madi ké tout moun kônê kédènié prié-a ap-fèt, madâm ni kouté bò-frè li ki di li sa-pa-kôn fèt. Épi li râvoyè dènié priè-a. You madi-a dènié moun réini, madâm-nâ di li râvoyé li. La-a, tou, gê dé msié ki parèt, you salié moun yo ki nâ-kay-la. Yo ofri yo chèy, yo chitâ. Gé yôn nâmésié yo, ki lévé, li di: "W-a-di té-gê yô dènié priè ki t-ap-fèt jodi-a." Madâm-nâ répôn: "Mwê râvoyé-l pou-démê." Lòt nòm lévé bwap souchèy li, li di ak-yô fòs "Sé-pa jodi-a mwê té-di pou-fè dènié prič-a?" La tou madâm-nâ mâdé "Ki moun ou yé?" Tou dé chèy yo vid. Madâm-nâ tôbé sâ-konésâs. Li mouri twa jou apré sa. Sé-mêm nòm ki té-mouri-a ki té-parèt ak-défê frè li, fè mâdâm ni ésplicasiô.

A dead person may set [lit. give] a day for them to make the last prayer for him, he may leave animals for them to kill for him. At a time like that, if they don't do what he wants, misfortune will befall the person who has the duty of the prayer.

One day, brother Ledan chanced to die; he had always told his wife, if he died [lit. he might die] on a Sunday, it was Tuesday she should hold the last prayer for him.

It happened to be a Tuesday when Brother Ledan died. They held the burial in the afternoon. As they began the prayers on Wednesday, the last prayer finished on Wednesday week. But as Brother Ledan had always said they should hold his last prayer on a Tuesday, his wife was quite willing to hold it Tuesday. One Tuesday, when everyone knew that the last prayer was being held, his wife heard her brother-in-law who told her that wasn't customarily done. Then she put off the last prayer. A Tuesday, when everybody was gathered together, the woman said she had put it off. Thereupon there were two men who appeared, [and] they greeted the people who were in the house. They offered them chairs, they sat down. There was one of the men who got up [and] said: "You said there was a last prayer which was being held today." The woman answered: "I put it off till tomorrow." The other man got up, bop! from his chair [and] said: "Wasn't it today I told you to hold the last prayer?" Thereupon the woman asked: "Who are you?" Both the chairs were empty. The woman fell unconscious. She died three days after that. It was the same man who had died, who appeared with his dead brother, to hold an accounting with his wife.

Calls of the Haitian Street Vendors

The Coffee and Rapadou Vendor

Min ra-pa-dou, min_ poud' ca-fé._____ Min ra-pa-dou, min ca-fé._____ Min ra-pa-dou, min_ poud' ca-fé.___

Here is rapadou (hardened brown sugar),
Here is powdered coffee.
Here is rapadou,
Here is coffee.
Here is rapadou,
Here is powdered coffee.

The Kerosine Vendor

Min l'huile, min l'huile, min ké-ro-sine quim-bé lan lampe.

From Les Voix de nos Rues, *by Rene Victor, Port-au-Prince, 1949.*

Here is oil,
Here is oil,
Here is kerosine
That lasts in lamps.

The Bread Vendor

Pain yo gros, yo bel, yo ra - lé pou cinq. Ma -
danm' té di m'con ça, si_m' pas vann la dé___ vo - rém'.

The bread is large,
It is fine,
It is well-pulled for five cob (centimes).
My mistress said
If I don't sell it
She will devour (punish) me.

The Broom Seller

Gros ba - lé, ti' ba - lé, gros ba - lé, ti ba - lé,
min ma - chann ba - lé, min ma - chann ba - lé.

Big brooms, small brooms,
Big brooms, small brooms,
Here is the broom-seller,
Here is the broom-seller.

SOME HAITIAN PROVERBS

Behind the mountains are mountains. (No matter how powerful some-one is, there are others with powers equal to his.)

The high tree says he sees far, the walking (travelling) seed says he sees farther. (The small and weak may have more sense than the large and strong.)

Excrement isn't sharp but it makes you limp. (Said about some un-pleasant affair you'd like to ignore but cannot.)

The bocor (medicine man) gives you a protective charm, but he doesn't tell you to sleep in the middle of the highway. (Even if you feel safe, don't take unnecessary risks.)

The bellowing bull is never fat. (Refers to a person who brags but ac-complishes little.)

The man's affairs aren't small, it's just that his pants are too tight. (Said of a person who may look ludicrous but who nevertheless is well off.)

The eyes see, the mouth is silent. (Don't talk about everything you ob-serve.)

Speaking good French doesn't mean you are smart.

Hit the dog but watch out for his master.

The stick that beats the black dog also beats the white dog. (A knife cuts both ways. It can happen to you also.)

The sheep's affair is none of the goat's business.

Iron cuts iron. (A person may be strong but he's not invincible.)

The drummer can't dance. (Each person has his role. A man can't do too many things at once.)

On a bad day even clabbered milk can break your head.

Don't leave the donkey to beat the saddle basket. (Don't lose your head, you may lose the donkey.)

A donkey has children so it can rest its back.

The mapou tree falls, the goat eats the leaves. (When the mighty fall they are helpless before the weak. This proverb is also used to com-ment on ingratitude, for the goat eats the leaves that have given him shade.)

Stupidity doesn't kill you but it makes you sweat.

Prisons weren't built for dogs.

SOME HAITIAN RIDDLES

Gray horse mounted on his master. A tombstone.

A low obstacle, but the goats can't jump over it. The ocean.

Four bottles upside down. A cow's teats.

Two mothers carrying babies. One carries on the hip, the other on her head. A stalk of corn, a stalk of millet.

My father's chicken gives black eggs. A boll of cotton.

A golden needle that gets the president out of bed. Getting up to uri-nate.

My father's house is green outside, pink inside, and is full of black Haitians. A watermelon.

It is very small but it fills the room. An oil lamp.

It goes one way, it goes another way, it meets itself. A belt.

My father has three children. If one isn't there the other two don't do any work. The three stones of a fireplace. (The pot sets on three stones, the fire underneath.)

Water standing up. Sugar cane.

Two men hitting each other, neither gets hurt. Clapping hands.

Two women talking together in the market, but they don't shake hands. A woman's breasts.

Little man says, "You don't fear me but you walk around me just the same." Excrement.

Sergeant standing in the corner. A broom.

White man licking a black man's bottom. Fire under a pot.

The senators gather all dressed in black. Roasted coffee beans.

God sent me two bottles, one filled with sweet, one with sour. Life and death.

My father's horse is losing his teeth. A comb.

My grandfather's garden. In the daytime there's nothing there, but at night it's full of potatoes. Stars in the sky.

My father's sons wave their machetes in the air but they never cut one another. Blades of grass.

The bad-mannered boy points his finger at this person and that person. Palm fronds.

Meat underneath, meat on top, skin in the middle. A saddle.

NEGRO SONG POETRY IN PUERTO RICO

Although most of the song forms in Puerto Rico are shared, the common property of all ethnic and social groups, the bomba is almost exclusively a Negro tradition. Bombas are a special class of coplas, or popular songs, sung to accompany drum dances. The term bomba also refers to a type of drum of probably African origin, once constructed from a hollowed log but later made from barrel staves or a small barrel. By extension, the word refers to drums in general and the act of drumming. A drum dance is known as a baile de bomba, whose musical sound has much of the African quality of similar dances found elsewhere in the Caribbean.

Bomba dances are held on special festival occasions in predominantly Negro communities such as Loiza Aldea, not far from San Juan. The songs are generally short and do not have a classical form as do de-

cimas and aguinaldos. Nor do they have the tradition of the repeated
first line that characterizes Haitian songs and North American blues.
Their subject matter includes a wide variety of topics close to the experience of the singers, and frequently they express criticism or ridicule, or voice social comment. As in Afro-American songs heard elsewhere in the Western Hemisphere, there are frequent double enten-
dres, many of which would not be noted by outsiders. There is ample
evidence that bombas sung a century ago contained African words, expressions and idioms that have now faded away. For example, except
for the name Migué (Miguél), this old bomba defies translation:

> Aya, bombe, quinombó!
> Ohé, ohé mano Migué!
> Ayayá, sagú, carú!
> Ohé, ohé, quinombó!

Likewise, some of the decimas set down early in this century are in a
dialect once spoken by Afro–Puerto Ricans but no longer commonly
encountered.

Here is some of the Negro song poetry found in Puerto Rico, in free
translation:

When They Start the Fire (Bomba)

Cuando rompe el fuego
en cualquier bachata,
todo el mundo dice:
A bailar, muchachas.
¡ Ja, ja, ja, ja, ja, ja, ja!
¡ El pito!

When they light the fire
for the celebration,
everyone says:
Girls, come and dance.
Ja, ja, ja, ja, ja, ja, ja!
The whistle!

Mi mulata tiene
un pie chiquitito;
por eso le hago
zapatos bonitos.
¡ Ja, ja, ja, ja, ja, ja, ja!
¡ El pito!

My mulatto girl
has a small foot;
I make for her
beautiful shoes
Ja, ja, ja, ja, ja, ja, ja!
The whistle!

Mi mulata tiene
un baja-talle;
ella se lo pone
cuando va a la calle.
¡ Ja, ja, ja . . . etc.
¡ El pito!

My mulatto girl has
a low-necked dress;
she puts it on
when she goes in the street.
Ja, ja, ja . . . etc.
The whistle!

*The examples of bombas given here are from "Porto-Rican Folklore," by J.
Alden Mason, Journal of American Folklore, Vol. 31, No. 21, July–September
1918. The two examples of decimas were kindly contributed by Dr. Pedro
Escabí.*

The next stanza seems to have sexual innuendo:

Mi mulata tiene	My mulatto girl has
un buen pisa-pelo,	a good hair presser,
mi mulata tiene	my mulatto girl has
algo en el tablero.	something in the board.
¡ Ja, ja, ja . . . etc.	Ja, ja, ja . . . etc.
¡ El pito!	The whistle!

There Are Many Negroes Here (Bomba)

Hay muchos negros aquí;	There are many Negroes here;
al decirlo no me escondo;	I don't hesitate to say it;
que el que no tiene de congo	He who is not a Congo
tiene de carabalí.	is a Carabali.
¡ Jesucristo! qué me va espantar	Jesus Christ! It does not scare me
como hacen los negros para	when their mouths yawn open!
bostezar!	They open their mouths and say, ay, ay, ay
Abren la boca y hacen. Ay, ay, ay!	

When the White Man Plays the Drum (Bomba)

Cuando el blanco toca bomba	When the white man plays the drum
el Negro sale a bailar,	the Negro comes out to dance,
y coge su parejita	and he gets hold of his partner
y se pone a relajar.	and he begins the gaiety.

The Black Amelia (Bomba)

La negrita Amelia	The black girl Amelia,
ésa es mi mujer;	she is my woman;
yo la quiero,	I love her,
yo la quiero,	I love her,
yo la quiero.	I love her.
¡ Ay, ay, ay!	Ay, ay, ay!
¡ Ay, ay, ay!	Ay, ay, ay!

When a Negro Goes to a Dance (Decima)

This song is a social comment on something that occurred at a dance. The individuals concerned are probably known to the listeners, and the singer is holding the white father up to contempt and ridicule.

Cuando un negro va a un baile	When a Negro goes to a dance
y ve a una muchacha blanca	and sees a white girl there
manda a tocar una danza	he asks her to dance
como si fueran iguales;	as if they were equals;
y doe pronto llega el padre	suddenly her father arrives
y dice: " ¿ Que diache es esto?	and says: "What the devil is this?
en mi casa no hay respeto.	there is no respect for my house.
A mi hija vengo a buscar,	I have come to get my daughter,
porque no la dejo bailar	because I do not let her dance
con ese morcillo prieto."	with that black sausage."

A Black Man Stole a Chicken (Decima)

The word Negro is used in this song much as is common elsewhere in the Carribbean, to mean "man," rather than to emphasize race. Again, an incident is described and an action criticized, but there is a goodly portion of humor, with double entendre intended in the lines depicting a button snapping off and a chicken coming out.

Un negro como un caldero	A man as black as a kettle
una polla se robó	stole a chicken
y como nadie lo vió	and no one seeing him
cogió y se la echó en el seno.	he hid it inside his clothing.
Ese negro no era bueno	The Negro was not good
cuando se robe esa polla	when he stole that chicken
y se formó una tramolla:	and there was a big commotion;
le dieron un pescozón	someone gave him a hard slap
se le reventó el botón	and burst off a button
y se le salió la polla.	and the chicken came out.

FOUR TALES FROM GUADELOUPE
TRANSLATED FROM THE CREOLE

Woy, Who Knows?

A man named Manteau was accused of stealing a goat from his neighbor and was ordered to appear in court on a certain day. He quickly found a lawyer to plead his case for him. The lawyer questioned Manteau thoroughly. Convinced that Manteau had in fact stolen the goat, he decided to make the man appear simpleminded in court, and thus gain the sympathy of the judge. So he instructed Manteau to say nothing at all in court except, "Woy, who knows?" He said, "If they ask you your name, or how old you are, or anything else, say nothing but 'Woy, who knows?'"

The day of the hearing came. Manteau and his lawyer were in the courtroom, and so were Manteau's accuser and his lawyer. Manteau's accuser told his story, saying that he found the goat tied up behind Manteau's house. So the judge asked Manteau what he had to say. Manteau said, "Woy, who knows?" The judge asked again, "Did you steal the goat or not?" Manteau answered, "Woy, who knows?" The judge said, "How did the goat come to be at your house?" Manteau said, "Woy, who knows?" The judge said, "Have you ever been in trouble before?" And Manteau answered, "woy, who knows?"

The judge shook his head, saying, "This man is simpleminded. If he did in fact steal the goat, he didn't know what he was doing. The accuser has reclaimed the goat. Let the matter rest there. Let Manteau go."

So Manteau went free. And when they were outside the courthouse his lawyer said to him, "Well, you see how I managed your case. It is all over. Now there is the matter of the fee. It is five hundred francs." Manteau said, "Woy, who knows?" The lawyer said, "You can stop that now, the trial is over. We are talking about my fee." Manteau said, "Woy, who knows?" The lawyer said, "I would like to have my money today." Manteau said, "Woy, who knows?" The lawyer said, "Well, then, I must absolutely have the money tomorrow." Manteau said, "Woy, who knows?" The lawyer said, "When are you going to pay the fee?" Manteau answered, "Woy, who knows?"

Why People Do Not Live Again After Death

One day Cat met Dog, and they made conversation. They spoke of death, and Cat said, "Man is born, he dies, and when he dies he does not rise to live again." Dog said, "No, people die, they rise again." They argued. Cat said, "Tomorrow let us go and see what God has to say about the matter." Dog said, "Yes, let us go." But after Cat had left, Dog contrived to distract Cat on the journey. He placed bits of butter along the trail, thinking, "Cat will stop to eat some butter here, some butter there, and I will arrive at God's house first." Cat, on the other hand, placed fresh bones along the trail to distract Dog on the journey.

In the morning they set out. They came to where Dog had set out the butter, but the cat did not stop. They came to the place where Cat had put out a bone. Dog stopped. He could not resist the bone. He gnawed at it, while Cat went on. Each time Cat came to the butter he merely looked ahead and kept on the trail. But each time that Dog found a bone he stopped and gnawed on it. So it was that Cat arrived at God's house first.

He asked God whether man died and remained dead, or whether he arose and lived again. God said, "What is your position on this matter?" And Cat answered, "I contend that people die and do not arise from death, but remain dead." God replied, "Well, then let us leave it that way."

In time, Dog arrived. He put the same question to God. God said to him, "Well, the matter has been decided. Cat came. He contended that the dead should remain dead. I said, 'Very well, that is the way it will be.' You, Dog, you are too late. Coming along the trail you did not keep your mind on your purpose. You stopped here and there, wherever you smelled something to eat. Therefore it shall be as Cat has said. People shall die and not live again." (For an African comparison, see Appendix IX, p. 585.)

Oh, Misery!

A syrup vendor was travelling along the road one day when she came to a wet place and slipped. The jar of syrup she carried on her head fell to the ground and broke. She cried out, "Oh, misery! Oh, misery!" Seeing that there was nothing that could be done, she went on. But a monkey sitting in a nearby tree went down to investigate the cause of the commotion. He tasted the spilled syrup. It was sweet, sweet, sweet. Never had he tasted anything as good. He licked it from the ground until it was gone. Still he wanted more. He asked the cat where he might find some more of that wonderful Misery. The cat didn't know what he was talking about. He asked the donkey, the guinea fowl and the pig. He went everywhere searching for Misery, asking here, asking there. One day he asked the cow about it. The cow answered, "Only God knows what you are talking about." So the monkey decided he would go to God's house to procure some of that wonderful tasting food.

He dressed in his holiday clothes. He went along the road that led to God's house. He arrived. God was very busy, but he stopped long enough to ask the monkey what he wanted. The monkey said, "God, I'm sorry to disturb you. But there's something I have to have." God said, "What is it?" The monkey answered, "What I need is Misery." God replied, "People have come to ask for many things, but you are the first to ask for misery." The monkey said, "Oh, yes, I had it once before, and now I can't live without it." God said, "Well, it is a strange request. I am very busy right now. But take this key and open that large box over there. It contains what you are looking for."

The monkey took the key and went to the box, saying, "What an enormous supply of Misery God has in his house!" He opened the box. Three fierce dogs leaped out. The monkey turned and ran. The dogs pursued him down the trail from God's place. The monkey was in great fear. When he came at last to the big trees he swiftly climbed up and crouched in the topmost branches until the dogs went away.

Eventually the monkey came down. But the dogs were never far away, and time after time he had to seek safety in the tops of the trees. Whenever he heard the dogs coming he cried out, "Oh, misery!" Thus it was that the monkey learned the true meaning of the cry of the syrup vendor: "Oh, misery! Oh, misery!"

Rabbit Seeks Wisdom

Compère Rabbit one day went to ask God for wisdom. God said to him, "Every person already has a little wisdom." Rabbit answered, "It is true. Everyone has a little of it. But I want much wisdom." God pondered on the question. He said, "Very well. If you can meet the tests, I will give it to you." Rabbit asked, "What are the tests?" And God replied, "There are three impossible things. No one else has been able to do them. First, bring me the scales of the great ocean fish. Second, bring me milk from the wild cow. Third, bring me two teeth from the mouth of a living crocodile."

Compère Rabbit said, "It is nothing. I will get them." He went home. He took his drum. He went to the edge of the sea. He began to play his drum, calling for all the great fish to come and dance. Small fish appeared. They came out of the water and danced around Compère Rabbit. He said, "This dance is for the great fish of the sea. Surely there are others larger than you." Large fish appeared out of the water and joined the dance. Rabbit said, "Where is the greatest fish of all? Is he afraid to dance?" At last the great fish appeared, but he would not come out of the water. He simply watched the others dancing. So Rabbit said, "Great One, come and play the drum while I dance." The great fish came and played the drum while Rabbit danced. After a while Rabbit said, "Now I will play the drum while you dance." So Rabbit played the drum and the great fish danced. Then Rabbit said, "Now I will lie down and rest while you watch over me." He lay down and rested, and the great fish watched over him. After a while Rabbit said, "Now you lie down and I will watch over you." So the great fish lay down, but no sooner had he done so than Rabbit struck him a blow and killed him. He took the scales from the great fish to God, saying, "I believe you asked for these." And he recounted how he had obtained them.

After that, Rabbit went to the woods. He climbed a large tree and began calling for the wild cow to come and get him. The wild cow appeared, looking very angry. She said, "Who calls me in such a disrespectful way?" And Rabbit answered, "It is I, Compère Rabbit. I have just made a wager with people back home. They say you are strong enough to knock over a tree this size, and I say you are too weak. So tell me, what is the truth of the matter?" The wild cow answered, "You are wrong, wrong. I can do it." Rabbit said, "Is it really possible? But how can I take your word for it?" The wild cow said, "I will show you that my word is good." She put her head down and charged the tree in which Rabbit was sitting. The tree was a soft one, like cork, and the wild cow's horns went in deep. She could not pull her horns out. Rabbit said, "Oh, that was a good one. Try again." But the wild cow said, "I cannot remove my horns." Rabbit said, "Are you certain?" The wild cow answered, "I am certain." Then Rabbit came down. He had a small gourd with him. He milked the wild cow, and she could do nothing about it. He took the gourd of milk to God, saying, "I believe you asked for this." He told God how he had obtained the milk.

Rabbit then left God's place and went to his own house. There he asked his wife for soap, which he carried to a certain trail used by the crocodile. He soaped the trail from the top of the hill to the bottom, and at the bottom he placed a large rock. Then he called out to the crocodile, "Come quick! At the bottom of the trail there is a rabbit for you to eat!" And he lay down near the rock and pretended to be dead. Crocodile came out of his house at the top of the hill. He saw Compère Rabbit lying down below as if he were dead. He began to come down. He slipped on the soap. He could not keep from slipping. He slid faster and faster. And at the bottom he crashed against the large rock, which knocked two teeth from his jaw. Compère Rabbit jumped up, seized the two teeth and carried them to God's house. He said, "I believe you asked for these." God asked, "How did you get them?" And Rabbit told him.

God said, "You have done three impossible things. It required great wisdom to do what you have done. You already have what you came to get from me. I can add nothing to the cleverness in your head. But take care, Rabbit! Cleverness like this can kill you."

(For an African comparison, see Appendix X, pp. 586–87.)

TWO OLD SLAVE SONGS FROM CARRIACOU

This song recalls an event in slavery days, the sale of a husband and wife to different plantations, one in Trinidad and one in Haiti. Their children were left behind in Carriacou.

From "The Big Drum Dance of Carriacou," introductory notes by Andrew C. Pearse to record album by the same name, New York, Ethnic Folkways Library, 1956. These two translations from the original Creole vary somewhat from those given by Mr. Pearse.

Cry for me, Lidé, cry for me Maiwaz, oh!
Wail for me, Lidé, wail for me, oh, Maiwaz!
Lament, for we are going away!
Next Sunday the schooner sails to Haiti,
Friday it departs from there, oh, Maiwaz!
Whoever loves me, console my choldren for me!
Whoever loves me, console Zabette for me!
Whoever loves me, console Walter for me!

The following brief words speak of the homesickness of a slave, or, alternately, loneliness for deceased parents. Read one way, it suggests that her parents were left behind in Africa. But it was believed by many that when one died he returned to Africa (Guinea), and interpreted this way the song could be one of mourning for a dead father and mother.

Woyo, Maman, beautiful Louise, oh!
I want to go to Guinea to meet with my parents!
But the sea stands in my way!

THE BAMBOULA DANCE, MYTH AND REALITY

According to a number of early chroniclers, whoever had seen the Bamboula Dance had been spectator to unfettered human depravity. One interpreter of the Virgin Islands scene declared that the last "true" Bamboula Dance occurred in 1848, after which time it was diluted into something scarcely resembling its former self. As he described the dance before its reform:

"At these dances, a girl begins slowly, with the rhythms of the tambours, to disrobe as she dances before a group of men around the fire. When she is naked the music grows faster and she dances more wildly until she seizes a tame snake and holds it before her, often using the tail as a phallus. When everybody is thoroughly excited, the sacrifice is ready. It might be a child, or an animal, but the blood is smeared on everyone, who is thus bound to keep whatever compact has been made."[1]

George Cable[2] did not show so much imagination, but he adhered to the tradition of describing the Bamboula in New Orleans as a dance of wild abandon:

---

1. *The Virgin Islands and Their People,* by J. Antonio Jarvis, *Philadelphia, Dorrance and Co., 1944.*
2. *"The Dance in Place Congo," by George Cable,* Century Magazine, *February, 1886.*

"A sudden frenzy seizes the musicians. . . . What wild, what terrible delight! The ecstasy rises to madness; one—two—three of the dancers fall—*bloucoutoum! boum!*—with foam on their lips and are dragged out. . . . It was a frightful triumph of body over mind. . . ."

In reality, the Bamboula—known throughout the West Indies and in Louisiana, sometimes under different names—was a recreational dance of plantation workers and other country people. Even in the English-speaking islands, songs sung to Bamboula rhythms were frequently in the Creole language, indicating that the dance may have spread from such places as Martinique, Trinidad, Haiti or even the Louisiana mainland. Although it was a secular dance, it sometimes had an institutionalized function, providing an activity for people attending "last prayers" or a "nine-night" for a deceased person. The Bamboula was, and is, danced to the music of a single drum, which is usually played in a horizontal position with the drummer sitting astride it, and another musician beating sticks against the body of the drum. Although drumming is primarily a man's activity in the West Indies, at times of carnival in the Virgin Islands the Bamboula drum is sometimes played by women.

Songs heard at Bamboula dances may be old and well known or newly composed and topical. Subject matter may be in the Calypso tradition, or social complaint and criticism, or allude to personalities within the community. The following song, heard in St. Thomas, is in praise of a one-time chairman of the local legislative council:

> Good evening, dear chairman,
> Good evening, dear sir.
> What a privilege you have done to us,
> To take the old from the gutter.
>
> Good evening, Mr. Harris,
> Good evening dear sir.
> You will never want as long as you live,
> For you look to a home for the homeless.
>
> Good evening, Mr. Harris,
> Good evening, dear sir.
> If it wasn't for the God-damned lottery,
> This life would be murder.[3]

3. *From* Isles of Rhythm, *by Earl Leaf, New York, A.S. Barnes and Company, 1948.*

PREACHER TALES IN THE CARRIBEAN

The Responsive Congregation

Once upon a time a minister went to church, he had forget his glasses, so he said to the congregation, "Dear beloved people, my eyes are very dim, I can not see to read the hymn. I leave my glasses at home." The people start to sing,

> My eyes are very very dim,
> I can not even see to read the hymn.

The minister said, "I never told you that you must sing. I only say that my eyes were dim." They start,

> I never told you that you must sing,
> I only say that my eyes were dim.

The minister said, "What foolish people all you be! I'll take my hat and go." They start,

> What foolish people all you be!
> I'll take my hat and go.

The minister left and the whole congregation left behind him.

> The wheel bend and the story end.

(St. Croix)

The Parson's Beard

Once upon a time a woman went to church. So when the parson began to preach, the woman began to cry. The parson t'ought it was his sermon had touch her heart, so he told her when church out, to stay in.

She stayed. When the minister asked her what was the matter, she said, "Parson, I can't tell you."

He said, "Tell me, sister, and let me help you."

She said the second time, "Parson, I can't."

He said, "Tell me! Let me see what I can do for you."

Eight tales from Folk-Lore of the Antilles, French and English, *by Elsie Clews Parsons, Memoirs of the American Folk-Lore Society, Vol. XXVI, 1936. Reprinted by permission of the American Folklore Society.*

Then she said "Parson, every time I see your mouth going up and down, it put me n mind of the old ram goat that they steal f'om me."

> I step in a little butter.
> If the butter was little stronger,
> My story would of end a little longer.

(St. Croix)

Whatsoever in Thy Bosom

Once upon a time a man went to church. So he was living far, so he made some dumplin to take with him that when church out, he would have something to eat. And it happen that the minister's text was, "Whatsoever in they bussom, pluck it out!" The man had the dumplin' in his bussom, so he said, "Minister, I have three dumplin' and I can't give you any because it ishent enough." And the whole church was alarm.

> The wheel bend
> And the story end.

(St. Croix)

The Hymn

Once upon a time a man went to church. He was a bull miner so for many years he didn't go to church, but this was festival Sunday, so he determine to go this Sunday. So he paid a friend to work for him that Sunday. Now when you are a stranger and you go in any church the people always give you a book to follow the services.

Now the minister give out a hymn, and the hymn was Holy Holy Holy, Lord God Almighty! The man could not read. So he had a cow in his flocks name Marley and he began to sing, "Woah Marley, Woah Woah Woah Marley! Woah! If I come down there I'll cut Marley tail."

The parson had to stop him and said, "No friend, you are wrong, it's not that. The hymn is Holy Holy Holy."

He turn and told the minister, "Hold me, no hold, hell!" And he took his hat and leave, and the news spread all over the country. The story end.

(St. Croix)

Pack of Cards

Dere was a sergeant who went to church an' not having no prayer book it was a pack o' cards he had in his pawket. So he took dem out an' he follow his Mass by de cards. So one of his officers notice it and cyarry him up to de court. And dey ask him what was de meanin' of de pack dat he had in church, and he said de ace remoin him of one god, de t'ree, of de t'ree persons, de seven, of de sacraments, de five, of de five wirgins, de Jack, of Judas, de ten, de ten commandments, de king was King Soloman, de queen, de queen of Sheba, de four was de four evangelists. Den he get clear.

(St. Bartholomew)

The Parson's Hog

One day a man went to service and he put a penny in the plate the parson passed around. The parson told him come tomorrow for grace. He didn't understood what the parson told him. But the parson had a hog by the name of Grace. He didn't wait til the parson comes, he went in right to the pen and took the hog. When he reach home he kills it and start to cook. He give his son a bone, son went out in the street with the bone eatin'. Parson met him and ax him what is he eatin'? So he told the parson, "You told my father yesterday to come for Grace, when he came you was not there, so he took Grace, kill it and here am I now with Grace bone in my hand." Parson told the little boy, "Come to church tomorrow!" The boy went home and told his father what the parson told him and what he told the parson. Father said, "Go back to the parson and tell him you have no clothes, no shoes, and no hat, so you cyan not come to service tomorrow." The boy went and told the parson just what the father told him. The parson said to him, "I will give you everything just to come to service tomorrow to tell the truth and nothing but the truth." The parson said to him, "I will put you in the pulpit and you will tell all brothers and sisters what your father did." He said yes. So the parson invited all big folks to come and listen at the truth, nothing but the truth. The boy went home to his father and told his father the parson said he will give him everything just to tell the truth. The father said to the boy, "When you go in tomorrow, son, do as I tell you! You will say, " 'The parson says he is going to live with the sexton wife for all the days of his life.' " So the little boy did so, and all the people walked out the church and believe what the parson says no more.

(Guadeloupe)

Come In or Stay Out

Dere was an Irishman oncet, who was very fond of drinking hard. One day a minister says to him, "But stop, Michael! When you fellow drink so hard, how can you expect to get to Heaven when you die?" De Irishman say, "Oh, get away f'om me! When I die, I'll go to de gate of

Heaven. I'll push it in and haul it out and I will continue so until Saint Peter get displease' wid me an' say, 'Fah goodness sake, Michael, eider come in or stay out!' "

(Antigua)

My Name First

There were two Englishmen in Guadeloupe who didn't understand the Creole language. One was named Dominique, the other Maurencie. One day these two Englishmen went to Mass. As they entered the church they heard the priest call out, "Dominus vobiscum!"

When they left the church Dominique said, "The priest mentioned my name before yours."

Maurencie said, "Very well, Tomorrow I will go to Mass and you will go also. And you will hear my name mentioned before yours."

Maurencie went to the priest. He said, "Good day, Father, good day! Father, I came to ask you to mention my name in church tomorrow before Dominique's. I will give you five hundred francs and two carrés of land planted in grapes if you will call out my name before Dominique's."

"Yes," the priest said, "I will call out your name first."

The next morning when the Mass began the priest sang:

"Do you know that Maurencie has given me five hundred francs
And two carrés of land planted in grapes
To call out his name before Dominique's?"

And the congregation sang back in response:
"Oh, man, you are too stingy."

(Guadeloupe)

WEST INDIAN CALYPSO

The style of singing known as Calypso attracted the attention of the outside world as a genre belonging primarily to Trinidadians, but factually speaking it was a generalized form encountered widely in the English-speaking islands of the Caribbean. The style is rooted in folk songs that antedated what we know as Calypso, and some of its characteristics are shared with other West Indian song forms. One of the marks of the "true" Calypso, according to some older people who recall when Calypso was in its prime, is that the song presented one side of a debate or argument. On various festival occasions Calypso singers would gather to contest with one another. One singer would improvise a song on a selected topic, making some kind of debatable assertion—for example, that a man should only marry a woman with money. His adversary, singing to the same standard musical accompaniment (perhaps a guitar and rattle, or a small band) would counter with the proposition that a man should never marry a wealthy woman.

The improvised nature of these songs required a considerable knack for quick thinking, quick phrasemaking, and rhyming. The singers did not hesitate to use doggerel, well-worn clichés, erudite allusions, or fancy phrases that were not part of everyday speech. The words had to match the music, and where long words were used the singers sometimes had to cramp them into a space much too small. The test was to sing well, make the argument in a witty or broadly humorous way, and to fit the song into a pretty much predetermined form. As stated in one Calypso song:

> Veteran Calypsonians are known to be
> Men who can sing on anything instantaneously.

The origins of Calypso are not known in a precise way, but older people in Trinidad generally agree that English-language Calypso developed out of a Creole tradition. Some of the oldest known Calypso songs are in fact in the Creole language. As one song acknowledges:

> Would you like to know what is Calypso?
> It was sung by the Creoles years ago.

It was only when Calypso began to be sung in English that it became widely popular throughout the English-speaking West Indies and, on phonograph records, invaded the mainland.

Musically, Calypso belongs to a general category of West Indian traditions. It is a New World style compounded of a good many influences. Its structure ranges from rigid to free, and since its beginnings it has absorbed elements of various other types of singing. But to a conspicuous degree its substance reflects elements of the earlier Creole culture and even earlier African patterns. The content of Calypso songs may be social comment, gossip, complaint, recrimination, moralizing, personal adventures, women, current events, or perhaps mere vignettes. Seen this way, in terms of content they parallel the Blues of the American mainland, though differing in mood. As in the Blues, there is considerable sexual allusion and double entendre. And like the Blues, Calypso derives its essential substance from African songs of complaint, social comment and recrimination.

Professional Calypsonians sought names for themselves that could not be confounded with any other, names that sounded almost like royal titles. There were, for example, Houdini, Destroyer, The Growler, Lord Invader, Macbeth, Duke of Iron, Sly Mongoose, Lord Beginner, Lord Executor, Mighty Zebra, Mighty Terror, Black Czar, Sir Jablonski and, no doubt, hundreds of other such sonorous appellations.

The annual pre-Lenten Mardi Gras Carnival in Trinidad was the great event for Calypsonians. As seen by one observer in the 1930s:

> The Negroes of the island look forward to Carnival for months.
> For weeks every store on the island displays masks and the mak-

ings of costumes. Everyone, no matter how poor, manages somehow to invest. Blackface regalia is conspicuous by its absence.
Clown-white is the special favorite.

Half the population is costumed by daybreak of Mardi Gras
Monday, most of them with notable originality. One school of costume that is a conspicuous favorite bases its inspiration, by a curious inheritance, in the regalia of the long-dead Caribs who once
populated the island. They are elaborate affairs of turkey red, ca-
nary yellow and orange robes, sashes and flowing sleeves, the
whole topped by enormous paper headdresses in the form of tow-
ers, turreted castles and great ships. Others dress in white towel-
ing, wear pink paper ears and unconvincingly announce themselves as rabbits. Still others are gorgeous black bats with yellow
wings. Variety is endless; the congested streets of Port of Spain at
the height of the festivities a remarkable spectacle.

Typically, groups of celebrants form themselves into bands and
walk the streets begging and singing. Their musical instruments–
and, since they are Negroes, they produce real music from them–
are often nothing more than washboards scraped with an iron rod,
two hard sticks rapped together, gourds filled with seeds and big
graters scraped with a heavy nail. [See p. 4, Ed.] Their singing,
sometimes prepared a little in advance, often extemporized on the
spot, deals with anything and anyone that happens to occur to
them. Many calypso songs are therefore necessarily poor. Others
are ribald, effective, and extraordinarily brilliant. Prizes are award-
ed at each Carnival for the best.

So stimulating a custom is not to be set aside when the holiday is
over. Particularly gifted singers and composers have emerged, surrounded themselves with efficient bands, and become profession-
als. Now, through the whole year, every event that interests the
common people of the island finds its way quickly into the calypso
form.

On a recent visit to Trinidad I spent an evening at a large moving picture theater in Port of Spain where a half-dozen of the more
famous calypso singers were appearing. There were no other
whites in an audience of nearly a thousand. The conduct of the
affair was totally un-selfconscious.

A band of about ten players–sophisticated to the point of good
clothes, banjos, clarinets and saxophones–seated themselves in
kitchen chairs on the stage, then, one by one the stars came on and
sang their latest calypso compositions into a microphone. Their
noms-de-pièce had a Carnival character. On that evening I heard
Attila, The Lion, Houdini, Radio King, and Young Pretender.

The subjects they sang of were the recent resignation of a

Carnival description is from Caribbee Cruise, © *1938 by John Vandercook; renewed 1966 by John Christopher Vandercook and Margaret Vandercook. Reprinted by permission of Harcourt Brace Jovanovich.*

governor-general, a strike riot in the southern oil fields, a speech made at the last assemblage of the Legislative Council, the state of the cocoa market—none, one might think, rich in lyric or comic possibilities, yet all poignantly close to the interests and emotions of the audience. I was a complete outsider, in race, in experience. I knew little or nothing of the subjects discussed in the calypso singing. Yet, so magnificent was their rhythm, so vivid and original their style, and so sharp and infectious their wit, outsider though I was, I found myself completely enthralled. I was made to yell with laughter, my feet twitched responsively to the irresistible time, my palms became worn from applause.

Here was folk-music—spontaneous and unwritten—as it was meant to be. Here, as was the intention of song, the matter was life itself, its hourly, immediate events. The singers, queer, ill-assorted, oddly dressed colored men outwardly like any passers-by of the Port of Spain streets, seemed to me to be men of genius.

The conclusion of the performance was most remarkable of all. The stars, who previously had taken turns at the microphone, at last crowded round it in a body—and for twenty minutes engaged in a rapid-fire, completely extemporaneous, humorous cross-talk in *rhymed song*. It was an unbelievable achievement. I know no group of entertainers in America or England who could rely with such entire success upon their own unaided wits.

Small Island (DUKE OF IRON)

No flour, no rice in the land.
Why, because it's too many small island.
They come by the one and the two and the three,
Now I find them up inside my breadfruit tree.
Oh, Small Island, go back where you really come from,
Yes, Small Island, go back where you come from.
You come from Trinidad in a fishing boat,
Now you wearing a swagger coat.
Small Island, go back where you really come from.
You see them Bajan, they are the worst of all,
Hear they all talk, "Me no going back at all."
Well, in Barbados there was an old carterman,
In Trinidad they are a great big policeman.
Small Island, go back where you really come from.
Now we have a quelbo playing in the band
Running all about and saying he is a Cuban.
Play the violin is all that he know,
He run all about and say he'll pizzicato.
Small Island, go back where you really come from.
Now the Lord Invader is a smart fellow,

He tell the people that he is famous for Coca Cola.
Run all about and say he make his name
Fooling around with the women in Port of Spain.
Small Island, go back where you really come from.

Bamboo Dance (BLACK CZAR)

One night I took a chance
And I went to the Bamboo Dance.
Uh-huh, one night I took a chance
And I went to the Bamboo Dance.
Believe me, the rhythms they sound so sweet

Music notation by John Benson Brooks.

That I went to the dance walking on my feet.
Oh yes, join the Bamboo Dance,
Hold on your cap, take a chance!
Oh yes, join the Bamboo Dance,
Hold on your cap, take a chance!

Me, I didn't take no chance
The night that I went to this Bamboo Dance.
I was sitting in the far corner
And the old lady choose me for her partner.
Then she started wiggeewam,
É Lord, I think she was a wily one.
Then what she said:
Oh yes, join the Bamboo Dance,
Hold on your cap, take a chance!
Oh yes, join the Bamboo Dance,
Hold on your cap, take a chance!

In the middle of the night
Somebody went and doused out the light.
Everybody holding their post
Started to rub one another's nose.
The old lady said, partner hold me tight
And don't let go till they turn on the light.
That's what she said:
Oh yes, join the Bamboo Dance,
Hold on your cap, take the chance!
Oh yes, join the Bamboo Dance,
Hold on your cap, take the chance!

She said, this rhythm for two,
I love the rhythm from this here Bamboo.
This rhythm do make me feel glad,
It reminds me of my days from East Trinidad.
Then the old lady start to shake
And twisting her body round like a snake
And what she said:
Oh yes, join the Bamboo Dance,
Hold on your cap, take the chance!
Oh yes, join the Bamboo Dance,
Hold on your cap, take the chance!

I tell you I was ringing down wet
When I heard the rhythm from the clarinet.
É Lord, the melody get right in me bone
And I hear a noise from the saxophone.
The old lady said to me, bacchanal,
Young boy, don't stop it at all.

And what she said:
Oh yes, join the Bamboo Dance,
Hold on your cap, take the chance!
Oh yes, join the Bamboo Dance,
Hold on your cap, take the chance!

Subway Train (LORD INVADER)

When I first landed in the U.S.A.
Listen how I got lost on the subway.
When I first landed in the U.S.A.
Listen how I got lost on the subway.
I had a date with a chick and I went to Brooklyn,
But I couldn't find my way back the following morning.
I had money yet I had to roam,
And still I couldn't get a cab to drop me back home.

I met a cop and I told him I'm a stranger,
Lord Invader, a Calypso singer,
I live in Harlem and came here yesterday,
But now I want to go home and I can't find my way.
He told me to walk back three blocks and he further explained,
Go to subway and take the uptown train.
I got confused, I was in a heat,
I couldn't find my way to 125th Street.

I came out the subway and didn't know what to do,
Looking for someone to help me through.
You talk about people as bad as crabs
Is the drivers who driving the taxicabs.
Some passing you empty and yet they won't stop,
Some will say they have no gas or they can't make the drop.
I had money yet I had to roam,
But still I couldn't get a cab to drop me back home.

I consoled myself and started to walk,
I said that happens to persons born in New York.
So I decided to leave the girls alone,
If they wanted to see me they must come to my home.
Because New York is so big it takes a year and a day
For anyone to get accustomed to the subway.
I had money yet I had to roam,
And still I couldn't get a cab to drop me back home.

Dorothy, One Morning (MACBETH)

I went on a spree, one morning,
I went to see Dorothy, one morning,
But I met a collision,
It was me and a policeman, one morning.

I knock the door without any fear,
I said, "Dorothy darling, are you there?"
But I put myself in a calalou,
The police was knocking on the back door too, one morning.

She got right up and she turned the lock,
But at the back door was a different knock,
In march the branch of the law,
And said, "Macbeth, what you come for?" one morning.

I said, "I come here to cut my shine,"
But he said, "You come here for what is mine."
I had to appeal to sweet Dorothy,
She said, "Tonight let us sleep in three," one morning.

He said, "My boy, don't you contemplate,
For Dorothy is a heavyweight,
And if you are strong you can win this fight,
But I am going to box like Louis tonight," one morning.

So I went in a dream in the middle of the night,
I feel something was holding me tight,
I got up and I made a way-down caress,
And I found my head on the policeman's chest, one morning.

There is one thing, friends, I would like to know,
Why Dorothy treat Macbeth so,
She had Pacheco under the bed,
And Duke of Iron hit him in his head, one morning.

My Donkey Want Water (MACBETH)

Hold him Joe, hold him Joe,
Hold him Joe but don't let him go,
Will you hold him Joe but don't let him go.
My donkey want water, hold him Joe,
Better hold your daughter, hold him Joe,
For when my donkey want water, hold him Joe,
My donkey is bad, hold him Joe,
I'm from Fyzabad, hold him Joe,

My donkey want water, hold him Joe,
My donkey want water, hold him Joe.

I took me donkey to Sandigrad
And he bit off the hand of a obeah man,
This donkey of mine wouldn't work at all,
All he does is break the boards out the stall.
When he want his water, hold him Joe,
Better hold your daughter, hold him Joe,
When me donkey want water, hold him Joe,
My donkey is bad, hold him Joe,
I'm from Trinidad, hold him Joe,
Oh me donkey want water, hold him Joe.

The whole thing, friends, is true jealousy,
They want to take me donkey from me,
They want to put me donkey in pound for spite,
Just because they know me donkey can fight.
When he want his water, hold him Joe,
Better hold your daughter, hold him Joe,
My donkey is bad, hold him Joe,
I'm from Fyzabad, hold him Joe,
My donkey want water, hold him Joe.

The whole thing, friends, is true jealousy,
They want to take me donkey from me,
My donkey is a donkey, don't make no fun,
If you are not a good jockey you got to run.
When he want his water, hold him Joe,
Better hold your daughter, hold him Joe,
My donkey is bad, hold him Joe,
I'm from Trinidad, hold him Joe,
My donkey want water, hold him Joe,
My donkey want water, hold him Joe.

Matilda (DUKE OF IRON)

O, Lord, it is Matilda,
Believe me, friends, it is Matilda,
What it is at all, Matilda,
She take my money and run Venezuela.

CHORUS:
Matilda,
What it is at all, Matilda,
Lord, I got to fall,
Matilda, she take my money and run Venezuela.

Five thousand dollars, friends, I lost,
The woman even sell me cart and horse,
O, Lord, Matilda,
She take my money and run Venezuela.

(CHORUS)

The money was to buy me house and land,
Then she draft a serious plan,
O, Lord, Matilda,
She take my money and run Venezuela.

(CHORUS)

The money was quite inside my bed,
Chuck up the mattress below me head,
Don't you know that Matilda
Done find my money and run Venezuela.

(CHORUS)

Well I feel a jumbee shove my head,
He said, Boy, no money inside your bed.
Don't you know that Matilda
Done take your money and run Venezuela.

(CHORUS)

When I put in my hand it was all in vain,
On the spot I got a serious pain.
O, Lord, Matilda,
She take my money and run Venezuela.

(CHORUS)

So never, my friend, to love again,
Because all my money gone in vain.
O, Lord, Matilda,
She take my money and run Venezuela.

So Them Bad Minded (AGUINALDO HOOKER)

In every home that you can find,
There are people who have bad mind.
In every home that you can find,
There are people that have bad mind.

CHORUS:
Certain bad mind in a certain line,
Saying criticize the people who pass.
Certain bad mind in a certain line,
Saying criticize the people who pass.

You meek and you looking thin,
They say consumption in your skin.
You meek and you looking thin,
They say consumption in your skin.

(CHORUS)

You rosy and you big and fat,
They say dropsy in your skin.
You rosy and you big and fat,
They say dropsy in your skin.

(CHORUS)

You get up and go to church,
Instead of gospel you going to grind.
You get up and go to church,
Instead of gospel you going to grind.

(CHORUS)

You kneel in your home to pray,
They say a hypocrite you did play.
You kneel in your home to pray,
They say a hypocrite you did play.

(CHORUS)

From the album Caribbean Rhythms, *recorded in San Andres by Thomas J. Price, Jr., New York, Folkways Records, 1957. By permission.*

Stickman (AGUINALDO HOOKER)

> There was a big confusion,
> A certain preacher nigh rob a stickman.
> There was a big confusion,
> A certain preacher nigh rob a stickman.
> And when the question nigh rob pop up,
> The stickman decide to kill the preacher.
> The preacher say let him come let him come, I have no fear,
> I'm going to beat him, set on my way.
> And they shouted who-o-o-o-soever
> Say what the preacher' sermon,
> Preacher beat his try and the stickman
> Three hand jumping like a red beef boiling in pot.

> > CHORUS:
> > Singing Billy Dunne waille-o!
> > Billy Dunne ba moin par' commère!
> > Singing Billy Dunne waille-o!
> > Billy Dunne ba moin par' commère!

> A few people gather,
> Turn to the police to settle the matter.
> Before one policeman reach,
> The stickman in the preacher' skin like a leech.
> The preacher came inside like he crazy,
> Came back running with the stickman' money.
> Stickman say yeah, let him go.
> So I let that parson go free and everybody
> Join this melody.

> > (CHORUS)

> What's the cause of frightening,
> I thought this stickman was going to kill the parson.
> I turn and I tell Mabel
> Nothing in this world stronger than the Devil.
> The parson know he distraught that stickman
> And blaze the gown off him back.
> And they shouted who-o-o-o-soever
> Hear where the preacher' sermon.
> Preacher beat his try and the stickman,
> Three hand jumping like tiger running around the yard.

> > (CHORUS)

From Caribbean Rhythms, ibid. *By permission.*

All Day, All Night, Merriam (TRADITIONAL)

All day, all night, Merriam,
Sitting by the roadside digging sand.
All day, all night, Merriam,
Sitting by the roadside catching man.

Sound Bay gal don't eat at all, they buy their crayfish,
Sound Bay gal don't eat good food, they buy their crayfish,
Sound Bay gal don't eat at all, they buy their crayfish,
Sound Bay gal don't eat good food, they buy their crayfish.

SOME TALES WITH AFRICAN THEMES
FROM THE ENGLISH-SPEAKING ISLANDS

Any close examination of the thousands of
folk tales gathered in the Caribbean region
reveals numerous stories, plots and themes
with African antecedents. A few tales of this
genre are gathered here as examples, with
references to one or more of the African
variants.

The Three Companions (FROM ST. BARTHOLOMEW)

This tale, though the setting has been transformed and the details revised, is a New
World variant of a Mende story collected by
Leo Frobenius, which appears in Vol. 8 of
the Atlantis Series of *Volksmarchen und
Volksdichtungen Afrikas.* The Mende story
in English translation is to be found in *Afri-*

The stories, "The Three Companions," "Tar Baby," "Magic Flight," and "The
Things That Talked" are from Folklore of the Antilles, French and English, by
Elsie Clews Parsons, by permission of the American Folk-Lore Society.

can Genesis, **by Leo Frobenius and Douglas C. Fox.**

T'ree men went to seek deir fortunes, one a shoemaker, one a tailor, one a blacksmith. Dey went travellin' and dey found a great forest where dey built a little hut. And every day two would go out to seek deir fortune and leave one behin' to prepare deir food for dem. After de food was prepared each day, an ol' man wid great big oiyes and long beard would go to de hut, and tell de one dat remain, "Oh, I am so col'!" So he tell him come by de fire an' warm heself. An' he said, "Oh, I am so hungry!" Dat was de tailor. So he tol' him, "I have me comerade's dinner prepared, I will give you a little out of it." After he ate it he wanted more an' he tell him no, he could not give him any more. So he flew on him and he bet (beat) him and he took all de dinner and he eat it. So when his comerades come, he had nothin' to give dem. He tol' dem de story about de ol' man, but dey would not believe him. So de nex' day de shoemaker said he would remain and he would be sure to put up dinner for dem. So dis day, after de shoemaker had p'owide his food an' everyt'ing, up comes de ol' man again, but dis time he had two heads. He tol' him, "Oh, I'm so hungry again an' I'm so col'!" He tol' him to go to de fire an' warm himself, an' he gave him some food. When he was finished, he said he wanted more, an' he said he would not give him more. An' he done him de same, he flew on him an' he bet him an' he took de food an' eat it. Dis day de blacksmit' said he would remain, an' de oder two would go to seek deir fortune. So whoil dey was gone, and de blacksmit' had cook dinner for dem, up comes de ol' man, an' dis day he had t'ree heads. "Oh," he said, "I'm so cold an' so hungry!" De blacksmit' gave him some food, an' he said he wanted more. He told him no, he had but what he had put up fah his comerades. He wanted to treat him as he had done de oder two. But he took his blacksmit' hammer an' he flew on him, an' he knocked aff two of his heads. An' wid dat de ol' man went away an' he never seen him again. And after, all dey gain deir fortune an' went home very rich men.

Tar Baby: Eavesdropper: Without Scratching (FROM ST. CROIX)

> Here we have a tale with several themes widely known in West African lore: The tar baby, the seemingly impossible task of working in the field without scratching, and learning the secret of the taskmaster by eavesdropping. The Ashanti trickster Anansi (the Nancy of the Caribbean) figures in identical episodes.

Nancy is a wery wise man. He so wise and strong dat if he do any-
t'ing, anybody got to be satisfied. So Father Gad plant a whole field of
yam. When de yam grew an' commence now time to dig, Mister Nancy
is de firs' man find out dat it could be dig. Brer Nancy is a real big t'ief
man, you know. One night he start wid his bag an' went to de field
where de yam is. An' he dig his bag right up full wid yam. An' mind de
land is not his, he goin' to steal. After he t'ief de bag of yam, he start
now to hide it in his place where he live. So Nancy he run an' went in
de bush. An' it was reported to the Lard Fader Gad about it. An' de
Lard tell de watchman he mus' get two piece of board and put in de
middle of de groun' de shape of a man, wid tar. After dey put de tar
man in de groun', "Oh man, look a see man t'ief Fader God yam!" He
walk up to de tar man an' he commence to strike. He hit him wid de
first han', 'e fasten. 'E tek de left hand, knock 'e blow, 'e fasten. He tek
'e foot, 'e right foot to kick down de board, 'e fasten. Now he take 'e
head now and he bott de board and he head fasten. An' after he head
fasten, he stand to dat one place, he commence to sling heself, for t'ree
days.

After dat he sah a beautiful cock was passin'. He call out to de cock.
De cock say, "Nah, man, I have nut'in' to do wid you." He sah a bull
passin' again. De bull say, "Nah, man, I have nut'in' to do wid you."
He sah a sheep comin' passin'. "Nah, man, I have nut'in' to do wid
you." He stand again, he saw a beautiful ram goat and he beg to ram
goat, "Do, Ram Goat!" if he couldn't stand aff a little distance and bott
down de board for him. And so de ram goat do dat. An' when de ram
goat do dat, one foot loose, and de ram goat head fasten. So de ram
stand to de black board. And he get clear and he come down and he
take his knife and slash de ram goat skin off, and puts it in de bag an'
cyarry home.

An' after dat de nex' day he went to Fader Gad. He told Fader God,
"Fader Gad, I betch yer I tell yer what's in yer mind." And Fader Gad
say, "So you tell me what's in my mind? I betch yer you don't tell me.
Well, all right, go down de de blacksmith shop and mek dis and dat
and de oder!" An' he stand by skulking about de place only to catch a
little news, and he hear a little bird passin', and de bird say, "Fader
Gad, what you say to Nancy?"—"I told him to go down to de blacksmith and tell him to make t'ree dings, Moon, Sun, and Star." So
t'rough dat by standin' dere idle, he hear dat, and he start right down to
de blacksmith and say, "Blacksmith! Blacksmith! Make Moon, Sun,
and Star and let me cyarry it up!" An' de blacksmith go right off and
make Moon, Sun, Star, and hand them to him, and he was away wid it.
And when he went, he hand it to de Lard, and when he hand it to de
Lard, de Moon, Sun, Star commence to fight. De moon t'rew water and
de sun t'rew fire.

After he done that, Fader Gad said, "All right! Now, Nancy, what
you do for me? I want cher dat whole bush to clean off and I will give
yer de best bull in de pen." [One of the conditions, not made clear
here, is that Nancy is supposed to do this work without scratching
himself.] Then Fader Gad give him a bill an' a ax an' a shovel, an' he

went showing the bush. But de bush too bad, nothing but snake, Jack Spaniard, cow itch, all sarts of wa'min (vermin) in dat bush. First Snake began to call his foot, nex' Jack Spaniard commence to bitin' his face and swell it, de nex' cow itch commence to bite and teaze. So he break off in de work and went to Fader Gad. Fader Gad said, "Wid all dat, Nancy, tomorrow I goin' to send me dater to show you de work." (Nancy is a villain, you know.) De Lard send his dater to watch him work and den he commence to clatch (scratch). He is not to clatch at all, he is to work. And den he say,

"'E fatty fatty so, de bull
 'E speckle, speckle so
 'E 'cratch e, 'cratch e."

[By singing this song, Nancy pretends not to be really scratching, but to be imitating God's bull.]

De girl say yes. [That is, he has met the conditions.] So when he done, he went home. De Lard sent to de pen and put a rope 'pon de bull and hand it to him, Mr. Anancy. An' den de received de bull and he was away wid it in de bush, and de story was end.

Magic Flight

(FROM ST. CROIX)

The central themes of this story—impossible tasks given to the hero by the devil, and the flight from Hell and the pursuit—have numerous counterparts in African oral literature. Both themes, of course, are likewise known in European tales, and the provenience could therefore be a matter of dispute. The task of cleaning the dung heap, for example, might have come directly from Greek mythology (the Augean Stables). But the throwing of magic eggs to create a river and a wall and to turn the hero and heroine into mules is at least as African as European. (See notes on "Mérisier, Stronger Than the Elephants" in Appendix VI, pp. 579–582.) Also, there is a familiar African (as well as European) theme in the girl's admonition to the boy not to let a certain thing happen lest he lose all memory of her. The substitution of the devil and hell for some demonic African character and the African bush (or underworld) is frequently encountered in Afro-American folklore. In some such tales, this one included, the devil shows anxiety that the boy visitor to Hell

might take the place over. In one U.S. variant, the devil gives the boy a live coal and
tells him to go somewhere else and start his
own hell.

A bwiy an' his moder. Ev'y time his moder say, "Bwiy, go to Hell,"
an' he says, "One of dese days I gwine to Hell." So one day now he
start aff to go to Hell. He walk and he walk until he reach nearly to Hell
ground. When he reach he meet hoe digging cane hole wid nobody at
all only dey working deyself. An' dey all stan' up an' dey all say,
"Bwiy, bwiy, whey you goin'?" He say, "Me mama sent me to Hell an'
ah goin' to Hell." Dey say, "Go an, Bwiy, go an!" When he reach furder
he meet bill cutting cane widout anybody usin' dem. All de bills stand
right up an' say, "Bwiy, bwiy, whey you goin'?" He say, "Me mama
sent me to Hell an' ah goin' to Hell." Dey say, "Go an, Bwiy, go an!"
When he reach furder on he meet mill grinding cane, liquor run in. He
stan' up an' he say, "If I had somet'in' I would take a drink o' liquor,"
an' a big calabash roll cane meet him widout anybody bringin' de calabash. He take it up an' he drink de liquor. When he goin' furder he
meet de devil owerseeer. Devil owerseer say to him, "Bwiy, bwiy,
whey you goin'?" He say, "Me mama sent me to Hell an' ah goin' to
Hell." Den he meet de devil manja. De devil manja said to him, "Bwiy,
bwiy, whey you goin'?" He say, "Me Mama sent me to Hell an' ah
goin' to Hell."—"Das a good mama! Das a good mama!" Den when he
go furder an' he met de devil se'f an' de Devil said (in a deep voice),
"Bwiy, bwiy, whey you goin'?" He say, "Me mama sent me to Hell an'
ah goin' to Hell."

Den de devil had one dater. De dater name was Feng'kuma. An' de
wife name was Katroni. When he get down now, de devil said, "Ah
have t'ree tasks fah you." And de firs' task, de devil had a dung heap he
never havin' cleaned, an' de devil said, "By dis an' four o'clock I mus'
see f'am here to Windward Island." An' de bwiy start to cry, he didn'
know what to do. An' de gyirl come to ax he whey he name an' he say
he name' John. She ask him, "Whey me daddy say you mus' do?" An'
he tell her de task about de dung heap. An' she set down an' hold he
head til he drap asleep. An' after he drap asleep, she went in an' she
bring out a egg an' she say, "Dung heap, Dung heap, me daddy say, 'By
dis an' four o'clock mus' see f'am here to Windward Island.'" An' he
know not'in' about it. An' she wake he up an' say go tell he fader dat
dat task finish'. He went an' he tell de devil dat he finish. De devil say,
"Hum! Bwiy look like he know somet'ing." De nex' day now he had a
house of brass an' he tell him by dis an' four o'clock he mus' see who
will free him t'rough dose brass. John start to cry as usual but Feng-
'kuma come out an' ask what her fader tell him? He tell her. An' she
bring out a egg an' she say, "House of brass, House of brass, me daddy
say, 'By dis an' four o'clock you mus' see who will free him t'rough
you.'" An' den she went an' she wake John an' she tell him, "Go on an'
tell me fader dat de task finish'." Now de devil was so struck dat he
could but go an' consult de wife an' she say, "An' you say you ah Devil

but dat boy goin' to put you out of Hell!" Den de t'ird day now. Den was t'ree ol' mule an' since Hell den dey never come home, an' he say de boy mus' bring home de t'ree ol' mule. Well de boy start to cry as usual. Anyhow by de help of Feng'kuma again, she gi' a whistle. An' de boy blow de whistle, an' de mule come home pelting. De devil see dem come home, get frighten', consult de wife. She say, "An' you say you ah Devil but dat boy goin' to put you out of Hell!"

As dat was de las' task now, t'ought dey was to kill de bwiy. But by de help of Feng'kuma she tell him, "Don't go 'sleep six o'clock as usual. Stap outside." An' dey going to get away. De devil had t'ree harses, one name Debil Leper, one name' Debil Jumper, an' Debil Flyer. Before she get dese harses she spit all over his (her) room. At six o'clock when her moder call her, de spit ansah Mama. An' she say, "An' she goin' to call me tonight." Spit de room over. Now she get de Devil Leper an' gi' John de Devil Jumper, an' lef' Devil Flyer. Well, dey start to go an' dey go an' dey go an' dey go till marnin', an' de las' spit ansah an' Katroni jump out an' say "Ah tell you, Devil, dat boy goin' put you out of Hell goin' wid my pickny. Go bring ma pickny back to me." Devil now get on to Devil Flyer, an' he fly went to meet dem.

When dey look an' dey see comin', Feng'kuma had t'ree egg an' she bus' one of de egg, an' it come a river water. When de devil reach dere, he say, "My dater, my dater, how mus' I get over?" An' she say, "You drink, an' de ol' harse drink," an' he had to drink an' de old horse drink, an' dey could dry de river. Now he had to tu'n back to Hell an' tell he wife dat he didn' meet dem. An' she chase he again, dat he mus' bring her choil'. Den he had to tu'n back again. By dis time now de river dry. When dey see he comin', she bus' anoder egg. When she bus' de nex' egg, now it come a high wall he couldn' get over. He say, "My dater, my dater, how mus' I get over?" She say, "You climb, an' de ol' harse climb." Den he could get over dey gone all de time. He had to tu'n back again, an' he tell his wife he didn' meet dem, an' she chase he, he go. When he come now, dey reach out of devil land an' de only t'ing he see is four ol' mule. Den he tu'n back again, dat journey, he tell his wife he had not seen nutin' but four ol' mule. Well, she instruct him now, "Well, any time you meet four of dem bring dem home." But he didn't meet dem at all.

After dey reach out of Devil land de two harses wait back. An' dey two went alang to John home. An' dey had a banana warf, so she stopped dere an' she tell him, "When you reach home, don't let a dog jump on you less you forget me." Den John went home, an' de dag did jump on him an' he did forget her. An' she was to de gut side fah t'ree days an' never see John. On de fourt' day John went down to de gut to feed his fowls an' he see a pretty Domenica fowl dat he have never see yet. An' he said, "Das a pretty Domenica fowl! If I know who it belongs to, I will buy it." An' den she said, "John! John! 'tis you callin' de Domenica fowl. Ah tell you you would ha' forgot me." An' den John hol' out de han' an' ketch her, an' den she come to her natcheral farm (form). An' den dey went home an' dey get married an' dey celebrate deir wedding an' John say, "Dis is what I projuce f'om going to Hell."

An' dey live happily, an'
   De wheel ben'
   An' story en'.

The Things That Talked

(FROM NEVIS)

> Talking objects are not uniquely African, but
> this tale, along with other New World vari-
> ants, comes directly from an Ashanti story
> featuring a farmer who goes out to work in
> his field. (See Appendix XI, pp. 588–89, and
> the Surinam story, "Broken Pledge," p. 216.)

One time a mon plant some nuts, an' he say he ain't gone to reap dem
before de hard time come round, das October. An' famine meet him before October come, an' he take up he hoe, he basket, an' he dog, an' he
go, an' he go in de fiel'. He go in de fiel', de hoe say, "Me no goin' dig
none." Basket say, "Me no goin' carry none." De dog laugh. So de man
take up de hoe to knock de dog. Hoe stick say, "Take care, you make de
dog bite me." De man lef' de groun' an' run in. An' when he got certain
way, he met man wid a bundle o' wood. An' he put he case to de man.
An' de man wid wood ax him, "If dat he runnin' for?" An' de bundle o'
wood dat was on de man's head say, "How you mean for dat he run
him for?"

   My lead bend,
   My Nancy story end.

TALES OF CUCKOLDS AND RAKES (THE BAHAMAS)

Man from God

Dis was a man. He jus' got married, an' de woman dat he marry had her sweetheart befo'. So at sunset her husban' said he would go out huntin' for raccoon. An' as soon as he went, ups come de woman's sweetheart. An' de two went in de room an' whent to bed. Directly she heard a rock to de do'. Den she tol' de sweetheart he mus' run out an' get up in de chimlay. Dere he runs an' went up in de chimlay. An' she open de do' for her husban'. "Oh," he said, "my wife, I caught a fine raccoon to-night, caught a fine coon, an' I'm goin' to make a fine fire to-night, an' have it swinge."—"Oh, no!" she says, "don't make up fire to swinge it to-night. Wait until de mornin'."—"Oh, yes!" he say, "I'll swinge my coon to-night 'fore I sleep." She says, "Oh, no! I beg you not to swinge it to-night." Den he went out in de yard. An' he work up plenty trash, an' he bring it, an' he caught up a big fire in de chimney, an' whilst de smoke an' de heat was goin' up, heatin' de po' man up in de chimlay. He t'ought to say he mus' cry out, "A man from Gawd in de chimlay!" Den he cry out, "Man from Gawd, man from Gawd!" den he drop down on de man an' de coon. Flash he make. De man say, "You could drop from hell if you like, you wouldn' carry [take] my coon." An' de dart he make to run knock me here to tell dat lie.

Frightened Sweetheart

Now, this was a man. He married. His wife was a very bad wife, she had a sweetheart. Every time her husband go in the field and stay till evening, she get her sweetheart. One day her husband shoot four birds and went back in the field, and her sweetheart was passing and saw the birds hang up. He said, "Give me one o' these birds." She said, "Take one and leave three." He take all. When her husband come, she told him that the creature eat it. He kill all the creature in that place. Next day he shoot seven, and gone in the field. His wife sweetheart come and ask for one. She said, "Take one and leave six." He take all; and when she come out and see all the birds was gone, she run and get plenty onion, and cut it up and steam it down. When her husband he bring one stranger to eat, his wife carry in the dinner and call her husband outside the door, and said, "The knife is dull to cut the bird."

These five Bahamas tales are from Folk-Tales of Andros Island, Bahamas, by Elsie Clews Parsons, Memoirs of the American Folklore Society, Vol. XIII, 1918.

And he went back in and get the knife, and went out to sharp it. His wife run in and told the man that her husband is gone out to sharp the knife to cut out your two nut. He run out the house and run to go home. The woman ran to her husband, and said, "The man gone with all the birds." He run behind the man and hollered, "Leave the foot for me!" The man running and hollered, "Oh, my two nut is going to cut out!" And the man turn back to his wife, and said, "That man is gone." And I been right there, and said, "Man, you too fool!"

> He dart at me, and I fart.
> Cause me and him to part.

Bunday.

Husband in the Bag

Little Dick Milton been married, an' his wife play sick on him. An' she had a frien' she call de Arshman [Irishman]. He vill hide away by day. An' at night when she played sick, po' little Dick Milton had twenty miles to go to look for medicine to bring to his wife. De Arshman den he would come in. He'd use dis word, "Open book!"

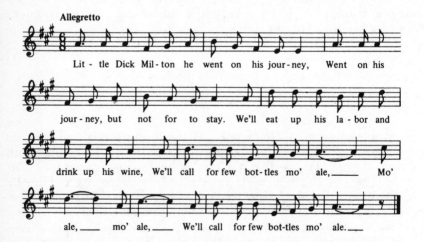

Allegretto

Lit-tle Dick Mil-ton he went on his jour-ney, Went on his jour-ney, but not for to stay. We'll eat up his la-bor and drink up his wine, We'll call for few bot-tles mo' ale,___ Mo' ale,___ mo' ale,___ We'll call for few bot-tles mo' ale.___

Nex' day Dick Milton return from his journey. "My wife, how you feelin' dis mornin'?"—"My deah, I'm jus' sick." He go again twenty miles mo'. On his way goin' he met up wi' an ol' man wi' his bag on his shoulder. "Where are you goin'?"—"I been two years travellin' for my wife for our heal'. No better yet." Says, "Jump'in dis bag here!" Now, de ol' Arshman he reach de house, say, "Open book!" De ol' man reached dis bag. "Good-evenin' frien's!" Come in an' sat down. De Arshman say to him, "Will you join us to dis sweet song?" He said,

"Yes." Dick Milton is in de bag now, listenin' to what his wife has been playin' sick for years:—

> "Little Dick Milton he went on his journey,
> Went on his journey, but not for to stay.
> We'll eat up his labor and drink up his wine,
> We'll call for few bottles mo' ale,
>   Mo' ale, mo' ale,
> We'll call for few bottles mo' ale."

Arshman sing,—

Call for Gran - ny Ma - ria, Gran - ny, gran - ny, oh!
Go, mod - er, you,— An' sen' for my gran - ny, oh!

He sprang up wi' his dagger out of de bag to chop off de Arshman head.

Tom Bell

Dere was a boy named Tom Bell. Now, dis boy was engaged to a young miss. After he done engage to dis miss, he done fall sick. Now, all his sick broke out in sores. So when he goin' out to visit de young miss, bein' bed-sores, de miss don' care settin' down close. He had no discourse. So he went to tell his fader dat de young miss would have no discourse wi' him. So his fader said, "Well, my son, you mus' get better." So his fader sen' him to de bes' doctor in dat county. An' after he been dere twelve months, he get better. He was a fifer befo' he gone. One even' he put on his clo'es (went out to meet the girl).

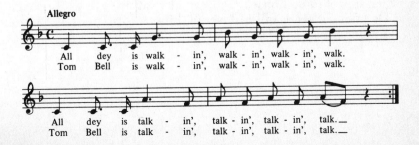

All   dey   is   walk - in',   walk - in', walk - in', walk.
Tom   Bell   is   walk - in',   walk - in', walk - in', walk.
All   dey   is   talk - in',   talk - in', talk - in', talk.—
Tom   Bell   is   talk - in',   talk - in', talk - in', talk.—

De girl didn' know de man. Nex' even' he walk a little furder. He commence to blow:

> "All dey is walkin', walkin', walkin', walk.
> All dey is talkin', talkin', talkin', talk.
> Tom Bell is walkin', walkin', walkin', walk.
> Tom Bell is talkin', talkin', talkin', talk."

Dis girl say, "Mus' see dat young one." Nex' even' he began to blow again:

> "All dey is walkin', walkin', walkin', walk.
> All dey is talkin', talkin', talkin', talk.
> Tom Bell is walkin', walkin', walkin', walk.
> Tom Bell is talkin', talkin', talkin', talk."

Nex' even' de girl say, "Mus' see who dat." Dress up. He come.

> "All dey is walkin', walkin', walkin', walk.
> All dey is talkin', talkin', talkin', talk.
> Tom Bell is walkin', walkin', walkin', walk.
> Tom Bell is talkin', talkin', talkin', talk."

Now, when he look, he see de girl comin'. She don' know de boy.

> "All dey is walkin', walkin', walkin', walk.
> All dey is talkin', talkin', talkin', talk.
> Tom Bell is walkin', walkin', walkin', walk.
> Tom Bell is talkin', talkin', talkin', talk."

When he see de girl:

> "All dey is walkin', walkin', walkin', walk.
> All dey is talkin', talkin', talkin', talk.
> Tom Bell is walkin', walkin', walkin', walk.
> Tom Bell is talkin', talkin', talkin', talk.

"Come heah, lub me girl, kiss me girl." De girl come nearer to him. Ax him to take a walk. "I'll fit out to take a walk wi' you home tomorrer evenin'." He fit out to take a walk nex' evenin'. He go to de girl house. Jus' when he get to de house, de girl moder fall in love wi' him right away. De younger sister fall in love wi' him too. An' her fader fall in love wi' de boy too—all. He get dem all in familee way—moder, two sisters, an' fader.

Charge the Engineer

Once was a time was an engineer-man. He didn't married, but he raise a boy wi' him, an' he put everyt'ing in dat boy's han'. He had an ol' woman named Grandy Boukee, an' he had a pretty house-girl name Liza Dilly. Dis girl been wi' him so long. Afterward dey foun' out dis girl big wi' chil'. De man said t'ain' him. He put it 'pon de boy. De boy say, "No, it ain' me." De boy cry. Nine mon' de girl had baby. Dey sen' for mantainance for de chil'. Dey sen' for de boy.

Allegretto

Gran - dee Bou-kee, Gran - dee Bou-kee, Gran - dee Bou-kee, mum,

Rise up me pil - low, Rise up me pil - low, Rise up me pil - low, mum.

Take de bunch o' key, Take de bunch o' key, Take de bunch o' key, mum.
O - pen box o' ches, O - pen box o' ches, O - pen box o' ches, mum.

Take sev - en poun, Take__ sev - en poun', Take__ sev - en poun', mum.

Mark de en - gi - neer, Mark de en - gi - neer, Mark de en - gi - neer, mum.

Das is none of mine, Das is none' of mine, Das is none of mine, mum.
Charge de en - gi - neer, Charge de en - gi - neer, Charge de en - gi - neer, mum.
Das is mars-ter chil', Charge de en - gi - neer, Charge de en - gi - neer, mum.

Amen to de buildin'. From dat day anybody can put a charge on any one.

OTHER TALES FROM THE ENGLISH-SPEAKING ISLANDS

Back in the Same Hole

One day b'o' Frawg was passin' by. He met a stone on top of a snake about two feet long. B'o' Snake ax b'o' Frawg to relieve in taking off dis stone off of him. B'o' Frawg did so. After b'o' Frawg take de stone off b'o' Snake, he was perishin' so long under de stone for somet'ing to eat, he want to eat de frawg. Frawg say, "Man, dat ain't right. I take de stone off you, you want to turn aroun' an' eat me." B'o' Frawg say, "Le' us go by de judge." Dey went by walkin', lookin' for some one to judge it. Dey buck up wid de sheep. Dey tol' de sheep how it happen. De sheep tol' him dat he couldn' judge it. He went up an' buck up to b'o' Hawk. He tol' b'o' Hawk how it happen. B'o' Hawk tol' him dat he couldn' judge it. B'o' Frawg say, "Let's go a little furder, den I may buck up wid some one who may judge it." Dey kep' on goin'. Dey buck up wid b'o' Cow. B'o' Frawg say to b'o' Cow, "You t'ink dis is right?" Say, "Ise goin' by. I met a big stone on de snake back. He ax me to take it off, an' I did so. After I finish, he turn aroun' an' want to eat me." B'o' Cow says, "I can't judge it here." Say, "Let us go back to de spot an' put it back. Le' me see how it been." B'o' Snake was quite agreeable to go back. When dey reach back to dis spot, b'o' Cow ax b'o' Snake to lay down how he been when b'o' Frawg take de stone off him. De snake lay down, an' 'pear stretch as he t'ought de cow was goin' to judge it in his behalf. De cow say to b'o' Frawg, "Put dat stone back on b'o' Snake an' le' me see how it ben." B'o' Frawg did so. B'o' Cow say, "Leave him dere now. Le' me see how he can manage." Dat's de reason why you see snake like to be in de wall to-day. Dat's de reason any frawg dey see dey eat um.

Fishing on Sunday

Once upon a time dere was a man who used to go fishin' ev'ry Sunday. Now, dis Sunday mo' dan all, when he caught fish, he foun' dat devil was in de boat. De devil said to de man, "Le' me an' you do de fishin' togeder." De man say, "Yes." Dey started fishin'. Dey caught plenty little small fishes, but de man ketch big fish. Now, when time for dem to come asho', de man share all de small fishes, an' was just goin' to share de big one. De devil said to de man, "Don' cut um, don' split um, but share um." De man say, "I don' know how you mean by 'don' cut um, don' split um but share um.'" De man started splittin' de

This group of tales is from Parsons, Folklore of the Antilles and Folk-Tales of Andros Island, Bahamas, previously cited.

fish. Devil say to de man, "I tell you don' cut de fish, don' split it, but share um." Man start off a-runnin'. De devil wait until de man reach jock to his house. De devil take his bill-hook an' bring de man back. De man commence cuttin' de fish in half. De devil say, "Don' cut um, don' split um, but share um." De man star' a-runnin' again. De devil wait until de man reach to his house, an' bring de man back, an' tol' de man to share de fish. De man say, "I can't share de fish." An' de devil say, "I goin' to share you." An' de devil swaller de man.

E bo ben,
My story en'.

She Sends for Her Husband

Once 'twas a time, a very good time,
Monkey chew tobacco an' spit white lime.

Dis was a woman. She was in fam'ly way, an' her husban' gone. An' when he gone, he get married over dere. De woman call b'o' Wood-Dove, an' he (she) say, "B'o' Wood-Dove, if I sen' you to call my husban', what you would say?" Say, "Hoom, hoom!" Woman say, "You won' do." Call Parakeet, say, "B'o' Parakeet, if I sen' you to call my husban', what you would say?" Say, "Tweet, tweet, tweet!" Woman say, "You won' do." Come a lovin'-bird now which you call hummin'-bird. Say, "If I sen' you to call my husban', what you would say?" Say,—

Say, "You will do." B'o' Hummin'-Bird start off. When he get to de firs' settlement, he say,—

"Wumb, wumb, wumb,
Captain, Lawyer, Baker,
Your wife in labor
Sence las' night."

"How long Captain Lawyer Baker pass here?"—"Jus' five weeks ago." He start off again.

> "Wumb, wumb, wumb,
> Captain, Lawyer, Baker,
> Your wife in labor
> Sence las' night."

"How long Captain Lawyer Baker pass here?"—"Jus' two weeks ago."

> "Wumb, wumb, wumb,
> Captain, Lawyer, Baker,
> Your wife in labor
> Sence las' night."

Dey was dancin'. An' when de bird sing, he say, "I hear some one call my name." He say, "Sing again." An' de bird did sing. An' he was dancin' wid his bride. An' he say, "If a man married an' have chilrun, an' got anoder woman an' love her, what mus' I do?" Dey says, "Go." He gone. De chil' what he gwoin' to call Jack he have chilrun beeg enough to tell me dat little storee.

The Cruel Friend

Once upon a time dere was two young men. One called Tom, an' de oder Sammy Lees. Sammy Lees had opinion dat he could beat Tom, an' Tom had opinion he could beat Sammy Lees. Now, de two gone in bush dis mornin' to shoot. Now, Sammy Lees start to shootin'. He shoot fifteen, he dropped ten. Tom started shootin'. He shoot twenty-five, drop ten. Sammy Lees startin' shootin' again. He shoot fifty. He drop forty-five. Tom started a-shootin'. He shoot fifteen. He drop one. After Tom see Sammy Lees beatin' him shootin' so much, Tom shoot Sammy Lees, but not dead. An' Sammy Lees' moder was something like a witchcraf'. Know Sammy Lees was shot. Ven' for him. Ven she reach de bush, she meet Sammy Lees in a deep hole. She wen' down an' took him up. Ven she took him out, she kyarry him home. Vwhen he reach home, fader, moder, sister, an' Tom who shot him, gether roun' him. Fader commence to sing,—

> "O my dear son, Sammy Lees!
> What shall you leave for thy dear father?"

Sammy Lees commence to sing,—

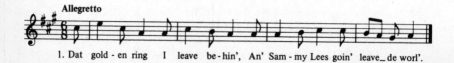

1. Dat gold-en ring I leave be-hin', An' Sam-my Lees goin' leave_ de worl'.

"Dat gol'en beaver I leave behin',
An Sammy Lees goin' leave de worl'."

De moder come an' started talkin' to Sammy Lees:

My dear son, Sammy Lees:
What shall you leave for thy dear mother?"

Sammy Lees commence to sing,—

"Dat golden slippers I leave behin',
An' Sammy Lees goin' leave de worl'."

De sister come,—

"O my dear brother, Sammy Lees!
What shall you leave for thy dear sister?"

Sammy Lees commence to sing,—

"Dat golden ring I leave behin',
An' Sammy Lees goin' leave de worl'."

Tom come, started singin',—

"O my dear frien', Sammy Lees!
What shall you leave for thy dear frien'?"

Sammy Lees commence to sing,—

"Dat hangin' gallus I leave behin',
An' Sammy Lees goin' leave de worl'."

An' Sammy Lees died right on dat. An' dey hang Tom. An' fader an'
moder an' sister lived right dere, an' lived in peace, died in peace, an'
buried in a spot o' candle-grease.

E bo ben,
Dis story en'.

Only One Mouthful

Dere was a drought cahl fah diggin' pon'. Bra Fowl say she cyant
cyarry load so she can't help clean de pond ketch water. After de pond
finish, rain come, water ketch in. Bra Fowl wid twelve chickens wan
day badly in need af water. She an' de chil'ren went down to de pond
an' dey look ahl around an' dey see no one. Dey all dip in deir mout' an'
take up one mout'ful af water. An' Fader God see dem an' say, "Ah, Bra

Fowl, I see you!" He held up his head within the time swallerin' an' said, "Lard, I only take one mout'ful." She dip in again. Fader God said, "Ah, Bra Fowl, I see you!" Within the time swallerin' she say, "Lard, I take two mout'ful," until she get to a dozen mout'ful an' was satisfy. From dat up to dis, fowl drinkin' water hol' up de head to Heaven an' said, "Lord, I drink one mout'ful."

JAMAICAN ALPHABET GAME

This is a form of ring game. The participants stand in a circle, and to the accompaniment of rhythmic handclapping each person, in turn, calls out his letter and improvises a phrase to characterize it, sometimes achieving a rhyme.

A signify ackee (1), qualify fish,
B signify bammie (2), work proper with pear,
C signify callalue (3), eat very nice,
D stand for dumpling, if it ever tie you'teet',
E is for elephant, big like Tacomah (4),
F is for fungi, it choke fever,
G is for Goozoo (5), all nigger papa,
I is the pronoun that you must learn,
J is for jackass, plenty go to school,
K is for Katy—she make me fool
L is for lawyer, them never walk straight,
M is for money, make you feel first-rate,
N is for Nancy—that's a girl have a mouth!
O favor C but a little more stout,
P for Puncheon-water (6), let you fight one another,
Q is for Quashie (7), Quabina oldest brother,
R is for room, let the best man fool,
S is for sugar, eat all you can,
T is for Thomas, is very unbelieving,
U is for Uncle Jacob, is very deceiving,
W is for women—follow them you fret,
X is a cross will favor ten,
Y is for yampe (8), a poor man's friend,
Z is for Zacheus, the smaltest of men.

From "Folk Games of Jamaica," by Martha Beckwith, in Jamaica Folklore.

Notes on the Jamaican words: (1) Ackee fruit boiled with fish is a popular Jamaican dish. (2) A favorite lunch of laborers. (3) Callalue (kalalu) is the familiar name of okra. (4) Tacomah is the local pronunciation of Intikuma, son of Anansi, the Ashanti spider trickster. He is, of course, very small. (5) Goozoo is a term used to designate witchcraft. (6) Puncheon water: rum. (7) Quashie: name designating a boy born on Sunday. (8) Yampe is a variety of yam. The letter V, obviously missing, was not in the original transcription.

ONE BRIGHT SUMMER MORNING

A BALLAD IN THE ENGLISH TRADITION, FROM TORTOLA, VIRGIN ISLANDS

Along with musical traditions of Spain, France, Denmark and the Netherlands, there have been preserved in the Virgin Islands some songs of English derivation. The following piece is a variant of an old English ballad, its phrases and images (as well as its meter) recalling the well-known western song, "Lonesome Cowboy."

> One bright summer morning
> As I were awalking,
> One bright summer morning
> As I were awalk',
> Whom should I meet there
> But a fair darling damsel,
> She was wrapped up in flannel,
> As cold as could be,
> She was wrapped up in flannel,
> As cold as could be.
>
> Oh come dearest mother
> And sit down beside me,
> Oh come dearest mother
> And pity my cry,
> For my poor heart is breaking,
> My poor head is bending,
> For I'm deep in salvation,

From the record album, Caribbean Folk Music, *New York, Ethnic Folkways Library, 1960. Reprinted by permission of Ethnic Folkways Library.*

And surely I must die,
For I'm deep in salvation,
And surely I must die.

Do send for the young man
That first introduced me,
Do send for the young man
That put me in shame,
Do send for the doctor
Although it is too late,
For I am a young girl
Adoggin' my pride,
For I am a young girl
Adoggin' my pride.

Six jolly young fellas
To carry my coffin,
Six jolly young ladies
To walk by my side,
With a bunch of green roses
To place on my coffin,
That the people might smell me
While passing along.

SOME BALLADS FROM THE BAHAMAS

While historical or tragic ballads are relatively uncommon in the Negro oral literature of the United States, they appear to have survived strongly in the Bahamas. The three Bahaman ballads given here—"The Sinking of the Pytoria," "Cecil Lost in the Storm," and "The Burning of Curry Camp"—display clear relationships with U.S. Negro singing styles, and also with English ballad tradition. In the song, "The Burning of Curry Camp," one can feel the imminent presence of English balladry. (See the music notation that precedes the text.) But "The Sinking of the Pytoria" closely resembles musically and structurally the Afro-American worksongs that were once commonly heard in the southern part of the United States, and which have a marked African character.

The Sinking of the Pytoria

From the album, Music of the Bahamas, *recorded by Samuel B. Charters, Folk-ways Records, 1959. Music notations by John Benson Brooks. Used by permission.*

In nineteen hundred and twenty-nine,
    Run come seek, run come seek,
Oh in nineteen hundred and twenty-nine,
    Run come seek, Jerusalem,
Somebody was seen a-leavin' out the harbor,
    Run come seek, run come seek.
Oh Lord, was three sails leavin' out the harbor,
    Run come seek, Jerusalem.
Oh Lord, I want you to tell me 'bout the three sails,
    Run come seek, run come seek.
Oh Lord, I want you to tell me 'bout the three sails,
    Run come seek, Jerusalem.
I want you to name those three sails for me,
    Run come seek, run come seek.
My Lord, I want you to name those three sails,
    Run come seek, Jerusalem.
Oh Lord, the *Result,* the *Myrtle* and *Pytoria,*
    Run come seek, run come seek.
Oh Lord, the *Result,* the *Myrtle* and *Pytoria,*
    Run come seek, Jerusalem.
Oh Lord, now they're leavin' out Nassau Harbor,
    Run come seek, run come seek.
Oh Lord, now they're leavin' out Nassau Harbor,
    Run come seek, Jerusalem.
Now God send the *Myrtle* into Blanket Sound,
    Run come seek, run come seek.

Ay, now God send the *Myrtle* into Blanket Sound,
   Run come seek, Jerusalem.
Now God send the *Result* into Staniard Creek,
   Run come seek, run come seek.
Now God send the *Result* into Staniard Creek,
   Run come seek, Jerusalem.
Oh Lord, now we leave the *Pytoria* on the ocean,
   Run come seek, run come seek.
Oh Lord, now we leave the *Pytoria* on the ocean,
   Run come seek, Jerusalem.
Oh now there's a dark cloud built up in the northeast,
   Run come seek, run come seek.
Oh now there's a dark cloud built up in the northeast,
   Run come seek, Jerusalem.
Lord now, the wind and the waves keep a-rollin' down,
   Run come seek, run come seek.
Yes Lord, now the wind and the waves keep a-rollin' down,
   Run come seek, Jerusalem.
Now *Pytoria* couldn't hold up for the channel,
   Run come seek, run come seek.
Lord, now, she's cut off from Standard Rock Channel,
   Run come seek, Jerusalem.
When she get opposite the channel,
   Run come seek, run come seek,
Oh Lord, Captain George was the captain,
   Run come seek, Jerusalem,
Lord, now, he spoke to the people on board her,
   Run come seek, run come seek.
Said, people, what we must do?
   Run come seek, Jerusalem.
Lord, now, those boys get confused in his mind,
   Run come seek, run come seek.
Oh Lord, now everybody get confused in his mind,
   Run come seek, Jerusalem.
Oh Lord, now, I got no channel here,
   Run come seek, run come seek.
Oh Lord, I got to go in the channel now,
   Run come seek, Jerusalem.
Lord now, the first sea hit the *Pytoria*,
   Run come seek, run come seek.
Thank God, everybody get confused,
   Run come seek, Jerusalem.
Oh Lord, now the second sea hit the *Pytoria*,
   Run come seek, run come seek.
Oh Lord, now she knock the little *'Oria* to Glory,
   Run come seek, Jerusalem.
Lord, she had thirty-four souls 'board her,
   Run come seek, run come seek.

(The transcription is unfinished, but the remaining lines of the song merely embellish the tragic denouement.)

The Burning of Curry Camp

Now I was on the bay, Lord,____ yes I____ saw a
fire,   I said to my Boss Man, Coak - ley Road on
fire,____ He said throw down this bag,____ boys,
throw down this bag, boys, you know-oh Ir - ving Mc - Fee; you know,
Cur - ry Camp burn - ed down.____ A- throw down the bag, boys,
don't you know we're on the Coak-ley Road,____ When I reached there____
____ saw John Rob-erts be - hind me,____ John____ Rob-erts is
my cou - sin, you know, he said un - to me, oh ____ good
Lord, Ir - ving Mc - Fee; Cur - ry Camp burned down.____
____ When I get on the porch, don't you know, I said to oth-ers at the
time,____ throw down your bag.____ Coak - ley
Road on fire____ say throw__ down this bag, boys,__
throw down this__ bag boys,__ you know Ir - ving Mc - Fee;__

Cur-ry Camp_ burned down. __ When I did reach there, don't you know, I said Un - to him now, _____ Throw down now the bag now, __ Call up the peo-ple on the farm, Six-ty-five peo-ple was work-in'___ in the for - est__ that day, Ir - ving Mc - Fee; __ Cur - ry Camp burned down.

Now I was on the bay, Lord, yes I saw a fire,
I said to my Boss Man, Coakley Road on fire,
He said throw down this bag, boys,
Throw down this bag, boys, you know—oh,
Irving McFee; you know, Curry Camp burned down.

A-throw down the bag, boys, don't you know
We're on the Coakley Road,
When I reached there, saw John Roberts behind me,
John Roberts is my cousin, you know,
He said unto me, oh good Lord,
Irving McFee; Curry Camp burned down.

When I get on the porch, don't you know,
I said to others at the time,
Throw down your bag, Coakley Road on fire,
Say throw down this bag, boys,
Throw down this bag, boys, you know,
Irving McFee; Curry Camp burned down.

When I did reach there, don't you know,
I said unto him now,
Throw down the bag now, call up the people on the farm,
Sixty-five people was working in the forest that day,
Irving McFee; Curry Camp burned down.

We throw down the bag, don't you know,
He put the whistle to his mouth, what he say?
The whistle did blow, in the forest,
(Spoken) This is what the whistle say:

When the whistle blow, glory my God,
Irving McFee; Curry Camp burned down.

Sixty-five people, don't you know,
Running on, out to Coakley Road,
Irving McFee said, won't you give me that losses,
What everybody have in this town, glory be to God,
Irving McFee; Curry Camp burned down.

Some say they lost eight pound,
Some say they lost six pound,
Some say they lost five pound,
Some say they lost four pound;
I lost an old coat, I give it for two pounds you know,
Irving McFee; Curry Camp burned down.

Cecil Lost in the Storm

Now in nineteen hundred and thirty-three,
On a blessed Sunday day, praise the Lord,
Some souls was crossing Jordan River's stream,
Cecil gone in the time of storm.

Tell you nineteen hundred and thirty-three,
On that blessed Sunday day, oh Lord,
Some souls was crossing Jordan River's stream,
Cecil gone in the time of storm.

I remember that boy and his mother had a talk,
He decide to go to Mastic Point,
Take his suitcase in his hand, walking down along the bay,
Cecil gone in the time of storm.

Lord, he get into the boat, yes he hoist the boat sail you know,
Start to go to Mastic Point,
When the boat get confound, poor Cecil get drowned,
Cecil gone, oh yes, Cecil gone.

I remember the time passed, for eight days time,
The boy now weren't turned back home any more,
When they make up in their mind to go to Blanket Sound land,
Cecil gone, oh yes, Cecil gone.

When they reach to Blanket Sound they met his uncle on the
    beach,
Say you ain't seen Cecil nowhere?
"I believe Cecil reach all the way to Nicholas Town,
Cecil gone, oh yes, Cecil gone."

I remember these questions what my friend now did say,
I believe Cecil now get drowned,
Oh blessed Lord, that my dearest friend is gone,
Cecil gone in the time of storm.

When they a week now around, bound to Blanket Sound land,
They met now his mother on the bay,
This is the question what Eudie now did ask,
Cecil gone in the time of storm.

I find the boat, I find the sail,
None of his body I behold.
I said, oh now my cousin, I believe Cecil drowned,
Cecil gone in the time of storm.

I remember that woman now, she fell on the bay,
She rolled all over the bay,
Said, I didn't know God would na answer my cry,
Cecil gone in the time of storm.

I remember that woman, Lord, she fell on the bay,
She rolled all over the bay,
Say, oh blessed Lord, there my youngest son was gone,
Cecil gone in the time of storm.

These the last words I remember what the woman did say,
Oh God, make peace with his soul,
If a man live in Christ, you sure will die right,
Cecil gone, oh yes, and he's gone.

AFRICAN-DERIVED RELIGIOUS
MOTIFS IN JAMAICA

Various cults and religious societies in Jamaica echo African belief systems of an earlier day. Among them are Kumina, the apparently related Maroon or Convince cult, Revival, Revival Zion and Pukumina (sometimes rendered as Pocomania). Worship in these and still other religious groups differs in numerous details, but they have conspicuous parallels: They supplicate pantheons of supernatural beings (deities, spirits and deceased ancestors); they consider mounting or possession of devotees by these beings to be direct contact with the world of the unseen; and in all of them there is ancestor veneration and placation.

Kumina has three ranks of beings who are appealed to and who may descend on devotees and possess them during religious services and dances—sky gods, earthbound gods and ancestral zombies (not to be confused with the zombies of Haitian tradition, though the name obviously has a common derivation.[1] The sky gods have appellations of various origins, some possibly African, at least one (Sango) definitely African, and others derived from biblical literature or created locally. Among the earthbound deities are many with Old and New Testament names and some whose provenance is not recognizable. The zombies—spirits of dead persons who in their lifetimes were possessed by deities—frequently bear names of remembered cult personalities.

The Maroon cult (which takes its name from the Maroons, slaves who escaped into the mountains in the seventeenth and eighteenth centuries to form their own free communities—see p. 158) is also called, variously, Convince, Convince Fankee and sometimes Bongo, though some investigators regard these groups as separate from one another. In many respects, the Maroon beliefs and practices are compatible with Kumina, and it is thought by some that Kumina has absorbed African elements originally preserved by the Maroons. They are close enough, in any event, so that Maroons sometimes participate in Kumina rites.

In Revival tradition, God the Father and God the Son are the dominant, though remote, forces of the universe, and under them is a class of biblical prophets and archangels who, through possession, make their presence known at rites and dances. Another class of spirits is composed of the four evangelists—Mark, Matthew, Luke and John—who rule the four corners of the earth. Still another class is composed of Jesus' disciples. And lastly there is a class of "shepherds" and "shepherdesses," the spirits of certain now dead cult leaders. The Revival Zion group includes among its pantheon of spirits Old Testament heroes and prophets, New Testament apostles, Jehovah, Jesus, the Holy Ghost, archangels, Satan and the dead ancestors. Pukumina has many of the characteristics of Revival and Kumina in its beliefs and practices.

Kumina is clearly the most African of the cults. Its followers claim that it is based on African traditions, and many of its beliefs and practices clearly reflect an African inheritance. Kumina people consider their group to be a "country," much as the Arara and Lucumi of Cuba and the Nago and Ibo cults of Haiti speak of themselves as "nations." The Kumina cult preserves within its ritual a vocabulary of presumed African words and expressions, a number of them authentically African. One investigator, Edward Seaga,[2] found that a substantial part of Kumina ritual words that he had set down were of Bantu origin, among them the following:

Nzambi (God)   yaaya (woman, old)

---

1. *This brief summary of Kumina is based primarily on "A Comparative Study of Acculturation in Morant Bay and West Kingston," by Joseph G. Moore and George Simpson, Zaire, November–December 1957 and No. 1, 1958. Beliefs and practices of this and other cults vary somewhat from region to region.*

2. Folk Music of Jamaica, *booklet accompanying record album of same title, New York, Ethnic Folkways Library, 1956.*

nbuta munta (man, old)	mbizi (meat)
ndumba (woman, young)	malavu (rum)
muana (baby)	wiza (come here)
mbolo (bread)	ntoto (earth)
mbeele (knife)	mbongo (money)

Elderly Kumina devotees mention as tribes (or nations) of their origin, or as bloodlines of their descent, Mondo(n)go, Moyenge, Machunde, Kongo and Mumbaka, all from Bantu areas of Africa, as well as Gaw, Ibo and Yoruba.[3]

Kumina ceremonies are held for mourning, betrothals, greeting an infant, nine nights, healing, and thanksgiving for benefactions received. Rites also may be conducted to solicit aid from gods and spirits in some particular endeavor—to win a lover, a lawsuit or a job, for example. Songs used in the ceremonies are mainly of two kinds, Bailo and Country (that is, nation). The Bailo songs are in English and are usually sung during the opening stage of the ceremonies before possessions take place, or during recreational breaks in the service. Country songs are sung in ritual (i.e., "African") language and are used to invoke, summon, placate or please the deities and the ancestral dead.

Musical instruments used for Kumina dances are comparable to instruments employed elsewhere in the Caribbean for African-style cult activities. According to Seaga:[4]

The main instruments used in Kumina are two types of drums: the Kbandu (Congo: mbandu), and the "Playing Cast." The former has a lower tone which is achieved either by making this drum a bit larger than the Playing Cast or by "heeling" it during play, that is, resting the heel against the drumhead.

These drums are made from small kegs or certain varieties of wood, primarily coconut. They are headed on one side only and always by goat-skin. The skin is attached to the drum by nails driven through a band which goes around the drum-head.

Both the Kbandu and Playing Cast are almost always less than one foot in diameter and two feet in length. The drummer sits astride the drum and plays it with the palms of his hands. The Kbandu keeps a steady beat while the Playing Cast adopts the particular rhythm used to charm a specific spirit, since all spirits are not charmed by the same rhythm. Usually four drums are used at the bigger rites. Two of these are Kbandu while the other two are Playing Casts. At any one time, however, there is likely to be only one Playing Cast in operation, the other being used as a Kbandu by heeling the drumhead. The reason for this is that the steady Kbandu beat is easily followed by a drummer while the polyrhythms of the Playing Cast drummer would conflict with those of a second such drummer unless one was able to duplicate the other accurately, a difficult feat. Hence, the two Playing Cast drum-

---

3. *Moore and Simpson,* ibid.
4. Folk Music of Jamaica, ibid.

mers in a group of four usually play as such in turns, and maintain a Kbandu beat at other times.

Other Kumina instruments include the Shakka, a small tin sheet with nail-punched holes over which a small strip of metal is scraped; gourds with stones which are shaken to provide a rhythmic beat; and sometimes metal triangles which are sounded by metal rods. Occasionally, a small stick about the diameter of a brush handle and less than eight inches in length is used to beat on the side of the drum behind the drummer. The player of this instrument, which is known as the "catta 'tick" (catta stick), sits astride the rear portion of the drum.

Despite a continuing acculturative process, the various African-style cults in Jamaica still retain strong elements of African belief systems. As analyzed by Simpson and Moore:

"In the framework of the sky gods, earthbound gods, and ancestral zombies, Cumina [Kumina] theology resembles West African and Congo religions. The names and duties of the Cumina gods are different, but their behavior and the theological rationale show little evidence of Christian Western European influence. . . . [Although] the names of the gods have changed in the shift from West Africa to Jamaica . . . the polytheistic orientation and the belief in the constant and direct intervention of the spirits in human concerns have been retained. . . . The public nature of spirit possessions, the methods of inducing and controlling possessions, and the behavior of possessed persons are derived from West African religions. . . . The use of drums and rattles, the emphasis in singing, foot patting, and 'spiritual' dancing during religious ceremonies are African retentions. Additional full or nearly full African retentions are found in revelation by the gods in giving remedies to men, and the throwing of food to the gods. . . ."[5]

Kumina Bailo Song

(A FRAGMENT)

> Wye, oh, Maroon gone, oh!
> Fare thee well, Maroon gone, oh!

---

5. *Ibid.*
Song text is from Seaga, ibid.

Maroon gone a Bungo Town to look 'pon de dead!
When him gone poor me one [lef'] ya, oh!

A bailo is a song sung at a Kumina gathering before possessions begin to take place, or during a rest period in the service. It thus reflects the lighter moments of the ceremony, and is comparable to certain dances and songs of Haitian religious rituals that are interspersed to relieve tensions. The term Maroon refers to a descendant of the Maroon community, composed of escaped slaves who set up free villages in the mountainous regions of Jamaica in the seventeenth and eighteenth centuries (see p. 158), or to a member of the Maroon cult. Bungo town is an unofficial designaton of a poor neighborhood of Kingston. Bungo is generally used to refer to communities or persons believed to follow African ways, and the leaders of Kumina and Maroon cult groups are called Bungo Men.

This bailo fragment is part of a song which states in various stanzas that the Maroon has "gone to catch a ghost," also called a duppy, signifying intent to work sorcery. The third line of the stanza shown here could not be verified through reference to the original tape recording, and is probably the collector's free rendition of its meaning.

THE RAS TAFARI MOVEMENT IN JAMAICA

In this description, Dr. George Eaton Simpson tells of the Jamaican cult that holds the conviction that West Indian blacks are reincarnations of the ancient Israelites, and that Haile Selassie, Emperor of Ethiopia (deposed in 1974), was the Living God. Ras Tafari was the name of the Emperor before he ascended the Ethiopian throne.

The Ras Tafari movement began to take shape about 1930. Although Marcus Garvey, founder of the Universal Negro Improvement Association, had no part in organizing this cult, he is highly respected by Ras Tafarians and is regarded as the forerunner of their movement. Mr. Garvey did advocate a mass migration to Africa, and his slogans:

"Africa for the Africans—At Home and Abroad" and "One God! One Aim! One Destiny!" are repeated at every Ras Tafari meeting.

Although groups have been formed in other parts of the island, the main Ras Tafari center is West Kingston, an economically depressed area at the edge of the capital. Cult members, some of whom have arrived only recently from country districts and many of whom are unemployed or underemployed, live in crowded one or two-room houses. The men who are employed are engaged in low-paid, unskilled or semi-skilled work. Women of the area find employment as domestic servants, street merchants, and shop-keepers. Those who are not fully employed "scuffle" for a living. This expressive term means: doing odd jobs, running errands, selling firewood, making baskets or other craft products for sale to tourists and Jamaicans, begging, gambling, stealing, pimping, prostitution; in short, doing almost anything that enables one to keep alive. Family life is unstable, recreation facilities are almost non-existent, and educational accommodations are inadequate.

ORGANIZATION OF RAS TAFARI GROUPS

In 1953, there were at least a dozen Ras Tafari groups operating in West Kingston, with memberships ranging from approximately twenty to one hundred and fifty or more. Among these groups were: United Afro-West Indian Federation, United Ethiopian Body, Ethiopian Youth Cosmic Faith, Ethiopian Coptic League, and the African Cultural League. The writer had close association with two of these groups and had some contact with members of the others.

The organization of Ras Tafari groups varies to some extent, but the usual officers are: President, Vice-President, Secretary, and Chairman. The President, the natural leader of the group, suggests group activities and, as a rule, presides at meetings. The Vice-President acts when the President is absent or incapacitated; the Secretary keeps the records, including minutes, roll-calls, and the contributions of members. The Chairman shares the leadership of meetings with the President. On one occasion the writer heard an argument as to whether a Ras Tafari group had one or two "systems of government." Finally it was agreed that there are two: a "material" system corresponding to the state, and a "spiritual" system corresponding to the church. The officers, however, are the same; they simply play different roles according to which "government" is operating at the moment.

It has been pointed out elsewhere that Ras Tafari groups "form, split, and dissolve, and some individuals accept cult beliefs without attaching themselves to an organization."[1] Unlike the leader-dominated

---

Extracted by permission of George E. Simpson and the Institute of Social and Economic Research from Social and Economic Studies, *Vol. 4, No 2 (June 1955).*

1. *G. E. Simpson, "The Ras Tafari Movement in Jamaica: A Study of Race and Class Conflicts,"* Social Forces, *34 (1955), pp. 167–70.*

Revivalist services in West Kingston, Ras Tafari meetings are conducted in an extremely democratic manner. Despite the emphasis which is placed on love and kindliness to fellow Ras Tafarians, there are some disagreements and rivalries between bands. Contrary to popular opinion, not all Ras Tafari groups favour beard wearing.[2] Groups vary somewhat on the question of whether it is of any use to try to improve conditions in Jamaica. According to some informants, Ras Tafari groups never hold a joint meeting, although, on occasion, when one body has a "function," individuals from other groups may attend. Although the basic principles are the same, some bad feeling has developed in the past because some groups have claimed to be better organized and better disciplined than others.

RAS TAFARIAN DOCTRINE

Six doctrines stand out in the Ras Tafari belief system. The first is that black men, reincarnations of the ancient Israelites, were exiled to the West Indies because of their transgressions. Second, the wicked white man is inferior to the black man.[3] Third, the Jamaican situation is a hopeless Hell; Ethiopia is Heaven. Fourth, Haile Selassie is the Living God. [This article was written before the deposition and death of the Emperor.—Ed.] Fifth, the invincible Emperor of Abyssinia will soon arrange for expatriated persons of African descent to return to the Homeland. Sixth, in the near future black men will get revenge by compelling white men to serve them.

2. *Since the beard has become the symbol of the Ras Tafari movement in the minds of most middle-class Jamaicans and visitors, further comment on this subject may be in order. Ras Tafarian arguments for beards include: (a) the beard is a part of Creation; (b) Haile Selassie wears a beard; (c) a beard indicates that a man belongs "to a certain philosophy"; and (d) some men cannot afford to shave. The main arguments of those who oppose beards are: (a) they are hard to keep clean; and (b) some criminals wear beards as a disguise, and Ras Tafari members get the blame for their misdeeds.*
3. *Usually the stereotype of the "white man" includes all whites regardless of nationality, but occasionally a distinction is made between Englishmen and Americans. The following cliché was heard on several occasions: "Americans tell you to stay here and they will stay there, but they make it possible for you to wear good clothes and to eat good food. The Englishman pats you on the back, but he puts food out of your reach." At one street meeting the Chairman began his remarks by saying: "Don't be afraid of this white man. He isn't an Englishman; he is an American. It is only the English that we fear." Another Chairman explained to the members of his group: "Mr. S. is not a real American. Only the American Indians are real Americans. He says that he is from Ohio, but he is an Englishman. I was born in Jamaica, but I am an Ethiopian." When asked to speak at this meeting, the writer remarked that there are good and bad men in every race. In reply the Chairman asked: "Are all white men bad? No, there are a few good white men. A good white man is the reincarnation of a good slave owner, the kind of man who bought a slave who was being beaten and then took good care of him." Repeated requests for permission to take photographs during the meetings of this group were denied. The most effective arguments against granting such permission were: "We don't know what is in the back of this white man's mind," and: "We signed a pledge never to do anything to please a white man and I, for one, am not going to break my oath." Although Ras Tafarians are extremely suspicious of white persons, and despite the fact that one of the main reasons for being of their movement is hatred of whites, the writer's impression is that most Ras Tafarians will respond favourably to a white person who is friendly.*

RAS TAFARI MEETINGS

Usually a Sunday night meeting at the headquarters of a Ras Tafari group in West Kingston begins with a song such as the following.

> Babel is raging
> Man is an angel and God is Our King.
> Kingdoms are falling,
> Read Revelation.
> The Negus is leading
> The Armageddon.
>
> We are appealing to every nation
> Who are oppressing
> The true sons of God.
> Man violating
> What God has spoken.
> The root of King David
> Brings Empress Menen.
> Be not a traitor,
> Get understanding,
> Love one another
> And honor your King.

Although each group is headed by a president, this officer is by no means the only speaker during a meeting. A speaker may follow the first song with remarks of this type:[4] "How did we get here?" Chorus: "The white man." "The white man tells us we are inferior, but we are not inferior. We are superior, and he is inferior. The time has come for us to go back home. In the near future, we will go back to Ethiopia and the white man will be our servant. The white man says we are no good, but David, Solomon, and the Queen of Sheba were black. The English are criminals and the black traitors (middle-class Jamaicans) are just as bad. Ministers are thieves and vagabonds. The black man who doesn't want to go back to Ethiopia doesn't want freedom. There is no freedom in Jamaica. Ras Tafari is the living God. Ras Tafari started Mau Mau. Ras Tafari says: "'Death to the white man!'" Chorus: "And to the black traitor!" "We believe in 'One God! One Aim! One Destiny!' We believe in Ethiopia for the Ethiopians . . ." Chorus: ". . . at home

---

4. *The members of the largest Ras Tafari group in West Kingston would not permit tape recordings of their speeches. The writer made as many notes as possible during meetings. The statements given here are almost* verbatim, *but some remarks are missing because it was impossible to record every sentence. Song titles were noted during meetings, but the words were dictated by leading Ras Tafarians during private interviews. The writer was unable to learn of any other white person, except one friend who accompanied him to a part of one meeting, who has attended closed meetings of a Ras Tafari group. He knows of only one middle-class Jamaican, a friend who was associated with the author in this study, who has been present at such meetings.*

and abroad." "The white man didn't teach us anything about Ethiopia. How do we know these things? Some ask if we get our knowledge from reading, or from visions, or from communication. No, we get these things directly. We have been with God from the beginning of Creation. We are reincarnations of the ancient Israelites. Why are we here? Because of our own stubbornness, because of our transgressions. We have suffered long enough. The time has come for us to go home and Haile Selassie, the Living God, will deliver us."

References to Ethiopia, the Homeland, may cause the presiding officer to lead the singing of a song of this type:

> Oh! Africa awaken, the morning is at hand.
> No more art Thou forsaken,
> Our bounteous Motherland.
> From far Thy sons and daughters
> Are hastening back to Thee.
> Our cry rings o'er the waters:
> Ethiopia now is free.

> CHORUS

> Ethiopia awaken
> And hear Thy children's cry,
> To God lift up Thine eyes.

> Oh land of perfect splendour
> Of bright blue skies above
> To Thee our best we tender
> Oh land of light and love.
> Some day we'll know Thy story
> And drink the cup of mirth
> Revive Thy ancient glory
> And bring the gods to earth.

> Oh bright and glorious country
> From where the sons of God
> Were called to foreign boundaries
> To bear the chastening rod.
> Torn from Thy blessed shelter,
> We too have suffered long
> Beneath the lash of welter
> And help to bear the cross.

A second speaker stands, removes his hat, and addresses the group along these lines: "If the Government wants a soldier, does he want a dead man?" Chorus: "No." "If the Governor wants someone to drive his car, does he want a dead man?" Chorus: "No." "What would God want with dead men? Heaven is a scheme of the English to make the black man think that white men and black men will be equal in the sky, but on earth the white man isn't going to give the black man anything. Everything the white man brings to us we find to be a failure. Only Ras Tafari can save us. You remember the foolishness that the teacher taught us. The two wickedest men are the police and the minister. Fraud has kept us back—the fraud of religion and politics. We want no more of the white man's indoctrination. Everything about the white man is false. He is a hypocrite, a murderer, a criminal thief. We understand what the white man has done to us and we are going to do unto them as they have done unto us."

The end of a speech calls for the group to participate in another song. This may be a Sankey such as: "Rejoice. Rejoice. The Lord Is King"; "By and By"; or "Day Is Dying in the West"; a Methodist hymn such as: "Let the Song Go Round the Earth"; "Jesus (with Negus substituted for Jesus) Shall Reign Where'er the Sun"; or "Hail to the Lord's Anointed"; or a Baptist hymn such as: "Jesus (Negus) the King".

The next speaker may use an article entitled "Modern Ethiopia" which appeared in the June, 1931, issue of the *National Geographic* magazine as his text. This article deals with the coronation of Haile Selassie as Emperor of Abyssinia, and it is often quoted almost sentence by sentence with appropriate interpretations by the speaker. The splendour of the coronation is dwelt upon, and emphasis is placed on the alleged bowing down of the kings and presidents of the earth before Haile Selassie. Haile Selassie's power, the speaker contends, is acknowledged by the mightiest rulers of the world. A speech of this type may be followed by several repetitions of a brief song called "The Lion of Judah Shall Break Every Chain."

> The Lion of Judah shall break every chain
> And give us a victory
> Again and again.

A fourth speaker may ask the Secretary to read a chapter from the Bible, interrupting him at the end of each verse, or of several verses, or even in the middle of a verse, to give his special politico-religious interpretation of the words. Among the favourite chapters of the Ras Tafaris are: Isaiah 43, 44, 47, 34, 3, and 9; Proverbs 8; Jeremiah 50, 51, 8, and 2; Amos 9 and 3; Malachi 1; Revelation 18, 17, 6, 5, 22, and 19; James 5; Lamentations 5; Joel 3 and 34; Zachariah 8 and 14; Micah 4; Deuteronomy 28, 30, and 4; Ezekiel 37 and 48; Daniel 2, 7, and 12; Leviticus 25; Psalms 87, 68, 48, 97, 99, 140, and 135; Genesis 2 and 18; Habakkuk 2 and 3; and the First Epistle of John 4. If the speaker has chosen Revelation 18, great stress will be laid upon the twenty-first verse: ". . . Thus with violence shall that great city Babylon be thrown down, and shall be found no more at all."

An appropriate song at this point would be: "Awake Sleeping Jews, Awake."

Oh Israel stand!
The land appear,
He now begins to rule.
The world gets fear.
Great kingdoms fall
At the sound of rabbi's voice.

CHORUS

Down in Abyssinia
Hear what a glorious cry.
All the people of the whole world
Going down before him to bow.
Great Ras Tafari, King of Kings
You come to reign.
Glory be to God our Father
Justice must be seen on Earth.

Can I forget his Covenant
He made with Israel once?
To Jacob's seed for evermore
His Covenant cannot break.

Sleeping Jews awake!
The Saviour comes.
He comes on earth to reign.
He comes to reign as King of Kings,
His promise cannot fail.

Our weeping stop,
Our mourning cease,
Our sighing turns to Psalms.
The fetters are broken,
The chain has dropped.
Poor Israel free at last.

The final speaker may proceed in this vein: "We are not here to compromise with black hypocrites or white demagogues. The white man
accuses the black man of being a thief, but the white man has stolen
continents and men. If the white man doesn't like us, why doesn't he
send us back to Africa? Today we see the downfall of England and the
rising of Ethiopia. Even British Guiana, a country that is smaller than
Jamaica, has defied England. We will co-operate with the Chinaman,
Chiang Kai-shek; we will co-operate with the Englishman, Winston
Churchill, but we want our own King." This speaker, as well as his
predecessors, may point from time to time to a large framed picture of
Haile Selassie.

After several announcements by the president, all stand, face the

East and close the meeting with the singing of the Ethiopian National Anthem and the Ethiopian prayer, both composed in West Kingston.

This is the anthem:

> Ethiopia, the land of our Fathers,
> The land where all God's love to be.
> As the swift bees to hive sudden gather,
> Thy children are gathered to Thee.
> With our Red, Gold, and Green floating o'er us,
> With the Emperor to shield us from wrong,
> With our God and our future before us,
> We hail Thee with shout and with song.

> CHORUS

> God bless our Negus, Negus I
> And keep Ethiopia free
> To advance with truth and right,
> To advance with love and light.
> With righteousness pleading,
> We haste to the cause.
> Humanity bleeding,
> One God for us all.

> Ethiopia, the tyrant is falling
> Who smote Thee upon Thy knees.
> And Thy children are lustily calling
> From over the distant seas.
> Jehovah the great one has heard us;
> He has heard our tears and our sighs.
> With the spirit of love he has brought us
> To be won through the coming years.

> Oh eternal Thou God of the Ages,
> Grant unto Thy sons that live
> The wisdom Thou gave to the sages
> When Israel was sore in need.
> Thy voice through the dim past has spoken;
> Ethiopia now stretch forth her hands
> By these shall our barriers be broken,
> God bless our dear Motherland.

This is the prayer:

Princes have come out of Egypt; Ethiopia now stretch forth her hands unto God. Oh Thou God of Ethiopia, Thy divine majesty, Thy spirit, come into our hearts to dwell in the paths of righteousness. Lead us, help us to forgive that we may be forgiven. Teach us love, loyalty on earth as to Heaven, endow us with Thy wisdom and understanding to do Thy will. Thy blessing to use that the hungry be fed, the naked clothed, the sick nourished, the aged protected, and the infants cared for. Deliver us from the hands of our enemies that we might prove fruitful for the last days. When our enemies are passed and decayed in the depths of the sea, in the depths of the earth, or in the belly of a beast, Oh give us all a place in Thy Kingdom for ever and ever. Selah.

A RAS TAFARI STREET MEETING

Street meetings are held once or twice weekly by each well-organized Ras Tafari group for the purpose of gaining converts. A typical street meeting attracts from one hundred to one hundred and fifty persons, and resembles a meeting at the group's headquarters. Members march to the designated street corner, bringing their paraphernalia in a push-cart. Photographs of Haile Selassie are hung on a stand, a rhumba box is placed on the sidewalk, and a large red, gold, and green banner mounted on a pole is held and waved by a flag-bearer. The caps, dresses, scarves, sashes, and robes worn by the members are of the same colors. One street meeting opened with the singing of a song about Haile Selassie.

> King Rasta is now on the wheel;
> The knowledge of truth is now flowing.
> If Israel can't hear they must feel.

> CHORUS

> Our Redeemer is calling us home.
> We see there is no truth in Rome.
> Our Heaven is in Ethiopia
> With King Rasta and Queen Omega.

> For centuries we have been downtrodden,
> We could not believe we were born.
> But we trust in King Ras Tafari
> For he is our guide and our shield.

Following the reading and interpreting of a chapter of Zachariah and the singing of a song entitled "Though the Battle May Be Hard and the Journey Long," the first speaker advanced from the semi-circle of members facing the crowd and made an appeal to the "black man." "Black man, a white man is here for our meeting tonight. He is a U.K. reporter. He knows that white men are devils. We ask you to be calm, to deny the things which are said against us. Thrones are toppling before the King of Kings and the Lord of Lords. Israel, what are you standing back for? What are you waiting for? This is the time. Read John 4. Time is gliding on. Marcus Garvey was an international figure. He brought a philosophy to the black man. Glory to God (pointing to a picture of Haile Selassie). The throne of Ethiopia is older than the throne of Saint George. It has existed since the beginning of time. Beloved Black people, the time of redemption is at hand. Our God and King is here to deliver us, and when we go back to that land no one will ever get us again. So, Black man, get in line. If you don't see me any more, meet me at the beautiful river." This last remark stimulated the singing of the hymn entitled "On the Banks of the Beautiful River."

A baton-carrying member wearing a red blouse stepped forward and launched into his speech: "I greet you all, white and black, in the name of Ras Tafari. Black men, you are full of sodomy, backbiting. You are liars, thieves, traitors, warmongers. That's why you were sent to Babylon. God is a philosophy. God is in human beings. Lift up your head, Black man. Do you see any resemblance between Jesus Christ and Ras Tafari? The spirit of David jump into Solomon, the spirit jump out of Solomon into Ras Tafari. Fifty-two nations bow down to Ras Tafari. This man is Jehovah God. Europe is for Europeans; Ethiopia for Ethiopians. Hear the voice of Ethiopia calling everyone. Black man, tuberculosis is white man's disease and there is no cure for it, but better food and living will prevent it. Black man, your children want education. The time is short. Today it is nation against nation. The King of Israel shall rule over all. Anyone who stands in the way will have to be moved. Jamaica was built up by black people and what have we got? Unite into one body and declare Ethiopia for Ethiopians, at home and abroad. The big, fat Negro (middle-class Jamaican) who stands in our way . . . there will be a remission of blood. Read Malachi 1:14—The deceiver's name shall be terrible. Strike Busta (Bustamante, leader of the Jamaica Labor Party and former Chief Minister), Manley (leader of the People's National Party and Chief Minister), Churchill and all who sit in the seats of the oppressors. Marcus Garvey was the spirit of the Word, the Sound, and the Power. Marcus Garvey laid the corner stone and the foundation. He was the world's greatest statesman and was sent by Ras Tafari to cut and clear.[5] We have the key. Read Jeremiah 8:21—'. . . I am black.' Read Revelation 6:15—"And the kings of the earth, and the great men, and the rich men, and the chief captains, and the mighty men, and every bondsman, and every free man, hid themselves in the dens and in the rocks of the mountains; and said to the mountains and rocks: Fall on us, and hide us from the face of him that sitteth on the throne, and from the wrath of the Lamb; For the great day of his wrath is come; and who shall be able to stand?" The appropriate song to follow this type of speech is entitled "He Comes to Break Up Oppression."

---

5. *An expression used by Jamaican revivalists to refer to ritualistic means of removing evil spirits.*

He (Haile Selassie) comes to break up oppression
To set the captives free
To take away transgression
And rule by equality.

CELEBRATION ON THE ANNIVERSARY OF
HAILE SELASSIE'S CORONATION

Ras Tafarians do not celebrate Christmas because they believe that Christ was born on April 1st. The latter date is regarded by them as the beginning of the year, and ceremonies are held during the day and in the evening. Emancipation Day, a Jamaican holiday, is not observed by Ras Tafarians because they hold that black men have not yet been emancipated. The anniversary of Haile Selassie's Coronation Day provides the occasion for the most important special celebration during the year. In 1953, this ceremony occurred on November 15. The evening program began with the singing of "When I Go to Zion I'll Never Leave Again."

When I go to Zion I'll never leave again.
When I go to Zion I'll never leave again.
I am going to the mansion
King Rasta come and prepare.
When I go to Zion I'll never leave again.

A special orchestra, which included the following instruments—two rhumba boxes, three guitars, two saxophones, one violin, one banjo, tambourines, and rattles—accompanied the singing. Special recitations, and songs by individuals and a quartette, were presented. Ten babies were dedicated to Ras Tafari, and a godfather and godmother were appointed for each baby. During this part of the ceremony, each mother handed her child to a male assistant of the Leader. This official took the baby in his arms, gently raised and lowered it several times, smiled and said: "The King (Ras Tafari) bless thee, keep thee, and make his face to shine upon thee, and give thee peace and life everlasting." Two collections were taken for the babies and the money was divided equally among the mothers. On this occasion ten speeches were delivered throughout the program. We shall cite only one speech: "Mr. S. is a brave man to come here, but remember that Satan is a brave man too. The Anglo-Saxons teach us ignorancy. Black man, be reasonable. Can you have a Queen without a King? I know that the Queen who is coming here doesn't care for me, so why should I adore her? The only future destination is with Ras Tafari. Where was God when the white man was raping India, Egypt and other countries? Haile Selassie is Jesus Christ reincarnated. He has a legion of angels [presumably his officials] around him. We are celebrating the coronation of Jesus Christ tonight, and for that we make no apology and no compromise. Mau Mau is a war between black men and white men. The white men throw bombs on the Mau Mau, but they can't hurt them because Haile Selassie controls the bomb. Mau Mau don't have guns; they use bows and arrows. The white man tells us to wait until Jesus comes, but we're not going to wait. The Minister of Education is going to prison. Our only hope is to go back to Africa. In the near future we are going back to our Homeland." The speech was followed by a brief song:

> I shall not die but I shall live
> Forever with the Lord.
> In these days I heard
> These prophets saying
> I shall live forever with the Lord.

ABOUT THE MAROONS OF JAMAICA

Like other parts of Afro-America, Jamaica had its share of slave runaways and insurrections. In time, as in the case of Surinam, nominally autonomous communities of former slaves came to exist. In the mountainous cockpit country even today, in the village of Accompong, there live descendants of runaways who contested for their liberty against Spanish and British colonial forces.

When Jamaica was taken over by the British from the Spanish in the year 1655, most of the Spanish inhabitants emigrated to Cuba. Many slaves that they left behind found sanctuary in the mountain fastnesses, joining other runaways that had preceded them. Thirty-five years later there was an insurrection in Clarendon Parrish, and more fugitives escaped into the mountains. Thus a number of communities of escaped slaves came into being. In the early eighteen hundreds the ex-slaves residing in Clarendon Parrish, who were now referred to as Maroons (from the French *marron* or the Spanish *cimaron*, meaning wild or fugitive), were organized under a chief named Cudjoe, whose two brothers, Accompong and Johnny, served as his assistants in the defense against the British. Many of the blacks in Cudjoe's region were Coromantes (Ashanti), but there appear to have been numerous Nagos, Mandingos, Angolas and others as well. Under Cudjoe's leadership, the fugitive community thrived and became nearly self-sufficient, frequently raiding white settlements when supplies ran low. Unable to cope adequately with the various groups of Maroons, Jamaican authorities signed a treaty with them in 1738 which for the time brought peace. It gave the Maroons of Trelawney Parrish unprecedented rights and privileges. It recognized them as self-governing, assigned land to them, specified their right to hunt, and acknowledged their right to travel and trade.[1] Later, these rights and privileges were given to other Maroon groups. In return, the Maroons agreed to return any runaway slaves that might seek sanctuary among them.

In the closing years of the eighteenth century, however, there were new frictions and forays. During these renewed hostilities, the Maroons living in the village called Accompong, after Cudjoe's brother, avoided conflict and remained faithful to their agreement with the British. Jamaican authorities attempted new negotiations, and this failing, they undertook an expedition to put down the Maroons once and for all. But the Maroons resisted strongly and turned back combined forces of British troops, Jamaican militia and free black auxiliaries. At last a body of Spanish hunters with trained dogs was brought from Cuba to hunt down and subdue the resisting blacks and at this point the Maroons surrendered, following which most of them were transported to Nova Scotia and, ultimately, to the British African protectorate of Sierra Leone. Some who were not deemed dangerous to the peace were allowed to remain in Jamaica, however, notably the people of Accompong, who had avoided hostilities with the British following the signing of the 1738 treaty.

Today, still, Accompong is recognized as a separate corporate entity, untaxed, allowed to select its own headmen (now called colonels), and possessing the right to hold its own courts and compel obedience to its own laws.[2]

Quadrille and Polka in Accompong

About thirty years ago, the dancer Katherine Dunham spent a month with the Maroons in Accompong. Out of that visit came a small book, in the form of a journal, called *Journey to Accompong*, from which this description of a Maroon dance is taken.

1. *Treaty details are from* American Negro Slavery, *by Ulrich B. Phillips, New York, Appleton, 1918.*
2. *Melville J. Herskovits,* The Myth of the Negro Past, *New York, Harper, 1941.*

. . . . We patiently sat and waited, and I had time to observe the gathering. Old women, young women and girl babies all wore clean white kerchiefs on their heads. . . . The regulation costume for women consisted of a loose sacklike gingham dress tied around the waist and falling well below the knee. The men wore blue denim or faded khaki trousers, and occasionally a white pair, straw hats, and perhaps a sack coat of some vintage past and forgotten. All were barefoot except the most prominent and affluent, such as council members and their immediate families, the shopkeeper, and young dandies of "cotin'" age who wished to make an impression.

Suddenly the hush into which we were rapidly falling was ruptured by a series of disharmonic chords and squeaks and loud thumps of the game leg [of the fiddler] and the bow on the floor. There was a moment of tension, a sigh, a violent expectoration over the pavilion railing, and the fiddler had "cum round." First he warmed up on a bit of this and that: improvisations, snatches of old English airs and Creole melodies. Meanwhile two lines formed, one of men, one of women. The men vied for partners, the women modestly looked down and fingered their dresses, and then as if by silent agreement, fiddler and dancers were under way. There was a great flourish of curtsies, and gradually it dawned on me that this was the Maroon version of the quadrille.

The dancers interested me more than the dance. As they swung into the second figure, the polka, I noticed that of the six women dancing, four were quite elderly, and all of the men except Shirly [a young boy] were well onto three-quarters of a century, if one could judge age by physical appearance. In my country these old women would be the dignified chaperons; here they were the belles of the evening. Before the night was over, I began to realize that, at the dances at least, the attitude of the Maroons toward their elders is that of many another primitive community—what the years heap upon one in infirmities, that much also do they add in knowledge and wisdom and perfection of artistry—"The Colonel would rudder dance with Mis' Ma'y den all dem young 'uns put togedder," Mai told me. And truly I marveled as I watched the wrinkled little bent figure suddenly straighten up as she tied her kerchief more tightly over her straggly gray knots, and step forth to take the Colonel's arm with all of the aplomb of a seasoned ballerina.

There were brief pauses for rum and to "kotch a bref." The music grew wilder, and even those of us who were observers were sweating with the excitement. The gentlemen no longer saluted the ladies with sweeping bows, but with a leap to the center of the square, a clicking of the heels high in the air, entre-sixes, backbends, and elaborate turns. The women's skirts began to climb, their eyes shone, their step was high and light, and the flashing of bare black calves brought about many a change of partner. The fiddler was inspired and became a veri-

From Journey to Accompong, by Katherine Dunham, New York, Holt, 1946. By permission of Katherine Dunham.

table orchestra as he swung from the stately "valse" into the sixth figure of the quadrille with much thumping of foot and bow, and frequent vocal accompaniment. Someone beat out the tempo with two sticks, the mouth harp joined in, and before I knew it the Colonel had passed Miss' Ma'y on and I was thick and fast in the throes of the "say-shay." This last figure of the set dance must undoubtedly be a Creole improvisation. Indeed it seems to have no place with the other conventional figures, variegated as they are. For the first time I begn to feel that the Maroons belonged to the sultry side of the Caribbean and that their Spanish and Indian and African ancestors must have known passions other than warfare.

TWO TALES FROM ACCOMPONG

AS SET DOWN BY KATHERINE DUNHAM

Fowl and Cockroach

Fowl 'en de cockruch frien'. De two of dem promis' to wuk one groun'. So dee start, en den one day de cockruch ve'y seeck. Ee so seeck. So ee tay in bed, en Bre' Fowl em bile tea en bile brekfus fe' Bre' Cockruch. Den Bre' Fowl 'im leave en go in fiel' en wuck de groun'. Et de same time, cockruch a fiddler, en ee smaht. Soon ez Bre' Fowl go wuck de fiel', Bre' Cockruch grab ee fiddle en commence for sing.

> "Bre' Foooooowwwl, I mak ya plan' dat groun',
>   Cok-a-teeeee,
> Bre' Foooooowwwl, I mak ya plan' dat groun',
>   Cok-a-teeeee."

So Bre' Fowl come home in de ebnin' en im see food wot ee bile in de mawnin' en ee tink Bre' Cockruch sic fer true. So eb'y day im bile brekfus, en eb'y day Bre' Cockruch grab 'ee fiddle en sing, en eb'y day

From Dunham, ibid., by permission of Katherine Dunham.

de fowl do all de wuck in groun' wot eem bof's s'pose to wuck. Den one day a frien' come in de fiel' en tell Bre' Fowl det Bre' Cockruch right hearty. So nex marnin', Bre' Fowl wan fer fin' out eeself. So ee bile de brekfus, same ez always, dem eem staht out fe wuk en lef' eem tings et de ben' en tuhn back. Ee peek in en ee see Bre' Cockruch singin' de song en fiddlin' like dis: [Here a lively imitation of the cockroach fiddling.]

> "Bre' Fooowwwlll, I mak' ya plan' dat groun'
>   Cok-a-teeee
> Bre' Fooowwwlll, I mak' ya plan' dat groun'
>   Cok-a-teee."

So Bre' Fowl ee so mad ee run in en peek eeem op en eat eem. En since dat day, never see cockruch een yahd what de fowl don' run up en peek eem up en eat eem!

Horse and Turtle

De hawse en de tuttle, eem mek bet fer see who git King'ton fus'! Ee who git King'ton fus' ee get bag uv salt. Now de tuttle eem smaht. Ee tek eem picknee [children] en drap one eb'y mile so en so [demonstrating the placing of the baby turtles at each milepost] en so—alla way King'ton. King'ton much much mile. So dey tuk out, en de fus' mile Hawse draw up et de milepos' en eem sing out real loud:

> "Wot occaaaaaaaasion
> Wot occaaaaaaaasion
> Wot occaaaaaaaaaaaasionnn,
>   En Hawse win race!"

But de picknee, eem answer:

> "On a road ta town
> On a road ta town
> Wot occaaaaasion,
>   En de Tuttle win race!"

So Hawse say, "Wot *dis!*" En ee pull out again en dis time ee trabble fas, en ee git to de milepos' en ee stop up short en ee sing out:

> "Wot occaaaaaaasion
> Wot occaaaaaaaaasion,
> Wot occcaaaaaaaaaaasionnnn,
>   En Hawse win race!"

En de picknee answer same ez before. So de Hawse es real mad wif eeself. Ee bop eeself pam! pam! pam! En ee tuk out agen. Ee draw up et de milepos', en dis time ee trabble so fas' ee out uv win'. Ee sing out real loud en quick:

> Wot occaaaaaasion
> Wot occcaaaaaaasion
> Wot occccaaaaaaaasionnnn
> En Hawse win race!"

En de picknee answer:

"En Tuttle win de race!"

So dis time de hawse right skeered. Ee pull out agen, en im put on spur, en im *trabble!* Im pas' lots milepos' en im no top fer eat ner fer drink eder. Em trabble fas', fas', fas', en af'er em pass lots milepos', em draw up right *'bom!* En em commence fer sing out real loud, "Wot occccaaaaaasion. . . ." En im all out uv bret'. En de nex' lil' picknee answer from behime pos':

"En Tuttle win de race!"

So de hawse ee say, "Great Fadder! Wot dis! De tuttle on eem belly, en me on me legs, en de tuttle win de race!" En ee bop eeself right hahd, *bie! bie! bie!* en eem pull out en eem gollop en gollop en gollop. De hawse don' stop for eat cawn, en ee don' stop fer drink watah. Eee jus' gollop. Now don' be two miles fer get ta King'ton. Ee sing out, "Wot occaaassssssion," en eem win' so sho't eem hah'dly kin sing. En de las lil' picknee answer right quick, "En de Tuttle win de race."

En de hawse tuk out agen, but dis time he wuk so hahd det ez ee reach King'ton ee hoof bus' en ee drap ded in de road.

SOME TRINIDADIAN HEALING REMEDIES

Folk remedies for commonplace ailments are known to many of the older generation in Trinidad. Ingredients that go into various "teas" potions and ointments—leaves, roots and barks—sometimes can be found growing wild in the countryside, or they can be purchased in stores and markets. For those whose illnesses do not respond to traditional home treatment, there are, of course, medical doctors, but nu-

merous people resort to healers who may be leaders of Afro-Trinidadi-
an cults or, in some cases, who are merely country people with a special knowledge of curing. The anthropologist George E. Simpson notes
that healers sometimes wear robes, the style and color of which have
been revealed to them in visions. "Frequently the healer grasps a ro-
sary in one hand during the session, and the client may be asked to
hold one or more lighted candles. A smoking incense pot may be
swung back and forth at the outset to purify [the surroundings]. At
some point the healer may go into a trancelike state and speak in the
'unknown tongue.'" Here are some of the remedies traditionally prescribed:

Colds. Various types of colds loom large in the total volume of complaints of lower class Trinidadians.

> Ordinary cold. Boil water cress and water grass to make a tea.
>
> Cough. Boil whole papaw (papaya), small calabash, cereal bush,
> Christmas bush, chandelier (shandella) [*Leonotis
> nepetifolia*], and rock sage. Strain the tea and add sugar, hon-
> ey, paregoric, olive oil, and soft candle (tallow).
>
> Cold in head. Make a paste of soft candle, mustard powder, and
> black pepper. Cut hair at center of head, apply paste, and cov-
> er spot with a thyme leaf. Patient perspires and cold leaves his
> head.
>
> Cold in head. Remove brain from head of goat that has been killed
> at a ceremony for Ogun (St. Michael) and put it in a bottle
> with ground guinea pepper, puncheon rum, ground spice, and
> ground clove. Add rum to the bottle from time to time.
>
> A bad cold. Hang a loaf of unleavened bread where cockroaches
> travel. Wash bread in a little water and squeeze water out of
> bread. Put sweet oil (olive oil) in pot with onions and to-
> matoes. When pot is dry, add a little water from the bread. Eat
> the browned onions and tomatoes.
>
> Cold in the blood. Make tea of tapanna leaves. Seat patient out-
> doors in the open air and have him drink glass of tea. Patient
> then lies down, covers up with a blanket, and perspires freely.
> Boil coffee and onion together, squeeze lime juice into coffee,
> and add a pinch of salt.

"Not feeling well"—(Sickness in General).

> Gereytoute tea is a "cure-for-all," an "old time" medicine.
>
> Soak isinglass crystals, gum of dragon, catscratch gum, and gum
> swatil in a glass of water until they dissolve. Add claret wine,
> spirits of asefesita (asafetida), and phosphorene.

---

*This list of remedies was compiled by George E. Simpson in 1960, and is ex-
tracted from his article, "Folk Medicine in Trinidad,"* Journal of American
Folklore, *October–December 1962, Vol. 75, No. 298. By permission of Dr.
Simpson and the* Journal of American Folklore.

This *tesan* (medicine) is a mixture of bush and drugstore ingredients. The bush ingredients include these roots: Cousin Mahoe [*Urena lobata*], minnie, coconut, man-better-man, male papaw, gully, white physic nut, red physic nut, and longbeth [lapit]. Drugstore ingredients include: tilly flowers, beacou leaves, senna pods, senna leaves, sosofa (susufoi) bark, calomel flowers, rhubarb powder, and jallop powder. Boil together the bush and drugstore ingredients. To the tea add Epsom salts for a woman and Glover salts for a man.

Fever.

Boil bonna bean leaves (two green and one yellow) with a green lime cut in halves. Add a little salt and puncheon rum to this tea.

Boils.

Apply a poultice made of soft candle, brown sugar, and brown soap.

Dysentery.

Cut rachette (prickly pear—a type of cactus) leaves into thin slices and heat them over a fire. Put hot leaves in a cloth and tie around the bowels (waist) to draw heat out.

Put chopped rachette leaves in a mug and pour boiling water over them. Drink tea after it has cooled.

Mash ripe bananas, put in cloth and tie around waist.

Pour boiling water in a mug containing devil grass. Drain off the tea and drink.

Stomachache; stomach gas; dyspepsia.

Chew guinea pepper with obi seed and swallow mixture.

Boil together some guava leaves and black sage leaves and add spirits of asefesita (asafetida).

Tea made by boiling Cousin Mahoe leaves.

Tea made by boiling dogbush (Da Chien) leaves.

Tea made of lemon grass and the following leaves, guava, soursop, avocado.

Same as above except that Cousin Mahoe and dogbush leaves are included.

Drink blood of goat that has just been killed.

Goat's brain mixed with rum, olive oil, and sugar.

Rheumatism.

Coconut oil as a lubricant or as a drink.

Muscular pains.

Sheep's brain and olive oil.

Cuts.

Put ground balsam leaves and young cocoa pods on cut and place piece of a rotten Banana stump on top of the mixture. Cut is not washed before mixture is put on. Banana stump will drop off within two or three days. Mixture will stay on until cut heals.

Swollen feet.

Hold front feet of frog with one hand and back feet with other and rub body of frog on the patient's leg. Tie frog securely and hang it in a tree. Frog dies and dries up and the swelling goes down.

Whooping cough.

Put molasses in a tin with tallow and olive oil and heat until the tallow melts. Stir and cool mixture. Give one teaspoon three times a day.

Weak eyes.

Heat Wonder-of-the-World [Kalanchoe] leaves over a fire and squeeze juice from them. For a week put a few drops in eyes each morning. Wild plantain (planta) leaves may be substituted for Wonder-of-the-World.

Worm fits.

Crush some worm grass (fit weed) in a pan of warm water and add wood ashes and salt. Bathe child with this mixture and boil some worm grass separately, add a pinch of salt, some grated nutmeg, a little rum, and some olive oil, and give the child a glass of the tea to drink.

Sprained wrist or ankle.

Grind Bois Flot leaves and a piece of ginger together and add a little vinegar to make a poultice. Place on piece of brown paper and tie paper on wrist or ankle.

Backache.

Tie a strip of matapel vine around waist (bark has a milk which makes it stick to skin). Sprinkle corn meal on piece of cloth, fold cloth in half and soak it in vinegar, puncheon rum, and water. Fold cloth again and place it over strip of vine. Bark will draw moisture from cloth. When cloth dries, soak it again, keeping it on back for a day or so. When cloth is taken off, bark will stick to skin. When bark falls off, the backache is cured.

Marasma (blood disease of children).

Grind honeysuckle leaves into a little water and mix with goat's milk. Have child drink this mixture for three or four days and then give him a purgative made of castor oil, senna, baby oil, sea water, and lime juice.

Maljo.

A child gets maljo when a person with a "bad eye" looks at a child and says: "Oh, that is a beautiful child." The child refuses to eat or drink, cries continually, and "pines away." It may have "an attack of fever." To find out if a child has maljo, put a branch of sweet broom in its hand or on its chest. If the sweet broom withers immediately, the child has maljo. To "cut" maljo, put a piece of indigo blue in a saucer and pour holy water on it. Put a branch of sweet broom, some lanebwah and gully root leaves in jar of water and add some of the blue water and a pinch of salt. Bathe the child with this solution. Mix spirits of asefesita (asafetida) and olive oil in saucer containing indigo blue water and make the sign of the cross on the child's forehead, on the soles of his feet, on his chest, and on his back. Annoint him with the liquid left in the saucer.

Thrush (sore mouth).

Put ground dogbush leaves in a plain piece of cloth and squeeze some lime juice on cloth. Scrub baby's mouth with cloth until it bleeds. Do this for four days.

Asthma.

Swallow heart of morocoy (land turtle).

Swallow liver of young Trinidad black bird (known as "old witch").

Boil together the following ingredients, strain the tea and give it to the patient to drink: one-half pound of onions, three snails, three cockroaches, some Christmas bush leaves, and some cereal bush blossoms.

Put yon tasso root, sarsaparilla root, young calabash, wild thyme leaves, petit baume leaves, mango bark, guava bark, cedar bark, coconut roots, coconut bark, green lime cut into pieces, lemon glassia leaves, and lemon grass in a large jar. Cover the jar, put it in a hole in the earth, cover jar with earth and leave it in the ground for two or three weeks. Strain and bottle the medicine.

Boil Bahama grass and coconut fiber together, add green rock sage leaves, and give that to sick person to drink. Roast rosemary bush and wild okra seeds together and grind them into a powder. Put powder in a tin or bottle with a tight cork. Add piece of menthol to the powder and have patient inhale that when he drinks the Bahama grass-coconut fiber tea.

Sores.

Bathe sores with sheep's blood.

Cut skin from a frog, especially from the frog's belly, and spread it over the sore. Leave it on skin for three days.

Boil physic nut bush and soak center of a loaf of bread in water. Make a poultice of physic nut leaves, bread, and olive oil. Wash sore with physic nut water. Put poultice on cloth and tie cloth on sore. Put on fresh poultice three times day. When poultice is taken off, wash sore with physic nut water. On the fourth day, paint sore with a feather dipped in carbolic oil and put fresh poultice on. May take two weeks to heal a bad sore.

Patient goes to a person on whom Michael manifests. Healer burns to ashes a piece of bone taken from a goat's head, grinds ashes to a fine powder, sprinkles powder on a piece of wool cloth and shakes out the cloth. Finest powder sticks to the cloth. The cloth is placed on the ulcer for four or five minutes. Cloth is removed and a feather is used to paint foot with olive oil. Physic nut leaves are boiled and the water is used to wash sore. A dry (brown) banana leaf is kept on ulcer for three days. When leaf drops off, ulcer is sprinkled with a mixture of powder from the bone of a goat's head and arrowroot powder.

Yaws.

For a child who has yaws, dig a hole in the earth, pour water into it, and stir mud until it becomes a paste. Put child in hole, and daub him with the mud. Put him in a place where others will not step on dirt that falls off and in that way get yaws. Repeat this procedure for two or three days and then give the child a dose of castor oil. On the following seven days, give the child a tea made of albay leaves. On the eighth day, grind leaves of the wakoo bush and longbeth (lapit) leaves in some water and bathe the child. Anoint him with lard and sugar of lead mixed together.

Aphrodisiac.

Boil together marbay bark, anise seeds, and nutmeg mace (skin covering the nutmeg shell). Sweeten with sugar and drink wine glass every day.

Trouble in urinating.

Boil leaves or root of gully root for a tea or put slices of the root in dry vermouth for a week.

Roast several thorns of lengwah grass and wild okra seeds (gumbo maize). Grind thorns and seeds together and make a tea. Strain tea and ask patient to drink it without sugar two or three times a day.

Boil roucou [*Bixa orellana*] leaves and to the tea add sapidillo seeds and wild coffee seeds (cafe zeb peean) which have been heated and ground together.

Menstrual troubles.
  Menstrual pain.
    Pound herbe-à-femme leaves, squeeze juice from leaves, add
    honey and olive oil, and take internally. Variation:boil leaves
    and drink tea.
    Boil one treff leaf (very bitter) and drink tea.
  Hemorrhaging during menstrual period.
    Boil together: a small maromay (milkweed) plant, mashupon
    leaves, and wild okra. Cool and drink tea.

Increasing milk supply of nursing mother.
  Boil vevenlatehaywhat (rat-tail) leaves. Cool the tea and give it to
    the mother without sugar three times a day. Mother must not
    nurse baby the first day. On the second day have mother drink
    a tea made of olive leaves and cow's milk. On the third day,
    she will be able to nurse the baby.

Venereal disease.
  Make tea of the following ingredients: Yon tasso root, sarsaparilla
    root, minnie root, gully root, zeb-a-femme root, wild coffee
    root, graveyard bush leaves, St. John's leaves, senna leaves,
    the inside of a young calabash, and sosofa bark. Strain tea
    through a clean cloth and add Epsom salts. Let mixture stand
    for three days until it has an acid taste. Take one wineglass ev-
    ery three days.
  Boil leaves with thorns of "Old Lady" (Ti Mawee) bush with Red-
    head roots. Cool, strain, and drink. After the "venereal" has
    been cured, mix water from boiled senna pods with Epsom
    salts and drink this mixture every other day for a week or so.

Abortion.
  Slice green pineapple with skin on and boil it with the navel (flow-
    er) of the silk fig (type of banana). Drink tea for two or three
    days.
  Boil together leaves of Dr. Barr bush (very bitter) and zeb-a-pick
    leaves. Add a little wood ashes to water. Strain and drink for
    two days. This is a stronger medicine than [the above] and it
    acts faster.
  Boil small pod of red cocoa (Caracas cocoa) and a piece of red cot-
    ton cloth, add black pepper and a little puncheon rum. This is
    a weaker medicine and it acts more slowly—after six or seven
    days.
  Crush majaycobwit leaves (bad scent) and squeeze juice in water.
    Add enough salt to water to make briny solution. This remedy,
    used for five months' pregnancies, is dangerous, and a medi-
    cal doctor may have to be called in. A high fee is charged for
    this treatment.

Diabetes.

Boil breadfruit leaves and drink water when thirsty.

Grate a little of an avocado seed in a glass of water and drink the water every other day.

Boil Coreyelee leaves and drink one tumbler every night before going to bed. Note: Breadfruit leaf water and avocado seed water can be used during the same period of time; or breadfruit leaf water and Coreyelee water can be used at the same time. Do not use all three at the same time. If Coreyelee water is not helping the patient, change to avocado seed water and breadfruit water.

Grate two or three obi seeds in a mixture of rum and water. Put in a bottle to soak for two or three days. Take one-half wineglass every night.

SONG OF A HOUSEHOLD SLAVE IN MEXICO

EIGHTEENTH CENTURY

I was born in Havana, called Domingo,
born black as jet;
with bad luck, all the more black
because I never knew my parents.

Francisquío, Francisquío,
Your master says he is going to sell you.

Ai, Senora! and why?

Because you do not know how to beat
the mamey jelly.

Beat, you! I will beat!
Beat, you! I will beat!

From "Algo del Folklore Negro en Mexico," by Vincente T. Mendoza, in Miscelanea de Estudios Dedicados a Fernando Ortiz por sus Discipulos, Colegas y Amigos, *Havana, 1956.*

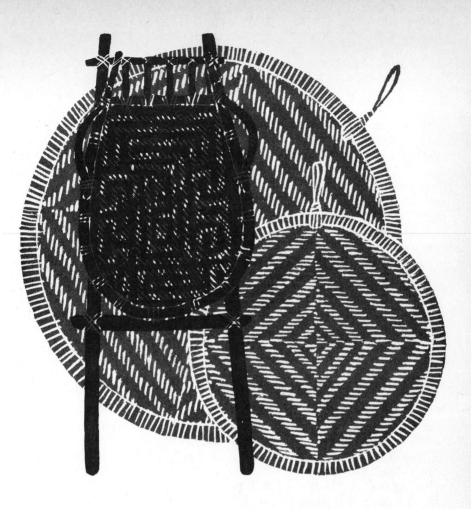

THE BLACK CARIBS OF BRITISH HONDURAS[1]

The phenomenon of the Black Caribs is unique in the Americas. Their origin, according to chroniclers of the seventeenth century, is connected with the shipwreck of two Spanish slave ships off the West Indian island of St. Vincent in the year 1635. An unknown number of Africans made their way ashore to the island, which was at that time populated by Carib Indians, successors to earlier Arawaks. These Africans were joined, over a period of time, by slave fugitives from other West Indian islands, and by the closing years of the seventeenth century between three and four thousand of them were settled there, but already, apparently, there had been considerable intermarriage with the

The substance of this background of the Black Caribs is extracted mainly from The Black Carib of British Honduras, *by Douglas MacRae Taylor, New York, Wenner-Gren Foundation for Anthropological Research, 1951; and from* The Black Caribs of Honduras, *by Doris Stone, New York, Ethnic Folkways Library, 1952.* [1]British Honduras gained independence in 1981 and is now called Belize.

Carib population. The largest part of the black community on St. Vincent in earlier days was male, and the men sought wives from among the Caribs, generally taking them by force. By the middle of the eighteenth century the Indian population had greatly diminished, due not only to difficulties with the blacks, but to constant harassment by Europeans who were endeavoring to establish claims to the various islands. But the blacks, now racially blended and included by European chroniclers under the Carib designation, survived and, to a point, flourished. At the three-quarter mark of the eighteenth century, most of the "Carib" population of St. Vincent was black, or at least it was a racially amalgamate group with obvious African, rather than Indian, physical characteristics.

Curiously enough, the classification of these people as Caribs, while inaccurate in a racial sense, was more correct than not in a cultural sense. Inasmuch as it was the blacks who seemed to be dominating the Indians on the island, and who survived while the Indians faded, it might have been expected that the Black Caribs would have retained strong elements of African culture. But by the late eighteenth century it was clear that, regardless of their dominant racial characteristics, the Black Caribs were culturally more Carib than anything else. they had taken over, along with Carib wives, a Carib way of life. They spoke the Carib language, though perhaps innovatively and with the intrusion of non-Carib vocabulary. They lived very much according to Carib custom, and adopted Carib beliefs and religious rituals as their own. Thus the "conquerors" in the contest between the Africans and the Caribs were conquered by the culture of the defeated.

Britain formally annexed St. Vincent in 1763, but the French continued their efforts to gain control of the island. They succeeded in winning the mostly Black Carib population to their side, and took the island from the British. But in 1873 the Treaty of Versailles returned St. Vincent to England. And this time the British, determined to consolidate their control, deported the Black Caribs to Roatan, one of the Bay Islands of Honduras.

Spain considered this region her own. Angered by the dumping of an alien population on Roatan, the Spanish sent an armed force against the Black Caribs. But the attackers were met, not with weapons, but with expressions of friendship. The Spanish governor then invited the Black Caribs to the mainland as a security precaution, and most of them accepted. When at last Spain was driven out of this region, some of the Black Caribs went east to the territory of the Mosquitias, but the great portion went to the Crown Colony of British Honduras. The Black Caribs today have settlements along the coast from Stann Creek in British Honduras to Black Creek in Honduras.

As They Were Seen in the Year 1700

The island of St. Vincent was visited in the year 1700 by the chronicler Jean-Baptiste Labat. As he saw them, the Caribs and the blacks were living in separate settlements, and such relations as they had with one another appear to have been troubled. The Caribs complained bitterly about their treatment at the hands of the numerically superior Africans:

[St. Vincent] is the center of the Carib Republic: the place where the savages are most numerous—Dominica not approaching it. Besides the savages, this island is also inhabited by a very great number of fugitive negroes, for the most part from Barbados, which, being to windward of Saint Vincent, gives the runaways every possible facility for escaping from their masters' plantations in boats or on [papyrus] or rafts, and taking refuge among the savages. The Caribs formerly brought them back to their masters, when they were at peace with them, or took and sold them to the French or to the Spaniards. I don't know for what reason they have changed their method, nor what has induced them to receive these negroes amongst themselves and to regard them as belonging to one and the same nation. They regret it now very much and very unavailingly, for the number of negroes has increased to such an extent, either by those born in the country or by those come from Barbados to join them, that it much surpasses that of the Caribs, so that the negroes have forced them to share the island and to relinquish the windward side to them. But it is not even that which mortifies the savages most, but the frequent kidnapping of their wives and daughters, whom the negroes seize whenever they want, and whom it is not possible to recover from their hands, because, being more numerous and more daring, they care nothing for the Caribs, whom they ill-treat and may one day oblige to go in search of another island, if indeed they so much as leave them their liberty and do not rather force them to work as their slaves, which might well happen. It would appear that they foresee and fear this eventuality. They put up with the negroes' outrages impatiently, complain bitterly of their ingratitude, and often beg the French and English to rid them of these dangerous guests; but up to now they have not dared to take arms and to join forces with the Europeans, who, having as much interest as they in the destruction of this refuge for their fugitive slaves, would have given them powerful aid in freeing themselves from these bad neighbours." [1]

The Black Caribs Today

The Black Carib language is even more hybrid than the people and is further complicated by a male and female tongue. This is not to be confused with genders which exist in both dialects. Each language is stocked with borrowed terms from French, Spanish, and English.

---

1. *Jean-Baptiste Labat,* Nouveau Voyage aux Isles de l'Amérique, *The Hague, 1724.*

From Stone, ibid. By permission of the Ethnic Folkways Library.

These have been incorporated into the grammar as stems to which are added the gender, tense, etc. Most words are polysyllabic and the majority end in a vowel. Red Carib, which has a certain percentage of Arawak, forms the base of the speech. A more exhaustive linguistic study is necessary to distinguish the extent to which African elements remain.

The woman's language is disappearing in the villages where non-Carib peoples are close neighbors.

Many details of the Black Carib life suggest their South American background. Traces of the couvade are still discernible. After childbirth both the father and the mother adhere to a diet, but the mother resumes her normal work at the end of three days while the father refrains from fishing and his accustomed tasks for three weeks, staying in or near the hammock. The method of planting, the preference for tubers, the use of a magical stone in curing, the ancestor cult, and some of their legends also point to the south.

On the whole, the life of this people is closely bound to the sea and their culture is that of an islander. Boats, primarily dug-out but also planked, are their one universal means of transportation. They are built of mahogany or cedar and vary in size from that for a single person to a small sailing vessel. It is interesting to note that the translation of the Black Carib word for train is land boat. Women often accompany the men fishing but do not go alone in a boat.

The mainstays of Black Carib diet are fish and shell fish, cassava, and coconuts. The man fishes with hook and line and a cast net. He downs the forest preparatory to burning the brush, which along with planting and harvesting is done by women. Besides cassava, sweet potatoes, malanga, plantains, and pineapples are usually grown. Hunting is done infrequently and restricted to small animals.

Coconut water and the grated meat are used in the majority of dishes, while cassava not only furnishes the bread but also is fermented and supplies a beer or chica. The preparation of this bread is a group affair. The women grate the tubers over a large wooden trough on individual plank graters set with small rocks. They accompany the work with songs known as áhorohani or grating songs. The residue is put into hollow tubes woven of reeds, and then made into flat cakes and baked on iron griddles. The bread is especially suitable for canoe trips and damp weather.

These people do not marry outside their racial group. A man usually has a woman in each Black Carib village. His obligation to a woman is to supply her with fish and to give her a house. The building of the home, however, is a community affair in which the greater part of the village including small children join. The houses are oval or rectangular and are generally made of palm wood or with a cane framework faced with mud, a dirt floor, and a palm leaf roof. There are some cane and plank houses but these are in the minority.

The soul plays a basic part in Black Carib ceremonials. Their three main rituals are chiefly concerned with the family dead, for although they are nominally Roman Catholic or Protestant, the ancestor cult predominates their beliefs. Spirits, both of family and of outsiders, are fundamental in curing the sick. The most important ritual is known as "refreshing the dead soul" or amuiadahani which through the scent of offertory food propitiates the spirits. It is distinct from other ancestor rites in that it concerns only the immediate family and is carried out without song or music. Prayers in a neighboring church are said in connection with this. The Cugú and the Dógo rites are also greatly concerned with ancestors. They require the presence of buiai or shaman and have songs but the Dógo has, in addition, drums and a dance.

There are two kinds of sickness, both due to spirits, the difference being that one is the resuult of the family dead who have not been properly attended while the other is due to evil spirits, generally mafia. The buiai is necessary to cure the second type, whereas the first is dealt with in amuiadahani rites. The buiai works with spirit helpers and exercises his powers with the aid of the rattle, song, and drum.

Diviners (surusia), both men and women, or soothsayers whose job entails duties such as pointing out the whereabouts of lost objects and people, and who cure with herbs and medicines, also form a part of Black Carib culture. Aside from these, the Roman Catholic priests and occasionally a Protestant pastor guide the spiritual life of these people and in a sense are responsible for the Black Carib's apparent conformity with his non-Black Carib neighbors.

The mediums of music and dance again recall the curious cultural mixture that distinguishes these people. Black Carib music is strongly derivative of West Africa, but the more ancient dance steps, done in a circle or Indian file, suggest the rain forest homeland of their Carib and Arawak ancestors. The wooden drum—covered with hide and played by hand without sticks both in a single steady rhythm and in a polyrhythm—the gourd rattle, pebble or grain filled, and the guitar and flute, borrowed from his non-Black Carib neighbor but never used in ceremonial song and dance, form the principal musical backgroud to this outward manifestation of his emotions. Almost all important acts of everyday life such as bread-making, house-building, as well as ceremonial occasions and curing the sick or honoring the dead, have song or a dance and song connected with them. Among what can be classed as religious or semi-religious songs are those known as abaimahani. This type of song is considered the property of the individual female who composes it or to whom it appears in a dream. It is sung by the owner in a Dógo rite to honor the request of a dead relative and sung by a group of women either with or without drums. It is used to help cure the sick, to calm the disgust or anger of another person, or simply to recount an ancient or past happening. Some abaimahani songs become so popular that they are heard repeatedly at these rites, fame gathering with their spread through the Black Carib villages.

When singing such songs the women stand in one or two rows or in a semi-circle. Each participant holds the thumb of her neighbor or puts an arm around the shoulders of the women beside her. All keep time by rhythmically swaying the body. Either manioc beer or aguardiente (sugar cane alcohol) is continually passed down the line and the singers drink as they desire.

One of the gayest Black Carib celebrations takes place during the period between Christmas and New Year and is known as Janqunu or Guana-Naragua. Both names signify maskers or masquerade. Although the first is possibly a non-Black Carib word it has been incorporated into the man's language in Honduras. It is a carnival with drums, revelry, painted and masked faces, and costumes adorned with shell anklets, necklaces, etc. There are a series of acts and songs in connection with this festival which include Ulliamo, Maladuana and Ladino.

A Black Carib Tale of the Constellations

The Carib and other related Indians apparently had a well developed mythology relating to the stars and the stellar constellations. They called Orion's Belt by the name Ebedimu; the Pleiades, Sirigo; and stars from Scorpio, Sagittarius and Capricornus were grouped under the name Bagamu. The names of thirteen Carib months describe or allude to these or other constellations, and the year is marked by the passing of Sirigo, the Pleiades, identified with the month of May. The Black Caribs retain some of the Indian sky mythology in their tales and in their reckoning of time. The Black Carib word for Sun, Euiu, also means day, and comes from the men's language; the word Hati, or moon, also means month, and comes from the women's language. The following story relates events with which the various constellations are associated.

There are six brothers. The youngest of them was called Bagamu (Scorpio, Sagittarius, Capricornus); the next was called Ebidimu (Orion's Belt); the third was Sirigo (the Pleiades); the fourth was Urau; and there were two others. It is said that a certain girl was in love with Ebedimu, and she arrived in front of the school one day with melons to

---

Rephrased from The Black Carib of British Honduras, *by Douglas MacRae Taylor.*

sell. The children who were playing in the yard began to throw stones at her. Bagamu was one of those who were throwing, and when he threw his stone the girl dropped her melons, breaking them. The girl said she would let the affair pass only on one condition—if Bagamu's brother Ebedimu would marry her.

So Ebedimu agreed to this. They were married. And some time after, Ebedimu took his wife with him when he went fishing. But every fish he caught was bitten in two before it came from the water. And when they returned from the fishing, Ebedimu consulted an old diviner who concluded that the girl and her mother were not human beings. The diviner advised Ebedimu to henceforth bind his fish hooks with wire. Ebedimu's wife asked for the reason for this binding of the hooks with wire, and he replied that in time she would know.

The next day he went fishing again. His mother-in-law helped him carry his fishing gear to the boat and said she would meet him on his return. He went out to fish. The first fish he caught was bitten in two. The second fish was a huge shark. Ebedimu cut the shark into many small pieces and threw them back into the sea; but every piece he threw into the water turned into a whole shark, and the many sharks around his canoe created a turbulence. Ebedimu feared that his canoe would be overturned. He cut his anchor rope and returned to the shore. He went to his house. His wife said, "You have killed my mother." Ebedimu said this could not have happened, for his mother-in-law had helped him load his canoe, and she had said she would meet him on his return. His wife continued to accuse him, and turning into a shark she began to chase Ebedimu. Unable to catch him, she went to the school to wait for his younger brother, Bagamu. Because he did not run swiftly enough, the shark bit off one of Bagamu's legs, and after that she went into the sea and disappeared.

Then Sirigo heard of the affair and he became angry with Ebedimu. That is why the two constellations, Sirigo and Ebedimu, keep their distance from each other when they rise from the sea into the sky. Urau (name of the tenth month, or October) heard of what happened; and for this reason, sharks are scarce in the month of Urau.

Black Carib Rituals

The African influence on Black Carib religious life seems clear even though there are no allusions to the West African or Bantu deities that are so prominent in other parts of Afro-America. There are concepts and details in Black Carib ritual which tell us that while they have inherited much from the Red Carib, they have also retained substantial elements of African tradition. The following description of Black Carib rites by Douglas MacRae Taylor reveals something of the African connection in the services for ancestors, the mounting or possession of participants by ancestor spirits, the behavior of possessed persons and the feeding of the dead.

THE AMUIADAHANI RITE

No opportunity to witness the first of these rites, the amuiadahani, or "refreshing" of the dead soul, was found. It is, informants said, an intimate affair of the dead person's immediate family, and takes place in the privacy of their home. A rectangular pool some six by four feet and about one foot in depth is dug in a corner of the house. Into this, by means of calabash-dippers (rida), those present pour a mixture of water and fine, half-baked manioc meal (sibiba). The dead person's suit or gown which was kept especially for this occasion is hung out upon a line over the pool; and the women and men by turns line up and sing in unison their supernaturally inspired songs of recollection and appeasement, as at the opening and close of the dogo rite to be described below.[1] There are no drums, no dancing, no feasting of the living or of the dead; and the presence of a buiai is not required.

THE CUGU RITE

The cugu, or "feeding" of the dead, is performed, likewise without drums or dances (except in so far as the gestured songs mentioned above may be referred to as such), in the home of the person whose affliction has occasioned the offering of the rite; but it is a considerably more important affair than the amuiadahani. All direct descendants together with any surviving siblings of the dead person or persons for whom the rite is given and of their siblings are, children excepted, in duty bound to attend, and to bring such contributions in the form of drink, fish, meat, or other foodstuffs as may be acceptable to the dead. These must be cooked without salt. The presence of a buiai is essential: first, to discover the details of the spirits' wishes; then, to see that

The section on Black Carib rituals is from The Black Carib of British Honduras, by Douglas MacRae Taylor, New York, Wenner-Gren Foundation for Anthropological Research, 1951. It is reprinted here by the kind permission of Dr. Taylor and the Wenner-Gren Foundation.

these are carried out with due and proper ceremony; and lastly, to ascertain whether satisfaction has been given. Concurrently with the cugu, wherever this is possible, a mass for the soul or souls of the dead concerned is given in the local church. However, apart from the limitations imposed by the absence of drums and by the fact that this rite lasts only one day, the ceremonies of the cugu are identical with those of the dogo; and the description of the latter to be given below will serve for both rites.

THE DOGO RITE

It is not always convenient or even possible to give a dogo rite soon after learning that it is being "sought." A special hall (dabuiaba) or ancestor-house (gaiunare)—both terms being used interchangeably—has to be built; money must be found for buying pigs, for rum, and for the buiai's [Shaman's] fee; food has to be grown, and the attendance of the other participants assured. Although the latter are the same, in theory, as for a cugu, the dogo is in general much better attended; and relatives will flock from distances of over a hundred miles, if proper time and notice be given, for this three-day celebration. In such cases, it is considered sufficient to make a promise to hold the dogo, say a year hence, in order to obtain temporary surcease from further sanctions on the part of the spirit or spirits of the dead. This is manifested by the hanging up of a number of openwork, hexagonal-weave baskets called uguagai (of the type described by Roth as "quakes"), in which, on fulfilment of the promise, the food offerings for the dead will be buried, and those for the hiuruha sunk in the sea. Today at least, this type of basket serves no other discoverable purpose among the Black Carib, and consequently has few makers. All those required during my stay in the Colony had to be ordered from the Republic of Honduras. Sometimes, one informant said, three little model dugouts are made and hung up together with the uguagai, to be released on the sea when the promise has been fulfilled.

The ancestor-house (gaiunare or dabuiaba) is built like any dwelling house, except that it is without a partition, and has two additions: a small room or sanctuary (called gule) built into the back, where the buiai "works," and where the tables on which the offerings are displayed (called madudu) are placed; and an open-sided shed (called dubase) in front, where the visiting participants may hang their hammocks. The size of the ancestor-house is said to vary with the importance of the gathering expected; those seen had a main hall some fifteen by thirty feet, which was extended fore and aft by dubase and gule of twenty and six feet in length respectively, thus giving an overall length of fifty-six feet. These latter structures were somewhat lower and slightly narrower than the main building, which had each of its long sides pierced by a door and, between it and the gule, by a window. At either end, doors gave access to the gule and to the dubase, respectively, the latter being flanked by two small windows, one on each side.

When this and all other preparations have been completed and a day set, three canoes (or two if the dogo is to be a small one), each containing a captain (aronei) a sailor, and three women, are sent out to the Cays for crabs, fish, and other seafood without which the rite is unthinkable. The people who undertake this task are known as adugahatiu (or idugahatu) "purveyors." If, as is generally the case, the rite is set to begin on a Monday morning, the canoes will leave on the previous Friday, and not reappear until the appointed hour. The buiai will arrive not later than the Saturday to install himself and his paraphernalia, and to be ready to hold the first arairaguni, literally: "descension" (of the spirits), on the Sunday evening. Boatloads of out-of-town guests arrive at frequent intervals all day Sunday and well into the night. By seven thirty that evening, there is usually a fair gathering seated on the low planks that have been placed across logs along either side of the hall; and before the next day breaks, there may be over two hundred guests. By some, it is considered unlucky not to attend any dogo which may be held in the district; and my Carib hostess in Hopkins once related how she had felt strange all one day since a butterfly (or urigabagaba) "pitched at her" in the morning, and she remembered that a dogo (or was it a cugu?) was then taking place in Stann Creek. This, although she was unrelated to the family and had, therefore, no obligation of attending the rite. She was convinced that the butterfly had been sent as a warning from the gubida. Others, on the other hand, say that a butterfly which alights on a person is the spirit-double of a friend: if white, it annouces a visit; if black, it warns of a coming calamity. This is but one example in many of divergence in beliefs and attitudes.

CEREMONIES, SONGS AND DANCES

Although the dogo proper does not commence until the morning, members of the household giving the rite and those of the guests who have arrived from other places rarely sleep that Sunday night. About seven thirty in the evening, the shaman (buiai) emerges from the sanctuary (gule), where his hammock has been slung, sits down in a corner facing the hall, and in the almost total obscurity begins to sing very quietly, as if to himself. One after the other, members of the audience join in, also very softly. These songs of invocation are unlike any others that are sung in the course of the ancestral rites or elsewhere, and contain some words which only buiai claim to understand, and others which, though comprehensible to all, are pronounced in an unusual way. One such song begins: "I sing alone; I sing, I sing, O my helper, ho! I sing alone, sing for help; ho! Speak to me, Udurei; cross over, wafted on the air; ho! Bear down upon them; cross over! Approach, spirit: hasten!" The word ahambue, "spirit," which occurs in the last phrase, has ahambue as its normal form; even so, it belongs to rather "technical jargon," and might refer to a spirit-helper, to another of the hiuruha, or to one of the gubida. At all events, the call is answered by both the shaman's helper and, accompanied and introduced by the latter, the ancestral spirit or spirits for whom the rite is to be given. In a quavering voice, the latter enquire whether this and that favorite grandchild be present; and these answer: ina, naruguti "present, grandfather," or ina, nagoto "present, grandmother," as the case may be. It may be noted that the word ina, the old Island Carib answer to a greeting of welcome, is completely obsolete in other contexts. For the rest, grandfather is mainly concerned to know that his favorite foods and dishes will be prepared, and that the rite will begin punctually at six o'clock on the following morning and be carried out to its full length of three days. The women, who, at a conservative estimate, outnumber the men in the proportion of four to one, generally spend the rest of the night dancing abaimahani.

Although often referred to as a dance, the abaimahani is in reality a gestured song, sung in unison by a group of women, and repeated over and over again. As few as five or as many as thirty women stand in line, clasping each other by the thumb. As they sing, they swing their arms and bodies rhythmically and flex their knees, bending slightly forward, now to the left, and now to the right hand. Should a large number of women wish to participate, two rows are formed, facing each other at a distance of a few feet. Manioc beer (hiu) is passed round from time to time; occasionally a man will go down the lines with a bottle of rum (binu), serving a small dram in a calabash cup (rida) to each woman who wants it. The abaimahani are thought of as only semi-sacred songs of recollection and appeasement. They are also employed as curing songs at joint visits to the sick; and the women have no hesitation in singing them outside of the rites when so requested by a stranger, although it would hardly strike them to do so for their own or for other Caribs' entertainment. Many women have their own abaimahani, which are therefore, in a sense, their private property. But no woman objects to another singing her songs any more than a poet objects to another reciting his verse, although, naturally, both like to have their authorship recognized. Moreover, while well-liked abaimahani may be repeated for a considerable number of years and become known over a fairly wide area, it is usual for new ones to be "given" in dreams to one or two of the participants on the occasion of each dogo. These are known as uianuy, and are considered to be a valuable contribution to the rite. The example whose words I have attempted to translate below was brought from Livingston, Guatemala, for a dogo given at Hopkins in May, 1947.

> Iriyuna's call rang above me; heigh-ho!
> Iriyuna's call rang above me; ho-heigh,

Iriyuna's call rang above me, ho-heigh,
And dawn lit the sky up above me: great Iriyuna!

Where will the dawn break upon me? Heigh-ho!
When will the dawn break upon me? Ho-heigh!
Dawn in the path will overtake me, ho-heigh,
Nearing the ancestor-hall: ah, woe are we!

Where will the evening befall me? Heigh-ho!
When will the evening befall me? Ho-heigh!
Eve on the beach will enfold me, ho-heigh,
When from the deep thou wilt behold me: wellaway!

I'll tell thee a little; heigh-ho!
A little to thee I'll explain; ho-heigh!
A little to thee I'll explain, ho-heigh,
Of what caused my trouble and pain.

Long before the appointed hour of six in the morning, the beach is
crowded with people on the lookout for the first appearance of the
canoes bearing the adugahatiu with their catch; while in the ancestor-
house, the drummers busy themselves adjusting their instruments and
practising their rhythms. There are three drums (garauau) of the hollow-log type, each made from a single piece of mahogany (or, more
rarely, of Cedrela odorata), and with a deer skin (lura usari) stretched
across one end and held in place by a hoop of bush cord (mibi), to
which guy ropes are attached. All three drums are cylindrical, having
the same diameter throughout. The largest, known as lanigi, "its
heart," measures some thirty inches in height by twenty in diameter;
and is flanked on left and right by two smaller ones: lafurugu, "its double," and laorua, "its third," of eighteen and sixteen inches in diameter, respectively.

The canoes of the adugahatiu appear with the sun, coming from the
south and traveling in line, parallel with the shore. They are carrying
no sail; but the masts are up, and each is beflagged. Their occupants returned with them from the cays yesterday evening, and camped over-
night behind a headland some miles distant, so that this solemn entry
might be achieved. They paddle past the crowd in front of the ancestor-house, and continue northward for some three hundred yards; then
veer out to sea a little way, turn south, and finally west, to beach their
craft at the feet of the waiting buiai, who shakes his big rattle (maraga)
over them in blessing, and proceeds to supervise the landing and dis-
posal of the catch. There is no particular dress for the officiating buiai.
He wore, in one instance, a black shirt with a black kerchief knotted
sailor-fashion about his neck, a wide-brimmed straw hat, and carried a
peeled stick at his side like a baton. All the occupants of the boats are
decked out in palm-leaf crowns, and their captains (aronegu) wear
palm-leaf skirts in place of trousers. While the others spring ashore, the

latter sit on the prows of their canoes, holding the rudder in one hand, a paddle in the other; until their turn comes to be carried thus, in the arms of some willing helper, one by one to the accompaniment of drum and rattles, to be placed in the new hammocks which have been slung against their coming in the ancestor-house. The boats are drawn up on the sand, but remain masted. Then the procession, headed by the buiai with his rattles and the drummers with their drums suspended by a strap from their necks, enters the dabuiaba ("hall") by way of the hammock-shed (dubase) to the refrain of: ge-banu bisisira, sai-banu buma-ragali uauni-ne, uabuiere, eie, u-mama-o! "shake thy rattles, swing thy big rattle over us, O our shaman, O mama, ho!" (if the last phrase has any meaning, it was not discovered). The dogo has begun.

The members of the family giving the rite wear, in the case of the women, a sort of long white shift, sash, and kerchief, all stained to an orange-red by a preparation called suruguli, which is made with rocou (Bixa orellana, Carib: guseue); while their menfolk are in ordinary clothes, but smear their faces, hands, and feet with the same paint. The latter sometimes, especially when they sing their arumahani, also don wide red and green ribbons over each shoulder and under the opposite arm, baldric-wise, crossing on back and chest. Women not of the lineage generally wear ordinary red kerchiefs on their heads, but have no other special mark or garb. While dancing, men and women alike all carry a narrow strip of cotton cloth, about eighteen inches long, passed over the middle finger of the right hand; these they wave left and right like censers during the ceremonies of placation (amalihani or mali) to be described below. Such strips are called ahuragole, "fans"; but when they are stained with rocou, as are those carried by the family and others attached to the drums, they are referred to as galatu, "it has something in it."

Drum rhythms are always produced with the hands alone, and are, in the case of dogo and mali, synchronic; although polyrhythms are known, and are employed in some secular dances, such as "Punta." For the dogo dancing itself, with which the greater part of the rite is occupied, a steady and monotonous rhythm consisting of one heavy and five light beats is kept up; while during the mali, this changes to a quicker, one-heavy-and-three-light beat. In both cases, the dance step is the same: with the weight of the body resting on one foot, the other advances slightly, rubs back and forth a couple of times in rapid succession, then the weight is shifted and the same process repeated with the other foot; the knees are flexed, and the upper part of the body bent slightly forward. In this way, they progress energetically but very slowly round the hall, one behind the other in several tightly packed concentric rings, singing the while; and turning about all together on a signal given at regular intervals, to continue the dance in the opposite direction.

Crabs, fish, lobsters, conches, and whatever else the adugahatiu have succeeded in capturing, have been placed in an elongated pile down the center of the hall; and remain there during the opening song, to be removed afterwards for cleaning and cooking. In each of the four corners, half a dozen sacrificial cocks are tied awaiting slaughter; while others, throughout most of the first day, are kept tucked under the arms of their dancing donors, who provoke them every now and then to renewed crowing. There was no pile of upturned earth covered with a mat and surrounded by drink offerings, such as Conzemius describes under the name of lanigi dogo, "the heart of the dogo," though older informants claimed to have seen it at rites held in Honduras. The words of an old, but still current, dogo song seem to refer to this custom: "There is much that is wrong with thee: thou dost not believe. If so be that thou'lt not believe, grandchild, then weeping in the dance, with thee all covered in red, we'll turn up the earth."

Each successive phrase of a dogo song is repeated about half a dozen times; and the whole song gone over again and again, until the drummers tire and break up the rhythm by a series of disconnected beats. One such dance lasts from twenty minutes to more than half an hour. It is a striking feature of many of these songs, that they make symbolic use of a number of nautical terms, comparing the movements of the dancers to the maneuvers of a dugout canoe at sea. Thus, for example, iriragua, "to glide," or "to ride the waves"; adaiagua, "to veer and come up to the wind—to luff"; aragaca, "to unloose" or "to sail down wind." The dogo step itself is also referred to in songs as "sharpening the feet."

During much of the dancing, the buiai remains in the sanctuary, resting in his hammock or preparing for the next ceremony; but occasionally he or his assistant (gulegi) will emerge to conduct and enliven the drumming and dancing with the rattles (sisira). For the ceremony of placation (mali), his presence is essential. Facing the big drum, he begins to shake his rattles, now deliberately, now with a shrill insistence; holding them sometimes at arm's length, by his side or above his head, and keeping them shoulder-high at others; while the people revert to their song of acclamation: ge-banu bisirira uauni-ne, uabuieire, uadoneme me! sai-banu bumaragali uabulugugee, "shake thy rattles over us, our shaman, that we may be equiped; swing thy big rattle above our heads!" At the signal for the mali, which the buiai gives by announcing: "heart-drummer, thou'lt placate our grandmother!" the rhythm changes; the drummers rise from their seats and advance with prancing steps; while the people range themselves behind; and the buiai, walking backward so as to face the drummers and the people, continues to lead with his rattles. The details of this ceremony appear to differ somewhat with different officiants. The drummers and the company behind them, in one dogo that was witnessed, sidled counter-clockwise four times round the hall, beginning on the south side, and stopping before each successive door and window. In another, they danced down the length of the hall to the east door (giving onto the hammock-shed), back to the west (the entrance to the gule), and hence to the south and north doors; repeating this performance four times, but neglecting the two windows giving onto the hammock-shed. But whatever the order or direction followed, the drums are lowered to the ground at each station; while the buiai shakes his rattles over them, and the people, bending low and wafting their cotton-strip "fans" without discontinuing the dance step, sing: iaua iaiaua no e! iaua iaiaua uo, aie-ieie! uagoto uamalihaiau, iaiaua uo; iaua iaiaua uo ie! iaua iaiaua uamalihaiau, aie-ieie!

The word uamalihaiau, "we are placating her," is replaced in the third verse by maniguati, "quietly—hush" and in the fourth by uaragaca, "we unloose," or "we sail down wind." At the word maniguati, the people lower their voices, and the rest of the verse is sung in a whisper. This song appears to be traditional; and it is worth noting that the term uagoto, "our grandmother," is never, as far as could be discovered, replaced by another, such as uaruguti, "our grandfather," even when only male spirits are being placated. The meaning of the rest is obscure: iaiaua is said to be a "dogo word" for "grandmother" or "dead grandmother," although ordinarily it means "pineapple"! Iaua, phonetically [iyawa], means "shade," "shadow," "reflexion," "image," "picture," "photograph"; but pronounced iaua [iyawa], as in the song, with the stress on the initial vowel, it has no known meaning today. However, it seems probable that, etymologically, both these terms meant "that which comes back again," like French revenant. The remainder of the utterance is exclamatory, except for uo, which is vocative.

The number of placations made during any particular dogo rite apparently depends to some extent upon the wealth of the family giving it; but it must be, it would appear, a multiple of eight. For every one performed, each of the drummers receives a "chaparita" (quarter pint, or eighth of a litre) of rum and a candle, both or either of which may be consumed on the spot, or taken home later at choice. In those rites witnessed, either sixteen or thirty-two placations were made in all. These were divided among eight periods of six hours, extending from six o'clock Monday morning until six o'clock Wednesday morning, so that either two or four placations took place during each period. Moreover, the direction of the dancing—clockwise or counter-clockwise round the hall—was reversed at the beginning of each new period. When the placations of the family giving the rite have been fulfilled—or even before then should time permit and the drummers be willing—"extras" may be given by members of other families anxious to placate their own gubida, but unable or unwilling to go to the expense of an independent rite for the time being.

Every placation (mali) ends with a sort of general caper round the hall, to the refrain of: idenderu tugura buga: dende, dende, dende uamutiha; dende, dende, dende uamania! The meanings of idenderu and of its root dende are far from clear. Some say that these forms have reference to the sacrificial cocks; others that they are a sort of salutation. A tentative but by no means certain translation is: "It was powerful in times past; we had power, power, power; let us have power, power, power!"

POSSESSION BY ANCESTRAL SPIRITS

Spirit possession, though not essential to the success of this rite, is rarely lacking from its performance. None is exempt, in theory, from this phenomenon; but it is evident that those most susceptible to it are young women between the ages of eighteen and twenty-five. It may manifest itself at any time or place during the three days that the rite lasts; though it appears to be most frequent among the dogo dancers in the dabuiaba during the latter part of the first day. It may be significant in this connection that the participants in the rite are not fed until the second day; although many, of course, bring their own food with them. It is also remarkable that those who become possessed outside the ancestor-house, unless they are observed and immediately dragged in to dance before the drums, always rush to throw themselves into the sea.

Three stages of possession are recognized terminologically: adereba, "to stiffen," is employed to describe a slight jerkiness of movement and fixity of gaze; agoburiha, "to be 'be-anciented,' " indicates a state of full possession; and aueha, "to pass out," explains itself, and is a stage not reached in every case. Nor is the initial stage always observed: a girl may be sitting or standing at one side, quietly watching the dancers, suddenly to plunge into the throng with a yell, fully possessed and careless of whom she may upset. But more often it is one of those already dancing, who, on reaching that end of the hall, withdraws from the round to dance alone before the drums. Gradually her movements get more intense, and her eyes take on a glassy stare. One by one, others drop from the round, make space for her, and gather to watch. Her friends may come running with a long, wide skirt such as old women ordinarily wear, and forcibly change her into this; tying her head with a kerchief, and removing her shoes should that not already be done (all but a few of the younger people are barefoot all the time). The only reason given for this was that of modesty—so that the girl might not expose herself during her possession.

The possessed girl may pause in her dance to impersonate the deceased ancestor whose spirit has entered her. The latter may have been known to most of those present, or may have been dead so long that even his or her name is forgotten. One girl was seen possessed by a certain Mr. John, who, it was said, had been a buiai. She walked with the gait of an old man, tried to arrange her skirt to resemble a pair of trousers, and, amid general laughter, made several passes at her own mother. Then she broke off into a wild and impromptu song, which she interrupted several times to shout (in Carib): "They're MY ancestors— YOUR ancestors!" Another, who had evaded all attempts to change her skirt, kept up her dancing before the drums continuously; and ended with something like a Russian trepak, until, falling, she continued to dance on her knees, and finally collapsed face foremost with arms outstretched before her. She was lifted up by her comrades, and placed in one of the hammocks slung for that purpose in each corner of the hall. Here she appeared to come to in about fifteen or twenty minutes' time. The buiai then went and sat beside her, patted her arm, and talked to her quietly for a few moments. But some time after he had gone, she began to moan and to toss herself up and down; whereupon two other girls helped her out of the hammock and, supporting her under each arm, danced with her between them.

Spirit possessions that threaten to become too violent, or those of persons not members of the family by their own gubida, may be restrained. This is done by rubbing the face of the possessed persons with rum, by fanning them with the cotton-strip fans to placate the possessing spirit, by giving them a drink called lihigu, which is generally held in readiness by the officiating buiai, and by other methods. Many reliable informants said that possessed girls frequently get up and dance on the upper tie beams (idanu) of the roof, performing acrobatic feats that would be quite impossible for them in their normal state. But in the only attempt of this kind witnessed, the girl was held back while the shaman lit a bue cigar and puffed its smoke onto the back of her head. Another case of restraint was that of a woman of middle age, who, together with her brother, was giving the rite. Exceptionally, it is not unlikely in her case that alcohol had something to do with the "possession"; but the treatment, if not the cause, was orthodox. It was on the afternoon of the third day of the rite. This woman, together with a large number of others, had been dancing abaimahani continuously for several hours. Most of them were exhausted, and had retired to rest or to eat; but she insisted on going on, and about five other women had remained to humor her. Despite this, the good woman complained that she was being abandoned, cursed her companions volubly for a lazy lot of good-for-nothings, and taking one mouthful of rum after another, spat it out again over the patient women. Finally she was shuffled into a hammock where she continued to sing and to jig. A female buiai was sent for, came, and tried the more usual methods of restraint. Finding these ineffectual, she undid the woman's sash, removed all her other red-stained garments forcibly, and redressed her in her everyday clothes. The reddened sash, shift, and kerchief were then entrusted to a third woman, with detailed instructions from the female shaman as to where and how to wash the rocou (Bixa orellana) out of them, so that the ancestral spirit tormenting her patient might be compelled to depart from her.

Most Caribs believe—and impartial observation tends to justify their belief—that persons manifesting spirit-possession are, on the whole, genuine; although a few may counterfeit this state in order to call attention to themselves, or because they may, while possessed, call for and be given rum. One young man related how his girl friend, to his horror, had been possessed at the very first dogo she attended, when she was only seventeen. Immediately upon her recovery she had left the hall, because, as she explained when he found her again outside, she felt so ashamed of herself. He had then persuaded her to go home (a distance of several miles), which she did, albeit somewhat reluctantly. But later, he discovered that she had sneaked out of the house afterwards, and returned by herself to the dogo. This girl, as well as others, explained their experience by saying that they had lost all consciousness of their whereabouts; and had seen themselves surrounded on all sides by short little people, some of whom were dancing on the tie beams (idanu). One little man in a red breech-clout (uaigu) had taken her by the hand, said this particular girl, and compelled her to dance; and all else had disappeared until, on coming back to consciousness, she found herself lying in a hammock, with people fanning her. All informants were agreed that a person can be possessed only by the spirit of one of his or her gubida, although not necessarily by one for whom the rite is being given at the time.

Some Black Carib Proverbs

You are like a hoe—everything goes to yourself.
By no means, said the booby-bird.
Spider brought the poverty of the country to town.
This cow has soiled its own tail, all the more readily will it soil the savanna.
If you stumble in a path, don't go tread it again.
Don't go by those roads which have thorns on them.
Don't trouble with poverty when poverty doesn't trouble with you.
Earthenware pot is jealous of cauldron, but they are the same as to their boiling.
Cooking a cow's skin with borrowed water is impossible.
You cannot dance until dawn with a borrowed drum.
_____ does not weep over prickles, her weeping is over the length of life.
Feet do not spurn the road.
When rain is falling, the doorstep is wet; in dry weather the doorstep is dry.
A man's death means the overgrowing of his door with grass.
If you were to proceed slowly, you might find an ant's stomach.

SURINAM: COAST PEOPLE AND BUSH NEGROES

"There are men on the upper river and
there are men on the lower river also."—
Djuka proverb

Surinam, Guiana and French Guiana, clustered on the northeast
shoulder of South America, have an intertwined history in the conflict-
ing efforts of Britain, France and the Netherlands to achieve colonial
dominance in this region. And there is a fascination in the central role
of Africans and their descendants in the shaping of these colonies, Surinam in particular. Today the urbanized, more coastally located people of African descent constitute about forty percent of Surinam's population, and the so-called Bush Negroes, descendants of revolted
slaves, about ten percent. A large portion of the eighteenth century in
Surinam was marked by warfare between the escaped Africans and the
settlers. Numerous expeditions were sent against the Bush Negroes in

the hope that they could be suppressed. For, having escaped and set up villages deep within the upriver forests, the Africans frequently raided European settlements and plantations for supplies, sometimes as military reprisals. Not only did the raiders take such booty as food, firearms and gunpowder, they also took as many of the slaves as they could liberate, and thus increased their capability for future depredations against the whites. There were, as a consequence, numerous moments during the eighteenth century when the colonists believed that the very survival of Surinam was at stake. Expeditions mounted against the Bush Negroes, and some other African goups as well, were either total failures or merely temporary successes.

At last, in 1772, a major military expedition was sent from the Netherlands to subjugate the revolted Africans. What was to have been a fast, decisive blow against the Bush Negroes turned out to be a five-year campaign, during which the government forces tramped back and forth through jungle and marsh seeking the enemy, while succumbing to bad diet and all manner of tropical diseases. Now and again they found and burned an enemy village, and sometimes fought pitched battles, but the Africans had a way of disappearing, then coming back to fight guerrilla war or to rebuild their settlements. The five-year campaign took an enormous toll among the Dutch and mercenary troops. And when it was all over it could not be said that the Africans had been beaten. In the end it was a peace forged out of exhaustion and treaties or agreements with individual African leaders.

The Bush Negroes—the Djukas, the Saramaccas and others—lived in isolation from the whites and blacks of the coastal regions, and preserved ways and traditions of the African countries from which they had come. What they preserved, moreover, must now be considered archaic African culture that has changed little in the past two and a half centuries. The language spoken among the Djukas has a vocabulary with numerous words drawn from Dutch, English and French; but an impressive part of the language is African, not only in vocabulary but in structure and usage. Some of the vocabulary, as well as some customs, were taken over from the Indians with whom the Djukas came into contact in the jungle. But in a great many respects the Bush Negroes lived in conformity with customs, traditions and beliefs brought directly from African shores. And without parallel in other black communities in the Americas, the Bush Negroes and their descendants retained a woodcarving tradition. Bowls, combs, stools and other carved Djuka objects are distinctly reminiscent of carving in the Akan regions of West Africa, though they have a New World style of their own. Those Surinam blacks who did not join the revolted slaves in the bush were of course greatly influenced by European customs and traditions, and when manumission finally came they formed a culture with a different center of gravity. There were influences not only fom Europe, but from Asia as well, for upon the breakup of the plantation system numerous indentured workers were brought to Surinam from Java and India. Yet with all the mixtures, the town Negroes still retain many ways that are more African than anything else, and an oral literature with clear African beginnings.

A member of the 1772 expedition against the revolted slaves was a British officer named Captain J. G. Stedman. He wrote an invaluable account of the expedition and the conditions out of which it arose, *Narrative of a Five Years' Expedition Against the Revolted Negroes of Surinam, in Guiana, on the Wild Coast of South America, from the Year 1772 to 1777.* Captain Stedman's interests went far beyond the expedition itself. He was a first-class observer and chronicler of the social scene, and among his descriptions are many that give a special insight into the attitudes and customs of both whites and blacks. Following are some excerpts from the Stedman book.

On the Capture and Transport of Slaves

From what I have learned by inquiry, from persons well informed on the subject, it clearly appears, that numbers of the negroes offered for sale have been taken in battles, and made prisoners of war; while many others have been scandalously kidnapped, and some others transported for offences, &c.; of all which shall produce a few examples in future.

These groups of people are marched from every inland part, to the factories erected by different nations upon the coast, where they are sold, or more properly speaking, bartered, like the other productions of their country, *viz.* gold, elephants teeth, &c. to the Europeans, for bars of iron, firearms, carpenters tools, chests, linens, hats, knives, glasses, tobacco, spirits, &c. Next they are embarked for exportation, during which time they, without contradiction, feel all the pangs that mental or corporeal misery can inflict. Being torn from their country and dearest connections, stowed hundreds together in a dark stinking hold, the sexes being separated: while the men are kept in chains to prevent an insurrection. In this manner are they floated over turbulent seas, not certain what is to be their destiny, and generally fed during the passage with horse-beans and oil for their whole subsistence. But these sufferings are often alleviated with better food by the more humane: so far, that none or few of the cargo die during the passage, and the whole crew arrive healthy in the West Indies. I even remember one instance, where the captain, mate, and most of the sailors, having expired at sea, so that the remaining few could not work the ship without the negroes assistance, yet these last having been well treated, helped at last to run the vessel on shore, by which means they not only saved many lives, but tamely and even cheerfully allowed themselves to be fetched and sold to any person who would please to buy them. . . .

No sooner is a Guinea ship arrived, than all the slaves are led upon deck, where they are refreshed with pure air, plantains, bananas, oranges, &c. and being properly cleaned, washed, and their hair shaved in different figures of stars, half-moons, &c. which they generally do the one to the other, (having no razors) by the help of a broken bottle and without soap. After this operation, one part of them is sent ashore for sale, decorated with pieces of cotton to serve as fig-leaves, arm-bands, beads, &c. being all the captain's property; while the others spend the day in dancing, hallooing, and clapping hands on board the vessel.

Having sufficiently described their figures after landing, we now may suppose them walking along the water-side, and through the streets, where every planter picks out that number which he stands in need of, to supply those lost by death or desertion, and begins to make a bargain with the captain. Good negroes are generally valued at from fifty to a hundred pounds each. Amongst these, should a woman chance to be pregnant, her price is augmented accordingly; for which reason I have known the captain of a Dutch Guinea vessel, who acknowledged himself to be the father, take advantage, with a brutality scarcely credited in the story of Inkle and Yarico, of doubling the value, by selling his own offspring to the best bidder; for which however he was highly censured by his companions.

The next circumstance that takes place before the bargain is struck, is to cause the negroes for sale, one after another, to mount on a hogshead or a table, where they are visited by a surgeon, who obliges them to make all the different gestures, with arms and legs, of a Merry-Andrew upon the stage, to prove their soundness or unsoundness; after which they are adopted by the buyer, or rejected, as he finds them fit for his purpose, or otherwise. If he keeps them, the money is paid down; and the new-bought negroes are immediately branded on the breast or the thick part of the shoulder, by a stamp made of silver, with the initial letters of the new master's name, as we mark furniture or any thing else to authenticate them properly. These hot letters, which are about the size of a sixpence, occasion not that pain which may be imagined, and the blisters being rubbed directly with a little fresh butter, are perfectly well in the space of two or three days. No sooner is this ceremony over, and a new name given to the newly-bought slave, than he or she is delivered to an old one of the same sex, and sent to the estate, where each is properly kept clean by his guardian, instructed and well fed, without working, for the space of six weeks; during which period, from living skeletons, they become plump and fat, with a beautiful clean skin, till it is disfigured by the inhuman flogging by some rascally proprietor, or rather his overseer. . . .

The negroes are composed of different nations or casts, such as the

Abo,	Congo,	Loango,	Pombo,
Conia,	Gango,	N. Zoko,	Wanway,
Blitay,	Konare,	Nago,	&c. &c.
Coromantin,	Riemba,	Papa,	

On Their Languages, Music and Customs

With the languages of the African negroes I am but little acquainted; as a specimen, however, I will insert a few sentences of that called the *Coromantyn,* upon the credit of my boy Quaco, who belonged to that nation, together with a translation in English; and only observe, that they break off their words very short, in a kind of guttural manner, which I cannot easily describe:—For instance—*"Co fa ansyo, na bara-mon bra,* Go to the river, and bring me some water."—*"Mee yeree, na-comeda mee,* My wife, I want some food."—So much for the Coroman-tyn language, as spoken by the negroes on the coast of Guinea.

But as to that spoken by the black people in Surinam, I consider my-self a perfect master, it being a compound of Dutch, French, Spanish, Portuguese, and English. The latter they like best, and consequently use the most. It has been already observed, that the English were the first Europeans who possessed this colony, hence probably the predi-lection for that language which they have still retained. In this mixed dialect, for which I have seen a printed grammar, the words end mostly with a vowel, like the Indian and Italian, and it is so sweet, so sonorous and soft, that the genteelest Europeans in Surinam speak little else; it is also wonderfully expressive and sentimental, such as, "Good eating, *sweety-muffo."*—"Gun-powder, *man sanny."*—"I will love you, with all my heart, so long as I live, *Mee saloby you, langa alla mee hatty, so langa me leeby."* "A pleasing tale, *ananassy tory."*—"I am very angry, *me hatty brun"*—"Live long, so long until your hair become white as cotton, *Lebee langa, tay, tay, ta-y you weeree weeree tan wity likee catoo."*—"Small, *peekeen."*—"Very small, *peekeeneenee."*—"Fare-well! Good-bye! I am dying, and going to my God, *Adioso, cerroboay, mee de go dede, me de go na mee Gado."* In this sample, many corrupt English words are perceptible, which however begin to grow out of use near the capital, but are still retained in the distant plantations; for instance, at the estate *Goet-Accoord,* in Cottica, I have heard an old ne-gro woman say, *"We lobee fo leebee togeddere,"* by which she meant, we love to live together; and at Paramaribo to express the same sent-ence, *"Wee looko for tanna macandera."*

Their *vocal music* is like that of the birds, melodious, but without time, and in other respects not unlike that of a *clerk* performing to the congregation, one person constantly pronouncing a sentence extem-pore, which he next hums or whistles, and then all the others repeat the same in chorus; another sentence is then spoken, and the chorus is a second time renewed, &c.

This kind of singing is much practised by the barge rowers or boat negroes on the water, especially during the night in a clear moonshine; it is to them peculiarly animating, and may, together with the sound of their oars, be heard at a considerable distance.

As a specimen, I have tried to set the following words to music, sup-posing a ranger going to battle, and thus taking leave of his girl:

Such is their vocal melody; and of their instrumental music, and dancing, which is perfectly to time, I shall speak hereafter, having already given a short account of that which is practised by the Loango negroes. That these people are neither divested of a good ear, nor poetical genius, has been frequently proved, when they have had the advantages of a good education. Amongst others, *Phillis Wheatley,* who was a slave at *Boston* in New England, learned the Latin language, and wrote thirty-eight elegant pieces of poetry on different subjects, which were published in 1773. . . .

To what I have already advanced, I may add, that all negroes firmly believe the being of a *God,* upon whose goodness they rely, and whose power they adore, while they have no fear of death, and never taste food without offering a libation. In the rivers *Gambia* and *Senegal* they are mostly Mahometans; but generally the worship and religious ceremonies of the Africans vary, as do the numberless superstitious practices of all savages, and indeed of too many Europeans. Perceiving that it was their custom to bring their offerings to the wild cotton-tree, I enquired of an old negro, why they paid such particular reverence and veneration to this growing piece of timber. "This proceeds (said he) massera, from the following cause: having no churches nor places built for public worship (as you have) on the Coast of Guinea, and this tree being the largest and most beautiful growing there, our people, assembling under its branches when they are going to be instructed, are defended by it from the heavy rains and scorching sun. Under this tree our gadoman, or priest, delivers his lectures; and for this reason our common people have so much veneration for it, that they will not cut it down upon any account whatever."

No people can be more superstitious than the generality of negroes; and their *Locomen,* or pretended prophets, find their interest in encouraging this superstition, by selling them *obias* or amulets, as I have already mentioned, and as some hypocrites sell absolution in Europe, for a comfortable living. These people have also amongst them a kind of *Sibyls,* who deal in oracles; these sage matrons dancing and whirling round in the middle of an assembly, with amazing rapidity, until they foam at the mouth, and drop down as convulsed. Whatever the prophetess orders to be done during this paroxysm, is most sacredly performed by the surrounding multitude; which renders these meetings extremely dangerous, as she frequently enjoins them to murder their masters, or desert to the woods; upon which account this scene of excessive fanaticism is forbidden by law in the colony of Surinam, upon pain of the most rigorous punishment: yet it is often practised in private places, and is very common amongst the Owca and Seramica negroes, where captains Fredericy and Van Geurick told me they had seen it performed. It is here called the *winty-play*, or the dance of the mermaid, and has existed from time immemorial; as even the classic authors make frequent mention of this extraordinary practice. . . .

But what is still more strange, these unaccountable women by their voice know how to charm the *ammodytes,* or *papaw* serpent, down from the tree. This is an absolute fact; nor is this snake ever killed or hurt by the negroes, who, on the contrary, esteem it as their friend and guardian, and are happy to see it enter their huts. When these sibyls have charmed or conjured down the ammodytes serpent from the tree, it is common to see this reptile twine and writhe about their arms, neck and breast, as if the creature took delight in hearing her voice, while the woman strokes and caresses it with her hand. . . .

Another instance of superstition amongst the negroes I must relate; there is a direct prohibition in every family, handed down from father to son, against the eating of some one kind of animal food, which they call *treff*; this may be either fowl, fish, or quadruped, but whatever it is, no negro will touch it; though I have seen some good Catholics eat roast-beef in Lent, and a religious Jew devouring a slice from a fat flitch of bacon.

However ridiculous some of the above rites may appear, yet amongst the African blacks they are certainly necessary, to keep the rabble in subjection; and their *gadomen* or priests know this as well as the infallible Pontiff of the Roman church. These illiterate mortals differ, however, in this respect from the modern Europeans, that whatever they believe, they do it firmly, and are never staggered by the doubts of scepticism, nor troubled with the qualms of consience; but whether they are, upon this account, better or worse, I will not pretend to determine.—I however think that they are a happy people, and possess so much friendship for one another, that they need not be told to "love their neighbour as themselves;" since the poorest negro, having only an egg, scorns to eat it alone; but were a dozen present, and every one a stranger, he would cut or break it into just as many shares; or were there one single dram of rum, he would divide it among the same number: this is not done, however, until a few drops are first sprinkled on the ground, as an oblation to the gods.—Approach then here, thou canting hypocrite, and take an example from thy illiterate sable brother!— From what I sometimes throw out, however, let it not be understood that I am an enemy to religious worship—God forbid! But I ever will profess myself the greatest friend to those whose actions best correspond with their doctrine; which, I am sorry to say, is too seldom the case amongst those nations who pretend most to civilization.

If savage nations be commonly generous and faithful, they are not, however, without their dark shades; and among these, the most conspicuous is a proneness to anger and revenge. I never knew a negro indeed forgive those who had wilfully offended him. The strength of this passion can only be equalled by their gratitude; for amongst them, it may be truly said, that

> "A generous friendship no cold medium knows,
> "But with one love, with one resentment glows."

Their abominable cruelties also, like those of all barbarous nations, are truly shocking. In the colony of Berbice, during the late revolt, they made no scruple of cutting up their mistresses with child, even in their master's presence, with many other savage devices too dreadful to relate.—In the art of poisoning, not even the *Accawaw* Indians are more expert; they can carry it under their nails, and by only dipping their thumb into a tumbler of water, which they offer as a beverage to the object of their revenge, they infuse a slow but certain death. Whole estates, as well as private families, have become the victims of their fury, and experienced their fatal vengeance, even putting to death scores of their own friends and relations, with the double view of depriving their proprietors of their most valuable possessions. These monsters are distinguished by the name of *Wissy-men*, perhaps from *wise*, or knowing, and by their fatal genius carry destruction to a most dreadful length before they are detected.

All barbarous and uneducated people have indistinct notions of property; nor can we wonder that slaves, who in their own persons suffer the most flagrant violation of every right, should be disposed to retaliate. The slaves on the plantations are therefore too commonly thieves, plundering whatever they can lay their hands upon with impunity; nor can any bounds be set to their intemperance, especially in drinking. I have seen a negro girl empty a china-bowl at one draught, containing two bottles of claret, which I had given her by way of experiment, till she could no more stand.

I should not forget to mention that the *Gango* negroes are supposed to be *anthropophagi* or cannibals, like the Caribbee Indians, instigated by habitual and implacable revenge. Amongst the rebels of this tribe, after the taking of Boucou, some pots were found on the fire with human flesh; which one of the officers had the curiosity to taste, and declared it was not inferior to some kinds of beef or pork. . . .

But from these deformities of character I will now relieve the attention of the reader, and proceed in justice to dispel the gloomy cloud, by introducing the sunshine of their virtues.

Their genius has been already treated of, so has their gratitude; which last they carry to such length, that they will even die for those who have shewn them any particular favour. Nothing can exceed the fidelity and attachment they have for those masters who use them well, which proves that their affection is as strong as their hatred. Negroes are generally good-natured, particularly the *Coromantyn,* and those of *Nago.* They are also susceptible of the tender passion, and jealousy in their breasts has produced the most dreadful effects. The delicacy of these people deserves likewise to be noticed: I do not remember, amongst the many thousands I have seen during several years residence among them, ever to have observed even an offer to kiss a woman in public. Maternal tenderness for their children is also natural to the females, for in general, during the two years which they usually suckle them, they never cohabit with their husbands; this they consider as unnatural, and prejudicial to the infants. . . . The cleanliness of the negro nation is peculiarly remarkable, as they bathe above three times a day. The *Congo* tribe in particular are so fond of the water, that they may, not improperly, be called amphibious animals.

The negroes are likewise spirited and brave, patient in adversity, meeting death and torture with the most undaunted fortitude. Their conduct, in the most trying situations, approaching even to heroism; no negro sighs, groans, or complains, though expiring in the midst of surrounding flames. Nor do I remember, on any occasion whatever, to have seen an African shed a tear, though they beg for mercy with the greatest earnestness when ordered to be flogged for offences which they are conscious deserve to be punished; but if they think their punishment unmerited, immediate suicide is too often the fatal consequence, especially amongst the *Coromantyn* negroes, who frequently, during the act of flagellation, throw back their heads in the neck, and *swallow their tongue,* which chokes them upon the spot, when they drop dead in the presence of their masters. But when negroes are sensible of having deserved correction, no people can be more humble, or bear their unhappy fate with greater resignation. The swallowing of the tongue, which they only practise during the moments of severe discipline, has of late been prevented in Surinam by the *humane* method of holding a firebrand to the victim's mouth, which answers the double purpose of burning his face, and diverting his attention from the execution of his fatal determination. Some have a practice of eating common *earth,* by which the stomach is prevented from performing its ordinary functions, and thus dispatch themselves without any immediate pain, but linger perhaps for a twelvemonth in the most debilitated and shocking condition. Against these ground-eaters the severest punishments are decreed by the laws, but without much effect, as they are seldom detected in this act of desperation.

On the Conditions of Slavery

The reader may remember that I have already introduced the slaves as landing from on board the Guinea ships, and generally shocking instances of debility and misery.

I have also observed, that under the care of some old negroes, appointed for that purpose, they soon become fat and sleek, and learn the language of the colony: they they are sent to work in the fields, to which they cheerfully submit; though I have seen some instances of newly-imported negroes refusing to work, nor could promises, threats, rewards, nor even blows, prevail: but these had been *princes* or people of the first rank in their native country, who by the casualties of war had the misfortune to become slaves, and whose heroic sentiments still preferred instant death to the baseness and miseries of servitude. Upon these occasions I have seen the other slaves fall upon their knees, and intreat the master to permit them to do the work required, in addition to their own tasks; which being sometimes granted, they continued to shew the same respect for the captive prince that he had been accustomed to receive in his own country. I remember once to have had a re-markable good-looking new negro to attend me, whose ankles and wrists being much galled by chains, I enquired the cause. "My father," said he, "was a king, and treacherously murdered by the sons of a neighbouring prince. To revenge his death, I daily went a hunting with some men, in hopes of retaliating upon his assassins; but I had the mis-fortune to be surprized, taken, and bound; hence these ignoble scars. I was afterwards sold to your European countrymen on the coast of Guiana—a punishment which was deemed greater than instant death."

The history of Quaco, my black boy, was still more extraordi-nary:—"My parents," said he, "lived by hunting and fishing: I was stolen from them very young, whilst playing on the sands with two lit-tle brothers; I was put into a sack, and carried for several miles. I after-wards became the slave of a king on the coast of Guinea, with several hundreds more. When our master died, the principal part of his slaves were beheaded and buried along with him; I, with some other children of my age, were bestowed as presents to the different captains of his army; and the master of a Dutch ship afterwards had me, in exchange for a musket and some gun-powder."

No sooner do these wretched strangers begin to flag at their labour, than whips, cow-skins, bamboos, ropes, fetters, and chains are intro-duced, until they are ready to sink under accumulated oppression. With some masters their tasks can never be performed, as they must toil on, day and night, even Sundays not excepted. I recollect a strong young negro, called *Marquis,* who had a wife he loved, with two fine children; he laboured hard, and generally finished his task of digging a trench of five hundred feet by four o'clock in the afternoon, that he might have some time to cultivate his little garden, and go to fish or fowl to support his beloved family: hard did Marquis strive to earn this additional pittance, when his *humane* master, apprized of his industry, for his encouragement informed him, that if he could delve five hun-dred feet by four o'clock, he could certainly finish six hundred before sun-set; and this task the unfortunate young man was condemned from that day ever since to perform.

In Surinam the slaves are kept nearly naked, and their daily food consists of little more than a few yams and plantains; perhaps twice a year they may receive a scanty allowance of salt fish, with a few leaves of tobacco, which they call *sweety-muffo,* and this is all: but what is pe-

culiarly provoking to them is, that if a negro and his wife have ever so
great an attachment for each other, the woman, if handsome, must
yield to the loathsome embrace of an adulterous and licentious manager, or see her husband cut to pieces for endeavouring to prevent it.
This, in frequent instances, has driven them to distraction, and been
the cause of many murders.

It is in consequence of these complicated evils, that so many also destroy themselves by suicide, run away to the woods to join their countrymen in rebellion, or if they stay, grow sad and spiritless, and lan-
guish under diseases, the effects of bad usage; such as the *lola,* which
is a white scorbutic spot that externally covers the body. The
crassy-crassy, or itch, which with us comes from poorness of diet, is of
course very common with them. The *yaws,* a most disagreeable disorder, by many compared to the veneral disease, which renders the patient a shocking spectacle, all covered over with yellow ulcers. . . .

Still more dreadful is the *boassy,* or *leprosy,* which is deemed incurable: the face and limbs in this complaint swell, and the whole body is
covered with scales and ulcers; the breath stinks, the hair falls off, the
fingers and toes become putrid, and drop away joint after joint. . . .

The *clabba-yaws,* or *tubboes,* is also a very troublesome and tedious
disorder; it occasions painful sores about the feet, mostly in the soles,
between the skin and the flesh. The usual remedy in this case is, to
burn out the morbid part with a red-hot iron, or cut it out with a lancet;
and then the warm juice of roasted limes is introduced into the wound,
though with great pain yet with great success. The African negroes are
also subject to many species of *worms,* both extraneous and internal,
owing to the wading much in stagnated waters, and to the crudity of
their diet. . . .

Besides these dreadful calamities, peculiar to themselves, the negroes are subject to every complaint common to the Europeans; who,
in their turn, are not exempt in Guiana from the afflicting and dangerous distempers I have just described.

It is therefore not to be wondered at if many of the plantations are
crowded with miserable objects left under the care of the *dressy negro*
or black surgeon only, whose whole skill consists in administering a
dose of salts, or spreading a plaster. As to the numbers who are ex-
coriated from their neck to their heel, by constant whipping, they may
cure themselves, or do their work without a skin, if they think proper.

Thus from accumulated miseries, some naturally succeeding from
the climate and their poor diet, but more from the inordinate cruelty of
managers, it must follow that numerous slaves become unfit for work,
many from weakness and depression of spirits, and others from extreme labour becoming old before their time. But for all these evils,
this plantation despot finds an infallible remedy, which is no other
than to put them to death at once: the loss does not affect him but his
master, and he is proud of shewing only such negroes as are able to do
their task, assuring their owner that they mostly died by the venereal
disease; and the word of the human carcase-butcher is quite sufficient,
as no negro is allowed to give evidence in any case whatever. Yet

should some fair European by accident prove the murder, the delinquent escapes, as I have observed, by paying a fine of £.50 and the value of the slave, if the owner requires it; and for this price of blood he may slaughter the poor wretches whenever a temporary passion or a habit of cruelty, which is too commonly generated in this situation, prompts his rage. . . .

By such inhuman usage this unhappy race of men are sometimes driven to such a height of desperation, that to finish their days, and be relieved from worse than Egyptian bondage, some even have leaped into the caldrons of boiling sugar, thus at once depriving the tyrant of his crop and of his servant.

From these sketches can it be a matter of surprize, that armies of rebels are assembled in the forest, and at every opportunity thirsting for revenge? . . .

In Surinam there are, upon an average, about 75,000 negro slaves, as I have stated; from which if we subtract children, and superannuated men and women, there will not be found above 50,000 really fit for labour. There are from six to twelve Guinea ships, that import from 250 to 300 slaves each from Africa annually: we may therefore compute the yearly importation at an average of 2,500, necessary to supply and keep complete the above 50,000; so that the annual deaths exceed the births by the number of 2,500, thought each man negro has a wife or two if he chuses, which is, upon the mass, just 5 *per cent.* and consequently proves that the whole race of healthy slaves, consisting of 50,000, are totally extinct once every twenty years.

A Surinam Obeahman

This African (for he was born on the coast of Guinea) by his insinuating temper and industry, not only obtained his freedom from a state of slavery, but by his wonderful ingenuity and artful conduct found the means of procuring a very competent subsistence.

Having got the name of a *lockoman,* or sorcerer, among the lower slaves, no crime of any consequence was committed, especially at the plantations, but *Gramman Quacy,* which signifies Great-man Quacy, was instantly sent for to discover the perpetrators, which he so very seldom missed, owing, in fact, to their faith in his sorceries, added to his penetrating look and authority among them, that he has often prevented farther mischief to their masters; and, for these services, occasionally received very capital rewards. The corps of rangers, and all fighting free negroes, are under his influence; to whom he sells his *obias* or *amulets,* in order to make them invulnerable, and, of course, to engage without fear: by which deceit he has most certainly done much good to the colony, and at the same time filled his pockets with no inconsiderable profit to himself; while his person by the blacks is adored and respected like a God. The trash of which his amulets are made costs him in reality nothing; being neither more nor less than a collection of small pebbles, sea-shells, cut hair, fish-bones, feathers, &c. the whole sewed up together in small packets, which are tied with a string of cotton round the neck, or some other part of the bodies of his credulous votaries.

But besides these, and many other artful contrivances, he had the good fortune, in 1730, to find out the valuable root known by the name of *Quacioe bitter,* of which he was actually the first first discoverer, and from which it took its name: and, notwithstanding this medicine is now less in repute in England than formerly, it is highly esteemed in many other parts of the world for its efficacy in strengthening the stomach and restoring the appetite. It has, besides this valuable property, that of being a powerful *febrifuge,* and may be successfully used when the bark is nauseated, as is frequently the case.

In 1761, it was made known to *Linnoeus* by Mr. *d'Ahlberg,* formerly mentioned; and the Swedish naturalist has since written a treatise upon it. By this drug alone Quacy might have amassed riches, were he not entirely abandoned to indolence and dissipation; the consequence of which is, a complication of loathsome distempers, of which the leprosy is one: and that disorder is, as I have already stated, absolutely incurable. Nevertheless his age, though he could not exactly ascertain it, must have been very great, since he used frequently to repeat that he acted as drummer, and beat the alarm on his master's estate, when the French commodore, *Jacques Cassard,* put the colony under contribution, in the year 1712. . . .

This very same week we had indeed a fresh proof of the good effects of Gramman Quacy's animating obias or amulets, a captain of the rangers, named *Hannibal,* bringing in the barbacued hands of two rebel negroes, which he had himself encountered and shot; and one of these hands proved to be that of the noted rebel *Cupido,* formerly taken in 1774, and brought to Colonel Fourgeoud in the forest, but from whom he had since that time, though loaded with chains, found means to run away. . . .

A Free Negro's Retort

I shall never have done mentioning the insolence of these savage brutes [plantation overseers], who mostly are the refuse of the earth, brought up in Germany, or elsewhere, under the cane of a corporal. "Well," said one of these miscreants ironically to an old *free* negro, "don't you believe that the monkies are a race of damn'd Christians, who have been thus transformed for shewing so much lenity to such as you?"—"No, sir," replied the black man, "we do not think that the monkies are damned Christians; but I, and all of us, believe that many who call themselves Christians are a pack of damn'd monkies."— Which pointed repartee afforded me infinite satisfaction.

On Some Rebel Chiefs and Their Villages

Captain Hannibal [a Negro ranger] . . . informed me, that the famous chief *Bonny* was supposed to be in person amongst the neighbouring rebels; and that he was born in the forest amongst them, notwithstanding his being a mulatto, which was accounted for by his mother escaping to the woods from the ill treatment of her master, by whom she was then pregnant. . . .

This sable warrior made me also acquainted with the names of several other rebel commanders, against whom he had frequently fought for the Europeans. Such as *Quammy,* who was the chief of a separate gang, and had no connection with the others; *Caromantyn, Cojo, Arico,* and *Joli-Coeur;* the two last being celebrated captains, whose revenge was insatiable against the whites, particularly *Joli-Coeur's,* who had I confess great reason, as has been already stated. The noted rebel negro *Baron,* he believed, was now serving also under the great chief *Bonny.*

He next proceeded to tell me the names of the principal rebel settlements, some of which were already destroyed, some now in view, and some of these were only known to us by name. These appellations were all very expressive indeed; and as they may serve in some measure to elucidate our enquiries concerning the negro nations, I have thought proper to give them a place in this narrative, with their meaning in an English translation; *viz.*

Boucoo	I shall moulder before I shall be taken.
Gado Saby	God only knows me, and none else.
Cofaay	Come try me, if you be men.
Tessee See	Take a tasting, if you like it.
Mele me	Do disturb me, if you dare.
Boosy Cray	The woods lament for me.
Me Salasy	I shall be taken.
Kebree me	Hide me, O thou surrounding verdure.

The others were:

Quammi Condre	From Quammi, the name of the chief.
Pinenburgh	From the pines or manicole-trees which formerly surrounded it.
Cara Condre	From the quantity of maize it afforded.
Reisee Condre	From the quantity of rice it produced.

Such were the names of the negro warriors, and their settlements.

Musical Instruments and Dances

Their instruments of music, which are not a little ingenious, are all made by themselves, and consist of those represented in the annexed plate. [The plate faithfully depicts the instruments being described.]

No. 1, which is called *qua-qua,* is a hard sounding-board, elevated on one side like a boot-jack, on which they beat time as on a drum, with two pieces of iron, or two bones.

No. 2, is the *kiemba-toetoe,* or hollow reed, which is blown through the nostrils, like the nasal flute of Otaheite: it has but two holes, one at each end, the one serving to sound it, the other to be touched by the finger.

No. 3, is the *Ansokko-baina,* which is a hard board, supported on both sides like a low seat, on which are placed small blocks of different sizes, which being struck with two small sticks like a dulcimer, give different sounds, that are not at all disagreeable.

No. 4, is the *great Creole drum,* being a hollow tree, open at one end, and covered at the other with a sheep-skin, on which they sit astride, and so beat time with the palms of their hands; answering the effect of the bass-viol to the *qua-qua* board.

No. 5, is the *great Loango drum,* being covered at both ends, and serves the same purpose as a bass drum.

No. 6, is the *Papa drum,* beaten as the others.

No. 7, is the *small Loango drum,* beaten together with the great one.

No. 8, the *small Creole drum,* for the same use.

No. 9, is called *coeroema;* this is a wooden cup, ingeniously made, covered also with a sheep-skin, and beaten with two small rods or drum-sticks, after the manner of the *qua-qua* board.

No. 10, is the *Loango-bania* [a sansa—Ed.]. This I thought exceedingly curious, being a dry board, on which are laced, and kept down by a transverse bar, different sized elastic splinters of the palm-tree, like pieces of whalebone, in such a manner that both ends are elevated by two other bars that are fixed under them; and the above apparatus being placed on.

No. 11, which is a large empty *callebash* to promote the sound [of the sansa]; the extremities of the splinters are snapt by the fingers, something in the manner of a piano-forte, when the music has a soft and very pleasing effect.

No. 12, is called by the negroes *saka-saka,* being a hollow gourd, with a stick and handle fixed through it, and filled with small pebbles and pease, not unlike the magic shell of the Indians. This they hold above their heads, and while they dance rattle it to measure.

No. 13, is a *conch,* or sea shell, which by blowing they sound, for pleasure, or to cause an alarm, &c. but is not used as an accompaniment to dancing.

No. 14, is called *benta,* being a branch bent like a bow by means of a slip of dry reed or warimbo; which cord, when held to the teeth, is beaten with a short stick, and by being shifted backwards and forwards sounds not unlike a jew's-harp. [A mouth bow—Ed.]

No. 15, is the *Creole-bania,* this is like a mandoline or guitar, being made of a half gourd covered with a sheep-skin, to which is fixed a very long neck or handle. This instrument has but four strings, three long and one short, which is thick, and serves for a bass; it is played by the fingers, and has a very agreeable sound, but more so when accompanied by a song.

No. 16, is the *trumpet of war,* to command advancing, retreating, &c. and is called by the negroes the *too-too.* [A side-blown trumpet—Ed.]

No. 17, is a *horn* used to supply the place of the other, or on the plantations to call the slaves to work.

No. 18, *is the Loango too-too,* or flute, which they blow as the Europeans do, after the common way. It has but four holes for the fingers, and yet they make it produce a variety of sounds.—Such are the musical instruments of our African brethren, to which they dance with more spirit than we do to the best band in Europe.

To what I have stated, I will only add, that they always use full or half measure, but never triple time, in their dancing music, which is not unlike that of a baker's bunt, when he separates the flour from the bran, sounding *tuckety-tuck* and *tuckety-tuck* ad perpetuum. To this noise they dance with uncommon pleasure, and most times foot it away with great art and dexterity.

Every Saturday evening, the slaves who are well treated close the week with an entertainment of this kind, and generally once a quarter are indulged with a grand ball, to which the neighbouring slaves are invited; the master often contributing to their happiness by his presence, or at least by sending them a present of a few jugs of new rum.

At these grand balls the slaves are remarkably neat, the women appearing in thier best chintz petticoats, and many of the men in fine Holland trowsers. So indefatigable are they at this diversion, that I have known the drums continue beating without intermission from six o'clock on Saturday night till the sun made its appearance on the Monday morning; thus had passed six-and-thirty hours in dancing, cheering, hallooing, and clapping hands. The negroes dance always in couples, the men figuring and footing, while the women turn round like a top, their petticoats expanding like an umbrella; and this they call *waey-cotto.* During this, the by-standing youths fill about the liquor, while the girls encourage the performance, and wipe the sweat from the brows and sides of the unwearied musicians.

It is indeed upon the whole astonishing to see with what good-nature and even good manners these dancing societies are kept up, of which I repeat it they are so fond, that I have known a newly-imported negro, for want of a partner, figure and foot it for nearly the space of two hours, to his shadow against the wall.

DJUKA SONG FROM THE SURINAM BUSH

Many songs of the Djukas, both music and words, are recognizable to the Ashanti and Fanti people of Ghana, though some Djuka songs show the influence of Dahomean and Yoruba cultures. This song is one of a class to which the term Apuku is applied. The term refers to the "little people" or beings that are supposed to inhabit the bush country. The words appear to be in the Tshi language, and include a reference to Aberu (Aberewa), one of the Ashanti deities.

> Let us sing,
> Let us sing well,
> Let us be united,
> People of Aberu.

SOME PROVERBS OF THE SARAMACCA BUSH-NEGROES OF SURINAM

If you sell your head, where will you put your hat when you buy it? (Don't do something that will put you at a disadvantage in the future.)

From Suriname Folk-Lore, *by Melville J. Herskovits and Frances S. Herskovits, New York, Columbia University Press, 1936. By permission of Columbia University Press.*

Even if his stomach is full he is not very fat. (Said of someone who is less worthy or substantial than he appears to be, or whose argument is not persuasive.)

Today is yours, but tomorrow is mine. (My chance is coming.)

The day a leaf falls in the water is not the day it spoils. (It is not over yet; do not be premature. A Haitian proverb says: "The day a leaf falls in the water is not the day it sinks.")

Still water has a deep bottom. (Said of a person or a situation that is more meaningful or dangerous than it appears.)

No one must die, yet the graveyard does not stand empty. (In the end, death comes to all.)

A chicken can lie about her eggs but she cannot deceive about her chicks. (One does not know what is in a person's mind, but a person's actions are revealing.)

A boat without a steersman floats aimlessly. (A village, or a family, must have a head.)

Mosquito says, "Mmmm, mmmm, you are a man, I cannot kill you.' (One must recognize the limits of his capabilities.)

Wash your hands thoroughly if you wish to eat with those who are important. (Deference to those who deserve it has its rewards.)

Telling the truth can dig a grave. (Said of a person whose candor put him in a bad situation.)

Be generous to people but do not take out your entrails for them. (There is a limit to accommodation.)

LOBI SINGI FROM PARAMARIBO

Lobi singi (literally love song or love singing) is an institutionalized form of social criticism and recrimination among the Nengere, or Negroes, of Surinam. It has varied purposes, the most common of which is to shame or embarrass a woman who has "stolen" another woman's husband or lover. If a woman is abandoned by her lover, she may decide on a lobi singi as a means of making her complaint known to the community at large, and as a way of persuading her successful rival to send the man home. The victimized woman, along with her friends and sometimes with local musicians, appears in her rival's yard, perhaps at the head of a procession. Facing the cabin of the offending woman they sing verses, newly improvised or borrowed, that criticize or ridicule her for taking a mate belonging to someone else. The songs may contain romantic statements, comparisons between the offended and offending persons, reflections on the nature of true love as opposed to temporary passion, harsh judgments about the husband-stealer, or comments on the man himself. The imagery draws on commonplace sights or proverbs for its substance, and on occasion has the feel of genuine poetry. Here are some examples of lobi singi.

A woman compares herself with the rival with whom her man has taken up:

> You are handsomer than I,
> You are fatter than I,
> But I am sweeter than you are.
> That is why my treasure [i.e., lover]
> My treasure cannot bear
>   To leave a sweet rose
> To come to the house of a crab Dinki.

Here a woman says that the man who has left her was worthless when they first came together and only after that became important:

> When I bought my cow, my cow,
> When I bought my cow,
> When I bought my cow, my cow,
> My cow had no horns.

An abandoned woman deprecates what her rival has to offer:

> A passionate love without anything
> Is wearying.
> It comes to resemble a rose
> With no fragrance.

The woman sings that her lover (or husband) is more than her rival can handle:

> What can an ant do
> With a cow's head?
> Ha! Ha!
> It must eat the meat
> And leave the bones.
> Ha! Ha!

In this song the woman says she refused to waste away simply because her man has left her:

Song texts are from *Herskovits, and Herskovits*, ibid. *By permission of Columbia University Press.*

> If a lover has loved me,
> And he loves me no more,
> I cannot drown myself in the river
> On that account.
> Ha! Ha!

This song warns that the man will be no more faithful to his new woman than he was to the old, and that he might even return to the one that was abandoned:

> No matter how long the road,
> How dark the night,
> It is not dark, it is not dark.
> Ha! Ha!
> The lover's path is not far away.

The woman asks her rival to be generous and send her man home:

> My dear, don't you feel how sweet love is?
> But my lover brings me no sweetness.
> I have [only] one lover.
> Look, return him to me again.

Here the abandoned woman compliments the one who has taken up with her man, saying that her rival can easily find other lovers:

> My lover left me.
> Leave him, let him go.
> Ha! Ha!
> Because you are the cakes.
> Ha! Ha!
> You are the bottle.
> Ha! Ha!
> Another will buy you,
> Another will buy you.
> Leave him, let him go.
> Ha! Ha!
> Another will buy you.

Again, the theme of transient passion as against true love:

> Pretty Miss, how am I to live?
> Pretty Miss, how am I to live?
> The gold chain around your neck
> Is very dazzling.
> Passionate love is something
> That goes away in a day like a blue flower.

It does not last long.
It does not last long.
It does not last long.
Ha! Ha!
Sweet love is something.

In this song an abandoned woman protests that, contrary to what has been said of her, she is an attractive person:

Wanton, how can you say I am not beautiful?
Two beautiful flowers bore me.
A rose-bud was my mother.
A bachelor-button was my father.
How can you say I am not beautiful?
Two beautiful flowers bore me.

Although it is primarily used as a public recrimination, the lobi singi sometimes serves other purposes. One such purpose is public confession. In the following song a woman deplores her former promiscuous life and announces her desire to begin a new way of living:

If I were a rich man
I would buy a large farm.
And what would I plant in it?
And what would I plant in it?
I would plant experience in it
So that when I went forth
Experience would be a perfume for my body.

SOME SURINAM TALES

Many of the folk tales of Surinam are widely known throughout the Carribean area, in particular those of the Anansi repertoire. Among them are stories that have changed little from their West African prototypes. The tale, "Dog Asks for a New Name," for example, is a variant of an Ashanti story collected by Rattray; "Grudging Hospitality" features Anansi in his traditional greedy and gluttonous African role; "The Feast on the Mountain and the Feast under the Water" is familiar to the Ashanti and other West Africans in virtually the same form as it is known to the people of Surinam; "Broken Pledge: All Things Talk" is a close Surinam variant of a tale told in Ghana; and "Trespassing on the Devil's Land" is almost identical to a story known to the Yoruba, the Ashanti, and other West Africans.

Why Cat and Dog Are Enemies

Anansi did not know how Dog's mouth worked. Then he called Dog "Friend-little-mouth." But now, when they went to eat together, if Dog made but two swallows he finished all the food. Anansi studied, and said, "Well, how is it that Dog's mouth works so? It does not look big from the outside, but it devours so." Now they gave a feast. Then Cat came to the table. But now when Cat came, she and Dog did not eat together. Just as Cat came to Dog's side, Dog bared his teeth at her. Instantly he saw how Dog's mouth worked. Now he said to Dog, said, "Yes, friend, I have been calling you 'Friend-little-mouth' for nothing, but I did not know that your mouth worked this way. Otherwise I would never have eaten together with you at the table. But now I have to thank Cat. She made me see today that that is how your mouth works."

And that is why when Cat and Dog come before a plate of food, Dog bares his teeth at Cat. They do not eat together. It is finished.

Dog Asks for a New Name

Dog could not walk the streets. People insulted him. They called him thief. So he went to God and he said, "Please, Master God, can you change the name of Dog for me?" So God, the Master, said to him, he said, "All right. I will see." So the Master took Dog and he took him away with him. He killed a fat cow and he said to Dog, he said, "Make a barbecue and let us barbecue the cow. Then I will leave you to watch the cow while it is being barbecued, but not a single piece must be missing." Dog said to God, he said, "Yes, Master, I will look after it well." But when the fire began to barbecue the cow, then the cow ran fat. Dog smelt the fat, and he licked his tongue because he longed for a piece of the cow. But he was afraid to eat it. But he waited and he waited so till . . . he could keep back no longer. He looked about him and he saw no one, so he took a piece of the meat and he ate it. Then he wiped his mouth, so that no one should see him.

These tales are from Herskovits and Herskovits, ibid., and are reprinted by permission of Columbia University Press.

The next day when God came Dog asked him, said, "Master, did I not look after the meat well?" God answered him, said, "Yes, you looked after it very well." Dog said, "Well, then you must change my name." The Master answered him, said, "Since you looked after the meat so well, I will change your name for you." Dog was happy so till. . . . He said, "Master, you are just and good to change my name. But tell me, what sort of name do I have now?" So God said to him, said, "You are not called Dog any more, but your name is Just-the-same-as-ever. Just-the-same-as-ever."

So Dog went about the streets, and the small boys in the street called after him, "Look, the thieving Dog." The Dog answered them, said, "I can take you to court, because I am no longer called Dog. My name is Just-the-same-as-ever, Just-the-same-as-ever." At once the boys called. "Yes, Just-the-same-as-ever, Just-the-same-as-ever, Dog lives by thieving!"

Why Dog Goes About Naked

A dance was going to be held. Dog had no clothes in which to go dancing. Then he borrowed a pair of breeches from Anansi. But when they went to dance, the breeches were too small for Dog. When Dog danced he spread his feet. The first time Anansi called him aside, and he said, "Friend, look out, you are tearing my breeches." He left him. When they danced again, Dog spread his feet again. Anansi called him again, and he said, "Friend, look out, you are tearing my breeches." But, when for the third time Dog spread his feet again, Anansi suddenly caught the breeches and pulled them from Dog's body.

That is why to this day Dog goes about naked.

Dog's Riddle

Dog said he did not let rice get by him. Now Anansi did not understand him. He said, "Friend Dog, what does that mean?" Dog said to him, said, "That means when someone gives you a plate of food, and you do not eat all, then when the food is carried outside, it isn't yours. Haven't you noticed, when someone gives me food I eat all of it?"

Grudging Hospitality

Anansi went about and ate with the other animals. But now he said to the other animals, said, one day he himself was going to have them come and eat with him. But when they passed, if they heard him talk to himself, then they must not come in, because he would be working at his work. But if they heard him remain silent, then they could come.

So one day the animals were passing, and they heard Anansi talking to himself. They did not go in, but all the same when Anansi ate, then he talked to himself so that the animals thought that he was working at his work. Then they did not go in.

But one day the animals were passing, and they heard him talking to himself. Now they said, "Today we must go and see what Anansi is doing." When they went in they found Anansi eating. They said, "Friend Anansi, did you say to us that when you talk to yourself you are at work, but when you are silent, then you are eating? So every day when we passed, we heard you talking." At once Anansi said to them, said. "Well friends, when my mouth says 'tya-kom, tya-kom', is it not work at which I am working? Well, when you eat your mouth is working, and when you are working, your mouth talks-talks."

The Feast on the Mountain and the Feast Under the Water

Anansi had a birthday. He was giving a feast. He invited all the animals to come and eat with him. Now, since all the animals came, Tortoise came, too. But Anansi did not want Tortoise to come and eat at the table. Before they went to eat, Anansi suddenly said, all the animals who were going to eat must wash their hands before they came to the table. Now Tortoise went to wash his hands, but as he walked back, his hands were dirty again. He washed his hands many, many times, but he could not walk any other way. So he did not eat at the table.

Tortoise went away. He said, "Anansi caught me, but I am going to get even with him."

Tortoise now had a birthday. He sent to call all the animals to come to his birthday party to eat with him. He knew that Anansi was going to come, too. That is why he was giving the feast under the water, because he knew that Anansi was light, and could not come under the water. That is why he did this, so that, he might catch Anansi. Now when all the animals began to arrive, Anansi could not go under the water. He went and borrowed a pair of breeches and a coat, and he dressed himself in that. He picked up many stones, and put them in his pockets, so that he might become heavy. But now when he was heavy enough, he went down into the water. When the table was set, all were to come and eat. All at once Tortoise looked, and saw that Anansi had put stones in his pockets. Immediately Tortoise said to them all, said, before they came to the table, all the people should take off their coats. So Anansi was troubled when he heard this. He studied, and said, "If I take off my coat, then I am going to come up on top again, because the stones which are in my pockets hold me." Now Anansi could not take off his coat. When Anansi came to the table, Tortoise at once said, "Didn't I tell you that all must take off their coats? You have to take off your coat. When you gave a feast you did what you liked. When I give mine I can do what I like, too."

So Anansi took off his coat. No sooner did he take it off, than he rose to the surface of the water. He did not get any food to eat. Greed caused this to happen to him. So when you eat, you must eat with others. It is finished.

Tables Turned: Cockroach Revenged on Anansi

Anansi asked the King if he might become a preacher. The King said let him first go one Sunday and preach a sermon in church. But when Anansi went the first day the King could not go to hear him preach. Then the King gave Anansi a black suit, and said to him, said, he must wear this the following week.

But now Anansi and Cockroach lived side by side. Beside the garden fence was a coconut tree, but it was on Cockroach's side. It was not a large tree, but it did have a coconut. This hung right on top of the fence, so that one part came on Anansi's side and one part came on Cockroach's side. Anansi took his hoe and cut it right in two. When Cockroach saw he had cut it, he said to him, said, "Well, how could you cut the coconut? The tree is in my yard, [and] you should not have cut it." Anansi said, "Well, didn't you see how it hung down so that one part was on your side, and the other part on mine?" Cockroach said, "All right. I will get even with you."

The Saturday before Anansi was going to preach in church, he said to his wife, said, let her hang up his black suit (for him) to air. His wife took the coat and hung it right on the fence. Now Cockroach took his knife, and he cut off that part of the coat which was on his side.

Now, Sunday morning the King went to church to hear how Anansi would preach. But Anansi could not come, because he did not have the black coat. And so the King had them take Anansi to prison.

Anansi said to Cockroach, said, "You! as long as I live, I won't forget you for what you did to me. You made me lose my job. Death will make me forget you."

Giants Cure Boastfulness

There was a man who thought he was better than all other men. He had a trumpet. Every day he blew his trumpet, and the trumpet said, "I am the man who surpasses all men." Then his wife said to him, said, "You must not blow the trumpet so."

One day, as he was blowing his trumpet, he heard another trumpet blow, saying, "Man surpasses man." Then he came out to go and see where the trumpet was being blown. He walked so till . . . he met an old woman. Then the old woman said to him, "You must go away. If you remain here, when my children come they are going to kill you." But he begged the old woman, he said, let her hide him. Then the old woman hid him.

When the first child came in the afternoon he brought ten buffaloes. The other came, he brought ten sacks of rice. The other brought four sacks of salt. But when they had cooked they ate. Then the mother said to them, said, "You do not know that you have a brother, but he has not been living here." Then they said, "Why have you never told us?" She said, "I was too sad to tell you." Then she said, "Well, if I let you see him, what will you do with him?" They said, "We shall rejoice with him." When the mother had him come, the first one took him and tossed him up in the air. When he fell down the other caught him and tossed him again. When he fell down again the other one caught him, then he tossed him again. Then he fell to the ground. At once he said, "Yes, I am not the only one who is a man. Man surpasses man."

Then he went home, and he told his wife what had happened. Then the wife said to him, said, "When Salamander's tail is cut off, he immediately finds a hole (in which to hide)."

Spreading the Fingers

In the early times Ba Yau was a plantation overseer. He had two wives in the city. But as he found things [provisions] on the plantation, he brought them to his wives. But when he brought [things], then he said to them, said, "When you eat, you must spread your fingers." But when he said this, the first one did not understand very well what that meant to say. He told the second wife the same thing, and that one understood. What that meant was that it was meant to say [that] when he brought them things, they were not to eat them alone, they were to give others half.

Now the one who did not understand what that said, then, in the afternoon when she cooked, she ate. Then she went outside, and spread her fingers, and said, "Ba Yau said when I eat I must spread my fingers." Because Ba Yau brought her much bacon and salt fish. She alone ate it. But when Ba Yau brought the things for the other one, she shared half with other people, because she had understood what the proverb had said.

Not long afterwards Ba Yau died. But when Ba Yau was dead, nobody brought anything to the wife who had spread her fingers in the air. She sat alone. But to the other one who had shared things with other people, many people brought things. One brought her a cow, one brought her sugar, one brought her coffee. So she received many things from others. Now one day, the one wife went to the other, and she said, "Yes, sister, ever since Ba Yau died, I have suffered hunger. No one brought me anything. But look, how is it that so many people have brought things to you?" Then the other one asked her said, "Well, when Ba Yau had brought you things, what did you do with them?" She said, "I alone ate them." Then the other one said again, "When Ba Yau said to you, said, 'You must spread your fingers,' what did you do?" She said, "When I ate, I spread my fingers in the air." The other one said, "So . . . . Well then, the air must bring you things, because you spread your fingers for the air. As for myself, the same people to whom I gave things, bring me things in return."

The proverb, when you eat you must spread fingers, means, when you eat, you must eat with people, you must not keep all for yourself. Otherwise, when you have nothing, nobody else is going to give you, because you had not given people what was yours.

The Fastidious Go Hungry

In early days you had many, many people who were running away. But now [once], several had run away. But when they ran away, they went into the bush, and there they suffered hunger, then they came upon a bunch of bush plantains, which they roasted. But now there was one man there who, when the plantains were being roasted, put his at the side of the fire. But now the others, before the plantains were well roasted, they ate them. Soon the others asked the man, they said, "Well brother, aren't you eating?" Then he answered them, he said, "Friends, let them get done, they are not well done yet." Then the others ate until they were full, but that one did not eat.

A little later, all at once they heard people coming to the bush to catch them. Instantly they all began to run. The man had no time to look after the plantains which he had put at the side of the fire. At once the others shouted to him, said, "Friend-Well-Done—o! How is it getting done?" So the others came to ridicule him, because he had put the plantains at the side of the fire to have them well done. And that is why they gave him the name Agari [Well Done].

The Preacher Traps a Thief

A preacher had an orange tree. Every day someone went to rob it. Then every week the preacher preached in church how they stole the oranges. Then he let it be known that he was going to catch the thief. Then one Sunday he took one of the oranges, and carried it to church. When he went to preach, then his text said "Thou shalt not steal." Then he said that he knew the thief, [for] he had dreamt that night of the thief. "See how he is looking at me, the thief! If I did not remember God, I would hit him with the orange." The thief ducked his head, and then all the people knew immediately that this was the man who had been stealing the oranges.

So the preacher caught the thief.

The Devil Complains

Well, the Devil said to someone said, no matter what good he did people, he did not have a good name. The Devil said, "All right, I will let you see this."

Now the Devil went to God, and he said to God let God put a big stone on the path, and he would put a sack of money, then they should see who would get the credit. Well, when they did this, then one day someone came by and he struck his foot on the stone. At once he said, "The Devil put the stone on the path and made me strike my foot!" Now another came by and he saw the money. He took the money, and at once he said, "Praise God! I say to you 'Many thanks,' [that] I found the money."

At once the Devil said, "You see, it is I who put down the money, but the man gives God thanks. And the person who put down the stone, he curses. So me he cursed, and he thanked God. So did I not tell you that I get no justice on earth?"

Proverb: Look where you stub your foot, but do not look where you fall down.

Broken Pledge: All Things Talk

A man found several peanuts. Then he planted them. But when he planted them, he said, as long as there was no birthday he would not dig up the peanuts. But now before the birthday, the peanuts were ripe, and he went to dig them up. At once the peanuts said, "That is not what you had said." His walking stick said, "I had heard. It is not what you had said." All the things in his house began to talk, "The peanuts are right. This is not what you had said."

The man began to run. As he ran he met a man who had a bundle of wood on his head. The man said, "Why do you run so?" He said to the man, "I planted peanuts and this is what I said, 'When my birthday comes, I will dig them up.' But when I went to dig them up, then instantly all the things in my house began to say, 'This is not what you had said. The peanuts are right.'" The man said, "Ah! that is why you run. I would not run for so silly a thing." Instantly the bundle of wood on top of his head cried out, said, "You lie, if it were you, you would run faster." At once the man shook with fear, he threw the wood down on the ground. The man said to him, "Well brother, you should do as you said. From such a thing you cannot run. You already run faster than I." It is finished.

(For a West African comparison, see Appendix XI, pp. 588–89.)

Trespassing on the Devil's Land

Mat' Luison was a devil. He lived at a certain place. But (one day) a man took his children and his wife, to go and make a field right there beside it. No sooner had they struck with a hoe than Luison asked, he said, "Who is there?" The man said, "It is I, Luangu." He said, "What have you come to do?" He answered him, said, "I have come to make a field." Luison said to his children, said, "Come, go help Mat' Luangu cut his field." Before Mat' Luangu cut down one tree, Mat' Luison and his children had cut the whole field. They went away.

The next day Mat' Luangu went back. Mat' Luison asked, "Who is there?" He said, "It is I Luangu." "What are you doing?" He said, "I am going to plant the field." Luison said to his children, let them come and help plant the field.

But now when they had finished planting, the crop became ripe. No sooner did Mat' Luangu go to cut a stalk of corn than Luison asked him, said, "What are you doing?" He said, "I am cutting a stalk of corn." Luison said to his children again, said, "Come, go help Mat' Luangu cut the corn." Before Mat' Luang' had cut a stalk of corn, Luison and his children had cut the whole field of corn.

The next day Mat' Luang went to cut a plantain. He went softly so Luison would not hear. But no sooner did he take hold of the plantain, than Luison asked him, said, "Who is there?" He said, "It is I, Luangu." "What are you doing?" He said, "I am cutting a plantain." Luison said to his children, said, "Come, go help Mat' Luangu cut plantains." Before Luang' had cut one plantain they had cut the whole field.

Then Mat' Luangu was angry. When he went home, then one of his children misbehaved. No sooner did he begin to beat the child than Luison asked, said, "What are you doing?" He said, "I am beating my child." Luison said to his children, "Come, go help Mat' Luangu beat a child." They went and they beat the child till they killed it.

So Mat' Luangu became afraid. He said to his wife, "Let us run away from here, because these are no good people here beside us." And so they went away and left Mat' Luison. Mat' Luison took all the crops of the field which they had planted.

The end.

(For African and West Indian comparisons, see Appendix XII, pp. 590–92.)

THREE PARTY SONGS FROM GUYANA

Ring Down Da Rumour

God mek a black man,
'E mek am in a day,
Forget to paint am white.

So bye-bye me honey,
For de ting is getting funny,
Ring down da rumour till morn.

God mek a white man,
'E mek am in a night,
Forget to paint am black.

So bye-bye me honey,
For de ting is getting funny,
Ring down da rumour till morn.

God mek a coolie,
'E mek am out o' troolie,
Ring down da rumour till morn.

So bye-bye me honey,
For de ting is getting funny,
Ring down da rumour till morn.

Johnny Fernandes (to the tune of Blow the Man Down)

Johnny Fernandes was a Putagee man,
Blow, blow, blow de man down!
Blow de man down wid a bottle o' rum,
Gie me some time to blow de man down!

Johnny kyan' read, Johnny kyan' spell,
Blow, blow, blow de man down!
Blow de man down wid a piece o' cow dung,
Gie me some time to blow de man down!

From a ms. collection of Guyana folk songs set down by Homer Gayne.

Magalena

> Lululu Magalena oh Lulu,
> Lululu Magalena Lu,
> Lululu Magalena oh Lulu,
> Come back tomorrow night
> We sah do dis ting.
> Seven long years we nah do dis ting, Lulu,
> Seven long years we nah do dis ting,
> Seven long years we nah do dis ting, Lulu,
> Come back tomorrow night
> We sah do dis ting.

FOUR AFRO-VENEZUELAN TALES

The Man, the Snake and the Fox

A man was returning to his conuco [a small homestead] when he discovered a large snake pinned down by a rock that had fallen on him. The snake groaned, "Good man, for the sake of the thing that you love most, get me out of this difficulty. I am a snake with a family."

"Get you out of that difficulty? To set you free so that you may bite me afterwards?" the man replied.

"Please, good man," the snake said. "I have no evil intentions toward you. I promise that I will not bite you."

These four Afro-Venezuelan tales were collected by Juan Pablo Sojo in Caracas and Curiepe in 1946, and have been made available through the kindness of Dr. Luis Felipe Ramon y Rivera and the Instituto Nacional de Folklore. English translations are by Esteban McCragh.

The man relented and removed the rock. The snake stretched its body and breathed deeply, while the man waited for words of gratefulness. But the snake raised its repulsive head and said, "Now I am going to bite you."

"Snake," the man protested, "this is an outrage. You made a promise."

"Don't you know, poor man, that good is repaid by evil?"

"No," the man said, "that is false."

"Very well, the snake said, "let us go and get the truth of the matter from anyone we meet on the road. If I am wrong, I will let you go free. But if I am right, disaster will fall on you."

They agreed to handle the situation this way, and went along the road together. They met a donkey grazing nearby.

The man asked, "Donkey, do you think that good should be repaid with evil?"

The donkey put down its ears and brayed. He said, "That is the way of the world, my friend. I have worked many years for my master. From dawn to dusk I have helped him in his tasks. What happens? He beats me with a stick until my body is red and raw. And now that I am good for nothing, he leaves me in this place where there is hardly any grass to eat."

"What did I tell you?" the snake said to the man, and it prepared to bite him.

"Wait," the man said, "let us ask someone else."

The snake agreed, and so they went on until they saw a fox fishing in a stream.

The man approached the fox, saying, "Tell me, Uncle, do you think good must be repaid with evil?"

The fox looked at the man and the snake for a while. Then he answered, "That depends, my friend. Let me hear first the reason for your question." After the man had related what had happened to him, the fox said, "Before I give an opinion I want to go with you to the place where this affair started."

So the three of them went to the place where the man and the snake had met. The fox said, "Now I want to see exactly how the snake was trapped under the stone." So the snake stretched out his body and the man replaced the stone on him. When the fox saw that the snake was firmly pinned down, he said to the man, "Leave him there, now, my friend, to wait for someone else to save him."

The man and the fox departed. The man tried to think of a way to express his thanks. He told the fox, "Because of your good deed, I would like you to come occasionally to my house. I will always have a chicken for you in the chest in my yard."

The fox was very pleased. The following day it went for its chicken, which it found where the man said it would be. The next day the fox came again for a chicken. He came, not occasionally, but every day. He came continually and took the chickens wherever he could find them. The man became desperate. He didn't know what to do. One hundred days passed, and the fox took away one hundred chickens. The man thought that the fox was abusing him for coming so often. Unless an end was put to the affair, the man thought, he would soon be ruined.

So the next day he placed in the chest not a chicken but two savage dogs. When the fox arrived he was happy. He said good morning to the man, and without waiting for an answer he went to the chest. When he lifted up the lid, the two dogs attacked him. He fled across the fields, the dogs following him. While running from his pursuers, the fox called out (to his legs):

> Stretch and contract,
> For everything in this world is cheating.

The Swordfish

A young boy and a young girl lived with their parents on a ranch. Every day the children went to the forest to get firewood. One day after a rain, the girl found a small pond among the bushes. In the pond was a little fish. The girl remained there watching the fish while her brother went on his way. After a while the girl began to sing this way:

> Con mi palanquilla,
> Sirena,
> Unangolá!
> Y mi maridito,
> Sirena,
> Un pejespá!

> With my little lever,
> Siren,
> *Unangolá!*
> And my little husband,
> Siren,
> A swordfish!

She repeated this song, and immediately the fish came to the surface, answering her, "Cayón, cayón, cayón, arrived!" Finding her at the pond, her brother asked her, "What are you doing, little sister?" She answered, "I am watching a little fish whom I am going to marry." They went back to the ranch, saying nothing more about the matter.

The next day they went again to the forest for firewood. The girl brought breadcrumbs to the pond for the fish, and again she sang her little song:

> Con mi palanquilla,
> Sirena,
> Unangolá!
> Y mi maridito,
> Sirena,
> Un pejespá!

The fish answered in the same way as before: "Cayón, cayón, cayón, arrived!"

Time passed, and things went on this way. Years went by. The pond had become large and deep, and the fish had grown to a great size. The girl had become a young lady. Her father grew suspicious because she spent so much time in the forest. He questioned the brother, who could no longer hide the secret. He told his parents that when his sister went to the forest for firewood she spoke with a very large fish in a deep pond.

The next day the parents followed the brother and sister into the forest. They saw how the sister called the fish to the surface by singing. After the young woman had left the pond, the father went to the water's edge and sang her song:

> Con mi palanquilla,
> Sirena,
> Unangolá!
> Y mi maridito,
> Sirena,
> Un pejespá!

But when the swordfish heard the deep voice of the father, he only descended lower in the water. Then the mother sang the song, imitating the voice of her daughter. The fish was deceived, and immediately came to the surface, answering, "Cayón, cayón, cayón, arrived!" And as soon as the fish appeared, the father killed it with his long knife. They took the fish from the water and carried it home. There they cut it up and cooked it for dinner. They hid the scales of the fish in a trunk belonging to their daughter.

When the girl came home from hunting firewood, it was time to eat. But the girl ate nothing, for she had no hunger. When she went to her room and found the fish scales in her trunk, her grief was great, for she realized that the swordfish, her little husband, had been killed. She went running to the pond and found that it had dried up. She placed the scales there and cried.

The parents, discovering that she had run away, went after her. They came to where the pond had been, and found it dry. The girl, they did not find her. They saw only her hair sticking out of the ground and gradually disappearing under the earth. They pulled on the hair to bring the girl back, but they accomplished nothing. Finally there was nothing left of the girl to be seen.

The Woman, the Giant and the Vulture

There was a woman who was very dissatisfied with her life because she found herself perpetually pregnant. She decided to go see God to ask him to relieve her of this constant punishment. She set out, and while she was on the road to Father God's house a giant saw her coming and called out to her, "Hello, good woman, where are you going?"

"Why," she said, "I am going to the house of Father God to find out why I have to be pregnant year after year."

The giant answered, "Oh, now that is something! I think I shall go along. I also have a complaint. I will find out why God made me so big."

And without any further discussion, they travelled along the road together. Further on they were greeted by a vulture. He said, "Hello, you two. Where are you going in such a hurry?"

The giant answered, "We are on the way to see Father God to get some explanations. I want to know why he made me so big, and this woman wants to know why she is always pregnant."

The vulture said, "Well, now, that is something! I am going with you. I would like to know why God made me so black."

So the three of them went on together until they reached heaven. St. Peter greeted them, and when he found out what they wanted he conducted them to God's house.

God listened first to the giant's complaint. He arose from his chair, saying, "Come with me." He took the giant into an adjoining room. He said, "Observe carefully what you see." Lying in the middle of the room was the body of a dead child.

The giant said, "A sad thing, but what is the meaning of it?"

"The meaning," God said, "is that if you had died when you were a small child you would not be here today complaining about your size."

Hearing this, the giant said no more.

Then God spoke to the woman and asked for her complaint.

"It is this constant state of being pregnant," the woman said. "Year after year I am pregnant. Why should I be punished this way?"

God led her outside into the yard. He said, "Observe what is going on out here."

All the woman saw were a hen and a rooster. The hen was running this way and that, pursued by the rooster. The hen jumped on a box and went over a fence. The rooster followed, not quite managing, however, to overtake her. On the other side of the fence, the hen ran one way and another until she came to a clump of bushes, and there she hid. The rooster could not find her, and he gave up the chase.

"I have observed it," the woman said. "What does it mean?"

"It means," God said, "that if you follow the good example of this hen you will not be pregnant all the time."

It was in this way that the woman and the giant received God's reply to their complaints.

(At this point, the narrator abruptly ended his story. after an expectant silence, one of his listeners called out, "And what about the vulture?" The narrator responded: "Lift up his tail and kiss his ass.")

The Rooster, the Goat and the Dog

In a certain house, there lived together a rooster, a goat and a dog. For differing reasons, the three of them decided that they would have to leave the place where they lived. The goat wanted to go because he was to be killed and eaten at a festival scheduled for the next day. The rooster wanted to go because he had been replaced by a younger rooster, and he knew he was destined to end up in the pot. The dog wanted to leave because he was ill-treated by his master and was always hungry. Therefore, they all went away together.

They came to a wide river which they had to cross, but looking at the farther bank they saw a very large tiger [jaguar?] peering at them from among the bushes. So the dog volunteered to go across first. He entered the water and swam to the far side as quietly as he could. When he reached dry land he discovered that what they had seen was only the head of a tiger, which had been cut off by a hunter. The tiger's body was lying nearby.

The dog returned to his friends with the good news. He instructed the rooster to get on his back, and he ferried him to the other side. Once more he returned and carried the goat across. Then the dog satisfied his hunger with tiger meat, while the rooster pecked at seeds lying on the ground and the goat grazed in the lush grass. When their hunger was appeased they were very contented with their lot. Without thinking much about the matter, they pulled the tiger's head to the foot of the tree where they intended to spend the night.

When darkness started to fall, the dog leaped into a low branch of the tree. The goat stood on his hind legs and the dog pulled him up by the horns. In a short flight, the rooster reached the branches. As they began to sleep, they heard noises in the bushes and became frightened. Looking down, they saw a pride of tigers coming out of the jungle. The tigers came straight to the tree that sheltered the three friends. One of the little tigers discovered the head that lay below the tree. He called out, "Mama! Here is father's head!" The female tiger came instantly and began to lament with loud cries. "Blessed be God!" she cried. "They have killed my husband! Ai! Ai! They have killed my loved one!" All the family threw themselves around with grief.

The goat, who was shaking with fear, began to fall from his perch in the tree. Seeing what was about to happen to the goat, the rooster clapped his wings against his sides, making a loud noise. The goat fell with a great crash among the tigers. And the dog shouted, with a loud voice, "Take the biggest!"

Hearing this, the tigers—believing that hunters were in their presence—put their tails between their legs and fled into the jungle.

The three friends, now safe, embraced one another and celebrated their triumph.

THE AFRO-VENEZUELAN MAMPULORIO

(DEATH WATCH FOR AN INFANT)

When a Negro child of tender age dies—generally a newborn baby—the Negroes of the Barlovento region stand wake by the tiny corpse which is bedecked and surrounded with flowers and lighted candles.

It is upon such an occasion that the song of the *mampulorio* is sung.

The country people believe and say that a dead child turns into an angel, and, therefore, this watch is called "watch for the little angel."

The "watches for the little angel" are not only celebrated by the Negroes but also by the people of the Adean region, who traditionally stand watch by newborn children who have died.

Among the Negroes of Barlovento (in the districts of Acevedo, Brión and Páez in the State of Miranda) and among practically all the peons in the neighboring cocoa plantations, the "watches for the little angel" have their peculiar characteristics.

The watch is celebrated on a chosen plantation. The dead child rests in a simple coffin, painted white, which is placed upon a table in the back of the room. Wild flowers, or flowers decorated with colored pa-

From the booklet by Juan Liscano and Charles Seeger accompanying the Library of Congress record album, Venezuelan Folk Music, *album XV of* Folk Music of the Americas.

per, ornamented candles and beadwork give the appearance of an altar upon which the coffin rests. The audience is seated in front of this improvised altar, and the musicians are gathered in a corner.

Suddenly, the monotonous song rises. A man steps forward into the center of the gathering, carrying a hat, which he places, successively, upon the knees of each of those present. Another man, who accompanies him, holds an elaborate candle in his hands. The first, after having put his hat upon the knees of one of the audience, commences to deposit in it a series of objects such as are enumerated in the accompanying song given below. The candle-bearer then takes his turn. He brings the candle close to the face of a member of the audience, twisting it in his hands, moving it back and forth. The member of the audience tries to blow it out. The song refers to this activity.

If the member of the audience does not succeed in putting out the candle, he must bring a gift which, at the end of the ceremony, he may redeem when he has complied with a previously imposed penance. In this way the *mampulorio*, a Negro funeral rite, may be compared with the "pledge games" which delighted our forefathers. This custom, however, is beginning to die out (repeated legal action has been taken to prohibit it)—particularly that aspect of the celebration involving the boiling of the corpse to delay decomposition, which affords opportunity to prolong the *velorio* for many days, in one ranch after another.

This death rite represents a profound sense of social protest. The people think, with bold reasoning, that the prematurely deceased child, through his death, escapes the bitter experience of having to grow up and become an adult. Therefore, rather than with tears, they celebrate his death with joy, as if it were liberation.

Exclaimed: Drums! Drums!
Sung to the accompaniment of maracas, drum and quatro:

For the sake of the blessed souls
                  Who are in purgatory,
Here is the candle
           (chorus) of the mampulorio
Here is the candle
           of the mampulorio
Here is the box of matches
                of the mampulorio
Here is the ring
           of the mampulorio
Here is the ring
           of the mampulorio
Ai, my little pullet
Went out to the street
And I pray to God
              that no one finds it
That no one finds it

                              that no one finds it
That no one finds it
                              that no one finds it
And here is the candle
                    of the mampulorio
And here is the guitar
                    of the mampulorio
And here is the candle
                    of the mampulorio
And here is the hibiscus
                    of the mampulorio
I pray to God
                    that no one finds it
No one finds it
                    no one finds it
Here is the candle
                    of the mampulorio
Here is the cigar
                    of the mampulorio
Here is the rose
                    of the mampulorio
Ai, for the blessed souls
Who are in purgatory
Here is the candle
                    of the mampulorio
Here is the rose
                    of the mampulorio
Here is the cigar
                    of the mampulorio
Here is the hibiscus
                    of the mampulorio
Here is the rose
                    of the mampulorio
For the blessed souls
Who are in purgatory
Put out the candle
                    of the mampulorio
It wasn't put out
                    and it wasn't put out
And it wasn't put out
                    and it wasn't put out
Put it out then
                    and it wasn't put out
Now he's lighting it
                    and it wasn't put out
Etc.

(Later, other objects of the mampulorio are mentioned, such as the hat and the maracas.)

THE MYTH OF MARIA LIONZA

The cult of Maria Lionza is a fascinating synthesis of numerous belief systems, some of them Venezuelan in origin, some foreign and exotic. Woven into Maria Lionza beliefs and rituals are African deities,
Catholic saints, Indian nature spirits, astrology, magic and spiritualism. Elements of Brazilian Shango rites and Cuban santeria have been
absorbed, as have many varied mystical and theological propositions
of uncertain origin.

The cult takes its name from a mythical or legendary woman of supernatural powers, envisioned as a queen-mother-goddess living in a
palace inside the mountains of Sorte. Surrounding her is her "court,"
composed of spirits, demigods and wild animals. It is believed that the
human spirits that comprise her retinue are the souls or afterimages of
persons who, when alive, sought favors from Maria Lionza, for which,
after death, they became her perpetual servants, slaves and vassals.
Maria Lionza rules the mountains, forests, rivers and lakes. She is a nature deity subservient only to God, both kind and harsh, and a source
of all good things wanted by humans. She is a protector of fish, of wild
animals and of plant life. Some of her devotees identify her with the
Virgin Mary, or with the Virgen de Coromoto, regarded as the protec-
tress of Venezuela. Her throne, say some, is made of snakes, and she is
guarded by the spirits of lions and goats. It is said that she is harsh
with hunters who needlessly kill wild animals, or with peasants who
burn down her forests.

Within the cult there is a belief in a number of "courts" other than
that of Maria Lionza herself, such as a court of the stars, a court of the
ancient Indian chiefs who resisted the Spanish conquistadores, and an
African court composed of Yoruba deities. There are also a court of Simón Bolívar, a celestial court and a Hindu court, among others.

Foremost among those who populate the African court are these sev-
en Yoruba deities:

Shango, also identified as Santa Barbara
Oshun, also called La Virgen de la Caridad del Cobre
Yemoja, also known as La Virgen de la Regla
Ogun, likewise called San Pedro

Extracted from a number of sources, but primarily from Maria Lionza, Mito y
Culto Venezolana, *by Angelina Pollak-Eltz, Caracas, 1972.*

Orula (Orunmila), identified with St. Francis of Assisi
Obatala, also called La Virgen de las Mercedes
Elegba or Eshu, messenger god, sometimes identified with Satan

In some localities there is the belief that certain black historical figures reside in one or another of the courts. Among these personalities are: Felipe, a Cuban who was prominent in the struggle for Cuban independence; Miguel, said to have been an instigator of an uprising among Venezuelan slaves in the year 1552; and Pedro Camejo, "the First Black," a leader in the struggle for Venezuelan independence and a companion of Simón Bolívar.

That the cult of Maria Lionza is an accretion of religious concepts and magical practices from many sources is obvious. But how or when the cult in its present form began remains pretty much a mystery. Some scholars in this field note that Lionza may be a corruption of la onza, the jaguar. Others observe that there was a Spanish woman by the name Maria Lionza in colonial times. But these and other clues have not led anywhere. What is generally agreed on is that the cult probably grew out of a tradition of the Caquetio Indians that the countryside was once ruled by a female nature spirit who protected the fish of the waters and the animals of the land. Several versions of this myth exist, including the following:

Before the Spanish conquest, a chieftain of the Caquetio people in the region of Nirgua (Yaracuy) had a beautiful daughter. This girl had very light-colored eyes, which marked her as a wife of the great anaconda snake which ruled the watery domains. The people wanted her to be killed, but the chief refused. A time came when she reached puberty, and her father was preparing a purification ceremony that would completely release her from the anaconda and other water spirits. Twenty-two Caquetio warriors were assigned to watch out for her safety.

But one day when all of the guards were asleep, the girl slipped out of her house and wandered to the edge of the lake. Now, she had never seen her face in a mirror, and she was fascinated to see it reflected in the water. The face she saw was beautiful, but her eyes resembled two very deep caves. The great anaconda who ruled the lake came to the surface and seized her, pulling her down, thrashing his tail about wildly. The thrashing tail sent floodwaters running over the land where the people lived, and drowned them or drove them away.

But the great anaconda was punished for his crime of stealing the girl. He swelled up till he filled the entire lake, and at last he burst and died. The chief's daughter became mistress of the lake and protector of the fishes. Later, her power extended over the forests and mountains, and she became the protector of creatures of the land.

Some of the attributes of this Indian nature spirit appear to have been inherited by the queen-mother-goddess Maria Lionza.

THREE AFRO-VENEZUELAN SONGS

Love Song

I have no sister,
I have no cousin,
I have a wound,
Maria, that is hurting me.

Last evening
When they thought I was dead,
With the light of your eyes
They brought me back to life.

Devotional

Jesus Christ be with me,
The mother who brought him into the world,
And the holy host
And the cross where he died.

Black was Santa Efigenia
The mother of San Benito;
Black were the three nails
With which Christ was nailed.

Carnival Song

From Barlovento to Caracas,
From the hacienda to the coconut grove,
We come prepared
For this beautiful festival.

From La Musica Afrovenezolana, *by Luis Felipe Ramon y Rivera, Caracas,
Universidad Central de Venezuela, 1971.*

They are the Negroes, they are the Negroes,
The Negroes from Cangalí
Who are coming to play
With the girls here.

BRAZIL: THE PALMARES STORY

The escape of slaves from the plantations of Surinam and the establishment of jungle settlements out of reach of the colonists had its
counterpart in seventeenth-century Brazil. Over a period of years thousands of blacks in Brazil fled from slavery into the forested wilderness,
where they collected in hamlets and villages, called quilombos, and set
about living as free people. The quilombos were scattered across a
wide expanse of territory, some of them remote from one another, and
many of them so isolated that their very existence was not known until
the following century, or even later. Numerous quilombos came into
being in the interior of what is now the state of Alagoas in northeastern
Brazil, a heavily forested area that gave the escapees a good measure of
security from pursuit and harassment until, in time, official government expeditionary forces were sent against them. Establishing a way
of life in the wilderness was difficult at best. But many of the refugees,
apparently, were first-generation Africans who had recollections of
comparable environments across the Atlantic, and old techniques were
employed in clearing land and growing food. Even so, the deprivations
were considerable, and the forest dwellers frequently sent raiding expeditions against the haciendas for food, tools and firearms. As in the
Dutch colony of Surinam, the raiding parties sometimes liberated
slaves from the haciendas and brought back girls and women for
wives. The depredations against the colonists caused considerable anxiety and concern among the whites.

In the first half of the century, perhaps as early as 1630 or 1640, the
separate quilombos in Alagoas began to merge into a political entity
that some historians have referred to as a kingdom, others as a confederation or republic. Collectively the settlements in the region were

---

*This account of Palamares is based on information from a number of sources,
but primarily from* The Negro in Brazil *by Arthur Ramos (translated from the
Portuguese by Richard Pattee), Washington, Associated Publishers, 1951, and
from* Brazil: People and Institutions, *by T. Lynn Smith, Baton Rouge, Louisiana State University Press, 1946.*

called Palmares, after the dense stands of palms that surrounded them. What was called Palmares in a generic sense was probably a loose confederation of quilombos, some larger and stronger than others, that functioned separately except in time of crisis. There is ample evidence that numbers of quilombos joined forces to oppose various expeditions sent against them by the Dutch and Portuguese. The fortunes of the quilombos ebbed and flowed. Old settlements were abandoned and new ones established. One quilombo, identified as New Palmares by chroniclers of the time, was said to have a long central street, two hundred twenty houses, fifteen hundred residents, a council building and a church. A quilombo called Cerca Real do Macaco, the capital of one group of settlements, was described by an unidentified chronicler as containing fifteen hundred houses within a high stockade of poles tipped with iron, and as being ruled by a king or chief by the name of Ganga Zumba, meaning Great Master. One of Ganga Zumba's nephews was Zambi, who played a central role in the final resistance against the Portuguese toward the end of the century.

According to available records, the Dutch—in temporary control of this region of Brazil—sent several military expeditions into the hinterland in the 1640s to destroy Palmares and disperse its population. Some of the quilombos were in fact attacked and burned, but their populations retired into the countryside and subsequently made new settlements. Following the expulsion of the Dutch from Brazil, frequent Portuguese expeditions sought to do what the Dutch had failed to accomplish. Quilombos were destroyed and their populations pursued, but the Portuguese seemed unable to achieve a military resolution. Finally the Portuguese governor, Pedro de Almeida, chose a peaceful course. He made peace with Palmares, the main terms being that the blacks would give up their arms in exchange for Almeida's promise of protection. Two emissaries of Ganga Zumba went to Recife and formalized the treaty.

But among the people of Palmares there were many who did not trust Portuguese intentions, and foremost in this group was Zambi, Ganga Zumba's nephew.[1] Zambi gathered a force, revolted against Ganga Zumba, killed him and took over the kingship. He then renewed hostilities against the Portuguese and for the next ten years things were much as before. In 1687 an expedition of bandeiras—Indian fighters—was sent against Palmares. The bandeiras located Zambi's

---

1. *In his book,* Brazil: People and Institutions, *T. Lynn Smith, in speaking of the Bantu cults of Brazil, says: "The great deity of Angola, Zambi or Nzambi, still lives in the macumbas in and about Rio de Janeiro under the names Zambi, Ganga Zumba and Gana Zona." Accordingly, if the statement is correct in all respects, Ganga Zumba and Zambi are one and the same. Ganga, or Nganga, is a Bantu word signifying doctor, conjuror or priest. And Zambi, or Nzambi, is a term heard throughout a large part of Central Africa to designate the supreme deity. It may properly be wondered at that any person, even a king, in Palmares would call himself Zambi. The chances are that the chronicler who recorded the names of the two Palmares leaders confused them with the names of the supreme deity who doubtless was frequently mentioned by the Bantu of that time in Brazil.*

quilombo but found it to be virtually impregnable. On their return home they described it as being more than a mile in circumference and surrounded by three palisades. Three armies totalling seven thousand men were then sent from Pernambuco, Alagoas and São Paulo to reduce the quilombo. The siege and fighting that followed lasted several months. When at last the beleaguered quilombo fell (in the year 1695 according to some records, in 1697 according to others) Zambi and his principal officers committed suicide by leaping from a high cliff. This event marked the effective end of Palmares, which had begun its life as a sanctuary for escaped slaves. But many other quilombos survive to this day in Amazonas, Maranhão and other frontier regions of Brazil.

AFRICAN RELIGIOUS SURVIVALS IN BRAZIL

The African religious impact on Brazilian life is evident on every side, particularly in Bahia, Rio de Janeiro and its environs, and Alagoas, but also in the interior—wherever, in fact, Afro-Brazilians lived in sufficient numbers to keep their traditions alive. While Brazil is overwhelmingly Catholic, this has in no way been an impediment to the survival of African religious beliefs. African religious traditions have permeated the Brazilian social scene to the extent that many whites pay respect to the African deities and seek the advice of Afro-Brazilian diviners and prophets. Africanisms have infiltrated rituals that are nominally Catholic; Christian saints have taken on at least some of the personalities and characteristics of African deities; and African concepts of the supernatural world have blended with Portuguese beliefs. As Arthur Ramos, writing in the 1930s, put it, "We [Brazilians] still live under the full domination of a magical world. . . . The medicine man, the fetisheer, has among our populations a prestige considerably greater than the directors of our destinies—it is necessary to have the courage to confess it. . . . The ebo [sacrifice] is an institution. The Negro carnival is our great festival."[1]

Within the numerous African and African-influenced cults in Brazil are to be found religious beliefs and practices from the Sudan, the Guinea Coast and Central Africa. There are the Gêge, whose rites are inherited from Dahomey; the Ketu, drawing on Yoruba traditions; the 'Jesha, also of Yoruba derivation, named after a still-extant Yoruba social-political organization; and the Congo-Angola cults which incorporate into their rites religious traditions from western Central Africa.

1. Ramos, ibid.

Nupe and other Sudanic religious survivals have been absorbed into the Ketu cycle of rituals, a not illogical phenomenon inasmuch as the Yoruba and Nupe live close to each other in Africa, and have intertwined histories. In addition, there are the Caboclo cults whose pantheons include deities of New World origin, gods with Indian or Portuguese names. Rituals of the Caboclo groups are compounded out of magico-religious elements gathered from many sources. There are also numerous hybrid, nominally Christian cults which have within them, perhaps in disguised form, concepts and rites of African beginnings; and still others within which African traditions are blended with spiritualism.

Melville and Frances Herskovits wrote of the various cult centers: "Those who by reason of traditional [African] conservatism, or some turn of good or ill fortune, hold to the belief that ancestral deities are active in the affairs of men, become associated with cult centers called condomblés, where African or African-like worship is carried on. These cult centers are so numerous, and their ceremonies so renowned throughout Brazil, that Bahia is often spoken of as 'the Rome of the Africanos.' In some of the condomblé houses, indeed, rituals are carried on with such nicety of African detail that they reproduce the worship of the areas of Africa which the Bahians identify as their 'nations.'"[2]

According to the Herskovitses:

"Worship in all these groups is based on the world-view that the destiny of the Universe is in the hands of deities that are everywhere the same, though the names they bear vary from region to region and from people to people according to the language that is spoken. The destiny of man, who is but a modest part of this Universe, is ruled by the same gods, but man enjoys the intercession of a hierarchy of ancestral dead, who in death as in life continue to be preoccupied with the well-being of the family to which they belong. Indeed, the gods appear to have given the ancient dead a certain autonomy in regulating the moral code of their descendants in the interest of human well-being, though they have not abrogated their own powers to regulate the conduct of the living members of each family. On the contrary, each individual has his or her god as a personal spirit.

"Man is not, however, a passive agent in relation to his destiny, for through divination he can discover the secrets of that destiny, and learn how to cause it to favor his ventures, his well-being, and his status in the group among which he lives. Thus the outcome of a journey, a marriage, a business undertaking may be threatened by the active disapproval or the indifference of his particular deity, or another of the powerful gods, or of the ancestors. The diviner will reveal whether

2. *Melville, J. and Frances S. Herskovits, "Afro-Bahian Religious Songs," article accompanying a record album by the same title, Washington, Music Division of the Library of Congress, 1947.*

these can be undertaken with safety and success by some act of propitiation of any of these forces to enlist active and favorable cooperation, and he will name the form this propitiation is to take.

"Initiation into the cult, the ultimate of several possible degrees of participation, demands a period of retreat in the cult-center for from more than a year for the intransigently orthodox Gêge to from four to six months for the Ketu and 'Jesha and Angola. It is only a matter of weeks, or even one week, for the Caboclo groups, though as the individual Caboclo center becomes more established, and the reputation of its cult-head grows, the term of initiation is extended, and many features of training are borrowed from the more orthodox 'African' cults.

"In each cult-group, mastery of esoteric knowledge is achieved over many years. The proverb, 'One climbs a ladder rung by rung,' is heard often in this connection. But whether extended training is given under initiation rites, in cult language, in cult song repertory, or in dancing, and whether the many complex rites that mark successive stages between the symbolic death and rebirth as a vehicle of a god are performed, certain 'preparation' is mandatory. The head must be ritually dedicated to the god so that he may descend there and take 'possession' of his devotee. She will have a new name, and for seven years will be known as *yawo*, 'bride,' or young initiate of the god. She will know the colors of her god, the foods he favors and abhors, and certain rules governing sexual continence in relation to this worship. She will understand the place of her god in the hierarchy of deities, and learn his emblems, his functions, and his powers. The Catholic saint with whom each god is equated in the thinking of all cult worshipers will be her special saint, and she will have chromolithographs of this saint at home. The tasks that may be performed by male gods and by female gods, the etiquette towards senior initiates, towards cult officials and the cult-head will all be taught her.

"Above all, however short her training, and how lacking in the valued mystical preparation which characterizes the orthodox cult houses, the initiate will know the drum rhythms of the god who rules the house she is associated with, and especially the rhythms of her own god that demand possession of her. With this will go an appreciable repertory of songs for all the gods, though not necessarily the more esoteric ones. For it is the rhythms identified with each god, and the songs that praise him that are a primary instrument in summoning him and enlisting his favors. It can well be said that in these cults no worship of the gods is possible without the rhythms that call and speak for the god, and the accompanying songs."[3]

Yoruba deities worshipped in Brazil include the following, all of them major gods of the Nigerian pantheon:

Olorun, the sky god
Orisha-Nla, or Obatala, shaper of human beings

---

3. *Herskovits and Herskovits*, ibid.

Shango, deity of the thunderbolt
Eshu, also called Legba, orisha of chance, Olorun's linguist and
    messenger
Ogun, deity of the forge, war and hunting
Yemoja (Yemanja in Brazil), a water deity
Oshun, a river goddess
Ochosi, patron of hunters
Ifa, a divining deity
Sonponno (Shapanan in Brazil), orisha of smallpox
Ibeji, protector of twins

Among the Bantu deities are Nzambi (or Zambi) Ampungu (or Mpun-
gu), a male sky god of the Bakongo, also known as Ganga Zumba and
Gana Zona; and Lemba.

Elements of African speech have survived strongly in Brazil, primarily in religious songs and rituals, and numerous African words have
become part of the country's language. Yoruba is perhaps the best preserved of the African languages, particularly within the cult setting,
but Fon (Dahomean) and dialects of Bantu from the lower Zaire (Congo) River region also persevere. Although fluency in the use of these
tongues is limited to a small number of cult priests and other officials,
many persons are familiar with elements of these languages that appear in songs.

KETU CEREMONY HONORING
THE DEITY YANSAN

Following is a typical Ketu ceremony for the Nago (Yoruba) goddess
Yansan, deity of the wind, as seen by Melville and Frances Herskovits[1]
in the early 1940s:

[Yansan's] metal is burnished copper, and her color flame. She is
equated with "Santa Barbara." Many gods accompany her. She is fiery,
a warrior-goddess, lover of many of the gods. Before dusk all the seats
are filled, and outside many persons are crowded about the open windows. Later more will join them to listen to the singing and to hear the
drumming. Inside, chairs are set out for distinguished visitors. At all
such rites it is good form to send invitations to the ranking cult-houses,
and friendly houses send representative delegations, which on important occasions, at prominent houses, will include the cult-heads themselves. They occupy these reserved places of honor, which are to one
side of the drums, the focus of the ceremony, for the gods come to
dance before the drums.

As night approaches, and the private rites of propitiating the
trickster-god, Eshu, guardian of roads and entrances, are completed,
the cult-head, gong in hand, takes his seat on a chair or a low stool beside the drums and begins the *shiré*, the opening of the "play" wherein

---

1. *From Herskovits and Herskovits*, ibid.

three songs are sung for each deity. There is some deviation in detail from "nation" to "nation" in this sequence, but at a Ketu cult-center the following can be taken as typical. First Ogun, god of metal and of war, who "opens the way," is sung for; then Oshossi, god of the hunt, and principal god of this particular house. Next, songs for Osain, god of leaves and healing, are heard; then for Oshunmare, the serpent-god of the rainbow; for Omolu, god of the earth, who is sometimes followed by Oba Oluwaye, his old father. Next in the sequence are songs for the "queens"—the female deities—Nana, the oldest, and mother of the earth-god, Omolu; Yemanja, goddess of the sea; Oshun, goddess of fresh water; Yansan, Oba and Eowa, the three warrior-goddesses. Then Shango, the god of thunder, and last of all, Oshala, father of the gods, are summoned with songs sacred to them.

By the time this cycle has ended, several possessions may have taken place among the dancers; and other possessions follow rapidly as the drums, unaccompanied, play the *adahun,* the rhythm that compels possession, "The voice you have got to say 'yes' to." In less than a minute the dancers, each in turn, sway to the rhythm, or spin about, then right themselves, their fixed, rigid facial expressions showing that their gods have now "descended" to their heads, as this possession experience is phrased.

The possessed initiates are then led out of the dancing space, where they will be robed as gods. They back out, and only turn when they have crossed the threshold that separates the dancing floor from the next room, since a god may not turn his back on the drums. During the interlude, any visiting initiate of another "nation" who has joined in the circle dance, now comes forward to hear the "voice" of her god expressed in the rhythms of her own "nation." Then, under possession, she too will be robed for her god in one of the appropriate costumes of the center giving the dance.

After perhaps an interval of half an hour, the best drummers assume places at the drums, while the cult-head, or the principal drummer takes over the gong. Confetti is passed around, and sometimes flowers. Then the march that heralds the coming of the gods begins. The spectators stand as they sing. The timing is handled with professional sureness of dramatic effect. Several times the song is repeated. Then in single file the gods enter.

Ogun, in green, as a male god, wears lace-edged pantalettes to the ankles under a short wide skirt, a bodice, and a cap as of an African prince. He carries a dagger. There may be several initiates for Ogun, and these follow by order of seniority of initiation. Next comes Oshossi in turquoise blue, horse's switch in one hand, and miniature bow and arrow in the other. Then Osain, god of leaves, with a raffia crown, Oshunmare the rainbow- and Omolu the earth-god, all with elaborate raffia woven headdress, the latter wearing one that completely covers his head and face with strands of raffia hanging thick to his waist. The "queens" are splendid—white and pale blue silk for Nana and Yemanja, respectively; gold for Oshun; Oba and Eowa in paler colors; crimson for Yansan. Their costumes, as that of Shango, god of thunder, follow the chromolithographs of the saints of the Church with whom they are identified. Oshala, aged and stooping, is in white, with a cloth falling over his head, silver staff surmounted by a dove in hand. Three times the gods circle the dancing space, while the confetti is thrown at them and, since it is Yansan's day, the flowers at Yansan. The ritual cries for the individual gods are shouted, and the gods step out of line to embrace the cult-head, and any one in the audience they select to honor.

Then the gods, beginning with Ogun, come forward to dance before the drums. Here is a display of such skill as gives fame to a cult-house. Again three songs are sung for each god—though some spirits beg the cult-head to allow them more and would dance interminably if not stopped—and then there is singing and dancing that specifically honors the god whose day it is. Later, still other deities, those of the visitors whose gods are not among the ones worshiped in the center giving the dance, are given their turn. And when, in the early hours of the morning, the gods no longer show by their tension a further need to dance, the rite comes quietly to a close.

SOME BRAZILIAN CULT SONGS
TO YORUBA DEITIES

Songs to Eshu

Ibarabo-o mojuba	O great one, I pay obeisance,
Iba koshe omo deko	A young child does not confront
Elegbara	The powerful one;
Omojuba	I pay obeisance
Elegba Eshu lona	To Elegba Eshu, who is on the road.

* * *

Odara kolori onejo	The good one, who has no head for dancing,
Sho-sho-sho abe	The stubborn knife
Kolori eni-ijo	Has no head for dancing.

* * *

Eshu tiriri	Eshu the awesome,
Bara abebe	O powerful knife!
Tiriri lona	The awesome one, on the road.

From Herskovits and Herskovits, ibid.

Songs to Oshosi

Odire-e odire	The family, the family,
Arere bare-o	The worthy and friendly,
Bare are-o	All the relations,
Arole (g)barajo	The head of the house gathers them together.

* * *

Oke	He calls,
Okeke ode	He calls like a hunter,
Oke	He calls.

* * *

Agogo olese	the bells on his feet,
Olesa, elese kuta	Feet, feet of stone.

Songs to Osain

Pelebe mi tobe-o	Flat is my knife,
Pelebe mi tobe-o	Flat is my knife,
Obe pelebe	The knife is flat;
Aku pelebe	Dull it is flat,
Ku aku pelebe	Dull or not it is flat.

* * *

Ere kanbi oje	Ere makes a noise like a bullroarer,
Arere ife-i	The sound of the whistle
E weti-ayo	Will go into his ears beseechingly.

* * *

Irere ijeje	The kindness of the seventh day,
Bakuroba	Never to leave the king,
Ibaribaba	The worshiper of the father,
Barisha	The worshiper of the god,
Ibari yeye	The worshiper of the savior,
Ibaba yeye	The father savior;
Mama aro	Without a hearth,
Afi kawa da she	We ourselves make ourselves
Omo 'Batala	Children of Obatala.

Songs to Yemoja

Ba uba-a	If we do not meet her,
Ba uba-a	If we do not meet her,
A woyo	Though we look for her long,
Sarele	We shall hasten to humble ourselves
Yewashe	Before our mother the lawgiver.

* * *

Awade	We have arrived,
Iyade lode	Our mother is outside.
Ba uba	Should we not meet her?

* * *

Onibo to ile	One who nourishes and protects the house
Aya onibo to ile	The wife of one who protects the house
Onibo iyawa	One who nourishes, the queen
Iya nibo ile	The mother who nourishes the household.

Songs to Oshun

Barewa lele	The beautiful one emerges,
Umale	The spirit-god,
Arele umawo	One of the family reincarnated.

* * *

Alabe Oshun	Honor to the knife of Oshun,
Oshun mirere-o	My good Oshun.

MELODY OF A BRAZILIAN CULT SONG

To the Yoruba Deity Oshun: 160

Transcribed by Alan P. Merriam. This notation appeared in Vol. I, No. 4 of
the African Music Society Journal. It is reprinted here by permission of Dr.
Merriam.

A CULT FESTIVAL, AS REPORTED IN THE PRESS

A news item about a festival for a Nago (Yoruba) deity, headlined, "Beach Blast Hails Goddess in Rio," and datelined Rio de Janeiro, December 31 (1974), had this to say about the event:

RIO DE JANEIRO, Dec. 31—Tens of thousands of white-robed voodoo believers jammed onto the famous Copacabana and Ipanema beaches tonight for the traditional New Year's Eve homage to Iemanja [Yemoja], the mystical goddess of the sea.

Brazilian followers of the voodoo cult called Umbanda—most of whom also are Roman Catholics—consider Iemanja equal in religious significance to the Virgin Mary.

Swarms of Rio residents and small bands of photo-snapping foreign tourists trudged through the sand for a closer look, as the spirit-worshipers threw flowers, small handmade boats and bottles of cachaca—a potent Brazilian rum—into the ocean as offerings to the allegedly influential voodoo goddess.

The cultists also tossed perfume, mirrors, talcum powder and bars of scented soap onto the waves, to appeal to Iemanja's reputed feminine vanity.

Legend says that if the gifts float out to sea, Iemanja has looked with favor upon the faithful and will grant a prosperous new year. If the offerings come back, it means she is displeased.

Because of the rough surf along Copacabana and Ipanema beaches, the New Year's Eve spirit offerings usually wash back on shore. Umbanda followers here conveniently overlook this drawback, however, and simply assume that Iemanja is on their side. . . .

A Rio Catholic priest and scholar, the Rev. Raymundo Cintra, calculates that more Brazilians actively practice voodoo than go regularly to Mass.

Nilo Maia, a self-styled "pai-de-santo" or Umbanda priest, told a visitor to the spot he had staked out in Copacabana for the Iemanja festivities, "I believe Umbanda will be Brazil's national religion in a few years."

The maker of a cheap brand of cachaca called Praianinha put out commercials on Rio radio stations urging people to buy its brew for Iemanja. "We respectfully salute the beliefs of 30 million Brazilians." the Praianinha spots declared.

The head of the Umbanda Spirit Congregation of Brazil, Tancredo Silva, warned, though, that too much cachaca could "distort the significance" of the Iemanja ceremony. He said he hoped the traditional beach ritual would not degenerate into an all-night drinking party. . . .

Most of those who paid homage to Iemanja were members of neighborhood Umbanda clubs which meet regularly throughout the year. Garbed in white robes and wearing symbolic beads and charms around their necks, they formed small groups in the sand, lit candles, smoked cigars, drank cachaca, beat drums, chanted spirit prayers and waited for midnight to begin the sea goddess ceremony.

The cultists included men, women and children of all races and income levels.[1]

---

1. The Washington Post, *Jan. 1, 1974.*

SOME WORDS OF AFRICAN ORIGIN
IN BRAZILIAN-PORTUGUESE SPEECH

caçamba—a bucket in a well
canga—a pouch or wallet
dengo—affected, presumptuous
cafuné—the gesture of snapping one's fingernail
        on the head of another person
lubambo—a fracas or plot
mulambo—a rag or cloth
caçula—youngest son
quitute—a dainty confection
mandinga—sorcery or witchcraft
muleque—young Negro (or by extension, a blackguard)
camondongo—a mouse
muganga—a grimace or contortion
cafajeste—a lowly person, one with bad manners
quibebe—paste of an edible gourd
quengo—a container made of half of a coconut shell
batuque—a Negro dance
banzo—melancholy, nostalgia
mucambo—a hut
bangue—a sugar canal, a sugar plantation, or a litter
bozo—a dice game
bunda—buttocks
zumbi—a night goblin
vatapa—paste made of manioc flour
banze—a commotion
mucama—a favored slave girl employed in the master's house
quindim—amorous longing, also a sweetmeat
catinga—a bad smell
mugunza—a dish made of corn and milk
malungo—comrade
birimbau—a low or despicable person
tanga—a slave garment worn from the waist to the knees
cachimbo—smoking pipe
candomblé—African religious rite

THE MAN WHO TOOK A WATER MOTHER FOR HIS BRIDE

The mãe d'agua, or water mother, is a familiar character in the beliefs of Afro-Brazilians. The water mother is a denizen of lakes
and rivers, in some tales malevolent, in others benign. In this story the water mother is
taken as a bride by a farmer on his promise
that he will never ridicule her for not being
human, a theme that is widely known in
Africa, Asia and Europe. For a West African
comparison, see Appendix XIII, pp. 592–95.

There was a poor country man named Domingos living alone in his
cabin not far from the edge of a certain river. He had no family whatever, and as for his garden, it barely produced enough to keep him alive.
No matter how he cared for his corn, it did not flourish. Other farmers
who lived near Domingos were also poor and wretched, but Domingos
was the most unlucky of them all.

One morning Domingos went to his corn to take a few ears to eat. As
he went from one stalk to another he noticed that some of the ears had
already been picked, and he wondered who had been heartless enough
to take the food from his mouth. The next day he went again to the field
and saw that more ears had been picked. Anger swelled in his breast,
and he swore to catch the thief and punish him. So that night he took
his cane knife and went out and hid in his cornfield at a place where he
could see to all sides. He put grass and straw over him so that he would
be invisible. He waited, while the night grew long and the moon
moved across the sky. Sleep was coming over him. His eyes began to
close. Then, on the side of the field near the river, there was the rustle
of someone walking through the cornstalks. Now he was awake. He
clutched his knife, thinking, "I will surely kill the one who is coming
to rob me." He heard the person approaching. He heard the sound of
an ear being broken from its stalk. He heard another ear being taken.
He saw the shadow of a person. He saw the person, and he left his hiding place and ran forward. What he found surprised him, for the one
taking his corn was a water woman who lived with others of her kind
in the depths of the river. He seized her, shouting and threatening
harm, but he did not strike the water mother. The moon was shining
brightly and he saw her beauty. He said, "Why do you steal the food
that barely keeps me alive?" She answered, "I was hungry, I meant you
no harm." He said, "I should punish you." But she answered, "Let me
go. I will return to the river. Henceforth I will go elsewhere for food."

Extracted from The Masters and the Slaves, *by Gilberto Freyre, New York, Alfred A. Knopf, 1946.*

Domingos' heart softened. It was warmed by the water woman's voice and her appearance. He said, "Why should I let you go?" She answered, "How would it benefit you to keep me?" And Domingos said, "Why, if I kept you I would not be alone. I would have a wife like anyone else." She said, "It is not possible. When has a water person ever married with a land person?"

But Domingos was captivated by her voice and her beauty. He asked her to remain. He supplicated her. At last, moved by the warmness of his entreaties, the water woman said: "We have been told by the old people that those who live on land and in the water cannot mix. Once before it happened that a young water woman was taken as a wife by a land person. At first all went well. But after a while the man began to abuse her. He did not treat her as well as in the beginning. And as time passed he began to ridicule her origins. He said with contempt, 'What can I expect from you, since you are a mere water woman?' And he spoke this way about her among the people of the village. And one night he beat her, saying, 'Water woman! What are you doing living in my house among humans?' She departed from his house then, she returned to the river. The water people said, 'It has always been this way. We must never try to live with the land people.' "

Domingos answered her, saying: "In my eyes you are not a water woman. You are only a woman. What do I care where you come from? Stay here with me, live in my house with me." And so the water woman stayed. She went to his house with him. She became his wife. And because of that, Domingos' fortunes changed. The corn in his field grew large ears. His goats and cattle multiplied. Other people who lived nearby began to praise Domingos for his industry. Whereas once he had been too poor to listen to, now they listened respectfully when he spoke, because he was a man of substance. Domingos built a new house. People came to him for help when they were in need. He had much surplus corn hanging from the branches of the large tree that shaded his roof. But Domingos never stopped to think about where his good fortune came from. He became arrogant. And one evening after he had been drinking to excess he began to abuse his wife. He said, "Our children are bad-mannered. Why have you set them such a bad example?" He said, "Why is it that while I work hard in the field you do nothing?" He said, "The people who live nearby, they say bad things about you. Why are you so careless in your ways?" Domingos went on this way, accusing her and abusing her, but she did not reply to him. And her silence angered Domingos still more. He said, "You are a sullen woman. Why don't you speak when you are spoken to?" Still his wife said nothing. And at last Domingos shouted at her, "Mãe d'agua! Water woman! You who came out of the river!"

When she heard these words, the water woman arose from where she was sitting. She went out the door of the cabin. Domingos followed her, shouting curses at the water people. But something happened to Domingos. He found that he could not walk, for his feet were rooted to the ground. He saw his wife go toward the river. One by one his children came from the house and followed their mother. When she reached the river's edge the woman went into the water and disappeared. Her children entered the water and disappeared. Domingos saw his goats and cattle going toward the river. One by one his goats entered the water. One by one his cattle entered the water. They descended. They were seen no more. Domingos cried out. He tried to follow, but he could not move from where he stood. Then he saw the corn ears that hung in his large tree begin to move. One by one the ears moved through the air as though they were flying. They went to the river. They went into the water and disappeared. And after that, Domingos' house and everything that was in it moved toward the river. Domingos called out, "My house! My house!" But the house went forward and entered the river. The fences Domingos had built to hold his cattle departed. The big tree that had shaded his house departed. The palms that grew all around departed. Everything that had belonged to Domingos departed and followed the water woman into the river. Only then did Domingo's feet become unrooted. He went here, he went there, looking for things that had once belonged to him.

Everything was gone. Domingos had nothing. And he lived to the end of his days as the poorest of all men.

BRAZIL: THE WAY OF BATUCADA

The word Batucada signifies music and dance of the streets, provocative drum rhythms, the samba. By extension it alludes to a class of indigent musicians and aficionados whose lives are devoted to gathering together at night in the back streets of the city, composing songs, and dancing to the sound of tamborines, drums of various kinds, African-style bells and the zanza bumba or *cuíca* (friction drum). To Brazilians

---

The Batucada songs included here are from a large collection recorded in 1941 and 1942 by Melville J. and Frances S. Herskovits in Bahia. The collection is now in the care of the Indiana University Archives of Traditional Music. Texts of the songs were transcribed, then translated into English, by Maria Madeiros, who also prepared background notes on which the above introduction is based. Miss Madeiros' English texts have been altered here and there by this editor to free them from the limitations of verbatim translation, and on occasion certain liberties have been taken to make the meaning more clear. The song texts are used by kind permission of the Indiana University Archives of Traditional Music.

it evokes a picture of people who avoid workaday tasks whenever possible, who sleep away their days and come to life when evening falls, who go endlessly from one lover to another, and who find no place in the mainstream of the city's activities. They are people of a subculture, outcasts in the sense that Gypsies were once relegated to the fringe of society in some countries, often suspected of petty crimes.

But among their own kind, those devoted to the way of Batucada are known for their singing and dancing, the songs they compose and their ability to express deep personal emotions. They are a kind of guild of the dispossessed for whom Batucada means spiritual fulfilment, whose playgrounds are the slum streets, and whose songs speak of the joy of living, of love, of remorse or guilt, of their inner conflicts and desires. Many of the songs heard in the Batucada are tangent statements, with allusions understood by only a few, giving them an esoteric quality that is accentuated in translation. Even so, there is a distinct feeling of poetry, and the singers may justly claim, as one song declares, that "our vagrant is an artist," and, as another states, "I have my worth."

The examples of Batucada songs given here were recorded in Bahia, to which place some of them had made their way from Rio de Janeiro (made evident by references to streets and neighborhoods of that city.)

Voice of the Backstreets

> Samba, voice of the slum,
> Our vagrant is an artist.
> The Batucada that shines
> In those parts of Batista[1]
> While the cuíca screams[2]
> Makes the people cry,
> Wakes up the sleeping,
> Raises up the sick.
> Come to "The Rabbit," [3]
> Listen to us!
>
> Speak, bad cuíca,
> Cabaça[4] and tambourine,
> Which make the glorious Samba!
> When day comes
> The mad throw rocks,
> The priest says mass.

---

1. *Batista: a street.*
2. *Cuíca: friction drum.*
3. *The Rabbit: allusion not understood.*
4. *Cabaça: calabash or gourd, probably a rattle.*

In Batista's Street

I know I am a vagrant, I know.
I know the way I do things.
Wait until day comes.
I know that our group is good.
It is good only to do Batucada.

Heavenly God, what is going to be?
My shoes have holes.
My hat fell down on the sand.
I go away.
I am going to do the Batucada
There in Batista's Street
Where the Samba has its home.

Why Do You Cry?

Sabía sang,
And I remembered
That you are going to sail,
And that you did not say you will come back.
Why do you cry?
I will cry, I will cry, I will cry.

There in slum's hill
Where the Bahia girl lives,
Woman does not ride a horse,
Nor does man look after chickens,
Nor does death get the men,
Nor does tumba[5] get the coconut.
The farm stands without an owner,
And one dies for the good of others.

I Will Reform

I have now changed my mind,
I am going to work,
Give up being a vagrant.
No one can change my mind.
I will. I will reform.

---

5. *Tumba: meaning unknown.*

I will regenerate myself.
I am going to leave the Batucada.
Oh, my God, what a sad destiny!

I will take my coat,
I go to the hill.[6]
In the batuque of my godmother
I will see the Samba
Where he is going to have a good time.

I Will Go Away

I am not going to work,
This word angers me!
I will not go, I am a vagrant.
I would rather die alone.
Oh, que tal, que tal.[7]

I will go away, I will go away
To the city of Lorena.
The vagrants sing the Samba,
I am sorry for the girl.

Playing my cuíca
And (wondering) whether Margarida will give me this pleasure
In the olive garden
Before the flowers bloom

And the bad cuíca,
Tamborine, war box, [8]
The vagrants sing the Samba
And I am sorry for the girl
And for the sadness of the world.

I will go away, I will go away
To the street of Batista
Playing a cabaca,
Playing my cuíca.

Playing my cuíca,
Everyone jumps.
I will call my girl
By the sound of the tamborine.

---

6. *The hill: the slum area.*
7. *Untranslated from the original.*
8. *War box: snare drum.*

Unfortunate Vagrant

Woman, one begs only to God,
Only to God, honey, to no one else.
I love a woman
And the tenderness she gives me.

Unfortunate vagrant,
In this world he shall not love.
Working for the future,
He does not prosper.

My God,
If the world comes to an end,
I have a woman
And she is going to leave me.

I Went to the Hill

I went to the hill
To enjoy the Batucada.
I went to the hill
To enjoy the Batucada.

When I arrived there
The group was animated.
They promptly gave me the tamborine
And I stayed on the hill
Until daybreak.
The day was breaking
When the Samba ended.
And those poor people
Cried when the Samba ended.

Where I Met You

It was in the wheeling of the Samba
That I met you.
Now you want to reject me,
But if you want to go away you can.
Later on
You will cry.
I will not miss you.
I have already sworn
Never again to take a woman from the Samba.

I Go to Lisbon

To love, to love as much as I love you!
I don't want to love anyone else.
Who gives you more than I give?
You can be sure you won't find anyone else.

I go away, I go to the city of Lisbon.
The vagrants sing the Samba
And the girls are nice.
I go away, I go away,
I've said that I will go.
I will take my woman with me,
Because she is my love.

The Sun Is Setting

There on the hill
The sun is setting.
There goes my sweetheart on the hill.
There goes the sun.
In God's name I swear
That these things make me angry.
When I am singing Samba,
The only thing I know is the Batucada.

You Want to Break Me

You gave me everything
Freely, without conditions.
Now you tell me
You like me very much.
Now, woman,
You want to break me up.

Sad Destiny (FRAGMENT)

I am going to leave the Batucada.
But, my God!
What a sad destiny!
It is killing me!

AFRO-AMERICAN LORE, ORAL LITERATURE
AND FOLK MUSIC IN THE UNITED STATES

It is amply obvious that African traditions have survived in the United States as they have almost everywhere that black communities are found. Some elements of African beginnings are conspicuous, some disguised or submerged; some are mere fragments of the originals, some overlaid with other traditions, some intricately interwoven with traditions and beliefs that came to the New World from Europe; and there are elements of the African inheritance that are more conceptual or attitudinal than visible.

We know that numerous tales associated with slave life or later plantation experiences came from Africa or were adaptations of African narrations; that U.S. Negro secular and religious music, while created under the influence of a variety of traditions, contain some characteristics that are clearly African; and that certain traditional African approaches to storytelling and music-making survive to the present day. There are remnants of African vocabulary and speech patterns, African work patterns, African social ways and manners, and African religious concepts and burial customs. But these elements are not found everywhere in the black community (or communities), and where they are found the proportions vary. What we loosely—and, surely, inadequately—term Negro or black culture contains a considerable inheritance from British, French and Spanish traditions, modified by contacts with other minorities and by social and historical experiences in the New World environment. Afro-American culture in the United States, however, is not African culture overlaid with a Euro-American veneer, nor is it a simple aggregate of African and European traits. It is a blend of traditions, ideas, concepts and attitudes on which American Negroes have drawn throughout their experiences in the Western Hemisphere. Afro-American culture in North America is as surely a product created on this side of the Atlantic as the Hispanic-American culture of the Southwest.

The Question of Survivals

The subject of the extent of African story survivals in the United States continues to be of great interest to many anthropologists and folklorists. One folklorist, Richard M. Dorson, tells of playing a series of recorded folk tales to a specialist in this field, who commented, "Those are some remarkable African tales." Later the recordings were played to another specialist who said, "Those are some remarkable European tales."[1] Dorson's point was that many U.S. Negro tales with counterparts in Africa are also well known in Europe, and that one must be wary of ascribing either African or European origins for them. What has to be considered, however, is not merely the classified story type or motif, but the specific use that has been made of it. Though its theme or plot may be common to Europe, Asia and Africa, a tale told in the Americas nevertheless may reveal its route to the New World by the clothes in which it is dressed. The classification of a theme or motif by no means reveals everything. There are some stories which, though they have counterparts in Europe, reflect African influence by their manner of telling, their characters, their structure, their imagery or explicit allusions. There are others whose inner characteristics point to European origin even though their themes are familiar elsewhere. As noted earlier, the Appendixes of this book contain African versions of a number of tales, legends or traditions extant among Negroes in the

1. American Negro Folktales, *by Richard M. Dorson. Greenwich, Connecticut, Fawcett, 1965.*

Western Hemisphere. They are not intended to stress the African connection above the European, but merely to demonstrate the fact of the connection.

Negro folk music in the United States also has been subjected to intensive scrutiny to determine the extent of its debt to Africa or to Europe. Negro spirituals, worksongs, blues, ballads and other forms have characteristics which distinguish them from the folk music of Africa and Europe, not only in their musical content but in their lyrical content as well, even though certain African and European elements may be recognized. The Africanist tends to take particular note of the African elements, while the Europeanist stresses elements that are recognizably European. But what we have, when all this has been accomplished, is a complex body of musical and musico-literary forms resulting from a quiet, unconscious blending process. Some rhythmic patterns may be suggestive of rhythms heard in the Caribbean or in Africa; certain musical and lyrical phrases, and certain themes or images, may echo others of English, Irish or Scottish tradition. But seen in its total context, U.S. Negro folk music is a separate and unique tradition developed out of diverse elements on the North American mainland.

With the civil rights movement in the 1950s there was in some quarters an ideological imperative to demonstrate that African survivals were enormously significant in American Negro life; and that, moreover, American blacks had a basically *different* culture characterized by inheritance, by a distinct New World experience, and even by genetic factors. Connections with Africa that not long before had been an embarrassment came to be lauded and valued, feted and, unfortunately, exaggerated. We are now at a stage where the African contribution to American life and culture needs no argument to support it. We can see Afro-American culture as an amalgam, just as the so-called "mainstream" culture is an amalgam. And it is clear that the body of concepts, beliefs, folkways, manners and attitudes pertaining to the black community is more "American" than it is any other single thing—if, indeed, the word American is truly definitive at all as applied to a description of culture. The American Negro with his particular threads of inheritance is as fully a New World cultural type as the white American who traces his philosophical ideas back to ancient Greece and his religious concepts back to the Semitic Middle East.

What, then, do we mean by Negro, or black oral literature in the United States? Simply stated, it is the oral literature shared widely (though not necessarily universally) by American blacks, whatever the origin of its multitudinous components. Generally speaking, it is an oral literature with a special personality, often containing implicit or explicit intellectual or emotional responses to the injustices and inequities inherent in the historic relationship of blacks to the mainstream culture. It contains elements of humor, irony, criticism and poetry that, in a literary sense, are uniquely expressed. It observes, it comments, it narrates. It ranges from humorous nonsense to profound and moving reflections on the human experience. Much of the Negro oral literature is a product of life in the cities, and reflects the struggles—and sometimes the triumphs—of the individual in the midst of a world he never made. But the roots of the literature are in the open fields of the southland, the sharecropped farms, the plantations of slavery and postslavery times, the small southern towns, and the little churches that were a focus of social contact as well as a vital source of emotional enrichment. As we read it today, this oral literature not only tells us much about the past, but also a great deal about the present.

Black, Afro-American or Negro?

In recent years writers, journalists, commentators and the press have tended to conform to the zealous proposition put forward by some that the word Negro is outworn and even opprobrious. Yet among American blacks generally, there is no apparent consensus on this basically ideological choice, and the words black, Negro and Afro-American all appear to be acceptable. These terms are used in this book interchangeably, except where the author finds one preferable to another. For example, to refer to black culture, black traditions, black music or black ideas suggests genetic rather than social forces at work, and the term Negro in these instances seems far more appropriate. The oral literature created and preserved by Afro-Americans will not be increased or diminished in any way by ideological preferences for black over Negro. As the Negro historian W. E. B. Du Bois wrote to a perplexed young man nearly a half century ago:

"You cannot change the name of a thing at will. Names are not merely matters of thought and reason; they are growths and habits. As long as the majority of men mean black or brown folk when they say 'Negro,' so long will Negro be the name of folks brown and black. . . .

"But why seek to change the name? 'Negro' is a fine word. Etymologically and phonetically it is much better and more logical than 'African' or 'colored' or any of the various hyphenated circumlocutions. Of course it is not 'historically' accurate. No name ever was historically accurate: neither 'English,' 'French,' 'German,' 'White,' 'Jew,' 'Nordic' nor 'Anglo-Saxon.' They were all at first nicknames, misnomers, accidents, grown eventually to conventional habits and achieving accuracy because, and simply because, wide and continued usage rendered them accurate. In this sense 'Negro' is quite as accurate, quite as old and quite as definite as any name of any great group of people. . . . If you do not believe in the necessity of such a name, watch the antics of a colored newspaper which has determined in a fit of New Year's Resolutions not to use the word 'Negro'!"

---

1. Crisis *magazine, March, 1928.*

The Matter of Vernacular

A problem that concerns collectors and transcribers of U.S. Negro lore—or that doesn't concern them enough—is the question of how precise and faithful one ought to be in representing the dialect. A majority of the earlier chroniclers of Negro tales and songs saw vernacular and pronunciation as integral to images, ideas and substance. The result was an inordinate stress on pronunciation, and orthography that bordered on the bizarre. Joel Chandler Harris, for example, was wont to have Uncle Remus say, "Brer Rabbit *wuz* goin' home," instead of "was," or "Brer Rabbit *bin* thinkin' 'bout this thing," instead of "been." He and others were likely to write *huzbin* for husband or husban'; *lizzud* for lizard or liza'd; *wut* for what or w'at; *sez* for says; *sezee* for says he; *youer* for you are or you're; *meezles* for measles, and so on. Yet, except in extreme cases, the dialect was not nearly as formidable or peculiar to the ear as it appeared on paper. The speech of whites normally was represented in traditional orthography, even though some of them pronounced various words much the same as did the blacks. A concept of quaintness dominated the transcription or rendering of Negro speech.

Some chroniclers did not limit their excesses to spellings. They devised mispronunciations and grammatical misconstructions of their own and attributed them to their Negro characters. These grotesque usages often overshadowed the content and meaning of stories and dialogues. This is not to imply that a genuine Negro vernacular did not exist, containing words, pronunciations, phrases and imagery not commonly heard in the speech of whites. It means only that the black vernacular (or regional vernaculars) was considerably abused by many chroniclers. Tales were often set down from memory, and memory could play false. The attempt to give the written story the feel imparted by a living narrator sometimes produced exaggerations, or a literary, stereotyped speech. And sometimes creative impulses in the transcriber added something extra.

Without detracting in the slightest from Joel Chandler Harris's enormous contribution to the field of Negro folklore, the question can still be asked: What part of Uncle Remus's dialogues were genuinely his own, and what part was the product of Harris's creative mind and his feel for Negro speech? It is no derogation of Uncle Remus to note that some of his dialogues, tales and pronouncements came from other blacks, and that Harris used the language freely and creatively in making it conform to the style of his narrator par excellence. Harris himself acknowledged that he selected the best variants of particular available tales. His guarantee was only that "each legend comes fresh and direct from the Negroes." Uncle Remus was the spokesman for them all, a literary figure created somewhat larger than life, a public entertainer whose sayings, witticisms and traditional stories were drawn from the common well of oral literature shared by the entire black community. And though Harris may have restructured the idiom here and there to make the dialogues flow, and though he may have imparted unnecessary quaintness to Negro speech from time to time, he unarguably had the feel of the vernacular, a feel that is conspicuously absent among many (though not all) of those who followed along the same trail.

There is of course the question of whether a good story needs to be retold in dialect at all. Stories have been translated from Hausa, Ibo, Yoruba, French, Italian, Russiian and other languages without any notable substantive loss. Wit and humor, except when based on wordplay or subtlety, are translatable, and social values and mores readily negotiate the distance between one language and another. It is difficult to explain, therefore, why a Negro tale or dialogue ought not to be rendered in conventional English, particularly when it is thought of as literature. Yet one recognizes that idiomatic usage, carrying with it fresh imagery and sometimes a near-poetic quality, can stimulate the mind and sharpen attention. Uncle Remus as a narrator figure would have been greatly diminished had he talked like the little white boy to whom he addressed his philosophy and tales. If a chronicler has not attempted to substitute a synthetic language for genuine idiom, and if he has not tortured word spellings to make Negro speech seem quaint, or fallen into the trap of thinking that the sound of the dialect is the essence of the tale, use of the vernacular has a good deal to be said for it. And it has to be faced, in any case, that most documenters of traditional Negro tales have used at least some degree of dialect, and it is on these documenters that one must draw. Indeed, some have done the job so well that the question of whether dialect should or should not have been used does not even come to mind.

THE SITUATION OF THE BLACKS AS SEEN BY NINETEENTH-CENTURY CHRONICLERS

Frederika Bremer's Impressions

Frederika Bremer, a Swedish writer and feminist, made extensive excursions to the cities and outlands of the United States during the years 1849, 1850 and 1851, observing life with the freshness of a chronicler from a

different part of the world. The record of
her travels and observations was published
in a two-volume book, *The Homes of the
New World; Impressions of America*, in
1853. It was a period when pressures against
slavery were mounting in the North, and
when the "peculiar institution," as Abraham
Lincoln referred to it, was being increasingly questioned in the South. It was only one
of the many subjects that interested Frederika Bremer, but the situation of the blacks
made a very strong impression on her. Following are excerpts from *The Homes of the
New World*.

Charleston, April 12th, 1850

. . . .When it began to grow dusk I turned back. I repassed the same
slave village. Fires blazed in the little houses, but every thing was
more silent and stiller than before. I saw a young negro with a good
and handsome countenance, standing thoughtfully under a peach-tree,
leaning against its bole. I accosted him, and asked him of one thing
and another. Another slave came up, and then still another, and the
conversation with them was as follows:

"At what time do you get up in the morning?"

"Before sunrise."

"When do you leave off in the evening?"

"When the sun sets—when it is dark."

"But when do you get time to look after your gardens?"

"We must do that on Sundays or at night, for when we come home
we are so tired that we could drop down."

"How do you get your dinners?"

"We have no dinner! It is all we can do if, while we are working, we
can throw a bit of bread or some corn into us."

"But, my friend," said I, now a little mistrustful, "your appearance
contradicts what you say; for you look in very good condition, and
quite brisk."

"We endeavor to keep ourselves up as well as we can," replied the
man by the tree; "what can we do unless we keep up a good heart. If we
were to let it droop, we should die!"

The others responded to the song of lamentation.

I bade them good-night and went my way, suspecting that all was
not true in the slaves' representation. But still, it *might* be true; it was
true, if not here, yet in other places and under wicked masters; it might
always be true in an institution which gives such irresponsible power
at will; and all its actual and possible misery presented itself to me,
and made me melancholy. The evening was so beautiful, the air so fra-
grant, the roses were all in blossom; nature seemed to be arrayed as a
bride; the heaven was bright; the new moon, with the old moon in her
arms, was bright in the firmament, and the stars came out, clear and
brilliant. The glory of the scene, and that poor, black, enslaved, de-

graded people—they did not at all agree! All my enjoyment was over.

I was glad, however, to have a man like Mr. Poinsett to talk with. And to him I confided, in the evening, my conversation and my thoughts. Mr. Poinsett maintains that the slaves have told me false-hoods. "One can never believe what they say," said he; adding, "that also is one of the evils of slavery. The people are made liars by it. Chil-dren learn from their parents to regard the white people with fear, and to deceive them. They are always suspicious, and endeavor by their complainings to get some advantage. But you may be sure that they have been imposing upon you. The slaves round here have a certain quantity of work set them for the day, and at this time of the year they have for the most part finished it by four or five o'clock in the after-noon. There is commonly kept on every plantation a male or female cook, who prepares the daily dinner at one o'clock. I have one for my people, and I have no doubt but that Mr.——also has one for his peo-ple. It can not be otherwise. And I am certain that you would find it to be so if you would examine into the affair."

Mr. Poinsett does not deny but that abuse and maltreatment of slaves has often occurred and still occurs, but public opinion becomes more and more sternly opposed to it. Some years ago extreme cruelty was practiced against the slaves on a plantation in the neighborhood by an overseer, during the prolonged absence in England of the owner of the plantation. The planters in the neighborhood united, wrote to him, told him that they could not bear it, and requested that the overseer should be removed. And this was done. Mr. P. considers that the system of slavery operates in many cases much more unfavorably on women than on men, and makes them not unfrequently the hardest masters.

* * *

Columbia, South Carolina, May 25th [1850]

One of my pleasures here has been to talk with an old negro called Romeo, who lives in a little house in a garden near, and which said gar-den he takes care of, or rather neglects, according to his pleasure. He is the most good-tempered, merriest old man that any one can imagine, and he has a good deal of natural wit. He was, in the prime of his life, stolen from Africa and brought hither, and he tells stories about that event in the most *naive* manner. I asked him one day what the people in his native land believed respecting life after death! He replied "that the good would go to the God of heaven who made them." "And what of the bad?" asked I. "They go out into the wind," and he blew with his mouth around him on all sides.

* * *

St. Louis, November 8th [1850]

Missouri is a slave state. But it seems at this moment to maintain the institution of slavery rather out of bravado than from any belief in its necessity. It has no products which might not be cultivated by white laborers, as its climate does not belong to the hot South. Missouri also sells its slaves assiduously "down South."

"Are you a Christian?" inquired I from a young handsome mulatto woman who waited on me here.

"No, Missis, I am not."

"Have you not been baptized? Have you not been taught about Christ?"

"Yes, Missis, I have a godmother, a negro woman, who was very religious, and who instructed me."

"Do you not believe what she told you about Christ?"

"Yes, Missis; but I don't *feel* it here, Missis," and she laid her hand on her breast.

"Where were you brought up?"

"A long way from here, up the Missouri, Missis; a long way off!"

"Were your owners good to you?"

"Yes, Missis; they never gave me a bad word."

"Are you married?"

"Yes, Missis; but my husband is a long way off with his master."

"Have you any children?"

"I have had six, Missis, but have not a single one left. Three are dead, and they have sold the other three away from me. When they took from me the last little girl, oh, I believed I never should have got over it! It almost broke my heart!"

And they were so-called Christians who did that! It was not wonderful that she, the negro slave, had a difficulty in *feeling* Christianity, that she could not feel herself a Christian. What a life! Bereaved of husband, children, of all that she had, without any prospect of an independent existence; possessed of nothing on the face of the earth; condemned to toil, toil, toil, without hope of reward or day of rest; why should it be strange if she became stupid or indifferent, nay, even hostile and bitter in her feelings toward those in whose power she is—they who call themselves her protectors, and yet who robbed her of her all? Even of that last little girl, that youngest, dearest, only child!

This pagan institution of slavery leads to transactions so inconsistent, so inhuman, that sometimes in this country, this Christian, liberal America, it is a difficult thing for me to believe them possible, difficult to comprehend how it can be a reality, and not a dream! it is so difficult for me to realize it. . . .

On the Mississippi, December 22nd [1850]

It was noon. The air became more and more delicious, and more and more animated became the scenes on the river-banks. Caravans of black men and women were seen driving out from the planter's house to the fields. After them came one or two buggies or cabriolets, in which were probably the overseers or the masters themselves. I gazed on the whole scene in that spirit of human love, in which to keep one's self, one believes, in good humor, the best of all men, and in which one endeavors to see every thing and all circumstances on the sunny side.

Two hours later I still sat aft on the piazza, and inhaled the same mild, delicious atmosphere, still beheld the same scene of southern beauty, but gazed upon it with a heart full of bitterness. Yes, for a dark picture had been unfolded before my gaze—a picture which I never shall forget; which perpetually, like a spectre of the abyss, will step between me and the memory of that enchanting veil which one moment captivated and darkened my vision.

I sat and gazed upon that beautiful scene as one looks at the scene of a theatre. I enjoyed with childish delight the decorations. Then came my new friend, the planter, and seated himself in an arm-chair on the piazza. We spoke a few words about the deliciousness of the air, which he enjoyed as much as I did. Then we sat silently contemplating the scenery of the shores. We saw the caravans of slaves and their overseers proceeding over the fields. I said to my neighbor in that spirit of human love which I have mentioned,

"There is a great deal more happiness and comfort in this life (the slaves' life) than one commonly imagines."

The planter turned to me his beautiful head with a glance which I shall never forget; there was astonishment, almost reproach in it, and a profound melancholy.

"Oh!" said he, in a low voice, "you know nothing of that which occurs on these shores; if you did, you would not think so. Here is much violence and much suffering! At this season in particular, and from the time when the cotton is ready to pluck, a great deal of cruelty is practiced on the plantations around here. There are plantations here where the whip never rests during all these months. You can have no idea of such flogging."

I will not repeat those scenes which the planter related to me, scenes which he himself had witnessed of violence, cruelty, and suffering during more than fourteen years, abominations which finally drove him thence, which drove him to sell his plantation, and leave the slave states forever. I will merely introduce some of this excellent man's words.

"I have known men and women who were actual devils toward their slaves—whose pleasure it was to torment them.

"People can flog a negro almost to death, and yet not let a drop of blood flow. The strip of cowhide which is used in doors can cause the most horrible torture without any mark being left.

"Women are not unfrequently the most horrible tormentors of the house-slaves, and I would rather be one of the field-hands than the house-slave of a passionate woman. The institution of slavery seems to change the very nature of woman.

"Slavery is destructive of the white. I have known young men and women, amiable in all respects, of the most attractive manners and dispositions, but toward their slaves they were unjust and severe.

"There are naturally exceptions. There are good and tender masters and mistresses, but they are few. The rule is, that slavery blinds and hardens the mind of the slave-owner from childhood upward.

"The state of things is considerably improved of late years, and still is improving. Light is beginning to enter this country... people are no longer afraid of speaking. A few years ago, if a person had published a seventh part of what I have now told you, he would have been shot without any further process. The slave-owner now acknowledges that the eye of the public is directed to him. It makes him more careful. Slaves, for the last ten or twelve years, have been better clothed and fed in this part of the country than they used to be; but sadly too much injustice and sadly too much cruelty exists still, and must always exist, so long as this institution lasts. And it is my conviction that it will soon become *"the question"*—the question of life and death within the American Union.

"Even now a man makes no demur about shooting down a negro whom he suspects of intending to run away, and the law is silent on all such acts of violence. I have seen many slaves severely wounded from having been shot at under such circumstances, but one only killed.

"Passion and insanity in the treatment of slaves are common. . . .

"The law is no protection to the slave. It is nominally so, but it is not any actual defense. The slave suffers from his master; the lawyers shut their eyes to the affair as long as they can; and the negro can not be a witness in a court of justice.

"They talk of public opinion; but public opinion is here, as yet, for the most part the product of demagogues. And the cotton interest is the only conscience. Many people see all this as very wrong, and deplore it, but they are silent, from the fear of involving themselves in trouble."

As Frederick Law Olmstead Saw the Slave States

In the middle and late 1850s, a journalist named Frederick Law Olmstead toured through the slave states recording his impressions of the conditions of life and the points of view of plantation owners, businessmen, farmers, slaves and freed blacks. Olmstead's chronicles were printed as articles in *The New York Times,* and later published in four compilations of these writings as books. While some southerners regarded Olmstead as a northern spy and troublemaker, he was generally applauded as an honest and accurate observer. He wrote with restraint, seeking not to overpaint his picture, but what he had to say of the condition of black slaves and poor whites, and of southern attitudes toward slavery, is considered to have added incentive to those who sought the end of slavery. Some of his articles read like vignettes without central meaning, but taken as a whole they were

**an exceedingly important social document.
The following extracts are from his *A Journey
in the Seaboard Slave States*, published in
1856.**

[Virginia] While calling on a gentleman occupying an honorable
official position at Richmond, I noticed upon his table a copy of Professor Johnson's Agricultural Tour in the United States. Referring to a
paragraph in it, where some statistics of the value of the slaves raised
and annually exported from Virginia were given, I asked if he knew
how these had been obtained, and whether they were reliable. "No,"
he replied; "I don't know anything about it; but if they are anything
unfavorable to the institution of slavery, you may be sure they are
false." This is but an illustration, in extreme, of the manner in which I
find a desire to obtain more correct but *definite* information on the subject of slavery is usually met, by gentlemen otherwise of enlarged mind
and generous qualities.

A gentleman who was a member of the "Union Safety Committee"
of New York during the excitement which attended the discussion of
the Fugitive Slave Act of 1850, told me that, as he was passing through
Virginia this winter, a man entered the car in which he was seated,
leading in a negro girl, whose manner and expression of face indicated
dread and grief. Thinking she was a criminal, he asked the man what
she had done:

"Done? Nothing."

"What are you going to do with her?"

"I'm taking her down to Richmond, to be sold."

"Does she belong to you?"

"No; she belongs to ——; he raised her."

"Why does he sell her—has she done anything wrong?"

"Done anything? No: she's no fault, I reckon."

"Then, what does he want to sell for?"

"Sell her for! Why shouldn't he sell her? He sells one or two every
year; wants the money for 'em, I reckon."

The irritated tone and severe stare with which this was said, my
friend took as a caution not to pursue his investigation.

A gentleman with whom I was conversing on the subject of the cost
of slave labor in answer to an inquiry—what proportion of all the stock
of slaves of an old plantation might be reckoned upon to do full
work?—answered that he owned ninety-six negroes; of these, only thirty-five were field hands, the rest being either too young or too old for
hard work. He reckoned his whole force as only equal to twenty-one
strong men, or "*prime* field-hands." But this proportion was somewhat
smaller than usual, he added, "because his women were uncommonly
good breeders; he did not suppose there was a lot of women anywhere
that bred faster than his; he never heard of babies coming so fast as
they did on his plantation; it was perfectly surprising; and every one of
them, in his estimation, was worth two hundred dollars, as negroes
were selling now, the moment it drew breath."

I asked what he thought might be the usual proportion of workers to slaves supported on plantations throughout the South. On the large cotton and sugar plantations of the more Southern States, it was very high, he replied; because their hands were nearly all bought and *picked for work;* he supposed, on those, it would be about one-half; but on any old plantation, where the stock of slaves had been an inheritance, and none had been bought or sold, he thought the working force would rarely be more than one-third, at most, of the whole number.

This gentleman was out of health, and told me, with frankness, that such was the trouble and annoyance his negroes occasioned him— although he had an overseer—and so wearisome did he find the lonely life he led on his plantation, that he could not remain upon it; and, as he knew everything would go to the dogs if he did not, he was seriously contemplating to sell out, retaining only his foster-mother and a body-servant. He thought of taking them to Louisiana and Texas, for sale; but, if he should learn that there was much probability that Lower California would be made a slave State, he supposed it would pay him to wait, as probably, if that should occur, he could take them there and sell them for twice as much as they would now bring in New Orleans. He knew very well, he said, that, as they were, raising corn and tobacco, they were paying nothing at all like a fair interest on their value.

Some of his best hands he now rented out to work in a furnace, and for the best of these he had been offered, for next year, two hundred dollars. He did not know whether he ought to let them go, though. They were worked hard, and had too much liberty, and were acquiring bad habits. They earned money by overwork, and spent it for whisky, and got a habit of roaming about and *taking care of themselves;* because, when they were not at work in the furnace, nobody looked out for them.

I begin to suspect that the great trouble and anxiety of Southern gentlemen is:—How, without quite destroying the capabilities of the negro for any work at all, to prevent him from learning to take care of himself.

¤ ¤ ¤

I learned that there were no white laboring men here [Virginia] who hired themselves out by the month. The poor white people that had to labor for their living never would work steadily at any employment. "They mostly followed boating"—hiring as hands on the bateaus that navigate the small streams and canals, but never for a longer term at once than a single trip of a boat, whether that might be long or short. At the end of the trip they were paid by the day. Their wages were from fifty cents to a dollar, varying with the demand and individual capacities. They hardly ever worked on farms except in harvest, when they usually received a dollar a day, sometimes more. In harvest-time, most of the rural mechanics closed their shops and hired out to the farmers at a dollar a day, which would indicate that their ordinary earnings are considerably less than this. At other than harvest-time, the poor white people, who had no trade, would sometimes work for the farmers by the job, not often at any regular agricultural labor, but at getting rails or shingles, or clearing land.

He did not know that they were particular about working with negroes, but no white man would ever do certain kinds of work (such as taking care of cattle, or getting water or wood to be used in the house), and if you should ask a white man you had hired to do such things, he would get mad and tell you he wasn't a nigger. Poor white girls never hired out to do servants' work, but they would come and help another white woman about her sewing or quilting, and take wages for it. But these girls were not very respectable generally, and it was not agreeable to have them in your house, though there were some very respectable ladies that would go out to sew. Farmers depended almost entirely upon their negroes; it was only when they were hard pushed by their crops that they got white hands to help them any.

Negroes had commanded such high wages lately, to work on railroads and in tobacco-factories, that farmers were tempted to hire out too many of their people, and to undertake to do too much work with those they retained, and thus they were often driven to employ white men, and to give them very high wages by the day, when they found themselves getting much behind-hand with their crops. He had been driven very hard in this way this last season; he had been so unfortunate as to lose one of his best women, who died in child-bed just before harvest. The loss of the woman and her child, for the child had died also, just at that time, came very hard upon him. He would not have taken a thousand dollars of any man's money for them. He had had to hire white men to help him, but they were poor sticks and would be half the time drunk, and you never know what to depend upon with them. One fellow that he had hired, who had agreed to work for him all through harvest, got him to pay him some wages in advance, (he said it was to buy him some clothes with, so he could go to meeting, Sunday, at the Court-House,) and went off the next day, right in the middle of harvest, and he never had seen him since. He had heard of him—he was on a boat—but he didn't reckon he should ever get his money again.

Of course, he did not see how white laborers were ever going to come into competition with negroes here, at all. You never could depend on white men, and you couldn't *drive* them any; they wouldn't stand it. Slaves were the only reliable laborers—you could command them and *make* them do what was right.

* * *

A well-informed capitalist and slave-holder remarked, that negroes could not be employed in cotton factories. I said that I understood they were so in Charleston, and some other places at the South.

"It may be so, *yet*," he answered, "but they will have to give it up."

The reason was, he said, that the negro could never be trained to exercise judgment; he cannot be made to use his mind; he always depends on machinery doing its own work, and cannot be made to watch it. He neglects it until something is broken or there is great waste. "We have tried reward and punishments, but it makes no difference. It's his nature and you cannot change it. All men are indolent and have a disinclination to labor, but this is a great deal stronger in the African race than in any other. In working niggers, we must always calculate that they will not labor at all except to avoid punishment, and they will never do more than just enough to save themselves from being punished, and no amount of punishment will prevent their working carelessly and indifferently. It always seems on the plantations as if they took pains to break all the tools and spoil all the cattle that they possibly can, even when they know they'll be directly punished for it."

As to rewards, he said, "They only want to support life, they will not work for anything more; and in this country it would be hard to prevent their getting that." I thought this opinion of the power of rewards was not exactly confirmed by the narrative we had just heard, but I said nothing. "If you could move," he continued, "all the white people from the whole seaboard district of Virginia and give it up to the negroes that are on it now, just leave them to themselves, in ten years time there would not be an acre of land cultivated, and nothing would be produced, except what grew spontaneously."

The Hon. Willoughby Newton, by the way, seems to think that if it had not been for the introduction of guano, a similar desolation would have soon occurred without the Africanization of the country. He is reported to have said:

"I look upon the introduction of guano, and the success attending its application to our barren lands, in the light of a special interposition of Divine Providence, to save the northern neck of Virginia from reverting entirely into its former state of wilderness and utter desolation. Until the discovery of guano—more valuable to us than the mines of California—I looked upon the possibility of renovating our soil, of ever bringing it to a point capable of producing remunerating crops, as utterly hopeless. Our up-lands were all worn out, and our bottom-lands fast failing, and if it had not been for guano to revive our last hope, a few years more and the whole country must have been deserted by all who desired to increase their own wealth, or advance the cause of civilization by a proper cultivation of the earth."

"But are they not *improving*?" said I; "that is a point in which I am much interested, and I should be glad to know what is your observation? Have they not, as a race, improved during the last hundred years, do you not think?"

"Oh, yes indeed, very greatly. During my time—I can remember how they were forty years ago—they have improved *two thousand per cent*! Don't you think so?" he asked another gentleman.

"Yes; certainly."

"And you may find them now, on the isolated old plantations in the back country, just as I recollect them when I was a boy, stupid and moping, and with no more intelligence than when they first came from Africa. But all about where the country is much settled their condition is vastly ameliorated. They are treated much better, they are fed better, and they have much greater educational privileges."

"Educational privileges?" I asked, in surprise.

"I mean by preaching and religious instruction. They have the Bible read to them a great deal, and there is preaching for them all over the country. They have preachers of their own; right smart ones they are, too, some of them."

"Do they?" said I. "I thought that was not allowed by law."

"Well, it is not—that is, they are not allowed to have meetings without some white man is present. They must not preach unless a white man hears what they say. However, they do. On my plantation, they always have a meeting on Sundays, and I have sometimes, when I have been there, told my overseer—'You must go up there to the meeting, you know the law requires it;' and he would start as if he was going, but would just look in and go by; he wasn't going to wait for them."

He then spoke of a minister, whom he owned, and described him as a very intelligent man. He knew almost the whole of the Bible by heart. He was a fine-looking man—a fine head and a very large frame. He had been a sailor, and had been in New Orleans and New York, and many foreign ports. "He could have left me at any time for twenty years, if he had wished to," he said. "I asked him once how he would like to live in New York? Oh, he did not like New York at all! Niggers were not treated well there—there was more distinction made between them and white folks than there was here. 'Oh, dey ain't no place in de worl like Ole Virginny for niggers, massa,' says he."

Another gentlemen gave similar testimony.

I said I supposed that they were much better off, more improved intellectually, and more kindly treated in Virginia than further South. He said I was mistaken in both respects—that in Louisiana, especially, they were more intelligent, because the amalgamation of the races was much greater, and they were treated with more familiarity by the whites; besides which, the laws of Louisiana were much more favorable to them. For instance, they required the planter to give slaves 200 pounds of pork a year; and he gave a very apt anecdote showing the effect of this law, but which, at the same time, made it evident that a Virginian may be accustomed to neglect providing sufficient food for his force, and that they sometimes suffer greatly for want of it. I was assured, however, that this was very rare—that, generally, the slaves were well provided for—always allowed a sufficient quantity of meal, and, generally, of pork—were permitted to raise pigs and poultry, and in summer could always grow as many vegetables as they wanted. It was observed, however, that they frequently neglect to provide for themselves in this way, and live mainly on meal and bacon. If a man does not provide well for his slaves, it soon becomes known, he gets the name of a "nigger-killer," and loses the respect of the community.

The general allowance of food was thought to be a peck and a half of meal, and three pounds of bacon a week. This, it was observed, is as much meal as they can eat, but they would be glad to have more bacon; sometimes they receive four pounds, but it is oftener that they get less than three. It is distributed to them on Saturday nights; or, on the better-managed plantations, sometimes, on Wednesday, to prevent their using it extravagantly, or selling it for whisky on Sunday. This distribution is called the "drawing," and is made by the overseer to all the heads of families or single negroes. Except on the smallest plantations, where the cooking is done in the house of the proprietor, there is a cook-house, furnished with a large copper for boiling, and an oven. Every night the negroes take their "mess," for the next day's breakfast and dinner, to the cook, to be prepared for the next day. Custom varies as to the time it is served out to them; sometimes at morning and noon, at other times at noon and night. Each negro marks his meat by cuts, so that he shall know it from the rest, and they observe each other's rights with regard to this, punctiliously.

After breakfast has been eaten early in the cabins, at sunrise or a little before in winter, and perhaps a little later in summer, they go to the field. At noon dinner is brought to them, and, unless the work presses, they are allowed two hours' rest. Very punctually at sunset they stop work and are at liberty, except that a squad is detached once a week for shelling corn, to go to the mill for the next week's drawing of meal. Thus they work in the field about eleven hours a day on an average. Returning to the cabins, wood "ought to have been" carted for them; but if it has not been, they then go to the woods and "tote" it home for themselves. They then make a fire—a big, blazing fire at this season, for the supply of fuel is unlimited—and cook their own supper, which will be a bit of bacon fried, often with eggs, corn-bread baked in the spider after the bacon, to absorb the fat, and perhaps some sweet potatoes roasted in the ashes. Immediately after supper they go to sleep, often lying on the floor or a bench in preference to a bed. About two o'clock they very generally rouse up and cook and eat, or eat cold, what they call their "mornin' bit"; then sleep again till breakfast. . . .

As to the clothing of the slaves on the plantations, they are said to be usually furnished by their owners or masters every year, each with a coat and trousers, of a coarse woolen or woolen and cotton stuff (mostly made, especially for this purpose, in Providence, R. I.), for Winter, trousers of cotton osnaburghs for Summer, sometimes with a jacket also of the same; two pairs of strong shoes, or one pair of strong boots and one of lighter shoes for harvest; three shirts; one blanket, and one felt hat.

The women have two dresses of striped cotton, three shifts, two pairs of shoes, etc. The women lying-in are kept at knitting short sacks, from cotton which, in Southern Virginia, is usually raised, for this purpose, on the farm, and these are also given to the negroes. They also purchase clothing for themselves, and, I notice especially, are well supplied with handkerchiefs which the men frequently, and the women nearly always, wear on their heads. On Sundays and holidays they usually look very smart, but when at work, very ragged and slovenly.

* * *

[*South Carolina*] I came upon two small white-topped wagons, each with a pair of horses feeding at its pole; near them was a dull camp fire, with a bake-kettle and coffee-pot, some blankets and a chest upon the ground; and an old negro, sitting with his head bowed down over a meal sack, while a negro boy was combing his wool with a common horse-card. "Good evening, uncle," said I, approaching them. "Good evening, sar," he answered, without looking up.

"Where are you going?"

"Well, we ain't goin' nower, master; we's peddlin' tobacco roun'."

"Oh! peddling tobacco. Where did you come from?"

"From Rockingham County, Norf Car'lina, master."

"How long have you been coming from there?"

"'Twill be seven weeks, to-morrow, sar, since we left home."

"Have you most sold out?"

"We had a hundred and seventy-five boxes in both wagons, and we's sold all but sixty. Want to buy some tobacco, master?" (Looking up.)

"No, thank you; I am only waiting here, while the coach changes. How much tobacco is there in a box?"

"Seventy-five pound."

"Are these the boxes?"

"No, them is our provision boxes, master. Show de gemman some of der tobacco, dah." (To the boy.)

A couple of negroes here passed along near us; the old man hailed them:

"Ho, dah, boys! Doan you want to buy some backey?"

"No." (Decidedly.)

"Well, I'm sorry for it." (Reproachfully.)

"Are you bound homeward, now?" I asked.

"No, massa; wish me was; got to sell our tobackey fuss; you don't want none, master, does you? Doan you tink it pretty fair tobacco, sar, just try it; it's right sweet, reckon you'll find."

"I don't wish any, thank you; I never use it. Is your master with you?"

"No, sar; he's gone across to Marion, to-day."

"Do you like to be traveling about, in this way?"

"Yes, master; I likes it very well."

"Better than staying at home, eh?"

"Well, I likes my country better dan dis; must say dat, master, likes my country better dan dis. I'se a free nigger in my country, master."

"Oh, you are a free man, are you! North Carolina is a better country than this, for free men, I suppose."

"Yes, master, I likes my country de best; I gets five dollar a month for dat boy." (Hastily, to change the subject.)

He is your son, is he?"

"Yes, sar; he drives dat wagon. I drives dis; and I haant seen him fore, master, for six weeks, till dis mornin'."

"How were you separated?"

"We separated six weeks ago, sar, and we agreed to meet here, last night. We didn', dough, till dis mornin'."

The old man's tone softened, and he regarded his son with earnestness.

"'Pears dough, we was bofe heah, last night; but I couldn't find dem till dis mornin.' Dis mornin' some nigger tole dar war a nigger camped off yander in de wood; and I knew 'twas him, and I went an' found him right off."

"And what wages do you get for yourself?"

"Ten dollars a month, master."

"That's pretty good wages."

"Yes, master, any niggar can get good wages if he's a mind to be industrious, no matter wedder he's slave or free."

"So you don't like this country as well as North Carolina?"

"No, master. Fac is, master, 'pears like wite folks doan ginerally like niggers in dis country; day doan ginerally talk so to niggers like as do in my country; de niggers ain't so happy hea; 'pears like de wite folks was kind o' different, somehow. I doan like dis country so well; my country suits me very well."

"Well, I've been thinking, myself, the niggers did not look so well here as they did in North Carolina and Virginia; they are not so well clothed, and they don't appear so bright as they do there."

"Well, massa, Sundays dey is mighty well clothed, dis country; 'pears like dere ain't nobody looks better Sundays dan dey do. But Lord! workin' days, seems like dey hadden no close dey could keep on 'um at all, master. Dey is a'mos' naked, wen deys at work, some on 'em. Why, master, up in our country, de wite folks, why, some on 'em has ten or twelve niggers; dey doan' hev no real big plantation, like dey has heah, but some on 'em has ten or twelve niggers, may be, and dey juss lives and talks along wid 'em; and dey treats 'um most as if dem was dar own chile. Dey doan' keep no niggers dey can't treat so; dey wont keep 'em, wont be bodered wid 'em. If dey gets a niggar and he doan behave himself, dey wont keep him; dey juss tell him, sar, he must look up anudder master, and if he doan' find hisself one, I tell 'ou, when de trader cum along, dey sell him, and he totes him away. Dey allers sell off all de bad niggars out of our country; dat's de way de bad niggar and all dem no-account niggar keep a cumin' down heah; dat's de way on't, master."

"Yes, that's the way of it, I suppose; these big plantations are not just the best thing for niggers, I see that plainly."

"Master, you wan't raise in dis country, was 'ou?"

"No; I came from the North."

"I tort so, sar, I knew 'ou wan't one of dis country people, 'peared like 'ou was one o' my country people, way 'ou talks; and I loves dem kine of people. Won't you take some whiskey, sar? Heah, you boy! bring dat jug of whiskey dah, out o' my wagon; in dah, in dat box under dem foddar."

"No, don't trouble yourself, I am very much obliged to you; but I don't like to drink whiskey."

"Like to have you drink some, massa, if you'd like it. You's right welcome to it. 'Pears like I knew you was one of my country people. Ever been in Greensboro' massa? dat's in Guilford."

"No, I never was there. I came from New York, further North than your country."

"New York, did 'ou, massa? I heard New York was what dey calls a Free State; all de niggars free dah."

"Yes, that is so."

"Not no slaves at all; well, I expec dat's a good ting, for all de niggars to be free. Greensboro' is a right comely town; tain't like dese heah Souf Car'lina towns."

"I have heard it spoken of as a very beautiful town, and there are some very nice people there."

"Yes, dere's Mr. ——, I knows him, he's a mighty good man."

"Do you know Mr. ——?

"O, yes sar, he's a mighty fine man, he is, massa; ain't no better kind of man dan him."

"Well, I must go, or the coach will be kept waiting for me. Good-by to you."

"Far'well, master, far'well, 'pears like it's done me good to see a man dats cum out of my country again. Far'well, master."

* * *

[Louisiana]When I left Mr. R.'s, I was driven about twenty miles in a buggy, by one of his house servants. He was inclined to be talkative and communicative; and as he expressed great affection and respect for his owner, I felt at liberty to question him on some points upon which I had always previously avoided conversing with slaves. He spoke rapidly, garrulously; and it was only necessary for me to give a direction to his thoughts by my inquiries, I was careful to avoid leading questions, and not to show such an interest as would lead him to reply guardedly. I charged my memory as much as possible with his very words, when this was of consequence, and made the following record of the conversation, within half an hour after I left him.

He first said that he supposed that I would see he was not a "Creole nigger"; he came from Virginia. He reckoned the Virginia negroes were better-looking than those who were raised here; there were no black people anywhere in the world who were so "well made" as those who were born in Virginia. He asked if I lived in New Orleans; and where? I told him that I lived at the North; he asked:

"Da's a great many brack folks dah, massa?"

"No; very few."

"Da's a great many in Virginia; more'n da is heah?"

"But I came from beyond Virginia—from New York."

He had heard there were a great many black folk in New York. I said there were a good many in the city; but few in the country. Did I live in the country? What people did I have for servants? Thought if I hired all my labor, it must be very dear. He inquired further about negroes there. I told him they were all free, and described their general condition; told him what led them to congregate in cities, and what the effect was. He said the negroes, both slave and free, who lived in New Orleans, were better off than those who lived in the country. Why? Because they make more money, and it is "gayer" there, and there is more "society." He then drew a contrast between Virginia—as he recollected it—and Louisiana. There is but one road in this country. In Virginia, there are roads running in every direction, and often crossing each other. You could see so much more "society," and there was so much more "variety" than here. He would not like now to go back to Virginia to live, because he had got used to this country, and had all his acquaintances here, and knew the ways of the people. He could speak French. He would like to go to New Orleans, though; would rather live in New Orleans than any other place in the world.

After a silence of some minutes, he said, abruptly;

"If I was free, I would go to Virginia, and see my old mudder." He had left her when he was thirteen years old. He reckoned he was now thirty-three. "I don't well know, dough, exactly, how old I is; but, I rec-'lect, de day I was taken away, my ole mudder she tells me I was tirteen year old." He did not like to come away at all; he "felt dreadful bad"; but, now he was used to it, he liked living here. He came across the Blue Ridge, and he recollected that, when he first saw it, he thought it was a dark piece of sky, and he wondered what it would be like when they came close to it. He was brought, with a great many other negroes, in wagons, to Lousville; and then they were put on board a steam-boat, and brought down here. He was sold to a Creole, and was put on this plantation, and had been on it ever since. He had been twice sold, along with it. Folks didn't very often sell their servants here, as they did in Virginia. They were selling their servants, in Virginia, all the time; but, here, they did not very often sell them, except they run away. When a man would run away, and they could not do anything with him, they always sold him off. . . .

He again recurred to the fortunate condition of the negroes on his master's plantation. He thought it was the best plantation in the State, and he did not believe there was a better lot of negroes in the State; some few of them, whom his master had brought from his plantation, were old; but altogether, they were "as right good a lot of niggers" as could be found anywhere. They could do all the work that was necessary to be done on the plantation. On some old plantations they had not nearly so many negroes as they needed to make the crop, and they "drove 'em awful hard"; but it wasn't so on his master's; they could do all the work, and do it well, and it was the best worked plantation he knew of. All the niggers had enough to eat, and were well clothed; their quarters were good, and they got a good many presents.

"Well, now, wouldn't you rather live on such a plantation than to be free, William?"

"Oh! no, sir, I'd rather be free! Oh, yes, sir, I'd like it better to be free; I would dat, master."

"Why would you?"

"Why, you see, master, if I was free—if I was *free*, I'd have *all* my time to myself. I'd rather work for myself. I'd like dat better."

"But then, you know, you'd have to take care of yourself, and you'd get poor."

"No, sir, I would not get poor, I would get rich; for you see, master, then I'd work *all de time* for myself."

"Suppose all the black people on your plantation, or all the black people in the country were made free at once, what do you think would become of them?—what would they do, do you think? You don't suppose there would be much sugar raised, do you?"

"Why, yes, master, I do. Why not, sir? What *would* de black people do? Wouldn't dey hab to work for dar libben? and de wite people own all de land—war dey goin' to work? Dey hire demself right out again, and work all de same as before. And den, wen dey work for demself, dey work *harder* dan dey do now to get more wages—a heap harder. I tink so, sir. I would do so, sir. I would work for hire. I don't own any land; I hab to work right away again for massa, to get some money."

Perceiving from the readiness of these answers that the subject had been a familiar one with him, I immediately asked: "The black people talk among themselves about this, do they; and they think so, generally?"

"Oh! yes, sir; dey talk so; dat's wat dey tink."

"Then they talk about being free a good deal, do they?"

"Yes, sir. Dey—dat is, dey say dey wish it was so; dat's all dey talk, master—dat's all, sir. . . ."

Frances Anne Kemble on the Selling of Slaves

Frances Anne Kemble, an English actress of considerable renown in her time, in 1834 married a Philadelphian named Pierce Butler, and a few years later went with him to live on his plantation in Georgia. Unlike Frederika Bremer and Frederick Law Olmstead, Miss Kemble lived in daily contact with the slaves, came to know them intimately as individuals, and became personally involved with their tribulations. While her husband seemed to see the conditions of slavery as a mere economic fact of life, perhaps sometimes a little disagreeable, Miss Kemble was revolted and deeply disturbed by her experience. In 1863 she published her *Journal of a Residence on a Georgian Plantation in 1838–1839*, a book that came to be a classic in its field. The following extract from her *Journal* is about the selling of

a slave family living on her husband's estate.
Pierce Butler is never referred to by name,
but as Mr. ——.

I have never questioned Psyche as to her sadness, because, in the first place, as I tell you, it appears to me most natural, and is observable in all the slaves whose superior natural or acquired intelligence allows of their filling situations of trust or service about the house and family; and, though I can not and will not refuse to hear any and every tale of suffering which these unfortunates bring to me, I am anxious to spare both myself and them the pain of vain appeals to me for redress and help, which, alas! it is too often utterly out of my power to give them. It is useless, and, indeed, worse than useless, that they should see my impotent indignation and unavailing pity, and hear expressions of compassion for them, and horror at their condition, which might only prove incentives to a hopeless resistance on their part to a system, under the hideous weight of whose oppression any individual or partial revolt must be annihilated and ground into the dust. Therefore, as I tell you, I asked Psyche no questions; but, to my great astonishment, the other day M—— asked me if I knew to whom Psyche belonged, as the poor woman had inquired of her with much hesitation and anguish if she could tell her who owned her and her children. She has two nice little children under six years old, whom she keeps as clean and tidy, and who are sad and as silent as herself. My astonishment at this question was, as you will readily believe, not small, and I forthwith sought out Psyche for an explanation. She was thrown into extreme perturbation at finding that her question had been referred to me, and it was some time before I could sufficiently reassure her to be able to comprehend, in the midst of her reiterated entreaties for pardon, and hopes that she had not offended me, that she did not know herself who owned her. She was, at one time, the property of Mr. K——, the former overseer, of whom I have already spoken to you, and who has just been paying Mr. —— a visit. He, like several of his predecessors in the management, has contrived to make a fortune upon it (though it yearly decreases in value to the owners, but this is the inevitable course of things in the Southern states), and has purchased a plantation of his own in Alabama, I believe, or one of the Southwestern states. Whether she still belonged to Mr. K—— or not she did not know, and entreated me, if she did, to endeavor to persuade Mr. —— to buy her. Now you must know that this poor woman is the wife of one of Mr. B——'s slaves, a fine, intelligent, active, excellent young man, whose whole family are among some of the very best specimens of character and capacity on the estate. I was so astonished at the (to me) extraordinary state of things revealed by poor Sack's petition, that I could not tell her that I had supposed all the negroes on the plantation were Mr. ——'s property, but that I would certainly inquire, and find out for her, if I could, to whom she belonged, and if I could, endeavor to get Mr. —— to purchase her, if she really was not his.

Now, E——, just conceive for one moment the state of mind of this woman, believing herself to belong to a man who in a few days was going down to one of those abhorred and dreaded Southwestern states, and who would then compel her, with her poor little children, to leave her husband and the only home she had ever known, and all the ties of affection, relationship, and association of her former life, to follow him thither, in all human probability never again to behold any living creature that she had seen before; and this was so completely a matter of course that it was not even thought necessary to apprise her positively of the fact, and the only thing that interposed between her and this most miserable fate was the faint hope that Mr.—— *might have* purchased her and her children. But if he had, if this great deliverance had been vouchsafed to her, the knowledge of it was not thought necessary; and with this deadly dread at her heart she was living day after day, waiting upon me and seeing me, with my husband beside me, and my children in my arms in blessed security, safe from all separation but the one reserved in God's great providence for all His creatures. Do you think I wondered any more at the wo-begone expression of her countenance, or do you think it was easy for me to restrain within prudent and proper limits the expression of my feelings at such a state of things? And she had gone on from day to day enduring this agony, till I suppose its own intolerable pressure and M——'s sweet countenance and gentle sympathizing voice and manner had constrained her to lay down this great burden of sorrow at our feet. I did not see Mr. —— until the evening; but, in the mean time, meeting Mr. O——, the overseer, with whom, as I believe I have already told you, we are living here, I asked him about Psyche, and who was her proprietor, when, to my infinite surprise, he told me that *he* had bought her and her children from Mr. K——, who had offered them to him, saying that they would be rather troublesome to him than otherwise down where he was going; "and so," said Mr. O——, "as I had no objection to investing a little money that way, I bought them." With a heart much lightened, I flew to tell poor Psyche the news, so that, at any rate, she might be relieved from the dread of any immediate separation from her husband. You can imagine better than I can tell you what her sensations were; but she still renewed her prayer that I would, if possible, induce Mr. —— to purchase her, and I promised to do so.

Early the next morning, while I was still dressing, I was suddenly startled by hearing voices in loud tones in Mr.——'s dressing-room, which adjoins my bedroom, and the noise increasing until there was an absolute cry of despair uttered by some man. I could restrain myself no longer, but opened the door of communication and saw Joe, the young man, poor Psyche's husband, raving almost in a state of frenzy, and in a voice broken with sobs and almost inarticulate with passion, reiterating his determination never to leave this plantation, never to go to Alabama, never to leave his old father and mother, his poor wife and children, and dashing his hat, which he was wringing like a cloth in his hands, upon the ground, he declared he would kill himself if he was

compelled to follow Mr. K——. I glanced from the poor wretch to Mr.
——, who was standing, leaning against a table with his arms folded,
occasionally uttering a few words of counsel to his slave to be quiet
and not fret, and not make a fuss about what there was no help for. I
retreated immediately from the horrid scene, breathless with surprise
and dismay, and stood for some time in my own room, with my heart
and temples throbbing to such a degree that I could hardly support myself. As soon as I recovered myself I again sought Mr. O——, and inquired of him if he knew the cause of poor Joe's distress. He then told
me that Mr. ——, who is highly pleased with Mr. K——'s past administration of his property, wished, on his departure for his newly-acquired
slave plantation, to give him some token of his satisfaction, and *had
made him a present* of the man Joe, who had just received the intelligence that he was to go down to Alabama with his new owner the next
day, leaving father, mother, wife, and children behind. You will not
wonder that the man required a little judicious soothing under the circumstances, and you will also, I hope, admire the humanity of the sale
of his wife and children by the owner who was going to take him to Alabama, because *they* would be encumbrances rather than otherwise
down there. If Mr. K—— did not do this after he knew that the man
was his, then Mr. —— gave him to be carried down to the South after
his wife and children were sold to remain in Georgia. I do not know
which was the real transaction, for I have not had the heart to ask; but
you will easily imagine which of the two cases I prefer believing.

When I saw Mr.—— after this most wretched story became known to
me in all its details, I appealed to him, for his own soul's sake, not to
commit so great a cruelty. Poor Joe's agony while remonstrating with
his master was hardly greater than mine while arguing with him upon
this bitter piece of inhumanity—how I cried, and how I adjured, and
how all my sense of justice, and of mercy, and of pity for the poor
wretch, and of wretchedness at finding myself implicated in such a
state of things, broke in torrents of words from my lips and tears from
my eyes! God knows such a sorrow at seeing any one I belonged to
commit such an act was indeed a new and terrible experience to me,
and it seemed to me that I was imploring Mr. —— to save himself more
than to spare these wretches. He gave me no answer whatever, and I
have since thought that the intemperate vehemence of my entreaties
and expostulations perhaps deserved that he should leave me as he did
without one single word of reply; and miserable enough I remained.
Toward evening, as I was sitting alone, my children having gone to
bed, Mr. O—— came into the room. I had but one subject in my mind;
I had not been able to eat for it. I could hardly sit still for the nervous
distress which every thought of these poor people filled me with. As he
sat down looking over some accounts, I said to him, "Have you seen
Joe this afternoon, Mr. O——?" (I give you our conversation as it took
place.) "Yes, ma'am; he is a great deal happier than he was this morning." "Why, how is that?" asked I eagerly. "Oh, he is not going to Alabama. Mr. K—— heard that he had kicked up a fuss about it (being in

despair at being torn from one's wife and children is called *kicking up a fuss*; this is a sample of overseer appreciation of human feelings), and said that if the fellow wasn't willing to go with him, he did not wish to be bothered with any niggers down there who were to be troublesome, so he might stay behind." "And does Psyche know this?" "Yes, ma'am, I suppose so." I drew a long breath; and whereas my needle had stumbled through the stuff I was sewing for an hour before, as if my fingers could not guide it, the regularity and rapidity of its evolutions were now quite edifying. The man was for the present safe, and I remained silently pondering his deliverance and the whole proceeding, and the conduct of every one engaged in it, and, above all, Mr. ——'s share in the transaction, and I think, for the first time, almost a sense of horrible personal responsibility and implication took hold of my mind, and I felt the weight of an unimagined guilt upon my conscience; and yet, God knows, this feeling of self-condemnation is very gratuitous on my part, since when I married Mr. —— I knew nothing of these dreadful possessions of his, and even if I had I should have been much puzzled to have formed any idea of the state of things in which I now find myself plunged, together with those whose well-doing is as vital to me almost as my own.

With these agreeable reflections I went to bed. Mr. —— said not a word to me upon the subject of these poor people all the next day, and in the mean time I became very impatient of this reserve on his part, because I was dying to prefer my request that he would purchase Psyche and her children, and so prevent any future separation between her and her husband, as I supposed he would not again attempt to make a present of Joe, at least to any one who did not wish to be *bothered* with his wife and children. In the evening I was again with Mr. O—— alone in the strange, bare, wooden-walled sort of shanty which is our sitting-room, and revolving in my mind the means of rescuing Psyche from her miserable suspense, a long chain of all my possessions, in the shape of bracelets, necklaces, brooches, earrings, etc., wound in glittering procession through my brain, with many hypothetical calculations of the value of each separate ornament, and the very doubtful probability of the amount of the whole being equal to the price of this poor creature and her children; and then the great power and privilege I had foregone of earning money by my own labor occurred to me, and I think, for the first time in my life, my past profession assumed an aspect that arrested my thoughts more seriously. For the last four years of my life that preceded my marriage I literally coined money, and never until this moment, I think, did I reflect on the great means of good, to myself and others, that I so gladly agreed to give up forever for a maintenance by the unpaid labor of slaves—people toiling not only unpaid, but under the bitter conditions the bare contemplation of which was then wringing my heart. You will not wonder that when, in the midst of such cogitations, I suddenly accosted Mr. O——, it was to this effect: "Mr. O——, I have a particular favor to beg of you. Promise me that you will never sell Psyche and her children without first letting me know of your intention to do so, and giving me the option of buying them." Mr. O—— is a remarkably deliberate man, and squints, so that, when he has taken a little time in directing his eyes to you, you are still unpleasantly unaware of any result in which you are concerned; he laid down a book he was reading, and directed his head and one of his eyes toward me and answered, "Dear me, ma'am, I am very sorry—I have sold them." My work fell down on the ground, and my mouth opened wide, but I could utter no sound, I was so dismayed and surprised; and he deliberately proceeded: "I didn't know, ma'am, you see, at all, that you entertained any idea of making an investment of that nature; for I'm sure, if I had, I would willingly have sold the woman to you; but I sold her and her children this morning to Mr. ——." My dear E——, though —— had resented my unmeasured upbraidings, you see they had not been without some good effect, and though he had, perhaps justly, punished my violent outbreak of indignation about the miserable scene I witnessed by not telling me of his humane purpose, he had bought these poor creatures, and so, I trust, secured them from any such misery in future. I jumped up and left Mr. O—— still speaking, and ran to find Mr. ——, to thank him for what he had done, and with that will now bid you good-by. Think, E——, how it fares with slaves on plantations where there is no crazy Englishwoman to weep, and entreat, and implore, and upbraid for them, and no master willing to listen to such appeals.

EPITAPH OF A SLAVE

Sunday
July 10, 1853
Peyton is no more
Aged 42
Though he was a bad man in many respects
yet he was a most excellent field
hand, always at his
post.
On this place for 21 years.
Except the measles and its sequence, the
injury rec'd by the mule last Nov'r and its sequence,
he has not lost 15 days' work, I verily believe, in the
remaining 19 years. I wish we could hope for his
eternal state.

Epitaph inscribed in a plantation diary, from American Negro Slavery, *by Ulrich Bonnell Phillips, 1918.*

TRADITIONS AND RECOLLECTIONS
IN THE SEA ISLANDS

Well into the first half of the twentieth century the coastal region of Georgia and South Carolina, particularly the offshore islands, remained in a state of cultural isolation from most of the mainland. The black islanders, in their rural environment, maintained a seemingly more tangible tie with their past than did most Negroes of the south, and spoke in a dialect, known as Gullah, which is believed by some scholars to contain remnants of some West African languages. Older people in the Sea Islands recalled traditions, customs and ways of doing things that generally had been forgotten in the mainland communities. They had recollections not only of African ancestors but of stories and tales told by those ancestors; of harvest celebrations related to similar celebrations in Africa; of burial rites that have long since gone out of fashion, in which people marched to the cemetery to the accompaniment of drums, stopped at the entrance of the graveyard to ask permission of the spirits to enter, and left dishes, pots, combs and other personal objects on the graves of the deceased. They "recollected" as fact tales about African slaves who soared into the air and flew back to Africa, and about hoes that worked by themselves in the fields. In the 1930s, The Georgia Writers' Project of the Works Projects Administration sent researchers to the islands to document traditions and beliefs. Much of what they found would have been characteristic of mainland Negro communities of an earlier day, but some things that they uncovered were unique to the islands. They found grave markers at Sunbury that were vividly reminiscent of markers seen in some regions of Africa. See photo illustration no. 2. They found a basket-weaving tradition, and some of the carved spoons, canes and other wooden objects made by the islanders were in an unquestionably African style. Here are some of the comments made by various Sea Island informants on their recollections and traditions.

About Sea Island Africans

"Now ole man Okra an ole man Gibson an ole Israel, dey's African an dey belong tuh James Couper an das how I knows em. Dey tell us how dey lib in Africa. Dey laks tuh talk. It funny talk an it ain so easy tuh unnuhstan but yuh gits use tuh it. Dey say dey buil deah own camp deah an lib in it.

"Ole man Okra he say he wahn a place lak he hab in Africa so he buil im a hut. I membuh it well. It wuz bout twelve by foeteen feet an it hab dut flo an he buil duh side lak basket weave wid clay plastuh on it. It hab a flat roof wut he make frum bush an palmettuh an it hab one doe an no winduhs. Massuh make im pull it down. He say he ain wahn no African hut on he place.

"Ole Israel he pray a lot wid a book he hab wut he hide, an he take a lill mat an he say he prayuhs on it. He pray wen duh sun go up an wen duh sun go down. Dey ain none but ole Israel wut pray on a mat. He hab he own mat. Now ole man Israel he hab shahp feechuh an a long pointed beahd, an he wuz bery tall. He alluz tie he head up a wite clawt an seem he keep a lot uh clawt on han, fuh I membuh, could see em hangin roun duh stable dryin.

"I membuh a ole uhmun name Daphne. He didn tie he head up lak ole man Israel. He weah loose wite veil on he head. He wuz shahp-fee-chuh too an light uh complexion. He weah one ring in he eah fue he eyes. I hab refrence to it bein some kine uh pruhtection tuh he eyes. Wen e pray, he bow two aw tree times in duh middle uh duh prayuh.

"We ain dance den duh way dey dances now. We dance roun in a succle an den we dances fuh prayin. I membuhs we use tuh hab drums fuh music an we beat duh drum fuh dances.

"Now, ole man Dembo he use tuh beat duh drum tuh duh fewnul, but Mr. Couper e stop dat. He say he dohn wahn drums beatin roun duh dead. But I watch em hab a fewnul. I gits behine duh bush an hide an watch an see wut dey does. Dey go in a long pruhcession tuh duh buryin groun an dey beat duh drums long duh way an dey submit duh body tuh duh groun. Den dey dance roun in a ring an dey motion wid duh hans. Dey sing duh body tuh duh grabe an den dey let it down an den dey succle roun in duh dance.

"Dey ain hab no chuch in doze days an wen dey wannuh pray, dey git behine duh house aw hide someweah an make a great prayuh. Dey ain suppose tuh call on duh Lawd; dey hadduh call on duh massuh an ef dey ain do dat, dey git nine an tutty [lashes].

"Dey ain marry den duh way dey do now. Attuh slabery dey hadduh remarry. Dey hab big baptizin in duh ribbuh lak dey do tuhday an dey dip em on duh ebb tuh wash duh sins away an duh preachuh he make a great prayuh tuh duh ribbuh.

Excerpts are from Drums and Shadows, Survival Studies Among the Georgia Coastal Negroes, by *The Savannah Unit of the Georgia Writers' Project, Works Projects Administration, with Foreword by Guy B. Johnson, Athens, University of Georgia Press, 1940.*

"Ole man Okra he a great un fuh buil drum. He take a calf skin an tan it an make duh side uh maple. Ise pretty sho it wuz maple. He stretch em obuh it good. It wuz bout eighteen inches wide an fifteen inches deep wen he finish it. He beat it wid a stick. Ole man Okra he sho kin chase a drum. Ole man Jesse he frum Africa, too, an he make he own drum.

"I know dat deah wuz a ole man, it bin so long I caahn relate his name, at duh plantation wut wehn roun wid ole man Okra an I membuh well he call all duh fish an ting uh duh ribbuh by duh name uh 'nyana' an den I heah pancake call 'flim.' Muh granmothuh Hettie, duh mothuh uh muh mothuh Bella, he come from Africa too an he huzbun come frum Africa. He name wuz Alex Boyd. Alex wuz bery small felluh but heaby an he ab dahk skin an shahp-feechuch. He talk African but he stuttuh so he dohn talk much roun us chillun, cuz we make fun at im, an as I say befo, I wuz small lad den. Alex wuz knock-kneed an he tie he head up in a clawt.

"Muh granmothuh tell some tings I membuh. He say he mus be bout tutteen aw foeteen wen dey bring im frum Africa. He say deah wuz great talk bout comin tuh dis country an some men tell em it would take only two aw tree days tuh git deah. Dey wuz all happy tuh come. Him an lot uh friens come tuhgedduh.

"Wen Hettie fus come, he say he feel worried cuz he couldn unnuhstan duh talk yuh an many udduh tings bein so diffunt frum he own country. He hab two sistuhs an tree brothuhs but dey couldn git a chance tuh come. He hab mo refrence tuh he mothuh dan tuh he fathuh. An he say dat in Africa he lib in a 'groun house.' It wuz a squeah house, an he say dat he didn lib close tuh a salt ribbuh but weah deah wuz a lot uh wile swamp. Wen he fus come tuh dis country, he didn unnuhstan bout fish. But he tell a lot bout monkey an parakeet. An, too, he say nuttn ebuh die way. Duh crops jis come back ebry yeah widout habin tuh be planted.

"Das all I membuh Hettie tellin bout Africa. Muh fathuh's fathuh come frum Africa too but wen muh fathuh Belali wuz a small young lad, muh granfathuh wehn tuh Dungeness on Cumberland Ilun tuh trade in slabes an nebuh wuz seen agen. It wuz muh fathuh Belali dat made rice cakes.

"Muh fathuh's mothuh lib at Altama. Huh name wuz Luna, but muh fathuh's fathuh wuz a unmarried man. Deah's many tings I do not membuh, it wuz sech a long time ago. I know dat wen deah wuz tuh be a buryin, dey alluz bury duh dead at night at duh plantation. Dey alluz come in frum duh tas [tasks] befo dahk.

"In doze days deah wuz no way tuh git tuh Savannah cep by boat an wen Mr. Couper wannuh go, he use a boat bout fifty foot long an bout six foot wide. He take six strong oahsmen an dey would make it in ten aw twelve hours. I heahd tell ub a house buil by a man frum Africa, wid cawn stalks an mud an wid a straw filluh."

(Ben Sullivan, St. Simons Island)

"I membuh ole Tom Floyd well. I bout fifteen wen he die. He wuz shawt an tick set. I tinks he wuz Ibo. He used tuh whoop an holluh. He say dey do da way in Africa. He was doctuh too an he could cut yuh wid a knife an cop yuh. I wish he wuz yuh right now tuh cop me. I sho needs it an it make yuh feel lots bettuh. I heah him talk plenty bout Africa but I caahn membuh so much ub it cuz uh wuz young boy den. He say he lib in a hut on a ribbuh an dey eat coconut an bread wut grow on a tree. Dey plant yam ebry seben yeah an dey dohn hadduh wuk it. Dey hab peanut an banana. He call it by anudduh name but I caahn membuh it. I seen plenty ub African people an dey all say dey plant duh crop an dey dohn hadduh wuk it. I heah lot ub em tell how dey git obuh yuh. Dey trap em on a boat wid a red flag. . . .

"We use tuh dance roun tuh a drum an a rattle goad. Dey could make good drum frum hawg an bass drum frum cow. Doze days dey ain only beat duh drum fuh dancin; dey beat it on duh way tuh duh grabe yahd. Dat wuz fuh duh det mahch wen dey use tuh carry duh body in a wagon. Dey hab lot uh singin den too an dey hab singin at duh baptizin."

(Floyd White, St. Simons Island)

"Deah wuz two countrymen wut bote come frum Africa libin on duh plantation. One ub dem die an dey bury um widout duh udduh knowin bout it. Pretty soon he lun bout ow he frien die an he make um dig um up. He say he wannuh say a few wuds tuh um. Dey dig up duh man an he speak tuh um an den put um back in duh grabe. It wuz all right attuh he say goodbye."

(Uncle Jonah, Sunbury)

"Muh gran Calina tell me how he got heah. He say he playin on beach in Africa, an big boat neah duh beach. He say, duh mens on boat take down flag, an put up big piece uh red flannel, an all chillun dey git close tuh watuh edge tuh see flannel an see wut doin. Den duh mens comes off boat an ketch um, an wen duh ole folks come in frum duh fiels dey ain no chillun in village. Dey's all on boat. Den dey brings um yuh."

(Phoebe Gilbert, Sapelo Island)

"Muh gran wuz Hestuh, Belali's daughtuh. She tell me Belali wuz coal black, wid duh small feechuhs we hab, an he wuz bery tall. She say Belali an all he fambly come on same boat frum Africa. Belali hab plenty daughtuhs, Medina, Yaruba, Fatima, Bentoo, Hestuh, Magret, and Chaalut.

"Ole Belali Smith wuz muh uncle. His son wuz George Smith's gran. He wuz muh gran Hestuh's son an muh mudduh Sally's brudduh. Hestuh an all ub um sho pray on duh bead. Dey weah duh string uh beads on duh wais. Sometime duh string on duh neck. Dey pray at sun-up and face duh sun on duh knees an bow tuh it tree times, kneelin on a lill mat. . . . (See p. 289.)

"Muh gran Hestuh say she kin membuh duh house she lib in in Africa. She say it wuz cubbuh wid palmettuh an grass fuh roof, an duh walls wuz made uh mud. Dey make duh walls by takin up hanfuls uh mud an puttin it on sumpm firm, sticks put crossways so. I membuh some pots and cups dat she hab made uh clay. She brung deze frum Africa. She membuh wut dey eat in Africa too. Dey eat yam an shuguh cane an peanut an bananas. Dey eat okra too. Yes'm, das right, dey calls it gumbo. Dey dohn hab tuh wuk hahd wid plantin deah. Jis go in woods an dig, an git big yam. Dey eat udduh roots too. Dey ain no flo tuh house. Dey sleep on hahd groun inside house. House wuz neah lill ilun weah dey ketch parrot and sell um. . . .

"She make strange cake, fus ub ebry munt. She call it 'saraka.' She make it out uh meal an honey. She put meal in bilin watuh an take it right out. Den she mix it wid honey, and make it in flat cakes. Sometime she make it out uh rice. Duh cake made, she call us all in an deah she hab great big fannuh full an she gib us each cake. Den we all stands roun table, and she says, 'Ameen, Ameen, Ameen,' an we all eats cake."

(Shad Hall, Sapelo Island)

"Ibo's Landing? Das duh place weah dey bring duh Ibos obuh in a slabe ship an wen dey git yuh, dey ain lak it an so dey all staht singin an dey mahch right down in duh ribbuh tuh mahch back tuh Africa, but dey ain able tuh git deah. Dey gits drown."

(Floyd White, St. Simons Island)

The Flying Africans

I membuhs one boatload uh seben aw eight wut come down frum Savannah. Dat wuz jis a lill befo duh waw. Robbie McQueen wuz African an Katie an ole man Jacob King, dey's all African. I membuhs um all. Ole man King he lib till he ole, lib till I hep bury um. But yuh caahn unduhstan much wut deze people say. Dey caahn unduhstan yo talk an you caahn unduhstan dey talk. Dey go 'quack, quack, quack,' jis as fas as a hawse kin run, an muh pa say, 'Ain no good tuh lissen tuh um.' Dey git long all right but yuh know dey wuz a lot ub um wut ain stay down yuh.

"Ain yuh heah bout um? Well, at dat time Mr. Blue he wuz duh obuhseeuh an Mr. Blue put um in duh fiel, but he couldn do nuttn wid um. Dey gabble, gabble, gabble, an nobody couldn unduhstan um an dey didn know how tuh wuk right. Mr. Blue he go down one mawnin wid a long whip fuh tuh whip um good. . . . Dey's foolish actin. He got tuh whip um, Mr. Blue, he ain hab no choice. Anyways, he whip um good an dey gits tuhgedduh an stick duh hoe in duh fiel an den say 'quack, quack, quack,' an dey riz up in duh sky an tun hesef intuh buzzuds an fly right back tuh Africa. . . . Dey sho lef duh hoe stannin in duh fiel an dey riz right up an fly right back tuh Africa.

"I ain seen um. I bin tuh Skidaway, but I knowd plenty wut did see um, plenty wut wuz right deah in duh fiel wid um an seen duh hoe wut dey lef stickin up attuh dey done fly way."

(Wallace Quarterman, Darien)

"Duh slabes wuz out in duh fiel wukin. All ub a sudden dey git tuhgedduh an staht tuh moob roun in a ring. Roun dey go fastuhnfastuh. Den one by one dey riz up an take wing an fly lak a bud. Duh obuhseeuh heah duh noise an he come out an he see duh slabes riz up in duh eah an fly back tuh Africa. He run an he ketch duh las one by duh foot jis as he wuz bout tuh fly off. I dohn know ef he wuz neah nuff tuh pull um back down an keep um frum goin off."

(Priscilla McCullough, Darien)

"Doze folks could fly too. Dey tell me deah's a lot ub um wut wuz bring heah an dey ain much good. Duh massuh was fixin tuh tie um up tuh whip um. Dey say, 'Massuh, yuh ain gwine lick me,' an wid dat dey runs down tuh duh ribbuh. Duh obuhseeuh he sho tought he ketch um wen dey get tuh duh ribbuh. But fo he could git tuh um, dey riz up in duh eah an fly way. Dey fly right back tuh Africa. I tink dat happen on Butler Ilun."

(Shad Hall, Sapelo Island)

Hoes That Work by Themselves

"I have heard about a magic hoe that folks put in the gahden. They speak certain words tuh it; then the hoe goes ahead and cultivates the gahden without anyone touching it. They jist tell it tuh do the wuk and it does it."

(James Collier, Brownville)

"Duh ole folks use tuh tell dat story bout de hoe wut could wuk by itsef. It stan right up in duh fiel widout nobody holdin tuh it. Das ef yuh knowd how tuh wuk it. Doze Africans knowd how tuh make dat hoe wuk an dey knowd how tuh wuk roots."

(Shad Hall, Sapelo Island)

Burial Traditions

"Use tuh alluz beat duh drum at fewnuls. Right attuh duh pusson die, dey beat um tuh tell duh udduhs bout duh fewnul. Dey beat a long beat. Den dey stop. Den dey beat anudduh long beat. Ebrybody know dat dis mean somebody die. Dey beat duh drum in duh nex settlement tuh let duh folks in duh nex place heah.

"Wen dey fix duh cawpse, dey put pennies on duh eyes an dey put salt on duh stomach tuh keep it frum purgin. Ebrybody put duh hands on um tuh say good-bye.

"On duh way tuh duh grabe dey beat duh drum as dey is mahchin long. Wen duh body is put in duh grabe, ebrybody shout roun duh grabe in a succle, singin an prayin. Each one trow a hanful uh dut in duh grabe."

(Alec Anderson, Possum Point)

"She [the informant's mother] die right in dis house. Dey measure uh wid a string. Dey beat duh drum tuh tell ebrybody bout duh settin-up. We all set up wid duh body. We hab a big wash pot full uh coffee an hab a big sack uh soda crackuh fuh duh folks. Ebrybody place dey han bery light on uh eahs an on uh nose an den dey say, 'Dohn call me. I ain ready fuh tuh go yit.'

"We bury uh by tawch light attuh dahk. Ebrybody mahch roun duh grabe in a succle. Ebry night attuh duh fewnul I put food on duh poach fuh duh spirit tuh come git it.

"In duh ole days dey beat duh drum tuh call duh people tuh duh fewnul. Dey beat it slow—boom—boom—boom. Wen dey wannuh stuhrup duh folks fuh a dance aw frolic, dey beats duh drum fas. Den dey knows it ain fuh no fewnul an dat it's fuh a good time. Duh people neahby, wen dey heahs it, beats deah drum an das how dey sends a message so udduh folks gits it.

"I kin membuh two kine uh drum. Deah wuz duh lill kittle drum. Hit wuz bout fifteen inches cross an tree an a half foot high. Dat wuz duh drum dey beat fuh a settin-up."

(Susan Maxwell, Possum Point)

"We didn alluz hab too much time fuh big fewnul in dem days cuz deah wuz wuk tuh be done an ef yuh ain do yuh wuk, yuh git whipped. Lots uh time dey jis dig a hole in duh groun an put duh body in it, but wenebuh we kin, we hab a settin-up. . . .

"Den dey would cook a regluh meal an dey would kill a chicken in front uh duh doe, wring he neck an cook um fuh duh feas. Den wen we all finish, we take wut victuals lef an put it in a dish by duh chimley an das fuh duh sperrit tuh hab a las good meal. We cubbuh up duh dish an deah's many a time Ise heah dat sperrit lif um. We ain preach duh sermon wen we bury um but we waits a wile so's all duh relations kin come. . .

"Dem dishes an bottles wut put on duh grabe is fuh duh sperrit an it ain fuh nobody tuh tech um. Das fuh duh sperrit tuh feel at home. Wen he die fah off, we bring um home tuh bury um, dohn leh no strainjuh be bury wid um. Yuh gib people wut ain belong tuh yuh anudduh piece uh ground tuh be bury in. We alluz hab two fewnul fuh duh pusson. We hab duh regluh fewnul wen yuh die. Den once a year we hab one big preachin fuh ebrybody wut die dat yeah."

(Jane Lewis, Darien)

"At duh fewnul, dey kills hawg an hab plenty tuh eat. Duh reason fuh dis is so dat sperrit hab plenty at duh las. Wen fewnul pruhcession gits tuh grabeyahd, dey stops. I ain know wy dey do it but dey stops at duh gate, and dey ax leab tuh come in. Deah ain nobody at duh gate, but dey alluz ax jis duh same. Dey say, 'Fambly, we come tuh put our brudduh away in mudduh dus. Plese leh us go tru gate.'"

(Katie Brown, Sapelo Island)

"Wen yuh hab a buryin, yuh alluz hab tuh ask leab tuh duh grabeyahd. Dey do dat tuh dis day. Yuh say, 'Fambly, please let us lay yuh brudduh in mudduh dus.'"

(Shad Hall, Sapelo Island)

"At duh time fuh buryin, duh drum would beat an all would lay flat on duh groun on dey faces befo duh body wuz placed in duh grave. Den all would rise and dance roun duh grave. Wen duh body wuz buried, duh drum would give signal wen all wuz tuh rise aw fall aw tuh dance aw sing."

(Tonie Houston, Tatemville)

"Yuh break duh dishes [placed on the grave] so dat duh chain will be broke. Yuh see, duh one pusson is dead an ef yuh dohn break duh tings, den duh udduhs in duh fambly will die too. Dey will folluh right long."

(Rosa Sallins, Harris Neck)

Putting on the Banjo

"Girls hab tuh be keahful den. Dey caahn be so triflin lak some ub em is now. In Africa dey gits punished. Sometime wen dey bin bad, dey put um on duh banjo. Dat wuz in dis country. Wen dey play dat night, dey sing bout dat girl an dey tell all bout uh. Das puttin uh on duh banjo. Den ebrybody know an dat girl sho bettuh change uh ways."

(Priscilla McCullough, Darien)

THE BILALI DOCUMENT

Bilali Mohamet, or Ben Ali Mohamet, was a Moslem slave on the Sapelo Island plantation of Thomas Spalding early in the nineteenth century. According to accounts in the 1930s by Sapelo Island residents claiming descent from Bilali, he and his family followed the way of Islam while other slaves retained elements of indigenous African religions or were taking up Christianity. Bilali appears to have been a man worth remembering. He was mentioned in various nineteenth-century writings, and oral recollections have survived for more than a century. One descendant, a great-granddaughter, recalled hearing it said that Bilali had been brought to Sapelo from Nassau, and that of numerous daughters, a number had African or Moslem names, including Yaruba (or Nyrrabuh, or Yarrabuh), Medina, Fatima and Bentoo (or Bintu). He spoke French, according to at least one recollection,[1] suggesting that before going to Nassau he had lived on a plantation in one of the French West Indian colonies. In various personal recollections he was described as kneeling to pray at sunup and sundown, prostrating himself three times to the east,[2] and as eating food that was prepared differently from that of other slaves. One writer described him as a very old man who was "head of a tribe," and who wore a cap resembling a fez.[3]

In 1930, the Georgia State Library received a thirteen-page document written in Arabic script that was believed to be Bilali's (or Ben Ali's) journal, in which he had set down his experiences as a slave since coming to the New World. Photocopies of this document were sent to a number of institutions in the United States, England, Egypt and South Africa which, seemingly, were unable to decipher it. But a member of the anthropology department at Northwestern University, Joseph Greenberg, took a copy with him on a field trip to West Africa in 1938, and he showed it to Hausa malams (learned men) in the city of Kano.

---

1. *Lydia Parrish,* Slave Songs of the Georgia Sea Islands, p. 27.
2. *Georgia Writers' Project,* Drums and Shadows, p. 166.
3. *Georgia Bryan Conrad,* "Reminiscences," Southern Workman, 1901, *according to Parrish,* ibid., p. 28.

These scholars were unable to make sense out of the writing and declared it to be the work of jinns (spirits). Dr. Greenberg later deduced that the writer had confused consonants; and when certain consonants were "corrected" there emerged the name Muhammad b. (ben, meaning son of) 'abdullah b. Yusuf b. 'ubaid. Despite a questionable sequence in the genealogy, Dr. Greenberg surmised that the name intended was 'abu Muhammed 'abdullah ben 'abi Zaid 'alqairawani, a native of Qairwan in North Africa and author of a well-known legal work, the *Risala.*

In Dr. Greenberg's own words: "When a handwritten copy of the *Risala* was procured and the 'diary' compared with this copy, it at once became apparent that the major portion of the document could be identified as a series of excerpts from the *Risala,* consisting of the title page, portions of the introduction and parts of the chapters dealing with ablutions and the call to prayer."[4] Although a small portion of the document remained unidentified, it is believed to be from the *Risala* or a similar work. The *Risala* was a product of the Malekite school of Islamic law, which was a western African variant, and the script of the Bilali document was of the Mahgrebine variety, also a product of the western regions of the continent, and so it was deduced that Bilali probably came from the Western Sudan or the areas to the north.

The reasons for the difficulties in deciphering the Bilali writing lay in part with the local variety of the language known to him. Dr. Greenberg conjectures that "at the time of the writer's departure from Africa he was still a young student. Books are first taught by oral memorization; and it is apparent that this manuscript was written by a man who had memorized the text, using a pronunciation of Arabic in which many consonants were not distinguished, making the errors that might be expected when he attempted to reproduce what he knew in writing."[5] (See Photo illustrations nos. 10 and 11.)

THE GULLAH SPEECH OF
THE COASTAL REGION

One of the earliest serious efforts to collect and document traditional Negro songs in the Sea Islands and the adjacent South Carolina and Georgia mainland was that of William Francis Allen, Charles Pickard Ware and Lucy McKim Garrison. Their collection of religious and secular songs, published in 1867 under the title, *Slave Songs of the*

---

4. Joseph Greenberg, "The Decipherment of the 'Ben-Ali Diary,' A Preliminary Statement," The Journal of Negro History, July 1940, pp. 373–74.

5. *Greenberg,* ibid., p. 374.

United States, became—and remains—a classic of its kind. It was far more than a compilation, for the authors were deeply interested in the setting which had produced the songs, as well as the cultural peculiarities of the relatively isolated region. The Gullah idiom in which many of the songs were phrased led them, inevitably, into an examination of speech patterns. (Gullah, or Gola, was frequently used in the islands as a term signifying "African.") In his introduction to the book, William Francis Allen devoted thirteen pages to analysis of the dialect. A century later students of the coastal speech were detecting numerous surviving Africanisms in Gullah, but in the nineteenth century it was taken for granted that most of the oddities of the dialect were corruptions of English. Despite his lack of appreciation for the extent of the African connection, Mr. Allen's purely descriptive account of Gullah was truly noteworthy. The following excerpts are from his introduction to *Slave Songs of the United States.*

It will be noticed that we have spoken chiefly of the negroes of the Port Royal islands, where most of our observations were made, and most of our materials collected. The remarks upon the dialect which follow have reference solely to these islands, and indeed most exclusively to a few plantations at the northern end of St. Helena Island. They will, no doubt, apply in a greater or less degree to the entire region of the southeasterly slave States, but not to other portions of the South. It should also be understood that the corruptions and peculiarities here described are not universal, even here. There are all grades, from the rudest field hands to mechanics and house-servants, who speak with a considerable degree of correctness, and perhaps few would be found so illiterate as to be guilty of them all.

Ordinary negro talk, such as we find in books, has very little resemblance to that of the negroes of Port Royal, who have been so isolated heretofore that they have almost formed a dialect of their own. Indeed, the different plantations have their own peculiarities, and adepts profess to be able to determine by the speech of a negro what part of an island he belongs to, or even, in some cases, his plantation. I can myself vouch for the marked peculiarities of speech of one plantation from which I had scholars, and which was hardly more than a mile distant from another which lacked these peculiarities. Songs, too, and, I suppose, customs, vary in the same way.

A stranger, upon first hearing these people talk, especially if there is a group of them in animated conversation, can hardly understand them better than if they spoke a foreign language, and might, indeed, easily suppose this to be the case. The strange words and pronunciations, and frequent abbreviations, disguise the familiar features of one's native tongue, while the rhythmical modulations, so characteristic of certain European languages, give it an utterly un-English sound. After six months' residence among them, there were scholars in my school, among the most constant in attendance, whom I could not understand at all, unless they happened to speak very slowly.

With these people the process of "phonetic decay" appears to have gone as far, perhaps, as is possible, and with it an extreme simplification of etymology and syntax. There is, of course, the usual softening of *th* and *v*, or *f*, into *d* and *b;* likewise a frequent interchange of *v* and *w*, as *veeds* and *vell* for *weeds* and *well; woices* and *punkin wine,* for *voices* and *pumpkin vine.* "De wile' *(vilest)* sinner may return." This last example illustrates also their constant habit of clipping words and syllables, as *lee' bro,'* for *little brother; plant'shun,* for plantation. The lengthening of short vowels is illustrated in both these (*a,* for instance, rarely has its short English sound). "Een (in) dat mornin' all day."

Strange words are less numerous in their *patois* than one would suppose, and, few as they are, most of them may be readily derived from English words. Besides the familiar *buckra,* and a few proper names, as Cuffy, Quash, and perhaps Cudjo, I only know of *churray* (spill), which may be 'throw'way;" *oona* or *ona,* "you" (both singular and plural, and used only for friends), as "Ona build a house in Paradise"; and *aw,* a kind of expletive, equivalent to "to be sure," as, "Dat clot' cheap." "Cheap aw." "Dat Monday one lazy boy." "Lazy aw—I 'bleege to lick 'em."

Corruptions are more abundant. The most common of them are these: *Yearde* (hear). "Flora, did you see that cat?" "No ma'am, but I yearde him holler." *"Sh'um,"* a corruption of *see 'em,* applied (as *'em* is) to all genders and both numbers. "Wan' to see how Beefut (Beaufort) stan'—nebber sh'um since my name Adam." *Huddy* (how-do?), pronounced *how-dy* by purists, is the common term of greeting, as in the song, "Tell my Jesus huddy O." "Bro' (brother) Quash sen' heap o' howdy." *Studdy,* (steady) is used to denote any continued or customary action. "He studdy 'buse an' cuss we," was the complaint entered by some little children against a large girl. "I studdy talk hard, but you no yearde me," was Rina's defence when I reproved her for not speaking loud enough. When we left, we were told that we must "studdy come back." Here, however, it seems to mean *steady. Titty* is used for mother or oldest sister; thus, Titty Ann was the name by which the children of our man-of-all work knew their mother, Ann. *Sic-a* or *sake-a,* possibly a condensation of *same* and *like.* "Him an' me grow up sic-a brudder an' sister." *Enty* is a curious corruption, I suppose of *ain't he,* used like our "Is that so?" in reply to a statement that surprises one. "Robert, you haven't written that very well." "Enty, sir?" John, it's going to rain to-day." "Enty, sir?" *Day-clean* is used for *day-break.* "Do, day-clean, for let me go see Miss Ha'yet; and de day wouldn't clean." *Sun-up* is also common. *Chu'* for "this" or "that there"; as "Wha' chu?" "See one knife chu?" *Say* is used very often, especially in singing, as a kind of expletive; "(Say) when you get to heaven (say) you 'member me." "Ain't you know say cotton de-de?" In the last sentence "de-de" (accent on first syllable) means "is there"—the first *de,* a corruption of *does* for *is,* will be explained presently; the other is a very common form for *dere,* there.

I do not remember any other peculiar words, but several words used peculiarly. *Cuss* is used with great latitude, to denote any offensive language. "Him cuss me 'git out." "Ahvy (Abby) do cuss me," was the serious-sounding, but trifling accusation made by a little girl against her seat-mate. *Stan'* is a very common word, in the sense of *look.* "My back stan' like white man," was a boast which meant that it was not scarred with the lash. "Him stan' splendid, ma'am," of the sitting of a dress. I asked a group of boys one day the color of the sky. Nobody could tell me. Presently the father of one of them came by, and I told him their ignorance, repeating my question with the same result as before. He grinned: "Tom, how sky stan'?" "Blue," promptly shouted Tom. *Both* they seldom use; generally "all-two," or emphatically, "all-two boff togedder." *One* for *alone.* "Me one, and God," answered an old man in Charleston to the question whether he escaped alone from his plantation. "Gone home one in de dark," for alone. "Heab'n 'nuff for me one" (*i.e.,* I suppose, "for my part"), says one of their songs. *Talk* is one of their most common words, where we should use *speak* or *mean.* "Talk me, sir?" asks a boy who is not sure whether you mean him or his comrade. "Talk lick, sir? nuffin but lick," was the answer when I asked whether a particular master used to whip his slaves. *Call* is used to express relationship; as, "he call him aunt." *Draw,* for receiving in any way—derived from the usage of drawing a specific amount of supplies at stated times. "Dey draw letter," was the remark when a mail arrived and was distributed among us whites. *Meet* is used in the sense of *find.* "I meet him here an' he remain wid me," was the cook's explanation when a missing chair was found in the kitchen. When I remarked upon the absurdity of some agricultural process—"I meet 'em so, an' my fader meet 'em so," was the sufficient answer. A grown man, laboring over the mysteries of simple addition, explained the gigantic answer he had got by "I meet two row, and I set down two." "I meet you dere, sir," said Miller frankly, when convinced in an argument. Too *much* is the common adverb for a high degree of a quality; "he bad *too* much" was the description of a hard master. *Gang,* for any large number; "a whole gang of slate-pencils." *Mash* in the sense of crush; "mammy mash 'em," when the goat had killed one of her kids by lying on it. *Sensibble* and *hab sense* are favorite expressions. A scholar would ask me to make him "sensibble" of a thing. "Nebber sh'um since I hab sense" (*i.e.,* since I was old enough to know). *Stantion* (substantial) was a favorite adjective at Coffin's Point. *Strain* is also a favorite word. "Dem boy strain me," explained Billy, when some younger boys were attempting to *base* him. "I don't want to give more nor fifty-five dollar for a horse," said Quash, "but if dey strain you, you may give fifty-six." "Dat tune *so* strainful," said Rose.

The letters *n, r,* and *y* are used euphonically. "He de baddes' little gal from 'ere to n'Europe," said Bristol of his troublesome niece Venus; "ought to put him on a bar'l, an' den he fall 'sleep an' fall down an' hut heself, an' dat make him more sensibble." "He n'a comin', sir," was often said of a missing scholar. At first I took the *n* for a negative. I set Gib one day to picking out *E's* from a box of letters. He could not distinguish *E* from *F,* and at last, discouraged with his repeated failures, explained, holding out an *F,* "dis y'ere stan'sic-a-r-*um*." (This looks like that.) It is suggested also that *d* is used in the same way, in "He d'a comin';" and *s,* in singing, for instance, "'Tis wells and good." So the vowel *a;* "De foxes have-a hole," "Heaven bell a-ring". . . .

It is perhaps not too strong to say that the field-hands make no distinction of gender, case, number, tense, or voice. The pronouns are to be sure distinguished more or less by the more intelligent among them, and all of these, unless perhaps *us,* are heard. *She* is rare; *her* still more so; *him* being commonly used for the third person singular of all cases and genders; *'em,* if my memory serves me rightly, only for the objective case, but for all genders, and both numbers. *He,* or *'e,* is, I should think, most common as possessive. "Him lick we" might mean a girl as well as a boy. Thus *we* is distinguished from *I* or *me,* and *dey* or *dem* from *him* or *dat;* and these are, I think, the only distinctions made in number. "Dat cow," is singular, "dem cow" plural: "Sandy hat" would mean indifferently Sandy's hat or hats.

I do not know that I ever heard a real possessive case, but they have begun to develop one of their own, which is a very curious illustration of the way inflectional forms grow up. If they wish to make the fact of possession at all emphatic or distinct, they use the word "own." Thus, they will say "Mosey house," but if asked whose house that is, the answer is "Mosey own." "Co' Molsy y'own" was the odd reply made by Mylie to the question whose child she was carrying. Literally translated, this is "Molsy's;" *Co'* is title, *y* euphonic. An officer of a colored regiment standing by me when the answer was made—himself born a slave—confessed that it was mere gibberish to him. No doubt this custom would in time develop a regular inflectional possessive; but the establishment of schools will soon root up all these original growths.

Very commonly, in verbs which have strong conjugations, the forms of the past tense are used for the present; "What make you leff we?" "I tuk dem brudder." Past time is expressed by *been,* and less commonly *done.* "I been kep him home two day," was the explanation given for a daughter's absence from school. "I done pit my crap in dee groun'." Present time is made definite by the auxiliary *do* or *da,* as in the [song] refrains "Bell da ring," "Jericho da worry me." "Bubber (brother) da hoe he tater." So *did* occasionally: "Nat did cuss me," complained one boy of another. It is too much to say that the verbs have no inflections, but it is true that these have nearly disappeared. Ask a boy where he is going, and the answer is "gwine crick for ketch crab" (going into the creek to catch crabs); ask another where the missing boy is, and the answer is the same, with *gone* instead of *gwine.* The hopeless confusion between auxiliaries is sometimes very entertaining: as "de-de," "ain't you know?" "I didn't been." "De Lord is perwide." "You'd better pray, de worl' da [is] gwine." "My stomach been-a da hut me."

Some of these sentences illustrate two other peculiarities—the omission of auxiliaries and other small words, and the use of *for* as the sign of the infinitive. "Unky Taff call Co' Flora for drop tater." "Good for hold comb" was the wisest answer found to the teacher's question what their ears were good for. "Co' Benah wan' Mr.— for tuk 'em down," was Gib's whispered comment when the stubborn Venus refused to step down from a bench. After school the two were discovered at fisticuffs, and on being called to account—"dat same Benah dah knock me," said Gib, while Venus retorted with "Gib cuss me in school."

It is owing to this habit of dropping auxiliaries that the passive is rarely if ever indicated. You ask a man's name, and are answered, "Ole man call John." "Him mix wid him own fat," was the description given of a paste made of bruised ground-nuts, the oil of the nut furnishing moisture. "I can't certain," "The door didn't fasten," "The bag won't full," "Dey frighten in de dark," are illustrations of every-day usage. . . .

In conclusion, some actual specimens of talk, illustrating the various points spoken of, may not be without interest. A scene at the opening of school:

"Charles, why did n't you come to school earlier?" "A-could n't come *soon* to-day, sir; de boss he sheer out clo' dis mornin'.'" "What did he give you?" "Me, sir? I ain't git; de boss he de baddest buckra ebber a-see. De morest part ob de mens dey git heaps o' clo'—more'n 'nuff; 'n I ain't git nuffin." "Were any other children there?" "Plenty chil'n, sir. All de chil'n dah fo' sun-up." "January, you have n't brought your book." "I *is*, sir; sh'um here, sir?" "Where is Juno?" "I ain't know where he gone, sir." "Where is Sam?" "He didn't been here." "Where is the little boy, John?" "He pick up he foot and run." A new scholar is brought: "Good mornin', maussa; I bring dis same chile to school, sir: *do* don't let 'em stay arter school done. Here you, gal, stan' up an' say howdy to de genlmn. Do maussa lash 'em well ef he don't larn he lesson." "Where's your book, Tom?" "Dunno, sir. Some-*body* mus' a tief 'em." "Where's your brother?" "Sh'um dar? wid bof he han' in he pocket?" "Billy, have you done your sum?" "Yes, sir, I out 'em." "Where's Polly?" "Polly de-de." Taffy comes up. "Please, sir, make me sensibble of dat word—I want to ketch 'em werry bad, sir, werry bad." Hacless begins to read. He spells in a loud whisper, "g-o; g-o; g-o—can't fetch dat word, sir, nohow. . . ."

One day when we returned from a row on the creek, to make a call, Dick met us with his face on a grin: "You seen him? you seen Miss T? *I* seen him. I tole him you gone wid intention call on she, but de boat didn't ready in time. He cotch you at Mr. H., on'y de horse bodder him at de gate." One of the boys came to me one day with the complaint, "Dem Ma' B. Fripp chil'n fin' one we book," *i.e.*, those children from Mr. T. B. Fripp's have found one of our books. "'E nebber crack 'e

bret," *i.e.*, say a word. "What make you don't?" "Mr. P. didn't must."
"I don't know what make I didn't answer." "How do you do to-day?"
"Stirrin;" "spared," "standin';" "out o' bed," (never "very well"). Or,
of a friend, "He feel a lee better'n he been, ma'am."

"Arter we done chaw all de hard bones and swallow all de bitter
pills," was part of a benediction; and the prayer at a "praise-meeting"
asked "dat all de white bredren an' sister what jine praise wid we tonight might be bound up in de belly-band ob faith." At a funeral in a
colored regiment: "One box o' dead meat gone to de grave to-day—who
gwine to-morrow? Young man, who walk so stiff—ebery step he take
seem like he say, 'Look out dah, groun', I da comin'." The following is
Strappan's view of Love. "Arter you lub, you lub, you know, boss. You
can't broke lub. Man can't broke lub. Lub stan'—'e ain't gwine broke.
Man hab to be berry smart for broke lub. Lub is a ting stan' jus' like tar;
arter he stick, he stick, he ain't gwine move. He can't move less dan you
burn him. Hab to kill all two arter he lub 'fo' you broke lub."

THREE TALES IN GULLAH DIALECT

Buh Rabbit and Buh Wolf Go Hunting

Buh Rahbit an' Buh Wolf all-two go fuh hunt deah. Buh Wolf got
plenty gunjuh [ginger cookies] an' 'e buy 'im one dog, but Buh Rahbit
ent got mo' 'n one gunjuh, so 'e buy 'im one dog haid. Dey ent gone too
long 'fo' Buh Wolf dog run a deah. Buh Rahbit say, "Come on, Buh
Wolf, my dog haid done ketch 'um," an' 'e run ahaid o' Buh Wolf an'
knock Buh Wolf dog off de deah an' fasten de dog haid on de deah, an'
w'en Buh Wolf git deh Buh Rahbit tell 'um, say, "Look, Buh Wolf, my
dog haid kill deah." Buh Wolf say, "Dog haid cyan' kill deah. Tek a
dog fuh kill deah." Buh Rahbit say, "Oh, yeh, dog haid kill deah. Yunnah shum [you see it] deh on de deah, enty [isn't it so]? 'E *my* deah, an'
I gwine git a cyaat [cart] fuh fetch 'um home." W'ile Buh Rahbit been
attah de cyaat, Buh Wolf been a-study. Finally at las' 'e yeddy Buh
Rahbit duh come wid de cyaat, an' 'e tek a piece o' grape-wine an' big-
gin fuh beat on a tree an' cry, "Please, Maussa, please don' beat we! My

*The three tales are from materials given to the author in manuscript form by
Guy B. Johnson in 1931.*

dog ent ketch yunnah deah. Buh Rahbit dog haid ketch dat deah. Oh, please, Maussa!" Buh Rahbit hice 'e yehs [raised his ears] an' listen. Buh Wolf keep on fuh hollah. Buh Rahbit jump off de cyaat and call out, say, "Oh, Buh Wolf, you lie. Whoebbah yeard of a dog haid ketch deah? Dog haid cyan' ketch deah, tek a dog fuh ketch deah." An' 'e run off an' lef' 'um fo' Buh Wolf.

Buh Deer and Buh Snail Have a Race

Buh Deah been a-boas' dat he de fastes' runnah een de worl'. Buh Snail say, "Buh Deah, I t'ink I run a race wid you." Dey all laugh at Buh Snail, but he say he want to try to beat Buh Deah, so dey 'p'inted de day fo' de race. Buh Deah come to de place weh dey gwine staart, but he not see Buh Snail. But Buh Snail, he deh, an' he crawl up easy-like undah Buh Deah tail. Fin'ly Buh Deah say, "Well, I wondah weh is dat Snail. I guess he don' wan' a-run no race." Buh Snail speak up an' say, "I'm hyuh, let de race staart." So Buh Deah went sailin' off down de road, an' soon he come to de finish place. Big crowd deh. Buh Deah say, "Hab anybody seen dat Snail?" Dey all laugh an' say dey ain' shum [see him]. So Buh Deah staart to set down, an' Buh Snail cry out, "Man, git up off-a me. I been hyuh long befo' you." So dey give de race to Buh Snail.

Playing Dead in the Road

Once a man been fishin' an had a cyaart load o' fish. Buh Rabbit lay down side o' de road like 'e daid. De cyaart go by, an' den Buh Rabbit run t'rough de woods an' lay down 'side de road again. Cyaart come along an' de man say, "How come so many rabbit daid een de road to-day. If I see anudder one, I pick um up." Buh Rabbit run roun' an' lay down 'side de road again. W'en de man come along, he say, "I never see so many daid rabbit. I t'ink I bigin to pick um up." So he pick up Buh Rabbit an' t'row 'im up on de cyaart wid de fish.

Buh Rabbit t'row off fish an' t'row off fish till he got all he want, den he jump off an' go back an' pick up de fish an' take um home. Buh Wolf come along an' see all de fish. He want to know how Buh Rabbit got um. Buh Rabbit say, "Man, I play like I daid, an' de man put me on de cyaart, an' I t'row off de fish." So nex' day Buh Wolf done de same trick. De man stopped de cyaart, say, "Well, Buh Rabbit fool me dat way, but you no fool me," an' he beat Buh Wolf to deat' an' carry 'im home fo' he chillun.

UNCLE REMUS CONFRONTED BY
THE COASTAL DIALECT

It is not clear whether Uncle Remus's response to hearing the coastal dialect was really his own, particularly since his chronicler, Joel Chandler Harris, was not there
when the confrontation took place. However, the dialogue testifies to the fact that
the inlanders regarded the seaboard speech
with amusement. This sketch comes from
Uncle Remus, His Songs and Sayings, by
Joel Chandler Harris, New York, Appleton,
1880.

The notable difference existing between the negroes in the interior of
the cotton States and those on the seaboard—a difference that extends
to habits and opinions as well as to dialect—has given rise to certain
ineradicable prejudices which are quick to display themselves whenever an opportunity offers. These prejudices were forcibly, as well as
ludicrously, illustrated in Atlanta recently. A gentleman from Savannah had been spending the summer in the mountains of north Georgia,
and found it convenient to take along a body-servant. This body-servant was a very fine specimen of the average coast negro—sleek, well-
conditioned, and consequential—disposed to regard with undisguised
contempt everything and everybody not indigenous to the rice-grow-
ing region—and he paraded around the streets with quite a curious and
critical air. Espying Uncle Remus languidly sunning himself on a corner, the Savannah darkie approached.

"Mornin', sah."

"I'm sorter up an' about," responded Uncle Remus, carelessly and
calmly. "How is you stannin' it?"

"Tanky you, my helt mos' so-so. He mo' hot dun in de mountain.
Seem so lak man mus' git need [underneath] de shade. I enty fer see no
rice-bud in dis pa'ts."

"In dis w'ich?" inquired Uncle Remus, with a sudden affectation of
interest.

"In dis pa'ts. In dis country. Da plenty in Sawanny."

"Plenty whar?"

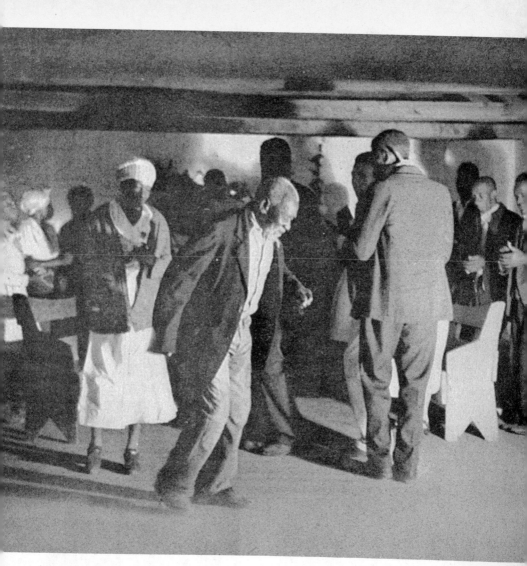

1.
Sea Islands, Georgia: The ring shout, a semireligious activity, preserves dance in disguised form as an aspect of religious expression. In Africa, dancing is an integral part of ritual. In the ring shout, however, any movements resembling overt dancing are prohibited. (See pp. 365–68.)

2, 3, 4.
A graveyard in Sunbury, Sea Islands, Georgia, in the 1930s: The markers are imaginative and seemingly innovative, but some of them reflect a survival of traditional African concepts.

5.
Bent-iron grave marker in burial ground of a church in Talladega National Forest, Alabama: The bent-iron rod appears to spell out the name Ford.

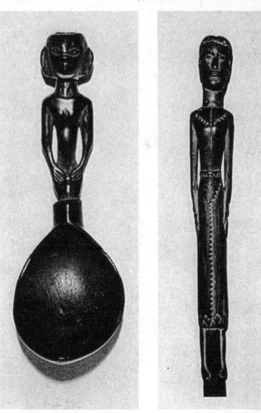

6, 7.
Carved spoon and head of walking stick: These carvings, photographed in Georgia in the 1930s, are believed to have been made by persons of African descent in the Sea Islands. The African influence is unmistakable.

8.
"The Fish Was This Big," sculpture photographed in Birmingham, Alabama, in the 1950s: It is made of stucco or cement.

9.
A Greenville, Mississippi, string base and its maker, Esau McGee.

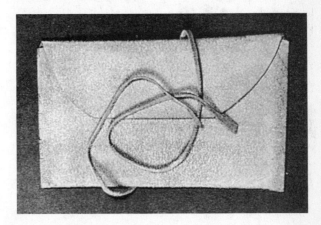

10, 11.
The Bilali or Ben Ali document: Written by a slave on Sapelo Island, Georgia, in the early nineteenth century, it was originally believed to be a journal, in Arabic script, of his early experiences in the New World. Later it was determined to be an Islamic religious work written down from memory. The document is now in the Georgia State Library, Atlanta. Some of the writing that appears faint is in reverse, showing through the paper from the opposite side of the page. (See pp. 289–90.) *Below,* outer covering of document.

12.
Cuban version of the African sansa: It is played with the thumbs.

13.
Masked figure of the Cuban Abakwa secret society: Abakwa, a fraternal organization with elaborate traditional rituals, is a direct descendant of the Egbo society of the Ekoi and Efik peoples of the Calabar Coast. (See pp. 20–25 and pp. 570–76.) This photo was taken under difficult circumstances, and the long conical crest of the mask is not visible.

14, 15.
Drums of the Cuban Arara cult, which preserves traditions of Dahomean religious worship. The drums reflect Dahomean style.

16.
Puerto Rican musicians with quatro and guitar: Many of their songs have religious content and are heard on festival occasions.

17.
Puerto Rican Bomba drummers: The Bomba Dance, still known in a few Puerto Rican communities, is in an African tradition. (See pp. 86–88.)

18, 19.
Above, the Haitian "mosquito drum": It is played by plucking its single string and varying the tone by pressure on the bow. The device is of African origin and was probably developed from a spring snare used for catching small game. *Below*, Haitian stamping tubes, made from sections of bamboo: They produce percussive tones when struck on the ground. Stamping tubes are also found in Venezuela. They are of African origin.

20.
Haitian ogan, a forged iron bell of Yoruba derivation.

21.
Haitian Marassas: Carvings representing twins and the deity of twins. The Haitian twin cult derives from Fon and Yoruba traditions.

22.
Haitian children playing the game called "Theater."

23.
Haitian religious service for the sea god Agwé: The ritual takes place at sea, where a sacrifice to Agwé is set adrift in a miniature boat. (See pp. 32–35.)

24.
Haitian service for the Ibo deities: The gods are fed by placing special food and drink in the two holes. The white flour designs on the ground and the patterns on the ollas have specific ritual significance.

25.
Haitian houngan, or cult priest: The rituals in which he officiates relate to Yoruba, Daho-mean, Ibo, and Bantu religious traditions. In his right hand he holds an asson, a sacred gourd rattle. In his left is a divining device.

26.
Ras Tafari leader in Jamaica: The cult has traditionally regarded Haile Selassie as God, and believes that blacks are reincarnations of the ancient Israelites. (See pp. 147–58.)

27.
Kumina drummers: The Kumina cult in Jamaica retains numerous elements of African religious beliefs, including a pantheon of deities, each with special attributes and powers.

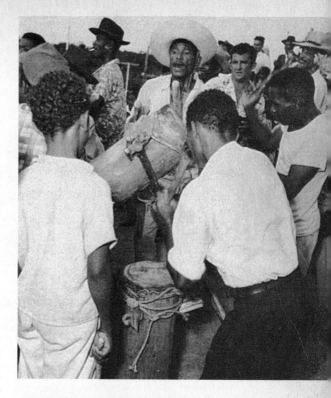

28, 29.
Players of Mina and Curbata drums
in the Venezuelan Festival of San
Juan: The drums are of African design and the music contains elements that are predominantly African.

30, 31.
Shrines of the Djuka bush people of Surinam: *Above,* in the foreground, the shrine of a deity called Aflamu, who is also known in Haiti. In the background, the shrine of another deity identified only as Vodun, a term that usually designates a generic group of gods. *Below,* the effigy or representation of Vodun as it appears within the shrine. (See p. 189 ff.) Djuka is a word that includes various Bush Negroes. These photos were taken in a village of the Aucaner tribe.

32.
Bush Negro carvings in Surinam: These combs are carved in a style that clearly reflects Akan (Ghana) tradition. The comb on the left is from the Saramaccaner tribe. The one on the right is from the Aucaner.

33.
A Djuka woodcarver: His tools are a machete and a common pocket knife.

34, 35, 36.
Candomblé in Bahia, Brazil: Rites of the Bahian Candomblés combine traditions of the Yoruba and the Fon peoples of West Africa, and retain numerous Fon and Yoruba deities. Names of some of these deities have undergone alteration through the years. Women who undergo ritual possession by the gods are called "daughters." *Upper left,* a daughter of Omolu. *Upper right,* a daughter of Oxum. *Below,* a daughter of Agum.

"Da plenty in Sawanny. I enty fer see no crab an' no oscher; en swimp, he no stay 'roun'. I lak some rice-bud now."

"Youer talkin' 'bout deze yer sparrers, w'ich dey er all head, en 'lev'm un makes one mouffle [mouthful], I speck," suggested Uncle Remus. "Well, dey er yer," he continued, "but dis ain't no climate whar de rice-birds flies inter yo' pockets en gits out de money an' makes de change derse'f; an' de isters don't shuck off der shells en run over you on de street, an' no mo' duz de s'imp hull derse'f an' drap in yo' mouf. But dey er yer, dough. De scads 'll fetch um."

"Him po' country fer true," commented the Savannah negro, "he no like Sawanny. Down da, we set need de shade an' eaty de rice-bud, an' de crab, an' de swimp tree time de day; an' de buckra man drinky him wine, an' smoky him seegyar all troo de night. Plenty fer eat an' not much fer wuk."

"Hit's mighty nice, I speck," responded Uncle Remus, gravely. "De nigger dat ain't hope up 'longer high feedin' ain't got no grip. But up yer whar fokes is gotter scramble 'roun' an' make der own livin', de vittles wat's kumerlated widout enny sweatin' mos' allers gener'lly b'longs ter some yuther man by rights. One hoe-cake an' a rasher er middlin' meat las's me fum Sunday ter Sunday, an' I'm in a mighty big streak er luck w'en I gits dat."

The Savannah negro here gave utterance to a loud, contemptuous laugh, and began to fumble somewhat ostentatiously with a big brass watch-chain.

"But I speck I struck up wid a payin' job las' Chuseday," continued Uncle Remus, in a hopeful tone.

"Wey you gwan do?"

"Oh, I'm a waitin' on a culled gemmun fum Savannah—wunner deze yer high livers you bin tellin' 'bout."

"How dat?"

"I loant 'im two dollars," responded Uncle Remus, grimly, "an' I'm a waitin' on 'im fer de money. Hit's wunner deze yer jobs w'at las's a long time."

The Savannah negro went off after his rice-birds, while Uncle Remus leaned up against the wall and laughed until he was in imminent danger of falling down from sheer exhaustion.

SEA ISLAND RIDDLES

Horse in de stable an' reinge [reins] outside.
    ('Tatuh in de bed and wine [vine] outside.)
Chip cherry up, chip cherry down, no man can climb chip cherry tree.
    (Smoke.)
Black hen set on de red hen nest.
    (Pot on de fiah.)

Some'tin' run all day an' all night an' nevah stop runnin'.
    (The river, time, wind.)
Rose in de gyaa'den an' rose outside. What one you take?
    (Rose in de gyaa'den is married gal, rose outside is unmarried gal.)

From "St. Helena Songs and Stories," by Guy B. Johnson, in Black Yeomanry, Life on St. Helena Island, by T. J. Woofter, Jr., New York, Holt, 1930.

SPIRITUALS AND RELIGIOUS EPICS

Negro religious songs include a wide range of styles, idioms, and substance. There are staid, square-measured songs that strongly reflect white hymns of an earlier day; rocking and reeling songs that truly shake the rafters; two-part prayer songs of polyphonous character; spirited tunes that are nothing less than marches; shouts that call for percussive effects by clapping and foot stamping; songs in which popular musical instruments such as tambourines, guitars, drums, and harmonicas provide instrumental dynamics; songs that are sung quietly and songs that put people on their feet; ecstatic moans and groans; reli-

From Negro Folk Music, U.S.A., *by Harold Courlander.* © 1963 by Columbia University Press. Reprinted here with emendations, deletions and new material by kind permission of Columbia University Press. All but one of the music notations are by John Benson Brooks.

gious songs of street singers that are almost indistinguishable from blues; strident gospel songs calling on sinners to reform; and songs which transpose scenes from the Bible into moving, immediate, colloquial, and, often, magnificently dramatic terms. So broad, indeed, is the realm of Negro religious music that the customary title "spiritual" is patently inadequate to describe it. In fact, this word is not used by some people who sing these songs, the term "anthem" being preferred. Although the range and variety to be found are considerable, most of them are within the limits of what we recognize as Negro religious and literary idiom.

Listening to Negro religious songs as they are sung in a great many churches, particularly in the South, one cannot fail to be impressed with an element that is best described as conservatism. In any community, there may be a large repertoire of religious songs upon which to draw. Selections are made according to circumstances—that is, songs appropriate to an occasion are sung. Despite an effect of spontaneity, innovation is not a daily phenomenon. Except in churches which favor the modern gospel-type song, old songs are called upon, and they are used in established ways, though there may be variations within the outer limits set by custom. A given piece may be sung "regular meter" or "long meter"; it may be done by a small choir in somewhat stilted fashion, perhaps with piano accompaniment, or it may be sung in free fashion by the entire congregation.

A good singing leader or a preacher can endow a song with a special, dynamic character. Songs may gradually move from one commuty to another, and a single church may have within its repertoire a number of variants of an old theme. But there is to be found nothing like the freedom of improvisation and invention that is characteristic of secular music. One perceives the richness of the oral literature only partially in the repertoire of a single community; its full implications lie in the composite picture. Some songs are heard in Mississippi and Texas that are not sung in Georgia and South Carolina, and many songs which are widely known throughout the country are sung differently in different places.

Many of the newer elements in Negro religious music come from individual street singers, gospel groups, and large urban churches. The religious street singers are fewer today than they once were. But it is inconceivable that countless performers such as Blind Willie Johnson did not affect more traditional styles of singing in churches. The gospel songs—composed or arranged airs—are among the most recent elements. They are self-consciously literary and formal, and many of them are designed primarily for performance by an individual singer or a choir. The urban churches have gone further in blending tradition with new styles than have the rural churches. Some urban services, in fact, are superproductions which employ professional gospel-type singers, instrumental ensembles, and even full-blown brass bands. This latter development is not altogether synthetic or illogical. A half century and more ago brass bands played at least a semireligious role in Negro life. In some regions of the South, particularly, bands of fraternal lodges participated conspicuously in funerals, beginning at the church and ending at the graveyard, and in other similar activities. The style of instrumental music in some contemporary churches where it is heard has been affected by both secular tradition and jazz. In some small rural churches, the presence of instrumental musical support is of long standing, and the use of such devices as guitars, drums, harmonicas and tambourines is regarded as traditional.

As for the main body of religious songs, we find in it a large number of themes projecting the Christian concepts of faith, love and humility, with considerable emphasis on salvation. Another large segment pinpoints events and stories recorded in the Old and New Testaments; if these songs are arranged in a somewhat chronological order, they are equivalent to an oral version of the Bible. Each song presents in a capsulized or dramatic form a significant Biblical moment. It has been possible for lay preachers of an earlier day to go from church to church armed only with a knowledge of these songs and their meanings and give sermons that have met the best existing standards.

Why did Negro oral religious literature take the particular form that it did, and why did it eventually diverge so much from the white tradition, in view of the fact that Negro Christian converts were presented with ready-made songs (white spirituals and hymns), an established way of singing them, and a preselected set of images and symbols? The answer must lie in an assumption that the materials thus made available were regarded as inadequate, in some respects, in relation to Negro tradition. For psychological and cultural reasons, the earliest Negro congregations found it necessary to remold these materials.

We can only speculate on the religious attitudes of the first few generations of Africans in the New World. But we have learned enough in recent times about African cultures to know that the slaves brought to the Christian service religious traditions of their own, as well as established methods of treating musical and invocational ideas. They had clear-cut concepts of the role of music in life. Music permeated virtually every important phase of living in Africa, from birth to death. Singing related to religious activity had a specific character and specific requirements. Most West and Central Africans had their own concepts of a supreme (though not necessarily exclusive) deity. In many instances, this deity tended to be somewhat remote, and their dealings—supplicative, invocational, and placative—were with lesser supernatural beings, including members of holy pantheons. These demigods were full of personality, their actions were as predictable or as unpredictable as those of humans, and many of them had epic histories. In religious rites, epic and dramatic actions of the demigods, as well as their special powers and attributes, were recalled and extolled. Those who served such deities sang songs of praise which alluded to their various powers, behavior and noteworthy deeds. Much of the oral religious literature of the African layman consisted less of "prayers" (as we think of them) than of dramatic statements, in the form of songs, relating to the deities.

Confronted with new religious patterns, the New World African found in the Bible prolific materials adaptable to the traditional dramatic statement and, occasionally, to the epic treatment. He felt impelled to translate and recast Biblical events into a dramatic form that satisfied his sense of what was fitting. The stories of the Bible thus transmuted became vivid images or, sometimes, poetry.

To enhance the drama, other subject matter was drawn from whatever portion of the Biblical literature, or whatever aspect of contemporary life, seemed suitable and useful. Thus there are interpolations from the New Testament into the Old, and from the Old into the New. Job, Jesus, Judas and Joshua may be found in the same song, along with the twentieth-century train that carries the sanctified. In some instances songs emerged in a form akin to the epic. Few Negro songs project mystical or abstract philosophical concepts. They tend to concentrate on particular events, episodes, stories, and revelations.

Any notion that Negro oral religious literature is primitive or naïve—an impression conveyed by numerous literary treatments—certainly does not survive careful reading or hearing. The song "All God's Children Got Wings," far from being quaint or childlike, is an expression of faith couched in symbols that were apparent to most preliterate slaves and, later, liberated Negroes. While some people must have taken the inherent promises of this song literally, for most Negroes the wings, harps and shoes must have conveyed simply the idea of relief from a hard and unrewarding life, either in this world or another. If Negro religious imagery is truly "naïve," then the burden of responsibility must be borne by the Bible, out of which the imagery is primarily extracted.

Negro religious literature, like the secular, is marked by an economy of statement, rich and fresh scenes, and the capacity to evoke recognition and response. The entire story of Jonah is presented in a song of fourteen lines, every one of which is visual and dramatic.[1] Many of the songs do not describe events so much as allude to them. Some telescope a variety of allusions into a few tight phrases.

There are certain standard images which are called upon again and again. The allusion to Elijah's chariot, for example, occurs frequently. The chariot represents not only Elijah's transportation to heaven, but the heavenly ascent of all who are saved. The image occurs, among other places, in "Job, Job"[2] and in "Rock Chariot, I told You to Rock,"[3] where the allusion to Elijah's chariot is clearly tied to each individual's fate:

> Rock, chariot, in the middle of the air.
> Judgment going to find me.
> I wonder what chariot comin' after me.
> Judgment going to find me.

---

1. See music notation no. 1 following this section.
2. See music notation no. 2 following this section.
3. See music notation no. 3 following this section.

The theme appears again in the song "Tip Around My Bed Right Easy":

> Jes' low down the chariot right easy,
>   Right easy, right easy,
> Jes' low down the chariot right easy,
>   Right easy, right easy,
> And bring God's servant home.

Another widespread image is that of the train, which represents more modern transportation to the same ultimate destination for those who have found salvation. Among many songs, it appears in "King David":

> Just as soon as you cease
>   Good Lord,
> Children, from your sins,
>   Good Lord,
> This-a train will start
>   Good Lord,
> To take you in. . . .[4]

The train motif has in it a certain excitement, an excitement that many people, regardless of backgound, have felt on seeing modern diesel or old-fashioned steam locomotives at close range. The impression that the snorting, smoking engines of an earlier day must have left on Negro song makers is evident in the frequent resort to this image, and in the excitement which it has the power to evoke. One ring shout actually takes on the driving character of a moving train, and it ties the train image to that of the chariot, for which it is only a modern substitute:

> Who's that ridin' the chariot?
> Well well well.
> One mornin'
> Before the evening
> Sun was going down
> Behind them western hills.
> Old Number Twelve
> Comin' down the track.
> See that black smoke.
> See that old engineer. . . .

In another song, the train has a slightly threatening character, with less glory and exaltation and more hint of judgment at the bar:

> Oh, the little black train is a-comin',
> I know it's goin' to slack;

---

4. See music notation no. 4 following this section.

You can tell it by its rumblin',
It's all draped in black.

The train we are singin' about,
It has no whistle or bell,
And if you find your station
You are in heaven or hell.

There's a little black train and an engine,
And one small baggage car;
You won't have to have much baggage
To come to the judgment bar.

The chorus of the song, interspersed between stanzas, goes:

There's a little black train a-comin',
Get all your business right;
There's a little black train a-comin',
And it may be here tonight.

From the spiritual "Every Time I Feel the Spirit" we have the lines:

Not but the one train on this track,
Not but the one train on this track,
Not but the one train on this track,
Runs right to Heaven and runs right back.

A song heard in the Georgia Sea Islands refers to a white horse in a somewhat similar context:

Loose horse in the valley.
    Aye.
Who goin' to ride 'im?
    Aye.
Nothin' but the righteous.
    Aye, Lord.
Time's drawin' nigh.

In recent days, some errant gospel songs have gone so far as to supplant the train with an airplane.

There are a good many other standard images of that type, including the wheel of Ezekiel and the gospel shoes.

Considerable attention has been paid to the possibility that a large number of spirituals were not what they seemed on the surface, but in actuality were songs full of hidden meanings, hints, messages and signals for slaves looking toward escape. The spiritual "Steal Away to Jesus," for example, frequently has been pointed out as a double-meaning song—ostensibly religious in intent, but in reality an invitation to the slaves to steal away to freedom:

> Steal away, steal away to Jesus,
> Steal away, steal away home.
> I ain't got long to stay here.
> My Lord calls me, he calls me by thunder,
> The trumpet sounds within my soul.
> I aint got long to stay here.

Similarly, the spiritual "Go Down, Moses" has been regarded as a significant double-meaning song:

> When Israel was in Egypt's Land,
>   Let my people go.
> Oppressed so hard they could not stand,
>   Let my people go.
> Go down, Moses, way down in Egypt's Land,
> Tell old Pharaoh, let my people go.

And a later stanza:

> No more shall they in bondage toil,
>   Let me people go.
> Let them come out with Egypt's spoil,
>   Let my people go.

Reminiscences of former slaves and the accretion of legend and hearsay have pinpointed Harriet Tubman, the Negro antislavery worker and unofficial "conductor" of the Underground Road, as the Moses of the song.

It is readily evident that songs of this kind could be interpreted in more than one way by the slaves. The situation of the Israelites in Egypt as described in the Old Testament was one with which people in bondage could easily identify themselves. It is a safe assumption that all Negro religious songs were understood by the slaves in the light of their own immediate condition of servitude. In singing of the Israelites' flight to freedom, or the promises inherent in the visions of St. John, or the prophecies of the prophets, or heavenly salvation, it certainly must have crossed their minds that there was a remarkable parallel to be seen. Songs about Moses and Joshua must have had a much more personal and immediate meaning to the Afro-American than to his white master. Indeed, one must consider the possibility that the appeal of Christianity to the New World African and his slave descendants lay to a significant extent in these obvious Biblical parallels.

Nevertheless, if songs of the type of "Steal Away to Jesus" and "Go Down, Moses" are to be considered conscious disguises for political, temporal meanings, a large part of the religious repertoire must be placed in the same category. Every reference to crossing the Jordan could be interpreted to mean escape to the North; every battle of the Israelites might be read to mean the battle for Negro freedom; every reference to Elijah's chariot or the gospel train could be seen as allusion to the Underground Railroad: and every trumpet blast interpreted as Emancipation Day. But such a notion would be difficult to accept. Negro religious activity and belief are not based on the principle of secular or situational parallels. Negro religious music must be considered to be, in the main, precisely what it purports to be.

It may well have been, as legend has it, that to some slaves Harriet Tubman was Moses. Yet in the semi-isolation in which many slaves found themselves, Harriet Tubman probably was not a household word, and "Go Down, Moses" must have been sung by some slaves in the belief that Moses meant simply Moses. A large number of spirituals and anthems were so worded that they could have a disguised meaning; but it is not safe to assume (or even take the word of persons who were born in slavery) that they were created as anything else but religious songs.

As suggested previously, it would be possible to put a large body of Negro religious songs together in a certain sequence to produce an oral couterpart of the Bible; if printed, they would make a volume fully as thick as the Bible itself. To see how this generalization works out in practice, it may be worthwhile to take a look at various examples.

In Genesis, we read: "And the eyes of both of them were opened, and they knew that they were naked: and they sewed fig leaves together and made themselves aprons. . . . And Adam and his wife hid themselves from the presence of the Lord God, amongst the trees of the garden. And the Lord God called unto Adam, and said unto him, Where are thou?" This story, on which so much of Christian theology turns, is told in song this way:

Oh, Eve, where is Adam?
Oh, Eve, Adam in the garden,
   Pinnin' leaves.
Adam in the garden,
   Pinnin' leaves.
Lord called Adam,
   Pinnin' leaves.
Adam wouldn't answer,
   Pinnin' leaves.
Adam shamed,
   Pinnin' leaves.
Adam?

Pinnin' leaves.
Adam!
   Pinnin' leaves.
Where't thou?
   Pinnin' leaves.
Adam naked,
   Pinnin' leaves
Ain't you shamed?
   Pinnin' leaves.
Lord I'm shamed,
   Pinnin' leaves.

Following closely on the heels of the Adam and Eve story in Genesis is the epic of the flood, told in broad and general terms, without the wealth of imagery, detail and poetry found in later portions of the Bible. But such details as there are in the original have provided inspiration for many Negro songs about Noah and the Ark, with dramatic images created by the songmakers themselves. Although the Bible states that Noah was instructed to make his craft out of gopher wood, this

song, found in Alabama, declares it was made in fact out of hickory
bark:

> Noah, Noah, who built this ark?
> Noah, Noah, who built this ark?
> Now who built this ark?
>
> Noah, Noah, built this ark,
> Built this ark out of hickory bark.
> Oh Lord, who built this ark?
> Noah, Noah, who built this ark?
> Who built this ark?
> Noah, Noah, built this ark,
> Built this ark without hammer or nails,
> Oh lord, who built this ark?
> Noah, Noah, who built this ark?
> Who built this ark?
>
> Called old Noah foolish man,
> Building this ark on this dry land,
> Oh Lord, who built this ark?
> Noah, Noah, who built this ark?
> Now who built this ark?
> Noah, No'.

In the Georgia Sea Islands, a quite different rendition known as
"Noah [pronounced Norah] Hoist the Window" was taken down by
Lydia Parrish. Although the structure of the song is different, and the
total effect is that of independent composition, the presence of identical lines suggest that the two versions had a common origin. The chorus and one stanza of the Sea Islands "Noah" are given here:

> Oh Noah, hoist the window,
> Oh Noah, hoist the window,
> Oh Noah, hoist the window,
> Hoist the window, let the dove come in.
>
> And the foolish man come ridin' by,
> Oh hoist the window, let the dove come in.
> Well he point his hand and he scorn at Noah,
> Oh hoist the window, let the dove come in.
> And he call old Noah the foolish man,
> Oh hoist the window, let the dove come in.
> You buildin' your ark on the hard dry land,
> Oh hoist the window, let the dove come in.

We have already taken note of a song dealing with the role of Moses.
Next comes Joshua, whose warlike accomplishments are the subject of

comment in many religious songs. Probably the best known is "Joshua Fit the Battle of Jericho," but it is not often that the words of that song are read in tranquility; too often the poetry is lost in the triumphant sweep and surge of the music. One version of "Joshua" is sung this way:

Chorus (after each stanza)
Joshua fit the battle of Jericho,
Jericho Jericho!
Joshua fit the battle of Jericho,
And the walls came tumblin' down!
That mornin',
Joshua fit the battle of Jericho,
   Jericho, Jericho,
   Joshua fit the battle of Jericho,
   And the walls came tumblin' down!

Good mornin' brother pilgrim,
Pray tell me where you bound,
Oh tell me where you travellin' to
On this enchanted ground.

My name it is Poor Pilgrim,
To Canaan I am bound,
Travellin' through this wilderness
On-a this enchanted ground.

You may talk about the King of Gideon,
You may talk about the man of Saul,
There's none like good old Joshua
At the battle of Jericho!

Up to the walls of Jericho
He marched with spear in hand.
Go blow them ram horns Joshua cried,
'Cause the battle is in my hand!

Then the lamb-ram-sheep horns began to blow,
The trumpets began to sound,
Joshua commanded the children to shout
And the walls came tumblin' down!

David is the protagonist of numerous songs, and around the scene of David playing his harp in the following piece there are woven various Biblical references and modern preachments; the final effect is a panorama with a great vista. There is an impression about this song that it was once smaller and more limited in scope, and that over the years it accumulated a number of themes which came from the preacher's pulpit.

1. King David was
      Good Lord
   That shepherd boy.
      Good Lord
   Didn't he kill Goliath
      Good Lord
   And he shout for joy.
      Good Lord

Well the tallest tree
   Good Lord
In Paradise
   Good Lord
Them Christians call it
   Good Lord
Their tree of life.
   Good Lord

Chorus (after each stanza)
Little David play on your harp,
   Hallelu, hallelu,
Little David play on your harp,
   Hallelu.
Didn't you promise to play on your harp,
   Hallelu, hallelu,
Didn't you promise to play on your harp,
   Hallelu.

2. Just watch the sun
      Good Lord
   How steady she run.
      Good Lord
   Don't mind, she catch you
      Good Lord
   With your works undone.
      Good Lord

3. You got a true way to find
      Good Lord
   Mister Hypocrite out.
      Good Lord
   At the first thing gwine
      Good Lord
   To church and shout.
      Good Lord
   You goin' to meet Mister Hypocrite
      Good Lord
   Comin' along the street
      Good Lord
   First thing he show you
      Good Lord
   His tongue in his teeth.
      Good Lord

4. Just as soon as you cease
      Good Lord

Children, from your sins,
   Good Lord
This-a train will start,
   Good Lord
It'll take you in.
   Good Lord
Way down yonder
   Good Lord
By Jordan Stream
   Good Lord
You can hear God's children
   Good Lord
Tryin' to be redeemed.
   Good Lord
Ain't Jordan wide,
   Good Lord
Old Jordan wide.
   Good Lord
Well none don't cross
   Good Lord
But the sanctified.
   Good Lord

5. Sister Mary goin' to heaven
      Good Lord
   On the springs of the sun.
      Good Lord
   When Mary got to heaven

Good Lord
Well her work was done.
  Good Lord
Just talk about me
  Good Lord
As much as you please,
  Good Lord
But the more you talks
  Good Lord
I'm goin' to bend my knees.
  Good Lord

6. Ever since my soul
  Good Lord
Children, been set free
  Good Lord
Satan act and lie
  Good Lord

At the root of the tree.
  Good Lord
Ain't Satan just like
  Good Lord
A snake in the grass
  Good Lord
He's always walkin'
  Good Lord
In a Christian's path.
  Good Lord
Old Satan got on
  Good Lord
Them iron shoes.
  Good Lord
It's you better mind
  Good Lord
Don't he step 'em on you.
  Good Lord[5]

The dramatic, epic-like saga of Samson, the half-tamed human lion, the "natural man" among Biblical heroes, has been recorded in a number of Negro religious songs, but the best known is one called "If I Had My Way." Over a period of time, many stanzas have appeared which were probably not a part of the "original" rendition. One version is sung like this:

Chorus (between stanzas, with variations)
He said, and if I had'n way, (×3)
I'd tear the buildin' down!
He cried O Lord,
O Lord,
O Lord Lordy Lordy,
O Lord!
He cried O Lord,
O Lord,
O Lord Lordy Lordy,
O Lord!
He said, and if I had'n my way, (×3)
I'd tear the buildin' down!

Delilah was a woman fine and fair,
A very pleasant lookin' with coal black hair.
Delilah she gained old Samson's mind
When he saw this woman and she looked so fine.

---

5. See music notation no. 4 following this section.

Oh whether he went to Timothy I can't tell,
But the daughters of Timothy they treated him well.
He supplied to his father to go and see,
Can't you get this beautiful woman fo me?

Stop and let me tell you what Samson done,
He looked at the lion and the lion run.
It's written that the lion had killed men with his paw,
But Samson had his hand in the lion's jaw.

Samson burned up a field of corn,
They looked for Samson but he was gone.
A-so many thousand formed a plot,
It wasn't many days 'fore he was caught.

They bound him with ropes, and while walkin' along
He looked on the ground, he saw an old jawbone.
He moved his arms, the rope popped like threads,
When he got through killin', three thousand was dead.

Samson's mother supplied to him,
Can't you find a wife among our kin?
Samson's father said it grieve your mother's mind
To see you marry a woman of the Philistines.

Another song about Samson deals with the haircutting episode:

Samson went out at a one time,
And he killed about a thousand Philistines.
Delilah fooled Samson and this we know,
For the Holy Bible tells us so.
She shaved off his head just as clean as your hand,
And his strength became as any other man's.

From the Second Book of Kings (2:11) comes the inspiration for the constantly recurring image of Elijah's chariot: "And it came to pass, as they still went on, and talked, that, behold, there appeared a chariot of fire, and horses of fire, and parted them both asunder; and Elijah went up by a whirlwind into heaven." In the song "Rock Chariot, I Told You to Rock" there are wedded symbols of salvation from various portions of the Old and New Testaments, including Ezekiel and the Revelation of St. John the Divine. Beginning with Elijah's chariot, the allusions turn to the gospel wheel of Ezekiel, gospel shoes, and the harps that are to be played on judgment day.

Rock, chariot, I told you to rock!
Judgment goin' to find me!

Won't you rock, chariot, in the middle of the air?
    Judgment goin' to find me!
I wonder what chariot comin' after me?
    Judgment goin' to find me!
Rock, chariot, I told you to rock!
    Judgment goin' to find me!
Elijah's chariot comin' after me!
    Judgment goin' to find me!
Rock, chariot, I told you to rock!
    Judgment goin' to find me!
Rock, chariot in the middle of the air!
    Judgment goin' to find me!
Wouldn't give you my shoes for your shoes!
    Judgment goin' to find me!
Wouldn't give you my robe for your robe!
    Judgment goin' to find me!
Wouldn't give you my crown for your crown!
    Judgment goin' to find me!
Wouldn't swap my soul for your soul!
    Judgment goin' to find me!
Rock, chariot, I told you to rock!
    Judgment goin' to find me!
Will you rock, chariot, in the middle of the air?
    Judgment goin' to find me!
Rock, chariot in the middle of the air!
    Judgment goin' to find me!
Wouldn't give you my wings for your wings!
    Judgment goin' to find me!
Wouldn't swap you my grave for your grave!
    Judgment goin'to find me!
Rock, chariot, in the middle of the air!
    Judgment goin' to find me!
I wonder what chariot comin' after me!
    Judgment goin' to find me!
Elijah's chariot comin' after me!
    Judgment goin' to find me!
That must be that gospel wheel!
    Judgment goin' to find me!
What wheel children is you talkin' about?
    Judgment goin' to find me!
Talkin' about the wheel in Jesus Christ!
    Judgment goin' to find me!
Every spoke is a human cry!
    Judgment goin' to find me!
Ain't you talkin' about the little wheel runnin' in the wheel?
    Judgment goin' to find me!
Them folks in Jesus Christ!
    Judgment goin' to find me!

> Wouldn't swap my wheel for your wheel!
>   Judgment goin' to find me!
> Wouldn't give you my Lord for your Lord!
>   Judgment goin' to find me!
> Ain't you got on them gospel shoes?
>   Judgment goin' to find me!
> I wouldn't swap my shoes for your shoes!
>   Judgment goin' to find me!
> I wouldn't give you my harp for your harp!
>   Judgment goin' to find me![6]

The reference to the wheel, syncretized with the chariot in the previous song, comes from one of Ezekiel's visions (1:16): "The appearance of the wheels and their work was like unto the color of beryl; and they four had one likeness; and their appearance and their work was as it were a wheel in the middle of a wheel." This image has been preserved in a well-known spiritual:

> Ezekiel saw that wheel
> Way up in the middle of the air.
> Ezekiel saw that.wheel
> Way in the middle of the air.
>
> And the big wheel run by faith
> And the little wheel run by the Grace of God,
> A wheel within a wheel
> Way in the middle of the air.

A song usually known as "Job, Job" is one of the outstanding epics of the Negro religious literature. Rarely heard twice the same way because of its length, its scope, and its rich fare, the song alludes to significant scenes scattered throughout the Old and New Testaments. Whether these scenes ever appeared in a more or less chronological order is not evident, but as now heard there is no rigid sequence. In the version given here, the song begins with Job in the first section; goes on in the second to tell about Judas, Pilate, and Pilate's wife; moves back to Joshua and the stopping of the sun in the third; follows in the fourth with scenes from the Revelation of St. John; continues with references to Gabriel in the fifth section; and in the sixth reproduces a vivid picture from the Book of Daniel. The choruses between stanzas vary, no two being exactly alike. They deal with Mt. Zion, the salvation train, judgment day, Elijah's chariot, and, finally, the resurrection. Partly chanted, partly sung, this synthesis of a number of earthly and celestial scenes has a certain poetic grandeur. It would seem that the song originated as a sermon, with the congregation giving vocal support in the affirmative exclamations ending each line and singing the short choruses.

---

6. *See music notation no. 3 following this section.*

Oh Job Job, good Lord,
Tell me how you feel, good Lord,
Oh what you reckon, good Lord,
That old Job supplied, good Lord,
That I'm feelin' good, good Lord,
Oh Job Job, good Lord,
Tell me how you feel, good Lord,
That-a Job supplied, good Lord,
I'm feelin' bad, good Lord,
Well what you reckon, good Lord,
Old Job said, good Lord,
Whilst I'm feelin' bad, good Lord,
I can't sleep at night, good Lord,
I can't eat a bite, good Lord,
And the woman I love, good Lord,
Don't treat me right, good Lord.

> Oh Rock Mount Zion, Rock Mount Zion,
> Oh Rock Mount Zion in that morning.
> Don't you hear the train comin',
> Hear the train comin',
> Don't you hear the train comin' in that mornin'.

Oh Pilate's wife, good Lord,
She dreamt a dream, good Lord,
'Bout a innocent man, good Lord,
Said who want to see, good Lord,
Old Pilate's work, good Lord,
Come and seek the man, ahuh,
Said give me water, good Lord,
I want wash my hands, good Lord,
I won't be guilty, good Lord,
'At a innocent man, Lordy.
That Judas was, ahuh,
Not a seasoned man, ahuh,
Forty piece of silver, ahuh,
Go count it out, ahuh,
Go way in the woods, ahuh,
I'm goin' suffer be hung, ahuh,
Before I be guilty, ahuh,
To this innocent man, ahuh,

> Don't you want to die easy,
> Don't you want to die easy,
> Don't you want to die easy in that mornin'.
> Don't you want to see Jesus,
> Don't you want to see Jesus,
> Don't you want to see Jesus in that mornin'.

Joshua was, ahuh,
Son of Nun, ahuh,
Prayed to God, ahuh,
Stop the sun, ahuh,
Lord oh Lord, ahuh,
Got my war cap, ahuh,
On my head, ahuh,
Lord oh Lord, ahuh,
Got my sword, ahuh,
Good and sharp, ahuh,
Lord oh Lord, ahuh,
Got my shoes, ahuh,
Good and tight, ahuh,
Sun stopped steady, ahuh,
Turn the light, ahuh,
Pale the moon, ahuh,
The sun steady, ahuh,
Work was done, ahuh.

> Rock Mount Zion,
> Rock Mount Zion,
> Oh Rock Mount Zion in that mornin'.
> Children you better get ready,
> You better get ready.
> Oh you better get ready in that mornin'.

God send angels, ahuh,
Heaven down, umn-hmn,
Go east angel, umn-hmn,
Veil the sun, umn-hmn,
Go east angel, umn-hmn,
Veil the moon, umn-hmn,
Sail back sun, umn-hmn,
Towards the heavens, umn-hmn,
Done your duty, ahuh,
Sail back moon, umn-hmn,
Drippin' blood, umn-hmn,
Done your duty, ahuh,
Go east angel, umn-hmn,
Hold the wind, ahuh,
God this mornin' umn-hmn,
Rule and chain, ahuh.
Go north angel, umn-hmn,
Hold the wind, umn-hmn,
Don't let it move, ahuh,
God this mornin', umn-hmn,
Rule and chain, umn-hmn,
Go west angel, umn-hmn,
Don't let it move, umn-hmn.

Say Rock Mount Zion,
Rock Mount Zion,
Oh Rock Mount Zion in that mornin'.
Don't you want to die easy,
Don't you want to die easy,
Oh you want to die easy in that mornin'.

God sent Gabriel, umn-hmn,
Go down Gabriel, ahuh,
Tetch the sea, ahuh,
Brace my feet, ahuh,
Water side, ahuh,
Brace my feet, ahuh,
Dry land, ahuh,
Blow loud Gabriel, ahuh,
Seven claps of thunder, umn-hmn,
Other than the one, ahuh,
Spoke to the clouds, umn-hmn,
Sail away clouds, umn-hmn,
Make up in chair, umn-hmn.

Swing low chariot,
Swing low chariot,
Oh swing low chariot in that mornin'.

See God that mornin', ahuh,
Filled up the air, umn-hmn,
Feet be movin', umn-hmn,
Feet be shinin', umn-hmn,
Like polished brass, umn-hmn,
Eyes be movin', umn-hmn,
Zig-zags of lightnin', umn-hmn,
Hair be rollin', umn-hmn,
Like pillars of cloud, umn-hmn,
Hair be shinin', umn-hmn,
Like lamb's wool, ahuh,
God this mornin', umn-hmn,
Rule and chain, umn-hmn.

Over yon comes Jesus,
Yon comes Jesus.
Oh yon comes Jesus in that mornin'.[7]

The story of Jonah and the Whale has inspired many Negro religious songs, most of which have common elements and common lines, suggesting that they may have developed from an early prototype. The

---

7. *See music notation no. 2 following this section.*

songmakers exploited to the full all of the dramatic potentials of the tale, condensing where useful, expanding and drawing out where artful. In the case of the Jonah song given here, the singer began with a prose narration of the story, much in the manner that it would be presented in the pulpit, and at the conclusion of the narration launched immediately into the singing.

Where the Bible says simply that "the Lord sent out a great wind into the sea, and there was a mighty tempest unto the sea, so that the ship was like to broken," this singer-narrator has angels hovering over the ship, fluttering their wings to get the wind down into it. The Bible says with brevity of statement: "Now the Lord had prepared a great fish to swallow up Jonah. And Jonah was in the belly of the fish three days and three nights." But the story teller brings a quality of theater to the event when he says: "And when he struck the water (slap!) a sudden mouth flew open like a ball of fire, and when last seen, Jonah, he was goin' through the water in the bowels of a whale." The story and song, as given by Richard Amerson of Halsel, Alabama, are as follows:

Jonah was a man, God told him to go over to Nineveh. God called him and spoke to him. And there was a ravine right across a big ocean of water over here. And He told him to go over there amongst them wild men and civilize 'em, preach to 'em. Jonah saw a . . . ship comin' down, and he thought he'd rather go and labor instead of goin' down amongst them men, and he went down there and got him a truck, and helped these people stack this cotton and stuff down there. And whilst bein' down in there amongst the laborin' men down in the ship he commenced to work a while. Jonah thought he'd stow on that ship, and wouldn't get on the ship they told him to get on. He got on the one he wanted to get on, say he wasn't goin' to preach, and hid down there.

And the captain came on up and locked the hull back up. 'Twas ever so many days, two-three days, and Jonah down there hid. They counted the men and thought the men was all out. But by the captain bein' a forgettin' man—and God was a forgiver, not a forgetter—he forgot Jonah, and God didn't forget him. That shows that you're bound to do what God send you to do. God intend for him to go over and preach gospel to the men and do what he say do. And he couldn't hide it from Him. And God command the ship to run for many miles, and after she run for many miles then she got to rockin'. The captain of the ship supplied to him down here, "What's the matter?" He said, "Let the oars up," and when they let the oars up on the ship it rocked worse. A little windstorm got in it. And the angels drooped their wings down and got the wind in and rocked it worse.

So the spirit of God was revealed in the angels, listen. God say his children can't stay anywhere but where he places 'em to stay. So when the ship began to rock again they got anxious and went down and got to movin' the bales of cotton and found a man, Jonah, lyin' fast asleep. . . . And two caught him by the legs and two by the hands, and before they have this ship destroyed by one man, they throwed him

overboard in the water. And when he struck the water (slap!) a sudden
mouth flew open like a ball of fire—it was a whale mouth flew open—
and when last seen, Jonah, he was goin' through the water in the bowels of the whale. And the whale, you could see so many miles of water
bustin' open, he cut the water half in two, he smote the water just like
Moses. That was a life-savin' boat God send to save his children anywhere, you know, that's for Jonah. And he struck the open water and
when last seen he was cuttin' the sea half in two a-goin'. And when he
stop he rest his breastplate over here in Nineveh. He went as far as he
could and got on a sand bar. And he opened his mouth and gapped,
and Jonah shot out alive. Then the whale turned around and went on
back, he had done what God told him to do.

And Jonah lay there so many days. The sun came to shine, the wind
and sand, and the sun begin to burn his face. Then come along a raven,
came a-flyin' alongside, see a gourd seed, and he picked it up like the
birds do, and he flew along and he got even with Jonah's head and the
gourd seed dropped right in that wet sand behind the sea. And so God
fixed it so . . . he strung up a little vine. And the vine went up [grew]
into a tree, and a great big limb of it came right over Jonah to shade
him.

And there came along a worm, came a-inchin' down there so many
miles, and every weed and stalk he saw, he wouldn't cut there. He
inched and he inched till he inched up where that gourd vine growed
over Jonah's head. And the inchworm sawed on it and sawed it
down. . . . So when it fell in his face it tickled Jonah, and Jonah woke
up. When Jonah woke up and came to power, he come up to the city to
become a preacher to them wicked men. You know what he do. Well,
he did what God told him to do, didn't he?

> Wake up Jonah, you are the man!
> Reelin' and a-rockin' o' the ship so long!
> Captain of the ship got trouble in mind!
> Reelin' and a-rockin' o' the ship so long!
> Let's go way down in the hull o' the ship!
> Reelin' and a-rockin' o' the ship so long!
> Let's search this ship from bottom to top!
> Reelin' and a-rockin' o' the ship so long!
> Then they found Brother Jonah lyin' fast asleep!
> Reelin' and a-rockin' o' the ship so long!
> Layin' way out yonder in the hull o' the ship!
> Reelin' and a-rockin' o' the ship so long!
> He said wake up Jonah, you are the man!
> Reelin' and a-rockin' o' the ship so long!
>
> Well they caught Brother Jonah by hands and feet!
> Reelin' and a-rockin' o' the ship so long!
> Well they pitched Brother Jonah up overboard!
> Reelin' and a-rockin' o' the ship so long!

Well the water whale came along swallowed him whole!
Reelin' and a-rockin' o' the ship so long!
Then he puked Brother Jonah on dry land!
Reelin' and a-rockin' o' the ship so long!
Then the gourd vine growed over Jonah's head!
Reelin' and a-rockin' o' the ship so long!
Then the inchworm come along cut it down!
Reelin' and a-rockin' o' the ship so long!
That made a cross over Jonah's head!
Reelin' and a-rockin' o' the ship so long![8]

The Book of Daniel has provided the substance for numerous Negro religious songs, many of which refer to Daniel's interpretations of King Nebuchadnezzar's dreams. One seemingly impossible task put on Daniel was not merely to interpret, but to describe, without being told, the very contents of a dream that greatly troubled the King. With divine assistance, Daniel narrates the dream and its meaning:

"As you watched, O king, you saw a great image. This image, huge and dazzling, towered before you, fearful to behold. The head of the image was of fine gold, its breast and arms of silver, its belly and thighs of bronze, its legs of iron, its feet part iron and part clay. While you looked, a stone was hewn from a mountain, not by human hands; it struck the image on its feet of iron and clay and shattered them. Then the iron, the clay, the bronze, the silver, and the gold, were all shattered to fragments and were swept away like chaff before the wind from a threshing-floor in summer, until no trace of them remained. But the stone which struck the image grew into a great mountain filling the whole earth. That was the dream. We shall now tell your majesty the interpretation. You, O king, king of kings, to whom the God of heaven has given the kingdom with all its power, authority, and honour; in whose hands he has placed men and beasts and birds of the air, wherever they dwell, granting you sovereignty over them all—you are that head of gold. After you there shall arise another kingdom, inferior to yours, and yet a third kingdom, of bronze, which shall have sovereignty over the whole world. And there shall be a fourth kingdom, strong as iron; as iron shatters and destroys all things, it shall break and shatter the whole earth. As, in your vision, the feet and toes were part of potter's clay and part iron, it shall be a divided kingdom. Its core shall be partly of iron just as you saw iron mixed with the common clay; as the toes were part iron and part clay, the kingdom shall be partly strong and partly brittle. As, in your vision, the iron was mixed with common clay, so shall men mix with each other by intermarriage, but such alliances shall not be stable: iron does not mix with clay. In the period of those kings the God of heaven will establish a kingdom

8. See music notation no. 1 following this section.

which shall never be destroyed; that kingdom shall never pass to another people; it shall shatter and make an end of all these kingdoms, while it shall itself endure for ever. This is the meaning of your vision of the stone being hewn from a mountain, not by human hands, and then shattering the iron, the bronze, the clay, the silver, and the gold. The mighty God has made known to your majesty what is to be hereafter. The dream is sure and the interpretation to be trusted."

The stone hewn from the mountain becomes the image on which all eyes are fixed as the congregation sings:

> Daniel saw the stone, hewn out the mountain,
> Daniel saw the stone, hewn out the mountain,
> Daniel saw the stone, hewn out the mountain,
> Tearing down the kingdom of this world.
>
> Have you seen that stone, hewn out he mountain!
> Have you seen that stone, hewn out the mountain?
> Have you seen that stone, hewn out the mountain?
> Tearing down the kingdom of this world.
>
> Yes I saw that stone, hewn out the mountain,
> Yes I saw that stone, hewn out the mountain,
> Yes I saw that stone, hewn out the mountain,
> Tearing down the kingdom of this world.
>
> You better seek that stone, hewn out the mountain,
> You better seek that stone, hewn out the mountain,
> You better seek that stone, hewn out the mountain,
> Tearing down the kingdom of this world.
>
> Jesus was the stone, hewn out the mountain,
> Jesus was the stone, hewn out the mountain,
> Jesus was the stone, hewn out the mountain,
> Tearing down the kingdom of this world.
>
> Going to preach about that stone, hewn out the mountain,
> Going to preach about that stone, hewn out the mountain,
> Going to preach about that stone, hewn out the mountain,
> Tearing down the kingdom of this world.
>
> Oh, that holy stone, etc.

Out of the imagery of the phrase, "Daniel saw the stone," numerous versions have been born, some more elaborate, some more simply stated. One such version goes:

Daniel saw that stone that came rollin' down the mountain,
Daniel saw that stone that came rollin' down through Babylon,
Daniel saw that stone that was hewn out of the mountain,
Tearing down the kingdoms of this world.

The episode of Daniel in the lion's den, from Daniel 6, is recalled in
the song:

Daniel was a Hebrew child,
Went to pray to the Lord a while.
The king at once for Daniel did send,
And he put Daniel down in the lion's den.
God told the angels the lions to keep,
And Daniel layed down and he went to sleep.

Out of Luke 16 comes the story of Lazarus:

"There was once a rich man, who dressed in purple and the finest
linen, and feasted in great magnificence every day. At his gate, covered
with sores, lay a poor man named Lazarus, who would have been glad
to satisfy his hunger with the scraps from the rich man's table. Even
the dogs used to come and lick his sores. One day the poor man died
and was carried away by the angels to be with Abraham. The rich man
also died and was buried, and in Hades, where he was in torment, he
looked up; and there, far away, was Abraham with Lazarus close
beside him. 'Abraham, my father,' he called out, 'take pity on me! Send
Lazarus to dip the tip of his finger in water, to cool my tongue, for I am
in agony in this fire.' But Abraham said, 'Remember, my child, that all
the good things fell to you while you were alive, and all the bad to Lazarus; now he has his consolation here and it is you who are in agony.
But that is not all: there is a great chasm fixed between us; no one from
our side who wants to reach you can cross it, and none may come from
your side to us.' 'Then, father,' he replied, 'will you send him to my father's house, where I have five brothers, to warn them, so that they too
may not come to this place of torment?' But Abraham said, 'They have
Moses and the prophets; let them listen to them.' 'No, father Abraham,'
he replied, 'but if someone from the dead visits them, they will repent.'
Abraham answered, 'If they do not listen to Moses and the prophets
they will pay no heed even if someone should rise from the dead.'"

Dip your finger down in the water
And cool my parchin' tongue,
Cause I'm tormented in the flame!

---

*"Poor Boy Lazarus" was recorded by Frederic Ramsey, Jr. Singer, Horace
Sprott.*

Well, poor boy Laz'rus . . .
> I'm tormented!

Yes, poor boy Laz'rus . . .
> I'm tormented!

Went to rich man Dives . . .
> I'm tormented!

Any crumb from your table . . .
> Dip your finger down and touch some water
> To cool my parchin' tongue,
> Cause I'm tormented in the flame!

Poor boy Laz'rus . . .
> I'm tormented!

Yes, poor boy Laz'rus . . .
> I'm tormented!

Went again to rich man Dives . . .
> I'm tormented!

No crumb did he find. . . .
> Dip your finger down (etc., with variations)

Poor boy Laz'rus . . .
> I'm tormented!

Poor boy Laz'rus . . .
> I'm tormented!

Say 'fore he die . . .
> I'm tormented!

I got a home on high . . .
> Dip your finger down (etc.)

Now, rich man Dives . . .
> I'm tormented!

Yes, rich man Dives . .
> I'm tormented!

Say before he die . . .
> I'm tormented!

I got a home in hell . . .
> Dip your finger down (etc.)

Well rich man Dives . . .
> I'm tormented!

Say Lord have mercy . . .
> I'm tormented!

Say Lord have mercy . . .
> I'm tormented!

Say Lord have mercy . . .
> Lord, dip your finger down (etc.)

Yes, rich man Dives . . .
> I'm tormented!

Say send poor Laz'rus . . .
> I'm tormented!

Oh send poor Laz'rus . . .
> I'm tormented!

With a little touch of water . . .
Dip your finger down *(etc.)*

The Gospel According to St. John, Chapter 4, tells that Jesus came to a well in Samaria, and engaged in conversation with a woman drawing water there. He spoke to her about the water of everlasting life which he had to offer, and she asked whether she might have some. "Jesus saith unto her, Go call thy husband and come hither. The woman answered and said, I have no husband. Jesus said unto her, Thou hast well said, I have no husband; for thou hast had five husbands; and he whom thou now hast is not thy husband: in that saidst thou truly. The woman saith unto him, Sir, I perceive that thou art a prophet." This human, intimate exchange, and the woman's report to the village on the event, is recorded in the following song:

When Jesus met the woman at the well,
Oh she went running to tell,
She said come to see a man at the well,
He told me everything that I done.

She cried oh, oh, he must be a prophet,
She cried oh, oh, he must be a prophet,
She cried oh, oh, he must be a prophet,
He told me everything that I done.

He said woman where is your husband?
She said that I don't have one.
He said woman you done had five,
And the one you got now ain't yours.

She cried oh, oh, you must be a prophet,
She cried oh, oh, you must be a prophet,
Oh, oh, you must be a prophet,
You told me everything that I done.

Oh he told me that Messiah was coming,
Oh he told me everything that I done.
Oh he told me that Messiah was coming,
Oh he told me everything that I done.

She cried oh, oh, *etc.*[9]

The song "Job, Job," which appears earlier in this chapter, refers to the episode of Pilate's washing his hands to symbolize his innocence

---

9. *See music notation no. 5 following this section.*

of the death penalty (Matthew, 27:14). The following song enumerates the events that followed, according to the gospel:

> Look how they done my Lord,
> Done my Lord, done my Lord,
> Look how they done my Lord,
> He never said a mumblin' word,
> Not a word, not a word did he say.
>
> Well they whupped him up Calvary,
> Calvary, Calvary, Calvary,
> They whupped him up Calvary,
> He never said a mumblin' word,
> Not a word, not a word did he say.
>
> Well they planted him a thorny crown,
> Thorny crown, thorny crown, thorny crown,
> They planted him a thorny crown.
> He never said a mumblin' word,
> Not a word, not a word did he say.
>
> Well they placed it on his head,
> On his head, on his head, on his head,
> They placed it on his head.
> He never said a mumblin' word,
> Not a word, not a word did he say.
>
> Well they speared him in the side,
> In the side, in the side, in the side,
> Well they speared him in the side.
> He never said a mumblin' word,
> Not a word, not a word did he say.

The story of the crucifixion and the resurrection was carried by word of mouth through the countryside, as recalled by the song "Somebody's Talking About Jesus." One stanza and chorus of the song goes:

> Everywhere I go,
> Everywhere I go my Lord,
> Everywhere I go
> Somebody's talking about Jesus.
>
> Well my knees been acquainted with the hillside clay,
> Somebody's talking about Jesus.
> And my head's been wet with the midnight dew,
> Somebody's talking about Jesus.

The memory of John the Baptist, who baptized Jesus, preaching in the wilderness, is evoked by this song:

> Wonder where is my brother gone?
> Wonder where is my brother John?
> He is gone to the wilderness,
> Ain't comin' no more.
> Wonder where will I lie down?
> Wonder where will I lie down?
> In some lonesome place Lord,
> Down on the ground.
> Wonder where will I lie down?
> In some lonesome place Lord,
> Down on the ground.[10]

Another song about John the Baptist demonstrates how singing and preaching can merge into an integral form. Except for the choral stanza, which is truly sung, the main body of this piece is Biblical prose chanted with a simple but emotionally charged rhythm, to guitar accompaniment. The words come almost unchanged from the Gospel According to St. Matthew. The rhythmic pauses in the song are a creative device on the part of the preacher-singer. They are suggested here by the way in which the lines are broken down. The story tells about Jesus' baptism by John, and about his forty days of fasting, and his temptation by Satan.

> John done saw that number
> Way in the middle of the air.
> John done saw that number
> Way in the middle of the air.
> Ee-ay-hay-ay.

> In those days came John the Baptist
> preachin' in the
> wilderness of Judea
> and sayin'
> repent ye,
> for the Kingdom of
> Heaven
> is at hand.
> For this is he
> that was spoken of
> by the prophet Esaias.

---

10. *See music notation no. 6 following this section.*

Hay-hay-ay.
His voice
the one
cryin' in the
wilderness,
prepare ye
the way
of the Lord and make
his
pathway straight and
the same John had his raiment of
camel hair
and a leather girdle
round his loins.

> John done saw that number, *etc.*

Jesus came from Nazarene
unto
Galilee
to be
baptised
of John
in Jordan
and
John said
unto him
come and talk to me
I need
to be
baptised
of thee and
Jesus said
unto
John
suffer it to be so for
thus it becomes us
to fill all righteousness.

> And John done saw that number
> Way in the middle of the air.
> John done saw that number
> Way in the middle of the air.
> Cryin' how long, how long, how long, my Lord,
> oh how long.

Ay
after Jesus was
baptised

of
John
straightway
out of the waters
looked and saw
heavens open
and the spirit
of God
came down and lit
a bow
on him,
and Jesus was
carried up
into the mountain
to be
tempted of the Satan
and when
he had fasted forty days and forty nights
the tempter
came unto him
and said,
If thou be the son of God
cast thy faith
cause these stones to be
made bread and
Je-eh-he-sus
said unto John *(sic)*,
Get behind me
for it is
written down here
not
tempt the Lord
thy God
but him only
thou shalt serve in faith.

And John done saw that number, *etc.*

Another song of this type, with a nearly identical chorus, refers not to John the Baptist but to St. John the Divine. It also has a preaching style of delivery, with sermonizing and singing interspersed. The various scenes which are depicted come from The Revelation. One half-sung sermonizing part goes:

There was a beast came out of the sea
Havin' ten horns and ten crowns,
On his horns was a-written blaspheme. . . .

A later section:

> God told the angel
> Go down about old John.
> Angel flew from the bottom of the pit,
> Gathered the sun all in her fist,
> Gathered the moon all round her wrist,
> Gathered the stars all under her feet,
> Gathered the wind all round her waist.

The Revelation of St. John the Divine, with all its spectacular, visionary, and poetic effects, evidently made a deep impression on the creators of Negro religious songs. Its free, cosmic and often wild and primitive imagery provided rich opportunities for sermons and for conveying, through musical statements, a spirit of wonder and awe. Chapter 12 of The Revelation begins: "And there appeared a great wonder in heaven; a woman clothed with the sun, and the moon under her feet, and upon her head a crown of twelve stars." This imagery is the basis of the song given above, which utilizes the original material in a free, poetic manner. That identical Biblical passages inspired different songmakers differently is evidenced by another anthem on the same subject:

> Wasn't that a wonder in the heaven?
> Wasn't that a wonder in the heaven?
> Mighty wonder in the heaven?
> That woman clothed with the sun,
> Moon under her feet!
>
> Read about the wonder in the heaven.
> Read about the wonder in the heaven.
> Mighty wonder in the heaven.
> That woman clothed with the sun,
> Moon under her feet.

In Chapter 20 of The Revelation, there are numerous references to the book of judgment, such as this: "And I saw the dead, small and great, stand before God; and the books were opened: and another book was opened, which is the book of life: and the dead were judged out of these things which were written in the books according to their works. . . . And whoever was not found written in the book of life was cast into the lake of fire." The song "It's Gettin' Late Over in the Evenin'" draws upon this theme for its substance:

> Lord it's gettin' late over in the evenin',
> Lord it's gettin' late over in the evenin',
> Children, it's gettin' late over in the evenin',
> Lord it's gettin' late over in the evenin',
> The sun most down.

Don't you seal up your book, John,
Don't you seal up your book, John,
Don't seal up your book, John,
Don't you seal up your book, John,
Till you can sign my name.

Spirit says seal up your book, John,
Spirit says seal up your book, John,
I want you to seal up your book, John,
I want you to seal up our book, John,
Don't write no more.

People, I just keep on tellin' you,
We just keep on a-tellin' you,
We just keeps on a-tellin' you,
Sinner, I just keep on a-tellin' you,
It's a God somewhere.

Children, you can come in my home,
You can come in my home,
Lord, you can come to my home,
You can come to my home,
Lord, and you'll find-a me there.

I'm goin' away to leave you,
I'm goin' away to leave you,
Sinner, I'm goin' away to leave you,
I'm goin' away to leave you,
And I can't stay here.

Lord, we got to make a move,
Lord, we got to make a move,
People, we got to make a move, move,
We got to make a move some day,
And we can't stay here.

Lord, we got to go to judgment,
We got to go into judgment,
People, we got to go into judgment,
We got to go into judgment,
Sister, and we can't tell when.

Chapter 5 of The Revelation begins: "And I saw in the right hand of him that sat on the throne a book written within and on the back side, sealed with seven seals." This passage is the inspiration for "John the Revelator," which opens with these stanzas:

Well, who's that a-writin'?
John the Revelator.

> Who's that a-writin'?
>   John the Revelator.
> Who's that a-writin'?
>   John the Revelator.
> Well, book of the Seven Seals.
>
> Tell me what's John a-writin'?
>   John the Revelator.
> What's John a-writin'?
>   John the Revelator.
> What's John a-writin'?
>   John the Revelator.
> Well, Book of the Seven Seals.

Other stanzas interpolate earlier Biblical events.

One of the most popularized of all spirituals, "Goin' to Shout All Over God's Heaven," also appears to derive from The Revelation. At various places in the book, there are references to wings, harps, robes, crowns, and other effects that are present at the scene of the final judgment, all of which are used to symbolize salvation:

> Ah you got shoes, I got shoes,
> All of God's children got shoes.
> And when I get to heaven goin' to try on my shoes,
> I'm goin' to shout all over heaven.
>
> *Chorus (after every stanza)*
> Oh heaven, heaven,
> Everybody talkin' about heaven aint goin' there,
> Heaven, heaven,
> I'm goin' to shout all over God's heaven.
>
> Well you got a robe, I got a robe,
> All of God's children got a robe,
> And when I get to heaven goin' to try on my robe,
> Goin' to shout all over God's heaven.
>
> Well you got a crown, I got a crown,
> All of God's children got a crown,
> And when I get to heaven goin' to try on my crown,
> Goin' to shout all over God's heaven.
>
> Well you got a harp, I got a harp,
> All of God's children got a harp,
> Ah when I get to heaven goin' to play on my harp,
> I'm goin' to shout all over God's heaven.

The certainty that those who lead a good Christian life will pass the test on judgment day runs through many spirituals and other religious songs, along with warnings to sinners that the time for repentance is short. How does one know for certain that his name appears in the list of the saved? The Revelation (21:12) says that 12,000 people from each of the twelve tribes are chosen, 144,000 in all. An angel shows John the New City, which "had a wall great and high, and had twelve gates, and at the gates twelve angels, and names written thereon, which are the names of the twelve tribes of Israel."

How'd you know your name been written down?
How'd you know your name been written down?
On the wall, oh, it's been written down.
On the wall, oh, it's been written down.
Oh the angel told me, been written down.
Oh the angel told me, been written down.
How'd you know your name been written down?
How'd you know your name been written down?
Well the Lord told me, been written down.
Well the Lord told me, been written down.
Be sure your name been written down.
Be sure your name been written down.
On the wall in heaven been written down.
On the wall in heaven been written down.
I know my name been written down.
I know my name been written down.
On the wall in heaven been written down.
On the wall in heaven been written down.
Aint you glad your name been written down?
Aint you glad your name been written down?

Among the finest of all judgment day songs is "Didn't You Hear?" The responsive part is sung like a clarion trumpet, and the entire scene projects a wildly joyous, cosmic New Year's Eve celebration with bells ringing, doves "moaning," ravens crying, horns blowing, harps playing, thunder rolling, lightning flashing, saints singing, brothers praying, sisters shouting, preachers preaching, and the organ playing. Note that the harp is "blown." To many rural people, as pointed out elsewhere, the heavenly harp is the mouth harp, or harmonica.

Didn't you hear my Lord when he called?
Yes I heard my Lord when he called!
Didn't you hear my Lord when he called?
Yes I hear my Lord call!
Didn't you hear my Lord when he called?
Yes I heard my Lord call!
My Lord callin', in my soul! (×4)

Didn't you hear them angels moan?
  Yes I heard the angels moan!
Didn't you hear them angels moan?
  Yes I heard the angels moan!
Angels moanin', in my soul! (×4)

Didn't you hear them turkle doves moan?
  Yes I heard the turkle doves moan?
Didn't you hear them turkle doves moan?
  Yes I heard the turkle doves moan!
Didn't you hear the heaven bells ring?
  Yes I heard the heaven bells ring!
The turkle doves moanin', my soul! (×6)
The angels moanin', my soul! (×2)

Didn't you hear the harp when it blowed?
  Yes I heard the harp when it blowed!
Didn't you hear them ravens cryin'?
  Yes I heard the ravens cryin'!
Didn't you hear that horn when it blowed?
  Yes I heard the horn when it blowed!
Didn't you hear my Lord callin'?
  Yes I heard my Lord call.
The turkle dove moanin', my soul! (×4)
The harp is blowin', my soul!(×2)
My Lord callin', my soul! (×2)

Didn't you hear that thunder roll?
  Yes I heard the thunder roll!
Didn't you see the lightnin' flashin'?
  Yes I see the lightnin' flash!
Didn't you hear them saints when they singin'?
  Yes I hear the saints when they sing!
Didn't you hear that brother pray?
  Yes I hear the brother pray!
Couldn't you hear them sisters shoutin'?
  Yes I heard the sisters shout!
Didn't you hear them preachers preachin'?
  Yes I heard the preachers preach!
Preachers preachin', my soul! (×2)
Sisters shoutin', my soul! (×2)
Thunder rollin', my soul! (×2)

Didn't you hear them organ playin'?
  Yes I heard the organ playin'!
Didn't you hear them horns blowin'?
  Yes I heard the horn when it blowed!

> Didn't you hear them saints singin'?
> Yes I heard the saints all singin'!
> Saints all singin', my soul! (×2)

Among the religious songs, there are, of course, many without direct allusion to BIblical scenes. Their themes are more generalized, or they may deal, for example, with the idea of death (usually accompanied by direct or indirect reference to salvation, or warnings to sinners), or Christian behavior. Inspiraton for many of these songs may have been in Biblical passages the identity of which is not readily recognized; or they may have been inspired by a local event or circumstance, or by sermons.

In the following song, "Got No Travellin' Shoes," the message is for everyone to be prepared for death by seeking salvation, and not to be caught unready:

> Death went out to the sinner's house,
> (Said) come and go with me.
> Sinner cried out, I'm not ready to go,
> I ain't got no travellin' shoes,
> Got no travellin' shoes,
> Got no travellin' shoes,
> Sinner cried out, I'm not ready to go,
> I ain't got no travellin' shoes.
>
> Death went down to the gambler's house,
> Called him come and go with me.
> The gambler cried out I'm not ready to go,
> I ain't got no travellin' shoes,
> Got no travellin' shoes, got no travellin' shoes,
> Gambler cried out, I'm not ready to go,
> I ain't got no travellin' shoes.
>
> Death went down to the preacher's house,
> Called him, come and go with me.
> The preacher cried out, I'm a-ready to go,
> I got my travellin' shoes,
> Got my travellin' shoes, got my travellin' shoes,
> The preacher cried out, I'm ready to go,
> I've got my travellin' shoes.

The song "This May Be Your Last Time" consists of a series of brief images dealing with Christian behavior, the unsanctified, the short time left to achieve salvation, and the final judgment:

Chorus (before each stanza, with variations)
This may be your last time, (×3)
May be your last time, I don't know.
Sister, this may be your last time,
This may be your last time, (×2)
May be your last time, I don't know.

Talk about me much as you please,
More you talk, I'll bend my knees.
May be your last time, I don't know.

Way down yonder by Jordan Stream,
Hear God's children tryin' to bend their knees.
May be your last time, I don't know.

Meet Mr. Hypocrite on the street,
First thing he show you, his tongue in his cheek.
May be your last time, I don't know.

Soon as you can cease from your sins,
Train goin' to stop and take you in.
May be your last time, I don't know.

Jordan deep, Jordan wide,
None don't cross but the sanctified.
May be your last time, I don't know.

If you want to go to heaven when you die,
Stop your tongue from tellin' lies.
May be your last time I don't know.

One of these mornin's, nine o'clock,
This old world begin to reel and rock.
May be your last time, I don't know.

Many souls [that] have never tried to pray,
Got sight of the Lord that day.
May be your last time, I don't know.

Another song, "Israelites Shouting," reflects on the death of various loved ones, all of whom now are "hidden behind God's altar," where they will remain until judgment day. The following stanzas are excerpted:

Oh I wonder where's my sister,
She's gone away to stay.
Got hidden behind God's altar,
She'll be gone till judgment day.

Chorus (after each stanza, with variations)
Goodbye, the Israelites shoutin' in the
Goodbye, the Israelites shoutin' in the heaven
Goodbye, the Israelites shoutin' in the heaven
Goodbye, the Israelites shoutin' in the
This day, the Israelites shoutin' in the heaven
This day, the Israelites shoutin' in the

Oh I wonder where's my father,
He's gone away to stay.
He left his church this mornin',
And now he can't be found.

Stanzas that follow name the mother and various other relatives, and
then:

God knows I am a Christian,
God knows I'm not ashamed.
Well the Holy Ghost is my witness,
The angels done signed my name.[14]

"The Sun Will Never Go Down," which appears to paint a picture of
life after death, has a haunting, slow melody, and the lyrics have a special poetic quality:

Oh the sun will never go down, go down,
Oh the sun will never go down, go down.
The flowers are blooming for evermore,
There the sun will never go down, go down.
Don't you feel like shouting sometimes, sometimes?
The flowers are blooming for evermore.
There the sun will never go down.

Don't you miss your mother sometimes, sometimes?
Don't you miss your mother sometimes, sometimes?
The flowers are blooming for evermore,
There the sun will never go down.

A good many religious songs, as we have noted, stress moral pressures on sinners or straying sheep. The epic-like "King David," a few
pages back, has interpolated parts of this kind, such as the lines:

You got a true way to find
Mr. Hypocrite out.
At the first thing [he's] gwine
To church and shout.

Another song notes that sinners, liars and gamblers need not expect mercy on judgment day:

> This train don't carry no sinners, this train!
> This train don't carry no gamblers, this train!
> This train don't carry no liars, this train!

The song "My God Aint No Lyin' Man" contains the verse:

> I got a home where the gambler can't go,
> I got a home where the gambler can't go,
> Oh, Jesus, Lord have mercy,
> I got a home where the gambler can't go.

Although the content of such songs is religious and the values specifically those of the church, one cannot help but be aware of their relationship to the traditional Negro song of social comment and criticism. The main difference is that the religious social comment usually has a generalized target, while secular social criticism is more often personalized. Religious social comment is a reflection of community attitudes toward a class or group of people who behave in a nonapproved way, while comparable secular songs, including blues, have more specific targets, or at least more specific protagonists. Nevertheless, many of the religious songs which comment on backsliding can be sung at times which give them a particular relevance. The partly preached, partly sung "God Don't Like It" concerns itself with church members that are addicted to corn liquor:

> *Chorus (×2 after each stanza)*
> Well God don't like it, no, no!
> God don't like it, no, no!
> God don't like it, no, no!
> It's a-scandalous and a shame!
>
> Some people stay in the churches,
> They settin' in a deacon's chair,
> They drinkin' beer and whisky,
> And they say that they don't care.
>
> Some people say that yellow corn
> Can make you the very best kind.
> They better turn that yellow corn into bread
> And stop that makin' shine.
>
> Some members in the churches
> They just send to testify,
> But when you come to find out,
> They're somewhere drinkin' shine.

> Now some people goes to church
> Just to speak their soul or mind,
> But when you come to find out,
> They been somewhere drinkin' shine.

In some versions of this song-sermon, a number of other subjects are commented upon, such as hypocritical preachers, church members who shout but don't put money in the collection box, vanity, loose living, lustful behavior, and people who don't return borrowed money.

The song "Scandalize My Name" comments on the behavior of people who gossip behind one's back:

> I met my sister the other day,
> I gave her my right hand,
> But as soon as ever my back was turned
> She scandalized my name.
>
> Now, do you call that a sister? No, no!
> Now, do you call that a sister? No, no, no!
> Now, do you call that a sister? No, no!
> She scandalized my name.
>
> Well, I met my brother the other day,
> I gave him my right hand.
> As soon as ever my back was turned
> He scandalized my name.
>
> Now, do you call that a brother? No, no!
> *Etc.*
>
> I met my preacher the other day,
> I gave him my right hand.
> As soon as ever my back was turned
> He scandalized my name.
>
> Now, do you call that a preacher? No, no!
> *Etc.*

Preachments of this kind are not essentially different from comments that turn up frequently in secular songs, both in the United States and the West Indies. The following Calypso-type song from San Andrés in the Caribbean, for example, is a comment on people who have "bad minds" and who are always making unfavorable remarks about others in the community:

> In every home that you can find,
> There are people who have bad mind.
> In every home that you can find,
> There are people who have bad mind.

Chorus (after each stanza)
Certain bad mind that sit and lie,
Sit and criticize the people who pass.
Certain bad mind that sit and lie,
Sit and criticize the people who pass.

(Each couplet is repeated to fill out a stanza)

You meek and you lookin' thin,
They say consumption in your skin.

You rosy and you big and fat,
They say dropsy in your skin.

You get up and you go to church,
Instead of gospel you goin' to grind.

You kneel in your home to pray,
They say a hypocrite you did play.

Except for the difference in idiom, this Calypso-type song might easily be taken for a United States Negro anthem. The song preceding it
could be sung to exactly the same Calypso beat and melody, and would
readily be accepted in this guise as within West Indian tradition.

It is only a small step from the moralizing religious song to the following blues:

Jimmy Bell's in town,
Lordy, walkin' round.
He got greenbacks enough, sweet babe,
To make a man a suit,
Make a man a suit,
Make a man a suit.
He got greenbacks enough, sweet babe,
To make a man a suit.

Jimmy Bell in the pulpit,
The Bible in his hand.
All them sisters sittin' back in the corner
Cryin' Jimmy Bell my man,
Jimmy Bell my man,
Jimmy Bell my man.
All them sisters sittin' back in the corner
Cryin' Jimmy Bell my man.

Jimmy Bell told the sexton
Go and tone that bell,
Cause some of these old members here

Sure is goin' to hell,
Sure is goin' to hell,
Sure is goin' to hell.
Cause some of these old members here
Sure is goin' to hell.

Etc.

In the theme of this song, one can appreciate how close Negro religious and secular literature can be. The singer includes the tune in his blues repertoire, yet in form it is not true blues; it is much closer to the form of the religious or secular ballad.

Various natural disasters, tragedies, and other events—including fires, floods, and crop failures—have been the inspiration of songs sung by religious street singers. One song of this kind is based on a windstorm which occurred in Terrebonne Parish, Louisiana, in the year 1909:

In the last day of September,
In the year nineteen nine,
God Almighty rose in the weather,
And that troubled everybody's mind.

The storm began on a Sunday,
And it got in awful rage.
Not a mortal soul
In the globe that day
Didn't have any mind to pray.
And God was in the windstorm
And troubled everybody's mind.

God Almighty and his ministers,
They rode up and down the land.
All God Almighty did that day
Was to raise the wind and dust.

God, he is in the windstorm and rain,
And everybody ought to mind.

A more recent topical event, the first Soviet rocket shot at the moon, was the springboard for this street gospel song recorded in New Orleans. Its allusions to modern technology contrast vividly with Biblical references:

Oh Russia, let that moon alone! (×2)
Moon ain't worryin' you!
Oh Russia, let that moon alone!
God told you go till the earth,

God didn't tell you to till the moon!
You got to let that moon alone!
Oh Russia, let that moon alone!
You can make your sputnickles
And your satellites,
You can't get God's moon!
Let God's moon alone!
The moon ain't worryin' you! (×2)
God told man to till the earth,
God didn't tell you to till the moon!
You better let God's moon alone!
The moon ain't worryin' you!
Oh [people] in Russia, get out on your knees and pray!
And let God's moon alone!
The moon ain't worryin' you! (×2)
God put the moon up there to give you light by night!
Oh let God's moon alone!

The Negro musical literature dealing with religious subject matter is rich and panoramic. It encompasses the anthems and spirituals with which we are largely familiar, chanted or half-sung sermons, improvisations by laboring gangs, the songs of itinerant street singers, and the spontaneous cries or hollers that are heard in the open fields. There is great variation among them in music and subject matter, but they all draw upon a common wellspring of inspiration and imagery. They are not all equally good or equally evocative. Each carries the mark of the feeling and genius that created it. Some achieve the level of pure or great poetry, while others contrive to make drama out of prosaic substance, and still others never quite manage to escape being doggerel. But the total picture is one of splendorous vision and a sensitive comprehension of the religious precepts out of which the vision derives.

AS THE SPIRITUALS ARE SUNG

1. Wake Up Jonah

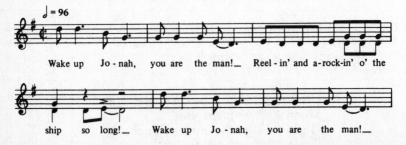

Wake up Jo-nah, you are the man!_ Reel-in' and a-rock-in' o' the
ship so long!_ Wake up Jo-nah, you are the man!_

Reel - in' and a-rock-in' o' the ship so long!__

Cap - tain of the ship got trou - ble in mind, __

Reel - in' and a - rock - in' o' the ship so long!__

Cap - tain of the ship got trou - ble in mind, __

Reel - in' and a - rock - in' o' the ship so long!__ Let's

go way down __ in the hull of the ship!__

Reel - in' and a - rock - in' o' the ship so long!__ Let's

search this ship from bot-tom to top!__ Reel-in' and a-rock-in' o' the

ship so long!__ Then they found broth-er Jo - nah ly - in'

fast a - sleep!__ Reel - in' and a - rock - in' o' the

ship so long!__ Lay - in' way out yon - der in the

hull of the ship!__ Reel - in' and a - rock - in' o' the

ship so long!__ He said wake up Jo - nah,

you are the man!__ Reel - in' and a - rock - in' o' the

ship so long!__ He said wake up Jo - nah, you are the man!__

Reel - in' and a - rock - in' o' the ship so long!__ Well they

2. Job, Job

Oh Job__ Job,__ tell me how you feel,__ good Lord,__

[Responsive:] good Lord,

oh what you reck - on that old Job sup - plied,__

good Lord,__

said I'm feel - in' good,__ good Lord,__

good Lord,

oh Job Job__ tell me how you feel,__

good Lord, __

that Job sup - plied, __ good Lord,__

good Lord,

I'm feel-in' bad,_____ good Lord,_____ well what you reck-on. good Lord,_____ old Job said,_____ good Lord,_____ whilst I'm feel-in' bad,_____ good Lord,_____ I can't sleep at night, good Lord,_____ I can't eat a bite,_____ good Lord,_____ said the wom-an I love,_____ good Lord,_____ don't treat me right,_____ Oh Rock Mount Zi - on, good Lord,_____ Rock Mount Zi - on, oh_____ Rock Mount Zi-_____ on in that mor - - - - ning. _____

3. Rock Chariot

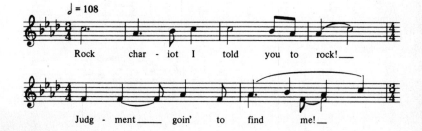

Rock char - iot I told you to rock!_____ Judg - ment_____ goin' to find me!_____

Rock char - iot I___ told___ you to rock!

Judg - ment___ goin' to find me!___

Rock char - iot I told you to rock!___

Judg - ment___ goin' to find me!___

Rock char - iot I told you to rock!

Judg - ment___ goin' to find me!___

etc.

4. King David

♩ = 96

King Da - vid was___ (good Lord)___ that shep-herd

boy___ (good Lord).___ Did - n't he kill Go -

li - ath (good Lord), ___ and he shout for joy___

___ (good Lord). ___ Well the tall - est tree___ (good Lord,)

play on__ your harp__
(hal - le - lu).__   Didn't you prom - ise to

play   on   your   harp,   hal - le - lu,
(hal - le -

etc.

did - n't you prom - ise to   play   on   your   harp   hal - le - lu.
lu),

5. When Jesus Met the Woman at the Well

♩ = 92 Orig.-1 st.

When Je - sus met the wom - an   at the   well,   oh, __

she   went   run - ning   to   tell.__   She said

come and   see   a   man__   at   the   well, __   He

told   me   ev - 'ry - thing__   that   I   done.__   She cried

oh, __   oh, __   he   must   be__   a   proph - et,   she cried

oh,   oh,   well,   he   must   be__   a   proph - et,   she cried

oh,_____   well,_____   he must (be) be   a   proph-et,   He

told   me   ev - 'ry - thing__   that   I   done._____   *etc.*

6. *Wonder Where Is My Brother Gone*

♩ = 80

Won-der where_____   is__ my broth-er gone?_____   Won-der

where_____   is my broth-er   John?_____   He is

gone to the wil-der-ness,__ ain't com-in' no more._____   Won-der where__

_____   will I__   lie down?_____   Won-der where__

_____   will I lie   down?_____   In some lone - some__

place Lord_____   down on__ the ground._____   Won-der where__

_____   will__ I lie   down?_____   In some

lone - some place Lord__   down__ on__ the   ground._____

FROM THE PULPIT

Sermon: Is God with Us?

(Heard by Frederika Bremer in Cincinnati in 1850)

. . . In the afternoon I went to the African Methodist Church in Cincinnati, which is situated in the African quarter. In this district live the greater number of the free colored people of the city. . . . I found in the African Church African ardor and African life. The church was full to overflowing, and the congregation sang their own hymns. The singing ascended and poured forth like a melodious torrent, and the heads, feet and elbows of the congregation moved all in unison with it, amid evident enchantment and delight in the singing, which was in it-self exquisitely pure and full of melodious life. . . .

After the singing of the hymns, which was not led by any organ or musical instrument whatever, but which arose like burning melodious signs from the breasts of the congregation, the preacher mounted the pulpit. He was a very black negro, young, with a very retreating fore-head, and the lower portion of the countenance protruding; on the whole, not at all good-looking. But when he began to speak, the con-gregation hung upon his words, and I could not but admire his flowing eloquence. He admonished the assembly to reflect on the present need of their brethren; to pray for the fugitive slaves, who must now, in great multitudes, leave their acquired homes, and seek a shelter out of the country against legal violence and legal injustice. He exhorted them also to pray for that nation which, in its blindness, would pass such laws and oppress the innocent! This exhortation was received with deep groans and lamenting cries.

After this the preacher drew a picture of the death of "Sister Bryant," and related the history of her beautiful Christian devotion, and applied to her the words of the Book of Revelation, of those "who come out of great afflictions." The intention of suffering on earth, the glorious group of the children of suffering in their release, and thanksgiving-song as represented in so divine and grand a manner in the pages of

From Homes of the New World: Impressions of America, *by Frederika Brem-er, New York, Harpers, 1853.*

Scripture, were placed by the negro preacher in the light as of noonday, and as I had never before heard from the lips of any ordinary ministers. After this the preacher nearly lost himself in the prayer for the sorrowing widower and his children, and their "little blossoming souls." Then came the sermon proper.

The preacher proposed to the congregation the question, "Is God with us?" "I speak of our nation, my brethren," said he; "I regard our nationality. Let us examine the matter." And with this he drew a very ingenious parallel between the captivity of the Israelites in Egypt and the negroes in America, and those trials by which Providence evinced His especial solicitude about the chosen people. After having represented the fate of the Israelites under Pharaoh and Moses, he went on to contemplate the fate of the negro people.

"How shall we know that God is with us? Let us look at the question thus."

He then boldly sketched out a picture of an enslaved people as oppressed in every way, but not the less "increasing in numbers and improving themselves, purchasing their own freedom from slavery (cries of 'Yes! yes!' 'Oh, glory!' throughout the church); purchasing land (shouts of joy); ever more and more land (increasing shouts); buying houses, large houses, larger and still larger houses (increasing jubilation and stamping of feet); building churches (still louder cries); still more and larger churches (louder and still louder cries, movement, stamping of feet, and clapping of hands); the people increasing still in number, in property, in prosperity, and in understanding, so that the rulers of the land began to be terrified, and to say, 'They are becoming too strong for us; let us send them over to Liberia!' (Violent fermentation and excitement.) This, then, will show us, my brethren, that God is with us. Let us not forsake Him; for He will lead us out of captivity, and make of us a great people!" (extreme delight and joy, with the cry of 'Amen!' 'Yes, yes!' 'Oh, glory!' and so on). The whole congregation was for several minutes like a stormy sea. The preacher's address had been a rushing tempest of natural eloquence. I doubt, however, whether his patriotism extended much beyond the moment of inspiration and of his pulpit; he was not a new Moses. Old Moses was slow of speech; he was a man of action.

This preacher was, however, the first negro from whom I had heard any distinct sentiment of nationality. The bill against fugitive slaves must mind what it is about, and what it may lead to.

John Jasper's Sermon on the Sun

John Jasper—"the unmatched Negro philosopher and preacher," as

---

The description of Jasper and the sermon text that follows are from John Jasper, the Unmatched Negro Philosopher and Preacher, *by William E. Hatcher, New York, 1908. The text as given here has been edited slightly for easier reading.*

he was styled by his appreciator, William E. Hatcher—was born in slavery and delivered his first sermon some twenty-five years before emancipation. As a slave preacher his reputation appears to have been widespread, and with the consent of his master he frequently travelled to distant places to sermonize at funerals and other special religious events. Jasper never had any schooling, and he learned to read the hard way. Hatcher described him as a rustic man, humble before the Lord but unflinching in his conviction that his preachments were God-given. When freedom came, Jasper continued to preach, his rustic style unchanged, and apparently he became a notable figure in Richmond and the surrounding Virginia countryside. By all accounts, he had a magnetic personality, the power of persuasion, and the ability to electrify his listeners.

According to Hatcher, his principal chronicler, many of the new breed of preachers in the vicinity of Richmond "resented Jasper's prominence and fame. They felt he was a reproach to the race, and they did not fail to fling at him their flippant sneers." Jasper did not take it meekly. "He looked this new tribe of his adversaries over and marked them as a calcimined and fictitious type of culture. To him they were shop-made and unworthy of respect. They called forth the storm of his indignant wrath. He opened his batteries on them, and, for quite a while, the thunder of his guns fairly shook the steeples on the other churches of Richmond."

What is known about John Jasper is mostly to be found in William Hatcher's biography about the black preacher. Hatcher himself was a white clergyman, pastor of the Grace Street Baptist Church in Richmond, and it was he who delivered the major eulogy when Jasper died at the age of eighty-nine. Set though he was against extravagance in preaching the scriptures, Hatcher acknowledged that he was fairly carried away when Jasper got to preaching, even when Jasper's propositions flew in the face of scientific knowledge, as in his sermon, "De Sun Do Move." That sermon appears to be the best known of Jasper's works, in part because it was delivered many times in one place or another, and in large measure because it was a valiant stand against heretics who denied that the sun moved, as the Scriptures maintained, and asserted that the earth rotated around it. Jasper seems to have gotten his ideas for the sermon from questions put to him by members of his congregation. By the time the Reverend Hatcher had a chance to hear "De Sun Do Move," the sermon was already a subject of contention between Jasper's defenders and detractors. He found a seat in the church firmly resolved not to be taken in by Jasper's eloquence about the motion of the sun. While he admired Jasper for all his personal attributes, he had no intention of being moved by his arguments. But after describing the sermon and the human scene, Hatcher declared: "I must make an admission. In the triumph of his ending, Jasper polled the crowd to see how his theory was prospering. He bade everybody who really endorsed his theory that the sun moved to show his hand. I stretched up my arm about four feet, and would have punched the ceiling with my fingers if it could have been done. Yes, I voted that the earth was flat and had four corners, and that the sun drove his steeds from the gates of the morning over to the barns in the West, and I never asked the question for a moment as to how the team got back during the night. Call me a hypocrite, if it will comfort you to do it; that's a very gentle way to speak to a reporter, but I was dead sincere. My vote was in favor of Jasper's logic, his genuineness, his originality, his philosophic honesty, and his religion."

Since all of Jasper's sermons were extemporaneous, it is clear that the text of "De Sun Do Move" is a reconstruction, written out of Hatcher's memory with the aid of a "friendly report" published in *The Richmond Dispatch*. As was usual for the times, the dialect was grossly overdone, with words misspelled for effect without regard to the fact that pronunciation had in no way been altered. For example, of was written as *uv*, was as *wuz*, been as *bin*, millions as *milyuns*, and so on. Some of these tortuous affectations have been eliminated from the text as reprinted here.

"Low me to say dat when I was a young man and a slave, I knowed nothin worth talkin bout concernin books. Dey was sealed mysteries to me, but I tell you I longed to break de seal. I thirsted for de bread of learnin. When I seen books I ached to git in to 'em for I knowed dat dey had de stuff for me and I wanted to taste deir contents, but most of de time dey was barred against me.

"By de mercy of de Lord a thing happened. I got a roomfeller—he was a slave, too and he had learned to read. In de dead of de night he give me lessons outen de New York Spellin Book. It was hard pullin, I tell you; harder on him, for he know'd just a little and it made him sweat to try to beat somethin into my hard head. It was worse with me. Up de hill every step, but when I got de light of de lesson into my noodle I fairly shouted, but I know'd I was not a scholar. De consequence was I crept long mighty tedious, gittin a crumb here and dere until I could read de Bible by skippin de long words, tolerable well. Dat was de start of my education—dat is what little I got. I make mention of dat young man. De years have fled away since den but I ain't forgot my teacher and never shall. I thank my Lord for him and I carries his memory in my heart.

"Bout seven months after my gittin to readin, God converted my soul and I reckon bout de first and main thing dat I begged de Lord to give me was de power to understand His Word. I ain't braggin and I hates self-praise, but I bound to speak de thankful word. I believes in my heart dat my prayer to understand de Scriptur was heard. Since dat time I ain't cared bout nothin 'cept to study and preach de Word of God.

"Not, my brothren, dat I's de fool to think I knows it all. Oh, my Father, no! Far from it. I don't hardly understand myself nor half of de things round me and dere is millions of things in de Bible too deep for Jasper and some of 'em too deep for everybody. I don't carry de keys to de Lord's closet and He ain't tell me to peep in and if I did I'm so stupid I wouldn't know it when I see it. No, friends, I knows my place at de feet of my Master and dere I stays.

"But I can read de Bible and get de things what lay on de top of de soil. Outen de Bible I know nothin extry bout de sun. I seen its course as he rides up dere so gran and mighty in de sky, but dere is heaps bout dat flamin orb dat is too much for me. I know dat de sun shines powerfully and pours down its light in floods and yet dat is nothing compared with de light dat flashes in my mind from de pages of God's book. But you knows all dat. I knows dat de sun burns—oh, how it did burn in dem July days! I tell you he cooked de skin on my back many a day when I was hoein in de corn field. But you knows all dat—and yet dat is nothing to de divine fire dat burns in de souls of God's chillun. Can't you feel it, brethren?

"But bout de course of de sun, I have got dat. I have done ranged through de whole blessed Book and scored down de last thing de Bible has to say bout de movement of de sun. I got all dat pat and safe. And lemme say dat if I don't give it to you straight, if I gits one word crooked or wrong, you just holler out, 'Hold on dere, Jasper, you ain't got dat straight, and I'll beg pardon. If I don't tell de truth, march upon dese steps here and tell me I's a liar and I'll take it. I fears I do lie sometimes—I'm so sinful, I find it hard to do right; but my God don't lie and He ain't put no lie in de Book of eternal truth and if I give you what de Bible say, den I bound to tell de truth.

"I got to take you all dis afternoon on an excursion to a great battlefield. Most folks like to see fights—some is mighty fond of gittin into fights and some is mighty quick to run down de back alley when dere is a battle goin on for de right. Dis time I'll 'scort you to a scene where you shall witness a curious battle. It took place soon after Israel got in de Promise Land. You 'member de people of Gideon make friends with God's people when dey first entered Canaan and dey was monstrous smart to do it. But, just de same, it got 'em in to an awful fuss. De cities round bout dere flared up at dat and dey all joined deir forces and say dey gwine to mop de Gideon people off de ground and dey bunched all dere armies together and went up for to do it. When dey come up so bold and brace de Gideonites was scared outen dere senses and dey sent word to Joshua dat dey was in trouble and he must run up dere and get 'em out. Joshua had de heart of a lion and he was up dere directly. Dey had an awful fight, sharp and bitter but you might know dat General Joshua was not dere to get whipped. He prayed and he fought and de hours got away too fast for him and so he asked de Lord to issue a special order dat de sun hold up awhile and dat de moon furnish plenty of moonshine down on de lowest part of de fightin grounds. As a fact, Joshua was so drunk with de battle, so thirsty for de blood of de enemies of de Lord and so wild with de victory dat he tell de sun to stand still till he could finish his job.

"What did de sun do? Did he glare down in fiery wrath and say, 'What you talking bout my stoppin for, Joshua? I ain't never started yet. Been here all de time and it would smash up everything if I was to start.' No, he ain't say dat. But what de Bible say? Dat's what I ask to know. It say dat it was at de voice of Joshua dat it stopped. I don't say it stopped; tain't for Jasper to say dat, but de Bible, de Book of God, say so. But I say dis; nothing can stop until it has first started. So I knows what I'm talkin bout. De sun was travellin long dere through de sky when de order come. He hitched his red ponies and made quite a call on de land of Gideon. He perch up dere in de skies just as friendly as a neighbor what comes to borrow something and he stand up dere and he look like he enjoyed de way Joshua waxes dem wicked armies. And de moon, she wait down in de low grounds dere and pours out her light and look just as calm and happy as if she was waitin for her escort. Dey never budged, neither of 'em long as de Lord's army needed a light to carry on de battle.

"I don't read when it was dat Joshua hitch up and drove on, but I suppose it was when de Lord told him to go. Anybody knows dat de sun didn't stay dere all de time. It stopped for business and went on when it got through. Dis is bout all dat I has to do with dis particular case. I done showed you dat dis part of de Lord's word teaches you dat de sun stopped, which show dat he was movin before dat and dat he went on afterwards. I told you dat I would prove dis and I's done it, and I defies anybody to say dat my point ain't made.

"I told you in de first part of dis discourse dat de Lord God is a man of war. I expect by now you begin to see it is so. Don't you admit it? When de Lord come to see Joshua in de day of his fears and warfare and actually make de sun stop stone still in de heavens so de fight can rage on till all de foes is slain, you're obliged to understand dat de God of peace is also de man of war. He can use both peace and war to help de righteous and to scatter de host of de aliens. A man talked to me last week bout de laws of nature and he say dey can't possibly be upset and I had to laugh right in his face. As if de laws of anything was greater dan my God who is de lawgiver for everything. My Lord is great! He rules in de heavens, in de earth and down under de ground. He is great and greatly to be praised. Let all de people bow down and worship before Him! Dere you are! Ain't dat de movement of de sun? Bless my soul! Hezekiah's case beat Joshua. Joshua stop de sun, but here de Lord make de sun walk back ten degrees; and yet dey say dat de sun stand stone still and never move a peg. It look to me he move round mighty brisk and is ready to go any way dat de Lord orders him to go. I wonder if any of dem philosophers is round here dis afternoon? I'd like to take a square look at one of dem and ask him to explain dis matter. He can't do it, my brothren. He knows a heap bout books, maps, figgers and long distances but I defy him to take up Hezekiah's case and explain it off. He can't do it, my brethren. De Word of de Lord is my defense and bulwark and I fears not what men say nor do—my God give me de victory.

"Low me, my friends, to put myself square bout dis movement of de sun. It ain't no business of mine whether de sun move or stan still, or whether it stop or go back or rise or set. All dat is out of my hand entirely and I got nothin to say. I got no the-o-ry on de subject. All I ask is dat we will take what de Lord say bout it and let His will be done bout everything. What dat will is I can't know except He whisper into my soul or write it in a book. Here's de Book. Dis is enough for me and with it to pilot me, I can't get far astray.

"But I ain't done with you yet. As de song says, dere's more to follow. I invite you to hear de first verse in de seventh chapter of de Book of Revelations. What do John, under de power of de Spirit, say? He says he saw four angels standin on de four corners of de earth, holdin de four winds of de earth and so forth. Low me to ask if de earth is round where do it keep its corners? A flat square thing has corners, but tell me where is de corner of an apple or a marble or a cannon ball or a silver dollar. If dere is anyone of dem philosophers what's been takin so many cracks at my old head bout here, he is cordially invited to step forward and square up dis vexin business. I hear tell dat you can't square a circle but it looks like dese great scholars done learn how to circle a square. If dey can do it, let 'em step to de front and do de trick. But, my brethren, in my poor judgment, dey can't do it; tain't in 'em to do it. Dey is on de wrong side of de Bible—dat's on de outside of de Bible, and dere's where de trouble comes in with 'em. Dey done got out of de breastworks of de truth and as long as dey stay dere de light of de Lord will not shine on deir path. I ain't care so much bout de sun, though it's mighty convenient to have it, but my trust is in de Word of de Lord. Long as my feet is flat on de solid rock, no man can move me. I's getting my orders from de God of my salvation.

"The other day a man with a high collar and side whiskers come to my house. He was one nice Northern gentleman what think a heap of us colored people in de South. Dey are lovely folks and I honors 'em very much. He seem from de start kinder strict and cross with me and after a while he broke out furious and fretted, and he says: 'Allow me, Mister Jasper to give you some plain advice. Dis nonsense bout de sun movin where you are gettin is disgracin your race all over de country and as a friend of your people I come to say it's got to stop.' Ha! Ha! Ha! Mars Sam Hargrovenever hardly smash me dat way. It was equal to one of dem old overseers way back yonder. I tell him dat if he'll show me I's wrong, I give it all up. My! My! Ha! Ha! He sail in on me and such a storm bout science, new discoveries and de Lord only knows what all, I never hear before and den he tell me my race is urgin me and poor old Jasper must shut up his fool mouth.

"When he got through—it look like he never would—I tell him John Jasper ain't set up to be no scholar and don't know de philosophies and ain't trying to hurt his people but is workin' day and night to lift 'em up but his foot is on de rock of eternal truth. Dere he stand and dere he is going to stand till Gabriel sounds de judgment note. So I say to de gentleman what scolded me up so dat I hear him make his remarks, but I ain't hear where he get his Scripture from, and that between him and de Word of de Lord, I take my stand by de Word of God every time.

Jasper ain't mad; he ain't fighting nobody; he ain't been appointed janitor to run de sun; he nothin' but de servant of God and a lover of de Everlasting Word. What I care bout de sun? De day comes on when de sun will be called from his race track and his light squincked out forever; de moon shall turn to blood and this earth be consumed with fire. Let 'em go; dat won't scare me nor trouble God's elected people, for de word of de Lord shall endure forever, and on dat solid Rock we stand and shall not be moved!

"Is I got you satisfied yet? Has I proven my point? Oh, ye whose hearts is full of unbelief! Is you still holding out? I reckon de reason you say de sun don't move is cause you are so hard to move yourself. You is a real trial to me, but, never mind, I ain't given you up yet and never will. Truth is mighty; it can break de heart of stone and I must fire another arrow of truth out of de quiver of de Lord. If you has a copy of God's Word bout your person, please turn to dat minor prophet, Malachi, what write de last book in de old Bible and look at first chapter, verse eleven. What do it say? I better read it for I got a notion your critics don't carry any Bible in deir pockets every day in de week. Here is what it says: 'For from de rising of de sun even unto de goin down of de same, My name shall be great among de Gentiles . . . My name shall be great among de heathen, says de Lord of hosts!' How do dat suit you? looks like dat ought to fix it. Dis time it is de Lord of Hosts himself dat is doin de talkin and He is talkin on a wonderful and glorious subject. He is telling of de spreadin of His Gospel, of de comin of His last victory over de Gentiles, and de worldwide glories dat at de last He is to get. Oh, my brethren, what a time dat will be! My soul takes wing as I anticipate with joy dat millennium day! De glories as dey shine before my eyes blinds me and I forget de sun and moon and stars. I just remembers dat long bout dose last days dat de sun and moon will go out of business, for dey won't be needed no more. Den will King Jesus come back to see His people and He will be de sufficient light of de world. Joshua's battles will be over. Hezekiah won't need no sundial, and de sun and moon will fade out before de glorious splendors of de New Jerusalem.

"But what de matter with Jasper? I most forgot my business and most gone to shoutin over de far away glories of de second comin' of my Lord. I beg pardon and will try to get back to my subject. I have to do as de sun in Hezekiah's case—fall back a few degrees. In dat part of de Word dat I'm given you from Malachi—dat de Lord hisself spoke—He declares dat His glory is gwine to spread. Spread? Where? From de rising of de sun to de goin down of de same. What? Don't say dat, does it? Dat's exactly what it says. Ain't dat clear enough for you? De Lord pity dese doubtin Thomases. Here is enough to settle it all and cure de worse cases. Walk up here, wise folks, and get your medicine. Where is dem high collared philosophers now? What dey skulkin round in de brush for? Why don't you get out in broad afternoon light and fight for your collars? Ah, I understand it; you got no answer. De Bible is against you and in your consciences you are convicted.

"But I hears you back dere. What you whisperin bout? I know! You say you sent me some papers and I never answer dem. Ha, ha, ha! I got 'em. De difficulty bout dem papers you sent me is dat dey did not answer me. Dey never mention de Bible one time. You think so much of yourself and so little of de Lord God and thinks what you say is so smart dat you can't even speak of de Word of de Lord. When you ask me to stop believing in de Lord's Word and to pin my faith to your words, I ain't goin to do it. I take my stand by de Bible and rest my case on what it says. I take what de Lord says bout my sins, bout my Saviour, bout life, bout death, bout de world to come and I take what de Lord say bout de sun and moon, and I cares little what de haters of my God chooses to say. Think dat I will forsake de Bible? It is my only Book, my hope, de arsenal of my soul's supplies and I wants nothin else.

"But I got another word for you yet. I done work over dem papers dat you sent me without date and without your name. You deals in figures and thinks you are bigger dan de archangels. Lemme see what you done say. You set yourself up to tell me how far it is from here to de sun. You think you got it down to a nice point. You say it is 3,339,002 miles from de earth to de sun. Dat's what you say. Another one say dat de distance is 12,000,000, another got it to 27,000,000. I hears dat de great Isaac Newton worked it up to 28,000,000 and later on de philosophers give another rippin rise to 50,000,000. De last one gets it bigger dan all de others, up to 90,000,000. Don't any of 'em agree exactly and so dey runs a guess game and de last guess is always de biggest. Now, when dese guessers can have a convention in Richmond and all agree upon de same thing, I'd be glad to hear from you again and I does hope dat by dat time you won't be ashamed of your name.

"Heeps of railroads has been built since I saw de first one when I was fifteen years old but I ain't hear tell of a railroad built yet to de sun. I don't see why if dey can measure de distance to de sun, dey might not get up a railroad or a telegraph and enable us to find something else bout it dan merely how far off de sun is. Dey tell me dat a cannon ball could make de trip to de sun in twelve years. Why don't dey send it? It might be rigged up with quarters for a few philosophers on de inside and fixed up for a comfortable ride. Dey would need twelve years rations and a heep of changes of raiment—mighty thick clothes when dey start and mighty thin ones when dey git dere.

"Oh, my brothren, dese things make you laugh and I don't blame you for laughing except it's always sad to laugh at de follies of fools. If we could laugh 'em out of countenance we might well laugh day and night. What cuts into my soul is dat all dese men seem to me dat dey is hitting at de Bible. Dat's what stirs my soul and fills me with righteous wrath. Little cares I what dey says bout de sun, provided dey let de Word of de Lord alone. But never mind. Let de heathen rage and de people imagine a vain thing. Our King shall break 'em in pieces and dash 'em down. But blessed be de name of our God, de Word of de Lord endureth forever! Stars may fall, moons may turn to blood and de sun set to rise no more, but Thy kingdom, oh, Lord, is from everlastin to everlastin!

"But I has a word dis afternoon for my own brethren. Dey is de people for whose souls I got to watch—for dem I got to stand and report at de last—dey is my sheep and I's deir shepherd and my soul is knit to dem forever. Ain't for me to be troublin you with dese questions bout dem heavenly bodies. Our eyes goes far beyond de smaller stars. Our home is clean out of sight of dem twinklin orbs. De chariot dat will come to take us to our Father's mansion will sweep out by dem flickerin lights and never halt till it brings us in clear view of de throne of de Lamb. Don't hitch your hopes to no sun nor stars. Your home is got Jesus for its light and your hopes must travel up dat way. I preach dis sermon just for to settle the minds of my few brethren and I repeats it cause kind friends wish to hear it, and I hopes it will do honor to de Lord's Word. But nothing short of de Pearly Gates can satisfy me and I charge, my people, fix your feet on de solid Rock, your hearts on Calvary, and your eyes on de throne of de Lamb. Dese strifes and griefs will soon get over; we shall see de King in His glory and be at ease. Go on, go on, ye ransomed of de Lord! Shout His praises as you go! And I shall meet you in de city of de New Jerusalem where ye shan't need de light of de sun—for de Lamb of de Lord is de light of de saints!"

Sermon: Behold the Rib

I take my text from Genesis two and twenty-one (Gen. 2:21)

> Behold de Rib!
> Now, my beloved,
> Behold means to look and see.
> Look at dis woman God done made,
> But first thing, ah hah!
> Ah wants you to gaze upon God's previous works.
> Almighty and arisen God, hah!
> Peace-giving and prayer-hearing God,
> High-riding and strong armed God
> Walking acrost his globe creation, hah!
> Wid de blue elements for a helmet
> And a wall of fire round his feet
> He wakes de sun every morning from his fiery bed
> Wid de breath of his smile
> And commands de moon wid his eyes.
> And Oh—
> Wid de eye of Faith
> I can see him

From Mules and Men, *by Zora Neale Hurston, New York, Harper and Row, Perennial Library Edition.*   *1935 by Zora Neale Hurston.*

Even de lion had a mate
So God shook his head
And a thousand million diamonds
Flew out from his glittering crown
And studded de evening sky and made de stars.
So God put Adam into a deep sleep
And took out a bone, ah hah!
And it is said that it was a rib.
Behold de rib!
A bone out of a man's side.
He put de man to sleep and made wo-man,
And men and women been sleeping together ever since.
Behold de rib!
Brothers, if God
Had taken dat bone out of man's head
He would have meant for woman to rule, hah
If he had taken a bone out of his foot,
He would have meant for us to dominize and rule.
He could have made her out of back-bone
And then she would have been behind us.
But, no, God Almighty, he took de bone out of his side
So dat places de woman beside us;
Hah! God knowed his own mind.
Behold de rib!
And now I leave dis thought wid you,
Standing out on de eaves of ether
Breathing clouds from out his nostrils,
Blowing storms from 'tween his lips
I can see!!
Him seize de mighty axe of his proving power
And smite the stubborn-standing space,
And laid it wide open in a mighty gash—
Making a place to hold de world
I can see him—
Molding de world out of thought and power
And whirling it out on its eternal track,
Ah hah, my strong armed God!
He set de blood red eye of de sun in de sky
And told it,
Wait, wait! Wait there till Shiloh come
I can see!
Him mold de mighty mountains
And melting de skies into seas.
Oh, behold, and look and see! hah
We see in de beginning
He made de beastes every one after its kind.
De birds that fly de trackless air,
De fishes dat swim de mighty deep—

Male and fee-male, hah!
Then he took of de dust of de earth
And made man in his own image.
And man was alone,
Let us all go marchin' up to de gates of Glory.
Tramp! tramp! tramp!
In step wid de host dat John saw.
Male and female like God made us
Side by side.
Oh, behold de rib!
And let's all set down in Glory together
Right round his glorified throne
And praise his name forever.

Sermon: The Poor-Rich and the Rich-Poor

(Delivered by a Minister in Cottonville)

"There is that maketh himself rich, yet hath nothing; and there is that maketh himself poor, yet hath great riches."—Prov. 13:7.

This proverb given by Solomon, the world's wisest man, expresses a bit of wisdom grasped by wise men of long ago. It should be thoughtfully considered today. It sets up a standard which is often overlooked. It tells us that there is a success which is failure, that there is wealth which is poverty; but there is a failure which is success, and there is a poverty which is wealth.

The poor-rich and the rich-poor. Paradoxical as this expression may seem, it is nevertheless true that one may be both rich and poor at the same time. In fact, it is not a rare thing for one who is poor in this world's goods to be truly "rich toward God." Neither is it an uncommon thing to find one who is rich in "the abundance of the things which he possesseth," but is indeed poor as regards spiritual riches.

I. THE POOR-RICH, WHO IS HE?

1. He who accumulates wealth but who is deaf to the cry of the poor.

From After Freedom, A Cultural Study in the Deep South, by Hortense Powdermaker, New York, Viking Press, 1939. "Cottonville" is a fictitious name for
the community where Miss Powdermaker conducted her study, probably Mt.
Bayou, Mississippi.

"He that hath pity upon the poor lendeth unto the Lord."—Prov. 19:17.

One commentator has said, "If you are satisfied with the security, down with the cash." Some of the rich seem to doubt the security.

The man of wealth who has not Christ, instead of possessing money, is possessed by his money. A rich man once said, "I owned $50,000 and was a happy man. Now $500,000 owns me. It says, 'Lie awake nights and worry.' It says, 'Run here,' and I run. It says, 'Trust in me,' and I trust in riches. I am rich, unhappy, and hanker for more." "But," he was asked, "why don't you give away the $450,000 and return to your happy state?" "Ah," said the man, "did you ever hold the hand of a galvanic battery? The more the juice the tighter you hold." Unconsecrated wealth brings poverty of soul. (Jas. 5:1–3.)

A man was once asked for a donation for some church purpose, but excused himself by saying, "I'm fattening a calf and when it's fat, I'll give the proceeds." This same excuse was given three times over in response to appeals. One day he was approaching church a little late, and heard the choir singing, "The half has never yet been told," and thought in the distance the words were, "The calf has never yet been sold." Conscience-stricken, he sold the calf, and gave the proceeds to the church.

2. He who gets riches but loses character. (I Tim. 6:19.)

In one room in a munition factory in Detroit thirty-five machinists were working. During the first five months of the war wages went up so that they were making an average of $40 a day. Of these thirty-five men, no less than fourteen who previously had been quiet, substantial citizens, good husbands, and loving fathers, became estranged from their wives during these prosperous months through their own folly. Fourteen broken homes out of thirty-five because of sudden riches!

Dr. Lorimer once asked a man why he did not join the church. The reply was that the dying thief did not join the church and he was saved. "Well," said the minister, "if you do not belong to a church, you help to support missions, of course?" "No," said the man, "the dying thief did not help missions, and wasn't he saved?" "Yes," said Dr. Lorimer, "I suppose he was, but you must remember that he was a dying thief, whereas you are a living one."

"For what shall it profit a man, if he shall gain the whole world, and lose his own soul?"—Mark 8:36.

3. He who has laid up treasures here upon earth but has nothing in the exchequer of Heaven.

He may be rich in earthly wealth, but poor in heavenly treasures; rich for time, but poor for eternity. Did I say rich for time? Nay, he gets the least out of this life, and has nothing beyond. A thoughtless man of the world said on a certain occasion, "It is hell to be poor." I responded, "No, it is not hell to be poor, but it is hell to be without God."

Naaman was rich, but he was a leper.

Dives was rich, but he was lost.

The young ruler who came to Jesus was rich, but he made the great refusal. Many today are rich but they are poor.

A ship bearing a hundred emigrants has been driven from her course and is wrecked on a desert island far from the tracks of man. There is no way of escape; but there are means of subsistence. An ocean, unvisited by ordinary voyagers, circles around their prison; but they have seed, a rich soil to receive it, and a genial climate to ripen it. Ere any plan has been laid or any operations begun, an exploring party returns to headquarters, reporting the discovery of a gold mine. Thither instantly the whole party resorts to dig. They labor successfully day by day and month by month. They acquire and accumulate large heaps of gold. But spring is past, and not a field has been cleared nor a grain of seed committed to the ground. The summer comes, and their wealth increases; but the store of food is small. In harvest they begin to discover that their heaps of gold are worthless. When famine stares them in their faces a suspicion shoots across their fainting hearts that the gold has cheated them. They rush to the woods, fell the trees, dig the roots, till the ground, sow the seed. It is too late! Winter has come, and their seed rots in the ground. They die of want in the midst of their treasures. This earth is a little isle, eternity the ocean around it; on this shore we have been cast. There is living seed, but gold mines attract us. We spend spring and summer there; winter overtakes us toiling there, destitute of the bread of life, forgetting that we ought to seek first the kingdom of God and His righteousness; and all these things shall be added unto us.

II. THE RICH-POOR, WHO IS HE?

1. He who gives his life for others.
"He that findeth his life shall lose it; and he that loseth his life for My sake shall find it."—Matt. 10:39
"There is that scattereth, and yet increaseth."—Prov. 11:24.
"Is your father at home?" I asked a little child on our village doorstep. "No," he said; "he's away." "Where do you think I could find him?" "Well," he said in a considering air, "you've got to look for some place where people are sick or hurt or something like that. I don't know where he is, but he is helping somewhere." And I turned away with this little sermon in my heart. If you want to find the Lord Jesus you've got to set out on a path of helping somewhere, or lifting somebody's burden, and lo! straightway one like unto the Son of man will be found at your side. We cannot always find Him whom our soul loveth, in worship or in ordinances or in sacraments or in still meditation; we can never find Him in selfish idleness or in worldliness or in self-indulgence; but on the contrary, like the little one's father, He is sure to be found helping somewhere.
2. He who grasps the great truth of stewardship.
The silver and gold are His. All is His. "All souls are mine." "Ye are not your own." I believe in tithing not as a legal obligation but as a Christian privilege.

In a recent periodical a minister gives the account of a good man in one of his charges who regularly gave every Sunday five dollars for the support of his church. A poor widow, also a member of the same church, supported herself and six children by washing. She was as regular as the rich man in making her offering of five cents per week, which was all she could spare from her scant earnings. One day the rich man came to the minister and said that the poor woman ought not to pay anything, and that he would pay the five cents for her every week. The pastor called to tell her of the offer, which he did in a considerate manner. Tears came to the woman's eyes as she replied, "Do they want to take from me the comfort I experience in giving to the Lord? Think how much I owe Him. My health is good, my children keep well, and I receive so many blessings that I feel I could not live if I did not make my little offering to Jesus each week."

If we play fair with God in a financial way we shall realize the truth of the proverb which reads, "The blessing of the Lord, it maketh rich, and He addeth no sorrow with it."—Prov. 10:22.

3. He who goes on day by day laying up treasures in the upper banking house of eternal revenue.

The Christian is rich in the things which money cannot buy—a contented mind, peace of heart, "joy unspeakable," rich in the love of God, the presence of Jesus, the comfort of the Holy Spirit, a hope that is big with immortality; rich in faith, rich in good works, poor, yet making many rich; having nothing yet possessing all things. He rejoices in the words of Paul, "For all things are yours."

Every Christian, though he may be classed as poor, is rich. He may be poor for time, but rich for eternity. Did I say poor for time? Nay, he gets the most out of this life, and has everything beyond. He is poor in property but rich in piety; poor in money but rich in heavenly grace.

"If a son, then an heir of God through Christ."—Gal. 4:7.

The poor woman who dwells in the hovel over yonder who can say, "Christ is mine," is richer than the English nobleman who owned the beautiful grounds and majestic woods as far as the eye could reach.

The richest man in town was not the town's wealthiest citizen but a very poor man who was a veritable saint.

So the Rich-Poor are those who sing with the poet:

"Lord, I care not for riches, neither silver nor gold:
I would make sure of Heaven, I would enter the fold.

"In the book of thy Kingdom, with its pages so fair;
Tell me, Jesus my Saviour, is my name written there?"

THE RELIGIOUS SHOUT

The shout is not, as the name might suggest, merely a loud vocalization of religious experience, but a religious or semireligious activity combining music, devotion, and movement. It is a cluster of thinly disguised and diluted elements stemming from West African religious practices. As described in the New York *Nation* of May 30, 1867:

"This is a ceremony which the white clergymen are inclined to discountenance, and even of the colored elders some of the more discreet try sometimes to put on a face of discouragement; and although, if pressed for Biblical warrant for the shout, they generally seem to think 'he in de Book,' or 'he dere-da in Matchew,' still it is not considered blasphemous or improper if 'de chillen' and 'dem young gal' carry it on in the evening for amusement's sake, and with no well-defined intention of 'praise.' But the true 'shout' takes place on Sundays or on 'praise'-nights through the week, and either in the praise-house or in some cabin in which a regular religious meeting has been held. Very likely more than half the population of the plantation-is gathered together. Let it be the evening, and a light-wood fire burns red before the door of the house and on the hearth. For some time one can hear, though at a good distance, the vociferous exhortation or prayer of the presiding elder or of the brother who has a gift that way, and who is not 'on the back seat,'—a phrase, the interpretation of which is 'under the censure of the church authorities for bad behavior;'—and at regular intervals one hears the elder 'deaconing' a hymn-book hymn, which is sung two lines at a time, and whose wailing cadences, borne on the night air, are indescribably melancholy. But the benches are pushed back to the wall when the formal meeting is over, and old and young, men and women, sprucely-dressed young men, grotesquely half-clad field hands—the women generally with gay handkerchiefs twisted about their heads and with short skirts—boys with tattered shirts and men's trousers, young girls barefooted, all stand up in the middle of the floor, and when the 'sperichil' is struck up, begin first walking and by and by shuffling round, one after the other, in a ring. The foot is hardly taken from the floor, and the progression is mainly due to a jerking, hitching motion, which agitates the entire shouter, and soon brings out streams of perspiration. Sometimes they dance silently, sometimes as they shuffle they sing the chorus of the spiritual, and sometimes the song itself is also sung by the dancers. But more frequently a band, composed of some of the best singers and of tired shouters, stand at the side of the room to 'base' the others, singing the body of the song and clapping their hands together or on the knees. Song and dance are alike extremely energetic, and often, when the

This description, except for the 1867 quotation, is from Negro Folk Music, U.S.A., *by Harold Courlander. New York, Columbia University Press, 1963, and is reprinted with the kind permission of the publisher. The quote from the* New York Nation *is from* Slave Songs of the United States, *by William Francis Allen, Charles Pickard Ware and Lucy McKim Garrison, 1867.*

shout lasts into the middle of the night, the monotonous thud, thud of the feet prevents sleep within half a mile of the praise-house."

In its customary form, the ring shout consists of a circle of people moving single file (usually counterclockwise) around a central point, to the accompaniment of singing, stamping, and heel clicking. In some instances, the participants tap (in effect, drum) on the floor rhythmically with sticks to produce percussion effects. The steps are akin to a shuffle, with free foot movement prohibited, and little versatility permitted. Sometimes, the clearly defined single file circle gives way to a sort of amorphous crowd moving around a central point. The tempo may build up gradually, singing interspersed with exclamations characteristic of some other Negro church services, until it reaches a tense peak close to an ecstatic breaking point. At the high point of the excitement, such exclamations as "Oh Lord!" and "Yes, Lord!" turn into nonsense sounds and cries; seemingly wild emotional responses, they nevertheless are related to the music as a whole, and no notation which omits them can give a fair picture of what is heard.

The tension generated in the course of the shout has certain approved outlets, such as ecstatic seizures or possessions, but the feet are required to be kept under control. A person who violates this commonly understood proscription by "crossing his feet"—that is to say, by "dancing"—is admonished or evicted from the service. One elderly man described his own unfortunate experience this way: "Well, don't you know, them folks all shouting, rockin', and reelin', and me in the middle; and I ask you if it wasn't the Holy Ghost that come into me, who was it? Those feet of mine wouldn't stay on the ground in no manner, they jumped around and crossed over, back and forth, and the next thing I know they turned me out of the church."

The shout is a fusion of two seemingly irreconcilable attitudes toward religious behavior. In most of Africa, dance, like singing and drumming, is an integral part of supplication. Not all religious rites in West Africa include dancing, but most of them do; certainly at some stage of supplication dancing plays an essential role. Among West Africans, dancing in combination with other elements is regarded as a form of appeal to supernatural forces, and this tradition remains alive in New World African cults in Haiti, Jamaica, Trinidad, and other West Indian islands. In the Euro-Christian tradition, however, dancing in church is generally regarded as a profane act. The ring shout in the United States provides a scheme which reconciles both principles. The circular movement, shuffling steps, and stamping conform to African traditions of supplication, while by definition this activity is not recognized as a "dance." However, if one violates the compromise by going too far, he has committed an irreverent act.

Anyone who sees a ring shout performed by older people is impressed by the motion patterns. Postures and gestures, the manner of standing, the bent knees, the feet flat on the floor or ground, the way the arms are held out for balance or pressed against the sides, the movements of the shoulders, all are African in conception and derivation. Some of the photographs published by Lydia Parrish in her book on the music of the Sea Islands, as well as her descriptions, reveal the extent to which some of the African dance motifs have been retained.[1] They show also that among the children most, if not all, of these motifs have disappeared. For the older people of the Sea Islands, there was a continuity of relatively undisturbed tradition once the original accommodation had been made between Euro-Christian and African elements. But the outer world has pressed in on the younger generations, and, although life has not changed as rapidly in the islands as it has in the towns and cities, the more archaic traditions are slipping away into the past.

It appears that emphasis on the more dramatic aspects of the ring shout by many writers has tended to obscure its essential meanings. While it is dance (contrary to the premise of the participants), it is not dance brought into religious activity from the secular world, either as a manifestation of revolt against the strictness of Christian concepts or as a means of retaining a pleasurable profane institution in disguise. When a congregation sings, "I'm going to shout all over God's Heaven," the allusion is not to disturbing the peace but to devotional activity including singing, rhythmic sound, patterned movement, and intense emotional expression—elements traditionally associated with worship.

Some of the choreographic aspects (as well as the sounds) of the shout are similar to those of the Revivalist cults of Jamaica, where, also, traditional elements are present. George E. Simpson describes a religious service in Kingston in a way that leaves little doubt of the similarity:

"Halfway through the service the leader may begin to circle counterclockwise the altar, or a table inside the church, or the 'seal' in the yard outside the church. The officers and leading members of the church, often up to twenty people, fall in behind him as all of them 'labor in the spirit.' . . . This 'spiritual' dancing is believed to increase the religious understanding of the participants."[2] As in the shouts, ecstatic seizures or possessions take place. The Jamaican revivalists have overlaid and disguised the African elements in their worship and hold themselves aloof from the so-called African cults such as the Kumina. Nevertheless, they form a bridge between the ring shout in the United States and the openly acknowledged African-style cult activities of the West Indies and, of course, Africa itself.

Songs used in the shout are of various kinds, some of them clearly religious in content, others drawing largely upon secular experience and imagery but given religious character by interpolations, responses, and underlying attitudes. As with other Negro songs, the statement or idea may be tangent or metaphoric. As the tempo and the emotions heighten, words may be improvised. Some of these songs are reputed to last

---

1. *Lydia Parrish,* Slave Songs of the Georgia Sea Islands, *plates 22, 23, 24, facing pages 128, 129, and 144.*
2. *George E. Simpson, introduction to the record album,* Jamaican Cult Music, *Ethnic Folkways Library FE 4461.*

more than an hour (some observers said as long as three hours), and the words may dissolve into expletives and unrecognizable syllables. Sometimes a second singing leader moves in to relieve the exhausted starting leader. Different leaders employ different styles. Some use a kind of rhythmic preaching style, some a kind of semimusical call, and others "sing" in the usual sense of the term.

Run Old Jeremiah

One of the most exciting recorded examples of a ring shout is "Run Old Jeremiah," recorded by John and Alan Lomax in Louisiana in 1934 for the Library of Congress. The recording begins after the singing is under way and ends before the piece is finished. This example has an overall character more "African" than many known African performances. Hand clapping and heel stamping produce powerful, driving rhythmic effects, with the short vocal responses sometimes tending more toward sounds than words. The words of "Run Old Jeremiah" are partly narrative and partly dramatic sound, with apparent improvisation as the singer strives to maintain his command of the situation, and repetition as he poises himself for a new thought or line. Partway through, a second leader takes over. Early in the recording, the responsive part consists of the words "Good Lord," sung in a growllike timbre. A little later, as the fervor and tempo increase, the words are replaced by less intelligible sounds, with slight pitch variations. These change briefly to moanlike sounds, and, shortly after the second leader has replaced the first, the chorus responds with a barklike "Yeah!" This again changes, with the mounting tension, to groans and high-pitched or falsetto yells and yelps.

Good Lord, by myself.(x5)
You know I've got to go.
You got to run.
I've got to run.
You got to run.
By myself.(x3)
I got a letter.(x2)
Ol' brownskin.
Tell you what she say.
"Leavin' tomorrow,
Tell you goodbye."
Oh my Lordy.(x6)
Well well well.(x2)
Oh my Lord.(x2)
Oh my Lordy.(x2)
Well well well.(x2)
I've got a rock.
You got a rock.
Rock is death.
Oh my Lordy.
Oh my Lord.
Well well well.
Run here Jeremiah.(x2)
I must go.
On my way(x4)
Who's that ridin' the chariot?(x2)
Well well well.

(Second leader takes over)
One mornin'
Before the evening
Sun was going down(x3)
Behind them western hills(x3)
Old Number Twelve

Soon soon soon.
Wah oh!
Well well well.
Ol' engineer,
I've got your life
In my hands.(x2)
Told your father.(x2)

Comin' down the track.(x3)
See that black smoke.
See that old engineer.(x2)
Tol' that old fireman
Ring his old bell
With his hand.
Rung his engine bell.(x2)
Well well well.(x2)
Jesus tell the man,
Say, I got your life
In my hand.
I got your life
In my hand.(x2)
Well well well.
(Ol' fireman told
Told that engineer
Ring your black bell
Ding ding ding.
Ding ding ding ding.
Ol' fireman say
. . .[1]
That mornin'.
Well well well.(x2)
Ol' fireman say,
Well well,
I'm gonna grab my
Old whistle too.
Wah wah ho!
Wah wah wah wah ho!
Wah wah ho!
Wah wah wah ho!
(Etc.)
Mmmmmmmmmmmm.

Well well well.
I was travellin(x2)
I was ridin(x3)
Over there.(x2)
Ol' engineer.
This is the chariot(x2)

---

1. *Three lines indistinguishable in recording.*

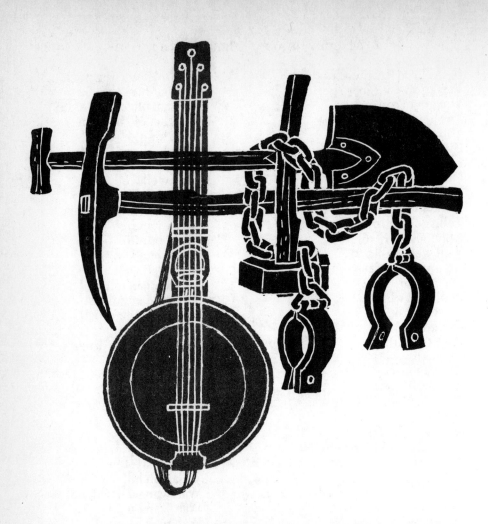

ON THE MAKING OF SONGS

While some latter-day blues singers have earmarked particular songs as their own creations, the authorship of spirituals, ballads, blues, and other song genres is generally unknown, as one would expect in something called folk music. Indeed, as far as blues are concerned, the music is borrowed freely by one song from another, as are a great many phrases and lines, and the same holds for many ballads. When a blues singer claims authorship to a certain song he is not really thinking of himself as a musical composer, but as one who has captured an idea or taken note of a certain happening or feeling and placed it in a setting. He is never held accountable for what he may have unconsciously borrowed from the common wellspring. The same attitudes pertain to ballad-making. Songs spontaneously generated to accompany track lining or woodcutting may surface again a hundred miles away as a guitar-accompanied ballad or blues. And a railroad song once sung to memorialize a train wreck in 1917 may reappear with a variety of changes to describe the derailing of an express in 1947. Authorship is applauded when it is known, but folk songs quickly become anonymous as they are absorbed into the common reservoir. People listening to a street-corner gospel singer are more impressed with his performance, or with what he (or she) conveys, than with the fact that the song is being heard for the first time. Folk songs are usually anonymous in the same way that traditional African wood sculpture is anonymous. The blues-gospel singer Blind Lemon Jefferson has often been referred to by latter-day blues singers with admiration. Blind Lemon may be presumed to have originated some of the songs in his repertoire, but it was his style of singing that attracted attention, not his authorship.

Many traditional black folk songs are so generalized in their statements that they can be readily applied to new happenings. But some are so specifically topical that they can refer only to a particular happening at a particular time. Thus, songs about the sinking of the *Titanic* and the gospel song, "Russia, Leave That Moon Alone," are so basically "historical" that they cannot be transposed to fit other events. Some older persons may recall who it was that sang a certain song for the first time in a certain place, but usually without any assurance that he composed it. The enriching process of songmaking has been going on for a very long while, but the men or women who made the songs, and the moments of original creation, are part of a hidden past.

The descriptions that follow tell us something about how songs were made and the circumstances surrounding them.

Bo-Cat

Pin Point [a community about nine miles southeast of Savannah on a peninsula overlooking Shipyard Creek] attained a certain measure of fame as the setting of the Bo-Cat murder in 1932. Limerick De Lanzy, a Pin Point man nicknamed Bo-Cat, killed his wife, Catherine, and dropped her corpse into the deep waters near Hell Gate. When the crime was discovered, the fact that it had taken place on Friday, the thiirteenth, loomed significant in the consciousness of the small community and in no time inspired a ballad. Attributed to no single author but apparently added to from time to time, the ballad now runs:

> On duh thuteent day ub May
> Yuh could heah ole Bo-Cat say,
> "Git muh deed an policy.
> Tun it in duh ashes way."

From Drums and Shadows, Survival Studies Among the Georgia Coastal Negroes, *Georgia Writers' Project, Athens, University of Georgia Press, 1940. By permission of the publishers.*

Den ole Catherine she begin tuh inquyuh.
Didn know ole Bo-Cat had dem in duh fyuh.
It a shame how Bo-Cat done he wife.

Put uh in duh boat,
Dey begin tuh float,
Dey float tuh duh Raccoon Keys.
He knock uh on duh knees.
Catherine holluh, "Wa-Wan-Wa."
Bo-Cat make uh "Na-Nan-Na."
It a shame how Bo-Cat done he wife.

He knock uh in duh bres
An duh oah done duh res.
It a shame how Bo-Cat done he wife.

He knock uh in duh back
An duh oah miss an crack.
It a shame how Bo-Cat done he wife.

Wen Bo-Cat wehn back home
He meet uh daughtuh all alone.
Uh daughtuh say, "Bo-Cat, Bo-Cat,
Weah my mama is?"
Bo-Cat tun right out he head
An he tro uh cross duh bed.
It a shame how Bo-Cat done he wife.

Dey got Bo-Cat in jail
Bout tuh hang im by duh rail
It a shame how Bo-Cat done he wife.

One of the Pin Point women, Margaret Snead, recalls vividly the events of the De Lancy crime.

"Wy, duh night fo Catherine De Lanzy wuz kill, she spen it in town wid me," said Margaret Snead. "Attuh dat night I didn see uh no mo. People from duh Pint come inquirin bout uh but nobody seem tuh know nuttn bout uh weahbouts. Bout two weeks latuh, a pahty uh wite mens out huntin come cross duh body at Raccoon Keys. Dis a ilun way beyon Hell's Gate. Mus be mohn twenny miles from duh Pint. I dohn see as ow nobody could carry a pusson dat fah jis tuh murduh em. Anyways, duh body wuz brung tuh duh city, an at duh unduhtakuh's office people went in tuh see ef dey could dentify it. Dis a hahd ting tuh do. She bin in duh watuh fuh days an days fo a high tide wash duh cawpse on sho. Duh body wuz caught tween two logs weah duh buzzuds went tuh wuk on it.

"I membuh a great big cawn wich she use tuh suffuh wid but couldn nebuh git rid ub. So I went in an had a look at duh foot, an sho nuff deah wuz dat cawn jis lak it use tuh be wen she wuz libe.

"Her ole huzbun, Limbrick De Lanzy, already wuz rested, an he git sen up fuh life. It wuz Friday, May duh thuteent, dat ole Limbrick carried Catherine off down duh ribbuh an murduh uh. A double bad luck, Friday an duh thuteent, das wy dey make up duh song."

"Was the body buried at Pin Point?" we were interested to know.

"Yes, it wuz, but we didn hab no settin-up cuz duh body wuz too fah gone. Dat wuz sad. Ebrybody lub Catherine an fuh uh tuh die an be buried widout a settin-up aw lettin anybody view uh face aw lay deah hans on uh wuz sho a pity.

"Ebrybody wuz at duh fewnul. Come frum miles roun tuh pay deah las respecks tuh a po wife murduhed by uh huzbun on Friday duh thuteent.

"Duh body wuz brung frum duh unduhtakuh's pahluh straight tuh Sweet Fiel ub Eden Chuch at duh Pint. Chuch so crowded yuh caahn hahdly see duh coffin up in front. We sing hymns, an den wen duh singin hab die out an yuh could heah jis a lill hummin heah an deah, somebody stan up an say, 'Catherine De Lanzy wuz a sistuh ub duh Lawd.' 'She sho wuz,' somebody else say. 'She wuz a chile ub Jesus and she walk in duh way ub righteousness.'

"Dis staht off duh whole congregation an mustuh bin neah a hundud people git up an gib testimony bout Catherine's goodness. Some people cry an scream wen dey tell duh congregation wut a fine uhmun she bin.

"Den duh remains wuz took tuh duh cimiterry neah duh chuch an buried. Duh whole time we sing hymns an sway tuh duh soun uh duh music. Ebrybody tro a hanful uh dut in duh grabe an wen duh grabe digguhs fix duh moun, we put some uh Catherine's tings on duh top. Deah wuz a lill flowuh vase wid duh bottom knock out, an a lamp chimney, an some puhfumery bottles, an duh pitchuh she made ice watuh in jis fo Bo-Cat tuk uh off. Den duh ministuh nounce dat duh fewnul suhmon wuz tuh be preach at duh annyul memorial wen dey pray fuh ebrybody who die durin duh yeah. An den das all an we wehn home."

Richard Creeks on Songmaking

Richard Creeks is the protagonist of the book, *The Big Old World of Richard Creeks*, set in the south in the first part of the twentieth cen-

From The Big Old World of Richard Creeks, © *1962 by Harold Courlander, Philadelphia, Chilton Press.*

tury. Rich is not a character transposed from real life so much as a composite, and some of his claims to have originated various songs were in fact made by several different men. But what Rich had to say on the subject of songmaking was really said by someone, and these excerpts from the book tell us something about how railroad songs, ballads, and blues came into being.

When you get around much like I did, you sooner or later get to work on the railroad, just like me. I worked at it some and then I didn't, but some men worked railroad all their lives. Some of them was pretty stout, too. Knowed one named Big Bill who'd lost five toes off his right foot when a handcar turned over on it. That was when he was young, but it never stopped him from being a railroad man, it just made him walk with a limp. He told me one time he could get me on the Yellow Dog and I went with him and he got me on. The boss, name of Mr. Reemer, looked me over that day and was kind of sad. He say, "Bill, we sure needs men on this gang, but we need them six-feet-four and not four-foot-six." Bill say, "Captain, this is a good boy. He can tamp ties, and if he don't line track like I know he can, I'll line for him." Boss said, "Bill, you knows we need stout men, not little runty ones, why you do this to me?" By this time Big Bill had the boss eating out of the pan, and say, "Captain, I'll guarantee that this boy Rich can make the other men do more work in less time." Boss said all right then, we going to try this boy, and he better do what you say.

That was my first railroad job. We worked up and down the line all summer. The track caller, he was the one that called the signals. When the men was lining track with iron bars, the track caller would sing out what to do and make it sound like music. When they was tamping the ties, this man would make up songs or else just sing old ones they liked. If they got in the spirit of it, it was a real sight. Of course, I was a good singer, and when our track caller don't show for work one day Mr. Reemer say to me, "Rich, you get over there and call track." So I did. Boss say, "Hold it right there. Get six bars. Put two bars on this side over here. All right now, shake it east. Shake it, boys, shake it. Give me what you got." First time I sung track I did some old songs the boys knew, and after that I got to making up some of my own. Most of the bosses on the railroad was nice men. They talked like they was mad but usually they wasn't, and you could make jokes with them. Lots of times you'd put the jokes in a song whilst lining track, like this:

> Oh the Captain can't tell
> Either day or night,
> Captain can't tell you
> If the track's lined right.
> N'Orleans, Louisiana, bam!
> Yakka yakka yakka,

N'Orleans, Louisiana, bam!
Yakka yakka yakka.

The bam was when they hit with a hammer, and the yakka yakka was
when they jiggled the track with their bars. Instead of N'Orleans, Louisiana, sometimes I would sing, "Big boy, let's move it," or something
like that.

One time I took a song and put Mr. Reemer's name in it. You don't
know for sure when you're joking around whether the boss going to act
mad or not, but when all the boys are feeling good and singing together, you can't help trying it. If it makes the boss mad it can make the
boys glad. Sometimes a track caller would sing something funny and
all the boys would get to laughing so hard they couldn't work. That's
the only thing ever really riled Mr. Reemer, when they was laughing
instead of working, but sometimes he'd laugh too, and then it was all
right. First song I made up with Captain Reemer in it went like this:

> Oh Captain Reemer,
> Where is your wife and children? Bam!
> What you doin' here, here,
> Captain what you doin' here?
> Oh Captain Reemer,
> Where in the world did you come from? Bam!
> Why'd you ever come here, here,
> Why'd you ever come down here?

There was an old song to the same tune, about a boy been chasing
two girls at the same time, name of Evalina and Mattie Campbell, asking them to take him in, but they don't say yes or no, just keep him
jumping. That one go like this:

> Evalina
> When you going to give me what I asked you?
> I don't know, know, know,
> Buddy, buddy I don't know.
> Hey, Mattie Campbell,
> When you comin' back over?
> Well I don't know, know,
> Buddy, buddy I don't know.

Lots of track callers knew that song and added their own words to it. I
sang one verse of it which was a joke on Captain Reemer:

> Oh Captain, when you get your section
> I want to be your straw,
> I'll marry your daughter
> And be your son-in-law.

That was one could of made Mr. Reemer mad, but it didn't, it just made him laugh. Quite a few years later I heard the men singing it over on the Southern Pacific, a little different but the same song.

Once a song is borned it's hard to stop it, specially if it's a natural song. I think some of them railroad songs will be going even after there ain't no more Yellow Dog Railroad. One song like that is about John Henry. I didn't make up that song, but I did sing it my own way, and the boys liked it. There's quite a few different ways to sing John Henry, and that's because every track caller got a different way of doing it. Some does it short and some long. The short ones is because they don't know all of it, just some parts. Mine was a long one, with everything that really happened.

Can't nobody claim a song for himself no more after it's started. When it just get borned it do everything its mamma and papa say do; after that it don't listen to nobody. Folks tell about a Negro back in slavery times, and his master was real hard on him. This poor boy, name of Coffee, he get the worst of everything. His old master, name of Colonel Robert Johnson he worked all his slaves hard, but he treat Coffee the worst, and every once in a while he throw in a good whuppin. Coffee had a pretty little wife, and the master took and sold her to another master down the river. Coffee beg with him not to do that, but all the Colonel say is it don't make no difference to him, he own her, and it going to teach Coffee a good lesson.

After that Coffee get the blues and don't care if he work or get whupped. One day the master say he had enough of Coffee, he going to sell him to another master over in Mississippi somewhere. Night before he was tooken off, Coffee put the banjo on Master Robert. That mean he made up a song about the master and sung it in the slave quarters. When you put the banjo on somebody, it tells all his meannesses and faults. It's like a judgment, and everybody listen to what you say. Well, Coffee put the banjo on the master, and it go like this:

> Well down on the Coosa River
> Year of eighteen and twenty-four,
> You ought to seen Master Robert
> With his fifty slaves and more.
>
> Promised them poor boys that when he die
> He going to free them all,
> But seem like that mean old man
> Had no intention of dyin' at all.
>
> Drove 'em in the turn row,
> Women just like the men,
> Say don't care if you walk or fall,
> Just keep agoin' till the cotton's in.

Older he get, the meaner he feel,
Teeth fell out, head got bald,
Says you better keep apickin'
Cause I got no notion of dyin' at all.

Face was old and ugly,
Toes was turned around,
Knees and back they get all bent
Till his coattails dragged the ground.

But old Master Robert 'fused to die,
Say he goin' to dry up first,
Says one more thing he got to do,
Going to drive the Niggers and make 'em work.

Well, the song was like that, and there was more to it—all about the man that sold poor Coffee's wife away from him. It get to be mighty popular around the plantation, and old master don't like it at all. Men was asinging it whilst cutting trees out in the woods. Women singing it out in the fields. Even the little children play games to that song. And Coffee, he sung it on the next plantation he went to, and the slaves over there liked it mighty fine. Pretty soon folks was singing it all up and down the river. Master Robert couldn't go nowhere amongst the slaves without hearing something of it, maybe just the tune without the words, like they was humming it.

One time Master Robert went down to the plantation where he had sold Coffee, and he ask the new master can he talk to him. They sent for Coffee out in the field, and when he come Master Robert say, "Coffee, that is a mean and miserable song you made up on me, and I want you to put a stop to it. Here is ten dollars in silver, and I don't want ever to hear that song no more." Coffee say, "Master, for the sake of this here ten dollars I won't sing that song no more. I mean it. But what can I do about them other folks that's singing it I don't know. You are a mighty important man around here, and if you can't stop all them folks from loud-mouthing up and down the river, how you expect a poor slave boy like me going to do it? 'Pear to me that what you got to do is go out and shoot that song down, now, cause it already been turned loose, and can't nobody tell it what to do." That's what I mean about how a good song don't belong to nobody in particular. . . .

We never wasted no chance to play pranks and get a good laugh on the job. One time we was lining track when Miss Judy and a white man with a beard that made him look like a sad goat came to see us whilst we was working near town. What they told the boss of our gang made us want to laugh. This man with the little goat beard was a song collector. He had a letter from the Governor of Alabama to whomsoever it may concern. The letter said to help him do whatever he do, but what he do was a new one on me. He said, "Gentlemen, I would be much obliged to you to let me hear you sing some work songs." I believe that was the first time in my life I ever heard a white man call Negroes gentlemen. Miss Judy said, "Bill, let this man hear you sing one of them fine songs of yours." Big Bill said yes'm, but we kept on working and didn't sing nothing. I was calling track, and the only song which come to mind was one I wouldn't dare sing in front of Miss Judy or no other white woman, so I just talked at the boys and didn't sing nothing. The man with the goat beard was standing there with a paper and pencil in his hand waiting, but we didn't sing. The boss had his hands on his hips waiting, and Miss Judy kept urging us on, but the only noise there was which came out of us was a lot of pig grunts.

This man waited till he couldn't wait no more; then he said, "Gentlemen, you know what kind of song I want to hear, the kind when you sing pick them up and lay them down and all that kind of stuff." So I started to sing track then, the way he said. I sang "Pick 'em up" and the boys all came back with "Lay 'em down." For ten-fifteen minutes we sang pick them up and lay them down, with a lot of rattle-dattle-dattle mixed up in it, whilst the man was making marks and putting words down on the paper. When we moved down to the next section, him and Miss Judy followed us, and we started over again with pick them up and lay them down. That's all they got out of us, till after a while they got tired and went away. Miss Judy was apologizing to the man. She said, "I don't know what gets into these Negroes, they always sing so pretty."

Soon as they was gone the boys fell down laughing, rolling all over the ground. The boss stood there laughing with us too; he knew a lot more about us than some folks did. We sat around snorting and howling, and Big Bill had tears running off his face. Then the boss said, "Well, come on, boys, you been laying your ass down on the ground long enough, now pick them up and let's get back to work." So we did, but every time I remembered the man making all those black marks on the paper every time we said pick them up or lay them down, I would cry and the rest of the men would catch it. In all my life I had heard of men making up songs and singing them, but not just collecting them. He never collected much from us.

After a while I sang some of my good songs for the men. There was one particular song I had, which was about a county farm prisoner in Alabama who run away and sent word to his woman. It was my own song, I had made it, and I can prove it by telling you what was behind it. It was a man from around Tuscaloosa name of Little Joe Brown, him and his woman Lucile. Little Joe got in a fight one Saturday night with another man who was hanging around Lucile, beat him up bad with a stove lid and in doing so, broke a plate glass window of a store. If he hadn't of broke that window they might of let him off, but the window belonged to a white man. Joe, he got sent to the county farm for three hundred and sixty-five days plus one, and before he went he pleaded with Lucile to wait for him, and not to take up with no one else or go back where she came from, which was Baltimore. When Joe broke out of the county farm he sent Lucile a message and told her to meet him at the waterfall, which she never did because she had took up with the man Joe beat up that night.

> Now your man done gone
> To the county farm
> Now your man done gone.
>
> Baby, please don't go
> Back to Baltimore
> Baby, please don't go.
>
> You know I loves you so
> So, baby, please don't go.
> Baby, please don't go.
>
> Turn your lamp down low
> And, baby, please don't go
> Baby, please don't go.
>
> I beg you all night long
> And night before
> Baby, please don't go.

That was the part before they took him off. When he say turn your lamp down low, that mean to keep on loving him and not to take up with no one else. When he sent her the message, it said:

> Now your man done come
> From the county farm
> Now your man done come.
>
> Now your man done come
> You better meet me at the waterfall,
> Now your man done come.
>
> Meet me at the waterfall
> And if you throw me off
> I'm going to walk your log.

When he say he would walk her log, that meant he would kill her if she don't come. It ain't in the song, but Lucile never did meet him cause she was gone, her and the other man. I heard that song many a time since then sung by good track callers, and they ain't none of them changed it much, because it was a natural song. Some men tell you that song was about a man in Texas or in Louisiana, but I know it was about Little Joe Brown, because I am the one who made it up.

Just the same it could have been about other men, because there was a lot of them went to county farms and come back to find their women had gone and left them. Half the songs you hear is about women who left their men or men who left their women, so I guess there is a lot of that going on. Almost every song that was sung, there was something behind it, but what that thing was sometimes got forgotten.

There was a lot of songs sung on the railroad that was made up on the state farms and the county farms. Most of those places was in Texas or Mississippi, because in Alabama they didn't like to hear no prisoners singing. They thought the men was too happy singing, and they didn't want no happy prisoners; they wanted them unhappy, because, after all, they done wrong and was being punished. But I can tell you one thing, the prisoners that could sing, they got a lot more work out of them than the ones in Alabama who they wouldn't let sing.

One of the songs was about a man who run away from a state farm down in Texas. They tracked him, but he outsmarted them because he fixed his shoes with a heel in front and a heel behind, and when they saw his tracks in the mud they didn't know whichaway he was going. They never did find him. There really was such a man, and he did do just what the song says. I talked to men who was down there in Texas when it happened and knew him by name.

One thing always got under our skin, that the white folks said all the Negroes is happy-go-lucky, they ain't got no cares or worries, they're always singing or loving or doing buck and wing. When I am singing it's not always because I am happy, but sometimes I feel so low I think I am going to die unless I can sing something. Some songs might of sounded happy to white folks but there wasn't no happiness in them at all, just a bad, sick feeling. That's what beats me about the Alabama prison farms not letting the men sing because they thought it meant they was too happy. Singing when you feel bad is what some folks call blues, but the blues you hear in town on talking machine records isn't nothing to the blues that is sung out in the open by a gang of men working together. Of course the songs we sung wasn't just that kind. Sometimes we would sing about something somebody we knew had done, good or bad. It could be to shame him or praise him. We would get to the boss this way, or maybe some white man who'd done bad to some Negro. Half the time nobody but the singers would catch on what it was all about.

I remember one man name of Hard Rock, born down in Galveston. He was an old man about sixty-five, but plenty stout. The boys got to telling about how much they could lift, and Hard Rock spoke up saying he could tote five cement bags at once, and that make close to five hundred pounds. The boys said hell, he couldn't do that, and Hard Rock said hell youself, I already done it. He said he done it in Galveston, where he was unloading for a construction job. "I put one sack of cement under my right arm," Hard Rock said. "I put another one under my left arm. That make two, don't it? Then I take hold of one sack with my right hand, catching it by the corner. Then I take another one by the corner with my left hand. And after that I just walked like this with all that cement to where the mixer was at." Rock walked around straddle legged like he was carrying all the stuff, and the men was about dying. One of them said, "Man, you can't count, you only got four sacks." Hard Rock stood still, said, "Boy, you are blind. Don't you see me holding one with my teeth?" That made the men whoop and holler, cause Hard Rock only had one tooth in the front of his mouth, the rest was all gums.

Maybe he could have done what he said, but not no more when he was sixty-five. Even so, one time I see two men wrastling with a long oak beam that was too much for them, and Hard Rock went over and took it away from them and brought it back balanced on his head. He was a real stout man for his age, but he was lazy, or maybe he just hated to break his back for somebody else making a lot more money than him. He used to sing a song about that, one he learned in the Texas State Farm. The way he sing it was like this:

> The Captain holler hurry
> I'm going to take my time.
> Says he's making money
> And trying to make time.
> Says he can lose his job
> But I can't lose mine.

The proudest thing Hard Rock had to tell about the way he fixed the road boss over in Texas State Farm was how he wheeled a wheelbarrow back and forth from the sand pit eleven-twelve times before he'd dump it where it was supposed to go, and the captain thought Hard Rock had toted that many loads. He'd go fill up his wheelbarrow again and make another eleven-twelve round trips with it before dumping. Hard Rock got the notion he was doing less work, too, but he wasn't, but it sure pleasured him to think about it. He was uglier than me and twice as old, but he must have had four or five women at one time in Mobile. Sometimes when he been drinking, Hard Rock got sullen and mean. He might go around all day without saying a word to nobody, and the boys would leave him alone.

One day we was quitting work and I asked him, "Hard Rock, you got the blues?" And he say, "It ain't blues I got, it's the blacks. When I'm feeling good it's the blues, but when I feel bad, blues are just happy to me." I asked him what his complaint was. Hard Rock say, "I feel bad cause I'm uglier than you, I got no money, the white folks says get off the sidewalk, I'm tired and sick of this town, and I can't stand the sight of all these people around here, black or white. And if it wasn't none of them things, I'd still feel the same way." What the matter with you is, I tell Hard Rock, is that you've got the blues. And he says don't tell me that, what I've got is the blacks, and that's worse cause there's no cure for it. Next time I see him, though, Hard Rock was acting happy and foolish again. I said to him, "Hard Rock, how come you so happy today when you was so mean and miserable yesterday?" And he say, "I got to, else I'm a dead man."

That's what happened, to him, too. He got mean and miserable one day and it never wore off. He went to a blind tiger and drank all night long and the next day too. Night after that he got in a fight in a pool hall and was stabbed to death. Some time after that when I remembered about it I made up a song about Hard Rock and sung it on the railroad. It was a natural song, and railroad men got to singing it all up and down the line. But they changed it some. It got to be "Hard as a Rock," and after that "Heart like a Rock." I heard this fifteen–twenty years later over in Arkansas, and they was singing it this way:

> Heart like a rock
> And a head like a marble stone.
> I gave that woman all I had
> Now she gone and throw me down.

The way I sang it was this:

> Hard Rock
> He stood alone.
> He had the blacks
> Said, man, I'm gone.
> Said when I feel thisaway
> My heart turn to stone.
> My gal Lucy tell me
> Going to throw me down.
> Ain't got a bed here
> In this old town.
> White folks around here
> Got me agoing.
> Well I got the blacks
> So I'll say so long.

A song like that has got lots of things in it when you know what's back of it.

EVOLUTION OF A PLANTATION SONG

>   The Lord made the bees,
>   The bees made the honey,
>   The Lord made man
>   And man made money.
> —Excerpt from an old English folk song

God makes man,
Man makes money.
> —Words from a Negro boatmen's song set down by
> Frances Anne Kemble in the mid-nineteenth century

>   De old bee make de honeycomb.
>   De young bee make de honey,
>   De niggers make de cotton an' corn
>   An' de white folks gits de money.
> —Words from a song transcribed by Joel Chandler Har-
> ris some forty years later

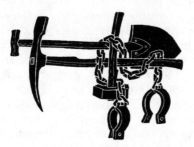

THE JOHN HENRY EPIC

If there is any single secular song that can safely be said to be known

The successive Negro songs are to be found in Miss Kemble's Journal of a
Residence on a Georgia Plantation, *New York, 1863, p. 218, and Joel Chandler Harris's* Uncle Remus, His Songs and His Sayings, *New York, 1880 and
1895, p. 197.*

From Negro Folk Music, U.S.A., *by Harold Courlander. © 1963 by Columbia
University Press. By permission of the publishers. The original text has been altered somewhat and material added.*

on every black railroad gang, by virtually all black ballad and blues singers, and in most black households in the rural southland, it surely is "John Henry" in one variant or another. The song appears in many lengths and forms. It is heard as a blues, a tragic ballad, work song, a washboard band air, an errant guitar or harmonica tune, and as a prose narration. White mountaineer musicmakers and sophisticated urban ensembles have adopted "John Henry" as their own.

Generally speaking, except for some of the extended spirituals and anthems, the epic concept, so widespread in Africa, was not carried over into the American Negro tradition. In the religious songs, of course, the heroic figures are Biblical characters and the great events are from the Old and New Testaments. In the songmaking process these figures and events were often transfigured into unique creations. But in secular songs and narrations here has been little that might be regarded as truly epic. In the more extended work songs one sometimes detects a near-epic—a story that moves in a heroic direction without quite escaping its episodic nature or achieving a larger-than-life, epic character.

But if any oral creation in the traditions of American blacks deserves the term "epic" it is the story of John Henry, a common man—not a ready-made Biblical hero—in contest with "the system," with technology, and with the very mountains that cast their daily shadows across the world in which common men live. In his own way, John Henry is as evocative as Jonah or Sampson, and some of the passages describing his courage, stubbornness, pride, strength, and downfall are as moving as any lines to be found in the spirituals. Some of the versions of the song are quite long, but none of them contains all of the elements of the legend. To comprehend the scope and meaning of John Henry one must see all the fragments, versions, variants, and allusions as part of a whole. Cumulatively, the John Henry legend contains numerous episodes, much genuine poetry, a glimpse of the human condition, and perhaps above all, the vision of a "natural man" (though an uncommonly strong one) enlarged to epic dimensions.

The story is about a railroad laborer who is convinced that no mechanical device such as a steam drill can ever replace a hard-working man in the building of a railroad, and who dies of exhaustion in his effort to prove his point. "Steam is only steam," he says in some of the songs, "but I'm John Henry and I'm a natural man." While the story centers on the dramatic contest between the man and the machine in the Big Bend Tunnel, there are lines and stanzas that flash back to John Henry's childhood and forward to scenes that follow his death. It is thought by some folklorists that the identity of the original John Henry has been established, and that he was, indeed, a track worker on the C and O Railroad. But the legend itself has grown to such dimensions that the individual who inspired it is no longer important.

Some versions contend that when John Henry was a baby he had a clear premonition of his life's work and the drama of his end:

John Henry was a little baby,
Settin' on his mamma's knee,
Said the Big Bend Tunnel on the C. and O. Line
Going to be the death of me,
Lord, going to be the death of me.

The details of the momentous struggle against the machine vary a great deal as the story is told, or the song sung, in different places at different times. Individual singers have imparted something of their own visions and dreams to the ballad. The substance of most versions, however, is the tale of the hammer man and spike driver who wielded a nine- (or twelve-, or twenty-) pound hammer as no one else ever did before or since. He could drive from both shoulders (that is, from either side), and he had so much stamina that he wore out his shakers (the men who held the drills for him). It is said that he could hammer all day without turning a stroke (striking a drill off-center).

One rendition has it that two crews of workmen competed in the Big Bend contest, one operating the steam drill, the other "shaking" for John Henry; at the end of thirty-five minutes the machine had drilled a hole nine feet deep, but John Henry had drilled two seven-foot holes, winning for himself a prize of one hundred dollars. But he was so exhausted from the contest that he died that night in bed. Other renditions say that he hammered himself to death right on the job: his eyes went dim, his arms grew weak, and he "died with his hammer in his hand." But the epic does not always end there. John Henry had a woman named, variously, Julie Anne, Mary Magdalene, Pearly Anne, Polly Anne, or Lucy Anne, who could handle a hammer as well as a man could. Hearing of John Henry's death, she went up on the mountain and took his place. And John Henry had a baby who said, "My daddy was a steel drivin' man, he died with his hammer in his hand, I want to die like Papa died."

John — Hen - ry said to the Cap - tain ___ that a
man is not ___ but a man. ___ Said be -
fore I let ___ this steam drill ___ beat me down ___ I'll

Notation by John Benson Brooks. The version given here was recorded by the author in Alabama in 1950.

man fell___ dead, says I'm go - in' where my man fell___

dead, says I'm go - in' where my man___ fell___ dead. He done

ham - mered his fool self to death, _____ he done

etc.

ham - mered his fool self to death.

John Henry said to the Captain
That a man is not but a man.
Said before I let the steam drill beat me down
I'll hammer my fool self to death.
I'll hammer my fool self to death.

John Henry had a little woman,
Well the dress she wore it's a-red like blood,
And the shoes she wore, it's a-red,
Well the hat she had on, it's a-red,
That woman's eyes they turned red with blood.
Well she come a'screamin' and a-cryin' that day,
Come a-walkin' down that railroad track.
The Captain supplied to the woman,
Said tell me woman, what's troublin' your mind.
Says I'm goin' where my man fell dead,
Says I'm goin' where my man fell dead,
Says I'm goin' where my man fell dead,
Says I'm goin' where my man fell dead.
He done hammered his fool self to death,
He done hammered his fool self to death.

John Henry had another woman,
Well her name was Pearly Anne.
Well Pearly Anne she heard about this man's death,
Well what you reckon she said?

Said before I stand to see my man go down,
Says give me a ten-pound hammer,
Goin' to hook it onto the right of my arm,
Goin' to bring me a nine-pound hammer,
Goin' to hitch it onto the left of my arm.
Before I stand to see my man go down,
I'll go down 'tween-a them mountains,
And before I stand to see (my) man go down,
I'll hammer just like a man,
I'm goin' to hammer just like a man,
I'm goin' to hammer just like a man,
I'm goin' to hammer just like a man
I'm goin' to whup-a this mountain down,
I'm goin' to whup-a this mountain down.
'E says I'll hammer my fool self to death,
I'll hammer my fool self to death.

John Henry had a little baby boy,
You could tote it in the pa'm o' your hand.
Well every time that baby cried,
He looked in his mother's face.
Well his mother looked down at her baby's face,
Said tell me son what you worryin' about?
The last lovin' words she ever heard the boy said,
Mamma I want to make a railroad man,
Mamma I want to make a railroad man.
I'm goin' to die like Papa died,
I'm goin' to die like Papa died.
Son, Papa was a steel-drivin' man,
Son, Papa was a steel-drivin' man
But he hammered his fool self to death,
But he hammered his fool self to death.

John Henry had another little baby boy,
He was lyin' in the cradle kickin' and cryin',
Every time Mamma rocked the cradle bump-de-bump-a-lump,
I want to make a railroad man,
Say I want to make a railroad man.
Goin' to die like Papa died,
I want to die like Papa died.
Son your Daddy was a steel-drivin' man,
Your Daddy was a steel-drivin' man.
But he hammered his fool self to death,
But he hammered his fool self to death.

When Henry was 'tween them mountains
The Captain saw him goin' down.
He supplied to Henry one day,

Tried to pacify his mind,
Says Henry you knows you's a natural man.
Well what you reckon he said?
Says the steam drill drive one hammer by steam,
Says the steam drill drive one by air.
How in the world you expect to beat steam down?
He says how in the world you expect to beat air down?
Henry supplied to the Captain that day,
Steam is steam, I know air is air,
Before I let the steam drill beat me down,
Say I'll die with these hammers in my hand,
I'm goin' to die with these hammers in my hand.
I'm goin' to hammer my fool self to death,
I'm goin' to hammer my fool self to death.

When Henry was 'tween them mountains,
His wife couldn't hear him cryin'.
When she went out 'tween them mountains,
Tried to git him to lay the irons down.
He supplied to his wife that day,
Said my knee bones begin to grow cold.
Said the grip of my hand's givin' out.
My eyes begin to leak water.
Say before I lay these hammers down,
I'll die with these hammers in my hand,
I'm goin' to die with these hammers in my hand.

Take John Henry to the cemetery,
Lay him in his lonesome grave.
While she walked up there to the foot of the grave,
Cast her eyes in her husband's face,
Come a-screamin' and a-cryin' that day.
Preacher looked around in the woman's face,
Tell me woman what you screamin' about?
Last lovin' words that she supplied to him,
'Taint but the one thing troublin' my mind,
That certainly was a true man to me,
That certainly was a true man to me.
But he hammered his fool self to death,
He hammered his fool self to death.

John Henry's wife was sittin' down one day,
Just about the hour of sun,
Come a-screamin' and cryin'.
Papa said, Daughter what's troublin' your mind?
I got three little children here,
Who goin' to help me carry 'em along?
Who goin' to shoe my children's feet?

Who goin' to glove my children's hand?
Who goin' to shoe my lovin' feet?
Who goin' to glove my lovin' hand?
Papa looked around in his daughter's face,
Tried to pacify his daughter's mind.
Daughter I'll shoe your lovin' feet,
Daughter I'll shoe your children's feet,
Daughter I'll glove your children's hands.
Brother he looked in his sister's face,
Tried to pacify his sister's mind,
Sister I'll kiss your rosy cheeks.
But you can't be my lovin' man,
Brother can't be my lovin' man.
Papa can't be my lovin' man,
Papa can't be my lovin' man.
'Cause you can't file the whole deal down,
Brother can't file the whole deal down,
Papa can't file the whole deal down,
Papa can't file the whole deal down.

John Henry in the Caribbean

A Jamaican call and response work song set down nearly a half century ago makes John Henry a local hero and gives the tragic drama a Jamaican setting, but the power of the mainland ballad comes through undiminished:

Ten poun' hammer kill John Henry,
  Somebody dying ebery day.
Tek de hammer and give it to de worker,
  Somebody dying ebery day.
Number nine tunnel, I will not work dere,
  Somebody dying ebery day.
St. Mary Mountain is a fruitful mountain,
  Somebody dying ebery day.
When me go home me will tell me mother,
  Somebody dying ebery day.
Me no born yah here, me come from yondah,
  Somebody dying ebery day.

From Black Roadways, A Study in Jamaica Folk Life, by Martha Beckwith, Chapel Hill, 1929.

The Birth of John Henry

> Many writers with a special interest in Negro
> life in the South have been inspired to use the
> John Henry legend creatively, bringing still
> new dimensions to the subject. One of the
> most successful efforts was by Roark Brad-
> ford, a Southern writer of distinction. The fol-
> lowing prose narration comes from his book,
> *John Henry.* It is the first chapter of the book,
> depicting John Henry's birth, his notable qua-
> lities, and the recognition given to the event
> by the elements. Mr. Bradford was an observ-
> ant student of black oral literature, and it is
> not easy to know what he, as a creator, may
> have contributed to the legend, and what may
> have come to him directly from the oral tradi-
> tion.

Now John Henry was a man, but he's long dead.

The night John Henry was born the moon was copper-colored and
the sky was black. The stars wouldn't shine and the rain fell hard.
Forked lightning cleaved the air and the earth trembled like a leaf. The
panthers squalled in the brake like a baby and the Mississippi River
ran upstream a thousand miles. John Henry weighed forty-four
pounds.

John Henry was born on the banks of the Black River, where all good
rousterbouts come from. He came into the world with a cotton hook for
a right hand and a river song on his tongue:

"Looked up and down de river,
  Twice as far as I could see.
Seed befo' I gits to be twenty-one,
  De Anchor Line gonter b'long to me, Lawd, Lawd,
  Anchor Line gonter b'long to me."

They didn't know what to make of John Henry when he was born.
They looked at him and then went and looked at the river.

"He got a bass voice like a preacher," his mamma said.

"He got shoulders like a cotton-rollin' rousterbout," his papa said.

"He got blue gums like a conjure man," the nurse woman said.

"I might preach some," said John Henry, "but I ain't gonter be no
preacher. I might roll cotton on de boats, but I ain't gonter be no cotton-rollin' rousterbout. I might got blue gums like a conjure man, but I
ain't gonter git familiar wid de sperits. 'Cause my name is John Henry,

---

From John Henry, *by Roark Bradford, New York and London, Harpers, 1931.*

and when fo'ks call me by my name, dey'll know I'm a natchal man."

"His name is John Henry," said his mamma. "Hit's a fack."

"And when you calls him by his name," said his papa, "he's a natchal man."

So about that time John Henry raised up and stretched. "Well," he said, "ain't hit about supper-time?"

"Sho hit's about supper-time," said his mamma.

"And after," said his papa.

"And long after," said the nurse woman.

"Well," said John Henry, "did de dogs had they supper?"

"They did," said his mamma.

"All de dogs," said his papa.

"Long since," said the nurse woman.

"Well, den," said John Henry, "Ain't I as good as de dogs?"

And when John Henry said that he got mad. He reared back in his bed and broke out the slats. He opened his mouth and yowled, and it put out the lamp. He cleaved his tongue and spat, and it put out the fire. "Don't make me mad!" said John Henry, and the thunder rumbled and rolled. "Don't let me git mad on de day I'm bawn, 'cause I'm skeered of my ownse'f when I gits mad."

And John Henry stood up in the middle of the floor and he told them what he wanted to eat. "Bring me four ham bones and a pot full of cabbages," he said. "Bring me a bait of turnip greens tree-top tall, and season hit down wid a side er middlin'. Bring me a pone er cold cawn bread and some hot potlicker to wash hit down. Bring me two hog jowls and a kittleful er whippowill peas. Bring me a skilletful er red-hot biscuits and a big jugful er cane molasses. 'Cause my name is John Henry, and I'll see you soon."

So John Henry walked out of the house and away from the Black River country where all good rousterbouts are born.

SOME TRADITIONAL BLACK BALLADS

As the term is used in regard to traditional songs in the black repertoire, "ballad" generally signifies a piece commemorating a noteworthy event, and usually it has a central figure who may or may not be a hero. In its more extended variants, "John Henry" is the ballad at its best. Numerous among the ballads are stories of bad men and killers.

While "Stagolee" (or "Stacker Lee") features a mean personality on whom little sympathy is wasted, some ballads are ambivalent in their sentiments, and others tend to excuse the criminal and the crime because of the circumstances. The ballad "Poor Lazarus" begins by identifying its hero as a bad man, but it is quickly turned around and he becomes the mourned victim when he himself is killed. In "The Ballad of Louis Collins," Louis is the victim of a shootout and becomes an object of sympathy, though nothing is said of the details leading to the fatal quarrel. A number of songs relate an event without particular reference to personalities, except perhaps in a peripheral way. Ballads may be short or long, though they are usually characterized by a regular stanza form and rhyming elements. To achieve the form and the rhyme, some of the songs resort to doggerel versifying, standard borrowable phrases, or well-worn clichés, but many of them have distinction and originality. Blues, work songs, and ballads may borrow themes and phrases from one another. Some work songs, except for the manner of singing, could well be classified as ballads. Usually the ballad per se is a single-voiced entertainment song with guitar or other instrumental accompaniment.

The Ballad of Louis Collins

Mrs. Collins weep, Mrs. Collins moan,
To see her son Louis leave his home.
Angels laid him away,
Angels laid him away,
They laid him six feet under the clay,
Angels laid him away.

Bob shot once and Louis shot two,
Shot poor Collins, shot him through and through.
Angels laid him away,
Angels laid him away,
They laid him six feet under the clay,
Angels laid him away.

Kind friends, oh wasn't it hard
To see poor Louis in a new graveyard?
Angels laid him away,
Angels laid him away,
They laid him under six feet of clay,
Angels laid him away.

Oh, when they heard that Louis was dead,
All the people they dressed in red.

As sung by John Hurt.

Angels laid him away,
Angels laid him away,
They laid him six feet under the clay,
Angels laid him away.

Frankie and Albert
(also known as Frankie and Johnnie)

The theme of "Frankie and Albert" has many precedents in English, Scottish, and other European balladry—the revenge of a scorned woman. But the setting for this drama is not a castle, and its characters are not nobility. It is a barrelhouse, or saloon, and the characters are a sporting man, a jealous woman, and a varied supporting cast from the wrong side of the railroad tracks. There are many versions of the ballad, and few singers have versions in common. Every rendition is an open invitation to improvise. The simple, regular stanzas, with second and fourth lines rhyming, and standard fifth refrain line, are easy to compose, and dead of spirit indeed is the singer who has done the song twice exactly the same way.

Some accounts say Frankie's revenge was carried out with a knife, others with a gun, the exact caliber of which is determined by the rhyme required—twenty-two, forty, forty-one, forty-four, or forty-five. Some singers prefer to have Albert meet his fate on the barroom floor, others in his room with his latest conquest, Alice Fry (or Bly, or Giles, or another similar sounding name).

Frankie was a good girl,
As everybody knows.
She paid a hundred dollars
For Albert's suit of clothes.
He was her man and he done her wrong.

Frankie went down to the corner saloon,
Wasn't goin' to be there long,
Asked the bartender had he seen her Albert,
'Cause he done been home and gone.
He was her man and he done her wrong.

Well, the bartender he told Frankie,
Can't lie to you if I try,
Old Albert been here an hour ago
And gone home with Alice Fry,
He was her man and he done her wrong.

Text of Frankie and Albert is somewhat of a composite, based on a rendition by John Hurt.

Frankie went down to Albert's house,
Only a couple of blocks away,
Peeped in the keyhole of his door,
Saw Albert lovin' Alice Fry.
He was her man and he done her wrong.

Frankie called out to Albert,
Albert said I don't hear.
If you don't come to the woman you love
Goin' to haul you out of here.
He was her man and he done her wrong.

Frankie she shot old Albert,
And she shot him three or four times.
Said I'll hang around a few minutes
And see if Albert's dyin'.
He was my man and he done me wrong.

An iron-tired wagon
With ribbons all hung in black
Took old Albert to the buryin' ground
And it didn't bring him back.
He was her man and he done her wrong.

Frankie told the sheriff
What goin' to happen to me?
Said looks like from the evidence
Goin' to be murder first degree.
He was your man and he done you wrong.

Judge heard Frankie's story,
Heard Albert's mother testify.
Judge said to Frankie,
You goin' to be justified.
He was your man and he done you wrong.

Dark was the night.
Cold was the ground,
The last words I heard Frankie say,
I done laid old Albert down.
He was my man and he done me wrong.

Last time I heard of Frankie
She was settin' in her cell,
Sayin' Albert done me wrong
And for that I sent him to hell.
He was my man and he done me wrong.

I aint goin' to tell no stories,
I aint goin' to tell no lies.
The woman who stole Frankie's Albert
Was the girl they call Alice Fry.
He was her man and he done her wrong.

Casey Jones

The ballad of Casey Jones, the railroad engineer who raced his locomotive against lost time and died in a wreck in the year 1900, is probably the most widely known song about American railroad disasters.
The original Casey Jones ballad (to the extent that it was original) is
generally attributed to Wallace Saunders, the Negro engine wiper who
took care of Jones' locomotive. Popularized versions of the song were
widespread in the first decade or so of the century and influenced the
development of still other versions. The song "composed" by Saunders was probably compounded, in part, out of a number of railroad
disaster songs already current among railroad men, both white and Negro.

While the hero of the song, Casey (John Luther) Jones, was white,
the best known variants bear the brand of Negro songmakers. There is
a curious mixture of Negro idiom and imagery with non-Negro
phrases, and sometimes there are interpolations of blueslike stanzas
which have no readily apparent relevance to the central theme. Such
additions helped the singers to gain time to think of new stanzas, as
well as to spin out the yarn to a length befitting an epic subject. Sometimes the inventions of the singers considerably distorted the character
of the hero and his family. There is considerable doggerel in most versions, rhyme being required. The following rendition of the ballad has
the feel of Negro style and invention. Stanzas such as the one referring
to Alice Spratt and the one mentioning the pension appear to be products of fertile imaginations and seem to have caused Mr. Jones' family
considerable discomfiture.

I woke up this mornin' four o'clock,
Mr. Casey told the fireman get his boiler hot.
Put on your water, put on your coal,
Put your head out the window, see my drivers roll, see my drivers
    roll,
Put your head out the window, see my drivers roll.

Lord, some people said Mr. Casey couldn't run,
Let me tell you what Mr. Casey done.

Introduction to and text of Casey Jones are from Negro Folk Music, U.S.A., *by
Harold Courlander,* © 1963 by Columbia University Press.

He left Memphis, was quarter to nine,
Got in Newport News it was dinner time, was dinner time,
Got in Newport News it was dinner time.

Lord, people said old Casey he was runnin' overtime,
And I'm nothin' losin' with the 109.
Casey said it ain't in line,
I run into glory 'less I make my time.
Said all the passengers better keep themselves hid,
I'm not goin' to shake it like Chaney did, like Chaney did,
I'm not goin' to shake it like Chaney did.

Mr. Casey ran his engine in a mile of the place,
Number Four stabbed him in the face.
The sheriff told Casey, well you must leave town.
For freedom of my soul I'm Alabama bound, Alabama bound,
For freedom of my soul I'm Alabama bound.

Mrs. Casey said she dreamt a dream,
In the night she bought a sewin' machine.
The needle got broke, she could not sew.
She loved Mr. Casey 'cause he told me so, told me so,
She loved Mr. Casey 'cause he told me so.

There was a woman named Miss Alice Spratt,
Said I want to ride with Casey 'fore I die,
I aint good lookin' but I take my time,
I'm a ramblin' woman with a ramblin' mind, got a ramblin' mind.
I'm a ramblin' woman with a ramblin' mind.

Casey looked at his water, water was low,
Look at his watch, his watch was slow.
On the road again,
Natural born leaf, goin' to roll again.

Lord, people tell 'bout the thought of home,
The manager fired Mr. Casey Jones, Mr. Casey Jones.
Mr. Casey said before he died, one more road that he want to ride.
People tell Casey which road is he?
The Southern Pacific and the Sancta Fee, Sancta Fee.

This morning I heard someone were dyin',
Mrs. Casey's children on the doorstep cryin',
Mamma, Mamma, I can't keep from cryin',
Papa got killed on a certain line, on a certain line,
Papa got killed on a certain line.

Mamma, Mamma, how can it be,
Killed my father in the first degree.
Children, children, won't you hold your breath,
Draw another pension from your father's death, from your father's
     death.
On the road again,
I'm a natural born leaf and on the road again.

Tuesday morning it look like rain,
Around the curve came a passenger train.
Under the pile laid Casey Jones,
Good old engineer, for he's dead and gone, dead and gone.
On the road again,
I'm a natural born leaf on the road again.

Betty and Dupree

Dupree was settin' in a hotel,
Wasn't thinkin' 'bout a dog-gone thing,
Settin' in a hotel,
Wasn't thinkin' 'bout a dog-gone thing.
Betty said to Dupree,
I want a diamond ring.

Dupree went to town
With a forty-five in his hand.
He went to town with
A forty-five in his hand.
He went after jewelry—
But he got the jewelry man.

Dupree went to Betty cryin',
Betty, here is your diamond ring.
He went to Betty cryin',
Here is your diamond ring.
Take it and wear it, Betty,
'Cause I'm bound for cold old cold Sing Sing.

Then he called a taxi
Cryin', drive me to Tennessee.
Taxi, taxi, taxi,
Drive me to Tennessee.
He said, drive me, bubber,
'Cause the dicks is after me.

From The Book of Negro Folklore, by Langston Hughes and Arna Bontemps,
New York, Dodd, Mead and Co., 1958.

He went to the post office
To get his evenin' mail.
Went to the general delivery
To get his evenin' mail.
They caught poor Dupree, Lordy,
Put him in Nashville Jail.

Dupree said to the judge, Lord,
I ain't been here before.
Lord, Lord, Lord, Judge,
I ain't been here before.
Judge said, I'm gonna break your neck, Dupree,
So you can't come here no more.

Betty weeped, Betty moaned
Till she broke out with sweat.
Betty weeped and she moaned
Till she broke out with sweat.
Said she moaned and she weeped
Till her clothes got soppin' wet.

Betty brought him coffee,
Betty brought him tea.
Betty brought him coffee,
Also brought him tea.
She brought him all he needed
'Cept that big old jail-house key.

Dupree said, it's whiskey I crave,
Bring me flowers to my grave.
It's whiskey I crave.
Bring flowers to my grave.
That little ole Betty's
Done made me her dog-gone slave.

It was early one mornin'
Jus about the break o' day,
Early, early one mornin'
Just about break o' day,
They had him testifyin'
And this is what folks heard him say:

Give my pappy my clothes,
Oh, give poor Betty my shoes.
Give pappy my clothes,
Give poor Betty my shoes.
And if anybody asks you,
Tell 'em I died with the heart-breakin' blues.

They lead him to the scaffold
With a black cap over his face.
Lead him up to the scaffold,
Black cap over his face.
Some ole lonesome graveyard's
Poor Dupree's restin' place.

The choir followed him
Singin' *Nearer My God to Thee.*
The choir followed him,
Nearer My God to Thee.
Poor Betty, she was cryin',
Have mercy on Dupree!

Sail on! Sail on!
Sail on, Dupree, sail on!
Sail on! Sail on!
Sail on, sail on, sail on!
I don't mind you sailin'
But you'll be gone so dog-gone long!

Poor Lazarus

A ballad about a man who broke into the commissary of a work camp
and robbed it, after which he escaped into the hills. The sheriff and his
posse pursued Lazarus and killed him. A good portion of the song elab-
orates the events following the encounter. This version of "Poor Lazarus," of which there are many, is a work song variant.

Oh, bad man Lazarus,
Oh, bad man Lazarus,
He broke in the commissary,
Lord, he broke in the commissary.

He been paid off,
He been paid off,
Lord, Lord, Lord,
He been paid off.

Commissary man,
Commissary man,
He jump out the commissary window,
Lord, he jump out the commissary window.

From Negro Workaday Songs, *by Howard Odum and Guy B. Johnson, Chapel
Hill, University of North Carolina Press, 1926.*

Commissary man swore out,
Lord, commissary man swore out,
Lord, commissary man swore out
Warrant for Lazarus.

Oh, bring him back,
Lord, bring him back,
Oh, Lord, Lord, Lord,
Bring Lazarus back.

They begin to wonder,
Lord, they begin to wonder,
Lord, they begin to wonder
Where Lazarus gone.

Where in the world,
Lord, where in the word,
Lord, where in the world
Will they find him?

Well, I don't know,
I don't know,
Well, Lord, Lord,
Well, I don't know.

Well, the sheriff spied poor Lazarus,
Well, the sheriff spied poor Lazarus,
Lord, sheriff spied poor Lazarus
Way between Bald Mountain.

They blowed him down,
Well, they blowed him down,
Well, Lord, Lord,
They blowed him down.

They shot poor Lazarus,
Lord, they shot poor Lazarus,
Lord, they shot poor Lazarus
With a great big number.

Well, a forty-five,
Lord, great big forty-five,
Lord, forty-five,
Turn him round.

They brought poor Lazarus,
And they brought poor Lazarus,
Lord, they brought poor Lazarus
Back to the shanty.

Old friend Lazarus say,
Lord, old Lazarus say,
Lord, old Lazarus say,
Give me a cool drink of water.

Before I die,
Good Lord, 'fore I die,
Give me a cool drink of water,
Lord, 'fore I die.

Lazarus' mother say,
Lord, Lazarus' mother say,
Nobody know the trouble
I had with him.

Since daddy died,
Lord, since daddy been dead,
Nobody know the trouble I had
Since daddy been dead.

They goin' to bury poor Lazarus,
Lord, they goin' to bury old Lazarus,
They goin' to bury poor Lazarus
In the mine.

Me and my buddy,
Lord, me and my buddy,
We goin' over to bury him
Half past nine.

Lazarus' mother say,
Look over yonder,
How they treatin' poor Lazarus,
Lord, Lord, Lord.

They puttin' him away,
Lord, they puttin' him away,
Lord, they puttin' Lazarus away
Half past nine.

The Sinking of the Titanic

The sinking of the *Titanic* in the year 1912, a catastrophe that received worldwide attention, produced numerous Negro ballads dealing with different aspects of the tragedy. Interest on the part of blacks was no doubt stirred by the fact that Jack Johnson, a black, and heavyweight boxing champion of the world, was denied passage on the *Titanic* because of his race. Allusion to the Johnson affair appears in some of the songs about the sinking, though others focus on the respective fates of the rich and the poor who shared the voyage. Many *Titanic* songs emerged in gospel singing and blues. Regardless of genre, virtually all of these songs and variants contained moral judgments, explicit or implied.

GOD MOVES ON THE WATER

Chorus (before each stanza)
God moves on the water,
God moves on the water,
God moves on the water,
And the people had to run and pray.

In the year of nineteen and twelve,
On April the thirteenth day,
When the great *Titanic* was sinkin' down,
Well the people had to run and pray.

When the lifeboat got to the landing,
The womens turned around
Cryin', look way cross that ocean, Lordy,
At my husband drown.

Captain Smith was a-lyin' down,
Was asleep for he was tired.
Well he woke up in a great fright,
As many gunshots were fired.

Well that Jacob Nash was a millionaire,
Lord, he had plenty money to spare.
When the great *Titanic* was sinkin' down,
Well, he could not pay his fare.

WASN'T IT SAD WHEN THAT GREAT SHIP WENT DOWN

On a Monday morning
Just about nine o'clock
The *Titanic*

Titanic *song texts are from* Negro Folk Music, U.S.A., *by Harold Courlander.* © 1963 *by Columbia University Press. By permission of the publishers.* "Fare Thee Well, Titanic" *was recorded by Frederic Ramsey, Jr.*

Began to reel and rock.
People a-kickin' and cryin'
Guess I'm goin' to die.

> *Chorus (after each stanza)*
> Wasn't that sad when that great ship went down,
> Sad when that great ship went down,
> Sad when that great ship went down.
> Husband and wife, children lost their life,
> Wasn't that sad when that great ship went down.

When that ship left England
Makin' for that shore
The rich paid their fares,
Would not ride with the poor.
Couldn't get boats a-lowered,
Fightin' at the door.

People on that ship
Long way from home,
There's prayin' all around me,
They know they got to go,
Death came a-ridin' by,
They know they got to die.

FARE THEE WELL, TITANIC

It was midnight on the sea,
The band was playing "Nearer My God to Thee,"
Fare thee, *Titanic*, fare thee well.

Titanic when it got here slowed,
Captain he hollered all aboard,
Fare thee, *Titanic*, fare thee well.

Titanic was comin' round the curve
When it run into that great big iceberg,
Fare thee, *Titanic*, fare thee well.

When the *Titanic* was sinkin' down,
They had them life boats all around,
Fare thee, *Titanic*, fare thee well.

They had them life boats all around,
Savin' the women and children and lettin' the men go down,
Fare thee, *Titanic*, fare thee well.

Jack Johnson wanted to get on board,
Captain he said I ain't haulin' no coal,
Fare thee, *Titanic*, fare thee well.

When he heard about that mighty shock,
Might o' seen a man doin' the Eagle Rock,
Fare thee, *Titanic*, fare thee well.

WORKSONGS: ROAD GANGS AND PRISON CAMPS

The old prison systems of the southern states and the still older traditions of gang singing combined to produce a special genre of work songs. The prisoners were segregated by race in the various so-called state farms and county farms, but little distinction was made between those convicted for large or small crimes. The farms were a labor repository. Sometimes the inmates were rented out to contractors, sometimes put to work on public projects such as road building, forest clearing, and land grading. The life was hard, confined, and unrelenting. For short-termers there was the hope of eventual release. For long-termers and lifers there was the dream of escape.

The work songs of the black prisoners sometimes had the characteristics of blues, sometimes of ballads, sometimes of spirituals. They were compounded out of bitterness, humor, hopelessness and the desire to survive. The foremost heroes and protagonists of the work songs were not barroom bad men, but prisoners who escaped from the state farms or the road gangs, men who took the ultimate risk. Some of them were successful, others were killed by their pursuers. Beside chronicling heroic events, the songs told of women, good lives gone wrong, complaints, camp bosses, preachers, and Christian salvation. Here and there a biblical scene was evoked as a parable or as a social comment. Out of their immediate experience, Negro prisoners created a rich and often poignant oral literature.

Don't You Hear My Hammer Ringing

This song begins with a kind of dedication to the captain, the steerer, and the sergeant who are in charge of the work gang. It is reminiscent

---

Song texts are from the record album, Negro Prison Camp Work Songs, *recorded by Toshi and Peter Seeger, John Lomax, Jr., Chester Bower and Fred Hellerman, New York, Ethnic Folkways Library, 1956. By permission of Folkways Records.*

in this respect of many West African songs that take note of important personages who may be listening. (Once the song is thus dedicated, any irony or criticism that may appear in the song later presumably will not cause hard feelings.) Following the introduction comes a section describing the prisoners' work, and the scene then shifts to the building of the Ark by Noah. Finally the subject reverts once more to the prisoners ringing in the bottom.

> I says I'm ringing in the bottom, (x2)
> I says I'm ringing for the captain,
> I says I'm ringing for the sergeant,
> I says I'm ringing for the steerer, (x2)
> I believe we ring for everybody. (x2)
> I'm going to tell you 'bout my hammer, (x2)
> Well, 'bout a-killing me, hammer, (x2)
> I says the captain's gone to Houston, (x2)
> He's coming back by Ramsey, [Ramsey State Farm],
> He's coming back by the Ramsey.
> He's gonna bring my partner, (x2)
> He's gonna give us both a hammer,
> And we're gonna live in the bottom.
> We're gonna walk to the live oak,
> Don't turn and walk away, sir,
> We're gonna walk to the gopherwood. (x2)
> Now, these words he did say, sir,
> He says ring old hammer. (x2)
> I says God told Norah
> About a rainbow sign,
> Well, there'll be no more water,
> Oh, there'll be no more water
> I b'lieve 'fore your next time, sir,
> Oh before next time, sir.
> Says he destroy this world, sir,
> Say he destroy this world, sir.
> Well, Norah, Norah,
> Oh don't you remember what I told you
> About a rainbow sign, sir.
> I'm gonna run and get some water
> Oh before your next time, sir.
> Well, old Norah got his hammer,
> Well, went marching to the bottom,
> And you can hear Norah's hammer,
> Well, you can hear Norah's hammer,
> Well, you can hear many ringing,
> Well, all over the land, sir.
> He's in the country too, sir.

And then the weaker generation,
Well, he asked old Norah,
Yes he asked old Norah,
Well, what in the world you gonna do, sir.
He's gonna build this-a ark-a.
Oh, tell me where you gonna build it.
Oh, just a mile from the river,
I'm gonna build this old building
So it'll float on the water
And on land, and, too, sir,
That's what I'm gonna do, sir.
Says you can hear Norah hollering,
Won't you ring, old hammer,
Now won't you ring, old hammer,
Why won't you ring in the timber,
Why don't you ring like you used to,
You used to ring like a bell, sir.
There ain't nobody's hammer (x2)
Nobody's hammer in the bottom
That ring like-a mine, sir.
I say that's all about the hammer,
'Bout a-killing me, hammer.
We're gonna ring this hammer,
I'm gonna ring it in the bottom.
I said, God got the key
And you can't come in, sir.
Why don't you ring old hammer,
Why don't you ring till your number,
Why don't you ring old hammer,
Old hammer won't you ring.

Lost John

One of the classic prison camp work songs, "Lost John," tells of an escaped prisoner who outwitted his pursuers by placing an extra heel on the front of each shoe. When his footprints were discovered, it was impossible to tell the direction of his flight. (As sung by a work gang, each line delivered by the singing leader was repeated by the chorus.)

One day, one day
I were walking along
And I heard a little voice
Didn't see no one.
It was old Lost John,
He said he was long gone
Like a turkey through the corn
With his long clothes on.

Had a heel in front
And a heel behind,
Well you couldn't hardly tell
Well you couldn't hardly tell
Whichaway he was goin'
Whichaway he was goin'.
One day, one day,
Well I heard him say
Be on my way
Be on my way
'Fore the break of day
By the break of day,
Got a heel in front,
Got a heel behind,
Well you can't hardly tell
Well you can't hardly tell
Whichaway I'm goin.'

At this point the song turns to commentary on the conditions which had driven Lost John to escape:

Oughta come on the river
Long time ago,
You could find a dead man
Right on your row.
Well the dog man killed him
Well the dog man killed him
'Cause the boy couldn't go
'Cause the boy couldn't go.
Wake up dead man,
Help me carry my row,
'Cause the row's so heavy
Can't hardly make it
To the lower turn row
To the lower turn row.
Oughta come on the river
Nineteen and ten,
Well the women was rolling
Just like the men.

Following another rendition of the escape story, there is more comment on prison camp life:

Oughta come on the river
Long time ago,
I don't know partner,
Say, you oughta know,

> You'd catch plenty trouble
> Everywhere you go
> Everywhere you go.
> One day, one day,
> Heard the captain say
> If you boys work,
> Gonna treat you mighty well,
> If you don't go to work,
> Says we may give you hell.

And at last a small note of hope:

> One day, one day,
> I'll be on my way
> And you may not never
> Ever hear me say
> One day, one day,
> I'll be on my way.

Here Rattler Here

The hero of the song "Here Rattler Here" is usually a man named Riley. The story recounts how he receives a letter telling him that his woman has died, and Riley tells his friends he is going to escape from the prison camp. Should the captain ask if he was running, they could say he was flying; should the captain ask if he was laughing, they could tell him Riley was crying. Riley takes off with the posse and the dog Rattler on his heels, but they never catch up with him and finally give up the chase. First comes a description of Old Rattler. Each line is followed by the choral response, "Here Rattler Here."

> Why don't you here, Rattler, here,
> Oh, don't you here, Rattler, here.
> This Old Rattler was a walker dog,
> Says he'll trail you 'cross a live oak log.
> Says Old Rattler hit the man's trail,
> Says he run and bit him on the heel,
> And you oughta heard that man squeal.
> You holler, here, here, Rattler,
> Hollerin' here, here, Rattler.
> Says Old Rattler was a walking dog,
> He could trail you 'cross a live oak log.

The story proper begins then with the discovery of Riley's disappearance:

> Says the captain come a-riding,

Asking where is that sergeant,
Says I believe there's a man gone.
Says the sergeant come riding,
Popping his whip upon the ground,
And Old Rattler turning round and round.
He said here Old Rattler,
Says Old Rattler, here's a marrow bone,
You can eat it, you can leave it alone.
I don't want no marrow bone,
I just want the man that's long gone.
Says Old Rattler went skipping through the morning dew,
And Old Rattler went to skipping through the morning dew,
And the sergeant pop the whip upon the ground,
And Old Rattler begin to turn round and round.
He cried, here Old Rattler,
Crying, here Old Rattler.

At this point there is a flashback to the scene in which Riley announces his departure:

Says Old Riley got worried,
He come running with a letter,
Says you ought to heard what that letter read.
Says Old Riley says that Irene's dead,
Say come home, pretty papa,
Yes, come home, pretty papa.
Says Old Riley he got worried,
Says to the captain that you was a-running,
You just tell him I was flying.
If he asks you was I laughing,
You can tell him I was crying.

Then follows the chase, but Riley has crossed the Brazos River and disappeared:

And it's here, Old Rattler,
And it's here, Old Rattler,
And Old Rattler got to the Brazos,
Well he left him there a-howling.
Old Rattler hollered, oooh, oooh, oooh, oooh!
He hollered, ooh, ooh, ooh, ooh!
And I heard the sergeant blowing his horn,
Oughta heard that sergeant blowing his horn,
Blowed it doo, doo, doo, doo!
Blowed it oo, oo, oo, oo!
Says I believe he crossed the river,
Believe he crossed the big Brazos.

He gonna give up Old Riley,
Take another day back on the way.
I'm going to call Old Rattler,
Hollering here, Rattler, here,
Won't you here, Rattler, here, here,
Won't you here, Old Rattler.

Grizzly Bear

This stirring prison camp work song heard in Texas, about an enig-
matic "grizzly bear," appears to be a tangent statement about events
that are not clearly spelled out. One informant in another area of the
South, who had served time in a Mississippi prison, declared the song
to be about a convict who escaped from a work gang and lived in the
woods, from where he made forages for food and other necessities.
Wild in appearance, he was nicknamed Grizzly (pronounced Grizzaly)
Bear, otherwise known as Jack of Diamonds (a term of anonymity), so
that his real name does not appear in the song. Nevertheless, some people expressed the opinion that the grizzly bear was really just a bear—a
view that doesn't seem to withstand the internal evidence of the song
text.

Each of the lines given here, sung by the leader, is repeated with minor variations by the group, which also comes in on the last two words
of the leader's lines.

Oh that grizzaly, grizzaly, grizzaly bear,
Tell me who was that grizzaly, grizzaly bear.
Oh Jack o' Diamonds was that grizzaly, grizzaly bear.
He had great long tushes like a grizzaly bear,
He made a track in the bottom like a grizzaly bear.
Well that grizzaly, grizzaly, grizzaly bear,
Tell me who was the grizzaly, grizzaly bear.
Jack o' Diamonds was the grizzaly, grizzaly bear.
He made a noise in the bottom like a grizzaly bear,
Well my mamma was scared of that grizzaly bear,
Well my papa went a-hunting for the grizzaly bear,
Well my brother wasn't scared of that grizzaly bear.
Oh the grizzaly, grizzaly, grizzaly bear,
Well I'm gonna kill that grizzaly bear.
Well the grizzaly, grizzaly, grizzaly bear,
Well I looked in Louisiana for the grizzaly bear.
Etc.

Captain Holler Hurry

The Cap - tain hol - ler hur - ry, _____ goin' to take my time. _____ Say the Cap - tain hol - ler hur - ry, _____ goin' to take my time. _____ Say he mak - in' mon - ey _____ and I'm tryin' to make time. _____ Say he can lose his job _____ but I can't lose mine. _____ I ain't got long to tar - ry, _____ just stop by here. _____ I ain't got long to tar - ry, _____ just stop by here. _____ Boys if ___ you got ___ long _____ you bet - ter move a - long. _____

From Negro Folk Music, U. S. A., *by Harold Courlander, New York, Columbia University Press, 1963. Notation by John Benson Brooks.*

SOME MISCELLANEOUS OLD BELIEFS

"Sometimes you hear a person say this ain't nothing but superstition. Once Mr. Russel told that to Tom Ibo. He said, 'Tom, you only got a superstition that the fence posts will come up if they're set out in the full of the moon.' Tom Ibo said to Mr. Russel, 'Yes, sir, I got a superstition that it's so and you got a superstition that it ain't so.' "
—Richard Creeks

There are a number of things that oughtn't to be done in the part of the month when the moon is full. If potatoes are planted in the full moon, they'll grow mostly to vines. If a roof is shingled in the full of the moon, the shingles are apt to curl up. If cement is laid in the full of the moon it won't set hard and is apt to crack. An ax sharpened in the full moon phase won't hold its edge, and it's the same way with a saw. Unless oak timbers are cut in the dark phase of the moon they may get soft and rot. If a cow is bred during the full moon its calf may be weakly, and the cow will be a poor milker.

It's a bad luck sign if someone steps over you when you are lying down (or if someone's shadow falls on you while you are lying down); if your face is brushed by a spider web; if a hen crows like a rooster; if you put your clothes on inside out; if you cross in front of a funeral procession; if you see a corpse in a mirror; if you sweep dirt out of a house or throw wash water at night and fail to say, "Excuse me, brother (or sister or friend)"; to start on a journey and have to turn back; to leave a chair rocking when you get up.

A white chicken in the yard keeps evil spirits away. A frizzled chicken will dig up lost objects, or a grigris planted there by one's enemies. If a rooster stands on the doorstep or porch and crows, it is a death omen.

It's a sign of impending death if a person kills a buzzard, counts mourners at a funeral, keeps a crutch of someone who has died, spends coins that have been on the eyes of a corpse, or crosses the road in the path of a funeral procession; if a dog howls in the dark of night, if a buzzard sits on a chimney, if a bluejay flies into someone's house, if a horse neighs outside a house where a wake is being held, or if a wasps' nest falls from one's house.

To cure a cow that has lost her cud, give her a greasy dishrag to chew on. To cure a cow that has an infection from scraping on barbed wire, apply a poultice of green cow manure to the wound.

To make a wart disappear, apply the milk of a milkweed; or, rub the wart with the bone of a dead horse, and throw the bone over your left shoulder. To counteract a snakebite, take a black chicken, split it down the middle and apply it over the bite.

A MISSISSIPPI SHARECROPPER, 1954

For the best part of the century that followed the Civil War, the black southern sharecropper was the symbol of the Negro's depressed status in the larger white world. The sharecropper paid his rent to the white landowner in crops and often went deeply into debt for food, seed, supplies, and farm tools. In many instances he made his purchases from what in effect was a company store, running up accounts that left him virtually penniless at the end of the year. On one hand threatened by eviction, on the other tied to his piece of land by necessity and debt, the sharecropper's condition epitomized the worst in the social and economic relationships between blacks and whites. All sharecroppers were not black, of course, and many white "croppers" found themselves much in the same predicament as Negro farmers.

But while sharecropping was considered to represent the hardest kind of rural life, the sharecropper's lot varied considerably from place to place and time to time. Some share-

From tapes in the collection of Moses Asch, by permission.

croppers, contingent on a variety of circumstances, fared as well as or better than some farmers who owned their own land. One such person was a Mississippi share-cropper named Charles Williams, who, seemingly, supported in handsome style a wife and twenty-four children. The passages that follow are excerpted from a taped conversation with Charles Williams in 1954.

I like this northern part of Mississippi. I'm a southern Mississippi raised fella, but I like the northern part of the state better. It's the yield of the land, you see, so much better than southern Mississippi. Oh, it's all right down there, but the land don't yield. I get one to two and a half bales an acre on this place. I'll get a hundred bales this year. You see, naturally, the government cut us and the dry weather cut us. I been cut two times. This year, 1954, I been cut twice, but I'll get over a hundred bales. I done got a hundred bales. There's been times when I didn't use no machine, and I'd say I picked ninety bales of cotton with my hands. Of course we got cotton pickin' machines in this country, the boss got it, in case we need it. You see, if this certain fella think he might pick his cotton with his hands, it's all right with the boss. But if there's to come on a rain in the late fall, it might last one day and it might last a week or two weeks. Late in the fall, that is. The boss man might come out there and talk with you, say do you think, now, you might get your cotton with your hands? He say, "Now I got a cotton pickin' machine, you don't have to strain about it and be worried about your cotton." They talk about it like this, and the boss say, "Why don't we just take the cotton machine and pick five bales real quick." And if that cotton hadn't been picked over, that machine would get five bales in less than five hours.

We boys got walkin' cultivators, we got two or three tractors that we use, they burn gas and oil. This mule we use with the walkin' cultivators, we might get in the middle of the cotton and we put maybe an eight- or ten-inch or maybe a twelve-inch point on the plow, and we set it as deep as the mules can pull it. As soon as we get over it we put our scratchers on it. We might take the walkin' cultivator and go over it again, then we carry [take] our mules to the barn. They're good mules all right, but I believe in the long run we're goin' to have to get more mules. I'm wearin' 'em out ginnin' cotton. Course mules can give you trouble. One day I went out in the field ridin', and I was settin' all cross-legged on that ol' mule. He was a young and fat-lookin' mule, and I jumped on him sideways and went on down that hill, and all at once when I knowed anything I was comin' down out of the air. Well, I had a son, a little bit of a boy, and when he saw me he come back and wanted to know what was the noise. I'd say I was fifteen feet in the air comin' down, and when I hit the ground that boy came runnin' back askin' me what was the matter. I told him I didn't know any trouble.

He said I had some mule trouble. I told him I don't know. That mule was a quarter of a mile from me, standin' up. Well, we didn't fool with the mules no more till the last of the crop. We used tractors. We use mules sometimes for plantin' cotton, for puttin' out fertilizer. We fertilize our cotton accordin' to the land. If we see an acre or two of this land that look like it need more fertilizer than this particular acre, we open up our distributing machine and do maybe two or three acres like that. When we get to the better land we begin cuttin' it off.

This fella I'm with [the landowner], I might say the company I'm with, we are gettin' along mighty good. There's ten crops I made here. He got some little children, and I have told him that if anything *should* happen that *could* happen, and he wouldn't be here, I'm goin' to look after his little children. He's got daughters, I think one ought to be about sixteen now, one ought to be around twelve, one maybe about ten. And I told him, now, I have been with him ten years, and *I* ain't goin' to get rid of *him*. I don't know what he gonna do to *me*. His name is Mr. M. P. Moore, I call him Mr. Hot Moore. That ain't his real name but around here they call him that. I wouldn't know just why they call him that. You see he's a kind of a northern Mississippi raised gentleman, and I'm a southern Mississippi raised fella. Well, me and him gettin' along just fine. We have conversations in the house here, me and him, we talk and we get along like brothers. You could tell we wasn't brothers only by the color. Me and him go out in the field after we leave the house here, talkin' about what he might want to do or what I might want to do. Whatever I think I might want to do to the land, why, it's perfectly all right with him. We decide on what this land might do and that land might do, or what kind of plowin' we goin' to do to this or what kind of machine we might put in that, or whether we ought to put on a cotton pickin' machine or ought to pick by hand, or what we ought to yield per hundred for handpicked cotton or for cotton picker cotton, how much fertilizer to use, and all that. We get together with it. Quite natural, we both agree on makin' this land yield as much as possible. I guess we get the best yield around here. I'd say we make a bale to two and a half bales an acre.

Natural, this is a big family we got here. Besides me and their mother we got twenty-four children in all, startin' with the oldest, he's twenty-two, down to the youngest, he's one. And they all consume a powerful lot of food and supplies. Lord, their mamma start at five in the mornin' cookin' breakfast, and if she's makin' flapjacks she's got five skillets goin' all at once on the stove. You see, I got a three-quarter-ton Ford truck which I bought new, brand new. It's just as good as new now. And I go into town to shop and get groceries, and when I come out of town that three-quarter truck, why you couldn't drop a dime in it, it wouldn't hit the bottom. Oh, man, you talkin' about those groceries. I couldn't say how many pairs of shoes, how many pairs of, say, blue jeans for the girls and boys. And lard by the fifties, flour by the barrel, hundreds of pounds of sugar, coffee by the fives, rice by the fifties, sardines and salmon by the cases, you see, like that, so forth and so on.

That's just for *this* month, one month, not any other month, just this *particular* month. It might be March or April or May or any month. I'd have a rough guess it would cost me, so far as I could say, in all it would cost me, doctor bills and all, would cost me over four hundred dollars a month all told, absolutely over four hundred dollars.

It don't worry me, I pay it in cash. And I got plenty of daughters and sons, and they want television, and natural I give it to 'em, you know. Try to do what I can. Boys, they want cars and buy 'em, pay cash and tear 'em up and then get 'em another one. The boy'll want a shotgun, the girl will want this, want that—it's expensive all right, a big family like this. But it don't worry me. Any hospital we want anywhere in the United States, we go to it. We have a chance to select our own hospital under the medical plan, quite natural. And I know lots of months it would take four hundred fifty dollars, I'd say at a rough guess, and some months according to how we might get sick and what medicine we might have to have, it might run to five hundred, but I never think about it. All those supplies, now, they don't last long. This is Sunday. If this was tomorrow which would be Monday, I might go to town and get two barrels of flour and come back. Well, all right, say now in one week one of them barrels is crippled. You'd better be lookin' at the other barrel, the one you hadn't turned over. I mean, the head part of the barrel if you had it turned down for safe keepin', you'd better be turnin' it up 'cause you goin' to have to soon open it. And I'd say a whole side of meat, it don't last long. You see, they all got good digestion, eatin' don't hurt 'em. They eat plenty meat, they eat plenty vegetables, I'd say all kinds, and eggs, chicken, and all that. And they're healthy. They eat good and they feel good and they get plenty sleep, they play plenty television shows, they go to plenty picture shows, go to schools and churches, and, oh, they're quite healthy.

And shoes? Oh, man, I could go to town tomorrow and if I wanted to buy some shoes, they'd say, "Well, all right, Charles, how many?" I'd tell 'em maybe five pair, let me look on my book, I'd tell 'em. I'd tell 'em, just give me a minute of time, let me get my book. To be correct, I'd say, it wasn't *five* pair but *six* pair I wanted. I'd say, all right, I got one stick in my pocket. All right, that one stick would buy six pairs of shoes. The first pair would be correct for the length of that stick, but I wouldn't know exactly what number it was. I tell 'em I want a shoe according to this stick. Well, all right, this merchant would put this stick in the shoe, and when I got to where this stick is a perfect fit, okay. Well then, I couldn't say just how far from the end is a notch, and right there I cut this stick off, and I hand him the stick the second time, and I tell him I want a pair according to how long the stick is now, and that's pair number two. Well, we'll fiddle around till he find a pair to fit that. And I cut it off again, that way, till I bought six pairs of shoes. The biggest number I bought, to my recollection, one time I went to town and I took a measure from one stick, absolutely, I bought fifteen pair of shoes from that one stick.

In this particular store where I generally do most of my tradin' they give five pounds of sugar for every five dollars that you spend cash. And one time I stood in there, about the last of November, they give me one hundred pounds of sugar free just for the shoes I bought, and I wasn't even started. I bought dry goods and stuff like that and they gave me another seventy-five or eighty pounds, I didn't even count it. Course, natural, we use a lot of sugar, least among the children. "Aw, I want some lemon cream," one of the boys says, and he'll put that in the refrigerator. Well, their ma may want strawberry cream, and some of 'em will want different flavored drinks, all like that, or one'll want a pie, or he'll want somethin' with different flavor. It takes quite a bit of sugar.

As for Christmas and how much it costs, it takes quite a bit. I'd have to kind of study myself a little on that. I'd have to take this book and ballpoint pen and look into it. A older boy, now, he wouldn't want to see Santa Claus, he just want five or ten dollars. But so many little ones, he or she might want Santa Claus to bring 'em a wagon or dolls. A kid don't know that racket about Santa Claus, but he knows he wants somethin'. This boy might want a bicycle, or he might want an expensive gun. When I go to the store to get all these things they need I don't quit till the record is run out for everybody, till I get everything from a package of cigarettes to a barrel of flour. I don't say I'm through with Christmas till every item is marked out. And when I say it would take me two or three days to get this, I say correct.

About whuppin' the children, you see it was like this. Naturally, you see, I was a man born back kind of early, back in 1908. Take my old Ford, you don't do that one the way you do *this* Ford. The first children, oh I whupped 'em, you see, because when I come on in my days I didn't get the schooling that my children gets. I didn't know like my children knows. Well, I whupped my oldest ones, you see I thought that is what it takes, but on down the line in years I found that teachin' would go further in raisin' a kid or young one. This whuppin' proposition, it's just now and then. And I hardly ever do whup one of 'em. I turn 'em over to their mother. She's a lady, and natural, she ain't as rough with 'em as I'd be. She take that young one and if she think he ought to have a little somethin' to kind of catch him up, let him know what he's doin' or who she is or who I am, she catch him up.

RECOLLECTIONS OF OLD MASTER AND JOHN

Old Master (sometimes rendered as Massa, Marster or Marse, and on occasion referred to as Old Boss) and John (now and then called George, Sam, or some other familiar name) are adversaries around whom innumerable tales, yarns, anecdotes, and jokes have clustered. John is usually a slave, though sometimes he is taken to be a post bellum black servant of a plantation owner. The difference is not meaningful, because the relationship between the protagonists is the same in both cases. Old Master is likely to be firm and demanding, even harsh and arbitrary, but he is also paternal and protective and sometimes manifests a genuine affection for John. John, also, is a combination of traits. He can be slow-thinking or swift-thinking. He is adept at getting into predicaments and at getting out of them. He is tolerant of Old Master and eager to please him; but he has mental reservations, and there are moments when he is stubborn, contemptuous, or rebellious. He accommodates to the foibles of Old Master but finds sly ways to chastise him or put him down. The two men are in continuous contest. In some yarns Old Master comes out on top, in others, John. John understands Old Master's weaknesses and strengths, but he usually plays this knowledge down to conform to the expected master-slave relationship, and often sounds obsequious or simple. Old Master, for his part, understands a good deal about John's character and motivations and appreciates his quick wit and cleverness. He is often in the process of peering behind what John says in order to discover what he means.

But the stories are told from the black man's point of view. They delight in making Old Master look a little (or very) foolish. And even when it is John who is the butt of the joke there is sometimes an irony that rubs off on Old Master. Now and then one senses that he is witnessing a human version of the war of wits between Brother Rabbit and Brother Fox. But the human version is far more subtle and contains endless social nuances. And from time to time, as in "John Saves Old Master's Children" (see p. 429), the story can have real bite or be exceptionally moving. The tales that follow are a sampling of the adventures, confrontations, defeats and victories of these two adversary companions.

Old Boss, John, and the Mule

Well, one time Old Boss had a man workin' for him named John. If they was anything this John liked best, it was sleepin'. He'd be up at cockcrow, all right, chop up a stack of stove wood, and get started out to the field.

First he'd hook up Old Boss' mule, talkin' sweetlike, "We goin' to plow a good stretch for Old Boss today, ain't we, Jim?" All that was just in case Old Boss might be watchin'. But when John got out there on the new ground he'd plow three-four furrows and then head for the big maple tree in the far corner. He'd tie the mule up and lay down in the shade and go to sleep. Every day it was like that. John couldn't wait to get up in the morning so's he could go out there and get some sleep.

After two-three days Old Boss say, "Ain't you got that field plowed yet, John?"

And John say, "Boss, that mule is the laziest, orneriest mule I ever work with."

Old Boss say, "John, you got to *encourage* him. Use the stick a little every once in a while."

Well, after that, when it was time to come home, John'd drive the mule up on the hill and whack him with a stick four-five times, hollerin', "Git movin', you lazy, good-for-nothin' mule! You give me a

This tale and the two that follow, "Old Boss and George" and "Old Master and Okra" are from Terrapin's Pot of Sense, © *1957 by Harold Courlander. Reprinted by permission of the publishers, Holt, Rinehart and Winston.*

mess of trouble today! When I say walk, *walk!*" Then he'd come in and take the harness off and get ready to eat.

But next mornin', naturally, he'd head for that big maple tree and do some more sleepin'.

One day when John was just settlin' down for shut-eye, the mule turned his head around and talked to him. He say, "Reckon it's about time I had a good talk with Old Boss."

Well, that John sat right up straight and looked around. Looked north and south, then up in the air, but he didn't see no one but the mule.

"Who said that?" John say.

"I said it," the mule say, "and I'm goin' to do it too."

John he commence to shake so hard he couldn't hardly get up.

"You the first mule I ever hear could talk," John say.

"You ain't heard no talkin' yet to speak of," the mule say. "I got a thing or two to put in Old Boss' ear."

"What you goin' to talk about?" John say.

"Plenty, that's what, plenty,"the mule say. "Goin' to mention how you get out here every mornin' and go to sleep in the shade, 'stead of workin'. Then on the way home you take me up on the hill and whup me with that stick, like I give you trouble all day. I'm goin' to give Old Boss somethin' to think on."

When John hear that, he got up and sold out, headed for home. Old Boss see him burnin' up the ground comin' in to the barn.

"What's up, John?" Old Boss say.

"Old Boss," John say, "I quit. I ain't goin' to drive no mule that talks. And besides that, if that mule tell you somethin' about me, it's a big lie."

John he went in the barn and sat down. Ain't nothin' Old Boss could say to make him go back after the mule. After a while he went himself, with his yellow dog runnin' along after him. Found the mule under the big maple tree, right where John left him.

"Hear you can talk," Old Boss say to the mule, but the mule don't say a thing, just grazin' in the grass.

Old Boss drive the mule home and put him in the barn.

Then he give John a good talkin' to, tellin' him if he don't mend his ways he goin' to have to get a new field hand.

All John would say was, "Boss, I don't fool around with talkin' mules."

"I'm pretty put out with you," Boss say and start on up to the house. Halfway there he shake his head, sayin', "Don't know what I'm goin' to do with that boy. Sure don't know."

Right then his yellow dog speak up, sayin', "Fire him, Boss. You got no choice."

"What's that?" Boss say, lookin' at the dog.

"Sure, fire him," the dog say. "When a man start to imagine things like that boy does, 'bout time to get rid of him."

Well, now, which one you think is the fool, John or Old Boss?

'Course, it don't say if Old Boss fired him or not. But if Old Boss is hearin' animals talk too, it don't hardly put him in a better position than John, do it?

(For an African comparison, see Appendix XI, pp. 588–89.)

Old Boss and George

I got another one to tell you about Old Boss and a different field hand, named George. Don't recall if George was before John or after John, Old Boss had so many.

George he had different habits, though. He could *work,* what I mean. He made Old Boss' mule really *walk,* practically wore him out. George was six feet four, wore number twelve shoes. Come cotton-pickin' time, George picked eight-nine hundred pounds of cotton without half-tryin'. When he was *tryin',* well, man, you never saw nothin' like it. Cotton bolls moved through the air so fast folks thought it was snowin'. If they was fence posts to be dug, this George dug 'em. If they was hoein' to be done, he hoed. Folks from all over use to tell Old Boss what a good worker this George was. Old Boss was proud about it too.

Soon one mornin' rain started to come down, and Old Boss figured there wouldn't be no field work done that day. So he called George out to the barn where he had six or seven sacks of potato seed. "George," he said, "might as well cut 'tato seed today. Leave the poor 'tatoes be. Put 'em in a pile over there. Pick out the good 'tatoes for seed and cut 'em in quarters. Put 'em right here in this tub."

Old Boss went back in the house and didn't hear no more from George. Two or three o'clock in the afternoon he say, "I sure forgot about George. He's out there in that barn still cuttin' seed 'tatoes."

When Old Boss get back to the barn, there was George settin' on the crate where he left him, right in front of the tub with a 'tato in one hand and a knife in the other. Old Boss looked in the tub. Saw five or six pieces of 'tato, that's all.

"George," Old Boss say, "You been cuttin' 'tato seed all mornin'?"

"Yeah," George say.

"Where they at?" Old Boss say.

"In the tub," George say.

"You mean that's all you done, George?" Old Boss ask him.

George he just hang his head.

"I'm sure disappointed," Old Boss say. "All the folks 'round here knows you're a steady worker. You can pick more cotton than just about anybody on the river. You can dig post holes like nobody's business. You're mighty stout with an ax in your hand too. You milk faster'n anybody I ever had 'round here. You walk that mule crazy with plowin'. How come you only got six bits of 'tato in that tub, George?"

Well, that George he just hang his head for true this time, hearin' Old Boss talk that way.

"Old Boss," he say, "I'm a real sorry man. I sure don't mind plowin' or cuttin' trees or pickin' cotton or mostly anything else. But there's one thing about it, this trying to make up my mind is too much for me."

Old Master and Okra

Old Master had to go down to New Orleans on business, and he left his number-one slave named Okra in charge of things. Okra declared to himself he goin' to have a good time whilst Old Master was away, and the thing he did the very first mornin' was to go out and tell the other slaves, "Now you get on with your affairs. Old Master gone to New Orleans and we got to keep things goin'."

Then Okra went in the kitchen to cook himself up some food, and in the process of doin' so he got ruffled and spilled the bacon grease on top of the stove. It burst up into a big fire, and next thing you know that house was goin' up in flame and smoke. Okra he went out the window and stood off a ways, lookin' real sorry. By the time the other hands got there, wasn't nothin' else to do *but* look sorry. They was so busy with lookin' that they never noticed that the sparks lit in the wood lot and set it afire too. Well, Okra ordered everybody out to the wood lot to save it, but by then the grass was sizzlin' and poppin', a regular old prairie fire roarin' across the fields, burnin' up the cotton and everything else. They run over there with wet bags to beat it out, but next thing they knowed, the pasture was afire and all Old Master's cattle was a-goin', throttle out and racin' for the Texas Badlands.

Okra went to the barn for the horses, but soon's he opened the door they bolted and was gone. "If'n I can get that ox team hitched," Okra said, "I'll go on down to Colonel Thatcher's place and get some help." Well, minute he started to put the yoke on them oxen, the left-hand ox lit out and was gone. The right-hand ox went after him, and the both of 'em just left Okra holdin' the ox yoke up in the air. When Old Master's huntin' dog see them oxen go off that way, he figured something was wrong, and he sold out, barkin' and snappin' at their heels.

'Bout that time Okra looked around and found all the slaves had took off, too, headin' North and leavin' no tracks. He was all alone, and he had to digest all that misery by himself.

Week or two went by, and Okra went down to meet the boat Old Master comin' back on. Old Master got off feelin' pretty good. Told Okra to carry his stuff and say, "Well, Okra, how'd things go while I was away?"

"Fine, just fine," Okra say. "I notice they're fixin' the bridge over Black Creek. Ain't that good?"

"Yeah," Old Master say, "that's fine, Okra, just fine. Soon's we get home I'm goin' to change my clothes and do some quail shootin'."

"Captain," Okra say, hangin' his head, "I got a little bad news for you."

"What's that?" Old Master say.

"You ain't neither goin' quail huntin'," Okra say, "your huntin' dog run away."

Old Master took it pretty good. He say, "Well, don't worry about it none, he'll come back. How'd he happen to run away?"

"Chasin' after the right-hand ox," Okra say. "That ox just lit out one mornin'."

"Where to?" Old Master say.

"I don't know where to," Okra say. "He was tryin' to catch up with the left-hand ox."

Old Master began to frown now, and he say to Okra, "You mean the whole ox team is gone? How come?"

"I was yokin' 'em up to go after Colonel Thatcher, after the horses bolted," Okra say.

"How come the horses bolted?" Old Boss say.

"Smoke from the pasture grass. That's what scared all your livestock and made 'em break down the fence and run for the swamp."

"You mean all my livestock is gone? Okra, I goin' to skin you. How'd that pasture get on fire?"

Okra he just stood there lookin' foolish, scratchin' his head. "Reckon the fire just came across from the cotton field, Captain," he say.

"You mean my cotton's burned!" Old Master holler. "How'd that happen?"

"Couldn't put it out, Captain. Soon as we see it come over there from the wood lot, we went down with wet bags but we couldn't handle it. Man, that was sure a pretty cotton field before the fire got there."

Right now Old Master was lookin' pretty sick. He talk kind of weak. "Okra, you tryin' to tell me the wood lot's gone too?"

"I hate to tell you, Captain, but you guessed it," Okra say, kind of sad. "Imagine, all them trees gone, just 'cause of one lonesome spark."

Old Master couldn't hardly talk at all now. He just whisperin'. "Okra," he say, "Okra, where'd that spark come from?"

"Wind blew it right from the house," Okra say, "it was when the big timbers gave and came down. Man, sparks flew in the air a mile or more."

"You mean the house burned up?" Old Master say.

"Oh, yeah, didn't I tell you?" Okra reply. "Didn't burn *up*, though, so much as it burned *down*."

By now Old Master was a miserable sight, pale as a ghost and shakin' all over.

"Okra, Okra," Old Master say, "let's go get the field hands together and do somethin'!"

"Can't do that," Okra say, "I forget to tell you, they's all sold out for Michigan."

Old Master just set there shakin' his head back and forth. "Okra," he say, "why didn't you come right out with it? Why you tell me everything was fine?"

"Captain, I'm sorry if I didn't tell it right," Okra say. "Just wanted to break it to you easy."

Old Master and the Bear

One day Ole Massa sent for John and tole him, says: "John, somebody is stealin' my corn out de field. Every mornin' when I go out I see where they done carried off some mo' of my roastin' ears. I want you to set in de corn patch tonight and ketch whoever it is."

So John said all right and he went and hid in de field.

Pretty soon he heard somethin' breakin' corn. So John sneaked up behind him wid a short stick in his hand and hollered: "Now, break another ear of Ole Massa's corn and see what *Ah'll* do to you."

John thought it was a man all dis time, but it was a bear wid his arms full of roastin' ears. He throwed down de corn and grabbed John. And him and dat bear!

John, after while got loose and got de bear by the tail wid de bear tryin' to git to him all de time. So they run around in a circle all night long. John was so tired. But he couldn't let go of de bear's tail, do de bear would grab him in de back.

After a stretch they quit runnin' and walked. John swingin' on to de bear's tail and de bear's nose 'bout to touch him in de back.

Daybreak, Ole Massa come out to see 'bout John and he seen John and de bear walkin' 'round in de ring. So he run up and says: "Lemme take holt of 'im, John, whilst you run git help!"

John says: "All right, Massa. Now you run in quick and grab 'im just so."

Ole Massa run and grabbed holt of de bear's tail and said: "Now, John you make haste to git somebody to help us."

John staggered off and set down on de grass and went to fanning hisself wid his hat.

Ole Massa was havin' plenty trouble wid dat bear and he looked over and seen John settin' on de grass and he hollered:

"John, you better g'wan git help or else I'm gwinter turn dis bear aloose!"

John says: "Turn 'im loose, then. Dat's whut Ah tried to do all night long but Ah couldn't."

Cussing Out Old Master

During slavery time two ole niggers wuz talkin' an' one said tuh de other one, "Ole Massa made me so mad yistiddy till Ah give 'im uh good cussin' out. Man, Ah called 'im everything wid uh handle on it."

This tale and the three that follow, "Cussing Out Old Master," "John Calls on the Lord," and "John Saves Old Master's Children," are from pages 100–101, 107–109, 96–99 and 121–122 of Mules and Men, *by Zora Neale Hurston. Harper & Row, Publishers, Perennial Library Edition. By permission of Harper & Row, Publishers, Inc. © 1935 by Zora Neale Hurston.*

De other one says, "You didn't cuss *Ole Massa*, didja? Good God! Whut did he do tuh you?"

"He didn't do *nothin'*, an' man, Ah laid one cussin' on 'im! Ah'm uh man lak dis, Ah won't stan' no hunchin'. Ah betcha he won't bother *me* no mo'."

"Well, if you cussed 'im an' he didn't do nothin' tuh you, de nex' time he make me mad Ah'm goin' tuh lay uh hearin' on him."

Nex' day de nigger did somethin.' Ole Massa got in behind 'im and he turnt 'round an' give Ole Massa one good cussin' an Ole Massa had 'im took down and whipped nearly tuh death. Nex' time he saw dat other nigger he says tuh 'im. "Thought you tole me, you cussed Ole Massa out and he never opened his mouf."

"Ah did."

"Well, how come he never did nothin' tuh yuh? Ah did it an' he come nigh uh killin' *me.*"

"Man, you didn't go cuss 'im tuh his face, didja?"

"Sho Ah did. Ain't dat whut you tole me you done?"

"Naw, Ah didn't say Ah cussed 'im tuh his face. You sho is crazy. Ah thought you had mo' sense than dat. When Ah cussed Ole Massa he wuz settin' on de front porch an' Ah wuz down at de big gate."

De other nigger wuz mad but he didn't let on. Way after while he 'proached de nigger dat got 'im de beatin' an' tole 'im, "Know whut Ah done tuhday?"

"Naw, whut you done? Give Ole Massa 'nother cussin'?"

"Naw, Ah ain't never goin' do dat no mo'. Ah peeped up under Ole Miss's drawers."

"Man, hush yo' mouf! You knows you ain't looked up under ole Miss's clothes!"

"Yes, Ah did too. Ah looked right up her very drawers."

"You better hush dat talk! Somebody goin' hear you and Ole Massa'll have you kilt."

"Well, Ah sho done it an' she never done nothin' neither."

"Well, whut did she say?"

"Not uh mumblin' word, an' Ah stopped and looked jus' as long as Ah wanted tuh an' went on 'bout mah business."

"Well, de nex' time Ah see her settin' out on de porch Ah'm goin' tuh look too."

"Help yo'self."

Dat very day Ole Miss wuz settin' out on de porch in de cool uh de evenin' all dressed up in her starchy white clothes. She had her legs all crossed up and de nigger walked up tuh de edge uh de porch and peeped up under Ole Miss's clothes. She took and hollered an' Ole Massa come out an' had dat nigger almost kilt alive.

When he wuz able tuh be 'bout agin he said tuh de other nigger; "Thought you tole me you peeped up under Ole Miss's drawers?"

"Ah sho did."

"Well, how come she never done nothin' tuh *you?* She got me nearly kilt."

"Man, when Ah looked under Ole Miss's drawers they wuz hangin' out on de clothes line. You didn't go look up in 'em while she had 'em on, didja? You sho is uh fool! Ah thought you had mo' sense than dat, Ah claire Ah did. It's uh wonder he didn't kill yuh dead. Umph, umph, umph. You sho ain't got no sense atall."

John Calls on the Lord

You know befo' surrender Ole Massa had a nigger name John and John always prayed every night befo' he went to bed and his prayer was for God to come git him and take him to Heaven right away. He didn't even want to take time to die. He wanted de Lawd to come git him just like he was—boot, sock, and all. He'd git down on his knees and say: "O Lawd, it's once more and again yo' humble servant is knee-bent and body-bowed—my heart beneath my knees and my knees in some lonesome valley, crying for mercy while mercy kin be found. O Lawd, Ah'm astin' you in de humblest way I know how to be so pleased as to come in yo' fiery chariot and take me to yo' Heben and its immortal glory. Come Lawd, you know Ah have hard time. Ole Massa works me so hard, and don't gimme no time to rest. So come, Lawd, wid peace in one hand and pardon in de other and take me away from this sin-sorrowing world. Ah'm tired and Ah want to go home."

So one night Ole Massa passed by John's shack and heard him beggin' de Lawd to come git him in his fiery chariot and take him away; so he made up his mind to find out if John meant dat thing. So he goes on up to de big house and got hisself a bed sheet and come on back. He throwed de sheet over his head and knocked on de door.

John quit prayin' and ast: "Who dat?"

Ole Massa say: "It's me, John, de Lawd, done come wid my fiery chariot to take you away from this sin-sick world."

Right under de bed John had business. He told his wife: "Tell Him Ah ain't here, Liza."

At first Liza didn't say nothin' at all, but de Lawd kept right on callin' John: "Come on, John, and go to Heben wid me where you won't have to plow no mo' furrows and hoe no mo' corn. Come on, John."

Liza says: "John ain't here, Lawd, you hafta come back another time."

Lawd says: "Well, then Liza, you'll do."

Liza whispers and says: "John, come out from underneath dat bed and g'wan wid de Lawd. You been beggin' him to come git you. Now g'wan wid him."

John back under de bed not sayin' a mumblin' word. De Lawd out on de doorstep kept on callin'.

Liza says: "John, Ah thought you was so anxious to get to Heben. Come out and go on wid God."

John says: "Don't you hear him say 'You'll do'? Why don't you go wid him?"

"Ah ain't a goin' nowhere. Youse de one been whoopin' and hollerin' for him to come git you and if you don't come out from under dat bed Ah'm gointer tell God youse here."

Ole Massa makin' out he's God, says: "Come on, Liza, you'll do."

Liza says: "O, Lawd, John is right here underneath de bed."

"Come on John, and go to Heben wid me and its immortal glory."

John crept out from under de bed and went to de door and cracked it and when he seen all dat white standin' on de doorsteps he jumped back. He says: "O, Lawd, Ah can't go to Heben wid you in yo' fiery chariot in dese ole dirty britches; gimme time to put on my Sunday pants."

"All right, John, put on yo' Sunday pants."

John fooled around just as long as he could, changing them pants, but when he went back to de door, de big white glory was still standin' there. So he says agin: 'O, Lawd, de Good Book says in Heben no filth is found and I got on dis dirty sweaty shirt. Ah can't go wid you in dis old nasty shirt. Gimme time to put on my Sunday shirt!"

"All right, John, go put on yo' Sunday shirt!"

John took and fumbled around a long time changing his shirt, and den he went back to de door, but Ole Massa was still on de doorstep. John didn't had nothin' else to change so he opened de door a little piece and says:

"O, Lawd, Ah'm ready to go to Heben wid you in yo' fiery chariot, but de radiance of yo' countenance is *so* bright, Ah can't come out by you. Stand back jus' li'l way please."

Ole Massa stepped back a li'l bit.

John looked out and says: "O, Lawd, you know dat po' humble me is less than de dust beneath yo' shoe soles. And de radiance of yo' countenance is so bright Ah can't come out by you. Please, please, Lawd, in yo' tender mercy, stand back a li'l further."

Ole Massa stepped back a li'l bit mo'.

John looked out agin and he says: "O, Lawd, Heben is so high and wese so low; youse so great and Ah'm so weak and yo' strength is too much for us poor sufferin' sinners. So once mo' and agin yo' humber servant is knee-bent and body-bowed askin' you one mo' favor befo' Ah step into yo' fiery chariot to go to Heben wid you and wash in yo' glory—be so pleased in yo' tender mercy as to stand back jus' a li'l bit further."

Ole Massa stepped back a step or two mo' and out dat door John come like a streak of lightning. All across de punkin patch, thru de cotton over de pasture—John wid Ole Massa right behind him. By de time dey hit de cornfield John was way ahead of Ole Massa.

Back in de shack one of de children was cryin' and she ast Liza: "Mama, you reckon God's gointer ketch papa and carry him to Heben wid him?"

"Shet yo' mouf, talkin' foolishness!" Liza clashed at de chile. "You know de Lawd can't outrun yo' pappy—specially when he's barefooted at dat."

(For comparison with West Indian variants, see Appendix XIV, p. 595.)

John Saves Old Master's Children

Ole John was a slave, you know. And there was Ole Massa and Ole Missy and de two li' children—a girl and a boy.

Well, John was workin' in de field and he seen de children out on de lake in a boat, just a hollerin'. They had done lost they oars and was 'bout to turn over. So then he went and tole Ole Massa and Ole Missy.

Well, Ole Missy, she hollered and said: "It's so sad to lose these 'cause Ah ain't never goin' to have no more children." Ole Massa made her hush and they went down to de water and follered de shore on 'round till they found 'em. John pulled off his shoes and hopped in and swum out and got in de boat wid de children and brought 'em to shore.

Well, Massa and John take 'em to de house. So they was all so glad 'cause de children got saved. So Massa told 'im to make a good crop dat year and fill up de barn, and den when he lay by de crops nex' year, he was going to set him free.

So John raised so much crop dat year he filled de barn and had to put some of it in de house.

So Friday come, and Massa said, "Well, de day done come that I said I'd set you free. I hate to do it, but I don't like to make myself out a lie. I hate to git rid of a good nigger lak you."

So he went in de house and give John one of his old suits of clothes to put on. So John put it on and come in to shake hands and tell 'em goodbye. De children they cry, and Ole Missy she cry. Didn't want to see John go. So John took his bundle and put it on his stick and hung it crost his shoulder.

Well, Ole John started on down de road. Well, Ole Massa said, "John, de children love yuh."

"Yassuh."

"John, I love yuh."

"Yassuh."

"And Missy *like* yuh!"

"Yassuh."

"But 'member, John, youse a nigger."

"Yassuh."

Fur as John could hear 'im down de road he wuz hollerin', "John, Oh John! De children loves you. And I love you. De Missy *like* you."

John would holler back, "Yassuh."

"But 'member youse a nigger, tho!"

Ole Massa kept callin' 'im and his voice was pitiful. But John kept right on steppin' to Canada. He answered Old Massa every time he called 'im, but he consumed on wid his bag.

Conversation About a Slave

CAP: Has you ever hear 'bout ole man Rebor an' he slave?

From Nigger to Nigger, *by E. C. L. Adams, New York, Scribners, 1928.*

VOICE: I is hear a heap 'bout ole man Rebor. He been a great friend to de niggers, dey tell me. Went 'gainst de white folks an' tooken up for de niggers in slavery time.

CAP: Dat's de trute an' I reckon some er de things he done were for de best, it matter not he intentions, but I has my own thoughts 'bout he reasons.

VOICE: Wuh is de tale 'bout de slave?

CAP:'Fore de war a fine gentleman from up North were visitin' ole man Rebor—us white folks ain' enter he house an' wouldn't 'low him in dey own—an' he see walkin' in de hall er ole man Rebor' house a nigger, a white nigger, you ain' kin tell him from a white man, an' de gentleman say:

"Who is dat man?"

An' ole man Rebor say:

"He is a nigger. One er my slave."

An' de gentleman say:

"I can't b'lieve it. He is a wonderful lookin' man. He look so distinguish."

An' ole man Rebor say:

"He is a slave, a loyal an' humble slave."

An' he wiggle he finger to de nigger an' say:

"Come here."

An' when de nigger come, ole man Rebor say:

"Open you' mout'."

An' when de nigger open he mout', ole man Rebor step up close to him an' spit down he th'oat an' say:

"I told you he were my humble slave."

VOICE: Wuh de gentleman say?

CAP: He ain' say nothin'. He turn he back an' walk out er ole man Rebor' house.

John Steals a Pig and a Sheep

Old Marster had some sheep, and a fellow named John living on the place, a tenant there, he got hungry and he stole the meat from Old Boss. Then he got tired of the sheep meat and stole him a pig. Old Marster come down night after he stole the pig, to get him to play a piece on the banjo. Old Marster knocked on the door, when John had just got through putting the pig away. So Old Marster come in and say, "Play me a piece on the banjo." John started to pick a piece on the banjo; while he's playing he looked around and sees a pig's foot sticking out, so he sings, "Push that pig's foot further back under the bed." (He was talking to his wife.)

"John Steals a Pig and a Sheep" and the next five tales—*"Baby in the Crib,"* *"The Yearling," "Old Marster Eats Crow," "John Praying"* and *"The Mojo"* are reprinted from American Negro Folktales, *compiled by Richard M. Dorson, Fawcett Publications, 1967. By permission of Richard M. Dorson.*

When he got tired of that pig meat he turned around and killed him another sheep. So he went back down to the barn and told Old Marster, "Another sheep dead, can't I have him?" Old Marster give him that sheep and he took that one home and ate it up. That made two that Old Marster had given him, so Old Marster got a watch out for him. John killed another one and went and told Old Marster again that a sheep had died. Old Marster told him, "You killed that sheep. What did you kill my sheep for?" John says, "Old Marster, I'll tell you; I won't let nobody's sheep bite me."

Baby in the Crib

John stole a pig from Old Marsa. He was on his way home with him and his Old Marsa seen him. After John got home he looked out and seen his Old Marsa coming down to the house. So he put this pig in a cradle they used to rock the babies in in them days (some people called them cribs), and he covered him up. When his Old Marster come in John was sitting there rocking him.

Old Marster says, "What's the matter with the baby, John?" "The baby got the measles." "I want to see him." John said, "Well you can't; the doctor said if you uncover him the measles will go back in on him and kill him." So his Old Marster said, "It doesn't matter; I want to see him, John." He reached down to uncover him.

John said, "If that baby is turned to a pig now, don't blame me."

The Yearling

In the old days the only things the slaves got good to eat is what they stole. Old Marster lost a yea'ling, and some of the preacher's members knowed its whereabouts. So Old Marster told him to preach the hell out of the congregation that Sunday, so that whosomever stole the yea'ling would confess having it.

The preacher got up and pernounced to the crowd: "Some of you have stole Old Marster's yea'ling. So the best thing to do is to go to Old Marster and confess that you stole the yea'ling. And get it off right now. Because if you don't, Judgment Day, the man that stole the Master's yea'ling will be there. Old Marster will be there too, the yea'ling will be there too—the yea'ling will be *staring* you in the face."

John gets up and says to the preacher, "Mr. Preacher, I understand you to say, Judgment Day, the man that stole Old Marster's yea'ling will be there, Old Marster will be there, the yea'ling will be there, yea'ling will be *staring* you in the face."

Preacher says, "That's right."

John replied then, "Let Old Marster git his yea'ling on Judgment Day—that'll be time enough."

Old Marster Eats Crow

John was hunting on Old Marster's place, shooting squirrels, and Old Marster caught him, and told him not to shoot there anymore. "You can keep the two squirrels you got but don't be caught down here no more." John goes out the next morning and shoots a crow. Old Marster went down that morning and caught him, and asked John to let him see the gun. John gave him the gun, and then Marster told him to let him see the shell. And Old Marster put the shell in the gun. Then he backed off from John, pointing the gun, and told John to pick the feathers off the crow, halfway down. "Now start at his head, John, and eat the crow up to where you stopped picking the feathers at." When John finished eating, Marster gave him the gun back and throwed him the crow. Then he told John to go on and not let him be caught there no more.

John turned around and started off, and got a little piece away. Then he stopped and turned and called Old Marster. Old Marster said, "What you want, John?" John pointed the gun and says, "Lookee here, Old Marster," and throwed Old Marster the half a crow. "I want you to start at his ass and eat all the way, and don't let a feather fly from your mouth."

John Praying

This old Boss-man said he was going to whip John within an inch of his life on Wednesday night. John started praying every day from Sunday to Wednesday. On Wednesday evening that was his last prayer. He told him, "Lord, I been praying every day since Sunday and you've never failed me. I want you to take me away this evening." The boys heard the prayer and they went down and climbed the tree with a ladder rope. So when John made his final prayer that night he said, "Lord I got to go, because I've only got fifteen minutes before my execution."

So they said, "Okay John, you'll have to come by way of the rope because my chariot is broke."

He said, "All right, Lord, let it down, I'm willing to go any way you carry me."

Little boys up in the tree put down the rope, said, "John, put your head in this loop." So they commenced tightening on the rope, and he commenced praying fast.

"O Lord, didn't you say you know everything? Well, don't you know damn well you choking me?"

The Mojo

There was always the time when the white man been ahead of the colored man. In slavery times John had done got to a place where the

Marster whipped him all the time. Someone told him, "Get you a mojo, it'll get you out of that whipping, won't nobody whip you then."

John went down to the corner of the Boss-man's farm, where the mo-jo-man stayed, and asked him what he had. The mojo-man said, "I got a pretty good one and a very good one and a damn good one." The colored fellow asked him, "What can the pretty good one do?" "I'll tell you what it can do. It can turn you to a rabbit, and it can turn you to a quail, and after that it can turn you to a snake." So John said he'd take it.

Next morning John sleeps late. About nine o'clock the white man comes after him, calls him: "John, come on, get up there and go to work. Plow the taters and milk the cow and then you can go back home—it's Sunday morning." John says to him, "Get on out from my door, don't say nothing to me. Ain't gonna do nothing." Boss-man says, "Don't you know who this is? It's your Boss." "Yes, I know—I'm not working for you anymore." "All right, John, just wait till I go home; I'm coming back and whip you."

White man went back and got his pistol, and told his wife, "John is sassy, he won't do nothing I tell him, I'm gonna whip him." He goes back to John, and calls, "John, get up there." John yells out, "Go on away from that door and quit worrying me. I told you once, I ain't going to work."

Well, then the white man he falls against the door and broke it open. And John said to his mojo, "Skip-skip-skip-skip." He turned to a rabbit, and ran slap out the door by Old Marster. And he's a running son of a gun, that rabbit was. Boss-man says to his mojo, "I'll turn to a greyhound." You know that greyhound got running so fast his paws were just reaching the grass under the rabbit's feet.

Then John thinks, "I got to get away from here." He turns to a quail. And he begins sailing fast through the air—he really thought he was going. But the Boss-man says, "I will turn to a chicken hawk." That chicken hawk sails through the sky like a bullet, and catches right up to that quail.

Then John says, "Well, I'm going to turn to a snake." He hit the ground and begin to crawl; that old snake was natchally getting on his way. Boss-man says, "I'll turn to a stick and I'll beat your ass."

(For an African comparison, see Appendix VI, pp. 579–82.)

The Single Ball

A white man liked to hunt deer, and he used to brag, too. He had a servant who always went with him in the woods to drive the deer. He was very fond of his Master, and he was ready any time to swear to the tale that the Master might tell about how many deer they killed and the way they killed them. One time this white man been telling some

From Negro Myths from the Georgia Coast, *by Charles C. Jones, Boston, Houghton, Mifflin and Co., 1888.*

friends how he shot a deer with his rifle, and when he went to examine him he found that the ball shot off the deer's hind foot and hit him in the eye. His friends couldn't see how that could happen, and didn't want to believe the tale. Then the hunter called on his servant to prove what he'd been saying. The servant said the same thing as his Master had said. Then the Master's friends asked him how the same ball could hit the deer in the hind foot and in the eye at the same time. The servant scratched his head, and then he answered: "Gentlemen, I expect that when Master fired at him, the deer must have been brushing a fly off his eye with his hind foot." That sort of satisfied the gentlemen and saved the white man's word.

After the gentlemen had gone, the servant called his Master to one side and said: "Master, I'm willing to back anything you say about hunting and killing deer, but let me beg you, next time you tell about how you shoot them, put the holes closer. This time you made them so far apart I had big trouble trying to get them together."

The Champion

The way it was, Old Master went out and bought him five hundred Negroes on this place. And the other captain over here bought *him* five hundred Negroes. And buying the five hundred Negroes, this master has a big Negro in there he said was stouter than any Negro that ever he bought, and he's the champion of that bunch. This master right across the fence on the next plantation told him he had one there, listen, was stouter than the one the first Master had there. "Well," he says, "the one I got will whip that one you got."

"Well," the first master says, "I'll bet you one thousand dollars that mine, listen, will whip that one you got, or else take his nerve so he won't fight." Said, "I'll bet you, understand, this hand of mine will fight this one of yours and whip him, or else I'll bet you five hundred dollars that when your hand gets there he won't fight mine."

Other one says, "When we goin' to meet?"

Says, "Well, Friday, let's meet 'em and let 'em fight." Say, "You have all your peoples on the place to meet 'em to fight, and I'm goin' to have all of mine to see to fight, and me and you goin' to be there."

Just before that Friday, next day, this first master's Negro said, "I don't believe I can whip this other champion over yonder, but I can fix it so you'll win the five hundred dollars if not the thousand. Just let me know where we goin' to fight at." He said, "Give me your shovel and give me your ax."

He went down in the woods and dug up a water oak, a common tree. He took a mule and drug it to a hole up there, and set it out in the hole.

This tale and the seven that follow are from the author's collection.

And when he set it in the ground he put some leaves around to make it look like the tree growed there. It wasn't goin' to wilt because it wasn't more than twenty-four hours before they going to fight. That tree looked alive. Then he taken all his wife's white clothes and put them around there and set out a wash tub.

The next day when the master from the other plantation came for the fight, the first master came with his champion with a grass line tied on him. There was a little place in the grass line where it was weak. The master walked his champion up to the tree and tied him to it. The other champion from the next plantation was walkin' loose.

His master supplied to the first one, "Is this the one goin' to fight my champion?"

Said, "Yeah."

Said, "Why you got him tied up that way?"

Said, "I'm scared he'll get frustrated and mad. He's ambitious and want to fight. I'm scared he'll get loose and jump on your champion and hurt him. He's so stout I have to tie him so I can talk to him."

This other champon that come from the other plantation, he tell his master, "Death ain't but death. I ain't goin' to fight no man they got to tie to a tree, else he'll kill me, so you might just as well shoot me down where I am."

The first master say, "You want to see how stout my champion is before they fight?"

Other one say, "Yeah."

He say, "Well then, I'll make him try out that rope a little." Says to his champion, "Bill, pull against that tree a little so's this other champion can see what you are."

Bill braced his feet and pulled, and the tree start to lean. All them Negroes from the other plantation backed up when they see that. Bill pulled some more, and the roots start to pop out of the ground.

The other champion got behind his master. Says, "Shoot me down, Master, cause that man goin' to kill me anyway. I ain't goin' to fight no man that pulls trees down by the roots."

His master say to the other one, "Your champion's scared mine 'bout to death. Don't let him pull no more."

But Bill gave another tug and that tree started to come down, and the rope broke at the thin place. He came runnin' at where the masters were standing.

The other master said, "And now I'm gettin' scared too. Hold him off. My champion ain't goin' to fight, so here's the five hundred dollars."

The first master tell all his hands to take Bill and hold him, and whilst they doin' that the Negroes from the other plantation just lit out for home.

Bill didn't think he could whip the other champion, but he worked it out so the other one was scared to fight him, and that's how his master won five hundred dollars in the bet.

Old Master and John Go Hunting

One time Old Master and John went out deer hunting. Old Master said, "John, there's a big six-point buck deer been seen over by the piney woods. We goin' to get that one today, and I'm goin' to mount the head and make it real pretty." John say it's all right with him. They went over toward the piney woods and Master say "John, I think I see that six-pointer out there. You see him too?" John say, "Well, maybe I do, but I can't rightly say for sure." Master tell him, "I see him, I surely do. I'm going after him. If he outruns me and comes this way, don't let him get by, you hear?" "Yes, Master," John tell him, "if that deer comes this way I'll shoot him." Master starts off. He say, "One thing, though, John, don't hit him in the head. Hit him in the middle. I got to mount that head and hang it on the wall." John say, "Yes, Master, I'm goin' to do just what you say."

So Old Master went off and left John standing there with the gun in his hands. He went down in the swamp and when he got near the piney woods he flushed the deer. It jumped around a little and then went running toward where John was waiting. That deer came right at John, and when it see him it turned a little and went right on past. John raised the gun, then he set it down. He just stood there. After a while Old Master came along tailing the deer. He was breathing hard. He say, "John! John! Get him, John!" When he see John standing there he say, "John, how come you didn't shoot? Didn't you see that deer come past?"

But John shook his head, say, "Deer? I ain't see no deer." Old Master was pretty put out about that. He say, "John, what you mean you didn't see no deer? He must have just about run over you." John shook his head again, and he talk pretty firm to Old Master. He say, "Old Master, you know I can recognize a deer, else why you bring me with you? Like I tell you, they wasn't no deer come this way." Old Master say, "John, didn't you see *anything* come this way? Didn't you see *anything* unusual?" "Oh, yes, I sure did see something *unusual*," John say. "I saw somebody running around with a cane-bottom chair on his head, but I ain't see no deer."

And that's how Old Master lost his six-point buck and didn't have the head hanging on his wall.

John's Watch

This man named John was walking on the road one time and he found a gold watch and chain lying there in the dust. He picked it up and polished it some, and he put it in his pocket and let the chain hang out, like Old Master did, but he couldn't read the time on it. So when he came to the barn Old Master was there, and John fiddled with the chain and said, "Well, I wonder what time is it now. Reckon I'll take a look." He pulled out the watch and examined. it. "Well, don't that beat all," he said, "just look at the time, will you."

Old Master, he said, "John, what you got there?" And John tell him, "Just my regular timekeeper, with the chain on it." Old Master tell him, "John, where you find that watch?" John say, "How you know I find it, master?" And Master say, "I sure know you didn't *buy* it, and I sure know you didn't have it *yesterday*, so I figure you got to have found it. Give it over here, John, let me see it." John gave Old Master the watch to look at. Old Master said, "Must be that some other Old Master lost this watch. Reckon I'll keep it and find out who owns it." John didn't like that. He said, "Master, if you take my watch how am I going to know what time of the day it is?" And Old Master tell him, "Now look here, John, you don't have to know what time of day it is, because I'll tell you. And another thing, you can't read the watch anyway."

John didn't like that, of course, because he like to have something around to tell the time, *just in case.* So one time he was in the field and he find a small turtle there, just about twice the size of the gold watch. He tied a string on it and put it in his pocket and let the string hang out like a chain. And that night when he get home to the barn he met Old Master, and Old Master see the string tied to his belt. Old Master say to hisself, "There John goes again. I'm going to get him this time." And he tell John, "Well, John, what time does your timepiece tell?"

John pulled out the turtle and took a good look at it. "'Cording to what it looks like," John said, "it's past six o'clock and kicking like the devil for seven."

The Ducks Get the Cotton

The way it was, this man named John sharecropped cotton for Old Boss, but whenever he sold his cotton it seemed like he owed Old Boss more than he got for it. If John made a hundred dollars on his cotton, well, then, Old Boss looked at his papers and made black marks all over 'em with his pencil. He'd say, "John, 'pears to me you got a balance to me of one hundred sixty-seven dollars and fourteen cents." And John'd say, "Old Boss, that seem a mite more'n I get for the cotton." Old Boss tell him, "Don't worry on it too long, John. Just give me the hundred and we'll let the rest on it ride over till next year."

Now, one time John was gettin' the wagon ready to take in some cotton and Old Boss come by. "That's a nice load of cotton you got there, John," he say. "How much you reckon as it'll bring?" But John was tired of that balance he always got on Old Boss's bookkeepin' books. He say, "Well, now, the way things is this year it's hard to tell." And Old Boss say, "John, what you mean it's hard to tell?" John scratch his head and look mournful. "They tell me," says John, "that they's a epidemic of ducks this year." Old Boss say, "That don't make no sense, John. What you mean about a epidemic of ducks?" "I can't rightly tell you 'bout that," John say, "but I just hear tell that the ducks is hell on cotton prices." "That's just nonsense, John," says Old Boss. "You just come on past my place on your way home and we'll settle up."

John went in to town, spent the day there and sold his cotton. He bought a few victuals at the town store and then come on back. When Old Boss saw him comin' along the road he went out to meet him. He said, "John, 'spect you did real good with your cotton. How much you make on it?" John say, "Old Boss, like I tell you, they's a duck epidemic goin' on over there, and I didn't come out good at all." "I heard you say about a duck epidemic before," says Old Boss, "and it don't make no more sense now than then. What you talkin' bout, John?"

"Well, to be particular short about it, Old Boss, I sold the cotton all right, and I had the money in my hand, but before I knowed it the ducks got it all. They deducks for the rotten bolls, they deducks for puttin' my wagon in the wrong place, they deducks for the commission, they deducks for the taxes, they deducks for this sugar and flour I bought, they deducks for this thing and that thing till by the time it's all over the ducks get it all. So I reckon we got to settle up some other time."

John said giddap and left Old Boss standin' side of the road. And when he get home he take his cotton money out of his shirt and put it in the jar. "All Old Boss want is to *settle up*," he say. "But what I need a little bit of is to *settle down*."

John Sharecrops for Old Boss

John, he heard they was an Old Boss up the river had twenty good acres to let out to a reliable man, and he went up there and told him he was as good a man as he could find to farm that land.

"You got credentials?" Boss ask him.

John say, "You mean something to tell how good I can work?"

"That's it," Boss tell him. "And I don't want no shiftless, stupid black man settin' on my place."

John show him the calluses on his hands, say, "Boss, these calluses is my credentials, and as to bein' stupid, anyone can tell you I'm a sharp man to come and sharecrop for you."

"Well, now," the Boss say, "we goin' to give it a try." He take John with him and they go down to the twenty acres. Now Old Boss can't think nothin' 'cept cotton, and he tell John this way: "We got to speak of the arrangements. You ready?"

John say, "Yes, Captain, I'm ready."

Boss say, "John, the arrangements is that we go half and half. That suit you?"

"Yes, sure suits me," John say.

"The way it is," Boss say, "I get the tops and you get the bottoms."

John ponder on it a while.

Boss say, thinkin' about all that cotton, "What's the matter, John, don't it suit you?"

John tell him, "Why, yes, sir, Captain, it suits me fine. We can shake hands on that."

They shake hands on it and Boss went on home.

John, he went to work on that land, plowed it all up and harried it. Then he plant. But he don't plant cotton like Boss has in his mind, he plant 'taters. And 'bout the time the 'taters has good green vines on 'em, John stop by Boss's house, say, "Captain, the crop is growin' mighty fine. You want to see how it looks?"

Boss say, "Yes, I'm comin' to look. Been meanin' to get down there long before this." When he get there he see John workin' in that great big 'tater patch.

"Captain," John tell him, "count of you ask for the tops and you give me the bottoms, you sure got you'self a mighty fine crop of greens. I goin' to bring them over in the wagon soon as I dig out the 'taters."

Boss, he got a real sad look on him. He say, "Well, John, you sure fix me that time. But I got one thing to tell you. Next year you better look out, cause I goin' to take the bottoms and you can take the tops."

John shake his head up and down. "That's sure a fair arrangement," he say, "and I'm ready to shake hands on it."

So they shake hands 'bout the next year's crop, and Boss went home.

Well the next year John don't plant 'taters, he plant the field with oats. This time the Boss don't stay away so long, and on the way down he meet with John on the road.

John say, "Captain, you come just at the right time. I sure want you to look at the crop. It's comin' along just fine."

When they was gettin' close to the field, John tell him, "Guess this year goin' to make you feel pretty happy, Captain, cause you takes the bottoms and leaves me the tops."

"Yes, John, this year I take the bottoms, but what you goin' to do with the tops sure mystifies me plenty."

Then they come to the field and Old Boss just stand there lookin'.

"That crop sure is pretty, ain't it?" John say. "Never did see a better stand of oats long as I been farmin'. You goin' to get a sizable lot of stalks, Captain. Reckon it goin' to make good straw to bed down the horses."

Old Boss shake his head, say, "John you outsmart me. You never said you was plantin' oats. But it goin' to be different next year. It goin' to be so different you ain't goin' to like it one bit. The way it goin' to be, John, is that I am goin' to take the tops *and* the bottoms and you get what is left. All you get is the middle. And if you ain't ready to shake hands on it right now you can pack up and get in your wagon and find you'self a home *elsewhere*."

John, he pondered some on that one.

"Well," Old Boss say, "what's it goin' to be?"

"Look like they isn't too much in it for me," John say, "but you been good to me on this place, Captain, and I goin' to take that proposition and shake on it."

Next year John plowed up all his twenty acres and harried the ground good, and after that he planted his crop. Old Boss was pretty busy with things, but round the middle of July he consider he better go over and see how John's field is doin'. He met John on the road again.

John say, "Old Boss, I was just on the way to get you. It's a real nice crop I got and I want you to see it."

And when they got to John's field, what you think Old Boss found? All John had planted was corn, twenty acres of it.

"You sure got a mighty fine stand of tassels above and stalks at the bottom," John say. "But me and my family prefers the ears in the middle. What kind of arrangement you want to make for next year?"

Old Boss say, "John, next year they ain't goin' to be no top, bottom or middle arrangement. I'll take same as you, just half and half."

John in Jail

One time Old Boss get a call from the sheriff, say that John was in jail and did Old Boss want him out on bail. Old Boss, he was mad that John give him so much trouble, but he got to get John out cause they was work to be done. So he went down to the sheriff's place and put ten dollars on the line, sign some papers and take John home with him.

"How come they put you in jail?" the Boss say.

"'Spect it was 'count of Miss Elizabeth's petunias," John say.

"Old Miss Elizabeth Grant? What's her petunias got to do with it?" Old Boss say.

"I hear tell Miss Elizabeth want a man to trim up her petunia garden," John say. "I got a little time now and then between workin' in the field, so I went up there to Miss Elizabeth's place to see could she use me. I knock on the back door and Miss Elizabeth come and ask me what I want. I tell her I'm the man to work in her petunia garden. She ask to see my testimonials, and that's when I make my mistake."

The Horsefly

John and Old Boss was taking a load of cotton to the auction, and whilst riding along, a horsefly came down on Old Boss and bit him in the back of the neck. Old Boss gave out a holler, saying, "What was that?"

John say, "Nothin' but a common horsefly, Boss."

Boss say, "John, that weren't no horsefly. Horseflies go after mules and jackasses."

"True, true," John say. "Howsoever, that one was a horsefly."

"Now listen, John, I say it weren't no horsefly," Old Boss say.

"Seem to me like it were," says John.

"John," Old Boss say, "you aren't calling me some kind of a mule or jackass, are you?"

"No, sir, Old Boss. You don't 'pear to be neither a mule or a jackass. Ain't nobody round here ever say anything like that. All I knows . . . ," John say. "All I knows. . . ."

"All you knows is *what?*" Old Boss say.

John scratched his head. "All I knows," he say, "is I never hear tell that a horsefly can be fooled 'bout such things."

John and the Blacksnake

One time John went down to the pond to catch him a few catfish. He put his line in the water, and cause the sun was warm John began to doze off a little. Soon as his head went down a little, he heard someone callin' his name, "John, John," like that. John jerked up his head and looked around, but he didn't see no one. Two-three minutes after that he heard it again, "John, John." He looked to one side and the other. He looked down at the water and he looked up in the air. And after that he looked behind him and saw a big old blacksnake settin' on a stone pile.

"Who been callin' my name?" says John.

"Me," the blacksnake tell him. "It's me that called you."

John don't feel too comfortable talkin' to a blacksnake, and he feel mighty uneasy about a blacksnake talkin' to him. He say, "What you want?"

"Just called your name to be sociable," blacksnake tell him.

John look all around to see was anyone else there. "How come you pick *me* to socialize with?"

"Well," blacksnake say, "you is the only one here, and besides that, John, ain't we both black?"

"Let's get it straight," says John, "they's two kinds of black, yours and mine, and they ain't the same thing."

"Black is black," blacksnake say, "and I been thinkin' on it quite a while. You might say as we is kin."

That was too much for John. He jumped up and sold out, went down the road like the Cannonball Express. And comin' down the road they was a wagon with Old Boss in it. Old Boss stop and wait till John get there. He say, "John, I thought you was down to the pond fishin' for catfish?"

John looked back over his shoulder, said, "I was, but I ain't."

Old Boss say, "John, you look mighty scared. What's your hurry?"

John say, "Old Boss, when blacksnakes get to talkin', that's when I get to movin'."

"Now, John," Old Boss say, "you know that blacksnakes don't talk."

"Indeed I know it," John say, "and that's why, in particular, I'm a-goin', cause this here blacksnake is doin' what you say he don't."

"'Pears to me as you been into that liquid corn again," Old Boss say. "I'm disappointed in you, John. You let me down."

"It ain't no liquid corn," John say, "it's worse than liquid corn. It's a big old blacksnake settin' on a rock pile down by the pond."

"Well," Old Boss say, "let's go take a look."

So Old Boss went with John back to the pond, and the blacksnake was still there settin' on the stones.

"Tell him," John said to the blacksnake. "Tell Old Boss what you told me."

But the blacksnake just set there and didn't say a word."

"Just speak up," John say, "tell him what I hear before."

Blacksnake didn't have a word to say, and Old Boss tell John, "John, you got to stay off that corn. I'm mighty disappointed in you. You sure let me down." After that Old Boss got in his wagon and took off.

John looked mean at the blacksnake. He say, "Blacksnake, how come you make me a liar?"

Blacksnake say, "John, you sure let *me* down too. I spoke with you and nobody else. And the first thing you do is go off and tell everything you know to a white man."

(For an African comparison, see Appendix VII, pp. 582–83.)

PLANTATION PROVERBS

Big possum climb little tree.
Dem what eats can say grace.
Old man Know-All died last year.
Better de gravy dan no grease 'tall.
Lazy folks' stomachs don't get tired (hungry).
Rheumatiz don't help at de log rollin'.
Mole don't see what his neighbor doin'.
(It) don't rain eve'y time de pig squeal.
Crow an' corn can't grow in de same fiel'.
Tattlin' 'oman can't make de bread rise.
Rails split 'fo' breakfast'll season de dinner.
Ef you want ter see you' own sins, clean up a new groun'.
Hog dunner (don't know) w'ich part un 'im will season de turnip salad.
It's a blessin' de white sow don't shake de plum tree.
(It's a) mighty po' bee dat don't make mo' honey dan he want.
Possum's tail good as a paw.
Dogs don't bite at de front gate.
Colt in de barley patch kick high.

From Uncle Remus, His Songs and His Sayings, *by Joel Chandler Harris. New York, D. Appleton and Company, 1880, 1895. Some of the seemingly excessive dialect has been moderated.*

Jaybird don't rob his own nest.
Pullet can't roost too high for de owl.
Meat fried 'fo' day won't last till night.
Stump water won't kyo [cure] de gripes.
De howlin' dog know what he sees.
Blind hoss don't fall w'en he follers de bit.
Hongry nigger won't w'ar his maul out.
Don't fling away de empty wallet.
Blacksnake know de way ter de hen's nest.
Looks won't do ter split rails wid.
Settin' hens don't hanker arter fresh aigs.
Tater-vine growin' while you sleep.
Hit take two birds fer to make a nest.
Ef you bleedzd ter eat dirt, eat clean dirt.
Tarrypin walk fast 'nuff fer to go visitin'.
Empty smokehouse makes de pullet holler.
W'en coon take water he fixin' fer ter fight.
Corn makes mo' at de mill dan it does in de crib.
Good luck say: "Open you' mouf en shet you' eyes."
Nigger dat gets hurt wukkin oughter show de skyars.
Fiddlin' nigger say hit's long ways ter de dance.
Rooster makes mo' racket dan de hen w'at lay de aig.
Meller mushmelon hollers at you fum over de fence.
Nigger wid a pocket-han'kcher better be looked atter.
Rain-crow don't sing no chune, but you can 'pend on 'im.
One-eyed mule can't be handled on de bline side.
Moon may shine, but a lightered knot's mighty handy.
Licker talks mighty loud w'en it git loose fum de jug.
De proudness un a man don't count w'en his head's cold.
Hongry rooster don't cackle when he fine a wo'm.
Some niggers mighty smart, but dey can't drive de pidgins ter roost.
You may know de way, but better keep you' eyes on de seven stairs.
All de buzzards in de settlement'll come to de gray mule's funeral.
You can hide de fire, but w'at you gwine do wid de smoke?
Termorrow may be de carridge-driver's day for ploughin'.
Hit's a mighty deaf nigger dat don't year de dinner-ho'n.
Hit takes a bee fer ter git de sweetness out'n de hoar-houn' blossom.
Ha'nts don't bodder longer hones' folks, but you better go 'roun' de
    graveyard.
De pig dat runs off wid de year er corn gits little mo' dan de cob.
Sleepin' in de fence-corner don't fetch Chrismus in de kitchen.
De springhouse may freeze, but de niggers 'll keep de shuck-pen warm.
'Twix' de bug en de bee-martin 'tain't hard ter tell w'ich gwineter git
    kotch.
Don't 'spute wid de squinch-owl. Jam de shovel in de fier.
You'd see mo'er de mink ef he know'd whar de yard dog sleeps.
Troubles is seasonin'. 'Simmons ain't good till dey 'er fros'-bit.

JUSTICE, INJUSTICE AND GHOSTS IN THE SWAMPS OF THE CONGAREE

The following sketches, dialogues, and tales were gathered and set down early in the twentieth century by Edward C. L. Adams. The setting was the rural area bordering the Congaree River in South Carolina. The form in which the yarns and observations are written—conversations and dialogues among a group of Congaree blacks of varying ages—gives special dimension to many of these sketches. One is not certain about how literally the dialogues and narrations were transposed to paper, and there is a sense that the "vernacular" might have been rendered a little more simply. But there is a persuasiveness about the sketches, and very real people emerge from them. There is a merging of history and folklore in the tales about ghosts and specters in the swamp, and a highly developed spirit of irony makes itself felt from time to time. The subjects to which the conversations address themselves range through conditions of slavery and the character of slave masters, justice and injustice, biblical themes, and the supernatural. Most of these stories do not appear to be part of the general, widespread repertoire of Afro-American oral literature, but seem to belong to the region of the Congaree where Mr. Adams gathered them.

Judge Foolbird

PERK: I been over to see de Jedge pass on Noah.
VOICE: Wha' Noah do?

From Congaree Sketches, Scenes from Negro Life in the Swamps of the Congaree and Tales by Tad and Scip of Heaven and Hell with Other Miscellany, *by Edward C. L. Adams, Chapel Hill, University of North Carolina Press, 1927.*

PERK: He been in ole man Hall Store, an' he say 'God-dam' to a nig-ger standin' dere, an' ole man Hall say he a Christian gentleman an' don' 'low no perfanity in he place of business—'git out!' An' Noah say, he ain't mean no harm, an' he walk out an' cross de big road. Atter while ole man Hall walk out an' follow him up an' he walk up to Noah an' bus' him over de head wid er axe halve an' beat him up an' de Po-lice 'rest both 'un em, an' Jedge Foolbird axe ole man Hall what de nig-ger do when he follow hm up and ole man Hall say 'He ain't do nu-thin', but he look like he goin' say sumpen,' and Jedge Foolbird fined Noah one hunnerd dollahs.

VOICE: What did he do wid ole man Hall?

PERK: He fine him fi' dollahs.

VOICE: 'Fore God! What make he fine ole man Hall fi' dollahs? Ain't he white folks?

PERK: Jedge Foolbird is de law, an' he goin' do what he goin' do. He de law, and de law is de law.

The Settin' Up

Dere was a fellow that went to one of he fren's settin-up, and dis fren' was laid out dead on de coolin-board, and in some shape he want-ed to go an' relieve him, an' he got down to prayer. Had a crowd of peo-ple there, too. He was prayin' dere wid he eyes shut, and he say, "Lord be wid dis deceased brother, he gone, he is dead; if it be thy will raise him; if it is not thy will, God, save his soul. God, he leaves all he sis-ters, he brothers, he companions here behind him. God, be wid him, have mercy on him, save his soul. Father, it is within they power to raise him, it is within they power to save him. Lord, go with his be-reaved family he leff behin'."

An' as he was down dere prayin', wid he eye shut, de man on de cool-in' board raise up, an' set up, an' de people saw him an' slipped out an' sneaked out, an' he still prayin' an' he raise up an open he eyes an' sawed no people but de dead man in front of him an' he backed off de dead man an' grabbed up a ax, an he say:

"If you don't wait till I git out of here I'll finish killin' you."

An' ever since den mens has been more perticular 'bout what dey ax God to do.

The Little Old Man on the Gray Mule

TAD: Wuh you run in here like you guh bus' your brains out fer? Is anything atter you?

BRUSER: I see sumpen en it frighten me.

TAD: Wuh you see?

BRUSER: I have been passin theu the Big Pea Ridge woods en I seems to hear the leaf cracklin'. I ain' know if I hear um ur no, but I sho I see sumpen, en I ain' know how I feel, en when I look I see a man runnin', wid he clothes tored mighty nigh off him en he eye red en he tongue hang out like dog. He look like he all tored up. And while I look he pass out of sight. Before I can get myself straight I seen a houn' dog wid he nose to de groun' trailin', and he pass on. And I see a pack of dog en dey pass me en dey all look like dey barkin' on a trail, but dey ain't make no soun'. And atter while here come a little man wid he long hair on his shoulder, yaller, ridin' a gray mule, and he bent over he mule en he look like he whoopin' to he dog, and he pass on, and de moon look brighter, and de tree shadder look darker, and de frosts on de leaf look like snow. And I ain' move for a while and it look like my heart guh froze I been so frighten. And den I lef' and I ain't want stay no longer, and I ain't wan' go dere no more.

VOICE: Who you reckon it been?

BRUSER: I ain't know.

OLD DANIEL: Is dis de fust time you hear about de old man wid he gray mule and he houn' dog, and de runnin' nigger?

TAD: Tell we.

OLD DANIEL: Way back in slavery time old Marster's Daddy had a little yaller nigger. De old folks says he had heap uh nigger. He had nigger he raise, and he had wild nigger, and when dese niggers been unruly and git punished some of dem run off and de little yaller nigger wid de gray mule's business been to run um wid he dog. Dat been he juty and dat been he pleasure, to say he ain' love nothen but he mule and he houn' and he old marster. And dey say dey ain' certain he love he old marster but he want to be friend wid him so he can have he pleasure. And in dem times in all de hours in de cold nights of winter and in de hot nights of summer and when de flowers is bloomin' or when de leaves is fallin' you could hear de little yaller man wid de gray mule whoopin' to he houn'. You could hear de dog trailin' and you knowed a nigger was in 'stress. And when he horn blow you knowed de race was done. And de little yaller man look kind and talk easy, and he look like he wouldn't harm nothen, but he heart, if he had a heart, been cruel as de teet' of de houn'.

TAD: Wuh make runnin' nigger wid houn' and punishin' 'um give him pleasure?

OLD DANIEL: Jesus knows. I ain' know. Ain't nobody know, but it is mighty hard to understand the minds of mens.

VOICE: Un' Daniel, wuh he runnin' nigger now fer?

OLD DANIEL: Dat he sperrit. And all you see, de nigger wid he tongue hangin' out, de little yaller nigger wid de gray mule, all dem is de sperrits of dead mens and beasts and dey'll never git no rest. Dey punishment is to keep on runnin'. Dey run in slavery days. Dey's runnin' now, and dey'll be runnin' when you is kivered up in de groun'. And dey can be seen in de dark woods when a bright moon is shinin' and de frost in on de leaf, and de people and critters of de worl' is asleep. Dey 'pears as a warnin' to mens.

The Lake of the Dead

TAD: De big swamp draws people like a trap draws flies, an' people dies in de big swamps like flies dies in traps. Dey's all kind o' unknown critters an' varmints an' trees an' herbs an' pison, an' you meets unknown men an' ain' know wey dey come from an' you ain't know wey dey gwine. Dey ain' right an' dey takes on de ways of things dat ain't nat'ral.

KIKE: Dey is dang'ous. Ole man July tells me dere is one place in de big swamp ain' nobody know wey it is, but if you wanders far enough an' long enough, you is sho to fin' it an' you don't come back.

TAD: I is heared 'bout dat place. It's a lake o' water wey all humans an' beasts perish on its shores.

KIKE: Tad, you sho is heared 'bout it. When I been chillun, de ole folks ain' 'lowed we to talk 'bout it, it was so fright'nin'. I heared it were a place wey nothin' can live, an' if it do live, it ain' never come back nat'ral. Humans loses dey minds, an' beasts never does act like other beasts, an' dey says its shores is strewed wid de dead, a hog one place an' a cow, here a little bird an' sometime it ain' nothin' but a bug. An' dead men lie dere, an' ain' nobody ever sees life cepen dreadful things.

Dey say dey is always one an' sometimes two or three buzzards walkin' through over an' 'round de dead. Sometimes a buzzard will be settin' on a log, an' sometimes day will be slowly walkin' 'round like dey ain' dere for no purpose but to make de place look more dreadful. Dey don't seems to have to eat de food dat's put 'efore 'em, an' dey looks like somen dat's dead wid de power to walk slow an' dey walks like dey counts dey footsteps, an' dey footsteps is de footsteps of de dead. Once in a while dey shake dey self an' streches out dey neck an' makes a sound dat makes your blood creep like dey was tryin' to make things as worse for your hearin' as it is dreadful for your eyes.

A beast will walk to de edge of de water an' raise his head an' poke he head way out an' look 'cross de lake, an' den he sinks down. Some beasts draws back, an' all seems to have de feelin' of another world creepin' on 'em. An' mens is de same way, but dey mind takes 'em wuh dey nature tells 'em to go back. Why it is an' wuh it is ain' nobody know, but don't seek it, my brother, don't seek it.

VOICE: Who guh seek such a place, Un' Kike?

KIKE: My brother, mens seeks many things an' strange places way dey got no business seekin', an' many falls into danger an' mens an' beasts stumble on hard things an' de big swamps breaks men. Some places is worser dan other places. Stay 'way, my brother, stay 'way from de path of de buzzard; for ef you walks in dey path an' wanders too far, you'll land on de shores of de Lake of de Dead, an' men has walked on de shores of dis lake.

Murder vs. Liquor

SCIP: Well, things is gettin' wusser.

TAD: How come?

SCIP: White folks been havin' such a time killin' niggers in self-defense dey gettin' a taste fer killin' white folks de same way.

TAD: Wuh you talkin' 'bout, Scip, hush!

SCIP: My mind has been runnin' on de law and de cotes. I just been ramblin' a little.

TAD: Wuh law and cotes, dey ain't never ought to have a law 'gainst killin' niggers.

SCIP: Dey claims to have a law against killin' both white folks and niggers, but sometimes de law protects 'em an' ain't l'um be try.

TAD: Dey send ole man Reuben to the penitentiary fer seven months fer a little liquor.

VOICE: Dey got to broke up liquor.

SCIP: Reuben were a nigger an' hab liquor an' dat were de jedge in de big cote. Ain't he de law?

TAD: How come you say ain't he de law, and wuh you talk 'bout liquor for? You started off talkin' 'bout murder, now you gone to liquor.

SCIP: Dey always punish fer liquor, an' de law 'lows killin', an' I ain't been talkin' 'bout no murder.

TAD: How come you say dat. You better hush your mout'.

SCIP: Ain't I hear de jedge tell de jury to bring in a verdict of not guilty. He tell 'em dey can't try dis man. He guh pertec' him kase de law got de right to go in anybody house, day or night, rouse him out, and kill him if he try to 'fend he-self. All de officer got to do is to tell de jedge he were huntin' liquor.

TAD: Ain't he got to find it?

SCIP;: He can say he find it. He can say wuh he have a mind to say.

TAD: Scip, you ain't talkin' 'bout de big cote, is you?

SCIP: No, I ain't talkin' 'bout de big cote. I jes sayin' de jedge is a great man and he can go against God if he got a mind to. He helt up de law, and de law is de law!

TAD: Have mercy! Jesus!

SCIP: De jedge guh say wuh he guh say, an' he guh do wuh he guh do, an' he guh broke up liquor.

TAD: How 'bout murder?

SCIP: I ain't say nothin' 'bout murder. I been talkin' 'bout liquor, an' de jedge is de law. When de jedge say dey ain't no murder, I ain't guh say dey is. De jedge know he business, an' I know mine, an' my business is to keep my eye wide open an' to keep my mout' shet tight, else if I got to open it I guh let my chune be he is a hones' jedge. He guh kill liquor! He guh kill liquor! He guh pertect everything in he cote from de louse in de witness box on uppass heself. He de law an' he guh broke up liquor. I ain' say nothin' 'bout no murder. Is killin' a man in he house at night murder when dey's huntin' liquor? It ain't matter how dey kill him if dey is huntin' liquor.

TAD: Scip, you is right. Murder is one thing, and liquor is another.

SCIP: An' de jedge is de jedge, an' de law mus' be helt up. De jedge is a great man. He is a hones' man. He know he business an' he guh broke up liquor.

Old Dictodemus

LEADER: Brothers and sisters, Brother March will preach to you tonight, and he words is always full of meanin' and dey ain't no fool words. Dey got dey meanin' and if you listen good, you will see he p'int. He tell you wuh he tell for de understandin' of colored folks. Brother March speaks our language and he speaks in words of wisdom.

BROTHER MARCH: 'Way back yonder when Paul and Jesus and other great mens was in de world and was trying' to save sinners from a burnin' hell, dere was men dat thought dey self bigger dan anybody else. Some un 'em had heared of Jesus, and some un 'em aint' know nothin' 'bout him, and if dey is know, dey try to discount him. But, my brothers, Jesus ain't been a man for nobody to discount. He were a man ain't never git mad; he was such a man he could grab a lion by de head and wring it off jes like you would wring a chicken's neck. He was such a man he could reach out one hand and grab de top off a mountain and throw it 'cross de world. Dat's de kind er man Jesus was.

And dere was a man in dem times dey called him Dictodemus. He were a great bad man. He defied God and man, all two un 'em, and laugh 'bout it. He was a man was always fightin' and beatin' up people but one day ole Dictodemus, dis great bad man, run into de wrong man—he met he match. He tried to put his self up against Capt'n Jesus. He ain't know it was Jesus, but it ain't take long to find out.

Well, Jesus ain't waste much time on Dictodemus, he had so much other things he was 'tendin' to. Ole Dictodemus got so humble he start to slippin' 'round at night tryin' to creep up to Jesus' tent, but Jesus run him off, he wants to git him when de right time comes. He wants to tes' him out.

One day he met Dictodemus in a lonely spot on de big road, and he stopped and had a talk wid him. Jesus been ridin' a little mule ain't no bigger dan a mouse, and he dismount and he say to Dictodemus, "Mount." And Dictodemus look at de little critter and sorter hold back, and Jesus say, "Mount." And Dictodemus mounted and rode a long distance into de holy city of Jerusalem, and when he git dere, de little mule stopped right in de heart of de city in de front of de temple, and Dictodemus say to de little mule, "Go on." And de little mule shake he self two or three times and started to buckin' and jumpin', and he th'owed Dictodemus clean out er sight, and when he landed he were on de back of sompen, he ain't know wuh it were. It had horns like a goat, but it ain't no goat; it had years like a cow, but it ain't no cow; it had a mouth like a hog, but it ain't no hog. And Dictodemus' mind been all angled up, he ain't know wuh it were; he ain't know wuh happen, he ain't know he self when Jesus appeared and hold up he hands and say, "Let dere be peace." And den he stepped back on he little mule and rode out to Jerusalem wid Dictodemus followin' behind on he foots tame as a dog.

EXCITED SISTER: (Shrieking at the top of her voice)
Oh, Lord! Oh, Lord! Oh, Lord, My Jesus!
It must a been a mule!
It must a been a mule!
It must a been a mule!
CONGREGATION: (Chanting):
It must a been a mule!
It must a been a mule!
It must a been a mule!

Ole Man Rogan

BALTI: Ain't had so much luck since we been fishin' here. Dis here place done fish out.

TUNGA: Less we lef' here and go to Boggy Gut. Ain't nobody fish much dere.

OLD BILL: I rudder stay here and don't have so much fish. I never is think too much of Boggy Gut.

TUNGA: How come you ain't want to go to Boggy Gut?

OLD BILL: Is you 'member hearin' 'bout Ole Man Rogan name call?

BALTI: I hear Ole Man Rogan name call, but ain't know nothin' 'bout him. Tell we.

OLD BILL: Ole Man Rogan nuse to sell nigger in slavery time. Dat's wey he nuse to fishin', and every time he come for res' he come to Boggy Gut. Ole Man Rogan a man wid curious ways. He ain't beat a nigger much, and he guin him plenty to eat, and he bring 'em here in drove and he have 'em chained together, but he have curious ways and he ain't have but one pleasure,—settin' fishin'. He always buy ooman wid chillun, and ooman wid husband, and ain't nobody can buy from Ole Man Rogan mother and chile or man and ooman. He great pleasure been to part. He always love to take er baby away from he ma and sell it, and take he ma somewhere else and sell her, and ain't luh 'em see one another again. He love to part a man and he ooman, sell de man one place and sell de ooman another, and dat look like all Ole Man Rogan live for, and when he ain't 'casion 'stress dat er way, he been onrestless. He love to see a man wid he head bowed down in 'stress, and he love to see chillun holdin' out dey arms cryin' for dey mother, and he always looked satisfied when he see tear runnin' down de face of er ooman when she weepin' for her chile.

And Ole Man Rogan die on Boggy Gut, and ever since den he sperrit wander and wander from Boggy Gut to de river and wander 'cross de big swamps to Congaree. Whether it be God or whether it be devil, de sperrit of Ole Man Rogan ain't got no res'. Some time in de night ef you'll set on Boggy Gut, you'll hear de rattle of chains, you hear a baby cry every which er way, and you hear a mother callin' for her chile in de dark night on Boggy Gut.

And you kin set on de edge of Boggy Gut and you'll see mens in chains bent over wid dey head in dey hands,—de signs of 'stress. While you sets you see de sperrit of Ole Man Rogan comin' 'cross de big swamps. You see him look at de womens and mens and chillun, and you see him laugh—laugh at de 'stress and de tears on Boggy Gut, and he laugh like he satisfied, but he ain't had no res'. And when he stayed a minute on Boggy But, to de river 'cross de big swamps and back again he wanders, on de edge of Boggy Gut.

The Yellow Crane

JUBE: Limus dead back in de swamp on Crane Lake.

SANDY: Wuh ail him?

JUBE: Him and Saber been seinin' back dere wid a gang of dem Free Issues, and dey all come out of de water. Limus stan' up on de edge of de lake and look out dere and look like he froze; he looked and stiffen he self and nod he head like he geein answer to somebody out in de water. Saber say he look like he git a call to come on and he ain't got to go less he gree, and he nod he head and stiffen he self like he see sompen ain't no human ever see 'efore, and den he shake all over and drap dead. And Saber say he ain't see a God's thing in dat lake but a monster big crane, a yaller crane.

He say it were a natural crane, but he been yaller wid eye like a goose, and he been dan a man and he had a bill longer dan de handle of a blacksmith's tongs. He say he noticed dat good, kase when Limus drap he seen him open he bill and work it like he were laughin'. He twis' he head dis way and dat and he ain't make a sound, but he wink he eye and ain't never shet it, but he half close it. It look like some kind of evil sperrit lookin' through a crack in de side of he head. He said dat ole bird guin him de ague.

Den he say dat crane rumple up he feather and shake he self. He start walkin' straight to wey Limus lay. He say he look at him good. He look like a crane and he look like a man, like a ole man yaller wid a beard, and he look evil and he look like de father of death. And he walk up to wey Limus lay and stoop down 'side him and put he head close to Limus' head like he listenin' to sompen. Den he twis' he head one side and look at him careful and laugh widout makin' a sound. Den he step 'cross Limus and put he foot on him like he scorn him, den he reach 'round his self like a man pullin' a cloak 'round him and walk out 'cross de big swamp wid he head drawed up. He look more sinful dan sin. He look satisfied and he look like he were in misery. Saber say he ain't know wuh to make of how he look, he look so much diff'ent kind of way.

SANDY: Wuh de ole Issue do?

JUBE: I axe Saber and he say he look and he seen all dem Issue walkin' off through de swamp, and dey ain't say nothin' and dey ain't look like humans. He say he ain't call 'em and ain't wan call 'em. He say de swamp look evil wid de yaller mud from de high water up on de trees higher 'an a man's head, and shadows from de trees and flies and things flyin' 'round. And up in de air a hawk been sailin' 'round and a buzzard way up dere in de sky; and through de yaller swamp de yaller crane and de goose eye yaller Issue was passin' in de distance mixin' wid everything else dat were yaller, and passin' dis way comin' into sight one minute and fadin' de nex' till dey all was swallowed up and everything were like it were not in a human world.

Saber say it were dreadful, and ef it had er las' much longer, he would er drap down dead like Limus done. He say he ain't know how he git home, and he know he days is shortened.

KIKE: You all ain't got no sense. You ain't heared 'bout de yaller crane of Crane Lake? Wuh you reckon dey call dat place Crane Lake for?

VOICE: Wuh?

KIKE: It been Crane Lake way back in slavery time when my granddaddy's pa been chillun, and it ain't never been no place for crane, scusin' de big yaller crane Saber see, and dat ain't been no crane.

Back in slavery time dey been a ole Issue who daddy sent him off to a furrin lan' for schoolin'. He sent him when he were chillun and he brung him back when he were a man. And dis here Issue been mighty smart wid heap er book and heap er larnin', and when he come back to de Sand Hill he been a doctor, and he live by he self. He had more sense 'an white folks and niggers both; he scorn everybody, nigger and white folks; and dey tells tales 'bout how he nuse to 'casion niggers to die. Dey say he ain't never miss a chance, and ain't nobody ketch him. White folks was feared on him wusser 'an nigger, and he look like he ain't got no nuse for Issue, but dey say he ain't harm 'em.

And he nuse to walk in de big swamp, and de ole folks says he would stan' on Crane Lake and laugh at he own weeked ways, and he were satisfied when some folks died; and he been full of misery for he self and everybody, but a real nigger were pison to him, and he were pison to de nigger. He hair were straight and he been goose eye and he look like a crane and he wored a long black cloak. He died on Crane Lake and many slavery time niggers die on Crane Lake, and dere is certain times when de yaller crane is seen, and a nigger always die and dey is enticed dere by Free Issues wid one excuse or another.

VOICE: Un' Kike, you done guin me a chill. Wuh he have 'ginst niggers?

KIKE: I ain't know. De ole folks says dat de way dey come to be Free Issues dat white womens were dey mammy and niggers were dey daddy, and de law ain't 'low de chillun of a white ooman to be a slave; and a new lookin' race of goose eye niggers was created, and dey had minds of dey own and ways of dey own. Dey was discounted by white folks and dey was scorned by niggers.

And now I done tell you de first start of Issues and dey creatin'. I ain't know no more and I ain't guh say no more.

Ruint

TAD: Is you hear de tale 'bout Ella?

VOICE: Wuh Ella?

TAD: Ella up to de white folks' yard.

VOICE: Wuh 'bout Ella?

TAD: You know Ella been raise up mighty proper. She ain' run 'round wid no mens. Ack like she ain' got no nuse for 'em.

SCIP: I ain' never pay no 'tention to no lie like dat. She ooman, ain't she? Mens is mens, ain't dey?

TAD: Well, she ack dat er way.

SCIP: She ack dat er way.

VOICE: Wuh de tale?

TAD: It ain't no tale. Ella been a apple in de white folks' yard. Dey 'pend on her. An' atter she been dere God knows how long, she disappear an' ain' say a word an' ain' nobody know wey Ella.

Well, all dese niggers had a excursion an' went to Wilmington, an' Janey—you know old man Jube' gal Janey—say she went on de excursion an' been standin' on de street cornder waitin' for de streetcar. An' she say she see a ooman all dress up wid fine clothes an' high-heel shoes wid ribbon all over her, an' more paint an' talcum powder 'an you ever heared of. An' she look at her an' she say it look like somebody she know. An' Janey say she walk up a little closer an' take her time an' look good. An' she say she walk up to de ooman an' say:

"Ain't dis Ella?"

An' de gal say:

"Sho', dis Ella."

An' Janey say:

"In de name er God, wey you been? Everybody been axen 'bout you."

An' Ella say:

"Ain't you hear de news? I been ruint."

From Nigger to Nigger, by E. C. L. Adams, New York, Scribners, 1928.

CHURCHES, PREACHERS, AND DEACONS

The church setting and the preacher have always had a strong attraction for the Negro storyteller, not only in the United States but in the English-speaking islands of the Caribbean as well. The church service was an occasion to see diverse people together, to measure them against each other and against what was known or surmised about their private lives. There was the bad neighbor, singing and clapping as loud as any other. Up front, a step or two from the mourners' bench, was the hypocrite. To one side, the liar and cheat, and to the other the proud. A showcase gathering of the saved and the undone sinners, of those who believed and those who came to play safe, and of those who came just to see what was going on. As Richard Amerson said (see p. 504), "We got everything in our church. We got some dogs in there. We got hogs in there. We got cows a-lowin' in there. . . ." The church elders, the deacon, the preacher, all were measured for their strengths and human weaknesses. For the storyteller the church was a bonanza, and with the seasoning of humor, any event, rumored or real, true or apocryphal, could be transformed into a yarn worth telling. The preacher, as the leader, invoker and interpreter, was the most vulnerable of all to caricature, but he frequently had the last word. In fact, it was a preacher in Alabama who told the story, "Devil in Church," and a preacher in Philadelphia who narrated "Balaam's Ass."

Devil in Church

Of all the places you expect you might meet up with the Devil, you never figure to see him in church, now, do you? But the Devil have a lot of experience, and he say you got to fight fire with fire, water with water, and wind with wind. He don't *have* to hang around places like Sodom and Gomorrah, 'cause he ain't needed there. Folks in those places already doin' his bad work for him. 'Nother thing, the Devil can't always go around *lookin'* like the Devil. If he did that, he ain't goin' to get nowhere. He got to pass himself off like ordinary people. Sometimes he even got to pray and shout like he been saved. Now there ain't

---

This tale and the two that follow, "Preacher and the Devil" and "What the Preacher's Talking About," are from Terrapin's Pot of Sense, © 1957 by Harold Courlander, by permission of Holt, Rinehart and Winston.

nothin' more against the Devil's nature than that, is there? I'll tell you what I mean.

Well, one day the Devil looked around and say, "Sure is quiet around here. Ain't nothin' bad happenin' today. Guess I'll make some trouble."

So he picked out one small half-sized Devil and tell him, "Boy, you go on up there and corrupt some folks today, make 'em mean and sinful. Get goin' now."

This Little Devil, he got dressed up, tucked his tail in good, and went up to find some folks to make 'em sinful. He got to town just about church time on Sunday. When he saw all the folks goin' into church, he say, "Looks to me like I got to go in there after those people."

So he went into church and sat down in the back row, waitin' till the service was over. Preacher preached, people moaned and shouted, and the Little Devil just sat and waited. When service was over, the Little Devil got busy runnin' around tryin' to corrupt folks by tellin' them to do bad things. But they didn't pay him no mind, sayin', "Don't believe we ever see you around here before, Brother." Well, the Little Devil got mighty discouraged after a while and went home.

"You corrupt a lot of good folks up there?" the Big Devil ask him.

"Uh-uh," the Little Devil say.

"Well," the Big Devil say, kind of mad, "what you spend all your time at?"

"I went up just like you told me," the Little Devil say. "All the folks were goin' to church, so I went in and sat in the back row till they got through. And then wouldn't no one talk to me after that."

Big Devil he just shook his head, lookin' kind of sad at the Little Devil, like he was pretty stupid. "Man," he say, "don't you know that if you goin' to get along, you got to fight fire with fire, water with water, iron with iron, and air with air? You got to do what the *other* folks do. If you goin' to church to do your work, you can't sit in the back row. You got to get up on the mourner's bench and shout and moan and groan with the rest of them. If you'd done that, wouldn't nobody have said they hadn't never seen you before. If you playin' baseball with the folks, you got to hit a home run to win their respect. If you doin' it with music, you got to make 'em dance. And if you doin' it in church, you really got to get sanctified. Man, you sure got a lot to learn."

Preacher and the Devil

If you goin' to stand there and allow as you saw a bear sittin' on Uncle Jim's porch readin' a newspaper, that calls for some close examination. Could be you got yourself *influenced* into thinkin' you saw it. Could be there was a real bear there too, but 'tain't likely. I see plenty of bears in my time, and ain't none of 'em learned their letters. The way

people are, they're always tryin' to see something other folks ain't seen,
and that's a powerful influence on the imagination. And if they gets a
little boost from the Devil, ain't no tellin' what they goin' to come up
with.

Like the time the Devil was moseyin' around tryin' to figure out
some devilment to do. He done so many devilments in his time he
couldn't hardly think of no new ones. Then he see the preacher comin'
along the road, and he say to himself, "Man, I got a good one to do on
the preacher. I'm goin' to get him to tell about the biggest lie folks
around here ever heard."

So he tucked his tail inside his clothes good and act mighty sweet.
When the preacher come along he say, "Mornin', Reverend, mighty
fine mornin'."

"Yeah, Brother, it sure is," Preacher say. "You a stranger 'round
here?"

"Just passin' through," the Devil say, "reckon I'll be around till
Monday or Tuesday."

"Well, ain't that nice," Preacher say. "You'll be right welcome at
church tomorrow."

"That's sure nice of you," Devil say. "What you going' to preach
on?"

"Brother," Preacher say, "David and Goliath is my text for tomorrow."

"That sounds fine to me," Devil say. "How big you 'spects that
Goliath was?"

"Well, Brother, he was sure bigger'n you or me. I reckon he might
have stood about nine feet tall."

Devil shook his head. "Well, that's a disappointment to me. You
know things was a lot bigger in them old days. Everything was different. Take Methuselah, now didn't he live nine hundred years? If you
say a man around here live to one hundred, that's pretty old; but if you
talkin' about Methuselah, one hundred years ain't nothin'. If you tell
folks that Goliath was only nine feet tall, they ain't goin' to be impressed. If you want to get that congregation of yours rockin' and reelin', you got to make things real big, what I mean."

Devil he went on talkin' this way, Preacher listenin' and takin' it all
in.

"I tell you what," Preacher say, "you goin' to be there tomorrow, you
just set in the front row and give me the nod. If you think somethin' got
to be a little bigger, bob your head up and down, and I'll be much
obliged."

"Fine," the Devil say, "I'll set right in the front row."

Next mornin' was Sunday and when the preacher get up there to
preach, he see this stranger sittin' right in the front row showin' all his
teeth.

Preacher open up his Bible, slap his hand on the table, and begin.

"This mornin' we goin' to talk about David the shepherd boy,"
Preacher say, "right from the First Book of Samuel. This boy David

was the son of Jesse; and he was pretty sharp. And the Philistines was comin' down on the Israelites, and they had a champion fighter 'mongst 'em name Goliath. Now, 'cordin' to the Good Book, the Philistines sent their champion out to the field to challenge the stoutest man 'mongst the Israelites to a fight. And he stood up there in the middle of the field and wasn't no Israelite wanted to fight him, 'cause Goliath was six cubits tall, and that make nine feet from head to toe."

Preacher he looked down in the first row to see what this stranger thinks, and he see the Devil bobbin' his head up and down. So the preacher think he can do a little better by Goliath, and he say: "Come to think of it, that nine feet was afore he was altogether full growed. He was eight cubits tall, and that make about twelve feet top to bottom." Preacher see the Devil still bobbin' his head. "But that was before he stretched himself out to his full height," Preacher tell the congregation. "You might say he was closer to fifteen or *twenty* feet altogether. Fact is, I'm pretty sure he was about as high as the steeple on the Presbyterian Church, and that was only when he was a little bit hunched down." Devil stopped bobbin' his head and showed his teeth, so Preacher relaxed a bit.

"Yes, Brothers and Sisters, and this man had a spear that weighed more'n fifty pounds, and the shaft was sixty feet long." Preacher looked down and see the Devil pushin' out his lips and shakin' his head up and down like he was mighty put out. So Preacher say: "But that's only 'cordin' to one way of lookin' at the matter. Another way of lookin' at it, that spear weighed around four hundred pounds and was as big around the shaft as that old elm tree out in front.

"Well, then, David the shepherd boy come out across the field with his slingshot and picked up a stone about as big as a buckshot . . ." Preacher see the Devil bobbin' his head like it was about to fall off. "Well, then, about as big as a watermelon," he say. Devil's head was still bobbin'. "Come to think of it, that stone was about as big as a bale of cotton, and if you figure the size of it, and made of stone all the way through, it must have weighed more'n a thousand pounds.

"And David the shepherd boy, only 'bout five feet four tall—or maybe only four foot five . . . or I guess you could say he was only about half that size—hit Goliath in the head with that stone from his slingshot and killed him dead. And when Goliath fell he was so tall he stretched out on the ground from Shochoh to Azekah."

Preacher looked sideways, and see the Devil bobbin' his head somethin' awful, so he say; "Old Goliath he stretched, you might say, from Shochoh to Jerusalem." Devil sat there still a-bobbin' away. "You might say Goliath stretched all the way from Shochoh to Mobile," Preacher say. "And if we don't adjourn this meetin' right now we goin' to have him layin' *right on top of us.*"

What the Preacher's Talking About

Now if a preacher can talk a lot, he can also talk a *little,* and I got in mind a particular preacher who come to church one Sunday mornin' and got up in the pulpit to preach. After the openin' prayer he stand up there, put on his specs, and open the book in front of him.

"Brothers and Sisters," he say, "good mornin' to you all. It's a sun-shiny world this mornin', and I likes the look of all those happy faces sittin' out there in front of me. Now I wonder if all you folks know what I'm goin' to preach to you about this day?"

Well, folks in church is always ready to answer the preacher, and they all call out, "No, Reverend, we don't know what you goin' to preach about."

When the preacher heard that, he took off his specs and look around the church, shakin' his head like he's mighty disappointed. He say, "Well, what use is it for me to preach to you, and you don't know what I'm talkin' about?" And he snap his book shut and went off the pulpit and went home.

Next Sunday the folks went to church early and stood around figurin' what to do. Lots of 'em come a long way to hear some preachin' and they don't want to be done out of it. After a while they got it all studied out what they goin' to tell the preacher that mornin'.

He gets up on the pulpit, lookin' in his book while the folks singin' the openin' prayer, then he stand up.

"Mornin' to you all, Brothers and Sisters, and a fine day it is. Now I ask you, do you know what I'm talkin' about this mornin'?"

That whole congregation holler back, "Yes, Reverend, we know."

When the preacher hear this, he snap his book shut and say: "'Pears to me that if you all know what I'm talkin' about, ain't no use of my sayin' a word."

And he went right off the pulpit, got in his carriage, and went home.

After that the congregation did some real serious studyin' about the situation. Looked like the preacher had 'em comin' and goin'. But next Sunday, when the service commenced, they was ready.

Preacher looked all around the church, from front to back and side to side. Then he put on his specs and say, "Mornin', Brothers and Sisters. Reckon you had somethin' to think on since I saw you last. Now I like to ask you, do you know what I'm talkin' about this mornin'?"

What happen then was one half the congregation rise up and say, "No, Reverend, we don't know what you preachin' 'bout this mornin'." And they sit down and the other half get up and say, "Yes, Reverend, we knows what you talkin' 'bout this mornin'."

Right then the preacher snapped his book closed and took off his specs again. "Seems to me," he say, "that half of you knows and half don't know. So if the half that knows will tell the half that don't know, it'll save me a powerful lot of time. So long."

The Bear Fight

Deacon Jones an' he gal live in a section of de country wey dere been a heap er bears. An' one night he been guine to an experience meetin', an' dere been two roads, an' he gal say:

"Papa, le's we don't go through de woods road, kaze I seen a bear dere today."

An' de deacon say:

"I ain' care notin' 'bout no bear. I a Christian an' loves God an' God loves me, an' I puts my trust in Him. I loves God. God is good. I'm guine through dem woods."

An' de gal say:

"Papa, le's we don't make no mistakes. Le's we go 'round."

An' de deacon say:

"I'm guine through dem woods. I trust God. I puts my faith in God. God is good an' will pertec' me."

An' de gal say:

"I ain' trustin' all dat. I'm guine 'round."

An' de deacon say:

"Well, I'm guine through de woods. God is my pertecter."

An' he went through de woods, an' de gal went 'round.

An' when de deacon git halfway through de woods, a bear jumped on him an' he had a terrible time fightin' wid dat bear. De bear tored mighty nigh all he clothes off, an' bit him up an' mighty nigh ruint him. But when he git loose, he made he way to de experience meetin'. An' when he git dere, dem niggers been tellin' 'bout dey experience wid God an' Jesus an de devil an' wid angels an' a passel er lies.

An' den dey spied Deacon Jones in de back er de congregation, an' dey call on him for his experience an' he say he ain' got nothin' to say. An' all dem brother an' all dem sister keep on hollerin' for him. An' atter while de deacon git up an' say:

"My brothers an' sisters, all I kin say is: God is good. God is good. I loves God. I sho' loves Him, an' I puts my faith in Him. God is good an' He'll help you in a lot er little things, but, my brothers an' sisters, good as God is, He ain' worth a damn in a bear fight."

Human Weakness

There was a big camp meeting going on over at Selma, one of the biggest they'd had for a long time. The preachers had come from all over, and they were spelling each other in the pulpit. First one would

From Nigger to Nigger, by E.C.L. Adams, New York, Scribner's, 1928.

"Human Weakness" and the five tales that follow—"The Card Game," "John and the Bear," "Go Down Below," "Balaam's Ass," and "Fattening the Calf"—are from the author's collection.

get up and give those people a sermon on Noah, then another would get up and preach on Jonah, and after him another one would preach on the Revelations of John the Revelator. The ones who weren't preaching at the moment sat behind and urged the preacher on. There was a lot of moaning, groaning, and jumping in the tent that day, and lots of folks being saved. After a while it got pretty hot, and the preachers gave a one-hour intermission so people could go get some lemonade and refresh themselves.

There were seven or eight preachers in the bunch, and they went next door, where they had pitched a small tent, and took off their coats and fanned themselves and had some lemonade. After they'd sat around a while, one of them said, "Brothers, we done a lot of talking this morning about the Good Book and human weakness. I got to say something on that. There ain't none of us is perfect in the sight of the Lord, and that includes us. I believe it would do us a powerful lot of good to humble ourselves and speak out on our own human weaknesses. Ain't that a fact?"

"Yes, Brother, it's the truth," the other preachers said, "ain't no one without a human weakness."

"Well, then," the first preacher said, "who want to begin?" Since no one else seemed ready to speak out on the subject of human weakness, he said, "Looks like I am the one got to get the ball rolling. Brothers, my human weakness is laziness. I can't tell you how lazy I get sometimes in doing the Lord's work. I don't mind putting in a *day,* mind you, but I get downright sluggish on the *overtime.* I surely got to reform myself."

"That," said another preacher, "ain't nothing at all compared to *my* human weakness, which is liquid corn. I just can't resist it. That's what my human weakness is all about, Brothers, and I'm a sorry man for it."

"Yes, that's bad, brother," another preacher said, "and I got something to match it. My weakness is gambling. That old Jack of Diamonds and Ace of Spades got me going. There ain't nothing makes me feel so good as playing cards at one dime a point. It sure give me shame to say it, but all Satan got to do is flash a deck at me and I'm lost."

"Brothers," the next preacher said, "we're all in need of reform, but of all the human weaknesses I heard of in here today, mine is the weakest. My problem is women. I just can't keep my mind off any good-looking gal, or any ugly gal neither. Seem like the Devil has got his hold on me for sure."

Every one of those preachers testified what was on his mind, all except one who never said a word. And at last the one who started the testifying in the first place said to him, "Well, Brother John, we heard from everybody except you. Ain't you going to join in?"

Brother John said, "Yes, I been thinking on it, but my weakness is a bad one."

"Ain't nothing too bad for the Lord to hear," the first one said. "Get on with it, Brother John."

Brother John said, "Brothers, my weakness ain't just *bad,* it's *terrible.*"

"Tell it out," one of the preachers said, "it'll wash your soul clean."

"I sure hate to tell you," Brother John said, "but my human weakness is *gossip,* and I can't hardly wait to get out of here."

The Card Game

They were having a big baptizing down by the riverside one time, and there was this boy named Billy. His mamma intended to see to it that Billy got baptized. Billy didn't care much for that because he didn't care whether he was saved or not. But his mamma said he got to do it, and she made sure he was there when the immersion began. There was a big crowd at the river, people who belonged to the church, and a great many of them were waiting their turn. Billy sort of faded out of sight. He and his friend Walt found a shady place in the trees, and Walt pulled out a deck of cards. They started playing poker, but they hadn't been at it long when Billy's mamma started to look for him. "That boy of mine got to be immersed," she said, "even if I have to drag him out in the river by myself."

After a while she came to the trees, and she kept calling out Billy's name. Billy and his friend Walt shoved their cards inside their shirts. When Billy's mamma found them she started scolding right away. She took her boy by the ear and marched him down to the water. "Get in there," she said, "and don't come back till you've been totally sanctified."

Two Brothers in Christ caught Billy by the arms and pulled him out to the deep water where the preacher was waiting. "Welcome, son," the preacher told him. "Welcome to the bosom of the church." And he took hold of Billy and pushed him down into total immersion, saying, "In the name of the Father. . . ." While Billy was still under water a card came loose from his shirt and floated to the top. It was an ace of hearts. Preacher looked at it then pulled Billy's head out. "In the name of the Son," he said, and pushed Billy's head down again. This time the ace of spades floated up and rode the river right under the preacher's nose. The third time Billy went down, with the preacher saying, ". . . the Holy Ghost," the ace of diamonds came out of his shirt.

Billy's mamma was standing there at the riverside and she saw those cards on top of the water. "Oh, my Lord," she said, "my poor boy Billy is lost forever!"

The preacher was standing there in the deep water studying those cards. And he said, "Sister, do not grieve so. With a hand like *that,* your boy Billy is *anything* but lost."

John and the Bear

There was this man named John who never went to church, and folks was saying he was an undone sinner. Fact is, John loved hunting more than being saved, and whilst other people was in church rocking and reeling he was out looking for rabbit and quail and such, or else sleeping on the riverbank. Soon one Sunday morning he took his shotgun and headed for the woods to hunt for something, but he didn't have no luck. Didn't see no rabbits or nothing else. So when he come to the river he lean his gun on a big tree there and laid down and shut his eyes. Before he know it he was asleep.

When John wake up he see a great big grizzly setting there twixt him and his gun. That bear was looking John over from head to feet making up his mind which end to tackle first. John stood up and backed off a little, but he couldn't get far that way cause the river was behind him. So he edged along the bank, inching himself away, and kept going like that till the bear got up and started to come after him. Then John sold out. He went tearing through the woods so fast he had to kick a couple of rabbits out of his way, but every time he looked back he saw that grizzly about four steps behind. Well, what he already done was nothing to what he started to do then. He was going so fast he sucked wind and leaves right off the trees. But when he looked around he saw the grizzly was still on his tail.

Now this John he ain't never prayed much in his life, but when he saw the way things was he just nachurly began to pray. He say, "Lord, get me out of this and I promise to go to church every Sunday!" He looked around and saw the bear still after him. Say, "Lord, I mean what I say! *Every* Sunday beginning *today!*" Well, he come out of the woods then right near the church. When he look around he see that bear was gone. And soon as he catch his breath he went on to the church and walked right in.

Preacher see John in the door. "Halleluja!" he say. "The lost is found, and the prodigal son is home to Jesus! Welcome, brother, welcome. But how come you here this morning, and why is you breathing so hard?"

John say, "Reverend, I just been chased five miles by a grizzly, and the Lord directed me here."

Preacher say, "Thank God you hear the Lord's voice, brother. But about that grizzly, maybe he didn't chase you as far as you say?"

"Five miles, Reverend," John say, "maybe six, and he was on my heels all the way."

"Come, come, brother," Reverend say. "Now, we knows how fast a grizzly can go and we knows how fast a man can go. Ain't no man can outrun a grizzly."

"In the ordinary sense a man can't outrun a grizzly, that's the truth," John say. "But you see, Reverend, in this case I was running on dry ground and that grizzly wasn't."

Go Down Below

There was this preacher, and he had one special sermon for the brothers and sisters, it was, "Sinners, if you want to find Jesus, go down below." That's from the Bible, directly. But this preacher never had no other text. He get up there every Sunday morning and say to the church, "What I'm going to preach about this morning is, 'Sinners, if you want to find Jesus, go down below.'" And it got so that the people knew the sermon from back to front, and whenever the preacher said, "Sinners, if you want to find Jesus," they sort of sung back to him, "Go down below." But they was some folks got pretty tired of that same old sermon, and they talked to the preacher about it. They said, "We sure like to find Jesus, but ain't there any other way? We sure like to hear a different sermon next Sunday."

The preacher tell them, "I appreciate your feelings on the subject, Brothers and Sisters, but I got one main text. Didn't John the Baptist have one main text, telling the people to repent because the Kingdom of Heaven is at hand? So do I have one great message to move you in the right direction, 'If you want to find Jesus, go down below.'" So that's the way it was next Sunday and the Sunday after that.

And there was a crow got in the church and made a nest in there, and it got used to hearing the words "go down below." One Sunday morning this crow fluttered down and set on the back of a chair next to where the preacher was preaching. He look the congregation over and say, "Go down below! Yaaak, go down below!" That's just what the preacher did. He left his Good Book right there on the pulpit and went down below where all the brothers and sisters was, and he kept right on going till he reached the door and just about tore the handle off getting out. The brothers and sisters about ran each other down following the preacher and they went through the door five at a time, with another five right on their heels, everybody shouting and crying "Amen!" and "Let me out next."

That talking crow got pretty upset with all the commotion and goings on, started to fly this way and the other, and he come down and set on a man's shoulder. He look the man in the face and said it again, "Go down below! Go down below!" This man's legs wanted to run but he couldn't move, just stood there like a fence post. The crow looked him in the eye and give him the text once more, "Go down below!"

The man tell him in a pitiful voice, "Thank you, Brother, but this ain't my regular congregation. Most times I go to the Primitive Baptist, and I reckon I can handle it better over there, cause they only got one preacher at a time telling the brothers and sisters what to do."

Balaam's Ass

One Sunday morning the preacher was sermonizing on Balaam and his ass. He say Balaam this and Balaam that, and his ass go this way and that way and don't do what Balaam want him to do, and Balaam hit his ass hard two-three times. And when the sermonizing was over and folks was leaving church, preacher stood at the door shaking hands, saying, "Come again next week, Brother, mighty fine to see you today Sister." Folks tell him, "Sure liked your sermon this morning, Reverend," and all that, until one man name of Jack Hawkins come along. This man been sitting all through the service looking sour about the whole thing. He tell the preacher, "Reverend, it was a powerful sermon you preach today, except for that one word."

"What word you talking about, Brother?"

"What I'm talking about, Reverend," Jack Hawkins tell him, "it's that word ass you been saying in your sermon. It surely surprise me to hear you saying it from the pulpit in the House of God."

Preacher put his hand on Jack Hawkins' shoulder. "Uncle Jack," he tell him, "don't think no more about it. That word don't mean what you think it mean."

"Don't it?" Jack say. "I am mighty glad to hear it. But what can it mean except what it mean?"

"In the Good Book," preacher tell him, "there is quite a few words that have a different sense. When the Good Book says *ass,* in particular when it speak of *Balaam's ass,* it don't mean what you got on your mind. What it really mean is a jack mule like the one you do your plowing with. When the Good Book say Balaam is riding on his ass, that mean his jack mule he is setting on. You get the point? When Balaam strike his ass he is encouraging his jack mule to move on. When Balaam get contrite and brush the dust off his ass, that mean he is grooming his jack mule. You got to know the language of the Good Book."

Jack Hawkins tell the preacher he is mighty glad to hear it, and how he sure enjoyed the sermon. After that he shake hands and go home in his wagon.

Well, about three-four weeks later something happened on Jack Hawkins' place. His jack mule took sick and died. Jack Hawkins' cotton was planted right to the fence, and he don't have any idea where he was going to bury that mule till his wife tell him, "Jack, bury it at the fence out by the road." So he take his shovel and went out to the fence and began to dig.

Just then the preacher come riding along in his gig. When he see Jack digging there he stop, say, "Morning, Brother, ain't it a mighty fine day for doing fine work?"

"It's a fact, Reverend."

"Ain't see you in church for a couple of weeks," preacher tell him. "Glad to see you are all right."

"Yes, Reverend, you might say as I am all right," Jack Hawkins say, his head down and digging.

"It's a blessing to see you working so," preacher said. "It's easy to see you don't let no grass grow under your feet. What are you digging there, a post hole?"

"Post hole?" Jack Hawkins say, scratching his head. "No, Reverend, this ain't no post hole. Leastwise that ain't what the Good Book call it."

Fattening the Calf

One time they was getting ready to build a new church to replace the old one, and the preacher made special mention every Sunday that it goin' to cost them some money. He tell the congregation they can put something in a special envelope and mark it "new church" and leave it on the table in a certain place, or they can give it to one of the brothers or sisters responsible for the collection. Some folks did one thing and some another, but this one man named Sam didn't do neither, and every time he hear the preacher say "new church" he pulled his head inside his collar like a terrapin. And after a while folks got to gossiping that Sam aint give nothin' to buildin' the new church, and it don't look like he goin' to do it at all.

But the preacher say, never mind, he goin' to have a little talk with Sam to agitate his conscience a little. And one time the preacher was out Sam's way and he stop to talk to him. He say, "Brother, you sure doing good with your crops and everything. Don't you feel like sharing a little with the Lord?"

Sam reckoned as he was nigh to cornered. He tell the preacher as how he lost one mule a couple of months ago, and another gone lame. Also his rheumatism been givin' him plenty trouble and he got to buy medicine for that, and the weevils got in his cotton, and hard cash money is hard to come by, all that sort of thing.

Preacher say ain't it too bad, some of the tests the Lord gives us, but he say Sam don't have to pay cash for the new church, maybe he just make a pledge.

When Sam hear that, he felt a mite better. He say, "Yes, Reverend, that's what I can do, make a pledge, long as it ain't cash. How do I do it?"

Reverend look around and his eyes fall on one of Sam's calves. "Well," he say, "there's that bull calf over there. He's mighty scrawny right now, but fat him up and he could bring a few dollars. Why don't you pledge that bull calf? In a few months or so, when you sell him, you can give the proceeds to the church fund."

"Yes, Reverend," Sam say, "I'll take a pledge on that." And after the preacher was gone, Sam slap his knees and tell hisself, "Well, I sure got out of that one."

A couple of months went by and that bull calf got bigger. Sam tell hisself, "Lessen I sell that calf I don't have to give no proceeds." One time a man say to Sam, "I hear you goin' to fat a calf and give the proceeds for the new church." One time a sister will tell him, "Ain't that nice about you sellin' a calf and givin' the proceeds." Seem like everybody know about it, but Sam don't sell the calf, just keep it.

Then one Sunday Sam went to church. He was a bit late, and he hear the choir already singing in there. When he got real close, he hear them sing: "The half has never been told." But from where Sam was, it sounded to him that they was singin': "The calf has never been sold."

Hearin' the words as he did, Sam stopped in his tracks. He said, "This proposition has got too big for me to handle." And after that, he went home, sold the calf and give the proceeds over to the preacher.

TESTING WITS: BUH RABBIT, BUH FOX, AND OTHER CREATURES

Animal tales in which the protagonists are in unending contest with one another are perhaps the best known of Afro-American narrations. In this instance the term Afro-American is particularly meaningful, for a considerable number of Buh (often rendered as Brer) Rabbit stories have recognizable African antecedents, and the rabbit inherits the trickster role of the African hare, tortoise, and spider. Some of Buh Rabbit's escapades and predicaments are virtually identical to those of Ijapa, the Yoruba tortoise, and Anansi, the Ashanti spider trickster. As in the African prototypes, many of Rabbit's confrontations are with the physically stronger and usually predatory creatures, with the fox, wolf, bear, and alligator replacing the lion, leopard, elephant, and other dangerous animals of the African bush. Among those tales of African origin the sometimes sophisticated preachment of the African original has tended to disappear, and a tale is likely to end with a summation such as, "Now, wasn't Buh Rabbit smart?" or, "That's the way it was. Who is the smartest now, Buh Rabbit or Buh Wolf?" But this diminution of moral emphasis also characterizes many animal tales heard in Africa today. Nevertheless, if anything has in fact been lost, the storytelling impulse has been very much alive throughout the years, and the basic rabbit-fox contest has inspired countless new tales related to New World life and the human condition.

The actions and traits of the animal actors often reflect human character and human whimsy. Rabbit, Wolf, and Alligator may be seen as human types, and, in particular situations, as individual human persons. There are tales in which Rabbit is the slave or sharecropper and Wolf or Bear the master or landowner. And there are some tales in which the animal characters play the same roles as do humans in others. In many stories Buh Rabbit does not appear at all, and the contest is between Hawk and Buzzard, for example, or Fox and Wolf, or Coon and Possum. Any commonplace animal tale is told different ways by different narrators, and the results are varied. An accomplished storyteller brings to his narration imagination and the arts of the theater. He may dramatize his characters, innovate and embellish, and the mere words of his narration in print seem impoverished by comparison with his original live performance.

Brer Coon Gets His Meat

Brer Rabbit an Brer Coon wuz fishermuns. Brer Rabbit fished fur fish an Brer Coon fished fur f-r-o-g-s.

Arter while de frogs all got so wile Brer Coon couldent ketch em, an he hadn't hab no meat to his house an de chilluns wuz hongry and de ole oman beat em ober de haid wid de broom.

Brer Coon felt mighty bad an he went off down de rode wid he haid down wundering what he gwine do. Des den ole Brer Rabbit wuz er skippin down de rode an he seed Brer Coon wuz worried an throwed up his years an say-ed:

"Mornin, Brer Coon."

"Mornin, Brer Rabbit."

"How is yer copperrosity segashuatin, Brer Coon?"

"Porely, Brer Rabbit, porely. De frogs haz all got so wile I cain't ketch em an I ain't got no meat to my house an de ole oman is mad an de chilluns hongry. Brer Rabbit, I'se got to hab help. Sumthin' haz got to be dun."

This tale, set down by A.W. Eddins, is from Publications of the Folk-Lore Society of Texas, No. I, *edited by Stith Thompson, 1916. The dialect is somewhat overdone in the writing, in the tradition of the times, but I have made no changes, preferring to let this fine example of oral narration speak for itself.—H.C.*

Old Brer Rabbit looked away crost de ruver long time; den he scratch his year wid his hind foot, an say:

"I'll tole ye whut we do, Brer Coon. We'll git eber one of dem frogs. You go down on de san bar an lie down an play des lack you wuz d-a-i-d. Don't yer mobe. Be jes as still, jest lack you wuz d-a-i-d."

Ole Brer Coon mosied on down to de ruver. De frongs hear-ed em er comin and de ole big frog say-ed:

"Yer better look er roun. Yer better look er roun. Yer better look er roun."

Nother ole frog say-ed:

"Knee deep, knee deep, knee deep."

An "ker-chug" all de frogs went in de water.

But Ole Brer Coon lide down on de san an stretched out jest lack he wuz d-a-i-d. De flies got all ober em, but he never moobe. De sun shine hot, but he never moobe; he lie still jest lack he wuz d-a-i-d.

Directly Ole Brer Rabbit cum er runnin tru de woods an out on de san bar an put his years up high an hollered out:

"Hay, de Ole Coon is d-a-i-d."

De ole big frog out in de ruver say-ed:

"I don't bleve it, I don't bleve it, I don't bleve it."

An all de littul frogs roun de edge say-ed:

"I don't bleve it, I don't bleve it, I don't bleve it."

But de ole coon play jes lack he's d-a-i-d an all de frogs cum up out of de ruver an set er roun whare de ole coon lay.

Jes den Brer Rabbit wink his eye an say-ed:

"I'll tell you what I'de do, Brer Frogs. I'de berry Ole Sandy, berry em so deep he never could scratch out."

Den all de frogs gun to dig out de san, dig out de san from under de ole coon. When dey had dug er great deep hole wid de ole coon in de middle of it, de frogs all got tired an de ole frog say-ed:

"Deep er nough,—deep er nough,—deep er nough."

An all de littul frogs say-ed:

"Deep er nough,—deep er nough,—deep er nough."

Ole Brer Rabbit was er takin er littul nap in der sun, an he woke up an say-ed:

"Kin you jump out?"

De ole big frog look up to de top of de hole an say-ed:

"Yes I kin. Yes I kin. Yes I kin."

Ole Brer Rabbit tole em:

"Dig it deeper."

Den all de frogs went to wuk an dug er great deep hole way down inside de san wid Ole Brer Coon right in de middle jest lack he wuz d-a-i-d. De frogs wuz er gittin putty tired an de ole big frog sung out loud:—

"Deep er nough. Deep er nough. Deep er nough."

An all de littul frogs sung out too:—

"Deep er nough. Deep er nough. Deep er nough."

An Ole Brer Rabbit woke up er gin and exed em:—

"Kin yer jump out?"

"I bleve I kin. I bleve I kin. I bleve I kin."

Ole Brer Rabbit look down in de hole agin an say-ed:

"Dig dat hole deeper."

Den all de frogs gin to wuk throwin out san, throwin out san, clear till most sun down and dey had er great deep hole way, way down in de san, wid de ole coon layin right in de middle. De frogs wuz plum clean tired out and de ole big frog say-ed:

"Deep er nough. Deep er nough. Deep er nough."

An all de littul frogs say-ed:—

"Deep er nough. Deep er nough. Deep er nough."

Ole Brer Rabbit peeped down in de hole agin an say:—

"Kin yer jump out?"

An de ole frog say:—

"No I cain't. No I cain't. No I cain't."

An all de littul frogs say:—

"No I cain't. No I cain't. No I cain't."

Den Ole Brer Rabbit jump up right quick an holler out:—

"RISE UP SANDY AN GIT YOUR MEAT."

An Brer Coon had meat fer sepper dat nite.

Brer Rabbit in the Well

"Brer Rabbit en Brer Fox wuz like some chilluns w'at I knows un," said Uncle Remus, regarding the little boy, who had come to hear another story, with an affectation of great solemnity. "Bofe un um wuz allers atter wunner nudder, a prankin' en a pester'n 'roun', but Brer Rabbit did had some peace, kaze Brer Fox done got skittish 'bout puttin' de clamps on Brer Rabbit.

"One day, w'en Brer Rabbit, en Brer Fox, en Brer Coon, en Brer B'ar, en a whole lot un um wuz clearin' up a new groun' fer ter plant a roas'n'year patch, de sun 'gun ter git sorter hot, an Brer Rabbit he got tired; but he didn't let on, kaze he 'feared de balance un um'd call 'im lazy, en he keep on totin' off trash en pilin' up bresh, twel bimeby he holler out dat he gotter brier in his han', en den he tak'en slip off, en hunt fer cool place fer ter res'. Atter w'ile he come 'crosst a well wid a bucket hangin' in it.

"'Dat look cool,' sez Brer Rabbit, sezee, 'en cool I speck she is. I'll des 'bout git in dar en take a nap,' en wid dat in he jump, he did, en he ain't no sooner fix hisse'f dan de bucket 'gun ter go down."

"Honey, dey ain't been no wusser skeer'd beas' sence de worril begin dan dish yer same Brer Rabbit. He fa'rly had a ager. He know whar he cum fum, but he dunner whar he gwine. Dreckly he feel de bucket

From Uncle Remus, His Songs and His Sayings, *by Joel Chandler Harris, New York, Appleton, 1880 (also 1895, 1908).*

hit de water, en dar she sot, but Brer Rabbit he keep mighty still, kaze he dunner w'at minnit gwineter be de nex'. He des lay dar en shuck en shiver.

"Brer Fox allers got one eye on Brer Rabbit, en w'en he slip off fum de new groun', Brer Fox he sneak atter 'im. He knew Brer Rabbit wuz atter some projick er nudder, en he tuck'n crope off, he did, en watch 'im. Brer Fox see Brer Rabbit come to de well en stop, en den he see 'im jump in de bucket, en den, lo en beholes, he see 'im go down outer sight. Brer Fox wuz de mos' 'stonish Fox dat you ever laid eyes on. He sot off dar in de bushes en study en study, but he don't make no head ner tails ter dis kinder bizness. Den he say ter hisse'f, sezee:

"'Well, ef dis don't bang my times,' sezee, 'den Joe's dead an Sal's a widder. Right down dar in dat well Brer Rabbit keep his money hid, en ef 'tain't dat den he done gone en 'skiver'd a gole-mime, en ef 'tain't dat, den I'm a gwineter see w'at's in dar,' sezee.

"Brer Fox crope up little nigher, he did, en lissen, but he don't year no fuss, en he keep on gittin' nigher, en yit he don't year nuthin.' Bime-by he git up close en peep down, but he don't see nuthin' en he don't year nuthin.' All dis time Brer Rabbit mighty nigh skeer'd outen his skin, en he fear'd fer ter move kaze de bucket might keel over an spill him out in de water. W'ile he sayin' his pra'rs over like a train er kyars runnin', ole Brer Fox holler out:

"'Heyo, Brer Rabbit! Who you wizzitin' down dar?' sezee.

"'Who? Me? Oh, I'm des a fishin', Brer Fox,' sez Brer Rabbit, sezee. 'I des say ter myse'f dat I'd sorter sprize you all wid a mess er fishes fer dinner, en so here I is, en dar's de fishes. I'm a fishin' fer suckers, Brer Fox,' sez Brer Rabbit, sezee.

"'Is dey many un um down dar, Brer Rabbit?' sez Brer Fox, sezee.

"'Lots un um, Brer Fox; scoze en scoze un em. De water is natally live wid um. Come down en he'p me haul um in, Brer Fox,' sez Brer Rabbit, sezee.

"'How I gwineter git down, Brer Rabbit?'

"'Jump inter de bucket, Brer Fox. Hit'll fetch you down all safe en soun'.'

"Brer Rabbit talk so happy en talk so sweet dat Brer Fox he jump in de bucket, he did, en, ez he went down, co'se his weight pull Brer Rabbit up. W'en dey pass one nudder on de half-way groun', Brer Rabbit he sing out:

> "'Good-by, Brer Fox, take keer yo' cloze,
> Fer dis is de way de worril goes;
> Some goes up en some goes down,
> You'll git ter de bottom all safe en soun'.'

"W'en Brer Rabbit got out, he gallop off den tole de fokes w'at de well b'long ter dat Brer Fox wuz down in dar muddyin' up de drinkin' water, en den he gallop back ter de well, en holler down ter Brer Fox:

" 'Yer come a man wid a great big gun—
W'en he haul you up, you jump en run.' "

"What then, Uncle Remus?" asked the little boy, as the old man paused.

"In des 'bout half n'our, honey, bofe un um wuz back in de new groun' wukkin des like dey never heer'd er no well, ceppin' dat eve'y now'n den Brer Rabbit'd bust out in er laff, en ole Brer Fox, he'd git a spell er de dry grins."

Terrapin's Pot of Sense

In the old days they was a big competition 'mongst the animals to see which one of 'em could collect the most good sense. Buh Coon, Buh Fox, Buh Guinea, Buh Geese, Buh Snake, and all the others went runnin' around pickin' up pieces of good sense on the ground or on the bushes or wherever they could find 'em. Buh Coon had a little pile of good sense in his place, Buh Rabbit had a little pile in his place, Buh Rooster had some in his place. Of course, they was all in such a hurry to outdo the other folks that some of the sense they picked up wasn't so good, and some was downright spoiled. But everyone was braggin' 'bout what a pile of sense he had back home. Trouble was, the places they had to keep it wasn't just right. Buh Possum's house had a leak in the roof, and everytime it rained, the water came drip, drip, drip, down on Possum's pile of sense. Buh 'Gator he put his sense in the nest where he keep his eggs, but every time the young ones hatch out they jump around and kick the good sense all over the place. Buh Rooster have his good sense in a nice pretty pile, but his wife, Sister Hen she's so nearsighted she can't tell sense from corn, and she was always a-peckin' at it. Buh Duck he want to fly South in the winter and don't know what to do with his pile of sense.

Well, Buh Terrapin he got a fine idea. He say, "Friends, what we need is a caretaker to take care of all the sense we gathered. You just bring it to me and I'll be the caretaker."

All the animals liked that idea, 'cause it eased their worries for 'em. So they all brought the sense they'd collected to Buh Terrapin, and he gave each and every one of 'em a receipt for it. Then he took all that sense and put it in a big iron cookin' pot.

Afterward he begin to study where could he hang the pot. At last he decided he goin' to hang it top of a great big sycamore tree safe and sound. So he took the pot in front of him and went to climb the tree

This story and the one following, "Buh Rabbit's 'Gator Fry," are from Terrapin's Pot of Sense, ©1957 by Harold Courlander, and are reprinted by permission of Holt, Rinehart and Winston.

with it. But he got a powerful problem, 'cause the pot was pretty big and Terrapin's legs was too short in the first place to be climbin' trees. Took Terrapin most of the day to get halfway up. All the critters was standin' around watchin' that pot of sense go up, sayin', "Hey there, Buh Terrapin, careful of that pot! It got my sense in it!"

Just afore nightfall a wind come up and begin blowin' things around. The top of the sycamore tree began to switch back and forth. Wind got stronger, and the top of the tree commence to whippin' around till Buh Terrapin couldn't hold on no more. He hollered, "Here I come!" and let go.

Buh Terrapin landed smack on his back and lay right there where he fall. The iron pot hit the ground and rolled this way and that. Naturally, everything that was in it got scattered all over. All the critters started to run around pickin' up pieces of sense. Everything was mixed up, and couldn't no one tell which was his and which was somebody else's. Didn't have time then to figure out what was good sense, or ordinary sense, or plain stupidity—everybody just grabbed.

And when they had they hands full and didn't know what to do with it, Buh Horse say, "I don't know what all you folks doin' with yours, but I'm puttin' mine in my head." And when he did that, the others say, "I'm puttin' mine in my head too," and they did the same as Buh Horse did. That's how come all the critters got sense in their heads. And they got good sense and bad sense as well. Some's luckier than others in what they picked up. Most everybody got a mixture, though.

When that part of it was all over, they saw Buh Terrapin still on his back, and they righted him. They saw his shell was all cracked from fallin' on the ground, just the way it's been ever since. They went away and left him. Terrapin he crawled around in the grass lookin' for bits of sense they'd left behind. He found some, but they hadn't left much for him. When you see Buh Terrapin crawlin' around in the grass nowadays, you can figure he's till lookin' for some scraps of sense.

That's a sad story for Buh Terrapin, ain't it? But some folks figure he had it comin', on account of they think he was fixin' to get all the sense for himself by appointin' himself caretaker.

(For an African comparison, see Appendix XV, pp. 595–96.)

Buh Rabbit's 'Gator Fry

One critter that always give Buh Rabbit a bad time is Buh Alligator. Buh Alligator he always talkin' real sweet, like, "Good evenin', how's all your folks doin' this evenin'?" And on Sunday Buh 'Gator always sittin' right up front in church prayin' and singin' with the most noise you ever heard. But the way he talks and prays ain't the way he acts. For one thing, he been eatin' Buh Rabbit's young ones, and Rabbit had just about enough of that. So he made a plot against Buh Alligator.

One mornin' he went down to the water where Buh 'Gator was always hangin' around, and say, "Mornin', Mr. Alligator. I came down to talk with you a little bit this mornin'."

Buh 'Gator he say, "What you got on your mind, Buh Rabbit?"

Rabbit say, "You know, we givin' a big eat over here today."

"That so?" Buh 'Gator say. "What you goin' to have for music?"

"Plenty," Buh Rabbit say. Buh Rabbit say. "Mr. Mockin'bird goin' to sing; Mr. Wrenbird goin' to sing; Mr. Turkledove goin' to moan, and Mr. Owl goin' to hoot for us. Mr. Turkey goin' to yelp. And Mr. Partridge goin' to sing *Pa-ta-da-hummm! Pa-ta-da-hummm!* Mockin'bird goin' to sing *Treedle-oo! Treedle-oo!* Jaybird goin' to holler *Jay! Jay!* Wrenbird holler, *Hyah! Hyah!* We goin' to get all them folks together to be our music, and they's goin' to be a mighty dance.

"Another thing," Buh Rabbit say, "Mrs. Possum goin' to bake paste for us. Mr. Coon goin' to run straight out there, back and forth, and Mr. Fox goin' to run 'round and 'round."

Mr. Alligator say, "That sure sounds like a big jamboree. I want to be in on that. Where's it goin' to be?"

"Right over there in that big straw patch," Rabbit say. "We want to make it right convenient for your whole family, Mr. Alligator. Goin' to have a table for you in that straw patch and you and your folks can just gather 'round it to eat. We goin' to make music down by the creek, give you the whole straw patch for your eatin'.

"Furthermore, we goin' to dance Bertillion," Rabbit say. Rabbit can dance mighty pretty, you know, turn double somersaults and all that. "Mr. Possum goin' to roll on the ground; Mr. Coon goin' to run; Dog goin' to bark and howl down there with pretty music; and birds goin' to be singin' overhead in the air. Mr. Wild Goose say he goin' to cackle mighty. Duck say he goin' to rock and walk and talk for us, so come on and hear all this music!"

Alligator say, "I'm comin' out then!" He commenced crawlin' out of the water with all his family—a big mess of alligators they was. They ganged up and came on up to the straw patch and sat around waitin' for the food and the music and dancin'.

"'Nother thing,'" Rabbit say, "we goin' to have fun at the first and Double Trouble on the last. When I holler 'Fun!' you look around and you'll see Double Trouble after it."

"What's this Double Trouble you talkin' about, Buh Rabbit?" Alligator say.

"We're savin' that for a surprise," Rabbit say.

Well, Rabbit he commence to dance Bertillion, *bzz bzz bzz,* like that, and Mr. Alligator and his folks get up and start to dance 'round and 'round too. Like Rabbit say, down by the creek Mr. Dog begin to bark and howl; Mr. Coon begin to run back and forth; Possum roll on the ground; Mockin'bird sing *Treedle-oo! Treedle-oo!* Turkledove moan, and Jaybird holler *Jay! Jay!* Mr. Partridge sing *Hummm! Pa-ta-da-hummm!* Wrenbird call *Hyah! Hyah!* Crow cawed, Turkey gobbled, Goose cackled, and Duck rocked and walked and talked. They made mighty music down there, you could almost hear it in Mobile.

And while all this was goin' on, Mr. Alligator and all his folks was dancin' Bertillion, 'round and 'round, waitin' for Rabbit to bring on the victuals.

But 'midst all this noise, Buh Rabbit slipped out with a match and set the whole straw field afire in a big ring around where the alligators was dancin'. In no time at all the smoke was goin' up; the birds disappear out of the air; geese stopped cacklin'; everybody stopped singin'; and Mr. Alligator holler, "Fire!"

Buh Rabbit holler, "Fun!"

Alligator holler, "Fire!"

Buh Rabbit holler, "Fun!"

Smoke gettin' blacker all around, and Mr. Alligator holler again, "Fire!"

Rabbit holler, "Fun!"

At last when that ring of fire get too hot, Buh Rabbit skipped off down by the creek.

"Fire!" Buh Alligator holler, runnin' 'round and 'round.

"Double Trouble!" Rabbit call back. "Buh Alligator, you been eatin' up my young 'uns, and now you got your Double Trouble!"

Well, in no time at all you could hear them alligators burning up in the straw patch, poppin' just like canebrake on fire.

And that's what happened when Buh Rabbit had enough of Mr. Alligator preyin' on his young 'uns. Now it don't pay to fool around with Buh Rabbit, does it?

Buh Buzzard and Salvation

Now, they was the two of them, Buh Hawk and Buh Buzzard. And one day, the way it was, Buh Hawk come a-flyin' over the cornfield, not flappin' his wings so much as settin' back and ridin' on the wind, lookin' things over down below to catch hisself some vittles to eat. And whilst he was doin' that he see Buh Buzzard settin' on the ground lookin' miserable, his head hangin' down, just about starvin' to death.

Buh Hawk sail over the place where Buh Buzzard was and call out to him, "*Kaaa, kaaa,* what you doin' down there, Buh Buzzard? Why ain't you up here like me lookin' for your dinner?"

Buh Buzzard is sure a sorry sight. He look up and say, "Buh Hawk, I'm just settin' here waitin', starvin' to death."

Buh Hawk supplied to him, "Well, what you waitin' on, anyway?"

Buh Buzzard tell him, "I'm waitin' on the salvation of the Lord to feed me, that's what I'm waitin' on."

When Buh Hawk hear that he let out with "*Kaaa, kaaa!*" He say, "Man, when you goin' to get some sense in you, Buh Buzzard? Don't you know you can't never just set and wait on the Lord's salvation to feed you? You got to go after it and get it yourself. You just keep settin' there and waitin' and you goin' to starve to death before tomorrow night."

Buh Buzzard tell him, "What you think I should do, Buh Hawk?"

This story and the one that follows, "Rail Fence," are based on narrations by Richard Amerson in 1950.

Buh Hawk hollered *"Kaaa!"* He say, "Don't you hear me hollerin'? I'm lookin' for my dinner. I'm goin' to have vittles in the next thirty minutes, Buh Buzzard. I'm goin' to chase Buh Rabbit out of the woods onto open ground where he got no place to hole up, and then I'm goin' to dive down on him and get him. After that you and me goin' to eat rabbit."

Buh Buzzard say, "Well, that's mighty nice of you, Buh Hawk, and I thanks you for it, but you know I can't eat fresh meat. I always got to let it set for a day or two to smell up and get seasoned."

Buh Hawk say, "Well, now, you sure goin' to die just waitin' on the salvation of the Lord. I see Buh Rabbit now, runnin' across that new ground. Keep your eye on me, watch me go down on him and get him."

Buh Hawk folded his wings in and dove down on rabbit, hollerin', "Here I go!"

Well, Buh Hawk came sailin' down out of the sky toward where Buh Rabbit was. Buh Rabbit see him comin', and just when Buh Hawk was about to grab him Buh Rabbit jumped into a hollow stump. Buh Hawk was goin' so fast he couldn't stop, and he went against the stump, listen, went right against that stump and broke his neck.

Buh Buzzard been watchin' everything. Buh Rabbit stick his head out of the hollow he was in and call to Buh Buzzard, "Come on, Buh Buzzard! Come and get him! Me and God will feed you!"

Buh Buzzard say, "Well, thank you, Lord, for answerin' my prayer. As soon as Buh Hawk stinks up a little and gets kind of seasoned I'll be there and eat him."

"You just do that," Buh Rabbit says, "you can count on me and God to feed you."

Rail Fence

There was that time, listen, when Buh Fox caught Buh Rabbit and tied him up for eatin' his young ones. Buh Rabbit say, "Well, you caught me all right, Buh Fox, just what you goin' to do with me?"

Buh Fox tell him, "You give me a mess of trouble, Buh Rabbit, and I don't know what I'm goin' to do with you yet. But you made me mad, and man, you are goin' to get it good. First of all, though, I'm goin' to take you over to Tuscaloosa and show the girls what I done caught."

Buh Rabbit say, "Yes, that's just fine, Buh Fox, just fine." He was studyin' hard on Buh Fox's proposition, though, all the time they was a-goin'. And when they come to a rail fence 'longside a big cornfield, he say to Buh Fox like this, he say, "Buh Fox, try the short cut. Ain't no use goin' round by the road, cause that's a long walk. We can go right through the rails here and save us a parcel of time."

"You think so?" Buh Fox say.

"I know so," Buh Rabbit say. "Just slack up on that rope a minute and I'll show you how we go through the rails."

Buh Fox, he don't put much trust in Buh Rabbit, and he held tight to the end of the rope but he slacked up on it a little, and that allowed Buh Rabbit to hop through a hole in the fence about halfway up. He say, "You see what I mean, Buh Fox? You can come right through that same hole."

Buh Fox scratch his head, lookin' at the hole. Said, "That hole look pretty small to me. Don't know as I can make it."

"Ain't no doubt you can make it," Buh Rabbit tell him. "Just to make sure, slack up on that rope a little more and I'll raise the rail for you."

Buh Fox slacked up some more on the rope, and Buh Rabbit raised the rail for him. Made just enough place for Buh Fox's head. "Come on, now, Buh Fox," he say, "let's move it."

Buh Fox ain't sure yet, and he stand there scratchin' his head. Buh Rabbit holler, "Well, doggone, look at them pretty girls from Tuscaloosa!"

"Where?" Buh Fox say. "Where?" And he put his head right through the hole to look.

Buh Rabbit pushed down on the rail instead of holdin' it up, and it squeezed down on Buh Fox's neck.

"Don't you see them pretty girls from Tuscaloosa?" Buh Rabbit say.

"Ouch!" Buh Fox say. "Hey, Buh Rabbit, you chokin' me!"

"That ain't what I asked you," Buh Rabbit say. "I asked if you see them pretty girls from Tuscaloosa."

Buh Fox was throwin' hisself around tryin' to get his head out of the fence. He's hollerin', "Ouch, Buh Rabbit, lean up on the rail, I believe you breakin' my neck!"

Buh Rabbit lean down on the rail with a little more weight. He say, "That ain't what I been askin' you, Buh Fox. What I want to know is do you see them pretty girls from Tuscaloosa?"

"Ouch!" Buh Fox says. "I believe I'm givin' out!"

"Reckon you better let go the rope," Buh Rabbit say.

Well, Buh Fox didn't know what he's doin' by that time and he let go the rope. Buh Rabbit, he just walked off, leavin' Buh Fox still in the rail fence, gaggin' and a-hollerin', his tongue hangin' out, just about choked to death.

Ain't that Rabbit a smart one?

The Magic Hoe

Bruh Rabbit and Bruh Wolf was always tryin' to git the best o' one another. Now Bruh Wolf he own a hoe and it work for crop all by itself.

From Drums and Shadows, Survival Studies Among the Georgia Coastal Negroes, Georgia Writers' Project, Athens, University of Georgia Press. Reprinted by permission of the publishers.

Bruh Wolf just say, "Swish," to it. Then he sit down in the field and the hoe do all the work.

Bruh Rabbit he want that hoe. He hide behind bush and watch how the wolf make it work. One day when the wolf away, Bruh Rabbit he steal the hoe. He go to he own field and he stand the hoe up and he say, "Swish." The hoe start to work. It work and work. 'Fore long the crop is done finish. Then rabbit want hoe to stop, and he call out and he call out but hoe keep right on workin'. Bruh Rabbit don't know what word to say to stop it. Pretty soon the hoe cut down all Bruh Rabbit's winter crop and still it keep on workin' and workin'. Bruh Rabbit wring he hands. Everything he has is gone. Just then Bruh Wolf come along and he laugh and laugh out loud when he see how Bruh Rabbit steal he hoe and how it done ruin all the crop. Bruh Rabbit he keep callin' out, "Swish, swish," and the hoe go faster and faster. When he see Bruh Wolf, he ax 'im to make the hoe stop. Bruh Wolf won't say nothin' at all cause he mad that Bruh Rabbit steal he hoe. Then after a time he say, "Slow, boy," and the hoe he stop workin'. Then Bruh Wolf he pick up he hoe and carry him home.

(For an African comparison, see Appendix XVI, p. 596–97.)

Between Two Dinners

Buh Wolf, him binner inwite ter two dinner de same day an de same time: one gen by Cooter Bay, and de tarruh by John Bay. Dem bin bredder, and dem lib on two seprite road wuh jine at de fork. Buh Wolf, him so greedy him cept bofe inbitation. Wen de time come fuh go, eh dress ehself up and eh light out. Wen he get ter de place way de road fork, eh stop and eh consider. Eh want fuh tek bofe road and go ter de two dinner. Eh cant tak one and leff tarruh. Eh gone down one road; eh tun back; eh tan ter de fork. Eh tek tarruh road; eh come back ter de fork; eh tan day gen. Eh state off; eh tun back. Eh state off gen; en tun back gen. Eh can't mek up eh mine which dinner fuh tek and which dinner fuh leff. Eh hanker arter bofe. Eh wase eh time. Wile dis bine a guine on, de people bin a eat at bofe de dinner.

Bimeby yuh come some er dem, wuh bin eat dinner with Cooter Bay, duh mek dem way home. Dem see Buh Wolf duh tan in de fork er de road, and dem hail um, an dem say: "Hi! Buh Wolf, wuh you duh do yuh?" Buh Wolf, him mek answer: "Me guine ter Cooter Bay fuh dine long um." Den dem tellum say de dinner done ober; dat dem just come from day, and dat dem bin hab plenty er good bittle fuh eat. Buh Wolf rale cut down case eh loss one dinner.

Eh hop off and mek fuh John Bay house fuh get de tarruh dinner. Eh yent bin gone no destant before eh meet dem people duh comin back

From Negro Myths from the Georgia Coast, by Charles C. Jones, Boston, Houghton Mifflin, 1888.

wuh bin gone fuh eat dinner long John Bay. Dem tell um de dinner done ober, and eh mights well tun back. Buh Wolf outdone. Eh so greedy eh couldn't mek up eh mine which dinner fuh tek. Eh tink eh guine git all two, and eh yent git none. Eh gone home dat bex an hongry eh ready fuh kill ehself.

People wuh wunt mek up dem mine in time wuh dem mean fuh do guine git leff.

(For an African comparison, see Appendix XVII, pp. 597–98.)

Catching the Snake and the Yellowjackets

Buh Rabbit greedy fuh hab mo sense den all de tarruh animel. Eh yent lub fuh wuk, and eh try heap er scheme fuh git eh libbin outer edder people by fool um.

One time eh gone ter one wise Cunjur Man fuh larne um him way, and fuh git him knowledge, so him kin stonish tarruh people and mek dem bliebe say him bin wise mo ner ebrybody. De Cunjur Man larne um heap er curous ting. At las Buh Rabbit ax um fuh gen um eh full knowledge. De Cunjur Man say: "Buh Rabbit, you hab sense nough aready." Buh Rabbit keep on bague um, and den de Cunjur Man mek answer: "Ef you kit ketch one big rattlesnake an fetch um ter me live, me guine do wuh you ax me fuh do."

Buh Rabbit git ehself one long stick and eh gone der wood. Eh hunt tel eh fine one whalin ob er rattlesnake duh quile up on one log. Eh pass de time er day berry perlite wid um, and arterwards eh bet de snake say him yent bin es long as de stick wuh him hab een him han. Buh Rattlesnake laugh at um, and eh mek answer dat eh know eh yiz long mo na de stick. Fuh settle de bet Buh Rattlesnake tretch ehself out ter eh berry lenk on de log, and Buh Rabbit pit de pole long side er um fuh medjuh um. Man sir! befo Buh Rattlesnake fine out, Buh Rabbit slip one noose roun eh neck and fasten um tight ter de een der de pole. Buh Rattlesnake twis ehself, and wrop ehself roun and roun de pole, and try fuh git eh head loose, but all eh twis and tun yent do um no good. An so Buh Rabbit ketch um, and cahr um ter de Cunjur Man.

De Cunjur Man rale surprise, and eh say: "Buh Rabbit, me always bin yeddy say you bin hab heap er sense, but now me know dat you got um. Ef you kin fool Rattlesnake, you hab all de sense you want."

Wen Buh Rabbit keep on bague de Cunjur Man fuh gie um mo sense, de Cunjur Man answer: "You go fetch me er swarm er Yaller Jacket, and wen you bring um ter me, me prommus you teh gie you all de sense you want."

From Jones, ibid.

Ebrybody know say Yaller Jacket was den warse, an bee, an hornet. Eh sting so bad, and eh berry lub fuh drap topper ebryting wuh come close eh nes, and dout gie um any warnin. So wuh Buh Rabbit do? Eh gone an eh git one big calabash, and eh crape um out clean, and eh cut one hole een um, and e pit honey een um, an eh tie um on de een er one long pole. Den eh hunt tel eh fine er Yaller Jacket nes, and eh set de calabash close by um dout worry de Yaller Jacket, an eh leff um day, and eh tan off an watch um. Bimby de Yaller Jacket scent de honey, and dem come out de nes and gone een de calabash fuh eat de honey. Wen de calabash full er Yaller Jacket, Buh Rabbit slip up and stop de hole, and cahr um ter de Cunjur Man. De Cunjur Man mek er great miration ober wuh Buh Rabbit bin done, and eh say: "Buh Rabbit, you is suttenly de smartest of all de animel, an you sense shill git mo and mo ebry day. Mo na dat, me gwine pit white spot on you forrud, so ebrybody kin see you hab de bes sense een you head." And dat de way Buh Rabbit come fuh hab er leely tuff er white hair between eh yez.

(For an African comparison, see Appendix X, pp. 586–87.)

Terrapin Shows His Strength

"Brer Tarrypin wuz de out'nes' man," said Uncle Remus, rubbing his hands together contemplatively, and chuckling to himself in a very significant manner; "he wuz de out'nes' man er de whole gang. He wuz dat."

The little boy sat perfectly quiet, betraying no impatience when Uncle Remus paused to hunt, first in one pocket and then in another, for enough crumbs of tobacco to replenish his pipe. Presently the old man proceeded:

"One night Miss Meadows en de gals dey gun a candy-pullin' en so many er de nabers come in 'sponse ter de invite dat dey hatter put de 'lasses in de wash pot en b'il' de fier en de yard. Brer B'ar, he holp Miss Meadows bring de wood, Brer Fox, he men' de fier, Brer Wolf, he kep' de dogs off, Brer Rabbit, he grease de bottom er de plates fer ter keep de candy fum stickin', en Brer Tarrypin, he klum up in a cheer, en say he'd watch en see dat de 'lasses didn't bile over. Dey wuz all dere, en dey wern't cuttin' up no didos, nudder, kaze Miss Meadows, she done put her foot down, she did, en say dat w'en dey come ter her place dey hatter hang up a flag er truce at de front gate en 'bide by it.

"Well, den, w'iles dey wuz all a settin' dar en de 'lasses wuz a bilin'

From Uncle Remus, His Songs and Sayings, *New York, 1880, 1895.*

en a blubberin', dey got ter runnin' on talkin' mighty biggity. Brer Rabbit, he say he de swiffes'; but Brer Tarrypin, he rock 'long in de cheer en watch de 'lasses. Brer Fox, he say he de sharpes', but Brer Tarrypin, he rock 'long. Brer Wolf, he say he de mos' suvvigus, but Brer Tarrypin, he rock en he rock 'long. Brer B'ar, he say he de mos' stronges', but Brer Tarrypin he rock, en he keep on rocking'. Bimeby he sorter shet one eye en say, sezee:

"'Hit look like 'perently dat ole hardshell ain't nowhars 'longside er dis crowd, yit yer I is, en I'm de same man w'at show Brer Rabbit dat he ain't de swiffes'; en I'm de same man w'at kin show Brer B'ar dat he ain't de stronges',' sezee.

"Den dey all laff en holler, kaze it look like Brer B'ar mo' stronger dan a steer. Bimeby, Miss Meadows, she up'n ax, she did, how he gwine do it.

"'Gimme a good strong rope,' sez Brer Tarrypin, sezee, 'en lemme git in er puddle er water, en den let Brer B'ar see ef he kin pull me out,' sezee.

"Den dey all laff g'in, en Brer B'ar, he ups en sez, sezee: 'We ain't got no rope,' sezee.

"'No,' sez Brer Tarrypin, sezee, 'en needer is you got de strenk,' sezee, en den Brer Tarrypin, he rock en rock 'long, en watch de 'lasses a bilin' en a blubberin'.

"Atter w'ile Miss Meadows, she up en say, she did, dat she'd take'n loan de young men her bed-cord, en w'iles de candy wuz a coolin' in de plates, dey could all go ter de branch en see Brer Tarrypin kyar out his projick. Brer Tarrypin," continued Uncle Remus, in a tone at once confidential and argumentative, "weren't much bigger'n de pa'm er my han', en it look mighty funny fer ter year 'im braggin' 'bout how he kin out-pull Brer B'ar. But dey got de bed-cord atter w'ile, en den dey all put out ter de branch. W'en Brer Tarrypin fine de place he wanter, he tuck one een' er de bed-cord, en gun de yuther een' to Brer B'ar.

"'Now den, ladies en gents,' sez Brer Tarrypin, sezee, 'you all go wid Brer B'ar up dar in de woods en I'll stay yer, en w'en you year me holler, den's de time fer Brer B'ar fer ter see ef he kin haul in de slack er de rope. You all take keer er dat ar een',' sezee, 'en I'll take keer er dish yer een',' sezee.

"Den dey all put out en lef' Brer Tarrypin at de branch, en w'en dey got good en gone, he dove down inter de water, he did, en tie de bed-cord hard en fas' ter wunner deze yer big clay-roots, en den he riz up en gin a whoop.

"Brer B'ar he wrop de bed-cord roun' his han', en wink at de gals, en wid dat he gin a big juk, but Brer Tarrypin ain't budge. Den he take bof han's en gin a big pull, but, all de same, Brer Tarrypin ain't budge. Den he tu'n 'roun', he did, en put de rope cross his shoulders en try ter walk off wid Brer Tarrypin, but Brer Tarrypin look like he don't feel like walkin'. Den Brer Wolf he put in en hope Brer B'ar pull, but des like he didn't, en den dey all hope 'im, en, bless grashus! w'iles dey wuz all a pullin', Brer Tarrypin, he holler, en ax um w'y dey don't take up de slack. Den w'en Brer Tarrypin feel um quit pullin', he dove down, he did, en ontie de rope, en by de time dey got ter de branch, Brer Tarrypin, he wuz settin' in de aidge er de water des ez natchul ez de nex' un, en he up'n say, sezee:

"'Dat las' pull er yone wuz a mighty stiff un, en a leetle mo'n you'd er had me,' sezee. 'Youer monstus stout, Brer B'ar,' sezee, 'en you pulls like a yoke er steers, but I sorter had de purchis on you,' sezee.

"Den Brer B'ar, bein's his mouf 'gun ter water atter de sweetnin,' he up'n say he speck de candy's ripe, en off dey put atter it!"

"It's a wonder," said the little boy, after a while, "that the rope didn't break."

"Break who?" exclaimed Uncle Remus, with a touch of indignation in his tone—"break who? In dem days, Miss Meadow's bed-cord would a hilt a mule."

This put an end to whatever doubts the child might have entertained.

TESTING WITS: HUMAN VS. DEMON

The following tale about Wiley and the Hairy Man has all the feel of the old rural South, the country cabin, the riverbank swamps, and the backland speech, and it has, as well, a certain lyrical style. But it is one of those stories decorating and embellishing a folklore theme of considerable age—the hunter and his dogs who save him from a malevolent creature of the forest (an ogre, a man-eating monster or demon, or a witch). Countless tales are told in Africa and Europe about a man who climbs a tree to escape the forest demon, and who is finally saved by his dogs. In this instance the demon is the Hairy Man, who has prototypes in some African lore.

Wiley and the Hairy Man

Wiley's pappy was a bad man and no-count. He stole watermelons in the dark of the moon, slept while the weeds grew higher than the cotton, robbed a corpse laid out for burying, and, worse than that, killed three martins and never even chunked at a crow. So everybody thought that when Wiley's pappy died he'd never cross Jordan because the Hairy Man would be there waiting for him. That must have been the way it happened, because they never found him after he fell off the ferry boat at Holly's where the river is quicker than anywhere else. They looked for him a long way downriver and in the still pools between the sandbanks, but they never found pappy. And they heard a big man laughing across the river, and everybody said, "That's the Hairy Man." So they stopped looking.

"Wiley," his mammy told him, "the Hairy Man's done got yo' pappy and he's go' get you 'f you don't look out."

"Yas'm," he said, "I'll look out. I'll take my hound dogs ev'rywhere I go. The Hairy Man can't stand no hound dog."

Wiley knew that because his mammy had told him. She knew because she was from the swamps by the Tombigbee and knew conjure. They don't know conjure on the Alabama like they do on the Tombigbee.

One day Wiley took his axe and went down in the swamp to cut some poles for a hen-roost and his hounds went with him. But they took out after a shoat and ran it so far off Wiley couldn't even hear them yelp.

"Well," he said, "I hope the Hairy Man ain't nowhere round here now."

He picked up his axe to start cutting poles, but he looked up and

From the manuscripts of the Federal Writers' Project of the Works Progress Administration for the State of Alabama, attributed to Donnell Van de Voort. The style of the narration suggests a creative contribution by the writer, but the intrinsic elements of the story are traditional. Reprinted from A Treasury of American Folklore, *by B. A. Botkin, with the permission of Crown Publishers.*

there came the Hairy Man through the trees grinning. He was sure ugly and his grin didn't help much. He was hairy all over. His eyes burned like fire and spit drooled all over his big teeth.

"Don't look at me like that," said Wiley, but the Hairy Man kept coming and grinning, so Wiley threw down his axe and climbed up a big bay tree. He saw the Hairy Man didn't have feet like a man but like a cow, and Wiley never had seen a cow up a bay tree.

"What for you done climb up there?" the Hairy Man asked Wiley when he got to the bottom of the tree.

Wiley climbed nearly to the top of the tree and looked down. Then he climbed plumb to the top.

"How come you climbin' trees?" the Hairy Man said.

"My mammy done tole me to stay 'way from you. What you got in that big croaker-sack?"

"I ain't got nothing yet."

"Gwan 'way from here," said Wiley, hoping the tree would grow some more.

"Ha," said the Hairy Man and picked up Wiley's axe. He swung it stout and the chips flew. Wiley grabbed the tree close, rubbed his belly on it and hollered, "Fly, chips, fly back in yo' same old place."

The chips flew and the Hairy Man cussed and damned. Then he swung the axe and Wiley knew he'd have to holler fast. They went to it tooth and toe-nail then, Wiley hollering and the Hairy Man chopping. He hollered till he was hoarse and he saw the Hairy Man was gaining on him.

"I'll come down part t'way," he said, "'f you'll make this bay tree twicet as big around."

"I ain't studyin' you," said the Hairy Man, swinging the axe.

"I bet you cain't," said Wiley.

"I ain't go' try," said the Hairy Man.

Then they went to it again, Wiley hollering and the Hairy Man chopping. Wiley had about yelled himself out when he heard his hound dogs yelping way off.

"Hyeaaah, dog, Hyeaaah," he hollered. "Fly, chips, fly, back in yo' same old place."

"You ain't got no dogs. I sent that shoat to draw 'em off."

"Hyeaaah, dog," hollered Wiley, and they both heard the hound dogs yelping and coming jam-up. The Hairy Man looked worried.

"Come on down," he said, "and I'll teach you conjure."

"I can learn all the conjure I wants from my mammy."

The Hairy Man cussed some more, but he threw the axe down and balled the jack off through the swamp.

When Wiley got home he told his mammy that the Hairy Man had most got him, but his dogs ran him off.

"Did he have his sack?"

"Yes'm."

"Nex' time he come after you, don't you climb no bay tree."

"I ain't," said Wiley. "They ain't big enough around."

"Don't climb no kind o' tree. Jes stay on the ground and say, 'Hello, Hairy Man.' You hear me, Wiley?"

"No'm."

"He ain't go' hurt you, chile. You can put the Hairy Man in the dirt when I tell you how to do him."

"I puts him in the dirt and he puts me in that croaker-sack. I ain't puttin' no Hairy Man in the dirt."

"You jes do like I say. You say, 'Hello, Hairy Man.' He says, 'Hello, Wiley.' You say, 'Hairy Man, I done heard you 'bout the best conjure-man 'round here.' 'I reckon I am.' You say, 'I bet you cain't turn yo'self into no gee-raff.' You keep tellin' him he cain't and he will. Then you say, 'I bet you cain't turn yo'self into no alligator.' And he will. Then you say, 'Anybody can turn theyself into somep'n big as a man, but I bet you cain't turn yo'self into no 'possum.' Then he will, and you grab him and throw him in the sack."

"It don't sound jes right somehow," said Wiley, "but I will." So he tied up his dogs so they wouldn't scare away the Hairy Man, and went down to the swamp again. He hadn't been there long when he looked up and there came the Hairy Man grinning through the trees, hairy all over and his big teeth showing more than ever. He knew Wiley came off without his hound dogs. Wiley nearly climbed a tree when he saw the croaker-sack, but he didn't.

"Hello, Hairy Man," he said.

"Hello, Wiley." He took the sack off his shoulder and started opening it up.

"Hairy Man, I done heard you 'bout the best conjure-man round here."

"I reckon I is."

"I bet you cain't turn yo'self into no gee-raff."

"Shux, that ain't no trouble," said the Hairy Man.

"I bet you cain't do it."

So the Hairy Man twisted round and turned himself into a gee-raff.

"I bet you cain't turn yo'self into no alligator," said Wiley.

The gee-raff twisted around and turned into an alligator, all the time watching Wiley to see he didn't try to run.

"Anybody can turn theyself into somep'n big as a man," said Wiley, "but I bet you cain't turn yo'self into no 'possum."

The alligator twisted around and turned into a 'possum, and Wiley grabbed it and threw it in the sack.

Wiley tied the sack up as tight as he could and then he threw it in the river. He went home through the swamp and he looked up and there came the Hairy Man grinning through the trees.

"I turn myself into the wind and blew out. Wiley, I'm go' set right here till you get hongry and fall out of that bay tree. You want me to learn you some more conjure."

Wiley studied a while. He studied about the Hairy Man and he studied about his hound dogs tied up most a mile away.

"Well," he said, "you done some pretty smart tricks. But I bet you cain't make things disappear and go where nobody knows."

"Huh, that's what I'm good at. Look at that bird-nest on the limb. Now look. It's done gone."

"How I know it was there in the fus' place? I bet you cain't make somep'n I know is there disappear."

"Ha ha," said the Hairy Man. "Look at yo' shirt."

Wiley looked down and his shirt was gone, but he didn't care, because that was just what he wanted the Hairy Man to do.

"That was jes a plain old shirt," he said. "But this rope I got tied round my breeches been conjured. I bet you cain't make it disappear."

"Huh, I can make all the rope in this country disappear."

"Ha, ha ha," said Wiley.

The Hairy Man looked mad and threw his chest way out. He opened his mouth wide and hollered loud.

"From now on all the rope in this country has done disappeared."

Wiley reared back holding his breeches with one hand and a tree-limb with the other.

"Hyeaah, dog," he hollered loud enough to be heard more than a mile off.

When Wiley and his dogs got back home his mammy asked him did he put the Hairy Man in the sack.

"Yes'm, but he done turned himself into the wind and blew right through that old croaker-sack."

"That *is* bad," said his mammy. "But you done fool him twicet. 'F you fool him again he'll leave you alone. He'll be mighty hard to fool the third time."

"We gotta study up a way to fool him, mammy."

"I'll study up a way tereckly," she said, and sat down by the fire and held her chin between her hands and studied real hard. But Wiley wasn't studying anything except how to keep the Hairy Man away. He took his hound dogs out and tied one at the back door and one at the front door. Then he crossed a broom and an axe handle over the window and built a fire in the fireplace. Feeling a lot safer, he sat down and helped his mammy study. After a little while his mammy said, "Wiley, you go down to the pen and get that little suckin' pig away from that old sow."

Wiley went down and snatched the sucking pig through the rails and left the sow grunting and heaving in the pen. He took the pig back to his mammy and she put it in his bed.

"Now, Wiley," she said, "you go on up to the loft and hide."

So he did. Before long he heard the wind howling and the trees shaking, and then his dogs started growling. He looked out through a knot-hole in the planks and saw the dog at the front door looking down toward the swamps, with his hair standing up and his lips drawn back in a snarl. Then an animal as big as a mule with horns on its head ran out of the swamp past the house. The dog jerked and jumped, but he couldn't get loose. Then an animal bigger than a great big dog with a long nose and big teeth ran out of the swamp and growled at the cabin. This time the dog broke loose and took after the big animal, who ran back down into the swamp. Wiley looked out another chink at the back end of the loft just in time to see his other dog jerk loose and take out after an animal, which might have been a 'possum, but wasn't.

"Law-dee," said Wiley. "The Hairy Man is coming here sho'."

He didn't have long to wait, because soon enough he heard something with feet like a cow scrambling around on the roof. He knew it was the Hairy Man, because he heard him damn and swear when he touched the hot chimney. The Hairy Man jumped off the roof when he found out there was a fire in the fireplace and came up and knocked on the front door as big as you please.

"Mammy," he hollered, "I done come after yo' baby."

"You ain't go' get him," mammy hollered back.

"Give him here or I'll bite you. I'm blue-gummed and I'll pizen you sho'."

"I'm right blue-gummed myself," mammy sang out.

"Give him here or I'll set yo' house on fire with lightnin'."

"I got plenty of sweet milk to put it out with."

"Give him here or I'll dry up yo' spring, make yo' cow go dry and send a million boll weevils out of the ground to eat up yo' cotton."

"Hairy Man, you wouldn't do all that. That's mighty mean."

"I'm a mighty mean man. I ain't never seen a man as mean as I am."

"'F I give you my baby will you go on way from here and leave everything else alone?"

"I swear that's jes what I'll do," said the Hairy Man, so mammy opened the door and let him in.

"He's over there in that bed," she said.

The Hairy Man came in grinning like he was meaner than he said. He walked over to the bed and snatched the covers back.

"Hey," he hollered, "there ain't nothin' in this bed but a old suckin' pig."

"I ain't said what kind of a baby I was givin' you, and that suckin' pig sho' belonged to me 'fo' I gave it to you."

The Hairy Man raged and yelled. He stomped all over the house gnashing his teeth. Then he grabbed up the pig and tore out through the swamp, knocking down trees right and left. The next morning the swamp had a wide path like a cyclone had cut through it, with trees torn loose at the roots and lying on the ground. When the Hairy Man was gone Wiley came down from the loft.

"Is he done gone, mammy?"

"Yes, chile. That old Hairy Man cain't ever hurt you again. We done fool him three times."

Wiley went over to the safe and got out his pappy's jug of shinny that had been lying there since the old man fell in the river.

"Mammy," he said, "I'm goin' to get hog-drunk and chicken-wild."

"You ain't the only one, chile. Ain't it nice yo' pappy was so no-count he had to keep shinny in the house?"

MORALIZING TALES

Although the theme of numerous Afro-American animal stories is the victory of the clever over the stupid, or of the weak over the strong, many of them concern themselves with social behavior. In the manner of certain African stories, they are prologues to a pedagogic or moralizing peroration, or to an aphorism. The content may be adventure, humor, and entertainment, but the interpretation, whether explicit or implied, is serious. One narrator of moralizing tales frequently added as a final statement the phrase, "That's it exactly, and I'm not preachin', I'm teachin'."

Over the years, no doubt, many stories have lost their explanatory endings, leaving only the adventures and escapades behind, but others retain their explicit moralizing character. The moralizing tales that follow, unless otherwise indicated, come from *Negro Myths from the Georgia Coast,* by Charles C. Jones. The book was published in 1888, when this type of story was more readily encountered than it is now. The Jones versions are "in the vernacular," which is to say in dialect. Because dialect was somewhat (or grossly) overdone in writings of the period, and also because of the difficulties the originals would present to most readers, the language of the Jones versions has been discreetly moderated into more conventional speech, without (it is hoped) loss of flavor, color, or sense.

The Dying Bullfrog

Once old Bull Frog was very sick and expecting to die. All his friends in the pond gathered around him and his family to nurse him and to take a last look at him. That old Frog had a young wife and a heap of young children. He was very troubled in his breast about who was going to mind his family after he was gone. When his voice began to fail him and just before he died he said: "My friends, who is going to take my wife when the breath leaves this here body?"

His friends all hollered out at the top of their voices: "Me me! Me me! Me me!"

Then he inquired: "Which one of you is going to mind my little children?"

For some time he didn't hear any answer; and then the answer came back to him, one by one, from all over the pond, and in a deep voice: "Not me! Not me! Not me!"

A heap of people are willing to notice a pretty young widow, but they don't want to bother themselves with another man's children.

Buh Raccoon and Buh Possum

Buh Raccoon asked Buh Possum why it was, when the dogs tackled him, that he doubled himself up and covered his eyes with his hands, and wouldn't fight like a man and whup the dogs. Buh Possum grinned and showed his teeth like a fool. He said when the dogs caught him they tickled his ribs so hard with their mouths that he had to laugh, and so he forgot to fight.

The cowardly man has all kinds of lies to tell to excuse himself.

Two Friends and the Bear

Two friends, they were on a journey together. They had to go through a thick swamp that was full of bear and other varmints. They promised to stand for one another, and to help one another out if the varmints should attack them. They didn't get halfway through the swamp when a big black bear jumped out of the bushes and made for them. Instead of standing by his friend, one of the men left and climbed a tree. The other man had heard that bears wouldn't eat dead people, so he lay down on the ground and held his breath and shut his eyes, and made out that he was dead.

The bear came up to him, and smelled him, and turned him over, trying to find out if he was breathing. When he found out the man wasn't breathing, he went off a little way and watched him. Then he turned back and smelled him again and looked at him closely. At length he made up his mind, said the man was really dead, and with that he left for good and went off in the woods.

All this time the other friend who was squinched up in the tree was watching what was going on. He was so scared he wouldn't do anything to help his friend, or try to run the bear off. When he saw that the bear was gone for sure, he hollered to his friend on the ground, said, "What the bear been telling you? Him and you seemed like you were having a close conversation."

Then his friend down below answered, "He been telling me never to trust anyone who calls himself a friend, and who runs like a coward as soon as trouble comes."

The Eagle and His Children

The eagle, he is a wise bird. He makes his nest on a tall pine tree close to the river or the sea, where nothing can get at it. He is satisfied with two children. He takes care of them. Every hour he fetches them snakes and fish, and he guards them from wind and rain and fowl-hawks, and makes them grow fast. When their wings are covered with feathers and are strong enough for them to fly, what does Buh Eagle do? He won't leave those children in the nest to get lazy and live on their father and mother, but he takes them on his wings, and they sail over the sea, and he tells those children: "The time has come for you to make your own living. I've fed you long enough. Now you have to look out for yourselves."

With that he flies out from under them, and the young birds, when they find out their father or mother isn't going to carry them any further, and that they have to shift for themselves, they try their wings and sail off in the elements to hunt food.

People ought to take notice of Buh Eagle and do as he does. When your children get big enough to work, make them work. Don't let them sit around the house doing nothing and expecting their fathers and mother to find food and clothes for them. If you do, your children are going to make you ashamed, and they will turn out very trifling. They will keep you dead-poor, too. Do the same as Buh Eagle. Mind your children well when they're little; and soon as they're big enough to work, make them work.

Chanticleer and the Barnyard Rooster

You never saw a finer bird than Buh Chanticleer. His feathers glisten like silver in the sun. He steps high and he isn't afraid of anything. When he crows you can hear him all through the settlement. The hens all love him and run after him whenever he calls. He can lick all those other roosters; and just as soon as he makes a motion at them, they all run.

Before this was known, there was a big Yellow Rooster in the gang who tried to spite Buh Chanticleer, and he bragged that he could lick him. They fought. The big Yellow Rooster couldn't stand up to Buh Chanticleer. Buh Chanticleer gaffed him, he pecked him in the back, he knocked him over, and he ran him out of the yard.

After that, the Yellow Rooster was afraid to come near Buh Chanticleer. He ran every time he saw Buh Chanticleer walking toward him, but he had to find a way to bedevil Buh Chanticleer. He went way off, and every time he heard Buh Chanticleer flap his wings and crow, he did the same. Early one morning when Buh Chanticleer crowed for day, the big Yellow Rooster, he crowed too. This thing bothered Buh Chanticleer, and he wanted to kill him. He tried hard to think of a way to do it. One day one of the hens that belonged to Buh Chanticleer's family gave him a plan. Then Buh Chanticleer sent for Buh Fox. Buh Fox came, and Buh Chanticleer said to him, "You want a fat rooster to eat?" Buh Fox answered, "Yes, I'd be very glad to get one, and a heap of thanks to you."

Then Buh Chanticleer told him to come the first moonlight night and he'd show him the way to get a good supper. Buh Fox was happy and promised to come. And he did come the first moonlight night, and Buh Chanticleer went with him and pointed out the big Yellow Rooster sleeping in a low cedar tree. Buh Fox crept up easy, and grabbed Yellow Rooster and ate him. When he was finished eating he licked his mouth. Buh Chanticleer asked, "How'd you like him?" Buh Fox answered, "I liked him very well. He was fat. He was sweet. I liked him so much I want more." With that, and before Buh Chanticleer could make out what he intended to do, Buh Fox jumped on Buh Chanticleer and mashed him to death and ate him up.

When you want someone to do you a service, call on your friend. Don't trust your enemy to do it.

Buh Lion and Buh Goat

Buh Lion was out hunting, and he spied Buh Goat lying on top of a big rock. Buh Goat was working his mouth and chewing. Buh Lion crept up to catch him. When he got close he noticed Buh Goat good. Buh Goat kept on chewing. Buh Lion tried to figure out what Buh Goat was chewing. He didn't see anything but the naked rock that Buh Goat was lying on. Buh Lion was astonished. Buh Goat kept on chewing, chewing, chewing. But Lion couldn't make it out. He came close and said, "Hey, Buh Goat, what are you eating?" Buh Goat was scared when Buh Lion rose up before him, but he kept a bold heart, and he answered, "I'm chewing on this rock, and if you don't get out of here, when I'm through I'm going to eat you." When Buh Lion heard that he said to himself, "If Buh Goat can chew rock what can he do to me?" And he departed. Buh Goat's big words saved him. He was a bold man. A bold man gets out of his difficulties, a coward loses his life.

Buh Turkey Buzzard and the Rain

Buh Turkey Buzzard, he hasn't any sense at all. You watch him.

When the rain pours down, he sets on the fence and squinches himself up. He draws in his neck and tries to hide his head, and he looks that pitiful you're real sorry for him. He half cries, and says to himself: "Never mind, when this rain is over I'm going to build a house right off. I'm not going to let this rain lick me this way any more."

When the rain has gone, and the wind blows, and the sun shines, what does Buh Turkey Buzzard do? He sets on the top of a dead pine tree where the sun can warm him up, and he stretches out his wings, and he turns round and round so the wind can dry his feathers, and he laughs to himself, and he says: "This rain is over. It ain't going to rain no more. No use for me to build a house now."

A careless man is just like Buh Turkey Buzzard.

Buh Fox Says Grace

Buh Squirrel was very busy gathering hickory nuts from the ground to put away to feed himself and his family in the winter. Buh Fox been watching him, and before Buh Squirrel see him he slipped up and grabbed him. Buh Squirrel, he was that scared he trembled all over, and he beg Buh Fox to let him go. Buh Fox tell him, say he been trying to catch Buh Squirrel a long time, but Buh Squirrel have such sharp eyes, and keen ears, and spry legs that he managed to dodge him; and now, when he got him at last, he means to kill Buh Squirrel and eat him.

When Buh Squirrel find out that Buh Fox isn't going to pity him and turn him loose, but that he's fixing to kill him and eat him, Buh Squirrel say to Buh Fox: "Don't you know they say nobody ought to eat vittles before he says grace over 'em?"

Buh Fox answered: "That's so." And with that he put Buh Squirrel in front of him, and he fall on his knees, and cover his eyes with his hand, and he turn in to say grace.

While Buh Fox do this, Buh Squirrel managed to slip away; and when Buh Fox open his eyes he see Buh Squirrel had run up a tree where he couldn't touch him.

Buh Fox saw he couldn't help himself, and he called after Buh Squirrel: "Never mind, Boy, you done got away now, but the next time I clap this hand on you I'm going to eat you first and say grace afterward."

The best thing for a man is to make sure of his vittles before he says thank you for them.

Knee-high Man Wants to Be Sizable

De knee-high man lived by de swamp. He wuz alwez a-wantin' to be big 'stead of little. He sez to hisself: "I is gwinter ax de biggest thing in dis neighborhood how I kin git sizable" So he goes to see Mr. Horse. He ax him: "Mr. Horse, I come to git you to tell me how to git big like you is."

Mr. Horse, he say: "You eat a whole lot of corn and den you run round and round and round, till you ben about twenty miles and atter a while you big as me."

So de knee-high man, he done all Mr. Horse tole him. An' de corn make his stomach hurt, and runnin' make his legs hurt and de trying make his mind hurt. And he gits littler and littler. Den de knee-high man he set in his house and study how come Mr. Horse ain't help him

From Stars Fell on Alabama, *by Carl Carmer, New York, Farrar and Rinehart, 1934; republished by Doubleday, 1952. Reprinted by kind permission of Carl Carmer.*

none. And he say to hisself: "I is gwinter go see Brer Bull."

So he go to see Brer Bull and he say: "Brer Bull, I come to ax you to tell me how to git big like you is."

And Brer Bull, he say: "You eat a whole lot o' grass and den you bellow and bellow and fust thing you know you gits big like I is."

And de knee-high man he done all Brer Bull tole him. And de grass make his stomach hurt, and de bellowing make his neck hurt and de thinking make his mind hurt. And he git littler and littler. Den de knee-high man he set in his house and he study how come Brer Bull ain't done him no good. Atter wile, he hear ole Mr. Hoot Owl way in de swamp preachin' dat de bad peoples is sure gwinter have de bad luck.

Den de knee-high man he say to hisself: "I gwinter ax Mr. Hoot Owl how I kin git to be sizable," and he go to see Mr. Hoot Owl.

And Mr. Hoot Owl say: "What for you want to be big?" and de knee-high man say: "I wants to be big so when I gits a fight, I ken whup."

And Mr. Hoot Owl say: "Anybody ever try to kick a scrap wid you?"

De knee-high man he say naw. And Mr. Hoot Owl say: "Well den, you ain't got no cause to fight, and you ain't got no cause to be mo' sizable 'an you is."

De knee-high man says: "But I wants to be big so I kin see a fur ways." Mr. Hoot Owl, he say: "Can't you climb a tree and see a fur ways when you is clim' to de top?"

De knee-high man, he say: "Yes." Den Mr. Hoot Owl say: "You ain't got no cause to be bigger in de body, but you sho' is got cause to be bigger in de BRAIN."

Reform Meeting

One time there was a big gatherin' of animals and fowls and birds to talk about everybody behavin' better. Instead of talkin' about doin' better, they start to tell what other folks doin' bad. Buh Hyena up and complained about the way Buh Buzzard was carryin' on. Seems his complaint was Buzzard was gettin' there first to eat. Then Buh Wildcat complained about the troublesome mice and rats. 'Pears like he liked to eat mice and rats real good. Then Buh Tiger up and groaned about the rabbits, sayin' they was the worst of all.

Old Buh Coon he couldn't stand the way the talk was goin', and he called the meetin' to order. "Friends," Buh Coon say, "we all got to do a lot better or we're goin' to end up in bad shape. What have you all got to say about reformin' ourselves?"

Buh Tiger he talk right up. "I'm for reform," he say. "I see Buh Coon stealin' corn every night, and it got to stop."

Then Sister Cow come in with, "I'm for reform too. Buh Tiger he got the blood of my young ones in his mouth, and it got to stop."

This story comes from an old Livingston, Alabama, newspaper, and was discovered by Ruby Pickens Tartt. It also appears in Terrapin's Pot of Sense, © *1957 by Harold Courlander. By permission of Holt, Rinehart and Winston.*

Buh Elephant say his piece then: "Look who talkin' about things which got to stop. Sister Cow is eatin' up all the grass, and leave nothin' for the Elephant."

Buh Wolf chime in with his song, sayin', "Men are goin' around carryin' guns and knives, and it isn't safe no more to go after 'em."

Buh Coon he call the meetin' to order again. "We got to have less complaints and more reform," he say. "Who is got somethin' to suggest?"

Well, Buh Deer pop right up and say all the animals got to stop eatin' meat. Buh Wolf don't like that proposition, and he say what's needed is for all the animals to stop eatin' grass. Sister Chicken she say they all miss the main point, which is that they got to kill all the snakes. Then Buh Fox say, "No, I rent my cave to the snakes. What we got to do is kill all the worms." The birds don't like that at all, figurin' to starve if the worms are killed. So they all kept at it, everybody tryin' to keep what was good for himself and get rid of what his neighbor wanted.

At last old Buh Coon rise up and say: "Now if any of you folks are agreeable to get rid of something you like for *yourself,* say so." But didn't nobody say a word, just set so quiet you could hear the potato vines growin'.

"This is sure a sinful world we are livin' in," Buh Coon say, "but when everybody just find fault with everybody else, it's time to quit and go back where you come from. You got to begin charity next door. But if you want to *reform,* it's got to begin at home."

Buh Fox's Number Nine Shoes

You children ever study about how come Buh Rabbit generally get the best of things, particularly with Buh Fox? You'd think Buh Fox goin' to learn a few tricks, the way Rabbit always outsmartin' him. Buh Fox sort of figure it that way too, and that's why he never give up tryin' to out-trick Buh Rabbit. Just about everything Buh Rabbit do in his dealin's with Buh Fox is a little different. He never do the same trick twice, and that's the secret of it. Every time Fox get the worst of it from Rabbit, he say, "Man, I'm goin' to remember that trick. Rabbit ain't *never* goin' to catch me with it again." Well then, next time it's a different trick Rabbit does. Fox is smart enough in his way. He never make the same mistake twice. But just the same, every one of his mistakes has a big resemblance to all the others.

That's the way it was the time Fox had Buh Rabbit holed up in a hollow log. Log had a hole at both ends, but Fox wouldn't go in either way 'cause he's afraid Buh Rabbit go out the other way. So he just set there waitin'. He say, "Buh Rabbit, come on out. Ain't no use hidin' in there, 'cause if you do I'll just starve you to death."

This story and the one that follows, "The Well," are from Terrapin's Pot of Sense, © 1957 by Harold Courlander, *and are reprinted by permission of Holt, Rinehart and Winston.*

Buh Rabbit say, "I don't know about that, Mr. Fox. Reckon I can wait just as long as you."

So Buh Fox just wait, settin' there in the hot sun with his tongue hangin' out. Rabbit don't mind it where he's at, it's nice and cool in there. Buh Fox commence to get hungry.

After a while Rabbit say, "Mr. Fox, you must get mighty tired eatin' nothin' but rabbit and chicken. How'd you like to try a big mess of fish for a change?"

"Well," Fox say, "what you got on your mind?"

"The way it is," Buh Rabbit say, "Buh Bear went fishin' this mornin', and pretty soon he's comin' home with a cartful. Man, it sure makes my mouth water."

"Mine too," Fox say, "but you made a big fool of me before, Buh Rabbit, and I ain't takin' no chances. Besides, ain't nobody can get them fish away from Buh Bear."

" 'Cept me," Rabbit say, "But if you don't want to go partners on this trick, don't make no difference to me. I got a big pile of greens in here and I'm fixed to stay a couple of weeks."

"I'll tell you what," Buh Fox say. "You come on out and we'll get the fish."

Buh Rabbit say, "How I know you ain't foolin' me, Buh Fox? I think I'm goin' to hole up here for a while."

"Come on, Rabbit," Fox say. "You got my mouth waterin' for fish."

So Buh Rabbit come out of the log. He say, "You stay here in the bushes and keep quiet. I'll go down the road a ways and wait for Buh Bear."

Fox he suspicious what Rabbit goin' to do, but he set in the bushes while Rabbit went down the road. When Rabbit see Buh Bear comin' along with his load of fish, he took off one of his shoes and set it right in the middle of the road, and then he hid himself in the grass. Pretty soon Buh Bear get there hollerin' giddap to his mule. When he see that one lonesome shoe there in the road he stop. "That shoe might just fit me," Bear say, "but what good is one shoe?" After that he left the shoe where it was and went on his way with his cartload of fish.

Well, Buh Rabbit take that shoe, the very same one, and run way 'round the field till he get ahead of Buh Bear again, and he put the shoe back in the road. When Buh Bear get there he say, "What you know, there's the other one!" And he left the cart right where it was and went back to get the first shoe.

Soon as he's gone, Buh Rabbit put his shoe on and take all the fish out of Buh Bear's cart. He gave some to Buh Fox and headed home with all the rest.

Now Buh Fox see everything that Buh Rabbit do. "That's a mighty smart trick," he say, "I think I can do it myself." So next day he wait for Buh Bear to come along with a load of fish, and he put one of his own shoes, number nine, out in the road where Buh Bear will see it. Buh Bear he been fooled once, but he been doin' some thinkin' since he lost all his fish the day before. So when he see Buh Fox's shoe, he pick it up and throw it in the cart. Don't wait to find the other one.

Buh Fox he run way ahead of the cart, and of course he's only got one shoe left now, so he puts that one in the road and wait for Mr. Bear to come along. Naturally there wasn't no purpose in it any more, but Buh Fox didn't get the point of it. When Buh Bear come along, he stop just long enough to pick up the other shoe.

"Well, now, I got a mighty fine pair of number nines," Bear say. "Giddap, mule."

Fox find out he's got no shoes at all, and no fish either. So he run after Bear, sayin', "Mornin', Buh Bear. You happen to find a nice pair of shoes this mornin'?"

"Maybe I did," Buh Bear say. "What size you wear?"

"Number nine," Fox say.

"I learned a lot about shoes since yesterday," Bear say, "Come on here and tell me are these shoes yours."

"Yeah, they sure look like my shoes, Buh Bear," Fox say.

"Look close," Bear say.

Buh Fox put his nose right up there. "They're mine all right," he say.

Bear grab Fox by the scruff of the neck. "You got my fish yesterday, Buh Fox," he say, "and I got you today!"

Well, the whuppin' Bear gave Buh Fox was a sight to see. Fox yelpin' and hollerin', Buh Bear cuffin' him first on one side then the other, and red fur flyin' every-which-way. When Fox got out of there he was a sad sight. Had to go home and grow a new coat of fur, and ain't *nobody* see him for four weeks and seven days.

Like I said before, the moral is—it don't do you no good to learn the right trick at the wrong time. Trouble with Buh Fox, if he'd done that trick on *Wednesday* 'stead of *Thursday* he'd made good on it. *Time* is one element you can't fool around with.

The Well

One time the rivers and lakes and everything dried up on account of there wasn't no rain. You might say it was the worst dry spell they ever had, and it was gettin' mighty difficult even to get a drink of water anywhere. So all the animals got together in a big meetin' to discuss the situation.

"It's sure bad for me and my family," Buh 'Gator say, "we ain't got no water to crawl in, and we can't take this hot sun."

"We're worse off than you," Buh Catfish say, "we floppin' around in the mudholes and pretty soon they goin' to be altogether dried up, the way things are goin'."

Buh Wasp say, "Where's that mud at? I'm lookin' for a little bit of wet mud to make my nest out of, but can't find it. Everything turn to sand around my place."

"Never mind about these particulars," Buh Coon say, "the main problem is what we goin' to drink. Anybody got any suggestions?"

"Milk," Buh Calf holler, "I goin' to drink milk."

"No, you ain't," Sister Cow say. "If I don't get no water soon, you ain't goin' to have no milk neither."

"What we got to have is a well," Buh Coon say. "Everybody want to drink water can help dig it."

Right then and there everybody went to work. There was some powerful diggers 'mongst them animals. Mr. Ground Hog, he's a natural-born digger. So's Mr. Mole. Sister Chicken scratched away. Buh Bull pawed the ground. Buh Horse kicked up the dirt. Buh Dog had lots of experience, and he went to it with his two front feet, stickin' his nose down in the hole every once in a while to see could he smell water. Buh Worm wriggled down and loosened the dirt. Buh Crow come down and picked up the loose stones and flew off with 'em. Mr. Fox, he's a diggin' man too, and he pitched in. Only one of all those animals didn't join in the diggin'. That was Buh Rabbit. He just set off to one side in the shade, watchin' the rest of 'em work.

After a while Buh Coon say, "Mr. Rabbit, how come you ain't diggin' with the rest of us?"

Rabbit, he say, "I don't need no well for myself, Buh Coon. I can lick the dew off the grass, that's plenty water for me."

"Well, there's one thing about it," Coon say, "ain't *nobody* drinks from this well but the ones who *digs* it."

"Yeah," the other critters say, "if Buh Rabbit ain't goin' to dig, he can't have no water."

After a while they hit water gravel, and the water came and filled up the hole. Let me tell you, all them animals was real happy with that. Everybody what wanted a drink came and took it. Buh Wasp took some water off and made some mud of his own and went to work buildin' his nest. Buh Catfish hauled some water off in a pail and poured it in the mudhole where his young ones was livin'. Alligator took some and splashed it on himself to cool off.

Next mornin' when they came back again, they find Buh Rabbit's tracks there. This makes all the folks real mad, 'cause Rabbit ain't done nothin' toward the diggin' of that well. They say, "What we need is a watchman to keep Mr. Rabbit away." So they 'pointed Buh Bear watchman. When night come, Buh Bear sat down by the well and waited. Buh Rabbit hidin' in the bushes, but he don't come out. After a while Buh Bear fall asleep. Then Rabbit come and get a drink and go away.

In the mornin' the animals come and say, "You seen Buh Rabbit last night?"

"Uh-uh, I ain't seen 'im," Bear say.

"Man, you must have been asleep," they say. "There's his tracks."

Next night they 'point Buh Wolf as watchman, but he fall asleep too. In the mornin' they find Buh Rabbit's tracks again.

"Seems to me we got to have somethin' better," Buh Coon tell all the folks. "I recommend we 'lect Buh Bullfrog as watchman."

"Me too," the animals holler, and they made Bullfrog the watchman.

That night Bullfrog sit by the well, watchin' with them big round eyes. Every time his eyes begin to close he holler, "I'm gone!" and jump in the water to freshen himself up.

Every time Rabbit think the watchman is asleep, he begin to creep up on the well, and Bullfrog holler, "Here he is! Here he is!"

Then Rabbit got to skedaddle to the bushes again.

Now I ask you, you ever see a rabbit drinkin' at the well? You sure don't, and you never will. And you ever figure why there's a frog in every well? He's the watchman, that's why, and he keeps Rabbit away. Almost every night you can hear Bullfrog holler, "Here he is! Here he is!" Or once in a while he says, "I'm gone!" and jumps in the water to wake himself up. That's the reason we got frogs in wells, and it's the main reason Buh Rabbit got to get up real early in the mornin' and lick the dew off the grass, like he boasted he could do.

There's just one more point about all this. I guess you never give much studyin' to why that long-handled pump out there screeches like anything sometimes, and other times it don't. Fact is, it pick up from where Buh Bullfrog left off. Every time it screeches when you pump it, that's because Buh Rabbit is loiterin' around waitin' to get a drink. If you listen good you can hear what that screech say—"Quit hangin' around! Quit hangin' around!"

Point is, no matter how sharp you are, you got to keep on the good side of people, else your smart ways goin' to get you in difficulty. There's a lot to bein' sharp, and maybe you can use it against one critter at a time and come off good, but when it comes to bein' sharp against the whole community at once, it don't pay off.

THE BEGINNING OF THINGS

Origin of the Races,

ACCORDING TO UNCLE REMUS

One night, while the little boy was watching Uncle Remus twisting and waxing some shoe-thread, he made what appeared to him to be a very curious discovery. He discovered that the palms of the old man's hands were as white as his own, and the fact was such a source of wonder that he at last made it the subject of remark. The response of Uncle Remus led to the earnest recital of a piece of unwritten history that must prove interesting to ethnologists.

"Tooby sho de pa'm er my han's w'ite, honey," he quietly remarked, "en, w'en it come ter dat, dey wuz a time w'en all de w'ite folks 'uz

From Uncle Remus, His Songs and His Sayings, *by Joel Chandler Harris, New York, 1880, 1895.*

black—blacker dan me, kaze I done bin yer so long dat I bin sorter bleach out."

The little boy laughed. He thought Uncle Remus was making him the victim of one of his jokes; but the youngster was never more mistaken. The old man was serious. Nevertheless, he failed to rebuke the ill-timed mirth of the child, appearing to be altogether engrossed in his work. After a while, he resumed:

"Yasser. Fokes dunner w'at bin yit, let 'lone w'at gwinter be. Niggers is niggers now, but de time wuz w'en we 'uz all niggers tergedder."

"When was that, Uncle Remus?"

"Way back yander. In dem times we 'uz all un us black; we 'uz all niggers tergedder, en 'cordin' ter all de 'counts w'at I years fokes 'uz gittin' 'long 'bout ez well in dem days ez dey is now. But atter 'w'ile de news come dat dere wuz a pon' er water some'rs in de naberhood, w'ich ef dey'd git inter dey'd be wash off nice en w'ite, en den one un um, he fine de place en make er splunge inter de pon', en come out w'ite ez a town gal. En den, bless grashus! w'en de fokes seed it, dey make a break fer de pon', en dem w'at wuz de soopless, dey got in fus' en dey come out w'ite; en dem w'at wuz de nex' soopless, dey got in nex', en dey come out merlatters; en dey wuz such a crowd un um dat dey mighty nigh use de water up, w'ich w'en dem yuthers come 'long, de morest dey could do wuz ter paddle about wid der foots en dabble in it wid der han's. Dem wuz de niggers, en down ter dis day dey ain't no w'ite 'bout a nigger 'ceppin de pa'ms er der han's en de soles er der foot."

The little boy seemed to be very much interested in this new account of the origin of races, and he made some further inquiries, which elicited from Uncle Remus the following additional particulars:

"De Injun en de Chinee got ter be 'counted 'long er de merlatter. I ain't seed no Chinee dat I knows un, but dey tells me dey er sorter 'twix' a brown en a brindle. Dey er all merlatters."

"But mamma says the Chinese have straight hair," the little boy suggested.

"Co'se, honey," the old man unhesitatingly responded, "dem w'at git ter de pon' time nuff fer ter git der head in de water, de water hit onkink der ha'r. Hit bleedzd ter be dat away."

The Deluge,

ACCORDING TO UNCLE REMUS

"One time," said Uncle Remus—adjusting his spectacles so as to be able to see how to thread a large darning needle with which he was patching his coat—"one time, way back yander, 'fo' you wuz borned, honey, en 'fo' Mars John er Miss Sally wuz borned—way back yander 'fo' enny un us wuz borned, de anemils en de creeturs sorter 'lecshuneer roun' 'mong deyselves, twel at las' dey 'greed fer ter have a 'sembly. In dem days," continued the old man, observing a look of incredulity on the little boy's face, "in dem days creeturs had lots mo' sense dan dey got now; let 'lone dat, dey had sense same like folks. Hit was tech en go wid um, too, mon, en w'en dey make up der mines w'at hatter be done, 'twant mo'n menshun'd 'fo' hit wuz done. Well, dey 'lected dat dey hatter hole er 'sembly fer ter sorter straighten out marters en hear de complaints, en w'en de day come dey wuz on han'. De Lion, he wuz dar, kase he wuz de king, en he hatter be der. De Rhynossyhoss, he wuz dar, en de Elephent, he wuz dar, en de Cammils, en de Cows, en plum down ter de Crawfishes, dey wuz dar. Dey wuz all dar. En w'en de Lion shuck his mane, en tuck his seat in de big cheer, den de sesshun begun fer ter commence."

"What did they do, Uncle Remus?" asked the little boy.

"I can't skacely call to mine 'zackly w'at dey did do, but dey spoke speeches, en hollered, en cusst, en flung der langwidge 'roun' des like w'en you' daddy wuz gwineter run fer de legislater en got lef'. Howsomever, dey 'ranged der 'fairs, en splained der bizness. Bimeby, w'ile dey wuz 'sputin' 'longer one er nudder, de Elephent trompled on one er de Crawfishes. Co'se w'en dat creetur put his foot down, w'atsumever's under dar wuz boun' fer ter be squshed, en dey wa'n't nuff er dat Crawfish lef' fer ter tell dat he'd bin dar.

"Dis make de udder Crawfishes mighty mad, en dey sorter swarmed tergedder en draw'd up a kinder peramble wid some wharfo'es in it, en read her out in de 'sembly. But, bless grashus! sech a racket wuz a gwine on dat nobody ain't hear it, 'ceppin may be de Mud Turkle en de Spring Lizzud, en dere enfloons wuz pow'ful lackin'.

"Bimeby, w'iles de Nunicorn wuz 'sputin' wid de Lion, en w'ile de Hyener wuz a laughin' ter hisse'f, de Elephent squshed anudder one er de Crawfishes, en a little mo'n he'd er ruint de Mud Turkle. Den de Crawfishes, w'at dey wuz lef' un um, swarmed tergedder en draw'd up anudder peramble wid sum mo' wharfo'es; but dey might ez well er sung Ole Dan Tucker ter a harrycane. De udder creeturs wuz too busy wid der fussin' fer ter 'spon' unto de Crawfishes. So dar dey wuz, de Crawfishes, en dey didn't know w'at minnit wuz gwineter be de nex'; en dey kep' on gittin madder en madder en skeerder en skeerder, twel bimeby dey gun de wink ter de Mud Turkle en de Spring Lizzud, en den dey bo'd little holes in de groun' en went down outer sight."

"Who did, Uncle Remus?" asked the little boy.

"De Crawfishes, honey. Dey bo'd inter de groun' en kep' on bo'in twel dey onloost de fountains er de earf; en de waters squirt out, en riz higher en higher twel de hills wuz kivvered, en de creeturs wuz all drownded; en all bekaze dey let on 'mong deyselves dat dey wuz bigger dan de Crawfishes."

Then the old man blew the ashes from a smoking yam, and proceeded to remove the peeling.

"Where was the ark, Uncle Remus?" the little boy inquired, presently.

"W'ich ark's dat?" asked the old man, in a tone of well-feigned curiosity.

"Noah's ark," replied the child.

"Don't you pester wid ole man Noah, honey. I boun' he tuck keer er dat ark. Dat's w'at he wuz dar fer, en dat's w'at he done. Leas'ways, dat's w'at dey tells me. But don't you bodder longer dat ark, 'ceppin' your mammy fetches it up. Dey mout er bin two deloojes, en den agin dey moutent. Ef dey wuz enny ark in dish yer w'at de Crawfishes brung on, I ain't heern tell un it, en w'en dey ain't no arks 'roun', I ain't got no time fer ter make um en put um in dar. Hit's gittin' yo' bedtime, honey."

SOME FAMILIAR PROVERBS

Jest countin' stumps don't clear the field.
Don't tell the white man has he forgot his hat, he'll jest say, "Nigger, bring it here."
No use singin' spirituals to a dead mule.
Wagon makes the loudest noise when it's goin' out empty.
A woman who know how to cook is mighty pretty.
Talkin' 'bout fire doesn't boil the pot.
Takin' your cat to church for salvation may please the deacon but it make all the other folks laugh.
When the preacher come by for Sunday dinner it make the chickens cry.
Old Used-to-Do-It-This-Way don't help none today.
Flies can't fall in a tight-closed pot.
Death don't see no difference 'tween the big house and the cabin.
Ain't no use askin' the cow to pour you a glass of milk.
Can't break the plow point twice.
Hand plow can't make furrows by itself.
Dog don't get mad when you says he's a dog.
Galluses (or belt) is small but it help keep you warm.
Buzzard ain't circle in the air jest for fun.
Can't sit on the bucket and draw water at the same time.

AN ALABAMA STORYTELLER AND BARD

In communities whose literary riches are mainly oral, and whose traditions are passed on from one generation to another "mouth to ear," as it is said, almost anyone can tell a story, but there are always a select few who stand out as masters of the narrative arts. In the American rural south the role of the storyteller of distinction slowly gave ground in this century to radio, television, and other mass media of communication. Like John Henry in contest with the steam drill, the itinerant narrator and entertainer found himself outmoded. But some of them, such as Richard Manuel Amerson, went on to the end believing in themselves, telling their tales and yarns, their hard-to-believe stories and literary lies, their preachments and their truths, on whatever street corner or in whatever cabin they happened to find themselves.

Rich Amerson, of Sumter County, Alabama, was by occupation—that is to say, whatever job he could get—a poor farmer, a lumberjack, a storm-pit builder, a track liner, a lay preacher. He sermonized when it was called for, counteracted conjur, sang religious songs, blues, and ballads, and recited personal adventures, both real and apocryphal. He was known in small towns throughout western Alabama, in some communities in Mississippi, and to at least a few people in Texas. He was a singing leader in railroad and logging gangs and a Saturday night entertainer. He gave whatever was wanted. If people wanted a harmonica tune, he was ready. If they wanted a sermon instead, he gave it. If he himself felt like it, he did a buck and wing dance. His stories ranged from personal narratives to tales of slave days to Brer Rabbit. One of Amerson's blues ballads, "Black Woman" (see p. 524) has been spoken of as one of the finest examples known in this genre.

Amerson was something more than a raconteur and living storehouse of tales. He was a man whose sense of poetry could not be diminished by the harshness of life. He saw the world the large way, a gift to which many aspire but few achieve. "I can look and I can see," he said, "that's the biggest part of it all. Sumter County is full of people looking back and forth, but what do they see, I ask you? And do they understand what they see? What good is it to be born if you don't understand what you see? In the ordinary sense I can't neither read *nor* write. But the sense God gave you don't depend altogether on schooling. I was schooled in hard work, and I read with a hoe and write with a plow. I ain't proud to be poor, but I ain't too poor to be proud. And I'm not too poor to be rich in values. Music is in everything you see and hear. Railroad, now that's music, isn't it? And church, that's music too, isn't it? And if you come right down to it, music is church too. Some folks, now, they won't sing no sinful songs. The way I see it, if a song is in you you got to sing it, and it's just another aspect of the Holy Spirit. When life is big, music is big."

The Amerson texts are from Negro Folk Music of Alabama, *a six-record set of recordings made by Harold Courlander in Alabama in 1950. New York, Ethnic Folkways Library, 1956, 1960.*

Some of Amerson's epic religious songs are included in the section, "As the Spirituals Are Sung" (see p. 342). Here are some of his yarns, tall tales, and preachments.

Chicago and Rome

(Coupled here are the great Chicago fire— begun, according to tradition, when Mrs. O'Leary's cow kicked over a kerosine lamp— and the Capitoline geese, which, according to legend, saved Rome from the Gauls circa 390 B.C. In Amerson's rendition Rome becomes a biblical city, and its inhabitants Christians, with the threat to first-born males interpolated from *Exodus*.)

The kick of a cow burned up the city of Chicago. That's a city, ain't it? And the cackle of the geese saved the city of Rome. You hear me talkin' to you here, black man, don't you? Now listen, I want to make that plain, don't I? Chicago has been a fine city, covered all over just like sheep's wool. And they wasn't allowed to drop a match nowhere. And there was a woman had a gentle cow, known not to kick. And she was in a hurry to fix her husband's breakfast, to milk. She set the lamp at the back of her heels to milk two teats, and the cow kicked the lamp over, and it burned up the whole city, and it exploded. That's why I meant the kick of a cow burned up Chicago.

I said the cackle of the geese saved the whole city of Rome. The city of Rome was full of boy children. And it come a group of men to destroy them boy children, wasn't it? And it was a lake down there just before they got a mile or so of the city. And the men who have the guns to destroy 'em come at four o'clock at that lake, and some geese come up in front of them and cackle, and they thought it was a pair of angels from Christ that wanted them not to do it. And the cackle of the geese saved the city of Rome, didn't it? Directly.

River, Creek, Sun, Moon

(This appears to be a very old riddle, with the sun represented as a male and the moon as a female who replenishes the rivers.)

> The river's all muddy
> And the creek gone dry.
> If it wasn't for the women
> The men would all die.

What you reckon. . . . Talk black, Richard, talk. Somebody tell me whether I'm right or wrong. Don't want to tell you my black self. I said the river's all muddy, if the creek goes dry, if it wasn't for the women the men would all die. God sends sunshine, the devil sends rain. If it didn't never rain three hundred and sixty-five days the sun would set the world afire. And if the moon didn't never change, that's the woman didn't rain, it wouldn't be no water in the creeks and neither the rivers, would it, and the men would all die. That's what I'm talkin' about. The moon's a woman and the sun's a man. Glory halleluja, that's directly.

The Draft Board

There was this time I was turned down by the draft board. You want to hear about it?

The first thing they asked was my occupation, and I told 'em, "Eatin'." And next they asked me where was I borned at. I told 'em I was born twelve miles out of Livingston, but I didn't know if that was counted by white folks or Negroes. The next thing they asked me was what day was I born. And I told 'em I didn't know if it was day or night, I hadn't heard my mamma or papa say nothin' about it. I told 'em I couldn't write. They gave me a picture of a rabbit with one leg and no head and told me to do whatever I thought best about it. I took a pencil and marked that paper till it got black and then tore it up. Well, I didn't like it, that's why I do it, because he told me to do whatever I thought best about it. And that was the best I knowed to do about it.

Well, they asked me what military service was, and I told 'em, "Eatin'." I said, "Directly, that's all I know about it." They had me in a race after that, runnin' to try me out. I run alongside my buddy and my buddy fainted. And when my buddy fainted I fainted too and fell on 'im. He puffed and blowed and I puffed and blowed. And I heard somethin' comin', like a horse arunnin'. And I got up and looked and picked up my buddy and says, "There's a white man comin' with a big horse his mouth wide open, and a forty-five and a blackjack." And when I got up he ask me had I got cool, and I said, "Yes, sir." That cured me, that got me cool.

But after that they tell me, "Richard Amerson, you been turned down for military service." And that's how come I never made it in the army. Now which one of us was the sharpest?

The Visit to Dr. Readys

I learned there was a whole lot to bein' ugly. But I offered eighteen dollars to change my countenance and be pretty. We got a doctor come in Mississippi State about fifteen years ago. I've heard him called Dr. Readys. You've heard of him, didn't you? Says he could cure anything a man wasn't born with. Well I liked that better than I did anything di-

rectly on earth as ever I heard. When I heard of him I like to shouted.
And I supplied to my sisters, "Thank God. You always been better
lookin' than I am, but I'm goin' to be the best lookin' man now, because I can pay eighteen dollars and get back like I have been born."

She supplied, "Bud, you was the prettiest baby of all Mamma's children."

And I says, "Now, I got five sisters livin' and I'm uglier than all of
'em, and I'm goin' now to see about it."

So a car full of we men got in the car and drove up to Dr. Readys'
office, where I got that paper from. And we lined up and walked up to
that gentleman. When he got through with everybody, doctorin' on
'em, he says "Now Rich Amerson, number one, walk up and give me
your complaint here."

I says, "My complaint is, Doctor, my mother mothered fifteen children, and I was the prettiest baby that's born, prettier than all the children. Since then I'm the ugliest thing in the bunch." Say, "I want to
know, can you cure me and get me back pretty like I was. I'm a sick patient."

The answer he supplied to me, "I'm not God."

"Well," I says, "you are. I been through your paper say you can cure
what a man wasn't born with." I say, "By that, you can cure me, listen,
back pretty like I was."

Doctor said, "Come out of the office over here by your paper."

And I said, "Another thing. I'm now an undone sinner." I says, "I'm
sick. Can you give me advice in here. If you can't cure this face and
make it look beautiful, can you make the soul beautiful? Can you give
me a little taste of medicine here will cure this sinsick pain, and let me
be born again? And then I'm pretty again."

He ordered me out of his office, says, "I'm not God."

I say, "Listen, then, don't make the express that you can cure what a
man wasn't born with."

"That's directly," he says. "Who you think, now, is the fool, me or
you?"

I said, "Me."

He said, "I'm the fool, and I give it to you."

And he shook hands and I walked out.

Excerpt from an Amerson Street Corner Sermon

We got everything in our church. We got some dogs in there. We got
hogs in there. We got cows a-lowin' in there. We got dogs a-barkin'.
You want to hear the voice of what I mean? Listen right close. When
you walk into church, if your shoes look bad you goin' to hear a Negro
say, "Umn!" Wasn't that a hog grunt? That grunt like a hog, didn't it?
And if you don't mind, you hear somebody way over there, "Aa-kaa-
kaa-kaa-kaa-kaa-kaa!" Didn't that cackle like a hen? I said they had
chickens in there, didn't they? Yes, sir. After while you goin' to hear

sounds like dogs growlin' in there, didn't they? Your preacher goin' to holler, "Hey-ey-ey-ah!" Then he go to say, "Yah-ah-ah." Ain't that a dog growlin'? That's a dog, ain't it? Now we got a ball game, somebody's hollerin' in there. After a while a sister jump up and shoutin', "Hey-ey-ey!" Isn't that just like the squall of a ball game?

THE TUB WITH THE ANCIENT ANTECEDENTS

One of the commonly seen instruments of street musicians in days not long past was the "washtub bass," also known as a "tub," a "drum," and a "gutbucket" (that is, a bucket plus a gut string). It was used to provide a small range of bass tones for a musical ensemble that often included a washboard scraper, metal percussion (perhaps a frying pan) and a guitar. The washtub bass is simply an inverted washtub (or an appropriate substitute) to the center of which a cord is attached. The other end of the cord is fastened to the top of a broomstick, the free end of which is braced against the lip of the inverted tub so that the cord is taut. Plucking or slapping the cord produces a musical tone, with the tub acting as a resonating chamber. Pressure against the stick varies the tautness of the cord and produces different tones. The tub player usually stands with one foot on its edge to keep it firmly on the ground. Sometimes a second player beats a rhythm on the metal "drumhead."

This instrument is an improvisation only in the sense that available modern materials have been adapted to an old use. The ancestor of the washtub bass is found not only in West and Central Africa but also in Afro-American communities in the West Indies. The African device was an apparent development of the spring snare, used for capturing small game. In its more primitive form, the resulting instrument was an earth bow, constructed in the following manner. A hole was dug in the earth next to a small green sapling, or a green stick was imbedded in the ground next to the hole. The hole was then covered with a bark or hide membrane, which was pegged down at the edges or held in place by stones. The sapling was bent over the hole and fastened by a cord to the center of the membrane covering. The taut cord was played by rubbing, plucking, and tapping, and a second player sometimes beat a rhythm on the membrane with sticks. A portable variant used a wooden box instead of a hole in the ground for a resonating chamber.

Extracted from Negro Folk Music, U.S.A., *by Harold Courlander,* ©*1963 by Columbia University Press. By permission of Columbia University Press.*

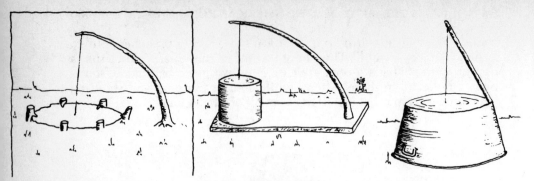

Evolution of the Gutbucket or Washtub Bass: *Left,* an earthbow, an African device developed from an animal snare. It is also known in Haiti and possibly elsewhere in Afro-America. *Middle,* a portable version found in the Caribbean, made of board, an inverted can and a bent stick. *Right,* the U.S. gutbucket, devised from an inverted washtub and a broomstick.

Both of these forms have survived in Haiti, with pails or large tins substituting for the wooden box.

The morphology of the American washtub bass leaves little doubt of its African ancestry. Not only is the basic structure of the instrument noteworthy, so is its manner of playing, which is virtually identical with the African technique. Add to this the frequently seen second player beating on the drumhead with sticks, and it is very difficult indeed to conclude anything but that the "makeshift" tub is in reality an instrument with a long history.

The emergence of the double bass viol in jazz band settings as a slapping and plucking instrument is an associated musical phenomenon. The method of playing on the strings is closely related to that of playing the tub, and the instrument has the same role in relation to the other instruments—that of providing varying bass tones. The plucking of the bass viol and the cello is certainly nothing new, but the concept of the bass viol as an instrument which is not bowed at all is not in the European tradition.

THE CAROLINA YELL AND OTHER CRIES AND CALLS

More than a hundred years ago, in 1853, a correspondent of the New York *Daily Times,* Frederick Olmstead, heard and wrote about what he

Extracted from Negro Folk Music, U.S.A., *by Harold Courlander,* © 1963 *by Columbia University Press, by permission of the publishers.*

called "Negro jodling" or "the Carolina yell." The scene was in South Carolina, nighttime along the railroad tracks:

"At midnight I was awakened by loud laughter, and, looking out, saw that the loading gang of negroes [slaves hired out to the railroad] had made a fire and were enjoying a right merry repast. Suddenly one raised such a sound as I had never heard before, a long, loud, musical shout, rising, and falling, and breaking into falsetto, his voice ringing through the woods in the clear, frosty night air, like a bugle call. As he finished, the melody was caught up by another, and then, another, then by several in chorus. When there was silence again, one of them cried out, as if bursting with amusement: 'Did yer see de dog?—when I began eeohing, he turn roun' an' look me straight into der face; ha! ha! ha!' and the whole party broke into the loudest peals of laughter, as if it was the very best joke they had ever heard."[1]

The Negro cries and calls of the open spaces are known by different names in different places. Sometimes they are called "corn field hollers," "cotton field hollers," or just "hollers." In Alabama, the term "whooping" is used, and it sometimes appears in songs ("Don't you hear me whoopin', oh, baby!"). According to one chronicler, some regions refer to the cries as "loud mouthing."

The cry does not have to have a theme, or to fit into any kind of formal structure, or to conform to normal concepts of musical propriety. It is often completely free music in which every sound line, and phrase is exploited for itself in any fashion that appeals to the crier. It may be short and sharp, with an abrupt end, or it can waver, thin out, and gently disappear into the air. It may consist of a single musical statement or a series of statements, and may reflect any one of a number of moods—homesickness, loneliness, lovesickness, contentment, exuberance. The clue often lies in the words as well as the music. One cry, heard in Alabama, went like this:

Ay-oh-hoh!
I'm goin' up the river!
Oh, couldn't stay here!
For I'm goin' home!
So bad, I'm so far from home!
And I can't get there for walkin'!
I want to go home so bad partner!
I'm goin' up the river, but I can't stay here!
I'm goin' home, woh!
I won't get back till July and August.
I won't get there till fall.
My boat up the river.
But I can't stay here, want to go back!
Oh Lord!

1. Frederick Law Olmsted, "Journey in the Seaboard Slave States," in The Slave States Before the Civil War, edited by Harvey Wish, New York, Putnam's, 1959, pp. 114–115.

An elderly woman of eastern Alabama whose father was born a slave in that area remembered and was able to sing some of the field calls she heard as a child. As distinguished from cries, these calls all had some kind of communicative purpose. They conveyed simple messages, or merely made one's whereabouts known to friends working elsewhere in the fields. According to a number of aged informants, calls of this kind had great importance to slaves who were confined by their work to particular fields, and who were not free to socialize at times of their own choosing with friends in other fields or on neighboring plantations.

Sometimes, just for the comfort of making one's presence known to others, a field hand would give a wordless call such as this one:

And from a distance, in identical musical phrasing, would come the answer: "Yeh-ee-ee, yeh-hee! Yeh-ee-ee, yeh-hee!"

When the father called to his children for assistance in the fields, it sounded like this:

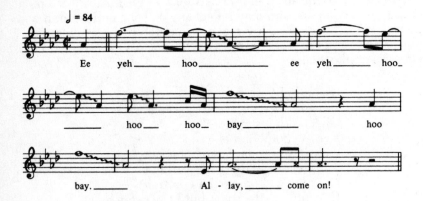

Young people seeking companionship or love might give the following call:

In slavery days, the field calls doubtless had a special importance that they lacked later. They were a means by which the slaves could keep in touch with one another, and perhaps get around regulations of the overseer that isolated one work party from another. In early slave days, these calls undoubtedly were in African dialects, insofar as actual words were used, and they must have been a source of irritation to white overseers who could not understand them.

In the farm fields of the present day, as on the old plantations, the water carrier is in constant demand. The call for the water boy (or girl), in one or another of its many variants, is well enough known that it has been interpolated into theater music and used by the concert recitalist. The water call given here was recorded in Alabama in 1950.

that I feel, little wa - ter time, hey,

lit - tle wa - ter boy, lit - tle wa - ter time, hey,

lit - tle wa - ter boy. Wa - ter on the wheel

how does the sun shine that I

feel, lit - tle wa - ter boy.

BLUES

Seen as oral literature, the traditional blues form is a vehicle used to express regret, remorse, or discontent with life. It tells the world about one's misfortunes, airs complaints against a person or a community, points a finger at someone who has caused suffering or injury, articulates a sense of injustice, or communicates a feeling of abuse, unhappiness, or melancholy. Men or women who have been unfaithful, or who have gone away or who have treated one badly are the subject of many blues. Others comment on poverty, sickness, lonesomeness, prison life, and even bedbugs. A blues song may contain tangent allusions to persons and events, and readily recognizable sexual innuendo. On occasion it may strike a light or humorous note. While it often borrows clichés and standard well-worn lines from other songs, it can also be reflective, philosophical, and poetic.

It is believed by some that the blues emerged into something like its present form at a particular time, possibly in the early years of this century or the closing years of the last, shaped out of the music of religious songs, work songs and field calls. Yet Africa and the Caribbean have songs comparable to the blues in their subject matter, and ultimately blues have to be recognized as a development of the traditional African song of gossip, complaint or recrimination. Musically, the blues contains melodic, tonal and rhythmic elements commonplace in work songs, spirituals, gospel songs, game songs and field cries. But there is every indication that it coexisted, by whatever name it was called, with these other forms early in the African experience in the New World. Its social function and its thematic content persuasively relate it to its African prototype and vitiate the supposition that it may be a product of late evolution in the New World setting. What has evolved is merely a conventionalized structure into which expressions of complaint and recrimination may be fitted. Though conventionalized, its form is far from rigid. As has been noted elsewhere:

What seems to be evident is that the blues stanza framework *tends* toward eight or twelve bars. In actual rendition, however, especially of songs that haven't been frozen into notations or popularized by performances on recordings, the blues stanza can be presented in eleven, thirteen, fourteen, fifteen, or seventeen bars. One rural blues heard in the South appeared to have twenty-two bars, and another contained twelve and a half bars. Certain blues songs are done in such free style as to fall into no clear-cut bar pattern at all. A contention that any blues song not cast into a twelve or eight bar form is "primitive" or "undeveloped" does not take into account the basic freedoms of folk music. The only consideration of a blues singer is that his song should sound "right," and there is ample elbow room within the limitations of what is effective for a good many types of things. The eight or twelve bar blues is probably no more traditional, and certainly no more "correct," than other variants. We are on firm ground if we think of the blues as a variable form centering in the neighborhood of twelve bars, with the swinging pendulum of improvisation or variation capable of producing a number of possibilities.

Concerning the lyrics of the blues, a number of characteristics stand out. Often, though not always, there is an original statement which is repeated, possibly with a slight word change or an added expletive, followed by another statement that supplements or rounds out the first. A blues song may consist of a series of stanzas which embellish or develop (or repeat) the theme put forward in the first stanza. They give more details of the story, or reflect upon it with different metaphors and images.

An element of rhyming is present in many, if not most, blues songs. Typical is a four-line stanza in which the second and last lines rhyme, or a six-line stanza in which the fourth and sixth rhyme. Sometimes the rhyme is determined by local speech dialect, and is not readily apparent when written. "Radio" may be rhymed with "more" ("mo'"), and "line" with "cryin'." Occasionally the rhyme is impure enough to be only suggested, and other times the rhyming effect is achieved by repetition of the same word. But there are blues in which other combinations of lines are rhymed, or in which no audible rhyme appears at all. Thus, the concept of rhyming is commonplace, but it is loosely conceived and not indispensable.

Another frequent characteristic of blues singing is the dropping or cutting off of the voice in the middle or near the end of a line, so that the burden of completion lies entirely on the instrumental accompaniment. When I asked one singer whether he had forgotten the words or was resting his voice, or whether he had some other reason for doing this, he replied: "No, I just step aside and let the guitar say it." Using this device to an extreme, a singer may articulate a few words at the beginning of a line or stanza and thereafter rely on humming or wordless open throat sounds, except where he withdraws his voice altogether. In such cases, the voice tends to become, in effect, accompaniment to the instrument. This relationship between voice and instrument has been widely observed in West Africa.

One may reasonably suspect that the partially articulated line of the traditional blues style is a carry-over from the responsive form which is so fundamental in Negro tradition. In numerous church and gang songs, for example, the statement of the leader is completed by the second singer or chorus.[1]

About Women

WHAT DO I WANT WITH A WOMAN LIKE MY GAL

What do you want with a bad rooster,
Won't crow for the dawn of day?
What do you want with a bad rooster,
Won't crow for the dawn?
What do I want with a woman like my gal,
Won't do nothin' I say?

I'm goin' to buy me a bulldog,
Chain him in my backyard.
Goin' to buy me a bulldog,
Chain him in my backyard.
And I'm goin' to tell my woman
Ain't gonna have nothin' she starts.

Say hey now, listen little gal,
What have you got on your mind?
Say now, little gal,
What have you got on your mind?
You tryin' to quit me or let me alone,
Or leave me all out and dyin'?

---

1. *Negro Folk Music, U.S.A., by Harold Courlander, New York, Columbia University Press, 1963, pp. 126–127.*

BIG FOOT MAMMA

Big foot mamma, and all the neighborhood.
Say listen big foot mamma, and all the neighborhood.
After she got all the money I made around,
Then she moved to the piney woods.

I'll tell you one thing now, gal, it's all 'round the neighborhood.
I'll tell you one thing now, gal, it's all in my neighborhood,
After she done got my money,
She moved to the piney woods.

Now the cook's in the kitchen pickin' over collard greens,
Says the cook's in the kitchen pickin' over collard greens.
And the white folks out in the parlor playin' cards
And the cook's gotta pick 'em clean.

Says my gal's got a mojo, boy she keep it hid.
Says my gal's got a mojo, oh she keep it hid.
But I got somethin' right in my pocket
To find old mojo with.

CUSTARD PIE BLUES

I'm goin' to tell you somethin', baby.
Ain't goin' to tell you no lies.
I want some of that custard pie.
You got to give me some of it,
You got to give me some of it,
You got to give me some of it
Before you give it all away.

Well, I don't care if you live across the street,
When you cut your pie
Please save me a piece.
I want some of it,
I want some of it
Before you give it all away.

I want to tell you, baby, it's understood,
You got the best pie
In this neighborhood.
I gotta have some of it,
I gotta have some of it,
I want some of it
Before you give it all away.

AVALON ON MY MIND

This song is generally attributed to a blues singer named Mississippi John Hurt, a native of Avalon, Mississippi. Interviewed on radio, Mr. Hurt recalled: "Well, I farmed, worked on the railroad, I worked on WPA projects and I worked with the U.S. Engineer Corps on the river, and when Thomas B. Hoskins discovered me I was a herdsman, tending a man's cattle. Had lots of cattle, my employer, and I'd feed them cattle and when one strayed from the drove I'd round him up and get him back in line. Well, [Mr. Hoskins] got ahold of one of my old O.K. records someplace, he told me, in music research. They also buy old records, you know, anywhere they can find them. And he got to know about me from one of my old records. He had it playing and said, 'Ah, wish we could have got over to him.' Says, 'Wonder if we can't get over to him.' 'I don't know, let's see.' It was all on the record, Mississippi John Hurt, Avalon, Mississippi. Somehow he overlooked it, I guess, believed it was Avalon, Georgia, and he went to the wrong state, Georgia, looking for me. They told him down there, 'If you're lookin' for that fellow, he dead, been dead.' He said, 'Well, I don't know, thought maybe he's down here.' Said, 'No, he's been dead.' So he came back home and got to playing the record again, said, 'Sure wish we could have got hold of him.' And then lifting the record off after he got through playing, why, he noticed it said Mississippi John Hurt, Avalon, Mississippi. Said, 'Oh, look here.' His partner, the president of this outfit, said, 'What have you found?' Said, 'This says Mississippi John Hurt. We haven't been to Mississippi.' Says, 'No, but no use in goin', he's dead.' But he says, 'I'm goin' to investigate this, I'm goin' to see.' Said, 'I'm takin' off for Mississippi next week.' And he got the record and the map together. And so he taken off and he didn't say anything more until he hit Mississippi. This town he hit in Mississippi was Granada, and he stopped there and asked for some information. Said, 'Is there a place on this highway between here and Greenwood by the name of Avalon?' They told him, 'Yeah, about twenty-four miles down the road there. That's the distance from Granada to Avalon.'" This is John Hurt's song about his home town."

> Avalon's my home town, always on my mind,
> Avalon's my home town, always on my mind,
> Pretty mammas in Avalon, women there all the time.
>
> Left Avalon this mornin' 'bout half past nine,
> Left Avalon this mornin' 'bout half past nine,
> Says come back, Daddy, let me change your mind.
>
> Hate to tell you, pretty Mamma, but you have got to know,
> Hate to tell you, pretty Mamma, but you have got to know,
> I'm leavin' Avalon, not comin' back no more.

When I left Avalon, throwin' kisses and wavin' at me,
When I left Avalon, throwin' kisses and wavin' at me,
Says come back, Daddy, and stay right here with me.

Left New York this mornin' 'bout half past nine,
Left New York this mornin' 'bout half past nine,
Pretty mammas in Avalon, women there all the time.

It's one thing I can't understand,
It's one thing I can't understand,
So many pretty mammas in Avalon, and I'm just one man.

I'M GOIN' TO THE RIVER

Well I'm goin' to the river, carry my rockin' chair,
Well I'm goin' to the river, carry my rockin' chair,
Well I'm goin' to the river, carry my rockin' chair,
And if the blues overtake me I'm gonna rock on away from here.

Gonna tell you somethin' dear God told the Jews,
Gonna tell you somethin' dear God told the Jews,
Gonna tell you somethin' dear God told the Jews,
That if you don't want me, what do I want with you.

Well I'm goin' away, gal, what you want me to bring you back?
Well I'm goin' away, what you want me to bring you back?
Well I'm goin' away, what you want me to bring you back?
Most any old thing you think your man would like.

Well run here, mamma, sit on daddy's knee,
Well run here, mamma, sit on daddy's knee,
Well run here, mamma, sit on daddy's knee,
Your man's in love with you now, gal, can't you see?

A MAN AIN'T NOTHIN' BUT A STUPID FOOL

Yes, a man ain't nothing but a stupid fool
To think he got a woman all by himself.
Yes, a man ain't nothing but a stupid fool
To think he got a woman all by himself.
Well, I say, soon as his back is turned
You know she cuttin' out with somebody else.

Yes, man ain't nothing but a crazy fool
To give one woman all his pay.

Yes, man ain't nothing but a crazy fool
To give one woman all his pay.
Well, I say, soon as his back is turned
Yes, you know she get out and throw it all away.

Homesick, Broke and Far from Home

ROLLIN' STONE

> Well, my mother told my father
> Just before I was born,
> You got a boy child comin', Lord,
> Goin' to be a rollin' stone,
> Goin' to be a rollin' stone.

POOR BOY A LONG WAYS FROM HOME

Poor boy, poor boy,
Poor boy a long ways from home.

I was down in Louisiana doin' as I please,
Now I'm in Texas, I got to work or leave.

Poor boy, poor boy,
Poor boy a long ways from home.

If your home's in Louisiana what you doin' over here?
Say my home ain't in Texas and I sure don't care.

Poor boy, poor boy,
Poor boy a long ways from home.

I don't care if the boat don't never land,
I got to stay on water as long as any man.

Poor boy, poor boy,
Poor boy a long ways from home.

And my boat came a-rockin' just like a drunken man,
Says my home's on the water and I sure don't like land.

Poor boy, poor boy,
Poor boy a long ways from home.

CAIRO STREET BLUES

I was standin' on Cairo Street one day,
I was standin' on Cairo Street one day,
I was standin' on Cairo Street one day,
One dime is all I had.

I bought the mornin' News,
I bought the mornin' News,
I bought the mornin' News,
Then I bought just a cig' or two.

What do you want your friend to be bad like Jesse James,
What do you want your friend be bad like Jesse James,
What do you want your friend be bad like Jesse James,
To have two big shooters, try to rob a passenger train.

RED RIVER BLUES

Which-a-way, which-a-way does that blood red river run?
Which-a-way, which-a-way does that blood red river run?
Runs from my back window straight to the rising sun.

Had the blues from my childhood, they're gonna follow me till I
    die.
Had the blues from my childhood, they're gonna follow me till I
    die.
I've had the blues so bad till I couldn't do nothin' but cry.

Jails and County Farms

LOWDOWN LONESOME CELL

I'm tired of sleepin' in a lowdown lonesome cell,
I wouldn't a-been here if it hadn't been for Nell.

Lay 'wake at night and just can't eat a bite,
Used to be my rider but she just won't treat me right.

A red-eyed captain and a squabblin' fore [man],
A mad dog sergeant, and he won't knock off.

I ask the government to knock some days off my time,
The way I'm treated I'm 'bout to lose my mind.

I wrote to the governor please turn me loose,
But I didn't get no answer, I know it ain't no use.

GOT NOBODY TO HELP ME PLEASE

Well I'm sittin' down in jail, down in jail on my knees,
Well I'm down in jail, down here on my knees,
And I got nobody to come and help me please.

Well I'm goin' goin' baby, don't you want to go?
Well I'm goin' now baby, don't you want to go?
I'm goin' to take you across the water where the monkey man
    can't go.

Say, listen now, baby, where'd you stay last night?
Say, listen now, baby, where'd you stay last night?
Well the reason I ask you, you ain't talkin' right.

Well I'm gonna tell you somethin' baby I want you to under-
    stand,
Well I'm gonna tell you somethin' I want you to understand,
I thought you was one kind of woman had one kind of man.

Well I'm worried here, worried everywhere,
Well I'm worried here, worried everywhere,
But I've just started home and I won't be worried there.

You can feed me on corn bread and beans,
Says you can feed me on corn bread and beans,
But I ain't gonna be treated this this old way.

LEVEE CAMP BLUES

Oh, that ole gal of mine stays out all night long;
Oh, that ole gal of mine she stays out all night long;
Oh, I can't do nothin' with you, woman, no matter what the pore
    boy do.

Oh, Captain, Captain, oh, you better count your men;
Oh, Captain, you better count your men;
Oh, some gone to the bushes, oh Lord, and some gone in.

Oh, I can eat more chicken, boy, than the cook can fry;
Oh, I can eat more chicken, boy, than the cook can fry;
Oh, I can pop more leather than the contractor can buy.

Oh, it's pay day tomorrow, oh, buddy, how you know?
Oh, it's pay day tomorrow, oh, buddy, how you know?
Oh, I know boys, 'cause the captain he told me so.

MEET ME IN THE BOTTOMS

Notation by John Benson Brooks, from Negro Folk Music, U.S.A., by Harold Courlander,   1963 by Columbia University Press.

I see her ev' - ry day.

BIG BRAZOS RIVER

Ummmmmmmm! Big Brazos, here I come!
Ummmmmmmm! Big Brazos, here I come!
You know I'm gonna do time for another man
When there ain't anything this poor boy done!

You ought to been on the Brazos in 1910,
Bud Russel drove pretty women just like he done ugly men.
Ummmmmmmm! Big Brazos, oh Lord yes, here I come.

Figure on doing time for another man
When there ain't nothing this poor boy done.

You know my mamma called me, I answered "Mam?"
She said, "Son, you tired of working?" I said, "Mamma, yes I
    am."
My papa called me, I answered, "Sir?"
"If you're tired of working, why the hell you goin' to stay there?"

I couldn't. . . . ummmmmmmm,
I just couldn't help myself.
You know a man just can't help feelin' bad
When he's doin' time for someone else.

ELECTRIC CHAIR BLUES

I'm goin' to shake hands with my partner, ask him how come he
    here.
Goin' to shake hands with my partner, ask him how come he
    here.
I had a wreck with my family, lead me to the 'lectric chair.

I seen wrecks on the ocean, wrecks on the deep blue sea,
I seen wrecks on the ocean, wrecks on the deep blue sea,
But not like that wreck in my heart that brought my 'lectricuted
    daddy to me.

Good bye pretty mamma, fare you well and good bye,
Good bye pretty mamma, fare you well and good bye,
They send me a special delivery letter and I got to leave you now.

Want to tell you somethin' 'bout wrecks on the deep blue sea,
Want to tell you somethin' 'bout wrecks on the deep blue sea,
They ain't nothin' to the wreck that brings my 'lectricuted daddy
    to me.

A TALKING PRISON BLUES

Lord, I feel so bad sometimes,/ seems like that I'm weakenin' every day./ You know I've begin to get grey since I got here,/ well a whole lot of worry causin' of that./ But I can feel myself weakenin',/ I don't keep well no more,/ I keeps sickly./ I takes a lot of medicine, but it looks like it don't do no good./ All I have to do is pray,/ That's the only thing'll help me here./ One foot in the grave, look like,/ and the other one out./ Sometime look like my best day/ got to be my last day./ Sometime I feel like I never see/ my little old kids any more./ But if I don't never see 'em no more,/ leave 'em in the hands of God./ You know about my sister,/ she like a mother to me./ She do all in the world that she can./ She went all the way along with me in this trouble/ till the end./ In a way/ I was glad my poor mother had 'ceased/ because she suffered with heart trouble,/ and trouble behind me,/ sure would-a went hard with her./ But if she were livin'/ I could call on her sometime./ But my old father dead too./ That make me be motherless and fatherless./ It's six of us sisters,/ three boys./ Family done got small now,/ looks like they're dyin' out fast./ I don't know,/ but God been good to us in a way,/ 'cause old death/ have stayed away a long time now.

Sung:

Lord, my worry sure carryin' me down.
Lord, my worry sure is carryin' me down.
Sometimes I feel like, baby, committin' suicide.
Yes, sometime I feel, feel like committin' suicide.
I got the nerve if I just had anything to do it with.
I'm goin' down slow, somethin' wrong with me.
Yes, I'm goin' down slow, somethin' wrong with me.
I've got to make a change while that I'm young.
If I don't, I won't ever get old.

From the album, Angola Prisoners' Blues, *recorded by Harry Oster and Richard Allen, Louisiana Folklore Society. Notation is by Mieczyslaw Kolinski, from* Negro Folk Music, U.S.A., *by Harold Courlander, New York, Columbia University Press, 1963.*

Lord, my wor-ry___ sure is car-ryin' me
down.___ Some-times I feel like,___
ba-by, eh,___ com-mit-ting su-i-cide.
Yes,___ some-times I feel,___ feel like___ com-
mit-ting su-i-cide. I got the nerve,___
if I just had,___ anything to do it with.___
I'm___ go-in' down slow,
some-thin' wrong with me.___

Two Free-Form Blues

Two of the finest examples of extended, "free-form" blues to be encountered are "Black Woman," which can be described as a field blues,
and "Motherless Children," which could well have been a field blues
in the beginning but which came in time to be part of the repertoire of
urban street singers.

"Black Woman" is characterized by a simplicity of conception, humming and "moaning," occasional use of falsetto, a rhythmic "ah
hmmm" (like that sometimes heard in Negro preaching), indirect statements or tangent allusions, and the impression that the singer is singing to himself. A number of phrases and images in the song are free

currency out of which many blues have been constructed, but they are woven together into a drama that is persuasive and haunting.

"Motherless Children" was sung in various styles, some of them more akin to gospel songs than to blues. The version given here is that of a now famous street bard of earlier days, Blind Willie Johnson. One of the atypical characteristics of this blues is the absence of the first person plea for attention. Instead, the focus is on "motherless children."

BLACK WOMAN

Well I said come here Black Woman,
Ah-hmmm, don't you hear me cryin', Oh Lordy!
Ah-hmmm, I say run here Black woman,
I want you to sit on Black Daddy's knee, Lord!
M-hmm, I know your house feel lonesome,
Ah don't you hear me whoopin', Oh Lordy!
Don't your house feel lonesome,
When your biscuit roller gone,
Lord help my cryin' time don't your house feel lonesome
Mamma when your biscuit roller gone!
I say my house feel lonesome,
I know you hear me cryin' oh Baby!
Ah-hmm, ah when I looked in my kitchen Mamma,
And I went all through my dinin' room!
Ah-hmm, when I woke up this mornin',
I found my biscuit roller done gone!
I'm goin' to Texas Mamma,
Just to hear the wild ox moan,
Lord help my cryin' time I'm goin' to Texas
Mamma to hear the wild ox moan!
And if they moan to suit me,
I'm going to bring a wild ox home!
Ah-hmm I say I'm got to go to Texas Black Mamma,
Ah-hmm I know I hear me cryin', oh Lordy!
Ah-hmm I got to go to Texas Black Mamma,
Ah just to hear the white cow I say moan!
Ah-hmm, ah if they moan to suit me Lordy
I b'lieve I'll bring a white cow back home!
Say I feel superstitious Mamma
'Bout my hog and bread Lord help my hungry time,
I feel superstitious, Baby 'bout my hog and bread!
Ah-hmm, Baby I feel superstitious,
I say 'stitious Black Woman!

As sung by Richard Amerson of Halsel, Alabama. From Negro Songs of Alabama, © 1960 by Harold Courlander, published with the assistance of the Wenner-Gren Foundation for Anthropological Research, New York, 1960. Music notation by John Benson Brooks.

Ah-hmm, ah you hear me cryin',
About I done got hungry oh Lordy!
Oh Mamma I feel superstitious
About my hog Lord God its my bread.
I want you to tell me Mamma
Ah-hmm I hear me cryin' oh Mamma!
Ah-hmm I want you to tell me Black Woman,
Oh where did you stay last night?
I love you Black Woman,
I tell the whole wide world I do,
Lord help your happy black time I love you Baby,
And I tell the world I do!
Ah-hmm, I love you Black Woman,
I know you hear me whoopin'. Black Baby!
Ah-hmm, I love you Black Woman
And I'll tell your Daddy on you, Lord!

Well I said come here— Black Wo - man,___ Ah - hmm!

Ah - hmm! don't you hear me cryin' oh___

Lor-dy!_____ Ah - hmm, I say run

here Black Wo - man_____ I want you to

sit on Black Dad - dy's___ knee, Lord!___ Ah -

hmm, I know your house feel lone - some,____

oh don't you hear me whoop-in' oh___ Lor- dy!_____ Don't your

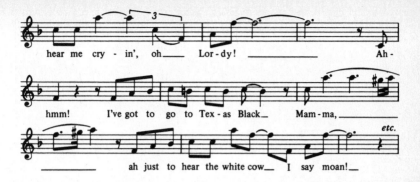

hear me cry - in', oh___ Lor - dy! _____ Ah-

hmm!   I've got to go to Tex - as Black___ Mam - ma, _____

_____ ah just to hear the white cow___ I say moan!___

MOTHERLESS CHILDREN

Well well well,
Ahhhhh,
Well motherless children have a hard time,
Motherless children have a hard time [when] mother's dead.
They don't have anywhere to go,
Wanderin' around from door to door,
Have a hard time.
Nobody on earth can take a mother's place, man,
When mother is dead, Lord,
Nobody on earth take mother's place when mother's dead,
Nobody on earth take mother's place [when she was startin'] fade
    away,
Nobody'll treat you like mother will, man.
Your wife your husband may be good to you
When mother is dead, Lord,
May be good to you, mother's dead,
But your husband may be good to you,
Better'n nothin' else, true but true,
Nobody treat you like mother will, man,
When mother is dead, Lord.
Lord Lord Lord,
Well ehhhh well,
Ahhhhh,
Well some people say that sister will do
When mother is dead,
That sister will do when mother is dead.
Some people say that sister will do,
But soon as she's married she'll turn her back on you,
Nobody treat you like mother will.
Ehhh, father will do the best he can
When mother is dead, Lord,

From Negro Folk Music, U.S.A., *by Harold Courlander,* © 1963 by Columbia
University Press. Music notation by Mieczyslaw Kolinski.

Will do the best he can when mother's dead.
Well he'll do the best he can,
It's no mistake about that Canaan Land,
Nobody treat you like mother will.
Ehhh, motherless children have a hard time
When mother is dead, Lord,
Motherless children have a hard time
Mother's dead.
Well they don't have anywhere to go,
Wanderin' around from door to door,
Well, a hard time.

well, the best he can___ when   moth-er's dead.

Well, he'll___   do   the   best   he   can, it's   no   mis-

take   a-bout that Ca-naan   Land.   No - bod - y   treat you like

moth - er   will_____   Eh,_____   moth - er - less

chil - dren have a   hard___   time_____   when moth-er   is

dead,__ Lord,   moth-er - less   chil-dren have a   hard___   time__

moth-er's dead.   Well   they don't   have   an - y

where   to   go,   wan - der - in' a-round   from___

door to   door,___   well, a hard___   time.___

BOASTING AND BIG OLD LIES

Heat

One boy says, "It's sure hot around here."
Another one says, "Hot? How come you call this hot? It's pure cool
to me. Down where I come from it's so hot you dassent leave your ham-

mer in the sun, cause the heat takes the temper right out of it."

"Hot? You call that hot?" another man say. "Why, down in the bottoms where my daddy lives all the fence posts bend over in the middle when the sun comes up, and the logs and stumps in the fields crawl away to find some shade."

"Well, that sounds kind of *warm* all right," someone say, "but it sure ain't hot. Down in my country when the dogs is chasin' cats down the main street they is all walkin'."

"I forgot to tell you one more thing about my place," says one. "Was so hot down there that when we pumped water nothin' but steam come out. So we had to catch that steam and put it in the ice house at night to turn it back to water."

"Speakin' of the ice house," says another, "we had to keep the popcorn there, else it popped right off the ears and covered the ground like snow."

"Well, that ain't much to mention," says one old boy, "where I come from the railroad tracks set out there in the sun long as they can stand it, then they burrow under the ground and don't come out till dark. That's how come the train don't go through till midnight."

"What you-all are talkin' about is plain cool to me," another man says. We got a creek down in my country that runs like the devil at night. But when the sun comes up in the morning this creek begins to get sluggish in the heat, and by ten o'clock it just stops in its tracks and don't move at all till the sun goes down."

"We got a creek too down on my daddy's farm," says one, "and if you go out there in the middle of the day you hear all the stones hollerin' something pitiful for somebody to come quick and throw them in the water."

"My mamma had a great big iron kettle," another man say, and she left it outside one time for just about ten minutes in the sun. And when she took it in it had great big water blisters on it."

"That does it," says another. "When *my* mamma left her iron kettle in the sun it melted down flat and she had to use it for a stove lid."

"Ain't you forget to hear about the big old swamp on my granddaddy's forty acres?" says this man who ain't said nothin' yet up to this point. "When it gets hot there that swamp rises up like a cake till it's thirty feet high, and it don't go down till the frost hits."

Well, about that time the first man to complain, he say, "The way it seem to me is where we're sittin' is just too cold, so somebody go and fetch my coat."

Mosquitos

"Mosquitos? Why, man, we got mosquitos down on the Brazos which can sting the bottom of your feet right through the soles of your shoes."

"Hmmm. They ain't mosquitos you talkin' about. Must be Georgia butterflies. Real mosquitos, mind you, real Georgia mosquitos is somethin' else. I once see a Georgia mosquito bore through the bottom of a iron griddle tryin' to get at a flapjack."

"Well, over there on the Black River they got mosquitos worth talkin' about. They don't never *light* on you so much as come down like a cannon ball. I was leanin' against a big old hickory tree one time when I hear this sound, *whmmmm!* from up in the sky, and I see these two 'squitos bearin' down on me 'bout seventy miles an hour. Just had time to slip around to the back of that hickory when they hit. Them pointy bills of theirs went right through the trunk and came out the other side. I quick took my eight pound hammer and bradded their bills down so they couldn't get out. Then I went around the other side and saw that when they hit they split the tree from the ground up to the first fork. That's what you call mosquitos."

"Don't know about that. They sort of sounds like 'squitos, but not so very. Now right up here in Pickens County we got mosquitos that sharpen they teeth on millstones and bore right through one thing goin' for another. I see one of 'em bore right through a hundred pound cake of ice to get at the iceman, and he had to wait till spring when the ice melt to get his bill out."

"Well, I knowed a mosquito to beat all them 'squitos you been talkin' about. He ain't satisfied with one thing at a time, he go after 'em in bunches. He fly right along with the Montgomery-Selma bus and wait till it get full. When he see that bus was loaded, then he come down on it and run his bill right through the top, expectin' to pick it up and tote it home for the whole family. And he would have done it, too, 'cept he came down so hard his bill went through the top and the floorboard and run right into the transmission. And that transmission just chewed up the 'squito's bill and spit it out. And if it hadn't been for that, this here 'squito would have had a whole busload of victuals."

Texas Sandstorm

I was coming through Texas, and I heard a roaring coming. And I discovered to people, "What is that roaring?" They said, "One of these sandstorms." I jumped on my horse, and put him at a high speed and run him about two miles, directly, as hard as he could go. And I saw the wind was going to overtake me. And I said 'taint no need of my getting destroyed, 'cause I got a storm pit right here in my mouth. I run that horse, and just ahead of me I had a hundred head of cows figuring to be destroyed in the wind. I took that horse and hovered all that hundred head of them cows, and I run them in this hollow teeth I had in my mouth. And I didn't want to leave the horse and the saddle out there, and I snatched the saddle off the horse and run him in there, and I chunked the saddle in there and I jumped in my black self. And I stayed in that hollow teeth until the storm was over with. And I taken

Narrated by Richard Amerson, 1950.

that teeth than when the storm was over with, and I spit enough posts out to put posts around ten acres of ground to wire my place in. And I taken the cow, one cow then, and skinned it and made shoes from number eight to number ten, enough for ten children. And I taken one of my shoes now and lived in it ten years for a house, a building. And I taken the horse' hoofs, listen, just the horse' hoof itself, you understand, and I farmed in it for my land, see. And I taken the horse's eye, understand, and I hung it up in the house and I used it for ten years for an electric light. And I took the holes, you know, where I get the eyes out of the head, and put it down and used it for my well. And that's why for the next twenty years me and my peoples done very well. And ever since that I been rich ever since on that farm.

RICHARD CREEKS ON CONJURING AND DOCTORING

. . . One more thing I did on my way to Mobile was some conjur business. An old man was sick, and his family found two sticks tied together in a cross shape on the front steps of their cabin. I told them I could counteract that conjur and they said to go ahead and do it. I told them first I had to have a black chicken and they got one for me. I went over in the woods by myself, killed it, roasted it, and ate the bones clean. When I come back I told them the old man needed a mojo. They gave me two dollars. I went back in the woods again and tied some stuff in a piece of cloth I tore out of my shirt. What was in that mojo wasn't nothing but crumbly leaves, dirt, an old penny, and stuff like that. Soon as I came back with the mojo—and you can believe it or not because it isn't no lie—the old man was crawling out of bed feeling fine. He took that mojo and put it in his pocket. I don't expect he's still alive, but if he is, he is probably still carrying around that piece of my shirt with my penny in it. On that piece of work I was a dollar ninety-nine and a chicken dinner ahead.

There are a good many folks carrying mojos around Alabama and Louisiana and Arkansas—you could fill the hold of a cotton boat with them. Some folks call them "greegrees." The conjur men who make them up put all kinds of things inside—dried blood, dirt from a graveyard, frizzled chicken feathers, dried-up bird feet, and things like that. I don't see nothing good about any of them. They all is fooling somebody. When that old man heard there was a bundle of crossed sticks in front of his cabin he was fooled sick, and when I ate his chicken and made him a package of leaves and dirt he was fooled well again.

From The Big Old World of Richard Creeks, © *1962 by Harold Courlander.*

There is a difference between conjuring and doctoring, and it ain't everybody knows the difference. For one thing, if a man gets a snake bite you take a black chicken, cut it in half with the feathers still on, and put it on the bite to draw the poison out. That ain't conjuring no more than what some white folks does. Mr. Russel, now, I'd say he's a smart man. Whenever one of his cows gets a fester on their legs from getting caught on the barbed wire, Mr. Russel has his man tie a green cow manure poultice over it. So you ask me how come that chicken has to be black, and I'll ask you how come that cow manure poultice has to be green. All that is doctoring—not conjuring or signs. There are people who don't want nobody else's shadow to fall on them if they are sleeping, cause it means bad luck, or they don't want nobody stepping over them when they are sitting or lying down. This is something else again. I don't think it's no different than what white folks says about covering clocks when somebody dies. . . .

If you plant potatoes in the full of the moon they'll grow to tops—all vines and nothing underneath. Potatoes have to be planted in the dark of the moon. Then there's shingles. If you're going to shingle a roof, you have to do it in the dark of the moon, else the shingles all going to curl up. Fence posts, they got to be set out in the dark of the moon, else they going to rise up and come loose. If you lay cement under a full moon, the moon will draw out all the strength and that cement is going to crack. Sharpen your axe in the full of the moon and it won't hold its edge. If you cut oak for timbers in the full of the moon they going to get soft and rot away. Breed a cow in the full of the moon and she going to be a poor milker. There's lots of things like that. Make butter in the full of the moon and like as not it'll turn watery.

The moon has got a power to it that you can feel. It ain't like the sun. When you in the moonlight you can feel it drawing on you. Folks say it is the moon makes the tides go up and down, that's the truth. If it can make the whole ocean come up and go down, I reckon it can do the same to a little pan of water. And if it can do that it can do the same thing to the sweat on your skin. Sometimes you hear a person say this ain't nothing but superstition. Once Mr. Russel told that to Tom Ibo. He said, "Tom, you only got a superstition that the fence posts will come up if they're set out in the full of the moon." Tom Ibo said to Mr. Russel, "Yes, sir, I got a superstition that it's so and you got a superstition that it ain't so."

SOME RING AND LINE GAMES FROM ALABAMA

Traditional ring and line games are largely a children's heritage. Unlike most traditions, they are not passed down from parents to children or teachers to students as much as from older children to younger. Although they are not as commonly encountered as they were a generation or two ago, they persevere strongly where they have not been crowded out by basketball, baseball, stickball and television. The ring and line games played by Negro children have both European and African ancestry. Some of them have words and tunes reminiscent of English game songs and folk songs; in others, the relationship between the singing, the handclapping and the body motions suggests African tradition. The songs themselves vary from the commonplace to the noteworthy. Some are recollections of events, such as the sinking of the *Titanic;* some are reflections on the social scene or comments on an individual's behavior; still others borrow lines from adult songs or contain words that defy comprehension.

The following games were observed and recorded in rural Alabama, but they may also be seen and heard, with minor variations (or none at all), in almost any large northern city.

LITTLE SALLY WALKER

> **Directions:** This is a partner-choosing game. The children stand in a line, except for one standing in front, facing them. This leader performs notions indicated by the song text, and finally "shakes" toward the chosen one, usually of the opposite sex.

Little Sal-ly Walk-er sit-tin' in a sauc-er,
cry-in' for the old man to come for the dol-lar.
Ride Sal-ly ride, put your hands on your hips,_ ah let your
back-bone slip, ah shake it to the east, ah shake it to the
west, ah shake it to the ve-ry one you love the best.

The songs were recorded by the author, and were notated by John Benson Brooks. Playing instructions were provided by Ruby Pickens Tartt of Livingston, Alabama.

Little Sally Walker
Sittin' in a saucer,
Cryin' for the old man
To come for the dollar.
Ride Sally ride,
Put your hands on your hips,
Let your backbone slip,
Shake it to the east,
Shake it to the west,
Shake it to the very one
You love the best.

MARY MACK

Directions: **The children usually stand in
lines facing each other. They all sing and
clap their partner's hands.**

Oh Mary Mack, Mack, Mack,
All dressed in black, black, black,
With silver buttons, buttons, buttons,
Up and down her back, back, back.

And I love coffee, coffee, coffee,
And I love tea, tea, tea,
And the boys love me, me, me.

I went to the river, river, river,
And I couldn't get across, 'cross, 'cross,

And I paid five dollars, dollars, dollars,
For the old grey horse, horse, horse.

And the horse wouldn't pull, pull, pull,
I swapped him for a bull, bull, bull,
And the bull wouldn't holler, holler, holler,
I swapped him for a dollar, dollar, dollar.

And the dollar wouldn't spend, spend, spend,
I put it in the grass, grass, grass,
And the grass wouldn't grow, grow, grow,
I got my hoe, hoe, hoe.

And the hoe wouldn't chop, chop, chop,
I took it to the shop, shop, shop,
And the shop made money, money, money,
Like the bees made honey, honey, honey.

See that yonder, yonder, yonder,
In the jay-bird town, town, town,
Where the women gotta work, work, work,
Till the sun goes down, down, down.

Well, I eat my meat, meat, meat,
And I gnaw my bone, bone, bone,
Well, good-bye honey, honey, honey
I'm going on home.

WATCH THAT LADY

Directions: **This is played as a ring game with one child in the center of the circle pretending to "hold that key." All of the children sing. The one in the center makes various motions, such as combing her hair, kneeling, standing on one foot, or shaking her body, and those in the circle try to imitate her.**

The children clap their hands, or sometimes hold their hands on their hips instead of clapping. Forms of this game are found in the West Indian islands of Jamaica, Trinidad and Martinique. In Haiti the game is known as "Théâtre."

I been all a-round my last___ time, last___ time,

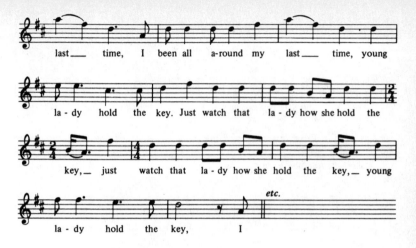

last___ time, I been all a-round my last___ time, young

la - dy hold the key. Just watch that la - dy how she hold the

key,___ just watch that la - dy how she hold the key,___ young

etc.

la - dy hold the key,   I

I been all around my last time, last time, last time,
I been all around my last time,
Young lady, hold the key.

Just watch that lady how she hold that key,
Just watch that lady how she hold that key,
Young lady, hold the key.

OLD LADY SALLY WANTS TO JUMP

Directions: **The children stand in two lines
facing one another. They all sing. Both rows
jump back and forth, each child with his feet
together. On the last line, "Old Lady Sally
want to bow," the lines jump forward and
each child bows to the one opposite him.
This is all sung and acted out very rapidly.
Old Lady Sally is an old woman who is still
trying to get a man. She goes "jump-ty jump"
to appear young and wear a red dress in the
latest style to catch one of the "many fishes
in the brook." The children think that she
should be ashamed of herself for not behav-
ing as an old woman should.**

Old la - dy Sal - ly wants to jump - ty jump,___ jŭmp - ty jump,___

Old lady Sally want to jump-ty jump,
Jump-ty jump, jump-ty jump.
Old lady Sally want to jump-ty jump,
And old lady Sally want to bow.

Throw that hook in the middle of the pond,
Catch that girl with the red dress on.

Go on, gal, ain't you ashame?
Shamed of what?
Wearing your dress in the latest style.

Many fishes in the brook,
Papa caught 'em with a hook.
Mamma fried 'em in a pan,
Baby eat 'em like a man.

Preacher in the pulpit,
Preaching like a man,
Trying to get to Heaven on a 'lectric fan.
Do your best, papa, daddy do your best.

ROSIE DARLING ROSIE

Directions: This is a partner-choosing game.
Two circles are formed, one within the other,
so that there is a lane between them. Children in the inside circle face those on the
outside. The leader, who stands to one side,
carries the burden of the song, and the others
sing the refrain, "Ha ha Rosie." On the
words "Grab your partner and follow me,"
she skips into the lane between the circles
and chooses a partner of the opposite sex.
The two then skip around the open lane, and
on the appropriate verse, the erstwhile leader
takes the vacant position and the boy becomes the new leader. The partner-choosing
routine continues until everyone has had a
chance to lead. At the conclusion, all eyes are
turned on the individual left without a partner, and the children sing:

Stop right still and study yourself,
See that fool where she (or he) got left.

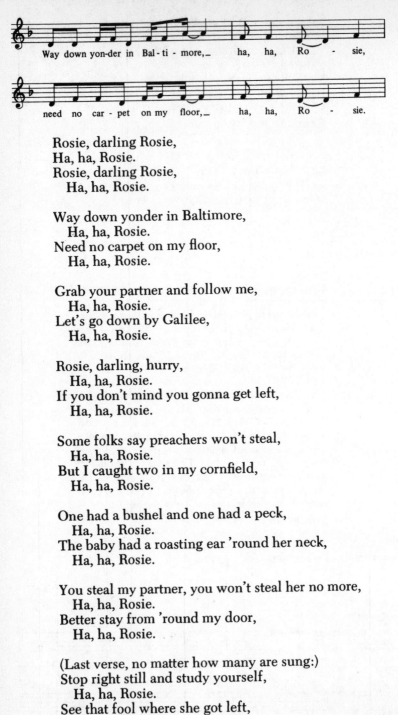

Way down yon-der in Bal-ti-more,— ha, ha, Ro - sie,

need no car-pet on my floor,— ha, ha, Ro - sie.

Rosie, darling Rosie,
Ha, ha, Rosie.
Rosie, darling Rosie,
  Ha, ha, Rosie.

Way down yonder in Baltimore,
  Ha, ha, Rosie.
Need no carpet on my floor,
  Ha, ha, Rosie.

Grab your partner and follow me,
  Ha, ha, Rosie.
Let's go down by Galilee,
  Ha, ha, Rosie.

Rosie, darling, hurry,
  Ha, ha, Rosie.
If you don't mind you gonna get left,
  Ha, ha, Rosie.

Some folks say preachers won't steal,
  Ha, ha, Rosie.
But I caught two in my cornfield,
  Ha, ha, Rosie.

One had a bushel and one had a peck,
  Ha, ha, Rosie.
The baby had a roasting ear 'round her neck,
  Ha, ha, Rosie.

You steal my partner, you won't steal her no more,
  Ha, ha, Rosie.
Better stay from 'round my door,
  Ha, ha, Rosie.

(Last verse, no matter how many are sung:)
Stop right still and study yourself,
  Ha, ha, Rosie.
See that fool where she got left,
  Ha, ha, Rosie.

AMASEE

> *Directions:* The children face each other in
> two lines. The leader sings the lines "Take
> your partner" and "Swing your partner"; the
> other children sing the refrain and clap their
> hands. Beginning with the head couple, each
> pair goes down between the rows, swinging
> partners on directions sung by the leader.

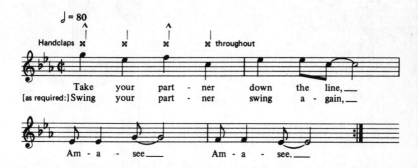

(The lines, "Swing your partner" and "Take your partner" are repeated
several times each, with the refrain, "Amasee" coming after each line.)

> Take your partner down the line,
>   Amasee, amasee.
> Take your partner down the line,
>   Amasee, amasee.
> Swing your partner, swing again,
>   Amasee, amasee.
> Swing your partner, swing again,
>   Amasee, amasee.

AFRICAN DANCING IN NEW ORLEANS

In the year 1819 the architect Benjamin Latrobe, visiting in New Orleans, encountered African-style dancing and music for the first time. Despite his distaste for what he saw and heard, Latrobe was a meticulous chronicler, and he left us one of the few reliable accounts of what these dances looked like. His sketches of musical instruments used by the slaves establish beyond doubt that those instruments were African in concept and construction, even though made, in all likelihood, in the environs of New Orleans. As he recorded the sights and sounds in his diary:

. . . This long dissertation has been suggested by my accidentally

From Impressions Respecting New Orleans: Diaries and Sketches 1818–1820, *by Benjamin Henry Boneval Latrobe.*

stumbling upon the assembly of negroes which I am told every Sunday afternoon meets on the Common in the rear of the city. My object was to take a walk with Mr. Coulter on the bank of the Canal Carondelet as far as the Bayou St. John. In going up St. Peters Street & approaching the common I heard a most extraordinary noise, which I supposed to proceed from some horse mill, the horses trampling on a wooden floor. I found, however, on emerging from the houses onto the Common, that it proceeded from a crowd of 5 or 600 persons assembled in an open space or public square. I went to the spot & crowded near enough to see the performance. All those who were engaged in the business seemed to be *blacks*. I did not observe a dozen yellow faces. They were formed into circular groups in the midst of four of which, which I examined (but there were more of them), was a ring, the largest not 10 feet in diameter. In the first were two women dancing. They held each a coarse handkerchief extended by the corners in their hands, & *set* to each other in a miserably dull & slow figure, hardly moving their feet or bodies. The music consisted of two drums and a stringed instrument. An old man sat astride of a cylindrical drum about a foot in diameter, & beat it with incredible quickness with the edge of his hand & fingers. The other drum was an open staved thing held between the knees & beaten in the same manner. They made an incredible noise. The most curious instrument, however, was a stringed instrument which no doubt was imported from Africa. On the top of the finger board was the rude figure of a man in a sitting posture, & two pegs behind him to which the strings were fastened. The body was a calabash. It was played upon by a very little old man, apparently 80 or 90 years old.

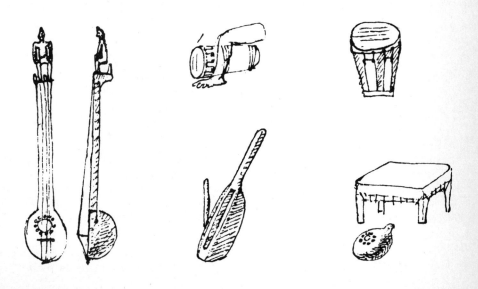

Benjamin Latrobe's notebook sketches of African musical instruments in New Orleans.

The women squalled out a burthen to the playing at intervals, consisting of two notes, as the negroes, working in our cities, respond to the song of their leader. Most of the circles contained the same sort of dancers. One was larger, in which a ring of a dozen women walked, by way of dancing, round the music in the center. But the instruments were of a different construction. One, which from the color of the wood seemed new, consisted of a block cut into something of the form of a cricket bat with a long & deep mortice down the center. This thing made a considerable noise, being beaten lustily on the side by a short stick. In the same orchestra was a square drum, looking like a stool, which made an abominably loud noise; also a calabash with a round hole in it, the hole studded with brass nails, which was beaten by a woman with two short sticks.

A man sung an uncouth song to the dancing which I suppose was in some African language, for it was not French, & the women screamed a detestable burthen on one single note. The allowed amusements of Sunday have, it seems, perpetuated here those of Africa among its inhabitants. I have never seen anything more brutally savage, and at the same time dull & stupid, than this whole exhibition. Continuing my walk about a mile along the canal, & returning after Sunset near the same spot, the noise was still heard. There was not the least disorder among the crowd, nor do I learn on enquiry, that these weekly meetings of the negroes have ever produced any mischief.

"VOODOO" RITUALS IN NEW ORLEANS

Most of the descriptions we have of African rituals that took place in New Orleans were based on hearsay, rumors and, unfortunately, total misunderstanding, not to mention the assumption that African practices were weird, wild, irrational and merely superstitious. Various documentations of dances and ceremonies were compounded out of nonsensical interpretations that undoubtedly had morbid appeal for readers. One of the ritual ceremonies which took place from time to time in New Orleans, according to the evidence, was the Dahomean Brulé Zin, or Canzo, an initiation of cult ser-

The Almanach *article appears in the original French in* Les Acadiens Louisianais et Leur Parler, *by Jay K. Ditchy, Washington, Institut Français de Washington, 1932.*

vitors into a higher status within the cult organization. As observed both in Dahomey
and in Haiti, the initiates were required to
show their mastery over fire by placing their
hands in a pot of boiling food and tasting its
contents. The "chroniclers" of this ritual in
New Orleans compensated for their failure
to grasp what was seen by adding substance
and interpretation from their own lurid imaginations, including naked orgies and human
sacrifice. One such description was this one,
which appeared in the *Almanach de la Louisiane* in 1866:

New Orleans presents the curious spectacle of this sombre cult
brought from barbarism into the middle of our enlightened religious
practices.

The black race, like all inferior and ignorant races, is naturally superstitious. In Africa it cultivates the most stupid fetishism. The most simple natural or scientific occurrences are beyond their intelligence and
are attributed to a malignant force. The slaves brought from the banks
of the Niger introduced and developed voodooism in Louisiana. Their
ceremony consists of invoking, by incantations, the force (or spirit) of
witchcraft and sorcery. This force or spirit is called *Grisgris*.
[Grisgris—greegree in English spelling—is an alternate term for a simple mojo or charm, not really the name of an African deity or spirit.—
Ed.] To obtain his favors, they gather in a secret place, make themselves absolutely nude, and light a large fire on which bubbles a pot
full of ingredients. Giving themselves up to dancing around the pot
like the sorcerers of Macbeth, they throw into it various animals and
snakes and unclean things, while mystically uttering sacramental
words.

After a time of cooking, during which the Voodoos work themselves
into an ecstatic state, the High Priest gives the signal for communion.
Then each one of the faithful in turn dips his fingers in the horrible
and nauseating food and puts it into his mouth after having made cab-
alistic signs on his forehead, his chest and shoulders. Once a year they
have a ceremony in each congregation with human sacrifices. The rite
calls for a child to be sacrificed in fire to the divine Voodoo. One of the
small unfortunates condemned by fate to be sacrificed succeeded one
day in escaping the sacrificial knife. He ran away and placed himself
under the protection of the police. Although the authorities have made
the greatest efforts for a long time to break up the Voodoos, they have
never been able to prevent them from gathering for the mysteries of the
night.

(For comparison with a realistically observed boiling pot ceremony
in Haiti, see Appendix XVIII, p. 598.)

CONGO SQUARE

George W. Cable's often-quoted description of the slave dances in the *Place Congo*, or Congo Square, was an imaginative reconstruction of something he himself had never seen. In his effort to bring alive the African-like activities that took place when the slaves came together for Sunday recreation, Cable did not spare the adjectives and adverbs. The slave's nature was "simple," "savage," "musical" and "superstitious." Drums "boomed" and wooden trumpets "blasted." Drummers played "madly with their fingers, fists and feet." The dancing was characterized by "ecstasy" rising to "frantic leaps," "frenzy" and "madness." Cable understood "African" to mean "untamed and licentious," and he did his literary best to portray a scene of physical and moral abandon. He put into the mouths of the dancing slaves songs that he and other collectors had gathered in quiet ways and which in some instances were sentimental, droll, or otherwise inappropriate to the savage scene he was painting. His English translations of those songs frequently were inaccurate or marred by an attempt to render them in Negro-English idiom. In short, his reconstruction of the African holiday events in Congo Square was made out of fragments of information and misinformation gathered from every possible source, including descriptions of life in Saint Domingue (Haiti) set down by Moreau de Saint-Méry more than three-quarters of a century earlier. Nevertheless, Cable's imaginative descriptions of events in Congo Square probably did more to keep the memory alive than any other writings on the subject. Despite their misunderstandings, distortions, sensationalism and romanticism, his descriptions have in them a feel for the African presence in Louisiana in the early years of the nineteenth century. From Cable's account, reconstructed out of other people's writings and recollections and embellished with his own emotions, come these scenes and vignettes of the dance spectacles in Congo Square:

From "The Dance in Place Congo," Century Magazine, February 1886.

Often the slave's attire was only a cotton shirt, or a pair of pantaloons hanging in indecent tatters to his naked waist. The bondwoman was well clad who had on as much as a coarse chemise and petticoat. To add a *tignon*—a Madras handkerchief twisted into a turban—was high gentility, and the number of kerchiefs beyond that one was the measure of absolute wealth. Some were rich in *tignons;* especially those who served within the house, and pleased the mistress, or even the master—there were Hagars in those days. However, Congo Plains did not gather the house servants so much as the "field hands."

Then came in troops. See them; wilder than gypsies; wilder than the Moors and Arabs whose strong blood and features one sees at a glance in so many of them; gangs—as they were called—gangs and gangs of them, from this and that and yonder direction; tall, well-knit Senegalese from Cape Verde, black as ebony, with intelligent, kindly eyes and long, straight, shapely noses; Mandingoes, from the Gambia River, lighter of color, of cruder form, and a cunning that shows in the countenance; whose enslavement seems specially a shame, their nation the "merchants of Africa," dwelling in towns, industrious, thrifty, skilled in commerce and husbandry, and expert in the working of metals, even to silver and gold; and Foulahs . . . of goodly stature, and with a perceptible rose tint in the cheeks; and Sosos, famous warriors, dexterous with the African targe; and in contrast to these, with small ears, thick eyebrows, bright eyes, flat, upturned noses, shining skin, wide mouths and white teeth, the Negroes of Guinea, true and unmixed, from the Gold Coast, the Slave Coast, and the Cape of Palms—not from the Grain Coast; the English had that trade. See them come! Popoes, Cotocolies, Fidas, Socoes, Agwas, short, copper-colored Mines—what havoc the slavers did make!—and from interior Africa others equally proud and warlike: fierce Nagoes and Fonds; tawny Awassas; Iboes, so light-colored that one could not tell them from mulattoes but for their national tattooing; and the half-civilized and quick-witted but ferocious Arada, the original voodoo worshiper. And how many more! For here come, also, men and women from all that great Congo coast—Angola, Malimbe, Ambrice, etc.—small, good-natured, sprightly "boys," and gay, garrulous "gals," thick-lipped but not tattooed; chattering, chaffering, singing, and guffawing as they come: these are they for whom the dance and the place are named, the most numerous sort of Negro in the colonies, the Congoes and Franc-Congoes, and though serpent worshipers, yet the gentlest and kindliest natures that came from Africa. Such was the company. Among these *bossals*—that is, native Africans—there was, of course, an ever-growing number of Negroes who proudly called themselves Creole Negroes, that is, born in America, and at the present time there is only here and there an old native African to be met with, vain of his singularity and trembling on his staff. . . .

The gathering throng closed in around, leaving unoccupied the circle indicated by the crescent of musicians. The short, harsh turf was the dancing floor. The crowd stood. Fancy the picture. The pack of dark, tattered figures touched off every here and there with the bright colors of a Madras *tignon.* The squatting, cross-legged musicians. The low-roofed, embowered town off in front, with here and there a spire lifting a finger of feeble remonstrance; the flat, grassy plain stretching around and behind, dotted with black stumps; in the distance the pale green willow undergrowth, behind it the *cyprière*—the cypress swamp—and in the pale, seven-times-heated sky the sun, only a little declined to south and westward, pouring down its beams. . . .

The singers almost at the first note are many. At the end of the first line every voice is lifted up. The strain is given the second time with growing spirit. Yonder glistening black Hercules, who plants one foot forward, lifts his head and bare, shining chest, and rolls out the song from a mouth and throat like a cavern, is a *candio,* a chief, or was before he was overthrown in battle and dragged away, his village burning behind him, from the mountains of High Soudan. [Actually, a *candio* or *canzo* was a person belonging to the highest level of servitors in the Vodoun or Dahomey cult.—Ed.] That is an African amulet that hangs about his neck—a *greegree.* He is of the Bambaras, as you may know by his solemn visage and the long tattoo streaks running down from the temples to the neck, broadest in the middle, like knife gashes. See his play of restrained enthusiasm catch from one bystander to another. They swing and bow to right and left, in slow time to the piercing treble of the Congo women. Some are responsive; others are competitive. Hear that bare foot slap the ground! one sudden stroke only, as it were the foot of a stag. The musicians warm up at the sound. A smiting of breasts with open hands begins very softly and becomes very vigorous. The women's voices rise to a tremulous intensity. Among the chorus of Franc-Congo singing girls is one of extra good voice, who thrusts in, now and again, an improvisation. This girl here, so tall and straight, is a Yaloff. You see it in her almost Hindoo features, and hear it in the plaintive melody of her voice. Now the chorus is more piercing than ever. The women clap their hands in time, or, standing with arms akimbo, receive with faint courtesies and head liftings the low bows of the men, who deliver them swinging this way and that.

See! Yonder brisk and sinewy fellow has taken one short, nervy step into the ring, chanting with rising energy. Now he takes another, and stands and sings and looks here and there, rising upon his broad toes and sinking and rising again, with what wonderful lightness! How tall and lithe he is. Notice his brawn shining through his rags. He too, is a *candio,* and by the three long rays of tattooing on each side of his face, a Kiamba. The music has got into his feet. He moves off to the farther edge of the circle, still singing, takes the prompt hand of an unsmiling Congo girl, leads her into the ring, and, leaving the chant to the throng, stands her before him for the dance.

Will they dance to that measure? Wait! A sudden frenzy seizes the musicians. The measure quickens, the swaying, attitudinizing crowd starts into extra activity, the female voices grow sharp and staccato, and suddenly the dance is the furious Bamboula.

Now for the frantic leaps! Now for the frenzy! Another pair are in the ring! The man wears a belt of little bells, or, as a substitute, little tin vi-als of shot, "bram-bram sonnette!" And still another couple enter the circle. What wild—what terrible delight! The ecstasy rises to madness; one—two—three of the dancers fall—*bloucoutoum! boum!*—with foam on their lips and are dragged out by arms and legs from under the tumultuous feet of crowding newcomers. The musicians know no fatigue; still the dance rages on. . . .

CREOLE TALES FROM LOUISIANA

The Irishman and the Frogs

Ein fois yavait ein l'Irlandais sou qui tapé révini village et té passé coté ein piti la rivière ou yé té gagnin boucou crapauds. Li tendé crapauds yé qui tapé dit: "Brum, brum, brum!" "Ah!" dit l'Irlandais la, tapé dit: "Rum, rum, rum, tolé mo rum, mo va donnin toi ein pé, mais faut to promette moin rende moin mo jug. *Mais di moin, est-ce que do l'eau la fond?"* . . .

Once upon a time there was a drunken Irishman who was returning to his village and who passed by a little river where were many frogs. He heard the frogs "Brum, brum, brum!" "Ah! said the Irishman, "you want my rum; I shall give you a little, but you must promise me to give back my jug. But tell me, is the water deep there?"

"Jou, jou, jou!" said the frogs. "Oh!" said the Irishman, "that is not very deep. Here is my rum." He threw his jug into the water and he waited a good while, then he said: "Well, gentlemen, send back my jug; it is late, I must go back home; they are waiting for me." But the frogs did not send back anything. Then the Irishman threw himself into the water that was very deep and came to his neck.

"Confounded liars," said the Irishman, "you told me the water would come to my knees *(genoux)*, and it is up to my neck."

As he was drunk, he was drowned.

The Marriage of Compère Lapin

Tim, tim! Bois sec! Cré coton! Compère Lapin, c'est ti bonhomme qui connin sauté.

These two tales are from Louisiana Folk-Tales, *by Alcée Fortier, Vol. II of the* Memoirs of the American Folk-Lore Society, *1895.*

Vous zotes doit rappeler, qué après yé té voyé Compère Lapin dans grands zerbes, comme li té chapé raide et comme li dit c'était la même so moman té fait li. Pour lors donc mo va dit vous qué même jou la Mamzelle Léonine couri joinde li et yé parti voyagé. . . .

Tim, tim! Bois sec. Cré coton! Compère Lapin [Rabbit] is a little fellow who knows how to jump!

You all must remember, after they had thrown Compère Lapin into the briers, how quickly he had run away, saying that it was in those very thorns that his mother had made him. Now then, I will tell you that on the same day Miss Léonine [Lioness] went to meet him, and they started travelling. They walked a long time, for at least a month; at last they reached the bank of a river which was very deep. The current was strong, too strong for them to swim over. On the other side of the river there was a pretty place; the trees were green and loaded with all kinds of fruits. Under the trees were flowers of every kind that there is in the world. When a person breathed there, it was as if a bottle of essence had been opened in a room.

Miss Léonine said: "Let us go to live there; besides, we cannot return to my father's. There, we shall be happy, and no one will bother us; but how shall we do to cross over to the other side?"

"Stop," said Compère Lapin, "let me think a moment," and then he began to walk and walk, until he saw a large piece of dry wood which had fallen into the water. "That is what I want," said he. He cut a tall pole, and then he mounted on the log and told Léonine to follow him. Poor Miss Léonine mounted also, but she was so much afraid that she was trembling dreadfully.

"Hold on well; you will see how we shall pass"; and he pushed with his stick. The log began to go down the current; they were going like lightning, and Lapin kept on paddling. They sailed for half a day before they were able to reach the other side, for the current was so strong that the log was carried along all the time. At last it passed very near the shore. "Jump, jump," said Compère Lapin, and hardly had he spoken than he was on shore. Miss Léonine finally jumped also, and they found themselves on the other side of the river. They were very glad, and the first thing they did was to eat as much as they could of the good things they found there. Then they took a good rest.

They found a pretty place to pass the night, and the next day, at dawn, they took a good walk. As everything they saw was so fine, they thought they would remain there to live. When they had run away, they had not been able to take any money with them, so they were without a cent. But God had blessed them, for they had come to a place where they did not need much money. They had already been there a good while, and they were quiet and contented, and they thought that they were alone, when one day, they heard, all at once, a noise, a tumult, as if thunder was rolling on the ground.

"What is that, my lord? Go to see, Compère Lapin."

"I, no, as if I am foolish to go, and then catch something bad. It is better for me to stay quiet, and, in that way, nothing can happen to me."

The noise kept on increasing, until they saw approaching a procession of elephants. As they were passing quietly without attacking any one, it gave Compère Lapin a little courage. He went to the chief of the elephants and told him that he asked his permission to remain in his country; he said that he came from the country of King Lion, who had wanted to kill him, and he had run away with his wife. The elephant replied: "That is good; you may remain here as long as you want, but don't you bring here other animals who know how to eat one another. As long as you will behave well, I will protect you, and nobody will come to get you here. Come sometimes to see me, and I will try to do something for you.'

Some time after that, Compère Lapin went to see the king of elephants, and the king was so glad when Compère Lapin explained to him how he could make a great deal of money, that he named immediately Compère Lapin captain of his bank and watchman of his property.

When Compère Lapin saw all the money of the king it almost turned his head, and as he had taken the habit of drinking since they had dug in his country a well, of which the water made people drunk, he continued his bad habit whenever he had the chance.

One evening he came home very drunk, and he began quarrelling with his wife. Léonine fell upon him and gave him such a beating that he remained in bed for three weeks. When he got up, he asked his wife to pardon him; he said that he was drunk, and that he would never do it again, and he kissed her. In his heart, however, he could not forgive Léonine. He swore that he would leave her, but before that he was resolved to give her a terrible beating.

One evening when Léonine was sleeping, Compère Lapin took a rope and tied her feet before and behind. In that way he was sure of his business. Then he took a good whip, and he whipped her until she lost consciousness. Then he left her and went on travelling. He wanted to go to a place where they would never hear of him any more, because he was afraid that Léonine would kill him, and he went far.

When Miss Léonine came back to herself, she called, she called; they came to see what was the matter, and they found her well tied up. They cut the ropes, and Léonine started immediately. She left her house, she travelled a long time, until she came to the same river which she had crossed with Compère Lapin upon the log. She did not hesitate, but jumped into the water. The current carried her along, and she managed, after a great many efforts, to cross over to the other side. She was very tired, and she had to take some rest; then she started to return to her father.

When her father saw her, he kissed her and caressed her, but his daughter began to cry, and told him how Compère Lapin had treated her. When King Lion heard that, he was so angry that all who were near him began to tremble.

"Come here, Master Fox; you shall go to the king of elephants, and tell him, that if he does not send Compère Lapin to me as soon as he can, I shall go to his country to kill him and all the elephants, and all the other animals, and everything which is in his country. Go quick!"

Master Fox travelled a long time, and arrived at last in the country where Compère Lapin was hidden. But he did not see him; he asked for him, but no one could give him any news of him. Master Fox went to see the king of elephants and told him what King Lion had said. The elephants hate the lions, so the king replied: "Tell your master that if he wishes me to break his jaw-bone, let him come. I shall not send anything or anybody, and first of all, get away from here quick. If you want good advice, I can tell you that you had better remain in your country. If ever Lion tries to come here, I shall receive him in such a manner that no one of you will ever return home."

Master Fox did not wait to hear any more; but he had no great desire to go back to his country, for he thought Lion would kill him if he returned without Compère Lapin. He walked as slowly as he could, and all along the road he saw that they were making preparations for war. He thought that perhaps the elephants were going to attack King Lion. He went on his way, and on arriving at a prairie he saw Compère Lapin, who was running in zigzags, sometimes on one side of the road, sometimes on the other. He stopped whenever he met animals and spoke to them, and then he started again as rapidly as before. At last Master Fox and Compère Lapin met, but the latter did not recognize his old friend.

"Where are you going like that, running all the time?"

"Ah!" replied Compère Lapin, "you don't know the bad news. Lion has declared war against all elephants, and I want to notify all mules, horses, and camels to get out of the way."

"But you, why are you running so? They are surely not going to make a soldier of you?"

"No, you believe that. Ah, well, with all your cunning you know nothing. When the officers of the king will come to get the horses and mules for the cavalry to go to war, they will say: 'That's a fellow with long ears; he is a mule; let us take him.' Even if I protest, and say that I am a rabbit, they will say: 'Oh, no! look at his ears; you see that he is a mule,' and I should be caught, enlisted, and forced to march. It seems to me that I know you, but it is such a long time since I have seen you. May God help me, it is Master Fox, my old friend!"

"Yes, yes, it is I, my good fellow. Well! what do you say about all that bad business?"

"All that is for a woman," said Compère Lapin; "we must try, my friend, to have nothing to do with that war."

"But what shall we do?" said Master Fox. "They will force us into it."

"No, you must be King Lion's adviser, and I will be that of King Elephant, and in that way we shall merely look on and let them fight as much as they want."

"You know," said Master Fox, "Léonine has returned to her father; and as you were not married before the church, I believe that Lion is about to marry her to one of his neighbors. Does it not grieve you, Compère Lapin, to think of that?"

"Oh, no; *ca zié pas oua tcheur pas fait mal* (we feel no sorrow for what we do not see)."

The two cunning fellows conversed a long time, for they were glad to meet after such a long absence. As they were about to part, they saw two dogs, that stood nose to nose, growling fiercely, and then turned around rapidly and began to smell each other everywhere.

"You, Master Fox, who know everything, can you tell me why dogs have the bad habit of smelling each other in that way?"

"I will tell you, Compère Lapin, why they do that. In old, old times, when there was but one god, called Mr. Jupiter, all the dogs considered their lot so hard and unhappy that they sent a delegation to ask Mr. Jupiter to better their condition. When they arrived at the house of the god in heaven, all the dogs were so frightened that they ran away. Only one remained; it was Brisetout, the largest dog of the party. He was not afraid of anything, and he came to Mr. Jupiter, and spoke thus: 'My nation sent me to see you to ask you whether you think that we are going to watch over our masters all day and all night, bark all the time, and then be kicked right and left and have nothing to eat. We are too unhappy, and we want to know if you will allow us once in a while to eat one of the sheep of our masters. We cannot work like this for nothing. What do you say, Mr. Jupiter?'

" 'Wait a moment. I shall give you such a reply that you will never wish to annoy me any more. I am tired of hearing all sorts of complaints. I am tired, do you hear?'

"Then Mr. Jupiter spoke a language that no one could understand, and one of his clerks went out to get something. He told the dog to sit down. Brisetout remained on the last step of the staircase. He thought that Mr. Jupiter was going to give him a good dinner; but the first thing he knew, the clerk returned with another man. They took hold of Brisetout, they tied him well, then they took a tin pan in which they put red pepper and turpentine. They rubbed the dog all over with the mixture; it burnt him so much that he howled and bellowed. When they let him go, Mr. Jupiter told him: 'You will give my reply to your comrades, and each one that will come to complain will be received in the same manner; you hear?'

"Ah, no, Brisetout did not hear; he ran straight ahead without knowing where he was going. At last he arrived at a bayou, fell into it, and was drowned.

"Some time after that, Mr. Jupiter did not feel well. He thought he would leave heaven and take a little trip to earth. On his way he saw an apple tree which was covered with beautiful apples. He began to eat some; and while he was eating, a troop of dogs came to bark at him. Mr. Jupiter ordered his stick to give them a good drubbing. The stick began to turn to the right and to the left, and beat the dogs so terribly, that they scattered about in a minute. There remained but one poor dog, who was all mangy. He begged the stick to spare him. Then Stick pushed him before Mr. Jupiter, and said: 'Master, that dog was so thin that I did not have the courage to beat him.' 'It is very well,' said Mr. Jupiter, 'let him go; but if ever any dog comes to bark at me again, I shall destroy them all. I don't want to be bothered by you, I say. You have already sent me a delegation, and I received them so well that I don't think they will like to come back to see me. Have you already forgotten that?' The poor lean dog replied: 'What you say is true, but we never saw again the messenger we sent you; we are still waiting for him.' Mr. Jupiter then said: 'I will tell you how you can find out the messenger you had sent to me: let all dogs smell one another, and the one which will smell turpentine is the messenger.'

"You see now, Compère Lapin, why dogs smell one another. It was all Mr. Jupiter's doing. Poor old fellow, he has now lost all his clients, since the pope ordered everybody to leave him, and he has had to close his shop. He left the heaven, and no one knows where he went to hide. You understand, Compère Lapin, people get tired of having always the same thing; so they took another religion, and I think that the one we have now is good."

"Thank you, thank you, Master Fox, for your good story; and in order to show you that I am your old friend, I will tell you what we can do. As I told you already, we must remain very quiet. As the elephants want to go to attack King Lion in his own country, they will make a bridge for the army to pass. When the bridge will be finished they will go straight ahead, without stopping anywhere, to attack King Lion, for they want to take him by surprise. Don't you tell that to anybody, you hear."

Compère Lapin and Master Fox then shook hands, and they parted. Master Fox went on his way, and Compère Lapin went to the king of elephants and asked him to give orders to all the carpenters and blacksmiths in the country to obey him. When all the workmen were assembled, Compère Lapin began to make the bridge, and soon finished it. On the side of the river which was in the country of the elephants, he made at the end of the bridge a large park. These were bars of iron planted in the earth; they were at least ten feet high, and so sharp that a fly could not touch one without being pierced through. Compère Lapin then covered the bars of iron with branches and brambles to make it appear like a patch of briers, in order that they might not know that it was a snare. Then he took four cows with their calves, and tied them in the very middle of the pit. Then he put in it red pepper, ashes, and tobacco snuff. Then he placed in the trap a great number of tubs of water, in which there was a drug that made people go to sleep right off. After he had finished all this, Compère Lapin said: "Now let King Lion come to attack us."

Master Fox was still travelling to render an account of his errand to King Lion; but he was so much afraid to return without Compère Lapin, that he concluded that it was better not to return at all. On his way he met a hen; he killed it, and covered an old rag with the blood. He tied his hind paw with the rag, and he began to limp, and jump on three feet. At last he met Bourriquet [Burro], to whom he said: "My dear friend, render me a little service; you see how sick I am. I pray you to go to King Lion, to tell him that I cannot come to see him. The elephants broke my leg because I had come to claim Compère Lapin."

"Oh, no!" said Bourriquet; "you were always against me with Compère Lapin. Go yourself."

"That is good," said Master Fox; *"c'est pas jis ein fois la bouche besoin manger* [I shall have my chance again, you will need me again]. If you knew what I have seen and what I know, you would listen to me."

"Well, tell me all," said Bourriquet; "and I will go, since you cannot walk."

"That is all right; listen well. The elephants intend to come to attack King Lion in his country. They are making a bridge to cross the river, and as soon as the bridge will be finished they will come immediately to surprise Lion. If the king understood his business, he would hasten to attack the elephants in their own country, before they come to lift him up before he knows it."

As soon as Master Fox had finished speaking, Bourriquet galloped away and went to King Lion, to whom he said what Master Fox had related to him. The king was so glad that he ordered some one to give Bourriquet a little hay to eat. Bourriquet was not very much pleased, and he began grumbling. "Don't you know, Bourriquet," said the king's servant, *"qué ein choual donnin to doite pas gardé la bride* [that you must not look at the bridle of a horse which was given to you]."

"Well," said Bourriquet, "I had expected a better reward, but I'll take that anyhow, because *ein ti zozo dans la main vaut mié qué plein ti zozos quapé voltigé dans bois* [a bird in the hand is better than two in the bush]."

All at once they heard a dreadful noise. It was King Lion, who was starting for the war with all the animals which he could find: tigers, bears, wolves, all King Lion's subjects were there. As to Master Fox, he had run back to notify Compère Lapin that the enemies were coming.

Miss Léonine was with the army, and her father used to tell her all the time: "I am glad that you came; Compère Lapin will have to pay for all his tricks; you must treat him as he treated you."

King Lion was at the head of the army, and coming near the bridge he saw Master Fox, who was lying in the road with his leg broken.

"Oh! oh!" said Lion, "this is the way they treated you! They shall have to pay for all that."

"Make haste," said Master Fox; "don't wait till they come to attack you; pass the bridge immediately; that will throw them in confusion."

The army went on. They all ran to pass over the bridge, King Lion at the head, with his daughter. As soon as they arrived at the place where the snare was, and they saw the cows and their calves, King Lion and his troops killed them and began to eat them. Then they quarrelled among themselves and began to fight. They scattered about the ashes, the red pepper, and the tobacco snuff, and were completely blinded. They fought terribly; they massacred one another; then those that were left drank the water in the tubs. Two hours later they were all sound asleep.

The elephants, which had remained prudently at a distance, hearing no more noise, came to the bridge. They killed all the animals that were left in Lion's army, and threw their bodies in the river. They flayed King Lion; they took his skin and sewed Bourriquet into it; then they tied some straw, covered with pitch, to Bourriquet's tail; they put fire to the straw, and they let him go to announce the news in Lion's country.

When Bourriquet passed on the bridge, he was galloping so fast that one might have thought that it was thunder that was rolling on the bridge, as if it were more than one hundred cart-loads. When Bourriquet arrived in his country his tail was entirely consumed by the fire, but he said that he had lost it in a battle. Although he announced very sad news, no one could help laughing at him: he was so funny without his tail, and so proud of his glorious wound.

As soon as all was over at the bridge, Compère Lapin went to get Master Fox, and took him to the king of the elephants. He presented him to his majesty, and told him that Master Fox was his good friend, and if the king wanted to accept his services, they would both be his very faithful subjects. The king of elephants said to them: "I believe that you are two cunning rascals, and that in my war with King Lion, Master Fox *té galpé avec chévreil et chassé avec chien* (had been on both sides of the fence); but all right, he may remain here, if he wants. As for you, Compère Lapin, I want you to get married. Here is Miss White Rabbit; she is rich, and will be a good match for you. Tomorrow I want to dance at the wedding."

The next day all the people assembled, and celebrated with great splendor the marriage of Compère Lapin with Miss White Rabbit. Master Fox was the first groomsman. Three weeks after the wedding, Mrs. Compère Lapin gave birth to two little ones; one was white and the other as black as soot. Compère Lapin was not pleased, and he went to see the king of elephants.

"Oh! you know nothing," said the king; "you are married before the church, and I will not grant you a divorce. Besides, I must tell you that in the family of Mrs. Compère Lapin it happens very often that the little ones are black. It is when the ladies are afraid in a dark night; so console yourself, and don't be troubled."

Compère Lapin consented to remain with his wife until death should part them, and that is how he married after all his pranks.

As I was there when all that happened, I ran away to relate it to you.

THREE CREOLE BALLADS

Among the traditional songs sung in the Creole language in former days are a number of ballads that do not belong to the English repertoire of neighboring regions of the South. Some of them are basically

European in form, others more related to an African-derived style. One of these ballads is about the battle of Chalmette in 1814. It is basically a personal account of a slave, who tells how he left his master at the scene of the fighting and made his own way to home and safety:

> *Fizi z'Anglé yé fé bim! bim!*
> *Carabin Kaintock yé fé zim! zim!*
> *Mo di' moin, sauvé to la peau!*
> *Mo zété corps au bord de l'eau;*
> *Quand mo rivé li té fé clair.*
> *Madam' li prend' ein coup d'colère;*
> *Li fé donn' moin ein quat' piquie*
> *Passeque mo pas sivi mouchie;*
> *Mais moin mo vo mie quat' piquié*
> *Passé ein coup d'fizi z'Anglé!*

> The English muskets went bim! bim!
> Kentucky rifles went zim! zim!
> I said to myself, save your skin!
> I ran along the water's edge;
> When I arrived at home it was day.
> Mistress flew into a rage;
> She had me whipped at the four stakes
> Because I didn't follow master;
> But for me the four stakes
> Are better than a shot from an English musket.

Following is a ballad about a Negro insurrectionist named Saint Malo, who was caught and hanged by the colonial authorities. The reference to the *cabildo*—the colonial council that administered Spanish rule of the colony—seems to date the event, if not the song itself, before 1803. As far as one can judge the song on the basis of words alone, it has a marked French character, and is quite similar in style to Creole historical ballads still extant in Haiti. Had it been composed in African tradition, its imagery and treatment would have been quite different. Certain scenes would have been alluded to briefly, there would have been a repetition of certain key lines, and many little observations made in the story would have been left to the imagination. The developing of details, and the tight and logical sequence of events mark the ballad as European in style, but the point of view is that of the Negro slave:

> *Aie! zein zens, vini fé ouarra*
> *Pou' pôv' St. Malo dans l'embas!*
> *Yé c'assé le avec yé chiens,*

The songs, collected by George Cable, appear in his article in Century Magazine, *February, 1886. His translations, which were inaccurate, have been revised.*

Yé tiré li ein coup d' fizi.
Yé halé li la cyprier,
So bras yé 'tassé par derrier,
Yé 'tassé so la main divant;
Yé marré li apé queue choual.
Yé trainein li zouqu'à la ville.
Divant michés là dans Cabil'e
Yé quisé li li fé complot
Pou' coupé cou à tout yé blancs.
Yé mandé li qui so compères;
Pôv' St. Malo pas di' a-rien!
Zize là li lir so la sentence,
Et pis li fé dressé potence,
Yé halé choual—ç'arette parti—
Pôv' St. Malo resté pendi!
Eine hèr soleil deza levée
Quand yé pend li si la levée.
Yé laissé so corps balancé
Pou' carancro gagnion manzé.

Aie! Young men, come to lament
For poor St. Malo out there!
They hunted him with dogs,
They fired guns at him.
They brought him from the cypress swamp,
His arms they tied behind his back,
They tied his hands in front;
They tied him to a horse's tail,
They dragged him to the city
Before the men of the Cabildo.
They accused him of a plot
To cut the throats of all the whites.
They asked him who his comrades were,
But poor St. Malo was silent.
The judge read out the sentence,
And then they prepared the gallows.
They drove the horse—the cart moved off—
And left poor St. Malo hanging there.
The day was an hour old
When they hanged him;
They left his body swinging
For the carrion crows to eat.

A song of Spanish colonial days that survived to the end of the nineteenth century is that of a slave escapee, addressed to a member of the Cabildo named General Florido. This song, as is evident, has a format which identifies it with Negro rather than French tradition. There is a statement, followed by a choral response, and a repetition. The second stanza, in the same pattern, gives a related allusion suggesting that the runaway slave was escaping by ship. Minute details of the event are regarded as of no importance, contrary to the French ballad's habit of spelling out a story in narrative form.

Oh Gén-é-ral Flo-ri-do! C'est vrai yé pas ca-pab' pren'
Yen a ein counan sur la mer! C'est vrai yé pas ca-pab' pren'

moin! Oh Gén-é-ral la Flo-ri-do! C'est
moin! Yen a ein cou-nan sur la mer! C'est

vrai yé pas ca-pab' pren' moin!
vrai yé pas ca-pab' pren' moin!

Oh General Florido,
It is true, you can't capture me!
Oh General Florido,
It is true, you can't capture me!

There is a ship on the ocean,
It is true, you can't capture me!
There is a ship on the ocean,
It is true, you can't capture me!

NEW ORLEANS SUPERSTITIONS

AS SET DOWN BY LAFCADIO HEARN

Lafcadio Hearn, whose late nineteenth century writings established him as a sensitive and romantic observer of life and traditions in Japan, the Caribbean and the American southland, was essentially a literary figure. He depended heavily on feelings and impressions, and whatever he witnessed of the life going on around him was material to be transmuted into something larger than life.

From "New Orleans Superstitions," by Lafcadio Hearn, Harper's Weekly, December 25, 1886.

But though a literary product was his objective, Hearn was, indeed, an observer, keen
and meticulous. In 1886 he wrote a piece for
Harper's Weekly on the subject of prevalent
superstitions in New Orleans. Although he
was not a folklorist, and although he was primarily speaking of the superstitions of
blacks, he astutely noted that what was called
voodoo (his spelling: voudoo) in New Orleans in the late nineteenth century was
largely unrelated to the West African religious system whose name it had borrowed.
And he observed, as well, that the superstitions held by many blacks were shared with
whites, and that many of these notions had in
fact come originally from Europe. Many of
the superstitious beliefs that he recorded
were again recorded by folklorists of a later
generation, testifying to his accuracy. Here
are some extracts from his *Harper's* article:

What is to-day called Voudooism in New Orleans means, not an African cultus, but a curious class of Negro practices, some possibly derived from it, and others which bear resemblance to the magic of the
Middle Ages. What could be more mediaeval, for instance, than molding a waxen heart, and sticking pins in it, or melting it slowly before a
fire, while charms are being repeated with the hope that as the waxen
heart melts or breaks, the life of some enemy will depart? What, again,
could remind us more of thirteenth-century superstition than the burning of a certain number of tapers to compel some absent person's return, with the idea that before the last taper is consumed a mysterious
mesmerism will force the wanderer to cross rivers and mountains if
necessary on his or her way back?

The fear of what are styled "Voudoo charms" is much more widely
spread in Louisiana than any one who had conversed only with educat-
ed residents might suppose; and the most familiar superstition of this
class is the belief in what I might call *pillow magic,* which is the supposed art of causing wasting sicknesses or even death by putting certain objects into the pillow of the bed in which the hated person sleeps.
Feather pillows are supposed to be particularly well adapted to this
kind of witchcraft. It is believed that by secret spells a "Voudoo" can
cause some monstrous kind of bird or nondescript animal to shape itself into being out of the pillow feathers—like the *tupilek* of the
Esquimau *iliseenek* (witchcraft). It grows very slowly, and by night
only; but when completely formed, the person who has been using the
pillow dies. . . .

Some say that putting grains of corn into a child's pillow "prevents it
from growing any more"; others declare that a bit of cloth in a grown

person's pillow will cause wasting sickness; but different parties questioned by me gave each a different signification to the use of similar charms. Putting an open pair of scissors under the pillow before going to bed is supposed to insure a pleasant sleep in spite of fetiches; but the surest way to provide against being "hoodooed," as American residents call it, is to open one's pillow from time to time. If any charms are found, they must be first sprinkled with salt, then burned. A Spanish resident told me that their eldest daughter had been unable to sleep for weeks, owing to a fetich that had been put into her pillow by a spiteful colored domestic. After the object had been duly exorcised and burned, all the young lady's restlessness departed. A friend of mine living in one of the country parishes once found a tow string in his pillow, into the fibers of which a great number of feather stems had either been introduced or had introduced themselves. He wished to retain it as a curiosity, but no sooner did he exhibit it to some acquaintance than it was denounced as a Voudoo "trick," and my friend was actually compelled to burn it in the presence of witnesses. . . .

Placing charms before the entrance of a house or room, or throwing them over a wall into a yard, is believed to be a deadly practice. When a charm is laid before a room door or hall door, oil is often poured on the floor or pavement in front of the threshold. It is supposed that whoever *crosses an oil line* falls into the power of the Voudoos. To break the oil charm, sand or salt should be strewn upon it. Only a few days before writing this article a very intelligent Spaniard told me that shortly after having discharged a dishonest colored servant he found before his bedroom door one evening a pool of oil with a charm lying in the middle of it, and a candle burning near it. The charm contained some bones, feathers, hairs, and rags—all wrapped together with a string—and a dime. No superstitious person would have dared to use that dime; but my friend, not being superstitious, forthwith put it into his pocket. . . .

The Negroes believe that in order to make an evil charm operate it is necessary *to sacrifice something.* Wine and cake are left occasionally in dark rooms, or candies are scattered over the sidewalk, by those who want to make their fetich hurt somebody. If food or sweetmeats are thus thrown away, they must be abandoned without a parting glance; the witch or wizard must not look back while engaged in the sacrifice.

Scattering dirt before a door, or making certain figures on the wall of a house with chalk, or crumbling dry leaves with the fingers and scattering the fragments before a residence, are also forms of a maleficent conjuring which sometimes cause serious annoyance. Happily the conjurers are almost as afraid of the counter-charms as the most superstitious persons are of the conjuring. An incident which occurred recently in one of the streets of the old quarter known as "Spanish Town" afforded me ocular proof of the fact. Through malice or thoughtlessness, or possibly in obedience to secret orders, a young Negro girl had been tearing up some leaves and scattering them on the sidewalk in front of a cottage occupied by a French family. Just as she had dropped the last leaf the irate French woman rushed out with a broom and a handful of salt, and began to sweep away the leaves, after having flung salt both upon them and upon the little Negress. The latter actually screamed with fright, and cried out, *"Oh, pas jeté plis disel après moin, madame! pas bisoin jeté disel après moin; mo pas pé vini icite encore."* (Oh, madam, don't throw any more salt after me; you needn't throw any more salt after me; I won't come here any more.)

Another strange belief connected with these practices was well illustrated by a gift made to my friend Professor William Henry by a Negro servant for whom he had done some trifling favor. The gift consisted of a "frizzly hen"—one of those funny little fowls whose feathers all seem to curl. "Mars'r Henry, you keep dat frizzly hen, an' ef eny niggers frow eny *conjure* in your yard, *dat frizzly hen will eat de conjure.*" Some say, however, that one is not safe unless he keeps two frizzly hens. . . .

The Negro's terror of a broom is of very ancient date—it may have an African origin. It was commented upon by Moreau de Saint-Méry in his work on San Domingo, published in 1796. "What especially irritates the Negro," he wrote, "is to have a broom passed over any part of his body. He asks at once whether the person imagined that he was dead, and remains convinced that the act shortens his life." Very similar ideas concerning the broom linger in New Orleans. To point either end of a broom at a person is deemed bad luck; and many an ignorant man would instantly knock down or violently abuse the party who should point a broom at him. Moreover, the broom is supposed to have mysterious power as a means of getting rid of people. "If you are pestered by visitors whom you would wish never to see again, sprinkle salt on the floor after they go, and sweep it out by the same door through which they have gone and they will never come back." To use a broom in the evening is bad luck: *balayer le soir, on balaye sa fortune* (to sweep in the evening is to sweep your good luck away), remains a well-quoted proverb. . . .

In New Orleans, among the colored people, and among many of the uneducated of other races, the victim of muscular atrophy is believed to be the victim of Voudooism. A notion is prevalent that Negro witches possess knowledge of a secret poison which may terminate life instantly or cause a slow "withering away," according as the dose is administered. A Frenchman under treatment for paralysis informed me that his misfortune was certainly the work of Voudoos, and that his wife and child had died through the secret agency of Negro wizards. Mental aberration is also said to be caused by the administration of poisons whereof some few Negroes are alleged to possess the secret. In short, some very superstitious persons of both races live in perpetual dread of imaginary Voudoos, and fancy that the least ailment from which they suffer is the work of sorcery. . . .

Here, as in other parts of the world, the crowing hen is killed, the hooting of the owl presages death or bad luck, and the crowing of the cock by day presages the arrival of company. The wren *(roitelet)* must not be killed: *c'est zozeau bon Dié* (it is the good God's bird)—a belief, I think, of European origin.

It is dangerous to throw hair-combings away instead of burning them, because birds may weave them into their nests, and while the nest remains the person to whom the hair belonged will have a continual headache. It is bad luck to move a cat from one house to another; seven years' bad luck to kill a cat; and the girl who steps, accidentally or otherwise, on a cat's tail need not expect to be married the same year. The apparition of a white butterfly means good news. The neighing of a horse before one's door is bad luck. When a fly bothers one very persistently, one may expect to meet an acquaintance who has been absent many years.

There are many superstitions about marriage, which seem to have a European origin, but are not less interesting on that account. "Twice a bridesmaid, never a bride," is a proverb which needs no comment. The bride must not keep the pins which fastened her wedding dress. The husband must never take off his wedding ring: to take it off will insure him bad luck of some kind. If a girl who is engaged accidentally lets a knife fall, it is a sign that her lover is coming. Fair or foul weather upon her marriage day augurs a happy or unhappy married life.

The superstitions connected with death may be all imported, but I have never been able to find a foreign origin for some of them. It is bad luck to whistle or hum the air that a band plays at a funeral. If a funeral stops before your house, it means that the dead wants company. It is bad luck to cross a funeral procession, or to count the number of carriages in it; if you do count them, you may expect to die after the expiration of as many weeks as there were carriages at the funeral. If at the cemetery there be any unusual delay in burying the dead, caused by any unlooked-for circumstances, such as the tomb proving too small to admit the coffin, it is a sign that the deceased is selecting a companion from among those present, and one of the mourners must soon die. It is bad luck to carry a spade through a house. A bed should never be placed with its foot pointing toward the street door, for corpses leave the house feet foremost. It is bad luck to travel with a priest; this idea seems to me of Spanish importation; and I am inclined to attribute a similar origin to the strange tropical superstition about the banana, which I obtained, nevertheless, from an Italian. You must not *cut* a banana, but simply break it with the fingers, because in cutting it you *cut the cross*. It does not require a very powerful imagination to discern in a severed section of the fruit the ghostly suggestion of a crucifixion.

Some other Creole superstitions are equally characterized by naïve beauty. Never put out with your finger the little red spark that tries to linger on the wick of a blown-out candle: just so long as it burns, some soul in purgatory enjoys rest from torment. Shooting-stars are souls escaping from purgatory: if you can make a good wish three times before the star disappears, the wish will be granted. When there is sunshine and rain together, a colored nurse will tell the children, *"Gadé! djabe apé batte so femme."* (Look! the devil's beating his wife!). . . .

Turning the foot suddenly in walking means bad or good luck. If the right foot turns, it is bad luck; if the left, good. This superstition seems African, according to a statement made by Moreau de Saint-Méry. Some reverse the conditions, making the turning of the left foot bad luck. It is also bad luck to walk about the house with one shoe on and one shoe off, or, as a Creole acquaintance explained it to me, *"c'est appeler sa mère ou son père dans le tombeau"* (It is calling one's mother or one's father into the grave). An itching in the right palm means coming gain; in the left, coming loss.

Never leave a house by a different door from that by which you entered it; it is "carrying away the good luck of the place." Never live in a house you build before it has been rented for at least a year. When an aged person repairs his or her house, he or she is soon to die. Never pass a child through a window; it stops his growth. Stepping over a child does the same; therefore, whoever takes such a step inadvertently must step back again to break the evil spell. Never tilt a rocking-chair when it is empty. Never tell a bad dream before breakfast, unless you want it "to come true"; and never pare the nails on Monday morning before taking a cup of coffee. A funny superstition about windows is given me in this note by a friend: *"Il ne faut pas faire passer un enfant par la fenêtre, car avant un an il y en aura un autre"* (A child must not be passed through a window, for if so passed you will have another child before the lapse of a year). . . .

If two marriages are celebrated simultaneously, one of the husbands will die. Marry at the time of the moon's waning and your good luck will wane also. If two persons think and express the same thought at the same time, one of them will die before the year passes. To chop up food in a pot with a knife means a dispute in the house. If you have a ringing in your ears, some person is speaking badly of you; call out the names of all whom you suspect, and when the ringing stops at the utterance of a certain name, you know who the party is. If two young girls are combing the hair of a third at the same time, it may be taken for granted that the youngest of the three will soon die. If you want to make it stop raining, plant a cross in the middle of the yard and sprinkle it with salt. The red-fish has the print of St. Peter's fingers on its tail. If water won't boil in the kettle, there may be a toad or a toad's egg in it. Never kill a spider in the afternoon or evening, but always kill the spider unlucky enough to show himself early in the morning, for the old French proverb says:

Araignée du matin—chagrin;
Araignée du midi—plaisir;
Araignée du soir—espoir

(A spider seen in the morning is a sign of grief; a spider seen at noon, of joy; a spider seen in the evening, of hope).

Some Creole Proverbial Wisdom

Ratte mangé canne, zanzoli mouri innocent.
Rat eats the sugar cane, the innocent lizard dies for it.
(A comment on injustice.)

Macaque dit si so croupion plimé ca pas gadé lezautt.
Monkey says that if his behind is bare it is nobody else's business.
(A comment on minding one's own affairs.)

Maringouin perdi so temps quand li piqué caïman.
Mosquito wastes his time trying to sting alligator.
(A comment on futile endeavors.)

Quand bois tombé, cabri monté.
When the tree has fallen even a goat may climb it.
(It is no achievement to take advantage of one who has become weak
    and defenseless.)

Faut pas marré tayau avec saucisse.
Do not tie up a dog with a chain of sausages.

Coupé zoré milet fait pas choual.
Cutting the ears of a mule will not make him a horse.
(Fundamental differences do not lie in appearances.)

Bouki fait gombo, Lapin mangé li.
Bouki makes the gombo but it is eaten by Rabbit.
(Said when someone steals an advantage from another's work.)

Cochon conné sir qui bois l'apé frotté.
Pig knows which tree to rub against.
(Said of someone who knows where his best interests lie.)

These Louisiana proverbs are from Gombo Zhèbes, *by Lafcadio Hearn, New
York, Coleman, 1885. The Author has retained Hearn's Creole spellings, but
has revised some of the English translations.*

APPENDIXES

APPENDIX I

THE DISTRIBUTION OF THE ORISHAS' POWERS: YORUBA VERSION

A Yoruba prototype of this Cuban tale is the following.

Numerous orishas were living on the earth, but they did not yet have all the powers for which they are now known. When knowledge was needed to accomplish an important thing, the orishas, like ordinary men, appealed to Olorun or to Orunmila for help. But one day the orisha called Oko thought, "Here I am, living among humans. But what distinguishes me? If the people need something they go to Orunmila for it. If I need something I also must go to Orunmila. Why should this be? If I had the knowledge of a certain thing people could call on me for help, and they would not have to importune Orunmila." Orisha-Oko went to where Orunmila was living on earth. He said, "I have no powers that distinguish me from the humans created by Obatala. You, Orunmila, who are spokesman for Olorun on earth, endow me with some special attribute. If this is done people can appeal to me for help in many things."

Orunmila pondered on what Orisha-Oko was asking. He said, "Yes, perhaps there is reason in it. Let me consider the matter." Orisha-Oko departed.

Now, the orisha called Ogun was thinking similar thoughts. "Am I not an orisha? I should have special powers greater than those of humans." He also went to where Orunmila was living. He said, "Whenever some important thing is required by the people they come to you. Their demands are heavy. It is Orunmila this and Orunmila that. Give me special knowledge of some kind so that I can do something to keep the world going."

Orunmila answered, 'Yes, I have been thinking about it. I will see what can be done."

The minds of the other orishas turned the same way. Eshu, who already had the knowledge of language, went to Orunmila seeking more knowledge. Shango went to Orunmila, Sonponno went to Orunmila, Olu-Igbo went to Orunmila, Osanyin went to Orunmila. And after them still more orishas went, all asking for a special gift of some part of Orunmila's understanding of the world and its forces.

Orunmila was distressed. He thought, "I hold all the orishas equal in my affection. If I give anything to one of them the others will surely complain that I denied something to them and they will hold it against me. There are many powers to be shared. To whom should I give one power or another?" Because the matter weighed heavily on him, Orunmila hardly touched his food. He could not sleep at night. His wives and servants worried about him. Orunmila took to walking by himself in the open country and pondering the question of how he might divide the powers among the orishas. He was walking in the fields this way one time when he met Agemo, the chameleon.

Agemo said to him, "You, Orunmila, spokesman for Olorun on earth, why are you so heavy with care?"

Orunmila answered, "One by one the orishas come to me, saying, 'Give me a special power so that I can relieve you of some of your burdens.' But there are so many powers, some great, some small. If I give something small it will be held against me. If I give something large to one, the others will resent it. I want to treat all the orishas equally. How can I do it so there will be harmony instead of dissension?"

Agemo said, "Perhaps it would be best to leave the distribution to chance. Return to the sky. Then send messengers to announce that on such and such a day you will pour the powers down on the earth. Let each orisha catch what he can or retrieve it from the place where it falls. Whatever powers an orisha collects in this way will be his. By sending your messengers you will have given everyone equal notice, and no one can say, 'Orunmila has neglected me.'"

On hearing Agemo's advice, Orunmila's mind rested, for now he saw how it could be done. He said, "Agemo, though you are small your name will be great. I will share out the powers and the knowledge by raining them on the earth."

Orunmila returned to the sky and prepared things. Then he sent messengers down to the places where the orishas lived. The messengers went from the house of one orisha to another. They said, "Orunmila has instructed us to announce that he will dispense the powers from the sky. On the fifth day following this one you are to go out into the open fields and wait. Orunmila will scatter the things you want. They will fall here, there and anywhere. Grasp what you can as it falls or retrieve it from the ground. One of you will acquire one thing, others will acquire others. In this way the special knowledge will be distributed, and no one can say Orunmila prefers one orisha over another."

The orishas said, "Orunmila does a good thing. Thank him for us. We will receive what he rains down on us."

On the fifth day they went into the open fields and waited. Then the powers began to fall from the sky. The orishas ran here and there with their hands outstretched. One orisha caught one thing, another caught another. Some of the powers eluded their hands and fell in the tall grass or among the trees. The orishas went searching in all directions. Now, some orishas were fleet while some were not. Some were more agile or stronger than others. Those who were swifter, or stronger or more persistent were able to get larger or more desirable portions of what Orunmila was bestowing. But everyone received something.

Because Eshu was one of the strongest, and because he did not hesitate to push anyone aside, he gathered a very large share of the powers, one of which was the capability of destroying anyone who offended him. He acquired the power of phallic strength and the power to deprive his enemies of their virility. He received the power of turning men back from their purposes and of turning order into disorder. And all these things were in addition to the power of language that he already possessed. Because of all these attributes possessed by Eshu, orishas and humans thereafter treated him with special respect and sought to avoid his enmity.

The orisha Shango, through what he picked up in the fields, became the owner of the lightning bolt, and therefore he acquired the name Jakuta, the Stone Thrower. Later, when he became the ruler of the city of Oyo, he was called Oba Jakuta.

Orisha-Oko received the power to make crops flourish, and human beings supplicated him to make their yams and grain grow.

Sonponno became the owner of smallpox, and both orishas and humans dreaded his power.

Osanyin acquired special knowledge of curing and divining, and Olu-Igbo became the orisha of the bush country and the forest.

Each orisha received something.

This is how the orishas who went to live on earth came by their special attributes.

APPENDIX II

OLOFIN PUNISHES BABALUAYE: A YORUBA COMPARISON

In Yoruba mythology, Olorun (Olofin in Cuba) is compelled from time to time to punish the orishas for their behavior. The following Yoruba story tells how Olorun punished Sonponno (Babaluaye in the Cuban version) for misbehavior at a social gathering.

The orishas who had settled in the land created by Obatala worked together in the fields and in this way demonstrated to humans the benefits of communal labor. They invented the game of ayo, or wari, so that they could amuse themselves in times of leisure. They introduced on the earth some of the ceremonies that they had performed when they had been living in the sky. They invented drums and other musical instruments and perfected singing and dancing. Life went on. It was good.

One year, at the time of the yam harvest, the orishas held a festival. They gathered in the center of their town to feast on game brought from the bush and crops brought in from the fields. A large amount of palm wine was prepared and placed in the center of the gathering in an earthen pot. The orishas ate, drank palm wine and danced.

Only one orisha, Sonponno, to whom had been given the secret of smallpox, did not dance. Sonponno had a wooden leg and had to move

(From Tales of Yoruba Gods and Heroes, © 1973 by Harold Courlander. Reprinted by permission of Crown Publishers.)

about with the aid of a walking stick. So he sat quietly while the festivities went on. But, like all the others, he frequently dipped his gourd into the pot of palm wine and drank. Everyone had much palm wine. They began to laugh. They began to speak loudly. There was shouting. When the orishas sang, their voices were not true. When they danced, their legs became unsteady and they staggered this way and that.

Someone noticed Sonponno sitting alone near the palm wine. He was offended. He said, "Why is it that Sonponno does not dance with us?" Others called out to Sonponno, urging him to get up and join them. "Join us, join us," they said, and some of them tugged at him to make him get up. But Sonponno sat without moving from his place. Because he was ashamed of his wooden leg he held back.

The others went on dancing and dipping their gourds in the palm wine. They began to taunt Sonponno. "Get up, get up," they called. "Do not sit there forever like a dead antelope."

Sonponno could no longer stand the taunts of the orishas. With the aid of his walking stick he stood up. He adjusted the flowing garment that he wore so it covered his wooden leg. Cautiously he joined the dancers. He commenced to dance. But he was unsteady from drinking so much palm wine. The others also were unsteady. They could not control their movements and they jostled one another this way and that. One of the orishas bumped into Sonponno. Sonponno sprawled on the ground and his wooden leg was exposed for everyone to see. The orishas laughed. Someone called out, "Wooden leg! Wooden leg!" Others joined in the taunting. They made a song out of the words.

Sonponno was overcome with shame. Then anger overtook him. He struggled to his feet. There was more laughter. Sonponno struck out with his walking stick. He struck one person, then another. The orishas were surprised. They were too befogged with palm wine to move away. Only when they felt the sting of Sonponno's stick on their backs did they begin to run. They scattered in all directions. The dancing came to an end, and Sonponno alone remained in the dance court.

The orishas went to their houses. Each person who had been touched by Sonponno's stick fell ill. Their eyes became red and sores broke out on their skin. News of the affair was carried to Obatala at a distant place. Obatala was angered. He said, "The orishas shamed Sonponno for something he could not help. They should not have done such a thing. But Sonponno should not have taken matters into his own hands. He should have come to me for justice. Those who ridiculed him have been punished by smallpox. But because Sonponno became the judge of his own affair he also must be punished."

Obatala dressed in his white clothes. In his hand he carried his cowtail switch ornamented with cowries, and he went to Sonponno's house to judge him. Sonponno saw Obatala coming, and he fled into the bush. On discovering that Sonponno had run away, Obatala proclaimed: "He has gone to the bush. Very well. There he must remain, for he cannot be trusted to live in the community."

From that time on, Sonponno never lived among other people, but by himself in the bush. Nevertheless, at one time and another he caused smallpox to come to orishas and humans. He was much feared, and for this reason people avoided calling him by his right name, Sonponno. They alluded to him by indirection, calling him Ile-Gbigbona, meaning Hot Ground; or as Ile-Titu, Cold Ground; or as Olode, Owner of the Public; or merely as Baba, meaning Father. Even those who worship him fear him, for still today he is the one who sends smallpox to torment people everywhere. And who knows the one he will touch with his staff? For it is said of Sonponno:

"He feasts with the father of the household, but he strikes down the father's son in the doorway."

APPENDIX III

AN ABAKWA INITIATION: THE EKOI-EFIK TRADITION

The Cuban Abakwa society is an inheritance from the Egbo society of the Ekoi and Efik peoples of the Calabar Coast. The following description of the Egbo society and its rituals was set down early in the twentieth century.

The whole country is honeycombed with secret societies, among which the Egbo Club is the most powerful. Before the coming of the white man this institution ruled the land, and even now it has more influence in many ways than government itself, and has caused endless difficulty to administrators.

The Ekoi claim to have originated the whole idea of such clubs, which have existed among them for centuries, and are mentioned in some of their very old folklore tales. Later on, the Ododop and other tribes near Iffianga, Akwa and Efut in the South Cameroons, started a similar society, which gradually became more powerful than the original Ekoi one, and therefore more costly to join. The Efiks of Calabar were not slow to perceive the advantage of such institutions, and so founded the Ekkpe Club, which, with the growing importance of their town through the coming of white men, soon became the wealthiest of all Egbo societies.

As the Efiks held the monopoly of the Calabar trade they and their club obtained great influence over the Ekoi, who found it adviseable to adopt many Efik customs and laws. This was especially the case with the Ekoi who live to the south of Oban, and therefore nearest to Calabar. Those to the north still keep their old Egbo practically unchanged, except the inhabitants of Ndebbiji, who have adopted that of the Ododop people, which is almost the same as the Efik one.

Calabar was practically the only place whence the Ekoi could obtain

---

(From In the Shadow of the Bush, *by P. Amaury Talbot, London, Heinemann, 1912.)*

guns and gunpowder. To reach it, they had to pass through Efik territory. The roads were picketed by the latter people, and it was imposible to reach the factories save by their goodwill. Even if some men from the interior managed to reach a white official and attempted to lay their grievances before him, the Efik interpreter took care that the true state of things should not be translated. If a case was tried in the Calabar courts the only chance which a "bush man" had of winning it was to enlist the help of some powerful Efik, and often the only way of doing this was to promise to become his "member." The arts by which Efik traders entrapped first one man and then the whole family, as slaves, were often cruel in the extreme. The only holds possessed by the Ekoi over their persecutors were that the Efiks feared their jujus and wanted the dried meat killed and preserved by Ekoi hunters. The establishment of a native court at Oban did not much improve matters. Indeed, in some ways, it made them worse, as the clerk who ruled it was always an Efik and arranged that judgment should be given in favor of his own people.

It is natural that the most powerful society should be called by the name of the most dreaded denizen of the bush, for "Egbo" is supposed to express to the Efik "Ekkpe" and the Ekoi "Ngbe," i.e., Leopard.

Possibly among the Ekoi, where totemism is still an article of belief, though most of them will deny the existence of any such idea, the Leopard Society originally consisted only of those who belonged to this totem. On account of the superior craft and power of the animal it would naturally draw to itself the largest following. Later, as totemism began to lose force, first one, then another prominent individual who was not, properly speaking, a "Leopard soul" might be allowed to join, until it gradually became open to all.

There are many indications which seem to place beyond doubt the fact that some form of totemism still enters into the ritual of the Egbo Society. For instance, at some of the bigger "plays," while the principal performers (or "images" as they are called) run up and down, now to the right, now to the left, the lesser personages form a circle, and keep time to a monotonous chant. In one case they sang:

"Okum ngbe ommobik ejennum ngimm, akiko ye ajakk nga ka ejenn nyamm."

The Egbo cannot walk straight, he is driven hither and thither by the movement of the beast.

On another occasion a prominent member of the Egbo, who had the reputation of knowing more Nsibidi—a primitive secret writing much used in this part of the world—than any man now alive, was asked to give me a little help in the study of this script. He refused point blank, though a good remuneration had been offered for his services. He added as an aside to another member of the society, with no idea that his words could be understood by [me], "If I taught him Nsidibi, he would know all the Egbo signs, and the secrets of the animals." He refused to give any further information, and soon after went away.

The importance of the society is obvious even to the most careless visitor to any land where it has gained a foothold, for the clubhouse is the principal building in every town. Even the smallest village has its Egbo shed, and when a town decides to migrate the first thing done, as soon as the fresh site is cleared, before even new farms are cut, or the land divided up, is to fix the position of the clubhouse. A small shed, called Ekpa Ntan (the house without walls) is erected to mark the spot where the Egbo house is to stand.

The many-sided character of Egbo may be judged from the immense powers which it has arrogated to itself in almost every direction. Under native rule it usurped practically all functions of government, made trade almost impossible for nonmembers, and exercised a deep influence on the religious and mystic side of the nation.

The ritual is certainly very ancient, and in it many juju cults are mixed. The name of Obassi is invoked before every sacrifice, and an oblation of food and drink laid in front of the Etai Ngbe (leopard stone), the cut stone usually found before the second pillar of the clubhouse.

It is difficult to discover more than the merest fragments of the secrets of Egbo, as any known informant would meet with a speedy death. Still from what has been gathered—mostly, as in the case already quoted, from snatches of song sung at different plays—there seems to be a close resemblance between these secrets and the Eleusinian and ancient Egyptian mysteries. Certainly a considerable amount of hypnotism, clairvoyance and spiritualism is taught, and only too many proofs have been given, that some of the powers of nature are known and utilized by initiates, in a way forgotten or unknown to their white rulers.

For instance, some of the esoteric members seem to have the power of calling up shadow forms of absent persons. Once an exhibition of this nature given in the central court of the compound of one of the head chiefs of Oban, was described to me.

It was midnight, and a bright moon was shining. Within the open space in the center of the compound a fire was burning. On this from time to time medicine was thrown, which caused clouds of smoke to rise. These died down, save for isolated puffs, which after a time assumed definite shape.

The spectators sat on the ground in a half-circle behind the fire, and facing a low mud wall, beyond which, against the background of the moonlit sky, dark silhouettes began to pass, each clearly recognizable as that of some person known to be absent at the time. There was no sign of any artificial means of producing these shapes, which continued to pass for about a quarter of an hour, at the end of which time they grew faint and at length faded.

The chiefs claimed to have the power of calling up the shadow shapes of white men, but no case in which this had actually been done was cited.

There are seven grades which the aspirant must pass before he can be admitted to the deeper teaching or the revelation of any save the lesser mysteries. All may be entered by young boys, should their fathers be rich enough to pay the necessary fees, but the secrets are not unfolded till middle age has been reached.

1. EKPIRI NGBE. Small Egbo.

2. EBU NKO (an old word, the meaning of which is not known). At a dance given by this grade, members must always wear their best clothes. Aspirants to each of these are marked with white chalk on both arms.

3. MBAWKAW (old Ekoi word adopted by Efiks). Aspirants to this are marked on the forehead with ekui (camwood dye). These three grades are called collectively Abonn Ogbe, i.e., Children of the Egbos. They are neither important nor expensive to enter.

4. NDIBU (old word, meaning unknown, equivalent to Efik Nyampke). This is the second division, and one to which it is accounted a great honor to belong. It is often called "The Mother of the Grades." Its president holds the second place in the whole society. If it was found necessary to expel a member who had reached this grade, death followed as a matter of course, lest any of its secrets should be revealed by the outcast.

When a man joins Ndibu the head chiefs and officials stay in the Egbo house, while the young men dance and play round the town. The best friend of the aspirant brings forward a calabash containing a leg of meat, and two bottles of palm wine. The postulant then enters the clubhouse, and sits down before the chief, who puts powder on his head, and recites all the names of the Egbo. The new member next rises and invokes the names in his turn, while after each the chiefs call out "Owe," i.e., Our Own. He then goes out and dances with the young men. The play is carried on for about eight days, during which time palm wine and meat are supplied to all.

At the present day at Oban, entrance to this grade costs about thirty pounds, which must be paid before full membership is allowed.

5. OKU AKAMA (The Priest Consents). This is not very expensive to enter, nor considered of much account, but it must be passed before further grades can be reached. The postulant is marked with yellow dye (ogokk) on the abdomen and the back of his shoulders.

The old Ekoi grade was called Asian, but when Oban adopted the Calabar Egbo, the Efiks insisted on this being suppressed.

6. ETURI (Metal or Brass Rod), Efik Okpokgo. In the old days during a play, all fires had to be extinguished and no noise of any kind was permitted in the town. Formerly very few men succeeded in reaching this grade, but now it is usually passed on the same day as

7. NKANDA, the highest and final grade. Oban took this from the Efiks, who again insisted on the destruction of the old Ekoi equivalent "Isong," and of another old grade "Mutanda," of slightly lesser importance.

Nkanda is more expensive than any other grade, and most men only enter late in life. When a man has succeeded in joining this high grade, he is rubbed on head and chest with yellow powder (ogokk). Five rings are made on front and back. Two yellow, one round each breast, a white one in the center some few inches below, and, beneath this again, two more yellow ones, forming a square with those on the breasts.

On the back the rings are arranged in the same way, but the central one is yellow and the four outer ones white. The arms are ornamented with alternate stripes of white and yellow, and till the last rite is finished, the man goes bare save for a long loincloth which reaches from waist to feet.

The chief of Nkanda is the president of the Egbo Lodge, and by far the most powerful man of the town. His office is sometimes hereditary, and only free-born chiefs can aspire to it. In olden days a slave could not join Egbo, lest he should reveal its secrets to a new master. He could, however, be present at most of the ceremonies if his owner was a member of Egbo, and permitted.

One of the chief insignia of the Nkanda grade is called the Ekabe (Efik Ekarra) Nkanda. This is a kind of hoop, covered with bright-colored cloth. The attendant whose duty is to carry this, performs many curious evolutions with it. He is obliged to hold back the Okum (or image) by its means if the latter, in a state of excitement, seems about to show himself to a nonmember, particularly a woman, at a time when this is not permitted. Should the Okum succeed in evading the vigilance of the Ekabe bearer, a cow is killed, and a feast provided for the members at the expense of the defaulting official.

Another symbol used by Nkanda and Ebu Nko alike is the Effrigi, a sort of wooden fan on which Nsibidi signs are inscribed.

The head priest of the whole Egbo Society is called Iyamba, the old Ekoi equivalent for which was Musungu.

Other officials are Murua, who carries the rattle during "plays," and Isua, the master of ceremonies for the Abonn Ogbe. The head of each grade is called Ntui (chief) and acts as treasurer.

Those who belong to the four higher grades, and have paid the fees in full, may join in another ceremony called Mariba, or Etem-I-Ngbe (The Bush Leopard). This is performed in the depths of the forest and with the greatest secrecy. It is during the Mariba that the successive mysteries are unveiled. The ceremony may also be performed at the funeral "customs" of very great chiefs.

The danger run by nonmembers on such occasions, before the coming of white rule, may perhaps be better understood by a case which happened not long before my arrival to start the District.

During the Mariba the sacred images, etc., are carried to a part of the bush where a little hut of green boughs has been built to receive them. Sentries are posted to keep all intruders from coming within a mile of this spot. On this occasion, however, two young girls, sisters, happened to have missed the patrol, and trespassed unwittingly within the sacred precincts, probably in search of nuts or bush fruits, which abound everywhere. They were caught by the sentries, brought before the Egbo, condemned to death, and hanged almost immediately. Their brother, who was a member of the highest grade of the society, was allowed, as a great favor, to be present at their death and afterwards to carry home the bodies to his family. Of redress, in such a case, there could be neither hope nor thought.

Sometimes rich and influential women are permitted to become honorary members of all grades, but they are never allowed to be full members, nor to know any of the mysteries.

Each grade has its particular dances and tunes, and each its own Okum Ngbe or Egbo image, which is never supposed to come out and show itself unless under direct inspiration to do so.

The so-called image is a figure robed from crown to heel in a long garment, of the color proper to the grade, and pierced with eyeholes. It usually bears on its head a wooden framework covered with skin and shaped like a human head, often with two faces, one male and the other female. This represents the omniscience of the Deity looking both ways, into the future and back to the past, as also the bisexual character shown in the oldest conceptions of Obassi Osaw and Obassi Nsi, Sky Father and Earth Mother.

The Okum runs up and down accompanied by two attendants clothed in gorgeous, close-fitting, knitted garments, usually of red, yellow and white. One of these carries a rod or whip, the symbol of the power of the society, with which, under native law, he had the right to flog to death any nonmembers who had seriously offended against its rules. The other bears the symbolic green boughs, which play so great a part in the lives of the Ekoi. At almost every important occurrence, from birth onward, green leaves of the kind proper to the event are used, and at the last are gently drawn over the face of a dying man, that his spirit may pass peacefully and without pain from this world to the next.

There is great rivalry between the different towns as to which can produce the most gorgeous robes for images and members. The financial state of a place can be told by a glance at one of the plays, as the local resources are strained to the utmost in the hope of outdoing neighboring towns. The chiefs of Oban volunteered the information that the play was so much finer on the second New Year after my arrival than formerly, because the opening of a government station had brought them an increase of wealth.

The most interesting figure in last New Year's dance, however, wore nothing either rich or attractive. This was the Ekuri Ibokk (Efik "Axe-Medicine"). It is a very old Ekoi juju, but was renamed a few years ago when the axe was placed between its jaws in addition to the other insignia.

The image was robed in a long gown of dark blue cloth, daubed with mud from the riverbed. This, to the Ekoi, as formerly to performers in the Greek Mysteries and to Flamen Dialis, is in itself a great juju. Over the robes of the image dark-spotted juju leaves were fastened here and there. On its head it bore a crocodile mask, carved in wood, perhaps a representation of Nimm herself. It was attended by two hunters armed with flintlock guns, a third bore a fishing net, and a fourth a curious earthen trumpet covered with leopard skin. The image was supposed to be deaf to human voices, and to hear only those of the bush beasts, save when awakened by the call of the trumpet. Ekuri Ibokk is the great "hunting juju" of the Ekoi, and had never before appeared to a European. It is the juju that is supposed to have the power of "smelling out" all others, and the axe in its jaws is a sign of its special fierceness. Powerful as it is, however, it is not proof against the very human weakness of wishing to have its photograph taken, and appeared, on this inducement, among its less exclusive brothers.

At such "plays" all the principal characters carry wands or whips, the symbol of the power of the society, which, as has already been mentioned, could be used to flog to death nonmembers who ventured outside their houses during an Egbo performance, or seriously offended in any way. Minor offenses were punished by fines, and from these the main revenues of the club were derived.

One great advantage to be gained from membership in the old days was the facility offered for the recovery of debts. A creditor brought his case before the Egbo Lodge in the debtor's town. The council considered the matter, and if the claim was thought justified, the club drum would be beaten through the streets, and the defaulter ordered to pay. He was also bound to provide a "dash" for the Egbo Society. Should he be unable to comply with both demands, his goods were seized, and, other means failing, himself or some of his family reduced to the position of slaves, in order to make good all liabilities.

APPENDIX IV

NANANBOUCLOU AND THE PIECE OF FIRE: AN ASHANTI VARIANT

The characters in this Haitian tale are all deities of the Dahomean and Yoruba pantheons. The theme of the tale appears in a number of West African stories. The following, in summary form, comes from the Ashanti:

Anansi had six sons, each of whom possessed a special power. There were Akakai, whose name signified "Able to See Trouble"; Twa Akwan, meaning "Road Builder"; Hwe Nsuo, meaning "Able to Dry Up Rivers"; Adwafo, meaning "Skinner of Game"; Toto Abuo, meaning "Stone Thrower"; and Da Yi Ya, meaning "Lie on the Ground Like a Cushion."

One day Kwaku Anansi went on a long journey. Several weeks passed, and he failed to return. Akakai, the son who had the ability to see trouble, announced that Anansi had fallen into a distant river in the middle of a dense jungle. Twa Akwan, the builder of roads, constructed a highway through the jungle, and the brothers passed through it to the edge of the river. Hwe Nsuo, who had the power to dry up rivers,

---

(Extracted from The Hat-Shaking Dance and Other Ashanti Tales from Ghana, *©1957 by Harold Courlander, by permission of Harcourt Brace Jovanovich.)*

dried up the river, and they found there a great fish which had swallowed Anansi. Adwafo, the skinner of game, cut into the fish and released his father. But as soon as they brought Anansi to the edge of the river, a large hawk swooped down out of the sky, caught Anansi in his mouth, and soared into the air with him. Toto Abuo, the stone thrower, threw a rock into the sky and hit the hawk, which let go of Anansi. And as Anansi dropped toward the earth, Da Yi Ya threw himself on the ground like a cushion to soften his father's fall. Thus Kwaku Anansi was saved by his six sons and brought home to his village.

Then one day when he was in the forest, Anansi found a bright and beautiful object called Moon. Nothing like it had ever been seen before. It was the most magnificent object he had ever seen. He resolved to give it to one of his children.

He sent a message to Nyame, the Sky God, telling him about his discovery. He asked Nyame to come and hold the Moon, and to award it as a prize to one of Anansi's sons—the one who had done the most to rescue him when he was lost in the river. The Sky God came and held the Moon. Anansi sent for his sons. When they saw the Moon, each of them wanted it. They argued. The one who had located Anansi in the jungle river said he deserved the prize. The one who had built the road said he deserved it. The one who had dried up the river said he deserved it. The one who had cut Anansi out of the fish said he deserved it. The one who had hit the hawk with the stone said he deserved it. The one who had cushioned Anansi's fall to earth said he deserved it. They argued back and forth, and no one listened to anybody else. The argument went on and on and became a violent squabble. Nyame, the Sky God, didn't know who should have the prize. He listened to the arguments for a long time. Then he became impatient. He got up from where he sat and went back to the sky, taking the Moon along with him.

And that is why the Moon is always seen in the heavens, where Nyame took it, and not on the earth where Anansi found it.

APPENDIX V

THE VOYAGE BELOW THE WATER: AN MBUNDU VERSION

In traditional Haitian belief, some of the spirits of the dead, though not all, go to live in a place described as being "below the water." There, in a different dimension, people go on much as they did when they were alive. The following comparable story comes from the Mbundu of Angola:

Mbanza (King) Kitamba kia Xiba, a chief who was at Kasanji, had built his village; he lived on. When he was thus, his head-wife, Queen Muhongo, died. They buried her; they wailed the mourning; it ended.

(From Folk-Tales of Angola, by Heli Chatelain, New York, Stechert (for the American Folk-Lore Society), 1894.)

Mbanza Kitamba said: "Since my head-wife died, I shall mourn; my village too, no man shall do anything therein. The young people shall not shout; the women shall not pound; no one shall speak in the village." The head-men said: "Master, the woman is dead; thou sayest, 'In village they shall not speak; I will not eat, not drink; not speak'; we never yet saw this." He, the king, said: "If you desire, that I laugh, that I talk, that in the village they talk, it shall be that you bring me my head-wife, Queen Muhongo." The head-men say: "King, the person is now dead; how can we fetch her?" He said: "If ye cannot fetch her, I am in mourning; in my village, no person shall talk."

The head-men consult among themselves, saying: "Let us seek a medicine-man." They send for the medicine-man; the calling-present to the doctor is a gun. The doctor has come; his cooking is a cow. The doctor said: "Tell, what you sent me for." They said: "The head-queen Muhongo is dead; King Kitamba says, 'I will mourn; in the village no one shall talk; if you want to talk, you must fetch me my head-wife, Queen Muhongo.' Therefore it is we sent for thee, thee, the doctor, that thou fetchest her, the head-queen, from Kalunga; that the people may rejoice."

The doctor said: "All right." He went through the country gathering herbs; he set a medicine-mortar outside, saying: "The king, he shall come and wash; all the people shall wash." The chief washed; all the people washed. The doctor said: "Dig ye a grave in my guest-hut, at the fire-place." They dug the grave; it is done.

He entered the grave with his little child, which had come with him. He told his wife, saying: "All days, do not wear a girdle; thou shalt tuck in only. All days thou shalt constantly put water on the fire-place here." The woman assented. The doctor said: "Cover ye it up." They filled it up, with the doctor and his child; they rammed it down as when there was the fire-place itself. They lived on. The wife always puts the water on the fire-place, all days.

The doctor, when he got into the grave, there opened a large road. He starts on the road; he goes ahead; his child walks behind. They walk a while; they arrive beside a village; that is at Kalunga-ngombe's. The doctor looks into the middle of the village; Queen Muhongo is yonder; she is sewing a basket. He arrives where Queen Muhongo is; Queen Muhongo turns her eyes. She sees a man who is coming, she says: "Thou, who art coming, whence comest thou?" The doctor said: "Thou, thyself, I have sought thee. Since thou art dead, King Kitamba will not eat, will not drink, will not speak. In the village they pound not; they speak not; he says, 'If I shall talk, if I eat, go ye and fetch my head-wife.' That is what brought me here. I have spoken."

The head-queen said: "Very well. Come look at that one; who is it sitting?" The doctor said: "I know him not." The head-queen said: "He is Lord Kalunga-ngombe; he is always consuming us, us all." She said again: "He yonder, who is he? who is in the chain." The doctor said: "He looks like King Kitamba, whom I left where I came from." The queen said: "He is King Kitamba. He is in the world not any longer; there lacks how any years, the chief will die. Thou, doctor, who camest to fetch me, we, here in Kalunga, never comes one here to return again. Take my arm-ring, that they buried me with; that when thou goest there, they accuse thee not of lying, saying, 'thou wentest not there.' The chief himself, do not tell it him, saying, 'I found thee already in Kalunga." She paused. She said again: "Thou thyself, doctor, I cannot give thee to eat here. If thou eatest here, thou canst return no more." The doctor said: "Well." He departed.

He arrives at the place here he got into the grave with his child, that he went with. The woman, who stayed on earth, kept putting water on the fire-place. One day, she looks at the fire-place; there are cracks breaking. A while, she looks: the head of the doctor has come out. The doctor throws his arms outside; he gets out; he is on ground. He takes the child by the arm; he sets him on ground. The child looks at sun; he faints. The doctor goes to the bush; he gathers herbs. He comes; he washes him. The son comes to. They slept.

In morning, the doctor says: "You, head-men of the town, who fetched me, come here that I report where I went." The head-men all come; he reports everything that the head-queen had told him. The doctor said: "Finished. Pay me now." The head-men said: "Well." They took two slaves; they paid him. The doctor went to his home.

The head-men reported to the chief, saying: "The doctor reported, saying, 'I went to Kalunga-ngombe's. The chief's wife, I found her, said, "Since thou didst die, the chief does not eat, does not drink; come, let us go." The queen returned to me, saying, "We, here, there comes not a person, to return any more. This my arm-ring, take it along, that they see thee not with lies."' That is what the doctor reported to us. Thou, king, we have spoken. The ring is here, which they buried the queen with." The chief said: "Truth; it is the same."

When they spent a few days, the chief, he eats; the chief, he drinks. They spent a few years, the chief died. They wailed the funeral; they scattered.

King Kitamba kia Xiba in Kasanji left this story.

APPENDIX VI

MÉRISIER, STRONGER THAN THE ELEPHANTS and THE MOJO: AN ASHANTI VERSION

The theme of the Haitian tale and the U.S. Negro variant—the magic flight—is familiar to the folklore of many peoples. The Haitian variant and the following one from Ghana have an additional element in common: they both feature the queen of elephants and the quest for a

(From The Hat-Shaking Dance and Other Ashanti Tales from Ghana, © 1957 by Harold Courlander, by permission of Harcourt Brace Jovanovich.)

coffin. In the U.S. Negro version the demon antagonist-pursuer is the white boss-man, and in place of the more usual quest we have master-slave conflict as the motivating force.

Once in Ashanti there was a man named Kofi, who wanted to marry the daughter of a great chief. Kofi already had one wife, but he wanted to take the chief's daughter as his second. There were many young men who wanted the chief's daughter, and her father couldn't make up his mind which of them should have her.

Then one day the chief's wife died. He called all the young men to his house. His stool was brought out, and he sat under the tree where he gave judgments. He announced that his wife had died, and he asked the men: "What kind of burial is fitting for the mother of the girl you wish to marry?"

Many of the men were silent, for they could think of nothing to say. But one spoke up, saying: "She should be buried in a coffin of aromatic wood." Another said: "Her body should be wrapped in cloth woven with gold." Others spoke, too, each in his turn. When the chief turned his eyes on Kofi, Kofi said: "She should be buried in a coffin made of the tail of the Queen of All Elephants."

The chief replied to Kofi: "Very well, I have heard. Bring me the tail of the Queen of All Elephants, and you shall have my daughter."

Kofi went to his house and took his weapons from the rafters. He took his spear, and he took his knife. His wife said, "Where are you going?"

And Kofi replied: "I am going for the tail of the Queen of All Elephants. When I bring it back, I will get the chief's daughter for my second wife."

His first wife was angry when she heard this. Kofi went away into the bush.

But he didn't know where the Queen of All Elephants lived. He went this way and that, but no one could tell him what he wanted to know. Then one day he met a sorcerer on the trail. He asked him: "Wherever will I find the Queen of All Elephants?" The sorcerer sat on the ground and made marks in the dust with his fingers. He threw cowrie shells on the ground and watched how they fell. He threw them seven times. At last he said:

"Go this way to the north, and that way to the west; go past the Town of the Dead, and beyond, and you will find the place of the Queen of All Elephants."

Kofi thanked him and paid him with a gold ring. The sorcerer said: "Here is a juju to help you." He tied the medicine bundle on Kofi's arm above the elbow. He opened his basket and took out four eggs. He gave them to Kofi, saying: "These eggs are powerful magic. Use them when you are in great danger."

Kofi went the way he had been directed. He went this way to the north, and that way to the west, and he passed the Town of the Dead without entering. At last he came to the elephant village.

Around the village was a fence of pointed stakes, and at the gate was a watchman. Kofi asked to enter the village, but the watchman refused, saying: "Why should you enter?"

"I need the tail of the Queen of All Elephants," Kofi answered.

"If you enter, the great elephants will destroy you," the watchman said.

"I have to enter," Kofi replied.

They talked this way, and at last the watchman said:

"Wait then until they are asleep. Then you may enter. They sleep in a great circle, with the Queen of the Elephants in the center. You will have to walk on the elephants who surround her to get to the Queen. Walk firmly. If you walk lightly, they will awaken."

When it was dark and the elephants were asleep, Kofi entered. He walked on the elephants firmly, and they didn't wake up. He came to the center and saw the great Queen sleeping. He took his knife and cut off her tail. Then he went out of the village in haste so they shouldn't catch him.

When morning came, the elephants awoke. They discovered the Queen's tail had been taken, and they made a great outcry. They rushed out in pursuit. They found the tracks of Kofi's feet in the grass, and they followed. They caught sight of him, and they ran swiftly. They came closer and closer.

Kofi ran, carrying the great elephant tail, but the angry elephants were swifter than he. And when they were very close and about to seize him, Kofi called to the juju which the sorcerer had given him, saying: "What shall I do?"

And the juju replied: "Throw an egg behind you."

Kofi took one of his magic eggs and threw it on the ground behind. It turned into a wide and mighty river. When the elephants came to its banks, they couldn't cross. But the Queen of All Elephants also had magic. She turned them all into crocodiles, and they swam to the other side.

Again they pursued Kofi. And once more when they were close upon him, he threw an egg behind him. Where the egg fell, there rose up a great mountain. The Queen of All Elephants still had magic. She turned herself and her friends into herons, which flew over the mountain. When they approached Kofi again for the third time, he threw another egg, and where it fell, there sprang up an impenetrable forest. And this time he left them behind.

He came to the village and brought the great elephant tail to the chief. The chief took it, saying: "This is indeed fitting for the burial of my wife. You will be my son-in-law."

So Kofi went home to his own house. He hung his weapons on the wall. He hung his juju on the wall. Afterwards he went out into the fields to see to his crops and to burn the dead grass.

Then he heard a great commotion; he saw a cloud of dust; and he saw the elephants coming. He shouted to his wife to bring his juju. She went to the house and brought it. But the elephants came faster than she. And just as they were about to seize him, Kofi shouted to his wife: "Throw me my juju!"

But she was angry with him for preparing to marry a second wife. She threw his juju into the fire.

Kofi felt the breath of the elephants upon him. He cried out to his juju: "What shall I do?"

His juju replied: "Turn into a hawk."

Kofi threw his fourth egg on the ground and turned into a hawk. He soared high in the air, and the elephants couldn't reach him.

In time, the great elephants went away. But Kofi was still a hawk. He called on his juju again and again for help, but it couldn't help him, because it had been consumed in the fire.

So it is that Akroma, the hawk, circles and hovers over a fire in the fields. He can never resist it, for it is really Kofi still waiting for his juju to tell him what to do.

APPENDIX VII

THE SINGING TORTOISE and JOHN AND THE BLACKSNAKE: MBUNDU AND NUPE COMPARISONS

The theme of a talking (or singing) animal or object that refuses to talk when its discoverer brings witnesses is widely known in Africa. An Ashanti tale in this vein has as its central object a singing tortoise, as in the Haitian story. Frequently the talking object is a skull. Just as the Haitian variant ends with a philosophical reflection ("Stupidity doesn't kill a Haitian, it makes him sweat"), the African skull tales usually conclude with the skull offering some bit of wisdom. In a U.S. Negro version, the skull says, "My big mouth done this to me, son. Your big mouth done this to you too." (See "The Skull" in *Terrapin's Pot of Sense,* by Harold Courlander, New York, Holt, Rinehart and Winston, 1957.)

The following African example comes from the Mbundu of Angola:

A young man started on a journey; he arrived in middle of the path. He finds a skull of the head of a person. They all used to pass it by there. But he, when he arrived there, he struck it with staff, saying: "Thou, foolishness has killed thee." The skull said: "I, foolishness has killed me; thou, soon smartness shall kill thee." The young man said: "I have met an omen; where I was to go, I will not go, but return hence at once. The head of a person has spoken to me!"

And he returned; arrived at home. He finds others, old men, says: "You, gentlemen, I have met an ominous wonder." The old men said: "What omen?" He says: "The head of a person has spoken to me." The people say: "O man, thou hast told a lie. We all of us, at same place we are wont to pass by the head. We never yet heard it speak; how has the

---

(From Folk-Tales of Angola, *by Heli Chatelain, New York, Stechert [for the American Folk-Lore Society], 1894.)*

head spoken to thee?" He said: "Let us go. When I beat it with staff, if it does not speak, I, cut off my head." They say: "All right."

The crowd starts with him; they arrive at the place; they found it. The young man beat it with his staff: "Foolishness has killed thee." The head kept silent. He beat it again, the second time, saying: "Foolishness has killed thee." The head kept silent. The crowd say: "O man! thou didst tell a lie." They cut off his head. When they finished cutting it off, the skull said: "I, foolishness has killed me; thou, smartness has killed thee." The people said: "Why, we killed him unjustly; the head of a person has spoken."

The young man found the head of a person, and he beat it, saying: "Foolishness has killed thee." The head of the person said: "Thou, soon smartness shall kill thee." Wits and foolishness, all are equal. The young man, his wits killed him.

Finished.

And a Nupe variant from Nigeria:

A hunter goes into the bush. He finds an old human skull. The hunter says: "What brought you here?" The skull answers: "Talking brought me here." The hunter runs off. He runs to the king. He tells the king: "I found a dry human skull in the bush. It asks you how its father and mother are."

The king says: "Never since my mother bore me have I heard that a dead skull can speak." The king summons the Alkali, the Saba and the Degi and asks them if they have ever heard the like. None of the wise men has heard the like and they decide to send a guard out with the hunter into the bush to find out if his story is true and, if so, to learn the reason for it. The guard accompany the hunter into the bush with the order to kill him on the spot should he have lied. The guard and the hunter come to the skull. The hunter addresses the skull: "Skull, speak." The skull is silent. The hunter asks as before: "What brought you here?" The skull does not answer. The whole day long the hunter begs the skull to speak, but it does not answer. In the evening the guard tell the hunter to make the skull speak and when he cannot they kill him in accordance with the king's command. When the guard are gone the skull opens its jaws and asks the dead hunter's head: "What brought you here?" The dead hunter's head replies: "Talking brought me here!"

(From African Genesis, by Leo Frobenius and Douglas C. Fox, New York, Stackpole, 1937.)

APPENDIX VIII

BOUKI AND TI MALICE GO FISHING: AN ASHANTI COMPARISON

In the Ashanti version of this story, the antagonists are Anansi, the spider trickster, and Anene, the crow:

Anansi invited Anene to work with him at setting fish traps. Anene agreed. They went together to the bush to cut palm branches to make their fish traps. Arriving there, Anansi said, "Give me the knife. I will cut the palm leaves and weave the traps. You, sit over there and get tired for me." Anene replied, "I do not want to get tired. Therefore I shall do the cutting and weaving. I will make the traps.You, go over there in that place and sit. You, you get tired. That is your part." So Anansi sat in the shade and dozed while Anene did the work. Sometimes he moaned, saying, "Oh, but the sun is hot! Oh, but the arms are weary!"

When the traps were finished, Anansi said, "Now I will carry the traps to the water. Come behind and feel the weariness for me." Anene said, "No, on the contrary, I will carry them. You may take the weariness." Anene carried the traps to the water, Anansi walking behind and groaning. Arriving at the water, Anansi said, "Well, I will go into the water and set the traps. If I should be bitten by a great fish, you can die for me." Anene replied, "No, no. It is I who shall set the traps." Anene set the traps. The two of them went home, each to his own house.

The next morning they returned to the water. They found fish in the traps. They started to divide the catch. Anansi said, "Oh, but the fish are small. You take all the small ones today, and I will take all the large ones tomorrow." Anene answered, "Anansi, I perceive your intention. Why should not I take the larger ones? No, you take all the small ones today, tomorrow I shall take the larger." They went home, Anansi with the fish, Anene with nothing.

They came again the next day. Anansi said, "The fish are somewhat larger. They are yours. But there are only a few. Tomorrow will be my turn. There will be more." Anene said, "Why should I take only a few and you many? You are exploiting me. You, Anansi, take the fish today and I will take my share tomorrow." Anansi took the fish. They went home.

Again they returned to the traps. They took out the fish. "A bad day," Anansi said, "small fish again. Take them, it is your turn. Tomorrow surely will be better." Anene protested, "No, indeed, the small fish are yours. Tomorrow I will take the larger ones."

It went on this way. Anansi took all the fish, while Anene took none. At last the traps began to rot. Anene said to himself, "Now I perceive it. Anansi has been getting everything, I have been getting nothing. It is time to bring this affair to an end." When they went again to the water, Anene said, "The traps are rotten. We can not catch with them any more. I will take them into town and sell them. That way I will get something for my work." Anansi answered, "Why should it be you? If the traps must be sold, it is I who will sell them." He pulled the rotten traps out of the water. He carried them to town. Anansi went through the marketplace calling out, "Here are rotten fish traps! I am selling rotten fish traps!" People in the market laughed at Anansi. But afterwards they became angry, saying, "He acts as though we were fools." Anansi continued to call out, "Get your rotten traps here!" The chief of the town heard about it. He sent for Anansi.

The chief said, "You with the rotten fish traps, what do you take the people for? Are you yourself a fool, or do you consider this to be a town of fools? No man wants a rotten trap. But you, vendor of rotten traps, you persist in insulting us." The chief called his guards. He instructed them. They took Anansi to the gates of the town. They whipped him and sent him away. He was ashamed. He hid in dark corners where people would not see him. So it is until now that the spider is found hiding in places where other people do not go.

APPENDIX IX

WHY PEOPLE DO NOT LIVE AGAIN AFTER DEATH: HOTTENTOT VERSION

Numerous variants of this tale are told in Africa. The following is a Hottentot version set down well over a century ago:

The Moon, it is said, sent once an Insect to Men, saying: "Go thou to Men, and tell them, 'As I die, and dying live, so ye shall also die, and dying live.'" The Insect started with the message, but whilst on his way was overtaken by the Hare, who asked: "On what errand art thou bound?" The Insect answered: "I am sent by the Moon to Men, to tell them that as she dies, and dying lives, they also shall die, and dying live." The Hare said, "As thou art an awkward runner, let me go." With these words he ran off, and when he reached Men, he said, "I am sent by the Moon to tell you: 'As I die, and dying perish, in the same manner ye shall also die and come wholly to an end.'" Then the Hare returned to the Moon, and told her what he had said to Men. The Moon reproached him angrily, saying, "Darest thou tell the people a thing which I have not said?" With these words she took up a piece of wood, and struck him on the nose. Since that day the Hare's nose is slit.

(*From* Reynard the Fox in South Africa, *by W. H. I. Bleek, London, 1864.*)

APPENDIX X

RABBIT SEEKS WISDOM and CATCHING THE SNAKE AND THE YELLOW JACKETS: ASHANTI VERSION

These stories are direct descendants of an Ashanti explanation of how Anansi, the spider trickster, came to be the owner of all tales.

In the beginning of things, all stories were called Nyankomsem, Nyame's tales. Now they are known as Anansesem, Anansi's stories, and this is how it came to be.

Anansi went to Nyame to ask that he be given the ownership of stories, and Nyame asked what Anansi was willing to give in exchange. Anansi said, "I am prepared to give whatever you ask." Nyame said, "I must have three things. First, a swarm of mmoboro, living hornets; second, Onini, the python; and third, Osebo, the leopard. In exchange for these things I will give you the right to call yourself the owner of all tales." Anansi said, "It is a modest price." Nyame said, "Many persons have tried to bring them, and all have failed." Anansi replied, "It is nothing."

He left Nyame's house and went home. He cut a gourd from a vine and made a small hole in it. Then he went into the bush where the hornets lived, singing, "The rain is coming, the rain is coming." The hornets said, "No water is falling." Anansi answered, "Soon, soon." He said, "If the water falls on you, go into this gourd and stay dry." He set the gourd on the ground and went away. Then he poured water on himself so that he was dripping. He returned to where the hornets were, saying, "See, back there where I was, the rain is falling. It follows me. Enter the gourd quickly and remain dry." The hornets entered the gourd, and when they were all inside, Anansi plugged the hole with grass. He took the gourd to Nyame. The Sky God accepted them, saying, "Yes, this is part of the price, but the other things are more difficult."

Anansi returned to the bush. He cut a long bamboo pole and went to where Onini, the python, lived. As he walked he talked to himself, saying, "My wife is wrong, and I am right. My wife says he is shorter, I say he is longer. My wife demeans him, I respect him." The python overheard Anansi's words. He said to Anansi, "What is the nature of your argument with your wife?" Anansi answered, "Why, we argued about you, Onini. I said you are long, long. My wife said you are short, short. I said you are longer than this pole, she said you are shorter than this pole."

The python said, "The test is simple, let us measure. Bring the pole here." So Anansi laid the pole on the ground. The python came and lay next to it. "You seem a little short," Anansi said. The python stretched himself out. "A little more," Anansi said, "you are still a little short." The python tried again. "No," he said, "I cannot stretch any further." Anansi said, "What happens is that when you stretch out at one end you get shorter at the other. Let me tie you in the front so that you don't slip back." He tied Onini's head to the pole. After that he went to the other end and tied the tail to the pole. And when that was done he tied the python in the middle. The python could not move. Anansi said, "Oh! My wife spoke true words, and I was wrong, for it is clear that you are shorter than the pole." He picked up the python, securely lashed, and carried him to Nyame. Nyame said, "It is a difficult thing you have accomplished." Anansi replied, "It was nothing." The Sky God said, "There is still another thing to accomplish." Anansi replied, "I will do it. It is nothing."

There remained only the leopard. Anansi went into the bush and dug a pit where the leopard frequently walked. He covered the pit with branches, then he placed small twigs and leaves on top, and he sprinkled them with dust so that the trap would not be perceived. After that, Anansi went some distance away and hid. When Osebo, the leopard, came walking in the darkness of night, with only a little of the moon throwing light, he stepped on the trap and fell to the bottom of the pit.

When morning came, Anansi went to the pit and saw the leopard down below. The leopard said, "I have fallen into this hole. Be a good friend and help me out." Anansi said, "Yes, one friend helps another. Yet if I bring you out, perhaps you will be hungry one day and eat me." The leopard protested strongly, saying, "No! I swear it!" So Anansi bent a tall sapling over the pit and tied it with vines. He tied another vine to the top of the sapling, and he dropped the loose end into the pit, saying, "Tie this to your tail." The leopard did as he was instructed. Anansi said, "Is it well tied?" The leopard answered, "Yes it is well tied." Then Anansi took his knife and cut the vine that held the sapling to the ground. The tree sprang up, jerking the leopard out of the pit. He hung twisting and turning in the air, helpless to defend himself. Anansi killed the leopard and carried him to the Sky God's house. He said, "This is the third part."

Nyame said to Anansi, "All the things I asked for, you have brought them. Therefore, from now on you will own all stories that people tell. Whoever tells a tale must acknowledge that it belongs to Anansi."

So it was that once all stories were called Nyankomsem, after Nyame who owned them, until Anansi earned them; and so it is now that all tales are called Anansesem.

APPENDIX XI

THE THINGS THAT TALKED; BROKEN PLEDGE: ALL THINGS TALK; and OLD BOSS, JOHN AND THE MULE: AN ASHANTI VERSION

A country man went out to his garden to dig up some yams to take to market. While he was digging, one of the yams said to him:

"Well, at last you're here. You never weeded me, but now you come around with your digging stick. Go away and leave me alone!"

The farmer turned around and looked at his cow in amazement. The cow was chewing her cud and looking at him.

"Did you say something?" he asked.

The cow kept on chewing and said nothing, but the man's dog spoke up.

"It wasn't the cow who spoke to you," the dog said. "It was the yam. The yam says leave him alone."

The man became angry, because his dog had never talked before, and he didn't like his tone besides. So he took his knife and cut a branch from a palm tree to whip his dog. Just then the palm tree said:

"Put that branch down!"

The man was getting very upset about the way things were going, and he started to throw the palm branch away, but the palm branch said:

"Man, put me down softly!"

He put the branch down gently on a stone, and the stone said:

"Hey, take that thing off me!"

This was enough, and the frightened farmer started to run for his village. On the way he met a fisherman going the other way with a fish trap on his head.

"What's the hurry?" the fisherman asked.

"My yam said, 'Leave me alone!' Then the dog said, 'Listen to what the yam says!' When I went to whip the dog with a palm branch the tree said, 'Put that branch down!' Then the palm branch said, 'Do it softly!' Then the stone said, 'Take that thing off me!' "

"Is that all?" the man with the fish trap asked. "Is that so frightening?"

"Well," the man's fish trap said, "did he take it off the stone?"

"Wah!" the fisherman shouted. He threw the fish trap on the ground and began to run with the farmer, and on the trail they met a weaver with a bundle of cloth on his head.

"Where are you going in such a rush?" he asked them.

"My yam said, 'Leave me alone!' " the farmer said. "The dog said, 'Listen to what the yam says!' The tree said, 'Put that branch down!'

(From The Cow-Tail Switch and Other West African Tales, by Harold Courlander and George Herzog,© 1975 by Harold Courlander. Reprinted by permission of Holt, Rinehart and Winston.)

The branch said, 'Do it softly!' And the stone said, 'Take that thing off me!'"

"And then," the fisherman continued, "the fish trap said, 'Did he take it off?'"

"That's nothing to get excited about," the weaver said, "no reason at all."

"Oh yes it is," his bundle of cloth said. "If it happened to you you'd run too!"

"Wah!" the weaver shouted. He threw his bundle on the trail and started running with the other men.

They came panting to the ford in the river and found a man bathing.

"Are you chasing a gazelle?" he asked them.

The first man said breathlessly: "My yam talked at me, and it said, 'Leave me alone!' And my dog said, 'Listen to your yam!' And when I cut myself a branch the tree said, 'Put that branch down!' And the branch said, 'Do it softly!' And the stone said, 'Take that thing off me!'"

The fisherman panted:

"And my trap said, 'Did he?'"

The weaver wheezed:

"And my bundle of cloth said, 'You'd run too!'"

"Is that why you're running?" the man in the river asked.

"Well, wouldn't you run if you were in their position?" the river said.

The man jumped out of the water and began to run with the others. They ran down the main street of the village to the house of the chief. The chief's servants brought his stool out, and he came and sat on it to listen to their complaints. The men began to recite their troubles.

"I went out to my garden to dig yams," the farmer said, waving his arms. "Then everything began to talk! My yam said, 'Leave me alone!' My dog said, 'Pay attention to your yam!' The tree said, 'Put that branch down!' The branch said, 'Do it softly!' And the stone said, 'Take it off me!'"

"And my fish trap said, 'Well, did he take it off?'" the fisherman said.

"And my cloth said, 'You'd run too!'" the weaver said.

"And the river said the same," the bather said hoarsely, his eyes bulging.

The chief listened to them patiently, but he couldn't refrain from scowling.

"Now this is really a wild story," he said at last. "You'd better all go back to your work before I punish you for disturbing the peace."

So the men went away, and the chief shook his head and mumbled to himself, "Nonsense like that upsets the community."

"Fantastic, isn't it?" his stool said. "Imagine, a talking yam!"

APPENDIX XII

TRESPASSING ON THE DEVIL'S LAND: AFRICAN AND WEST INDIAN VARIANTS

This story is found in a number of versions in West Africa, and has found its way to the West Indies as well as to Surinam. A Haitian variant, with Bouki as the central character, is to be found in *Uncle Bouqui of Haiti*, by Harold Courlander, New York, 1942. The following is a Yoruba version:

In a certain village there was a young man named Kigbo. He had a character all his own. He was an obstinate person. If silence was pleasing to other people, he would play a drum. If someone said, "Tomorrow we should repair the storage houses," Kigbo said, "No, tomorrow we should sharpen our hoes." If his father said, "Kigbo, the yams are ripe. Let us bring them in," Kigbo said, "On the contrary, the yams are not ready." If someone said, "This is the way a thing should be done," Kigbo said, "No, it is clear that the thing should be done the other way around."

Kigbo married a girl of the village. Her name was Dolapo. He built a house of his own. His first child was a boy named Ojo. Once when the time came for preparing the fields, Kigbo's father said to him: "Let us go out tomorrow and clear new ground."

Kigbo said: "The fields around the village are too small. Let us go into the bush instead."

His father said: "No one farms in the bush."

Kigbo said: "Why does no one farm in the bush?"

His father said: "Men must have their fields near their houses."

Kigbo said: "I want to have my fields far from my house."

His father said: "It is dangerous to farm in the bush."

Kigbo replied: "The bush suits my taste."

Kigbo's father did not know what else to say. He called Kigbo's mother, saying, "He wants to farm in the bush. Reason with him."

Kigbo's mother said: "Do not go. The bush spirits will make trouble for you."

Kigbo said: "Ho! They will not trouble me. My name is Kigbo."

His father called for an elder of the village. The village elder said: "Our ancestors taught us to avoid the bush spirits."

Kigbo said: "Nevertheless, I am going."

He went to his house. His wife Dolapo stood at the door holding Ojo in her arms. Kigbo said: "Prepare things for me. Tomorrow I am going into the bush." In the morning he took his bush knife and his knapsack and walked a great distance. He found a place and said: "I will make my farm here."

He began to cut down the brush. At the sound of his chopping many

(From Olode the Hunter and Other Tales from Nigeria, © *1968 by Harold Courlander. By permission of Harcourt Brace Jovanovich.)*

bush spirits came out of the trees. They said: "Who is cutting here?"

Kigbo said: "It is I, Kigbo."

They said: "This land belongs to the bush spirits."

Kigbo said: "I do not care." He went on cutting.

The bush spirits said: "This is bush-spirit land. Therefore, we also will cut." They joined him in clearing the land. There were hundreds of them, and the cutting was soon done.

Kigbo said: "Now I will burn." He began to gather the brush and burn it.

The bush spirits said: "This is our land. Whatever you do, we will do it, too." They gathered and burned brush. Soon it was done.

Kigbo returned to his village. He put corn seed in his knapsack. His father said: "Since you have returned, stay here. Do not go back to the bush."

His mother said: "Stay and work in the village. The bush is not for men."

Kigbo said: "In the bush no one gives me advice. The bush spirits help me." To his wife Dolapo he said: "Wait here in the village. I will plant. When the field is ready to be harvested, I will come for you."

He departed. When he arrived at his farm in the bush, he began to plant. The bush spirits came out of the trees. They said: "Who is there?"

He replied: "It is I, Kigbo. I am planting corn."

They said: "This land belongs to the bush spirits. Therefore, we also will plant. Whatever you do, we will do." They took corn seed from Kigbo's knapsack. They planted. Soon it was finished.

Kigbo went to a village where he had friends. He rested there, waiting for the corn to be grown. In his own village his wife, Dolapo, and his son, Ojo, also waited. Time passed. There was no message from Kigbo. At last Dolapo could wait no longer. She went into the bush to find her husband, carrying Ojo on her hip. They came to Kigbo's farm. The corn stalks were grown, but the corn was not yet ripe.

Ojo said: "I want some corn."

His mother said: "The corn is not yet ripe."

Ojo said: "I am hungry."

Dolapo broke off a stem of corn and gave it to him. The bush spirits came out of the trees, saying, "Who is there and what are you doing?"

She replied: "It is I, the wife of Kigbo. I broke off a stem of corn to give the little one."

They said: "Whatever you do, we will do." They swarmed through the field breaking off the corn stalks. Soon it was done, and all the broken stalks lay on the ground.

At this moment Kigbo arrived. He saw Dolapo and Ojo, and he saw all the corn lying on the ground. He said: "The corn is ruined!"

Dolapo said: "The bush spirits did it. I broke off only one stalk. It was Ojo's fault. He demanded a stalk to eat. I gave him a stalk, then the bush spirits did the rest." She gave Ojo a slap.

The bush spirits came out of the trees. They said: "What are you doing?"

Dolapo said: "I slapped the boy to punish him."

They said: "Whatever you do, we will do." They gathered around Ojo and began to slap him.

Kigbo shouted at his wife: "See what you have done!" In anger he slapped her.

The bush spirits said: "What are you doing?"

He said: "Slapping my wife for giving me so much trouble."

They said: "We will do it too." They stopped slapping the boy and began slapping Dolapo.

Kigbo called out for them to stop, but they wouldn't stop. He cried out: "Everything is lost!" He struck his head with his fist.

The bush spirits said: "What are you doing?"

He said: "All is lost. Therefore, I hit myself."

They said: "We will do it too." They gathered around Kigbo, striking him on the head.

He called out: "Let us go quickly!" Kigbo, Dolapo, and their son returned to the village, leaving the farm behind. He saw his father. Because of shame, Kigbo did not speak.

His father said:"Kigbo, let us go out with the men tomorrow and work in the fields."

Kigbo said: "Yes, Father, let us do so."

APPENDIX XIII

THE MAN WHO TOOK A WATER MOTHER
FOR HIS BRIDE:
A YORUBA COMPARISON

In the Nigerian town of Owo there is an annual festival, called Igogo (meaning bells). Bands of dancers and players of handbells go from place to place all day long soliciting gifts. The activities are led by priests who represent a search party that long ago went out to look for Orunsen, a missing wife of the ruler who then reigned over Owo. This is the story behind the festival:

The Oba in those days was man named Renrengenjen. It is said that he went hunting, and that when he was deep in the bush he discovered a deerskin hanging in the branches of a tree. The Oba recognized the skin as belonging to a deer-woman who had transformed herself into a human. It was widely known that animals of the bush sometimes removed their skins and took on human form so they could enter the town on market day. When they had finished their affairs in Owo they returned to the bush, put on their skins and again became bush creatures. Whenever strangers appeared in Owo's marketplace people ex-

(From Tales of Yoruba Gods and Heroes, © *1973 by Harold Courlander. by permission of Crown Publishers.)*

amined them closely for signs that they were antelopes, foxes or leopards in human disguise. If a hunting dog paid particular attention to a stranger people were likely to say, "Let us be careful. That person smells of the bush."

So when the Oba Renrengenjen found the deerskin he forgot about hunting. He wanted to see the deer-person who would come to reclaim the skin. He took the skin and rolled it up. He hung it on his back and climbed into a nearby tree from where he could see everything below. There he waited patiently. The sun moved in the sky. The shadows became long. At last he saw a woman coming from the town. As she approached, the Oba saw that she was beautiful. She arrived at the place where she had left the skin, but it was not there. She searched for it on the ground. She looked everywhere. Then she sat on the ground and began to cry.

Oba Renrengenjen descended from his tree carrying the deerskin. He went to where the woman was sitting, full of admiration for her beauty. She saw the skin he carried on his back and pleaded for it. The Oba spoke soft words to her, but she went on pleading. The Oba said, "Why do you want to return to the form of a deer? The human world is better. Our life is good. No one hunts us, because we are the hunters. Our fields provide plentifully for us, and we do not have to wander from place to place as the bush creatures must do. We have iron weapons, and therefore the leopards avoid us. Human beings have superiority over the animal world. Come back with me and live as my wife in Owo. I am the Oba of the town. Just as humans are supreme over animals, I am supreme over Owo. Just as I have everything I need, you also will have everything you need in life."

The Oba went on talking this way. And finally the deer-woman saw that he was determined. She said, "If the people of Owo learn that I am a deer-person they will ridicule me and make my life unbearable. No one must ever know that I came from the bush."

The Oba answered, "I will keep the secret. I will say that you are from a distant city. But what shall I call you?"

The deer-woman said, "My name is Orunsen."

The Oba brought her back to Owo. He hid the deerskin in the rafters of his house. He took Orunsen as his wife. She was first of all his wives in his affections.

His other wives kept asking the question, "Where does Orunsen come from? Her ways are strange to us."

And the Oba always answered, "She comes from a far-off place in the south."

Sometimes they asked Orunsen herself, and Orunsen also replied, "From the south."

Time went on. There was jealousy in the household. The Oba's other wives resented Orunsen. They made her life hard. But the Oba's affection for her was strong and he made her life worth living.

One day Oba Renrengenjen went on a long hunting expedition. His wives had much time on their hands. They prowled here and there looking for clues to Orunsen's origin. At last they found the deerskin that the Oba had hidden in the rafters. They brought it to Orunsen and taunted her. They cried, "Deer-woman!" and "Bush creature!" They no longer mentioned her name. They said, "Let the animal-with-the-skin-in-the-rafters do this," or, "Let Two Skins do that." They abused her endlessly. They spread the word in Owo that the Oba had taken a deer for his wife.

Orunsen said nothing in answer to the taunts she heard. She gathered her belongings and left Owo. She went into the bush. She disappeared.

When the Oba returned from his hunting expedition he looked at once for Orunsen, but she was not there. He asked his servants where she was. They said, "She went away into the bush." He asked his wives and they answered, "Oh, you mean, the deer-woman whose skin was hidden in the rafters? Yes, she went away to be with her own kind in the bush." They berated Renrengenjen for bringing an animal into the house to live with him.

The Oba was grieved. Without Orunsen his house seemed empty. He ordered that a search be made for Orunsen. His guards, his servants and his slaves went into the bush looking for her. They searched everywhere. And after many days of searching they returned to Owo, saying, "No. We went everywhere. We questioned everyone. We combed the bush. But Orunsen was not there."

The Oba said, "Return to the bush. Continue the searching. Do not come back to Owo without Orunsen."

But at this moment a voice was heard in the sky. It said: "Renrengenjen, abandon the search. Where I am now, you cannot find me. I have gone into the sky to live under the protection of Olorun. Here no one says, 'There goes the animal-woman.'"

The Oba's guards, his servants and his slaves, and his wives as well prostrated themselves on the ground.

The voice went on: "In my husband's absence his other wives took my skin from the rafters and ridiculed me before the whole town. For this reason I had to leave Owo. But Renrengenjen was good to me, and because of that I will be a benefactor of the town. Conduct annual sacrifices in my name. In exchange, Owo will flourish, no one will suffer poverty, and no woman will be barren."

Renrengenjen ordered the search ended. He went into his house and remained there many days without seeing anyone. He hardly ate. He lay on his bed silently, and his servants did not know whether he was asleep or awake. But in time the Oba came out into the world again and resumed his life.

He ordered the town to prepare a food offering for Orunsen. Cows, goats, bush cows and chickens were slaughtered for the sacrifice. Fish, kola nuts and palm oil were offered. Everyone in Owo participated. There were rituals and festivities. Songs were sung in praise of Orunsen. Bells were played in Orunsen's honor. In return, Orunsen gave prosperity and fertility to Owo.

This is how the Igogo festival began. It continues to the present day. When the priests go about playing their bells they are reenacting the long search for Orunsen in the bush. It is said that because Owo never forgets the annual ceremonies for Orunsen the people of the town continue to prosper.

APPENDIX XIV

JOHN CALLS ON THE LORD: A CARIBBEAN VARIANT

Many variants of this story are told in the Caribbean. A Haitian version, under the title, "Charles Legoun and His Friend," appears on p. 69. The following brief variant comes from the West Indian island of St. Kitts:

Dis is a fellah what name of Coffee. Ev'y time he's eat' his breakfas', he say, "Praise God, me belly full. Massah God, come fah Coffee, he mek Coffee belly well full." So a fellah was behin' his house, hear him. So one night he went an' he rap. He say, "Who is dat?" He say, "Me. Me, Master God."—"Why you come fah?"—"Come fah Coffee." He out de lamp. "Tell Massah God Coffee not dere."

APPENDIX XV

TERRAPIN'S POT OF SENSE: AN ASHANTI VERSION

Variants of this story are known in the West Indies, and African prototypes are found among the Yoruba, where the central character is also the trickster tortoise, and the Ashanti. In the Ashanti tale the central figure is Anansi, the spider:

Kwaku Anansi regarded himself as the wisest of all creatures. He knew how to build bridges, to make dams and roads, to weave, and to hunt. But he didn't wish to share this wisdom wth other creatures. He decided one day that he would gather together all the wisdom of the world and keep it for himself. So he went around collecting wisdom, and each bit he found he put in a large earthen pot. When the pot was full, Anansi prepared to carry it into a high treetop where no one else could find it. He held the pot in front of him and began to climb.

Anansi's son Intikuma was curious about what his father was doing, and he watched from behind some bushes. He saw Anansi holding the pot in front of him against his stomach. He saw that this made it hard

(From Folk-Lore of the Antilles, French and English, by Elsie Clews Parsons, New York, 1936.)

(From The Hat-Shaking Dance and Other Ashanti Tales from Ghana,© 1957 by Harold Courlander. By permission of Harcourt Brace Jovanovich.)

for Anansi to grasp the tree he was climbing. At last he couldn't keep quiet any longer and he said: "Father, may I make a suggestion?"

Anansi was startled and angry, and he shouted: "Why are you spying on me?"

Intikuma replied: "I only wanted to help you."

Anansi said: "Is this your affair?"

Intikuma said to him: "It's only that I see you are having difficulty. When you climb a tree, it is very hard to hold a pot in front. If you put the pot on your back, you can climb easily."

Anansi tried it. He took the pot from in front and put it on his back. He climbed swiftly. But then he stopped. He looked at Intikuma and was embarrassed, for although he carried so much wisdom in the pot, he had not known how to climb with it.

In anger, Kwaku Anansi took the pot and threw it from the treetop. It fell on the earth and shattered into many pieces. The wisdom that was in it scattered in all directions. When people heard what had happened, they came and took some of the wisdom Anansi had thrown away. And so today, wisdom is not all in one place. It is everywhere. Should you find a foolish man, he is one who didn't come when the others did to take a share of the wisdom.

This is the story the Ashanti people are thinking of when they say: "One head can't go into consultation."

APPENDIX XVI

THE MAGIC HOE: AN ASHANTI COMPARISON

In the beginning there was only one hoe in the world, and men worked their fields with a bush knife. For the coming of the hoe to Ashanti, Kotoko, the porcupine, is responsible, and Anansi, the spider, also played his part.

It is said that Kotoko and Anansi joined together to begin a new farm. When it was Anansi's turn to work, he took his family and went into the field and dug the earth with his bush knife. And when it was Kotoko's turn, he came to the field with a hoe.

He raised his hoe and struck it on the earth, singing:

> "Give me a hand, hoe of Kotoko, give me a hand!
> It is hot in the sun!"

The hoe leapt from Kotoko's hands and began to work in the field by itself. It cut up the earth over a great distance, and when night came, the porcupine said other words, and the hoe came to rest. When he went home, Kotoko took the hoe and hid it in his house.

But Kwaku Anansi, when he saw how the hoe labored, said: "Why

(From The Hat-Shaking Dance and Other Ashanti Tales from Ghana, ©1957 by Harold Courlander. By permission of Harcourt Brace Jovanovich.)

do I break my back? I shall get this hoe and let it work for me."

So early in the day, before the light came, Anansi went to Kotoko's house and stole the hoe from where it was hidden. He took it out to the field. He struck it on the earth and sang:

> *"Give me a hand, hoe of Kotoko, give me a hand!*
> *It is hot in the sun!"*

The hoe began to work. It turned and cultivated the earth while Anansi sat in the shade and rested. Anansi said: "Whoever had a thing like this before?"

The hoe moved across the field. All the earth was newly turned. Anansi was satisfied. He said to the hoe: "Stop now; the field is done." But the hoe didn't stop, because Anansi didn't know the right word. It went right on hoeing. It hoed itself into the dense brush, and still Anansi couldn't stop it. It hoed itself to the edge of the sea, and still it would not stop. It went across the sea and came to the Country of the White People.

And there the people liked it and fashioned other hoes after it. And when they had made many, they brought some of them across the sea to the Ashanti people. Thus today among the Ashanti there are numerous hoes, and men use them instead of the bush knife when they have to till the earth.

APPENDIX XVII

BETWEEN TWO DINNERS: ASHANTI VERSION

There was the Upper Village and the Lower Village, and it happened one time that both gave a feast on the same day. Anansi [spider], where he lived, heard of the feasts, and he decided to go to both of them. He went to the Upper Village to inquire when the food would be given out, but the people could not tell him. He went then to the Lower Village, asking everyone he met, "What time will the eating begin?" They answered, "Who can say with certainty?" So Anansi returned to the Upper Village, calling out, "Has the eating begun?" But the eating had not yet started, so Anansi hurried again to the Lower Village. Whomever he met, Anansi asked, "The feast, has it started yet?" They replied to him, "No, it has not begun. It will begin in time." From the Lower Village he hurried to the Upper Village, announcing, "A celebrated personage arrives. Let the food be served." But people said to him, "No, things are not yet beginning."

Now the Upper Village and the Lower Village were some distance from each other, and Anansi was wearing himself out with so much running back and forth. His son Intikuma said, "Why is it necessary to eat in both villages. It is better to settle for one or the other. Go to the Upper Village and wait there." His son Kwekutsin said, "Yes, make a decision. You can eat in the Lower Village." But Anansi said, "No, I

will go to the place where the food is served first, and after that I will
go to the other place."

He went to his house and procured two long ropes, after which he
went back to the main trail and stood halfway between the two villages. He tied the end of both ropes around his waist. The free end of
one rope he gave to Intikuma. The free end of the other he gave to Kwekutsin. He instructed his sons this way: Intikuma was to go to the Upper Village, Kwekutsin was to go to the Lower Village. When the food
was served in the Upper Village Intikuma was to pull on his rope.
When the food was served in the Lower Village Kwekutsin was to pull.
That way Anansi would know which village served first.

So Intikuma went to the Upper Village and Kwekutsin went to the
Lower Village, while Anansi stood in the middle. Time went by. Then
the food was served in the Upper Village and Intikuma began to pull.
At the very same moment, the food was served in the Lower Village
and Kwekutsin began to pull. They pulled very hard, and Anansi was
not able to move in one direction or the other. He tried to go to the Upper Village but he could not depart from the spot where he stood. He
tried to go to the Lower Village but he was unable to go that way either.
His sons pulled harder on the ropes. Only when the feasts were over
did they stop the pulling. Then they returned to where they had left
Anansi. They found him there. He had not moved up the trail or down
the trail. Where the ropes were tied around his waist he was very thin
from being squeezed. Above the ropes his body was puffed out, and below the ropes also his body was puffed out. This is the way Anansi
looked after the feasting was over. And this is the way Anansi remained
even to the present day.

APPENDIX XVIII

KANZO, THE BOILING POT CEREMONY

Observers and chroniclers of the African scene in New Orleans during and after the slavery period didn't seem to grasp the religious essence of the boiling pot ceremony, its solemnity or its meanings. Cable
thought that Kanzo (Candio, as he spelled it) was a title for a chief. The
Kanzo ritual was probably known in many part of French America
which had slaves from Dahomey. To measure the misunderstanding
that stands out so blatantly in the *Almanach de la Louisiane* article,
here is a description of the Kanzo rite in Haiti in this century, extracted
from the *The Drum and the Hoe, Life and Lore of the Haitian People*,©
1960 by Harold Courlander, by permission of the University of California Press and the Regents of the University of California.

To advance beyond the lowest status in the hounfor, the hounsi must
undergo the test of fire. This ritual is known as *kanzo,* meaning "to tie
fire." In the drama of the hounfor there are many tests and ordeals.
When certain loa enter, the mounted persons will eat broken glass.
Other loa will cause their "horses" to rub hot pepper in their eyes. Still

others will compel possessed persons to cut themselves with machetes. But these are bravado actions of the deities who have entered into the bodies of the servitors. The kanzo test is a formalized and premeditated ritual, in which it is demonstrated that the power of the cult—and the spirit of the individual—is superior to fire. Once having passed through this rite, the ordinary hounsi becomes a hounsi kanzo.

The kanzo ceremony—or, as it is known in some parts of Haiti, the brulé zin (the boiling pot)—is performed in diverse ways according to the tradition of the particular hounfor. But common to all is the dipping of the hands into boiling oil.

The common hounsi, the bossale, is prepared gradually for kanzo. In the course of certain rites she undergoes a smoke ordeal. On all fours, her head close to a fire, she must breathe in smoke without choking or coughing. When these and other tests indicate that she is ready, she will be permitted to undergo the rite of the brulé zin.

Near the town of Thomazeau in the Cul-de-Sac Plain I witnessed one of these rituals. It began with a dance, in which only the hounsi of the cult participated. They were all dressed in white. The chief drummer wore a woman's blouse, a kerchief on his head, and on top of that a woman's straw hat. He played alone while the houngan invoked the loa Legba. Then there were songs for Ogoun, and the dancing resumed.

The dance court was larger than average, about forty feet by sixty. Attached to the ever-present po'teau mitan or center post, were three oil lamps which threw a flickering light. At the entrance to the dance court a glowing-hot iron bar stood erect in a charcoal fire—the symbol of kanzo and of the loa Ogoun.

When the preliminary dances were over, the hounsi retired to one side of the court, where they sat in two rows facing the center.

Ritual rattle and bell in hand, the houngan took his place by the sacred center post. He was an elderly man with a gray beard. He wore a red kerchief like a turban around his head. He smoked a cigar, and in his free hand he held a bottle of rum. The red kerchief, the rum, and the cigar were all in honor of Ogoun. He moved back and forth across the center of the court, talking casually, even joking and laughing. The drums began again, on a signal from the houngan, and a number of visiting houngans and mambos came forward and began a stately Jenvalo dance. The backs of their hands touching their knees, their backs bent low, they moved slowly counterclockwise around the center post. The mambos outnumbered the houngans four to one. The hounsi sitting on the sidelines sang. The song was for Maîtress Ezilie. The houngan in charge stood by patiently, deep in thought. His assistant, the laplace, kept time with a small rattle and led the singing.

When the song came to an end, the visiting cult priests and priestesses retired from the dance ground. Again the hounsi danced. Afterward the houngan began to talk *langage*, twirling his bottle of rum about recklessly. He was speaking to a loa. The chief drummer beat out a salute to Ogoun. Then the houngan raised the bottle and placed it to his ear. It gurgled away, some of the liquid trickling down his face. He seemed to be swallowing the rum.

While all the hounsi, with bowed heads, sat on the ground, the houngan recited from the ritual of the Catholic service. Latin words, then Creole words in Latin cadences. After a while the houngan's assistant took over the recitation, and the hounsi answered him responsively. When the prayers were over, the hounsi arose and passed into the hounfor. The drums began a fast Nago rhythm, and the hounsi emerged with brilliant silk flags studded with tiny brass rivets. The houngan's chief assistants—the laplace and the houngénicon—carried military sabers upraised. The dancers circled in single file around the center post, a triumphal military heralding of the deity of war and the forge.

To the accompaniment of a crescendo of drums, the procession suddenly reversed its direction. Watching the upraised saber of the laplace for a signal, the hounsi reversed their direction again.

When the dance drama ended, the hounsi carried the flags back into the hounfor. Then they sat on the ground while the houngan came forward to the center post to make his ritual flour drawing. Holding the flour in his hand, he allowed a little of it to trickle out in a fine white line. He worked rapidly, with half-closed eyes, speaking *langage*. A complicated white geometric pattern grew on the earth around the center post. Among its intricate designs highly stylized phallic forms were discernible. When the houngan had finished the drawing, he wrote the name of the loa whom they were serving: Ogoun Badagry. Then the other houngans and mambos came forward, one at a time, to add to the design. When the vèvè was completed it covered virtually the entire dance court.

The laplace came from the hounfor with a bundle of brilliantly colored beads. He stood by the houngan at the center post. One by one the hounsi came before the houngan, dropped on their knees, and kissed the ground. Around each hounsi's neck the houngan placed a string of beads. He raised her, pirouetted her first to the right, then to the left. The pirouette was to encourage possession by the loa.

From the hounfor the hounsi now brought herbs and vegetables for the sacrifice. Baskets and bottles were set out neatly on the ground, along with bundles of sticks and the iron pots, or zins.

The dance was resumed in a single rotating line around the houngan and the ritual offerings. Two hounsi in the center of the circle built fires, one on each side of the court. Over the fires they set the ritual iron pots. They poured oil into the pots and began the preparation of ritual food balls, like dumplings, from the ingredients at hand. One by one they dropped the dumplings into the oil, which was soon boiling.

The drumming, singing, and dancing were sustained at a high tension. A second team of drummers took over without a break in the music. The dancers now were almost exhausted. With a quick motion, the houngan spilled some rum into one of the boiling pots. A blue alcohol flame shot high into the air. Some of the hounsi screamed but continued to dance. Three of them fell to the ground, their limbs jerking uncontrollably. The loa had entered. Two of the "mounted" hounsi arose and continued to dance, staggering and jerking across the dance court. The third had to be lifted and carried into the hounfor.

The man who was to undergo initiation was waiting in the djévo, a special room in the hounfor. For the past seven days he had lain on a mat in the djévo, in virtual isolation except for visits from the houngan and the laplace.

Now the kanzo initiate was brought out, completely covered with a white cloth. Only his hands and feet could be seen. With one hand on the shoulder of the laplace, who preceded him, he moved with the dancers in a circle around the two boiling pots. On the seventh circuit of the course, the laplace stopped him at the first pot. The houngan grasped the man's free hand and, bending down, dipped it into the boiling oil. There was no visible indication of pain. They moved to the second pot, and the man's hand was dipped again. They proceeded again to the first pot, where the dipping was repeated, then back again to the second pot. The neophyte's hand entered the boiling oil seven times in all. He made no sound, showed no resistance, no reflexes. Then the hounsi took him back to the hounfor. It was all over. After three days of isolation, they said, he would be kanzo. . . .

A SELECTIVE BIBLIOGRAPHY
OF WORKS CITED OR CONSULTED
IN THE PREPARATION OF THIS BOOK

THE CARIBBEAN AND LATIN AMERICA

Andrade, Manuel J. *Folklore from the Dominican Republic.* Memoirs of the American Folklore Society, Vol. XXIII, 1930.

Aretz, Isabel. *El Folklore Musical Argentino.* Buenos Aires: Ricordi Americana, 1952.

Aubin, Eugène. *En Haiti.* Paris, 1910.

Bascom, William. *Shango in the New World.* Austin: African and Afro-American Research Institute, University of Texas, 1972.

_____. "The Focus of Cuban Santeria," *Southwestern Journal of Anthropology,* Spring, 1950.

_____. "The Yoruba in Cuba," *Nigeria,* No. 37, 1951.

_____. "Two Forms of Afro-Cuban Divination," in *Acculturation in the Americas,* by Sol Tax, Twentieth Congress of Americanists, Chicago, 1952.

Beckwith, Martha. *Jamaica Anansi Stories.* Memoirs of the American Folklore Society, Vol. XVII, 1924.

Bickell, R. *The West Indies as They Are: or a Real Picture of Slavery in the Island of Jamaica.* London, 1825.

Botkin, B.A. *Lay My Burden Down.* Chicago: University of Chicago Press, 1945.

Charters, Samuel B. (compiler and editor). *Music of the Bahamas* (record album with explanatory notes). New York: Folkways Records, 1959.

Courlander, Harold. *The Piece of Fire and Other Haitian Tales.* New York: Harcourt Brace Jovanovich, 1964.

_____. *Haiti Singing.* Chapel Hill: University of North Carolina Press, 1939.

_____. *The Drum and the Hoe, Life and Lore of the Haitian People.* Berkeley:University of California Press, 1960.

_____. *Uncle Bouqui of Haiti.* New York: Morrow, 1942.

_____. "Musical Instruments of Haiti," *The Musical Quarterly,* Vol. XXVII, No. 3, July 1941.

_____. "Musical Instruments of Cuba," *The Musical Quarterly,* Vol. XXVIII, No. 2, April 1942.

_____. "Profane Songs of the Haitian People," *Journal of Negro History,* Vol. XXVII, No. 3, July 1942.

_____. "Gods of the Haitian Mountains," *Journal of Negro History,* Vol. XXIX, No. 3, July 1944.

_____. "Abakwa Meeting in Guanabacoa," *Journal of Negro History,* Vol. XXIX, 1944.

_____. "The Loa of Haiti: New World African Deities," *Miscelánea de Estudios Dedicados a Fernando Ortiz por Sus Discípulos, Colegas y Amigos.* Havana, 1955.

_____. "Vodoun in Haitian Culture," in *Religion and Politics in Haiti,* by Harold Courlander and Rémy Bastien. Washington: Institute for Cross-Cultural Research, 1966.

_____. "Haiti's Political Folksongs," *Opportunity,* April 1941.

_____. (compiler and editor). *Caribbean Folk Music* (record album with explanatory notes). New York: Ethnic Folkways Library, 1960.

Dallas, R.C. *History of the Maroons.* London, 1803.

Dark, Philip J.C. *Bush Negro Art.* New York: St. Martin's Press, 1973.

Deren, Maya. *Divine Horsemen, the Living Gods of Haiti.* London: Thames and Hudson, 1953.

Dunham, Katherine. *Journey to Accompong.* New York: Holt, Rinehart and Winston, 1946.

Eells, Elsie. *Fairy Tales from Brazil.* New York: Dodd, Mead and Co., 1917.

Escabí, Pedro. *Morovis: Vista Parcial del Folklore de Puerto Rico.* San Juan: Centro de Investigaciones Sociales, Facultad de Ciencias Sociales, University of Puerto Rico, 1975.

Freyre, Gilberto. *The Masters and the Slaves.* New York: Knopf, 1946.

Guirao, Ramon. *Cuentos y Leyendas Negras de Cuba.* Havana, date unknown.

Hall, Robert A. Jr., with the collaboration of Suzanne Comhaire-Sylvain, H. Ormonde McConnell and Alfred Métraux. *Haitian Creole.* The American Anthropological Association, Memoir No. 74, April–June 1953.

Herskovits, Melville J. *Life in a Haitian Valley.* New York: Knopf, 1937.

_____. "Wari in the New World," *Journal of the Royal Anthropological Institute,* Vol. LXII, January–June 1932.

_____. and Frances S. Herskovits. *Rebel Destiny, among the Bush Negroes of Dutch Guiana.* New York: McGraw Hill, 1934.

_____. *Suriname Folk-lore.* New York: Columbia University Press, 1936.

_____ and _____. *Trinidad Village.* New York: Knopf, 1947.

_____ and _____. (compilers and editors). *Afro-Bahian Religious Songs* (record album with explanatory notes). Washington: Music Division, Library of Congress, 1947.

Hyppolite, Michelson Paul. *Contes Dramatiques Haïtiens.* Port-au-Prince: Imprimerie de l'Etat, 1956.

Jarvis, J. Antonio. *The Virgin Islands and Their People.* Philadelphia: Dorrance, 1944.

Joel, Miriam. *African Traditions in Latin America.* Cuernavaca: Centro Intercultural de Documentacion, 1972.

Kahn, Morton. *Djuka, the Bush Negroes of Dutch Guiana.* New York: Viking, 1931.

Labat, Jean Baptiste. *Nouveau Voyage aux Isles de l'Amérique* (2 vols.). The Hague, 1724.

Lachatañeré, Romulo. "El Sistema Religioso de los Lucumis y Otras

Influencias Africanas en Cuba," *Estudios Afrocubanos,* Havana, 1945–1946.

Leyburn, James G. *The Haitian People.* New Haven: Yale University Press, 1941.

Liscano, Juan. *Folklore y Cultura.* Caracas: Editorial Avila Grafica, 1951.

―――― and Charles Seeger (compilers and editors). *Venezuelan Folk Music* (record album with explanatory notes). Washington: Music Division, Library of Congress, 1947.

Mendoza, Vincente T. "Algo del Folklore Negro en Mexico," *Miscelánea de Estudios Dedicados a Fernando Ortiz por Sus Discípulos, Colegas y Amigos,* Havana, 1956.

Merriam, Alan P. "Song of the Ketu Cult of Bahia," *African Music Society Journal,* Vol. 1, Nos. 3 and 4, 1956.

Métraux, Alfred. *Voodoo in Haiti.* New York: Oxford University Press, 1959.

Moore, Joseph G., and Simpson, George E. "A Comparative Study of Acculturation in Morant Bay and West Kingston," *Zaire,* Nos. 9 and 10, November–December 1957.

Ortiz, Fernando. *Los Negros Brujos.* Madrid, 1906.

――――. *Los Cabildos Afrocubanos.* Havana, 1916.

――――. *Los Negros Esclavos.* Havana, 1916.

――――. *La Africanía de la Música Folklórica.* Havana: Ediciones Cardenas y Cia, 1950.

――――. *Los Bailes y el Teatro de los Negros en el Folklore de Cuba.* Havana: Ediciones Cardenas y Cia, 1951.

――――. *Los Instrumentos de la Música Afrocubana* (4 vols.). Havana: Publicaciones de la Dirección de Cultura del Ministerio de Educacion, 1952.

――――. "La Música Sagrada de los Negros Yoruba en Cuba," *Estudios Afrocubanos,* Havana, 1938.

Parsons, Elsie Clews, *Folk-Lore of the Antilles, French and English.* Memoirs of the American Folklore Society, Vol. XXVI, 1936.

――――. *Folk-tales of Andros Island, Bahamas.* Memoirs of the American Folklore Society, Vol. XIII, 1918.

Pearse, Andrew C (compiler and editor). *The Big Drum Dance of Carriacou* (record album with explanatory notes). New York: Ethnic Folkways Library, 1956.

Pollak-Eltz, Angelina, *Maria Lionza, Mito y Culto Venezolano.* Caracas: Universidad Católica Andres Bello, Instituto de Investigaciones Históricas, 1972.

――――. *Cultos Afroamericanos.* Caracas: Universidad Católica Andres Bello, Instituto de Investigaciones Históricas, 1972.

――――. *Vestigios Africanos en la Cultura del Pueblo Venezolano.* Caracas: Universidad Católica Andres Bello, Instituto de Investigaciones Históricas, 1972.

――――. *Panorama de Estudios Afroamericanos.* Caracas: Universidad Católica Andres Bello, Instituto de Investigaciones Históricas, 1972.

Price, Thomas J. (compiler and editor). *Caribbean Rhythms* (record album with explanatory notes). New York: Folkways Records, 1957.

Price-Mars, Jean. *Ainsi Parla l'Oncle, Essais d'Ethnographie.* Port-au-Prince, 1928; and New York: Parapsychology Foundation, 1954.

Ramon y Rivera, Louis Felipe. *La Música Afrovenezolana.* Caracas: Universidad Central de Venezuela, 1971.

Ramos, Arthur. *O Negro Brasileiro.* Rio de Janeiro, 1934.

_____. *O Folk-lore Negro do Brasil.* Rio de Janeiro, 1935.

_____. *The Negro in Brazil.* Washington: Associated Publishers, 1939.

_____. *Las Culturas Negras en el Nuevo Mundo.* Mexico City: Fondo de Cultura Economica, 1943.

Revista de Téchnica Policial y Penitenciaria. Havana, 1936.

Rigaud, Odette Mennesson. "The Feasting of the Gods in Haitian Vodu," *Primitive Man,* Vol. XIX, Nos. 1 and 2, January and April 1941.

Rodrigues, José Honório. *Brazil and Africa.* Translated by Richard A. Mazzara and Sam Hileman. Berkeley: University of California Press, 1965.

Seaga, Edward (compiler and editor). *Folk Music of Jamaica* (record album with explanatory notes). New York: Ethnic Folkways Library, 1956.

Simpson, George Eaton. *The Shango Cult in Trinidad.* Rio Piedras: Institute of Caribbean Studies of the University of Puerto Rico, 1965.

_____. *Religious Cults of the Caribbean: Trinidad, Jamaica and Haiti.* Rio Piedras: Institute of Caribbean Studies of the University of Puerto Rico, 1970.

_____. *Caribbean Papers.* Cuernavaca: Centro Intercultural de Documentación, 1970.

_____. "Folk Medicine in Trinidad," *Journal of American Folklore,* Vol. 75, No. 298, October–December 1962.

_____. "The Ras Tafari Movement in Jamaica," *Social and Economic Studies,* University of the West Indies, Institute of Social and Economic Research, Vol. 4, No. 2, June 1955.

_____. "Four Vodun Ceremonies," *Journal of American Folklore,* April–June, 1946.

Smith, T. Lynn. *Brazil: People and Institutions.* Baton Rouge: Louisiana State University Press, 1946.

Stedman, Captain J.G. *Narrative of a Five Years' Expedition Against the Revolted Negroes of Suriname* (2 vols.). London: 1796, 1806.

Stone, Doris. *The Black Caribs of Honduras* (record album with explanatory notes). New York: Ethnic Folkways Library, 1952.

Tannenbaum, Frank. *Slave and Citizen, the Negro in the Americas.* New York: Knopf, 1947.

Taylor, Douglas MacRae. *The Black Carib of British Honduras.* New York: Wenner-Gren Foundation for Anthropological Research, 1951.

Vandercook, John W. *Caribee Cruise.* New York: Reynal and Hitchcock, 1938.

Victor, Rene, *Les Voix de Nos Rues.* Port-au-Prince: State Printing Office, 1949.

THE UNITED STATES

Adams, Edward C. L. *Congaree Sketches, Scenes from Negro Life in the Swamps of the Congaree and Tales by Tad and Scip of Heaven and Hell with Other Miscellany.* Introduction by Paul Green. Chapel Hill: University of North Carolina Press, 1927.

———. *Nigger to Nigger.* New York: Scribner's, 1928.

Allen, William Francis, with Charles Pickard Ware and Lucy McKim Garrison. *Slave Songs of the United States.* New York: A. Simpson and Company, 1867.

Botkin, B.A. *A Treasury of American Folklore.* Foreword by Carl Sandburg. New York: Crown, 1944.

———. *A Treasury of Southern Folklore.* New York: Crown, 1949.

———. "'Folk-Say' and Folk-Lore," in W. T. Couch, *Culture in the South.* Chapel Hill, 1934.

Bradford, Roark. *John Henry.* New York and London: Harpers, 1931.

Bremer, Frederika. *The Homes of the New World* (2 vols.). New York, 1868.

Brown, Ray. "Negro Folktales from Alabama," *Southern Folklore Quarterly,* June 1954.

Cable, G.W. *Creoles and Cajuns, Stories of Old Louisiana.* Garden City: Doubleday, 1959.

———. *The Grandissimes.* New York: Scribner's, 1899.

Carmer, Carl. *Stars Fell on Alabama.* New York: Farrar and Rinehart, 1934.

Courlander, Harold, *Negro Folk Music, U.S.A. New York: Columbia University Press, 1963.*

———. *The Big Old World of Richard Creeks.* Philadelphia: Chilton,1962.

———. *Terrapin's Pot of Sense.* New York: Holt, 1957.

———. *Negro Songs from Alabama.* Published with the assistance of the Wenner-Gren Foundation for Anthropological Research. New York, 1960. Republished with additional materials by Oak Publications, New York, 1963.

———. *Negro Folk Music of Alabama.* Introductory booklet accompanying record album by same title. New York: Ethnic Folkways Library, 1956.

Ditchy, Jay K. *Les Acadiens Louisianais et Leur Parler.* Washington: Institut Français de Washington, 1932.

Dorson, Richard M. *American Negro Folktales.* Greenwich: Fawcett (no date).

———. *Negro Folktales in Michigan.* Cambridge (Massachusetts), 1956.

Fortier, Alcée. *Louisiana Folk-tales. Memoirs of the American Folk-Lore Society,* Vol. II, 1895.

Georgia Writers' Project, *Drums and Shadows, Survival Studies among the Coastal Negroes.* Foreword by Guy B. Johnson. Athens (Georgia).

Greenberg, Joseph H. "The Decipherment of the 'Ben-Ali Diary,' A Preliminary Statement," *The Journal of Negro History*, Vol. XXV, No. 3, July 1940.

Harris, Joel Chandler. *Uncle Remus, His Songs and Sayings*. New York: Appleton, 1880.

Hatcher, William E. *John Jasper*. New York: Revell, 1908. University of Georgia Press, 1940.

Hearn, Lafcadio, *Gombo Zhèbes, Little Dictionary of Creole Proverbs*. New York: Coleman, 1885.

———. "New Orleans Superstitions," *Harper's Weekly*, Dec. 25, 1886.

Herskovits, Melville J. *The Myth of the Negro Past*. New York: Harper, 1941.

Hughes, Langston, and Bontemps, Arna. *The Book of Negro Folklore*. New York: Dodd, Mead and Company, 1958.

Hurston, Zora Neale. *Mules and Men*. Philadelphia: Lippincott, 1935.

Johnson, Guy B. "St. Helena Songs and Stories," in *Black Yeomanry, Life on St. Helena Island*, by T. J. Woofter, Jr. New York: Holt, Rinehart and Winston, 1930.

Jones, Charles C. *Negro Myths from the Georgia Coast*. Boston: Houghton Mifflin, 1888.

Kemble, Frances Anne. *Journal of a Residence on a Georgia Plantation*. New York: Harper, 1863.

Latrobe, B. H. B. *Impressions Respecting New Orleans*. Edited by Samuel Wilson, Jr. New York: Columbia University Press, 1951.

Odum, Howard, and Johnson, Guy B. *Negro Workaday Songs*. Chapel Hill: University of North Carolina Press, 1926.

Olmstead, Frederick Law. *A Journey in the Back Country*. New York: Mason Brothers, 1860.

———. *Journey Through Texas; or a Saddle-Trip on the Southwestern Frontier*. New York: Dix, Edwards and Company, 1857.

———. *A Journey in the Seaboard Slave States*. New York: Dix & Edwards, 1856.

Parrish, Lydia. *Slave Songs of the Georgia Sea Islands*. New York: Creative Age Press, 1942.

Phillips, Ulrich Bonnell. *American Negro Slavery*. Gloucester (Massachusetts): Peter Smith, 1959 (reprint).

———. *Plantation and Frontier Documents*, Vols. I and II of the *Documentary History of American Industrial Society*. Cleveland: 1909.

Powdermaker, Hortense. *After Freedom*. New York: Viking, 1939.

Puckett, Newbell N. *Folk Beliefs of the Southern Negro*. Chapel Hill, 1926.

Saxon, Lyle, *Old Louisiana*. New York: Century, 1929.

Smith, Reed, "Gullah," *Bulletin of the University of South Carolina*, No. 190, 1926.

Turner, Lorenzo D. "African Survivals in the New World with Special Emphasis on the Arts," *Africa from the Point of View of American Negro Scholars*. Paris: Présence Africaine, 1958.

Work, John W. *American Negro Songs and Spirituals.* New York: Howell, Soskin and Company, 1940.

AFRICA

African Arts (quarterly). Los Angeles: African Studies Center, University of California, Autumn 1967 (date of first issue) to Winter 1974.

Antubam, K. *Ghana's Heritage of Culture.* Leipzig : Kohler and Amelang, 1963.

Barker, W. H., and Sinclair, C. *West African Folk Tales.* London: George Harrap and Co. and Sheldon Press, 1917.

Bascom, William. *The Yoruba of Southwestern Nigeria.* New York: Holt, Rinehart and Winston, 1969.

_____. *Ifa Divination, Communication Between Gods and Men in West Africa.* Bloomington: Indiana University Press, 1969.

Beier, Ulli. *The Origin of Life and Death.* London: Heinemann, 1966.

Benton, P. A. *The Languages and Peoples of Bornu, Being a Collection of the Writings of P. A. Benton* (2 vols.). London: Frank Cass and Co., 1968.

Bérenger-Féraud, Laurent Jean-Baptiste. *Les Peuplades de la Sénégambie.* Paris, 1879.

_____. *Recueil de Contes Populaires de la Sénégambie.* Paris, 1885.

Bianco, F. M. *The African Saga.* Translated by Margery Bianco from *Anthologie Nègre,* by Blaise Cendrars. New York: Payson and Clarke, 1927.

Bleek, W. H. I. *Reynard the Fox in South Africa.* London: Trubner and Co., 1864.

_____ and Loyd, L. C. *Specimens of Bushmen Folklore.* London: George Allen and Co., 1911.

Brownlee, Frank. *Lion and Jackal, with Other Native Folk Tales of South Africa.* London: George Allen and Unwin, 1938.

Callaway, Henry. *Nursery Tales, Traditions and Histories of the Zulus, in Their Own Words.* Natal, 1868.

Cardinall, A. W. *Tales Told in Togoland.* Oxford: Oxford University Press, 1931.

Cendrars, Blaise. *The African Saga.* Translated from *L'Anthologie Nègre,* by Margery Bianco. New York: Payson and Clarke, 1927.

Chatelain, Heli. *Folk-Tales of Angola: Fifty Tales, with Ki-Mbundu Text, Literal English Translation, Introduction, and Notes.* Vol. I of the *Memoirs of the American Folklore Society,* Boston and New York: G. E. Stechert and Co., 1894.

Christaller, J. G. *Twi Mmebusem Mpensa-Ahansia Mmoaano (A Collection of Three Thousand and Six Hundred Tshi Proverbs in Use among the Negroes of the Gold Coast Speaking the Asante and Fante, i.e., the Akan Language).* Basel, 1879.

Cobham, Henry. "Animal Stories from Calabar," *Journal of the African Society,* Vol. IV, 1904–5 (pp. 307–9).

Courlander, Harold. *Tales of Yoruba Gods and Heroes*. New York: Crown Publishers, Inc. 1973.

———. *The King's Drum and Other African Stories*. New York: Harcourt Brace Jovanovich, 1962.

———, with Ezekiel A. Eshugbayi. *Olode the Hunter and Other Tales from Nigeria*. New York: Harcourt Brace Jovanovich, 1968.

——— and Herzog, George. *The Cow-Tail Switch and Other West African Stories*. New York: Holt, Rinehart and Winston, 1947.

——— and Leslau, Wolf. *The Fire on the Mountain and Other Ethiopian Stories*. New York: Holt, Rinehart, and Winston, 1950.

———, with Albert Kofi Prempeh. *The Hat-Shaking Dance and Other Ashanti Tales from Ghana*. New York: Harcourt Brace Jovanovich, 1957.

Cronise, Florence M., and Ward, Henry W. *Cunnie Rabbit, Mr. Spider and Other Beef*. London, 1903.

Dayrell, Elphinstone. *Folk Stories from Southern Nigeria*. London, 1910.

Dennett, R. E. "Note on the Folklore of the Fjort," *Publications of the Folklore Society*, XLI. London, 1898.

Doke, C. M. "Lamba Folk-Lore," *Memoirs of the American Folk-Lore Society*, Vol. 20, 1927.

Egharevba, Jacob Uwadiae. *Some Stories of Ancient Benin*. Benin, 1951 (2d ed.).

Finnigan, Ruth. *Oral Literature in Africa*. Oxford Library of African Literature. Oxford: The Clarendon Press, 1970.

Frobenius, Leo. *Atlantis, Volksmärchen und Volksdichtungen Africas*. Jena, 1926.

———. and Fox, Douglas C. *African Genesis*. New York: Stackpole, 1937.

Gutmann, B. *Die Stammeslehren der Dschagga*. Munich: C. H. Beck, 1923–38.

Henries, Doris Banks. *Liberian Folklore*. New York: The Macmillan Company, 1966.

Herskovits, Melville J. *Dahomey, an Ancient West African Kingdom* (2 vols.). New York: J. J. Augustin, 1938.

——— and Herskovits, Frances S. *Dahomean Narrative, a Cross-Cultural Analysis*. Evanston: Northwestern University Press, 1958.

Herzog, George, and Blooah, Charles. *Jabo Proverbs from Eastern Liberia*. Oxford: Oxford University Press, 1936.

Hollis, A. C. *The Masai, Their Language and Folklore*. Oxford: The Clarendon Press, 1905.

Huffman, R. *Nuer Customs and Folklore*. London: Frank Cass and Co., 1931.

Hughes, Langston. *An African Treasury*. New York: Crown Publishers, Inc. 1960.

Jacottet, E. *The Treasury of Ba-Sutu Lore*. London, 1908.

Johnston, H. A. S. *A Selection of Hausa Stories*. Oxford: The Clarendon Press, 1966.

Mbiti, John S. *Akamba Stories.* Oxford: The Clarendon Press, 1966.

Murgatroyd, Madeline. *Tales from the Kraals.* [South Africa] Central News Agency, 1944.

Nassau, Robert H. *Where Animals Talk.* London: Duckworth and Company, 1914.

Patterson, J. R., trans. *The Stories of Abu Zeid the Hilali.* London: Routledge and Kegan Paul, 1930.

Posselt, F. W. T. *Fables of the Veld.* Oxford: The Clarendon Press, 1929.

Radin, Paul, with Elinore Marvel and James J. Sweeney, *African Folktales and Sculpture.* New York: Bollingen Foundation, 1964.

Rattray, R. S. *Hausa Folk-Lore, Customs, Proverbs.* Oxford: The Clarendon Press, 1913.

_____. *Akan-Ashanti Folk-Tales.* Oxford: The Clarendon Press, 1931.

Roscoe, J. *The Baganda, an Account of Their Customs and Beliefs.* London: Frank Cass and Company, 1911.

Routledge, W. S. and K. *With a Prehistoric People: the Akikuyu of British East Africa.* London:Edward Arnold, 1910.

St. Lys, Odette. *From a Vanished German Colony, a Collection of Folklore, Folk Tales and Proverbs from South-West Africa.* London, 1916.

Shlenker, C. F. *A Collection of Temne Traditions, Fables and Proverbs.* London, 1861.

Schwab, George, "Bulu Tales," *Journal of American Folk-Lore,* Vol. XXXII, 1922.

Steere, Edward. *Swahili Tales, as Told by the Natives of Zanzibar.* London, 1870.

Talbot, P. Amaury. *In the Shadow of the Bush.* London: William Heinemann, 1912.

_____. *The Peoples of Southern Nigeria* (4 vols.). London, 1926.

Theal, G. McCall. *Kaffir Folk Lore.* London: George Allen and Unwin, 1886.

Thomas, Northcote W. "Thirty-two Folk-Tales of the Edo-Speaking Peoples of Nigeria," *Folk-Lore,* Vol. XXXI, 1920.

Torrend, J. *Specimens of Bantu Folklore from Northern Rhodesia.* London: Kegan Paul, Trench, Trubner and Company, 1921.

Tremearne, A. J. N. *Hausa Superstitions and Customs.* London: John Bale Sons and Danielson, 1913.

Vernon-Jackson, Hugh. *West African Folk Tales.* London: University of London Press, 1958.

Whitting, C. E. J. *Hausa and Fulani Proverbs.* Farnborough (England): Gregg, 1940.

INDEX